GRAND PRIX

GRAND PRIX

TREVOR R. GRIFFITHS

This edition first published in 1998 by
Motorbooks International Publishers & Wholesalers,
729 Prospect Avenue, PO Box 1, Osceola, WI 54020 USA.

First published in UK in 1992 by
Bloomsbury Publishing Plc,
38 Soho Square, London W1V 5DF
Second edition 1993
Third edition 1997

Library of Congress Cataloging-in-Publication Data Available.

ISBN 0-7603-0562-5

Designed by Geoff Green
Typeset by Hewer Text Composition Services, Edinburgh
Printed and bound in England by Clays Ltd, St Ives plc

Contents

Acknowledgements   vi

Introduction   vii

Points Scoring   ix

Part 1: The Results

1950–1997   1

Part 2: Drivers' Career Records

Abbreviations   486

Drivers' Results and Biographies A–Z   487

Part 3: Constructors' Records

Constructors' Records A–Z   557

Constructors' Championship   581

Constructors' Victories   581

Part 4: Grand Prix Winners

The World Champions   583

Wins per Driver   584

Race Winners   585

Select Bibliography   593

Acknowledgements

My greatest debts are to the drivers, constructors, teams and officials who have made my enjoyment of motor racing possible, to the journalists and historians who have recorded their activities, and to my brother and sister-in-law Geoffrey and Barbara Griffiths, who took me to the 1964 Italian Grand Prix, thereby fuelling a lifelong passion for motor racing. My research has been materially assisted by Valya Alexander, Ace and Derek McCarron, Tim Collings, and by the courteous, prompt and efficient service of Mike Kettlewell of Mill House Books. I am grateful to Michael Lomas, Archie A. Smith and J.A. Welch for drawing my attention to errors in earlier editions. I am very grateful to David R. Griffiths, Sara R. Griffiths and Irene Griffiths for their work on the project. I first shared my enthusiasm for motor racing with Kathy Rooney on 24 September 1972 – and I want to thank her for carrying on listening.

Trevor R. Griffiths
December 1997

Introduction

This new edition of *Grand Prix* now gives a complete set of results for all races counting towards the World Championship for Drivers and for Contructors revised and updated to the end of the 1997 season. With this book you can trace the developing careers of the great drivers from Fangio to Schumacher, race by race, as well as identify the unsung heroes who make up the grids. A unique feature of this book is that the driver biographies give the best results for *every* driver who participated in a race, not just those who finished in the first six. Brief seasonal summaries and full results for each championship set the scene and establish a context for the results, drawing attention to significant developments and personal milestones. Many books about grand prix racing concentrate on star drivers and constructors alone, but here you will find drivers such as Skip Barber, Carol Shelby or Jean-Louis Schlesser who achieved greater fame elsewhere, as well as Ascari, Clark, Lauda, Mansell, Moss, Prost, Senna and Stewart, and constructors such as ATS, Eurobrun, Gilby, Pacific, and Zakspeed, along with Alfa Romeo, Ferrari, Honda, Lotus, McLaren, Mercedes, Renault and Williams.

How to use this book

The book is divided into two main parts: full results for all races counting towards the world championship from 1950–1997, with brief seasonal summaries and world championship tables; and brief drivers' biographies with dates of birth and death (where known), first and last race started, highest race placing, record of championship positions, total of fastest laps and pole positions. Records are also given for constructors whose cars competed in grand prix. Tables of the winners of individual grand prix, world champions and champion constructors complete the book.

A driver's career can be traced in the results by using the biography to find out the first and last races competed in, and then looking at the intervening races.

Although there was virtually no overlap between competitors at Indianapolis and elsewhere in the championship, results are given here for the races from 1950 to 1960 that were included in the championship. Only Ascari of regular grand prix drivers actually competed at Indianapolis during the period, though Indianapolis driver Roger Ward competed in the 1959 US Grand Prix in a midget racer.

I have attempted to be as accurate as possible in giving reasons for retirement, but in many cases contemporary reports do not agree as to the primary cause of a retirement: in some cases the team may have given inaccurate information for their own reasons (eg, trying to confuse opponents, unwillingness to offend a supplier), and in other cases, no reason was given. Where drivers retired on the same lap it has not always been possible to determine which retired first. It has also not been feasible to include drivers who practised but failed to qualify for a race.

Since different conventions operated at different times for classifying drivers who were still running but had completed a small number of laps or who had retired after completing a substantial number of laps, I have usually given positions for all cars, whether retired or running, down to the last car still running, until the modern 90% rule was introduced in 1966. This does not, of course, make any difference to the point-scoring results. At Indianapolis all cars were classified, even if not running.

In the championship table, figures in brackets show the total number of points scored by a driver/constructor who scored in more races than were counted for that year's championship.

Points Scoring

The points scoring systems for both championships are as follows:

Drivers' Championship
1950–9
8 – 6 – 4 – 3 – 2 for 1st – 2nd – 3rd – 4th – 5th, with one point (shared if necessary) to the driver setting fastest lap. Until 1957 drivers sharing a car shared the points, although in some cases it was decided that a driver had not driven enough laps to score points. From 1950 to 1953 the best four results counted, from 1954 to 1957, the best five, in 1958 the best six, and in 1959 the best five.

1960
8 – 6 – 4 – 3 – 2 – 1 for 1st – 2nd – 3rd – 4th – 5th – 6th. The best six results counted.

1961–1990
9 – 6 – 4 – 3 – 2 – 1 for 1st – 2nd – 3rd – 4th – 5th – 6th. In 1961, 1962 and 1966, the best five results determined the championship; from 1963 to 1965, it was the best six. From 1967 until 1978 the championship was divided into two parts, with the worst result in each part being discarded. When there was an odd number of races, the first part of the year included more races. In 1979 the best four results in each half determined the championship positions; in 1980 it was the best five in each half. From 1981 to 1990, the best 11 results counted.

1991–
10 – 6 – 4 – 3 – 2 – 1 for 1st – 2nd – 3rd – 4th – 5th – 6th. All races counted.

Constructors' Championship

Scoring from 1958 to 1978 matched the pattern of the drivers' championship (though there was no point for fastest lap), with points going to the best placed car of each manufacturer. From 1979 all races counted and all cars finishing in the first six counted. The points for a winner were increased to 10 in 1991.

Part 1:
The Results

1950

The inaugural World Championship, to a formula which specified engine capacity of 1.5 litres supercharged or 4.5 litres unsupercharged, saw Alfa Romeo dominate with their supercharged 158, a well-developed pre-war design, which won all six European Grand Prix. Alfa drivers consequently dominated the championship with Farina edging out Fangio by virtue of his fourth place in Belgium. Although the Indianapolis 500, which ran to different regulations, was included in the championship series until 1960, it attracted very little European participation and, conversely, very few American Indianapolis drivers entered any grand prix. Etancelin, fifth in Italy, remains the oldest driver to score championship points.

British Grand Prix: Silverstone, 13 May 1950

70 laps of 2,89 mile/4.65 km circuit

Place	Driver	Car	Laps	Time/reason for retiring	Grid
1	Farina	Alfa Romeo	70	2h 13m 23.6s	1
2	Fagioli	Alfa Romeo	70	2h 13m 26.2s	2
3	R Parnell	Alfa Romeo	70	2h 14m 15.6s	4
4	Giraud-Cabantous	Talbot	68		6
5	Rosier	Talbot	68		9
6	Gerard	ERA	67		13
7	Harrison	ERA	67		15
8	Etancelin	Talbot	65		14
9	Hampshire	Maserati	64		16
10	Fry/Shawe-Taylor	Maserati	64		20
11	Claes	Talbot	64		21
12	Fangio	Alfa Romeo	61	oil pipe/con rod	3
13	Kelly	Alta	57		19
	Bira	Maserati	48	fuel feed	5
	Murray	Maserati	43	engine	18
	Crossley	Alta	42	transmission	17
	de Graffenried	Maserati	35	con rod	8
	Chiron	Maserati	23	clutch	11

British Grand Prix (cont)

Place	Driver	Car	Laps	Time/reason for retiring	Grid
	Martin	Talbot	7	oil pressure	7
	P Walker/Rolt	ERA	4	gearbox	10
	L Johnson	ERA	1	supercharger	12

Fastest Lap: Farina, 1m 50.6s. 94.04 mph/151.3 kph

Monaco Grand Prix: Monte Carlo, 21 May 1950

100 laps of 1.98 mile/3.18 km circuit

Place	Driver	Car	Laps	Time/reason for retiring	Grid
1	Fangio	Alfa Romeo	100	3h 13m 18.7s	1
2	Ascari	Ferrari	99		7
3	Chiron	Maserati	98		8
4	Sommer	Ferrari	97		9
5	Bira	Maserati	95		15
6	Gerard	ERA	94		16
7	Claes	Talbot	94		18
	Villoresi	Ferrari	62	rear axle	6
	Etancelin	Talbot	35	oil pipe	4
	Gonzalez	Maserati	0	fire	3
	Farina	Alfa Romeo	0	accident	2
	Fagioli	Alfa Romeo	0	accident	5
	Rosier	Talbot	0	accident	10
	Manzon	Simca-Gordini	0	accident	11
	de Graffenried	Maserati	0	accident	12
	Trintignant	Simca-Gordini	0	accident	13
	Harrison	ERA	0	accident	14
	Rol	Maserati	0	accident	17
	Schell	Cooper-JAP	0	accident	19

Fastest Lap: Fangio, 1m 51.0s. 64.09 mph/103.14 kph
*Nine cars were eliminated after Farina crashed on lap 1. Schell's Cooper was the first rear-engined car to start in a championship race.

Indianapolis 500: Indianapolis, 30 May 1950

200 laps of 2.5 mile/4.02 km circuit

Place	Driver	Car	Laps	Time/reason for retiring	Grid
1	Parsons	Wynn's Friction Proofing	138	2h 46m 56s	5
2	Holland	Blue Crown Spark Plug	137		10

Indianapolis 500 (cont)

Place	Driver	Car	Laps	Time/reason for retiring	Grid
3	Rose	Howard Keck	137		3
4	Green	John Zink	137		12
5	Chitwood/ Bettenhausen	Wolfe	136		9
6	Wallard	Blue Crown Spark Plug	136		23
7	Faulkner	Grant Piston Ring	135		1
8	Connor	Blue Crown Spark Plug	135		4
9	P Russo	Russo & Nichels	135		19
10	Flaherty	Granatelli-Sabourin	135		11
11	Fohr	Bardahl	133		16
12	Carter	Belanger	133		13
13	Hellings	Tuffy's	132		26
14	McGrath	Hinkle	131	accident	6
15	Ruttman	Bowes Seal Fast	130		24
16	Hartley	Troy Oil	128		31
17	Davies	Pat Clancy	128		27
18	J McDowell	Wales	128		33
19	Walt Brown	Tuffy's	127		20
20	Webb	Fadely-Anderson	126		14
21	Hoyt	Morris	125		15
22	Ader	Sampson	123		29
23	Holmes	Norm Olson	123	accident	30
24	J Rathmann	Pioneer Auto Repair	122		28
25	Banks/Agabashian	IRC	112	oil line	21
26	Schindler	Auto Shippers	111	universal joint	22
27	Levrett/Cantrell	Palmer	108	oil pressure	17
28	Agabashian	Wynn's Friction Proofing	64	oil line	2
29	Jackson	Cummins Diesel	52	supercharger	32
30	Hanks	Merz Engineering	42	oil pressure	25
31	Bettenhausen	Blue Crown Spark Plug	30	wheel bearing	8
32	D Rathmann	City of Glendale	25	stalled	18
33	Dinsmore	Brown Motor Co.	10	oil leak	7

Fastest Lap: Holland, 1m 09.8s. 129 mph/207.6 kph
* Race stopped after 138 laps due to rain.

Swiss Grand Prix: Bremgarten, 4 June 1950

42 laps of 4.52 mile/7.28 km circuit

Place	Driver	Car	Laps	Time/reason for retiring	Grid
1	Farina	Alfa Romeo	42	2h 02m 53.7s	2
2	Fagioli	Alfa Romeo	42	2h 02m 54.1s	3
3	Rosier	Talbot	41		10
4	Bira	Maserati	40		8
5	Bonetto	Maserati-Milan	40		12
6	de Graffenried	Maserati	40		11
7	Pagani	Maserati	39		15
8	Schell	Talbot	39		18
9	Chiron	Maserati	39		16
10	Claes	Talbot	39		14
11	Branca	Maserati	35		17
	Fangio	Alfa Romeo	32	valve	1
	Etancelin	Talbot	24	gearbox	6
	Martin	Talbot	18	accident	9
	Sommer	Ferrari	18	suspension	13
	Villoresi	Ferrari	8	transmission	4
	Ascari	Ferrari	3	oil pipe	5
	Giraud-Cabantous	Talbot	0	accident	7

Fastest Lap: Farina, 2m 41.6s. 100.78 mph/162.2 kph

Belgian Grand Prix: Spa, 18 June 1950

35 laps of 8.77 mile/14.12 km circuit

Place	Driver	Car	Laps	Time/reason for retiring	Grid
1	Fangio	Alfa Romeo	35	2h 47m 26s	2
2	Fagioli	Alfa Romeo	35	2h 47m 40s	3
3	Rosier	Talbot	35	2h 49m 45s	8
4	Farina	Alfa Romeo	35	2h 51m 31s	1
5	Ascari	Ferrari	34		6
6	Villoresi	Ferrari	33		4
7	Levegh	Talbot	33		10
8	Claes	Talbot	32		14
9	Crossley	Alta	30		12
10	Branca	Maserati	29		13
	Chaboud	Talbot	21		11
	Sommer	Talbot	19	engine	5
	Etancelin	Talbot	14	overheating	7
	Giraud-Cabantous	Talbot	1	engine	9

Fastest Lap: Farina, 4m 34.1s. 115.1mph/ 185.2kph

French Grand Prix: Reims, 2 July 1950

64 laps of 4.86 mile/7.82 km circuit

Place	Driver	Car	Laps	Time/reason for retiring	Grid
1	Fangio	Alfa Romeo	64	2h 57m 52.8s	1
2	Fagioli	Alfa Romeo	64	2h 58m 18.5s	3
3	P Whitehead	Ferrari	61		18
4	Manzon	Simca-Gordini	61		12
5	Etancelin/Chaboud	Talbot	59		4
6	Pozzi/Rosier	Talbot	56		14
7	Farina	Alfa Romeo	55	fuel pump	2
8	Giraud-Cabantous	Talbot	52		5
	Levegh	Talbot	36	engine	9
	Bonetto	Maserati-Milan	14	engine	17
	Claes	Talbot	11	overheating	16
	Rosier	Talbot	10	overheating	15
	R Parnell	Maserati	9	engine	10
	Rol	Maserati	6	engine	7
	Chiron	Maserati	6	engine	13
	Hampshire	Maserati	5	engine	11
	Sommer	Talbot	4	engine	6
	Gonzalez	Maserati	3	engine	8

Fastest Lap: Fangio, 2m 35.6s. 112.36 mph/180.8 kph
* Chaboud non-started, but shared with Etancelin.

Italian Grand Prix: Monza, 3 September 1950

80 laps of 3.9 mile/6.3 km circuit

Place	Driver	Car	Laps	Time/reason for retiring	Grid
1	Farina	Alfa Romeo	80	2h 51m 17.4s	3
2	Serafini/Ascari	Ferrari	80	2h 52m 36.0s	6
3	Fagioli	Alfa Romeo	80	2h 52m 53.0s	5
4	Rosier	Talbot	75		13
5	Etancelin	Talbot	75		16
6	de Graffenried	Maserati	72		17
7	P Whitehead	Ferrari	72		18
	Murray	Maserati	56	gearbox	23
	Harrison	ERA	51	radiator	21
	Sommer	Talbot	48	gearbox	8
	G Mairesse	Talbot	42		11
	Rol	Maserati	39		9
	Taruffi/Fangio	Alfa Romeo	34	valve	7
	Levegh	Talbot	29		20
	Fangio	Alfa Romeo	23	gearbox	1
	Claes	Talbot	22	overheating	22
	Ascari	Ferrari	21	engine	2
	Biondetti	Ferrari-Jaguar	17	engine	24

Italian Grand Prix (cont)

Place	Driver	Car	Laps	Time/reason for retiring	Grid
	Louveau	Talbot	16		14
	Comotti	Maserati-Milan	15		25
	Chiron	Maserati	13	oil pressure	19
	Trintignant	Simca-Gordini	13	water pipe	12
	Sanesi	Alfa Romeo	11	engine	4
	Manzon	Simca-Gordini	7	transmission	10
	Bira	Maserati	1	engine	15
	Pietsch	Maserati	0	engine	26

Fastest Lap: Fangio, 2m 00s. 117.4 mph/188.94 kph

World Championship 1950

1	Farina	30
2	Fangio	27
3	Fagioli	24 (28)
4	Rosier	13
5	Ascari	11
6	Parsons	8
7	Holland	6
8	Bira	5
9 =	Chiron, R Parnell, Rose, P Whitehead	4
13 =	Etancelin, Giraud-Cabantous, Green, Manzon, Serafini, Sommer	3
19	Bonetto	2
20 =	Bettenhausen, Chaboud, Chitwood	1

1951

Ferrari's newer, unsupercharged 4.5 litre cars offered a real challenge to the Alfas, which were nearing the end of their development potential. Although Alfas won four of the European races, with Fangio taking the championship, Ferrari's three victories spelled the end for the Alfas. BRM made their only championship appearance with the V16 at Silverstone, and the old, slow Talbots were increasingly outclassed. Fagioli remains the oldest driver to win a grand prix with his shared drive in France.

Swiss Grand Prix: Bremgarten, 27 May 1951

42 laps of 4.52 mile/7.28 km circuit

Place	Driver	Car	Laps	Time/reason for retiring	Grid
1	Fangio	Alfa Romeo	42	2h 07m 53.6s	1
2	Taruffi	Ferrari	42	2h 08m 48.9s	6
3	Farina	Alfa Romeo	42	2h 09m 13s	2
4	Sanesi	Alfa Romeo	41		4
5	de Graffenried	Alfa Romeo	40		5
6	Ascari	Ferrari	40		7
7	Chiron	Maserati	40		19
8	Moss	HWM	40		14
9	Rosier	Talbot	39		8
10	Etancelin	Talbot	39		12
11	Fischer	Ferrari	39		10
12	Schell	Maserati	38		17
13	P Whitehead	Ferrari	36	accident	9
14	Claes	Talbot	35		18
15	G Mairesse	Talbot	31		21
	Louveau	Talbot	30	accident	11
	Abeccassis	HWM	22	magneto	20
	Giraud-Cabantous	Talbot	13	ignition	15
	Villoresi	Ferrari	12	accident	3
	Gonzalez	Talbot	9	oil pump	13
	Hirt	Veritas	0	fuel pump	16

Fastest Lap: Fangio, 2m 51.1s. 95.18 mph/153.17 kph

Indianapolis 500: Indianapolis, 29 May 1951

200 laps of 2.5 mile/4.02 km circuit

Place	Driver	Car	Laps	Time/reason for retiring	Grid
1	Wallard	Belanger	200	3h 57m 38.05s	2
2	Nazaruk	Jim Robbins	200		7
3	McGrath/Ayulo	Hinkle	200		3
4	Linden	Leitenberger	200		31
5	Ball	Blakely	200		29
6	Banks	Blue Crown Spark Plug	200		17
7	Forberg	Auto Shippers	193		24
8	Carter	Mobilglas	180		4
9	Bettenhausen	Mobiloil	178	spun	9
10	Nalon	Novi	151	stalled	1
11	Force	Brown Motor Co.	142	engine	22
12	Hanks	Peter Schmidt	135	engine	12
13	Schindler	Chapman	129	engine	16
14	Rose	Pennzoil	126	accident	5
15	Faulkner	Agajanian Grant Piston Ring	123	crankshaft	14
16	Davies	Parks	110	rear axle	27
17	Agabashian	Granatelli Bardahl	109	clutch	11
18	Scarborough	McNamara	100	front axle	15
19	Mackey	Karl Hall	97	clutch	33
20	Stevenson	Bardahl	93	fire	19
21	Parsons	Wynn's Friction Proofing	87	magneto	8
22	Green	John Zink	80	engine	10
23	Ruttman	Agajanian Featherweight	78	crankshaft	6
24	Dinsmore	Brown Motor Co.	73	overheating	32
25	Miller	Novi	56	ignition	28
26	Walt Brown	Federal Engineering	55	magneto	13
27	Ward	Deck Manufacturing	34	oil line	25
28	Griffith	Morris	30	rear axle	18
29	Vukovich	Central Excavating	29	oil tank	20
30	Connor	Blue Crown Spark Plug	29	driveshaft	21
31	Hellings	Tuffanelli-Derrico	18	engine	23
32	J McDowell	W + J	15	fuel tank	26
33	Joe James	Bob Estes	8	driveshaft	30

Fastest Lap: Wallard, 1m 07.26s. 133.81 mph/215.345 kph

Belgian Grand Prix: Spa, 17 June 1951

36 laps of 8.77 mile/14.12 km circuit

Place	Driver	Car	Laps	Time/reason for retiring	Grid
1	Farina	Alfa Romeo	36	2h 45m 46.2s	2
2	Ascari	Ferrari	36	2h 48m 37.2s	4
3	Villoresi	Ferrari	36	2h 50m 08.1s	3
4	Rosier	Talbot	34		7
5	Giraud-Cabantous	Talbot	34		8
6	A Pilette	Talbot	33		12
7	Claes	Talbot	33		11
8	Levegh	Talbot	32		13
9	Fangio	Alfa Romeo	32		1
	Chiron	Maserati	27	piston	9
	Sanesi	Alfa Romeo	11	radiator	6
	Taruffi	Ferrari	8	rear axle	5
	Etancelin	Talbot	0	transmission	10

Fastest Lap: Fangio, 4m 22.1s. 120.5 mph/193.9 kph

French Grand Prix: Reims, 1 July 1951

77 laps of 4.86 mile/7.82 km circuit

Place	Driver	Car	Laps	Time/reason for retiring	Grid
1	Fagioli/Fangio	Alfa Romeo	77	3h 22m 11.0s	7
2	Gonzalez/Ascari	Ferrari	77	3h 23m 09.2s	6
3	Villoresi	Ferrari	74		4
4	R Parnell	Ferrari	73		9
5	Farina	Alfa Romeo	73		2
6	Chiron	Talbot	71		8
7	Giraud-Cabantous	Talbot	71		11
8	Chaboud	Talbot	69		14
9	G Mairesse	Talbot	66		19
10	Sanesi	Alfa Romeo	58		5
11	Fangio/Fagioli	Alfa Romeo	55		1
	Claes	Talbot	53	accident	12
	Rosier	Talbot	42	rear axle	13
	Etancelin	Talbot	36	inlet manifold	10
	Gordini	Simca-Gordini	26	valve gear	17
	Schell	Maserati	23	overheating	22
	Trintignant	Simca-Gordini	10	valves	18
	Ascari	Ferrari	9	gearbox	3
	Simon	Simca-Gordini	6	engine	21
	Manzon	Simca-Gordini	2	engine	23
	Marimon	Maserati-Milan	1	piston	15
	de Graffenried	Maserati	0	transmission	16
	P Whitehead	Ferrari	0	gasket	20

Fastest Lap: Fangio, 2m 27.8s. 118.3 mph/190.4 kph

British Grand Prix: Silverstone, 14 July 1951

90 laps of 2.89 mile/4.65 km circuit

Place	Driver	Car	Laps	Time/reason for retiring	Grid
1	Gonzalez	Ferrari	90	2h 42m 18.2s	1
2	Fangio	Alfa Romeo	90	2h 43m 09.2s	2
3	Villoresi	Ferrari	88		5
4	Bonetto	Alfa Romeo	87		7
5	R Parnell	BRM	85		20
6	Sanesi	Alfa Romeo	84		6
7	P Walker	BRM	84		19
8	Shawe-Taylor	ERA	84		12
9	P Whitehead	Ferrari	83		8
10	Rosier	Talbot	83		9
11	Gerard	ERA	82		10
12	Hamilton	Talbot	81		11
13	Claes	Talbot	80		14
14	Farina	Alfa Romeo	75	fire	3
15	Kelly	Alta	75		18
	Ascari	Ferrari	55	gearbox	4
	Fotheringham-Parker	Maserati	45	oil pipe	16
	Murray	Maserati	44	valve spring	15
	Chiron	Talbot	40	brakes	13
	John James	Maserati	22	radiator	17

Fastest Lap: Farina, 1m 44.0s. 99.9 mph/160.9 kph

German Grand Prix: Nürburgring, 29 July 1951

20 laps of 14.17 mile/22.81 km circuit

Place	Driver	Car	Laps	Time/reason for retiring	Grid
1	Ascari	Ferrari	20	3h 23m 03.3s	1
2	Fangio	Alfa Romeo	20	3h 23m 33.8s	3
3	Gonzalez	Ferrari	20	3h 27m 42.3s	2
4	Villoresi	Ferrari	20	3h 28m 53.5s	5
5	Taruffi	Ferrari	20	3h 30m 52.4s	6
6	Fischer	Ferrari	19		8
7	Manzon	Simca-Gordini	19		9
8	Rosier	Talbot	19		15
9	Levegh	Talbot	18		19
10	Swaters	Talbot	18		22
11	Giraud-Cabantous	Talbot	17	accident	11
12	Claes	Talbot	17		18
	Trintignant	Simca-Gordini	12	engine	14
	Bonetto	Alfa Romeo	11	magneto	10
	Hamilton	Talbot	11	oil pressure	20

German Grand Prix (cont)

Place	Driver	Car	Laps	Time/reason for retiring	Grid
	Simon	Simca-Gordini	11	engine	12
	Pietsch	Alfa Romeo	11	accident	7
	Farina	Alfa Romeo	7	overheating	4
	Etancelin	Talbot	3	gearbox	21
	Branca	Maserati	3	engine	17
	Chiron	Talbot	2	engine	13
	de Graffenried	Maserati	1	engine	16

Fastest Lap: Fangio, 9m 55.8s. 85.7 mph/137.9 kph

Italian Grand Prix: Monza, 16 September 1951

80 laps of 3.91 mile/6.3 km circuit

Place	Driver	Car	Laps	Time/reason for retiring	Grid
1	Ascari	Ferrari	80	2h 42m 39.3s	3
2	Gonzalez	Ferrari	80	2h 43m 23.9s	4
3	Bonetto/Farina	Alfa Romeo	79		7
4	Villoresi	Ferrari	79		5
5	Taruffi	Ferrari	78		6
6	Simon	Simca-Gordini	74		9
7	Rosier	Talbot	73		13
8	Giraud-Cabantous	Talbot	72		12
9	Rol	OSCA	67		15
	Fangio	Alfa Romeo	38	piston	1
	Manzon	Simca-Gordini	29	engine	11
	Trintignant	Simca-Gordini	29	piston	10
	Chiron	Talbot	22	ignition	14
	Levegh	Talbot	9	engine	17
	Swaters	Talbot	7	overheating	19
	Farina	Alfa Romeo	6	lubrication	2
	Claes	Talbot	4	scavenge pump	18
	de Graffenried	Alfa Romeo	1	supercharger	8
	P Whitehead	Ferrari	1	piston	16

Fastest Lap: Farina, 1m 56.5s. 120.97 mph/194.68 kph

Spanish Grand Prix: Pedrables, 28 October 1951

70 laps of 3.93 mile/6.32 km circuit

Place	Driver	Car	Laps	Time/reason for retiring	Grid
1	Fangio	Alfa Romeo	70	2h 46m 54.10s	2
2	Gonzalez	Ferrari	70	2h 47m 48.38s	3
3	Farina	Alfa Romeo	70	2h 48m 39.64s	4

Spanish Grand Prix (cont)

Place	Driver	Car	Laps	Time/reason for retiring	Grid
4	Ascari	Ferrari	68		1
5	Bonetto	Alfa Romeo	68		8
6	de Graffenried	Alfa Romeo	66		6
7	Rosier	Talbot	64		19
8	Etancelin	Talbot	63		13
9	Manzon	Simca-Gordini	63		9
10	Godia	Maserati	60		17
	Villoresi	Ferrari	47	ignition	5
	Simon	Simca-Gordini	47	engine	10
	Claes	Talbot	36	accident	15
	Taruffi	Ferrari	29	wheel	7
	Trintignant	Simca-Gordini	24	engine	11
	Grignard	Talbot	22	engine	17
	Giraud-Cabantous	Talbot	6	accident	14
	Chiron	Talbot	3	rocker	12
	Bira	OSCA	0	engine	18

Fastest Lap: Fangio, 2m 16.93s. 103.2 mph/166.1 kph

World Championship 1951

1	Fangio	31 (37)
2	Ascari	25 (28)
3	Gonzalez	24 (27)
4	Farina	19 (22)
5	Villoresi	15 (18)
6	Taruffi	10
7	Wallard	9
8	Bonetto	7
9	Nazaruk	6
10	R Parnell	5
11	Fagioli	4
12 =	Linden, Sanesi, Rosier	3
15 =	Ayulo, Ball, Giraud-Cabantous, de Graffenried, McGrath	2

1952

Alfa Romeo, unable to fund a new car, withdrew from racing, leaving Ferrari as the only serious Formula 1 contender. This led organizers to run their races for Formula 2, for 2 litre unsupercharged engines, which meant larger fields and a greater variety of cars, even if the victories all went to Ferrari. Ascari won the six grand prix he entered, missing the Swiss because he was at Indianapolis qualifying. Maserati and Gordini offered little challenge, but Mike Hawthorn's drives in his Cooper would earn him a works Ferrari drive in 1953. Fangio, badly injured in an early season crash, took no part in the championship. Ruttman remains the youngest driver to win a race counting for the championship.

Swiss Grand Prix: Bremgarten, 18 May 1952

62 laps of 4.52 mile/7.28 km circuit

Place	Driver	Car	Laps	Time/reason for retiring	Grid
1	Taruffi	Ferrari	62	3h 01m 46.1s	2
2	Fischer	Ferrari	62	3h 04m 23.3s	5
3	Behra	Gordini	61		7
4	Wharton	Frazer Nash	60		13
5	A Brown	Cooper-Bristol	59		15
6	de Graffenried	Maserati-Platé	58		8
7	Hirt	Ferrari	56		19
8	Brandon	Cooper-Bristol	55		17
	Bira	Simca-Gordini	51	engine	11
	Simon/Farina	Ferrari	50	magneto	4
	Schell	Maserati-Platé	30	engine	18
	Moss	HWM	23	withdrawn	9
	Macklin	HWM	23	withdrawn	12
	Manzon	Gordini	19	cooling damper	3
	Farina	Ferrari	16	magneto	1
	Collins	HWM	12	driveshaft, accident	6
	Abeccassis	HWM	13	driveshaft, accident	10
	Ulmen	Veritas	3	fuel tank	16

Swiss Grand Prix (cont)

Place	Driver	Car	Laps	Time/reason for retiring	Grid
	H Stuck	AFM	3	piston	14
	Rosier	Ferrari	2	accident	20
	de Terra	Simca-Gordini	0	magneto	21

Fastest Lap: Taruffi, 2m 49.1s. 96.3 mph/154.9 kph

Indianapolis 500: Indianapolis, 30 May 1952

200 laps of 2.5 mile/4.02 km circuit

Place	Driver	Car	Laps	Time/reason for retiring	Grid
1	Ruttman	Agajanian	200	3h 52m 41.88s	7
2	J Rathmann	Grancor Wynn's	200		10
3	Hanks	Bardahl	200		5
4	Carter	Belanger	200		6
5	Cross	Bowes Seal Fast	200		20
6	Bryan	Peter Schmidt	200		21
7	Reece	John Zink	200		23
8	Connor	Federal Engineering	200		14
9	Griffith	Tom Sararoff	200		9
10	Parsons	Jim Robbins	200		31
11	McGrath	Hinkle	200		3
12	Rigsby	Bob Estes	200		26
13	Joe James	Bardahl	200		16
14	Schindler	Chapman	200		15
15	Fonder	Leitenberger	197		13
16	E Johnson	Central Excavating	193		24
17	Vukovich	Fuel Injection	191	steering	8
18	Stevenson	Springfield Weld	187		11
19	Banks	Blue Crown Spark Plug	184		12
20	Ayulo	Coast Grain Co.	184		28
21	J McDowell	McDowell	182		33
22	Webb	Granatelli's Racing	162	oil pressure	29
23	Ward	Federal Engineering	130	oil pressure	22
24	Bettenhausen	Blue Crown Spark Plug	93	oil pressure	30
25	Nalon	Novi Pure Oil	84	supercharger	4
26	Sweikert	McNamara	77	differential	32
27	Agabashian	Cummins Diesel	71	supercharger	1
28	Hartley	Mel-Rae	65	exhaust	18
29	Scott	Morris	49	driveshaft	25
30	Miller	Novi Pure Oil	41	supercharger	27
31	Ascari	Ferrari	40	wheel	19
32	Ball	Ansted Rotary	34	gear case	17
33	Linden	Miracle Power	20	oil pump	2

Fastest Lap: Vukovich, 1m 06.6s. 135.14 mph/ 217.48 kph

Belgian Grand Prix: Spa, 22 June 1952

36 laps of 8.77 mile/14.12 km circuit

Place	Driver	Car	Laps	Time/reason for retiring	Grid
1	Ascari	Ferrari	36	3h 03m 46.8s	1
2	Farina	Ferrari	36	3h 05m 41.5s	2
3	Manzon	Gordini	36	3h 08m 14.7s	4
4	Hawthorn	Cooper-Bristol	35		6
5	Frere	HWM	34		8
6	A Brown	Cooper-Bristol	34		9
7	de Tornaco	Ferrari	33		13
8	Claes	Simca-Gordini	33		19
9	Brandon	Cooper-Bristol	33		12
10	Bira	Simca-Gordini	32		18
11	Macklin	HWM	32		14
12	Laurent	HWM	32		20
13	Legat	Veritas	31		21
14	O'Brien	Simca-Gordini	30		22
15	Gaze	HWM	30		16
	Montgomerie-Charrington	Aston-Butterworth	16	misfiring	15
	Behra	Gordini	13	accident	5
	Taruffi	Ferrari	13	accident	3
	Wharton	Frazer Nash	10	accident	7
	Rosier	Ferrari	5	transmission	17
	Collins	HWM	2	drive shaft	11
	Moss	ERA	0	gudgeon pin	10

Fastest Lap: Ascari, 4m 54s. 107.4 mph/172.9 kph

French Grand Prix: Rouen, 6 July 1952

3 hours on 3.17 mile/5.1 km circuit

Place	Driver	Car	Laps	Time/reason for retiring	Grid
1	Ascari	Ferrari	76	3 hours	1
2	Farina	Ferrari	76		2
3	Taruffi	Ferrari	75		3
4	Manzon	Gordini	74		5
5	Trintignant	Gordini	72		6
6	Collins	HWM	70		8
7	Behra	Gordini	70		4
8	Etancelin	Maserati	70		18
9	Macklin	HWM	70		14
10	Giraud-Cabantous	HWM	68		10
11	Fischer/Hirt	Ferrari	66		17
12	Comotti	Ferrari	63		16
	Bira	Gordini	56	rear axle	7
	Hawthorn	Cooper-Bristol	50	ignition	15

French Grand Prix (cont)

Place	Driver	Car	Laps	Time/reason for retiring	Grid
	de Graffenried/ Schell	Maserati-Platé	33	brakes	12
	P Whitehead	Alta	25	clutch	13
	Rosier	Ferrari	16	engine	9
	Claes	Simca-Gordini	14	con rod	20
	Schell	Maserati-Platé	6	gearbox	11
	Carini	Ferrari	1	head gasket	19

Fastest Lap: Ascari, 2m 17.3s. 83.1 mph/133.7 kph

British Grand Prix: Silverstone, 19 July 1952

85 laps of 2.93 mile/4.71 km circuit

Place	Driver	Car	Laps	Time/reason for retiring	Grid
1	Ascari	Ferrari	85	2h 44m 11s	2
2	Taruffi	Ferrari	84		3
3	Hawthorn	Cooper-Bristol	83		7
4	Poore	Connaught	83		8
5	Thompson	Connaught	82		9
6	Farina	Ferrari	82		1
7	R Parnell	Cooper-Bristol	82		6
8	Salvadori	Ferrari	82		19
9	Downing	Connaught	82		5
10	P Whitehead	Ferrari	81		20
11	Bira	Gordini	81		10
12	G Whitehead	Alta	80		12
13	Fischer	Ferrari	80		15
14	Claes	Simca-Gordini	79		23
15	Macklin	HWM	79		29
16	McAlpine	Connaught	79		17
17	Schell	Maserati-Platé	78		31
18	Bianco	Maserati	77		28
19	de Graffenried	Maserati-Platé	76		30
20	Brandon	Cooper-Bristol	76		18
21	Crook	Frazer Nash	75		25
22	Collins	HWM	72	misfiring	14
23	A Brown	Cooper-Bristol	69		13
	Hamilton	HWM	43	engine	11
	Moss	ERA	35	cylinder head	16
	Trintignant	Gordini	21	gearbox	21
	Gaze	HWM	19	head gasket	26
	Murray	Cooper-Bristol	13	spark plugs	22
	Manzon	Gordini	8	clutch	4
	Hirt	Ferrari	2	brakes	24
	Cantoni	Maserati	0	brakes	27

Fastest Lap: Ascari, 1m 52s. 94.08 mph/151.41 kph

German Grand Prix: Nürburgring, 3 August 1952

18 laps of 14.17 mile/ 22.81 km circuit

Place	Driver	Car	Laps	Time/reason for retiring	Grid
1	Ascari	Ferrari	18	3h 06m 13.3s	1
2	Farina	Ferrari	18	3h 06m 27.4s	2
3	Fischer	Ferrari	18	3h 13m 23.4s	6
4	Taruffi	Ferrari	17		5
5	Behra	Gordini	17		11
6	Laurent	Ferrari	16		17
7	Riess	Veritas	16		12
8	Ulmen	Veritas	16		15
9	Niedermayr	AFM	15		22
10	Claes	HWM	15		30
11	Klenk	Veritas	14		8
12	Klodwig	BMW	14		28
	Manzon	Gordini	8	lost wheel	4
	Heeks	AFM	6		9
	Gaze	HWM	5	gearbox	14
	Balsa	BMW	4		25
	Brudes	Veritas	4	engine	19
	Nacke	BMW	4	spark plugs	29
	Cantoni	Maserati	3	rear axle	26
	Krause	BMW	2		23
	Schoeller	Ferrari	2	shock absorber	24
	Aston	Aston-Butterworth	1	oil pressure	21
	Carini	Ferrari	0	brakes	27
	Pietsch	Veritas	0	gearbox	7
	Helfrich	Veritas	0		18
	Frere	HWM	0	de Dion tube	13
	Peters	Veritas	0		20
	Trintignant	Gordini	0	gearbox	3
	Bianco	Maserati	0		16
	Bonetto	Maserati	0	disqualified	10

Fastest Lap: Ascari, 10m 05.1s. 84.3 mph/135.7 kph

Dutch Grand Prix: Zandvoort, 17 August 1952

90 laps of 2.61 mile/4.19 km circuit

Place	Driver	Car	Laps	Time/reason for retiring	Grid
1	Ascari	Ferrari	90	2h 53m 28.5s	1
2	Farina	Ferrari	90	2h 54m 08.6s	2
3	Villoresi	Ferrari	90	2h 55m 02.9s	4
4	Hawthorn	Cooper-Bristol	88		3
5	Manzon	Gordini	87		8
6	Trintignant	Gordini	87		5
7	Hamilton	HWM	85		10

Dutch Grand Prix (cont)

Place	Driver	Car	Laps	Time/reason for retiring	Grid
8	Macklin	HWM	84		9
9	Landi/Flinterman	Maserati	83		16
10	Wharton	Frazer Nash	76	rear axle	7
11	Moss	ERA	72	engine	18
12	Van der Lof	HWM	70		14
	Downing	Connaught	26	oil pressure	13
	de Tornaco	Ferrari	18	valve	17
	Frere	Simca-Gordini	14	gearbox	11
	Behra	Gordini	9	carburettor	6
	Flinterman	Maserati	6	differential	15
	Bianco	Maserati	3	rear axle	12

Fastest Lap: Ascari, 1m 49.8s. 85.4 mph/137.5 kph

Italian Grand Prix: Monza, 7 September 1952

80 laps of 3.91 mile/6.3 km circuit

Place	Driver	Car	Laps	Time/reason for retiring	Grid
1	Ascari	Ferrari	80	2h 50m 45.6s	1
2	Gonzalez	Maserati	80	2h 51m 47.4s	5
3	Villoresi	Ferrari	80	2h 52m 49.8s	2
4	Farina	Ferrari	80	2h 52m 57.0s	3
5	Bonetto	Maserati	79		13
6	Simon	Ferrari	79		8
7	Taruffi	Ferrari	77		6
8	Landi	Maserati	76		18
9	Wharton	Cooper-Bristol	76		15
10	Rosier	Ferrari	75		17
11	Cantoni	Maserati	75		23
12	Poore	Connaught	74		19
13	Brandon	Cooper-Bristol	73		20
14	Manzon	Gordini	71		7
15	A Brown	Cooper-Bristol	68		21
16	Moss	Connaught	60	push rod	9
17	Bianco	Maserati	46	mechanical	24
18	Behra	Gordini	42	valve	11
19	Hawthorn	Cooper-Bristol	38		12
	Rol	Maserati	23	engine	16
	Trintignant	Gordini	4	valve gear	4
	McAlpine	Connaught	3	rear suspension	22
	Fischer	Ferrari	2	engine	14
	Bayol	OSCA	0	gearbox	10

Fastest Lap: Ascari/Gonzalez, 2m 06.1s. 111.76 mph/179.86 kph

World Championship 1952

1	Ascari	36 (53.5)
2	Farina	24 (27)
3	Taruffi	22
4=	Fischer, Hawthorn	10
6	Manzon	9
7=	Ruttman, Villoresi	8
9	Gonzalez	6.5
10=	Behra, J Rathmann	6
12	Hanks	4
13=	Carter, Poore, Wharton	3
16=	Bonetto, A Brown, Cross, Frere, Thompson, Trintignant	2
21	Vukovich	1

1953

Ferrari again dominated the championship, taking seven of the eight grand prix, although Fangio's Maserati challenge took him to second place in the championship and a win at Monza. Ascari stretched his unbeaten run to nine grand prix before Hawthorn broke the sequence at Reims. Farina is the oldest driver to win a race driving by himself.

Argentine Grand Prix: Buenos Aires, 18 January 1953

3 hours on 2.43 mile/3.91 km circuit

Place	Driver	Car	Laps	Time/reason for retiring	Grid
1	Ascari	Ferrari	97	3h 01m 04.6s	1
2	Villoresi	Ferrari	96		3
3	Gonzalez	Maserati	96		5
4	Hawthorn	Ferrari	96		6
5	Galvez	Maserati	96		9
6	Behra	Gordini	94		11
7	Trintignant/Schell	Gordini	91		7
8	J Barber	Cooper-Bristol	90		16
9	A Brown	Cooper-Bristol	87		12
	Manzon	Gordini	67	lost wheel	8
	Fangio	Maserati	35	prop shaft	2
	Bonetto	Maserati	32	transmission	15
	Farina	Ferrari	31	accident	4
	Menditeguy	Gordini	24	gearbox	10
	Birger	Simca-Gordini	22	crown wheel and pinion	14
	Cruz	Cooper-Bristol	20	lost wheel	13

Fastest Lap: Ascari, 1m 48.4s. 80.73 mph/129.92 kph

Indianapolis 500: Indianapolis, 30 May 1953

200 laps of 2.5 mile/4.02 km circuit

Place	Driver	Car	Laps	Time/reason for retiring	Grid
1	Vukovich	Fuel Injection	200	3 h 53m 01.7s	1
2	Cross	Springfield Weld	200		12
3	Hanks/Carter	Bardahl	200		9
4	Agabashian/ P Russo	Grancor-Elgin	200		2
5	McGrath	Hinkle	200		3
6	Daywalt	Sumar	200		21
7	J Rathmann/ E Johnson	Travelon Trailer	200		25
8	McCoy	Chapman	200		20
9	Bettenhausen/ Stevenson/Hartley	Agajanian	196	accident	6
10	Davies	Pat Clancy	193		32
11	Nalon	Novi Governor	191	accident	26
12	Scarborough/Scott	McNamara	190		19
13	Ayulo	Peter Schmidt	184	engine	4
14	Bryan	Blakeley Oil	183		31
15	Holland/ J Rathmann	Crawford	177	magneto	28
16	Ward/Linden/ Dinsmore	M A Walker	177	rear axle	10
17	Faulkner/Mantz	Auto Shippers	176		14
18	Teague	Hart Fullerton	169	oil leak	22
19	Webb/Thomson/ Holmes	Lubri-Loy	166	oil leak	18
20	Sweikert	Dean Van Lines	151	radius rod	29
21	Nazaruk	Kalamazoo	146	drive shaft	23
22	Flaherty	Peter Schmidt	115	accident	24
23	Hoyt/Stevenson/ Linden	John Zink	107	overheating	7
24	Carter	Miracle Power	94	ignition	27
25	P Russo	Federal Engineering	89	magneto	17
26	Parsons	Belond Exhaust	86	crankshaft	8
27	Freeland	Bob Estes	76	accident	15
28	Hartley	Federal Engineering	53	accident	13
29	Stevenson	Agajanian	42	fuel leak	16
30	Niday	Miracle Power	30	magneto	30
31	Scott	Belond Exhaust	14	oil leak	11
32	Thomson	Dr Sabourin	6	ignition	33
33	Linden	Cop-Sil-Loy Brake	3	accident	5

Fastest Lap: Vukovich, 1m 06.24s. 135.87 mph/218.66 kph
* Extremely hot weather led to many driver changes. Scarborough died of heat exhaustion.

1953

Dutch Grand Prix: Zandvoort, 7 June 1953

90 laps of 2.6 mile/4.19 km circuit

Place	Driver	Car	Laps	Time/reason for retiring	Grid
1	Ascari	Ferrari	90	2h 53m 35.8s	1
2	Farina	Ferrari	90	2h 53m 46.2s	3
3	Bonetto/ Gonzalez	Maserati	89		13
4	Hawthorn	Ferrari	89		6
5	de Graffenried	Maserati	88		7
6	Trintignant	Gordini	87		12
7	Rosier	Ferrari	86		8
8	Collins	HWM	84		16
9	Moss	Connaught	83		9
10	Villoresi	Ferrari	67	throttle	4
11	McAlpine	Connaught	64	engine	14
12	Schell	Gordini	60	transmission	10
13	Claes	Connaught	52		17
	Fangio	Maserati	36	rear axle	2
	Mieres	Gordini	28	transmission	19
	Gonzalez	Maserati	22	rear axle	5
	Wharton	Cooper-Bristol	18	suspension	18
	Salvadori	Connaught	13	valves	11
	Macklin	HWM	7	throttle	15

Fastest Lap: Villoresi, 1m 52.8s. 83.15 mph/133.82 kph

Belgian Grand Prix: Spa, 21 June 1953

36 laps of 8.77 mile/14.12 km circuit

Place	Driver	Car	Laps	Time/reason for retiring	Grid
1	Ascari	Ferrari	36	2h 48m 30.3s	2
2	Villoresi	Ferrari	36	2h 51m 18.5s	5
	Claes/Fangio	Maserati	36	accident – unclassified	10
3	Marimon	Maserati	35		6
4	de Graffenried	Maserati	35		9
5	Trintignant	Gordini	35		8
6	Hawthorn	Ferrari	35		7
7	Schell	Gordini	33		12
8	Rosier	Ferrari	33		13
9	Wacker	Gordini	32		15
10	Frere	HWM	30		11
11	A Pilette	Connaught	29		18
	Macklin	HWM	18	engine	17
	Farina	Ferrari	15	engine	4
	Fangio	Maserati	12	engine	1
	Gonzalez	Maserati	11	accelerator	3

Belgian Grand Prix (cont)

Place	Driver	Car	Laps	Time/reason for retiring	Grid
	Behra	Gordini	8	head gasket	14
	Collins	HWM	3	clutch	16
	Georges Berger	Simca-Gordini	2	engine	20
	Legat	Veritas	0	transmission	19

Fastest Lap: Gonzalez, 4m 34s. 115.3 mph/185.5 kph

French Grand Prix: Reims, 5 July 1953

60 laps of 5.19 mile/8.35 km circuit

Place	Driver	Car	Laps	Time/reason for retiring	Grid
1	Hawthorn	Ferrari	60	2h 44m 18.6s	7
2	Fangio	Maserati	60	2h 44m 19.6s	4
3	Gonzalez	Maserati	60	2h 44m 20.4s	5
4	Ascari	Ferrari	60	2h 44m 23.2s	1
5	Farina	Ferrari	60	2h 44m 26.2s	6
6	Villoresi	Ferrari	60	2h 45m 34.5s	3
7	de Graffenried	Maserati	58		9
8	Rosier	Ferrari	56		10
9	Marimon	Maserati	55		8
10	Behra	Gordini	55		22
11	Gerard	Cooper-Bristol	55		12
12	Claes	Connaught	53		21
13	Collins	HWM	52		17
14	Giraud-Cabantous	HWM	50		18
15	Chiron	OSCA	43		25
	Bonetto	Maserati	41	engine	2
	Moss	Cooper-Alta	37	clutch	13
	Bira	Connaught	28	differential	11
	Bayol	OSCA	17	engine	15
	Wharton	Cooper-Bristol	16	bearings	14
	Trintignant	Gordini	15	transmission	23
	Macklin	HWM	8	clutch	16
	Mieres	Gordini	3	rear axle	24
	Schell	Gordini	3	con rod	20
	Salvadori	Connaught	1	ignition	19

Fastest Lap: Fangio/Ascari, 2m 41.1s. 115.9 mph/186.5 kph

British Grand Prix: Silverstone, 18 July 1953

90 laps of 2.93 mile/4.71 km circuit

Place	Driver	Car	Laps	Time/reason for retiring	Grid
1	Ascari	Ferrari	90	2h 50m 00s	1
2	Fangio	Maserati	90	2h 51m 00s	4
3	Farina	Ferrari	88		5
4	Gonzalez	Maserati	88		2
5	Hawthorn	Ferrari	87		3
6	Bonetto	Maserati	82		16
7	Bira	Connaught	82		19
8	Wharton	Cooper-Bristol	80		11
9	Jimmy Stewart	Cooper-Bristol	79	accident	15
10	P Whitehead	Cooper-Alta	79		14
11	Rosier	Ferrari	78		24
	Rolt	Connaught	70	half shaft	10
	Villoresi	Ferrari	66	rear axle	6
	Marimon	Maserati	65	engine	7
	A Brown	Cooper-Bristol	61	fan belt	21
	Collins	HWM	56	accident	23
	Fairman	HWM	53	clutch	27
	Salvadori	Connaught	50	suspension	28
	de Graffenried	Maserati	33	clutch	26
	Macklin	HWM	30	clutch	12
	Behra	Gordini	29	fuel pump	22
	Ian Stewart	Connaught	25	engine	20
	Trintignant	Gordini	14	rear axle	8
	Hamilton	HWM	14	clutch	17
	Gerard	Cooper-Bristol	8	suspension	18
	Schell	Gordini	5	magneto	9
	Crook	Cooper-Bristol	0	fuel feed	25
	McAlpine	Connaught	0	split hose	13

Fastest Lap: Ascari/Gonzalez, 1m 50s. 95.79 mph/154.16 kph

German Grand Prix: Nürburgring, 2 August 1953

18 laps of 14.17 mile/22.81 km circuit

Place	Driver	Car	Laps	Time/reason for retiring	Grid
1	Farina	Ferrari	18	3h 02m 25s	3
2	Fangio	Maserati	18	3h 03m 29s	2
3	Hawthorn	Ferrari	18	3h 04m 08.6s	4
4	Bonetto	Maserati	18	3h 11m 13.6s	7
5	de Graffenried	Maserati	17		11
6	Moss	Cooper-Alta	17		12
7	Swaters	Ferrari	17		19
8	Ascari/Villoresi	Ferrari	17		1
9	Herrmann	Veritas	17		14

German Grand Prix (cont)

Place	Driver	Car	Laps	Time/reason for retiring	Grid
10	Rosier	Ferrari	17		22
11	Nuckey	Cooper-Bristol	16		20
12	Helfrich	Veritas	16		28
13	McAlpine	Connaught	16		16
14	Krause	BMW	16		26
15	Villoresi/Ascari	Ferrari	15	engine	6
16	A Brown	Cooper-Bristol	15	engine	17
17	Klodwig	BMW	15		32
18	Seidel	Veritas	14		29
	Marimon	Maserati	13	suspension	8
	Claes	Connaught	11		25
	Barth	EMW	11		24
	Karch	Veritas	10		34
	Heeks	Veritas	8		18
	Behra	Gordini	7	gearbox	9
	Schell	Gordini	6	head gasket	10
	Bira	Connaught	6	rocker	15
	Fitzau	AFM	3		21
	Adolff	Ferrari	2		27
	Bechem	AFM	2		30
	Bauer	Veritas	1		33
	Salvadori	Connaught	0	rocker	13
	Trintignant	Gordini	0	differential	5
	H Stuck	AFM	0		23
	Loof	Veritas	0	fuel pump	31

Fastest Lap: Ascari, 9m 56s. 85.612 mph/137.78 kph

Swiss Grand Prix: Bremgarten, 23 August 1953

65 laps of 4.52 mile/7.28 km circuit

Place	Driver	Car	Laps	Time/reason for retiring	Grid
1	Ascari	Ferrari	65	3h 01m 34.40s	2
2	Farina	Ferrari	65	3h 02m 47.33s	3
3	Hawthorn	Ferrari	65	3h 03m 10.36s	7
4	Fangio/Bonetto	Maserati	64		1
5	Lang	Maserati	62		11
6	Villoresi	Ferrari	62		6
7	Wharton	Cooper-Bristol	62		9
8	Landi	Maserati	54	gearbox	20
9	Sherrer	HWM	49		18
10	de Terra	Ferrari	48		19
	de Graffenried	Maserati	47	camshaft	8
	Marimon	Maserati	45	oil pipe	5
	Trintignant	Gordini	43	rear axle	4
	Behra	Gordini	36	oil pressure	12

Swiss Grand Prix (cont)

Place	Driver	Car	Laps	Time/reason for retiring	Grid
	Bonetto/Fangio	Maserati	28	valve	10
	Macklin	HWM	28	valve	15
	Hirt	Ferrari	16	oil	17
	Frere	HWM	1	con rod	16
	Rosier	Ferrari	0	accident	14
	Swaters	Ferrari	0	accident	13

Fastest Lap: Ascari, 2m 41.3s. 100.96 mph/162.48 kph

Italian Grand Prix: Monza, 13 September 1953

80 laps of 3.92 mile/6.3 km circuit

Place	Driver	Car	Laps	Time/reason for retiring	Grid
1	Fangio	Maserati	80	2h 49m 45.9s	2
2	Farina	Ferrari	80	2h 49m 47.3s	3
	Ascari	Ferrari	79	accident – unclassifed	1
3	Villoresi	Ferrari	79		5
4	Hawthorn	Ferrari	79		6
5	Trintignant	Gordini	79		8
6	Bonetto	Maserati	77	out of fuel	7
7	Mieres	Gordini	77		16
8	Mantovani/Musso	Maserati	76		12
9	Marimon	Maserati	75	accident	4
10	Maglioli	Ferrari	75		11
11	Schell	Gordini	75		15
12	Chiron	OSCA	72		25
13	Bira	Maserati	72		23
14	de Graffenried	Maserati	70	engine	9
15	A Brown	Cooper-Bristol	70		24
16	Moss	Cooper-Alta	70		10
17	H Stuck	AFM	67		29
18	Giraud-Cabantous	HWM	67		28
19	Rosier	Ferrari	65		17
20	Fairman	HWM	61		22
21	Wharton	Cooper-Bristol	57		19
22	McAlpine	Connaught	56		18
	Carini	Ferrari	40	mechanical	20
	Salvadori	Connaught	33	throttle	14
	Landi	Maserati	18	piston	21
	Bayol	OSCA	17	mechanical	13
	Fitch	HWM	14	engine	26
	Claes	Connaught	7	fuel pipe	30
	Macklin	HWM	5	engine	27

Fastest Lap: Fangio, 2m 04.5s. 113.2 mph/182.17 kph

World Championship 1953

1	Ascari	34.5 (46.5)
2	Fangio	27.5 (29)
3	Farina	26 (32)
4	Hawthorn	19 (27)
5	Villoresi	17
6	Gonzalez	13.5 (14.5)
7	Vukovich	9
8	de Graffenried	7
9	Bonetto	6.5
10	Cross	6
11 =	Marimon, Trintignant	4
13 =	Carter, Galvez, Hanks, Lang, McGrath	2
18 =	Agabashian, P Russo	1.5

1954

With the formula changing to 2.5 litres unsupercharged, Mercedes-Benz re-entered grand prix racing at the French Grand Prix with a streamlined single seater which Fangio took to a dominating win. Although the streamlined body was unsuitable for Silverstone, Mercedes produced a more conventional body and took three of the four remaining races. Fangio won the championship.

Argentine Grand Prix: Buenos Aires, 17 January 1954

3 hours on 2.43 mile/3.91 km circuit

Place	Driver	Car	Laps	Time/reason for retiring	Grid
1	Fangio	Maserati	87	3h 00m 55.8s	3
2	Farina	Ferrari	87	3h 02m 14.8s	1
3	Gonzalez	Ferrari	87	3h 02m 56.8s	2
4	Trintignant	Ferrari	86		5
5	Bayol	Gordini	85		13
6	Schell	Maserati	84		9
7	Bira	Maserati	83		8
8	de Graffenried	Maserati	83		11
9	Maglioli	Ferrari	82		10
	Hawthorn	Ferrari	–	disqualified, push start	4
	Behra	Gordini	–	disqualified, push start	15
	Marimon	Maserati	5	accident	6
	Mieres	Maserati	–	engine	7
	Daponte	Maserati	–	oil	16
	Loyer	Gordini	–	oil	14
	Rosier	Ferrari	2	accident	12

Fastest Lap: Gonzalez, 1m 48.2s. 80.8 mph/130 kph

Indianapolis 500: Indianapolis, 31 May 1954

200 laps of 2.5 mile/4.02 km circuit

Place	Driver	Car	Laps	Time/reason for retiring	Grid
1	Vukovich	Fuel Injection	200	3h 49m 17.27s	19
2	Bryan	Dean Van Lines	200		3
3	McGrath	Hinkle	200		1
4	Ruttman/Carter	Auto Shippers	200		11
5	Nazaruk	McNamara	200		14
6	Agabashian	Merz Engineering	200		24
7	Freeland	Bob Estes	200		6
8	P Russo/Hoyt	Ansted-Rotary	200		32
9	Crockett	Federal Engineering	200		25
10	Niday	Jim Robbins	200		13
11	Cross/Parsons/ Hanks/Linden/ Davies	Bardahl	200		27
12	Stevenson/Faulkner	Agajanian	199		5
13	Ayulo	Schmidt	197		22
14	Sweikert	Lutes Truck Parts	197		9
15	Carter/Teague/ Jackson/Bettenhausen	Auto Shippers	196		8
16	McCoy	Crawford	194		20
17	Reece	Malloy	194		7
18	Elisian/Scott	Chapman	193		31
19	Armi/Fonder	Martin Brothers	193		33
20	Hanks/Davies/ J Rathmann	Bardahl	191	spun	10
21	O'Connor	Hopkins	181	spun	12
22	Ward/E Johnson	Dr Sabourin	172	stalled	16
23	Hartley/Teague	John Zink	168	clutch	17
24	Thomson/Linden/ Daywalt	Chapman	165	stalled	4
25	Linden/Scott	Brown Motor Co.	165	torsion bar	23
26	Hoyt	Belanger	130	engine	30
27	Daywalt	Sumar	111	accident	2
28	J Rathmann/ Flaherty	Bardahl	110	accident	28
29	Bettenhausen	Mel Wiggers	105	bearing	21
30	Webb/Kladis	Advance Muffler	104	fuel pump	29
31	Duncan/Fonder	Ray Brady	101	brake cylinder	26
32	Parsons	Belond Exhaust	79	engine	15
33	Homeier	Jones & Maley	74	accident	18

Fastest Lap: McGrath, 1m 04.04s. 140.54 mph/226.17 kph

1954

Belgian Grand Prix: Spa, 20 June 1954

36 laps of 8.77 mile/14.12 km circuit

Place	Driver	Car	Laps	Time/reason for retiring	Grid
1	Fangio	Maserati	36	2h 44m 42.4s	1
2	Trintignant	Ferrari	36	2h 45m 06.6s	6
3	Moss	Maserati	35		9
4	Hawthorn/ Gonzalez	Ferrari	35		5
5	A Pilette	Gordini	35		8
6	Bira	Maserati	35		13
7	Mantovani	Maserati	34		11
	Frere	Gordini	13	engine	10
	Farina	Ferrari	13	ignition	3
	Behra	Gordini	11	suspension	7
	Marimon	Maserati	2	valve	4
	Swaters	Ferrari	0	engine	14
	Gonzalez	Ferrari	0	oil pipe	2
	Mieres	Maserati	0	fire	12

Fastest Lap: Fangio, 4m 25.5s. 118.97 mph/191.46 kph
* de Graffenried (Maserati) also participated as a camera car for a film.

French Grand Prix: Reims, 4 July 1954

61 laps of 5.16 mile/8.3 km circuit

Place	Driver	Car	Laps	Time/reason for retiring	Grid
1	Fangio	Mercedes	61	2h 42m 47.9s	1
2	Kling	Mercedes	61	2h 42m 48s	2
3	Manzon	Ferrari	60		12
4	Bira	Maserati	60		6
5	Villoresi	Maserati	58		14
6	Behra	Gordini	56		17
	Frere	Gordini	50	rear axle	19
	Trintignant	Ferrari	35	piston	9
	Rosier	Ferrari	27	engine	13
	Marimon	Maserati	27	gearbox	5
	Mieres	Maserati	24	piston	11
	Wharton	Maserati	19	transmission	16
	Schell	Maserati	19	fuel pump	21
	Herrmann	Mercedes	16	engine	7
	Salvadori	Maserati	14	transmission	10
	Gonzalez	Ferrari	12	engine	4
	Macklin	HWM	9	engine	15
	Georges Berger	Gordini	8	valve	20
	Hawthorn	Ferrari	8	engine	8
	Pollet	Gordini	8	engine	18
	Ascari	Maserati	0	engine	3

Fastest Lap: Herrmann, 2m 32.9s. 121.46 mph/195.5 kph

British Grand Prix: Silverstone, 17 July 1954

90 laps of 2.93 mile/4.71 km circuit

Place	Driver	Car	Laps	Time/reason for retiring	Grid
1	Gonzalez	Ferrari	90	2h 56m 14s	2
2	Hawthorn	Ferrari	90	2h 57m 24s	3
3	Marimon	Maserati	89		27
4	Fangio	Mercedes	89		1
5	Trintignant	Ferrari	87		8
6	Mieres	Maserati	87		30
7	Kling	Mercedes	87		6
8	Wharton	Maserati	86		9
9	A Pilette	Gordini	86		12
10	Gerard	Cooper-Bristol	85		18
11	Beauman	Connaught	84		17
12	Schell	Maserati	83		16
13	Marr	Connaught	82		22
14	Moss	Maserati	79	transmission	4
15	Thorne	Connaught	78		23
16	Whitehouse	Connaught	63	fuel system	19
17	Behra	Gordini	54	suspension	5
18	Salvadori	Maserati	53	gearbox	7
19	Bira/Flockhart	Maserati	44	accident	10
20	Gould	Cooper-Bristol	44		20
	Villoresi/Ascari	Maserati	40	con rod	26
	Riseley-Prichard	Connaught	40	accident	21
	R Parnell	Ferrari	25	water jacket	14
	Ascari	Maserati	20	valve	29
	Bucci	Gordini	17	accident	13
	Collins	Vanwall	16	head gasket	11
	Manzon	Ferrari	15	cylinder block	15
	P Whitehead	Cooper-Alta	4	oil pipe	24
	Rosier	Ferrari	2	engine	28
	Brandon	Cooper-Bristol	2		25

Fastest Lap: Ascari/Behra/Fangio/Gonzalez/Hawthorn/Marimon/Moss, 1m 50s. 95.79 mph/
154.16 kph

German Grand Prix: Nürburgring, 1 August 1954

22 laps of 14.17 mile/22.81 km circuit

Place	Driver	Car	Laps	Time/reason for retiring	Grid
1	Fangio	Mercedes	22	3h 45m 45.8s	1
2	Gonzalez/ Hawthorn	Ferrari	22	3h 47m 22.3s	5
3	Trintignant	Ferrari	22	3h 50m 54.4s	7
4	Kling	Mercedes	22	3h 51m 52.3s	20
5	Mantovani	Maserati	22	3h 54m 36.3s	13

German Grand Prix (cont)

Place	Driver	Car	Laps	Time/reason for retiring	Grid
6	Taruffi	Ferrari	21		11
7	Schell	Maserati	21		12
8	Rosier	Ferrari	21		16
9	Manzon	Ferrari	20		10
10	Behra	Gordini	20		8
	Bira	Maserati	18	steering	17
	Lang	Mercedes	10	spun/stalled	9
	Bucci	Gordini	8	lost wheel	14
	Helfrich	Klenk-Meteor	8	engine	19
	Herrmann	Mercedes	7	fuel pipe	4
	Frere	Gordini	4	lost wheel	6
	Hawthorn	Ferrari	3	rear axle	2
	Mieres	Maserati	2	fuel tank	15
	Moss	Maserati	1	big end	3
	A Pilette	Gordini	0	suspension	18

Fastest Lap: Kling, 9m 55.1s. 85.75 mph/137.99 kph
* Marimon (Maserati) killed in practice accident.

Swiss Grand Prix: Bremgarten, 22 August 1954

66 laps of 4.52 mile/7.28 km circuit

Place	Driver	Car	Laps	Time/reason for retiring	Grid
1	Fangio	Mercedes	66	3h 00m 34.5s	2
2	Gonzalez	Ferrari	66	3h 01m 32.3s	1
3	Herrmann	Mercedes	65		7
4	Mieres	Maserati	64		12
5	Mantovani	Maserati	64		9
6	Wharton	Maserati	64		8
7	Maglioli	Ferrari	61		11
8	Swaters	Ferrari	58		16
	Kling	Mercedes	38	fuel system	5
	Trintignant	Ferrari	32	engine	4
	Hawthorn	Ferrari	30	oil pump	6
	Schell	Maserati	22	oil pump	13
	Moss	Maserati	21	oil pump	3
	Wacker	Gordini	9	transmission	15
	Behra	Gordini	7	clutch	14
	Bucci	Gordini	0	fuel pump	10

Fastest Lap: Fangio, 2m 39.7s. 101.97 mph/164.11 kph

Italian Grand Prix: Monza, 5 September 1954

80 laps of 3.92 mile/6.3 km circuit

Place	Driver	Car	Laps	Time/reason for retiring	Grid
1	Fangio	Mercedes	80	2h 47m 47.9s	1
2	Hawthorn	Ferrari	79		7
3	Maglioli/ Gonzalez	Ferrari	78		13
4	Herrmann	Mercedes	77		8
5	Trintignant	Ferrari	75		11
6	Wacker	Gordini	75		18
7	Collins	Vanwall	75		16
8	Rosier	Maserati	74		20
9	Mantovani	Maserati	74		9
10	Moss	Maserati	71		3
11	Daponte	Maserati	70		19
	Ascari	Ferrari	48	valves	2
	Villoresi	Maserati	42	clutch	6
	Kling	Mercedes	36	accident	4
	Mieres	Maserati	34	suspension	10
	Musso	Maserati	32	transmission	14
	Manzon	Ferrari	16	engine	15
	Gonzalez	Ferrari	16	gearbox	5
	Bucci	Gordini	13	transmission	17
	Behra	Gordini	2	engine	12

Fastest Lap: Gonzalez, 2m 00.8s. 116.66 mph/187.75 kph

Spanish Grand Prix: Pedralbes, 24 October 1954

80 laps of 3.925 mile/6.32 km circuit

Place	Driver	Car	Laps	Time/reason for retiring	Grid
1	Hawthorn	Ferrari	80	3h 13m 52.1s	3
2	Musso	Maserati	80	3h 15m 05.3s	7
3	Fangio	Mercedes	79		2
4	Mieres	Maserati	79		11
5	Kling	Mercedes	79		12
6	Godia	Maserati	76		13
7	Rosier	Maserati	74		20
8	Wharton	Maserati	74		14
9	Bira	Maserati	68		15
	Mantovani	Maserati	58	accident	10
	de Graffenried/ Volonterio	Maserati	57	engine	21
	Herrmann	Mercedes	50	fuel injection	9
	Trintignant	Ferrari	47	gearbox	8
	Pollet	Gordini	37	mechanical	16

Spanish Grand Prix (cont)

Place	Driver	Car	Laps	Time/reason for retiring	Grid
	Schell	Maserati	28	rear axle	4
	Moss	Maserati	19	oil pump	6
	Behra	Gordini	16	mechanical	18
	Swaters	Ferrari	15	engine	19
	Ascari	Lancia	9	clutch	1
	Villoresi	Lancia	1	brakes	5
	Manzon	Ferrari	1	engine	17

Fastest Lap: Ascari, 2m 20.4s. 100.63 mph/161.95 kph

World Championship 1954

1	Fangio	42 (57.14)
2	Gonzalez	25.14 (26.64)
3	Hawthorn	24.64
4	Trintignant	17
5	Kling	12
6 =	Herrmann, Vukovich	8
8 =	Bryan, Farina, Mieres, Musso	6
12	McGrath	5
13 =	Marimon, Moss	4.14
15 =	Manzon, Mantovani	4
17	Bira	3
18 =	Bayol, Maglioli, Nazaruk, Pilette, Villoresi	2
23 =	Carter, Ruttman	1.5
25	Ascari	1.14
26	Behra	0.14

* Includes the point for fastest lap at British Grand Prix shared between Fangio, Gonzalez, Hawthorn, Marimon, Moss, Ascari and Behra.

1955

Mercedes again dominated the season, with Fangio taking four races, and his new team mate Moss the British Grand Prix. Ferrari won at Monaco after the Mercedes broke down and Ascari crashed into the harbour. Although he was apparently unscathed, he crashed fatally at Monza four days later. The disaster at the Le Mans Twenty Four Hour race on 11 June which killed Pierre Levegh and over 80 spectators led to the cancellations of four grand prix. Louis Chiron's start at Monaco made him the oldest driver to start a grand prix; he failed to qualify at Monaco as late as 1958.

Argentine Grand Prix: Buenos Aires, 16 January 1955

96 laps of 2.43 mile/3.91 km circuit

Place	Driver	Car	Laps	Time/reason for retiring	Grid
1	Fangio	Mercedes	96	3h 00m 38.6s	2
2	Gonzalez/ Trintignant/Farina	Ferrari	96	3h 02m 08.2s	1
3	Farina/Maglioli/ Trintignant	Ferrari	94		5
4	Herrmann/Kling/ Moss	Mercedes	94		10
5	Mieres	Maserati	91		16
6	Schell/Behra	Maserati	88		7
7	Musso/Mantovani/ Schell	Maserati	83		18
	Bucci/Schell/ Menditeguy	Maserati	54	fuel starvation	20
	Mantovani/Musso/ Behra	Maserati	54	mechanical	19
	Iglesias	Gordini	38	transmission	17
	Trintignant	Ferrari	36	valve	14
	Castellotti/Villoresi	Lancia	35	accident	12
	Moss	Mercedes	29	fuel vaporization	8
	Uria	Maserati	22	fuel starvation	21
	Ascari	Lancia	21	accident	3
	Bayol	Gordini	7	transmission	15
	Villoresi	Lancia	1	fuel pipe	11

Argentine Grand Prix (cont)

Place	Driver	Car	Laps	Time/reason for retiring	Grid
	Behra	Maserati	1	accident	4
	Kling	Mercedes	1	accident	6
	Birger	Gordini	1	accident	9
	Menditeguy	Maserati	1	accident	13

Fastest Lap: Fangio, 1m 48.3s. 80.8 mph/130 kph

Monaco Grand Prix: Monte Carlo, 22 May 1955

100 laps of 1.95 mile/3.15 km circuit

Place	Driver	Car	Laps	Time/reason for retiring	Grid
1	Trintignant	Ferrari	100	2h 58m 09.7s	9
2	Castellotti	Lancia	100	2h 58m 30.0s	4
3	Behra/Perdisa	Maserati	99		5
4	Farina	Ferrari	99		14
5	Villoresi	Lancia	99		7
6	Chiron	Lancia	95		19
7	Pollet	Gordini	91		20
8	Perdisa/Behra	Maserati	86	spun, stalled	11
9	Taruffi/Frere	Ferrari	86		15
10	Moss	Mercedes	81		3
	Ascari	Lancia	80	accident	2
	Schell	Ferrari	67	engine	18
	Mieres	Maserati	64	rear axle	6
	Bayol	Gordini	63	rear axle	16
	Fangio	Mercedes	49	transmission	1
	Manzon	Gordini	38	gearbox	13
	Simon	Mercedes	24	valve	10
	Hawthorn	Vanwall	22	throttle linkage	12
	Rosier	Maserati	8	fuel tank	17
	Musso	Maserati	7	transmission	8

Fastest Lap: Fangio, 1m 42.4s. 68.7 mph/110.57 kph

Indianapolis 500: Indianapolis, 30 May 1955

200 laps of 2.5 mile/4.02 km circuit

Place	Driver	Car	Laps	Time/reason for retiring	Grid
1	Sweikert	John Zink	200	3h 53m 59.53s	14
2	Bettenhausen/ P Russo	Chapman	200		2
3	Davies	Bardahl	200		10

Indianapolis 500 (cont)

Place	Driver	Car	Laps	Time/reason for retiring	Grid
4	Thomson	Schmidt	200		33
5	Faulkner/Homeier	Merz Engineering	200		7
6	Linden	Massaglia	200		8
7	Herman	Martin Brothers	200		16
8	O'Connor	Ansted-Rotary	200		19
9	Daywalt	Sumar	200		17
10	Flaherty	Dunn Engineering	200		12
11	Carter	Agajanian	197		18
12	Weyant	Federal Engineering	196		25
13	E Johnson	McNamara	196		32
14	J Rathmann	Belond Miracle Power	191		20
15	Freeland	Bob Estes	178	transmission	21
16	Niday	D-A Lubricants	170	accident	9
17	Cross	Belanger	168	engine	24
18	Templeman	Central Excavating	142	transmission	31
19	Hanks	Jones & Maley	134	transmission	6
20	Andrews	McDaniel	120	fuel pump	28
21	Parsons	Trio Brass	119	magneto	27
22	E Russo	Dr Sabourin	112	ignition	13
23	R Crawford	Crawford	111	engine	23
24	Bryan	Dean Van Lines	90	fuel pump	11
25	Vukovich	Hopkins	56	fatal accident	5
26	McGrath	Hinkle	54	magneto	3
27	Keller	Sam Traylor	54	accident	22
28	Ward	Aristo Blue	53	accident	30
29	Boyd	Sumar	53	accident	26
30	Elisian	Pete Wales	53	stalled	29
31	Hoyt	Jim Robbins	40	oil leak	1
32	Agabashian	Federal Engineering	39	spun	4
33	Reece	Malloy	10	engine	15

Fastest Lap: Vukovich, 1m 03.67s. 141.4 mph/227.5 kph

Belgian Grand Prix: Spa, 5 June 1955

36 laps of 8.77 mile/14.12 km circuit

Place	Driver	Car	Laps	Time/reason for retiring	Grid
1	Fangio	Mercedes	36	2h 39m 29s	2
2	Moss	Mercedes	36	2h 39m 37.1s	3
3	Farina	Ferrari	36	2h 41m 09.5s	4
4	Frere	Ferrari	36	2h 42m 54.5s	8
5	Mieres/Behra	Maserati	35		13
6	Trintignant	Ferrari	35		10
7	Musso	Maserati	34		7
8	Perdisa	Maserati	33		11

Belgian Grand Prix (cont)

Place	Driver	Car	Laps	Time/reason for retiring	Grid
9	Rosier	Maserati	33		12
	Kling	Mercedes	21	oil pipe	6
	Castellotti	Lancia	16	gearbox	1
	Hawthorn	Vanwall	8	gearbox	9
	Behra	Maserati	3	accident	5

Fastest Lap: Fangio, 4m 20.6s. 121.2 mph/195.06 kph

Dutch Grand Prix: Zandvoort, 19 June 1955

100 laps of 2.61 mile/4.19 km circuit

Place	Driver	Car	Laps	Time/reason for retiring	Grid
1	Fangio	Mercedes	100	2h 54m 23.8s	1
2	Moss	Mercedes	100	2h 54m 24.1s	2
3	Musso	Maserati	100	2h 55m 20.9s	4
4	Mieres	Maserati	99		7
5	Castellotti	Ferrari	97		9
6	Behra	Maserati	97		6
7	Hawthorn	Ferrari	97		5
8	da Silva Ramos	Gordini	92		14
9	Rosier	Maserati	92		13
10	Pollet	Gordini	90		12
11	Claes	Ferrari	88		16
	Trintignant	Ferrari	64	gearbox	8
	Manzon	Gordini	43	transmission	11
	Gould	Maserati	23	accident	15
	Kling	Mercedes	21	spun	3
	P Walker	Maserati	2	wheel bearing	10

Fastest Lap: Mieres, 1m 40.9s. 92.96 mph/149.6 kph

British Grand Prix: Aintree, 16 July 1955

90 laps of 3 mile/4.83 km circuit

Place	Driver	Car	Laps	Time/reason for retiring	Grid
1	Moss	Mercedes	90	3h 07m 21.2s	1
2	Fangio	Mercedes	90	3h 07m 21.3s	2
3	Kling	Mercedes	90	3h 08m 33.0s	4
4	Taruffi	Mercedes	89		5
5	Musso	Maserati	89		9
6	Hawthorn/ Castellotti	Ferrari	87		12

British Grand Prix (cont)

Place	Driver	Car	Laps	Time/reason for retiring	Grid
7	Sparken	Gordini	81		22
8	Macklin	Maserati	79		16
9	Wharton/Schell	Vanwall	72		15
	Trintignant	Ferrari	59	overheating	13
	Mieres	Maserati	47	piston	6
	J Brabham	Cooper-Bristol	30	valve	24
	McAlpine	Connaught	30	oil pipe	17
	Collins	Maserati	29	clutch	23
	da Silva Ramos	Gordini	26	engine	18
	Gould	Maserati	21	brakes	21
	Salvadori	Maserati	19	gearbox	20
	Rolt/P Walker	Connaught	18	throttle	14
	Marr	Connaught	17	accident	19
	Castellotti	Ferrari	16	transmission	10
	Simon	Maserati	15	gearbox	8
	Schell	Vanwall	13	accelerator	7
	Behra	Maserati	9	oil pipe	3
	Manzon	Gordini	4	transmission	11

Fastest Lap: Moss, 2m 00.4s. 89.7 mph/144.36 kph

Italian Grand Prix: Monza, 1 September 1955

50 laps of 6.21 mile/10 km circuit

Place	Driver	Car	Laps	Time/reason for retiring	Grid
1	Fangio	Mercedes	50	2h 25m 04.4s	1
2	Taruffi	Mercedes	50	2h 25m 05.1s	7
3	Castellotti	Ferrari	50	2h 25m 50.6s	4
4	Behra	Maserati	50	2h 29m 01s	5
5	Menditeguy	Maserati	49		14
6	Maglioli	Ferrari	49		10
7	Mieres	Maserati	48		6
8	Trintignant	Ferrari	47		13
9	Fitch	Maserati	46		18
	Hawthorn	Ferrari	38	gearbox mounting	12
	Kling	Mercedes	32	gearbox	3
	Musso	Maserati	31	gearbox	8
	Gould	Maserati	31	sump	19
	Moss	Mercedes	27	engine	2
	Pollet	Gordini	26	engine	17
	da Silva Ramos	Gordini	23	fuel pump	16
	Collins	Maserati	22	suspension	9
	Schell	Vanwall	7	de Dion tube	11
	Lucas	Gordini	7	engine	20
	Wharton	Vanwall	0	fuel injection	15

Fastest Lap: Moss, 2m 46.9s. 134.03 mph/215.7 kph

World Championship 1955

1	Fangio	40 (41)
2	Moss	23
3	Castellotti	12
4	Trintignant	11.33
5	Farina	10.33
6	Taruffi	9
7	Sweikert	8
8	Mieres	7
9 =	Behra, Musso	6
11	Kling	5
12	Davies	4
13 =	Bettenhausen, Frere, P Russo, Thomson	3
17 =	Gonzalez, Menditeguy, Perdisa, Villoresi	2
21	Maglioli	1.33
22 =	Faulkner, Herrmann, Homeier, Vukovich	1

1956

Mercedes had withdrawn, so Fangio joined Ferrari who had been given the Lancias when they withdrew for financial reasons. The main challenge to Fangio came from Moss at Maserati, and from his team mate Collins, although the British Connaughts, Vanwalls and BRMs showed some signs of promise. Moss and Collins each won two races, but Fangio's shared victory with Musso in Argentina made the difference.

Argentine Grand Prix: Buenos Aires, 22 January 1956

98 laps of 2.43 mile/3.91 km circuit

Place	Driver	Car	Laps	Time/reason for retiring	Grid
1	Musso/Fangio	Lancia-Ferrari	98	3h 00m 03.7s	3
2	Behra	Maserati	98	3h 00m 28.1s	4
3	Hawthorn	Maserati	96		8
4	Landi/Gerini	Maserati	92		11
5	Gendebien	Lancia-Ferrari	91		10
6	Uria/O Gonzalez	Maserati	88		13
	Moss	Maserati	81	engine	7
	Collins	Lancia-Ferrari	58	accident	9
	Piotti	Maserati	57	accident	12
	Menditeguy	Maserati	42	half shaft	6
	Castellotti	Lancia-Ferrari	40	gearbox	2
	Gonzalez	Maserati	24	valve	5
	Fangio	Lancia-Ferrari	22	fuel pump	1

Fastest Lap: Fangio, 1m 45.3s. 83.1 mph/133.7 kph

Monaco Grand Prix: Monte Carlo, 13 May 1956

100 laps of 1.95 mile/3.15 km circuit

Place	Driver	Car	Laps	Time/reason for retiring	Grid
1	Moss	Maserati	100	3h 00m 32.9s	2
2	Collins/Fangio	Lancia-Ferrari	100	3h 00m 39.0s	9
3	Behra	Maserati	99		4

Monaco Grand Prix (cont)

Place	Driver	Car	Laps	Time/reason for retiring	Grid
4	Fangio/Castellotti	Lancia-Ferrari	94		1
5	da Silva Ramos	Gordini	93		12
	Manzon	Gordini	90	transmission – unclassified	11
6	Bayol/A Pilette	Gordini	88		10
7	Perdisa	Maserati	86		7
8	Gould	Maserati	85		14
	Rosier	Maserati	72	engine	13
	Castellotti	Lancia-Ferrari	14	clutch	3
	Trintignant	Vanwall	10	overheating	6
	Schell	Vanwall	1	accident	5
	Musso	Lancia-Ferrari	1	accident	8

Fastest Lap: Fangio, 1m 44.4s. 67.39 mph/108.45 kph

Indianapolis 500: Indianapolis, 30 May 1956

200 laps of 2.5 mile/4.02 km circuit

Place	Driver	Car	Laps	Time/reason for retiring	Grid
1	Flaherty	John Zink	200	3h 53m 28.84s	1
2	Hanks	Jones & Maley	200		13
3	Freeland	Bob Estes	200		26
4	Parsons	Agajanian	200		6
5	D Rathmann	McNamara	200		4
6	Sweikert	D-A Lubricant	200		10
7	Veith	Federal Engineering	200		23
8	Ward	Filter Queen	200		15
9	Reece	Massaglia	200		21
10	Griffith	Jim Robbins	199		30
11	Hartley	Central Excavating	196		22
12	Agabashian	Federal Engineering	196		7
13	Christie	Helse	196		25
14	Keller	Sam Traylor	195		28
15	E Johnson	Central Excavating	195		32
16	Garrett	Greenman-Casale	194		29
17	Dinsmore	Shannon	191		33
18	O'Connor	Ansted-Rotary	187		3
19	Bryan	Dean Van Lines	185		19
20	J Rathmann	Hopkins	175	engine	2
21	Tolan	Trio Brass Foundry	173	mechanical	31
22	Bettenhausen	Belanger	160	accident	5
23	Elisian/E Russo	Hoyt Machine	160	brakes	14
24	Daywalt	Sumar	134	accident	16
25	Turner	Travelon Trailer	131	mechanical	24
26	Andrews	Dunn Engineering	94	transmission	20
27	Linden	Chapman	90	oil leak	9
28	Herman	Bardahl	74	accident	27

Indianapolis 500 (cont)

Place	Driver	Car	Laps	Time/reason for retiring	Grid
29	R Crawford	Crawford	49	accident	17
30	Boyd	Bowes Seal Fast	35	oil leak	12
31	Ruttman	John Zink	22	spun	11
32	Thomson	Schmidt	22	spun	18
33	P Russo	Novi Vespa	21	accident	8

Fastest Lap: P Russo, 1m 02.32s. 144.42 mph/232.42 kph

Belgian Grand Prix: Spa, 3 June 1956

36 laps of 8.77 mile/14.12 km circuit

Place	Driver	Car	Laps	Time/reason for retiring	Grid
1	Collins	Lancia-Ferrari	36	2h 40m 00.3s	3
2	Frere	Lancia-Ferrari	36	2h 41m 51.6s	8
3	Perdisa/Moss	Maserati	36	2h 43m 16.9s	9
4	Schell	Vanwall	35		6
5	Villoresi	Maserati	34		11
6	A Pilette	Lancia-Ferrari	33		15
7	Behra	Maserati	33		4
8	Rosier	Maserati	33		10
	Fangio	Lancia-Ferrari	23	transmission	1
	Trintignant	Vanwall	10	engine	7
	Scotti	Connaught	10	oil pressure	12
	Moss	Maserati	9	lost wheel	2
	Castellotti	Lancia-Ferrari	9	transmission	5
	Gould	Maserati	2	gearbox	14
	Godia	Maserati	0	accident	13

Fastest Lap: Moss, 4m 14.7s. 124.01 mph/199.58 kph

French Grand Prix: Reims, 1 July 1956

61 laps of 5.16 mile/8.3 km circuit

Place	Driver	Car	Laps	Time/reason for retiring	Grid
1	Collins	Lancia-Ferrari	61	2h 34m 23.4s	3
2	Castellotti	Lancia-Ferrari	61	2h 34m 23.7s	2
3	Behra	Maserati	61	2h 35m 53.3s	6
4	Fangio	Lancia-Ferrari	61	2h 35m 58.5s	1
5	Perdisa/Moss	Maserati	59		12
6	Rosier	Maserati	58		11
7	Godia	Maserati	57		16
8	da Silva Ramos	Gordini	57		13

French Grand Prix (cont)

Place	Driver	Car	Laps	Time/reason for retiring	Grid
9	Manzon	Gordini	56		14
10	Hawthorn/Schell	Vanwall	56		5
11	A Pilette	Gordini	55		18
	Simon	Maserati	45	mechanical	19
	Taruffi	Maserati	38	mechanical	15
	Gendebien	Lancia-Ferrari	37	clutch	10
	Villoresi	Maserati	21	brakes	9
	de Portago	Lancia-Ferrari	19	gearbox	8
	Trintignant	Bugatti	17	throttle	17
	Moss	Maserati	11	gear lever	7
	Schell	Vanwall	5	engine	4

Fastest Lap: Fangio, 2m 25.8s. 127.37 mph/204.98 kph

British Grand Prix: Silverstone, 14 July 1956

101 laps of 2.93 mile/4.71 km circuit

Place	Driver	Car	Laps	Time/reason for retiring	Grid
1	Fangio	Lancia-Ferrari	101	2h 59m 47s	2
2	de Portago/Collins	Lancia-Ferrari	100		12
3	Behra	Maserati	99		13
4	Fairman	Connaught	98		21
5	Gould	Maserati	97		14
6	Villoresi	Maserati	96		19
7	Perdisa	Maserati	95		15
8	Godia	Maserati	94		25
9	Manzon	Gordini	94		18
10	Moss	Maserati	93	rear axle	1
11	Castellotti/ de Portago	Lancia-Ferrari	92		8
12	Gerard	Cooper-Bristol	88		22
	Schell	Vanwall	86	fuel pipe	5
	Titterington	Connaught	74	con rod	11
	da Silva Ramos	Gordini	71	rear axle	26
	Trintignant	Vanwall	69	fuel line	16
	Collins	Lancia-Ferrari	63	oil pressure	4
	Salvadori	Maserati	58	fuel system	7
	Brooks	BRM	39	throttle, accident	9
	Rosier	Maserati	23	magneto	27
	Hawthorn	BRM	23	universal joint	3
	Halford	Maserati	22	piston	20
	Maglioli	Maserati	21	gearbox	24
	Scott-Brown	Connaught	16	axle	10
	Emery	Emeryson	12	ignition	23

British Grand Prix (cont)

Place	Driver	Car	Laps	Time/reason for retiring	Grid
	J Brabham	Maserati	3	mechanical	28
	Flockhart	BRM	1	engine	17
	Gonzalez	Vanwall	0	drive-shaft	6

Fastest Lap: Moss, 1m 43.2s. 102.1 mph/164.32 kph

German Grand Prix: Nürburgring, 5 August 1956

22 laps of 14.17 mile/22.81 km circuit

Place	Driver	Car	Laps	Time/reason for retiring	Grid
1	Fangio	Lancia-Ferrari	22	3h 38m 43.7s	1
2	Moss	Maserati	22	3h 39m 30.1s	4
3	Behra	Maserati	22	3h 46m 22.0s	7
4	Godia	Maserati	20		15
	Halford	Maserati	20	disqualified: push start	10
5	Rosier	Maserati	19		13
6	Volonterio	Maserati	16		18
	Milhoux	Gordini	15	engine	19
	de Portago/ Collins	Lancia-Ferrari	14	accident	9
	Villoresi	Maserati	13	engine	20
	Schell	Maserati	12	overheating	11
	Musso/ Castellotti	Lancia-Ferrari	12	accident	5
	Collins	Lancia-Ferrari	8	fuel leak	2
	Castellotti	Lancia-Ferrari	5	magneto	3
	Maglioli	Maserati	3	steering	6
	Gould	Maserati	3	oil pressure	12
	Salvadori	Maserati	2	rear suspension	8
	Manzon	Gordini	0	suspension	14
	Scarlatti	Ferrari	0	mechanical	16
	Piotti	Maserati	0	engine	17

Fastest Lap: Fangio, 9m 41.6s. 87.73 mph/141.19 kph

Italian Grand Prix: Monza, 2 September 1956

50 laps of 6.21 mile/10 km circuit

Place	Driver	Car	Laps	Time/reason for retiring	Grid
1	Moss	Maserati	50	2h 23m 41.3s	6
2	Collins/Fangio	Lancia-Ferrari	50	2h 23m 47s	7
3	Flockhart	Connaught	49		23

Italian Grand Prix (cont)

Place	Driver	Car	Laps	Time/reason for retiring	Grid
4	Godia	Maserati	49		17
5	Fairman	Connaught	47		15
6	Piotti	Maserati	47		14
	Musso	Lancia-Ferrari	46	steering – unclassified	3
7	de Graffenried	Maserati	46		18
8	Fangio/Castellotti	Lancia-Ferrari	46		1
9	Simon	Gordini	45		24
10	Gerini	Maserati	42		16
11	Maglioli/Behra	Maserati	41	steering	12
12	Salvadori	Maserati	41		13
	Schell	Vanwall	31	transmission	10
	Behra	Maserati	22	magneto	5
	Halford	Maserati	15	engine	21
	Trintignant	Vanwall	12	rear suspension	11
	Taruffi	Vanwall	11	suspension	4
	Castellotti	Lancia-Ferrari	8	puncture	2
	Manzon	Gordini	6	gearbox	22
	Villoresi/Bonnier	Maserati	6	engine	8
	de Portago	Lancia-Ferrari	5	puncture	9
	Leston	Connaught	5	torsion bar	19
	da Silva Ramos	Gordini	2	engine	20

Fastest Lap: Moss, 2m 45.5s. 135.4 mph/217.9 kph

World Championship 1956

1	Fangio	30 (33)
2	Moss	27 (28)
3	Collins	25
4	Behra	22
5	Flaherty	8
6	Castellotti	7.5
7 =	Frere, Godia, Hanks	6
10	Fairman	5
11 =	Flockhart, Freeland, Hawthorn, Musso	4
15 =	Parsons, Perdisa, de Portago, Schell	3
19 =	Gendebien, Gould, D Rathmann, Rosier, da Silva Ramos, Villoresi	2
25 =	Gerini, Landi	1.5
27	P Russo	1

1957

The Vanwall challenge became a reality in 1957, although Connaught was forced to withdraw for lack of funds and BRM remained unreliable. Fangio took his fifth, and final, championship, but the Vanwalls took three races. Fangio's drive at the Nürburgring, where he overtook Collins and Hawthorn on the penultimate lap after a pit stop had put him nearly a minute behind, was a classic.

Argentine Grand Prix: Buenos Aires, 13 January 1957

100 laps of 2.43 mile/3.91 km circuit

Place	Driver	Car	Laps	Time/reason for retiring	Grid
1	Fangio	Maserati	100	3h 00m 55.9s	2
2	Behra	Maserati	100	3h 01m 14.2s	3
3	Menditeguy	Maserati	99		8
4	Schell	Maserati	98		9
5	Gonzalez/ de Portago	Lancia-Ferrari	98		10
6	Perdisa/Collins/ von Trips	Lancia-Ferrari	98		11
7	Bonnier	Maserati	95		13
8	Moss	Maserati	93		1
9	de Tomaso	Ferrari	91		12
10	Piotti	Maserati	90		14
	Castellotti	Lancia-Ferrari	75	hub shaft	4
	Hawthorn	Lancia-Ferrari	34	clutch	7
	Musso	Lancia-Ferrari	30	clutch	6
	Collins	Lancia-Ferrari	26	clutch	5

Fastest Lap: Moss, 1m 44.7s. 83.58 mph/134.5 kph

Monaco Grand Prix: Monte Carlo, 19 May 1957

105 laps of 1.95 mile/3.15 km circuit

Place	Driver	Car	Laps	Time/reason for retiring	Grid
1	Fangio	Maserati	105	3h 10m 12.8s	1
2	Brooks	Vanwall	105	3h 10m 38.0s	4
3	Gregory	Maserati	103		10
4	Lewis-Evans	Connaught	102		13
5	Trintignant	Lancia-Ferrari	100		6
6	J Brabham	Cooper-Climax	100		15
	von Trips/ Hawthorn	Lancia-Ferrari	95	engine	9
	Scarlatti/Schell	Maserati	64	oil leak	14
	Flockhart	BRM	59	timing gear	11
	Menditeguy	Maserati	50	accident	7
	Bueb	Connaught	46	fuel tank	16
	Schell	Maserati	22	suspension	8
	Gould	Maserati	9	accident	12
	Hawthorn	Lancia-Ferrari	3	accident	5
	Collins	Lancia-Ferrari	3	accident	2
	Moss	Vanwall	3	accident	3

Fastest Lap: Fangio, 1m 45.6s. 66.62 mph/107.22 kph

Indianapolis 500: Indianapolis, 30 May 1957

200 laps of 2.5 mile/4.02km circuit

Place	Driver	Car	Laps	Time/reason for retiring	Grid
1	Hanks	Belond Exhaust	200	3h 41m 14.25s	13
2	J Rathmann	Chiropractic	200		32
3	Bryan	Dean Van Lines	200		15
4	P Russo	Novi Auto Air Conditioning	200		10
5	Linden	McNamara	200		12
6	Boyd	Bowes Seal Fast	200		5
7	Teague	Sumar	200		28
8	O'Connor	Sumar	200		1
9	Veith	Bob Estes	200		16
10	Hartley	Massaglia	200		14
11	Turner	Bardahl	200		19
12	Thomson	D-A Lubricants	199		11
13	Christie	Jones & Maley	197		33
14	Weyant	Central Excavating	196		25
15	Bettenhausen	Novi Auto Air Conditioning	195		22
16	Parsons	Sumar	195		17
17	Freeland	Ansted-Rotary	192		21
18	Reece	Hoyt Machine	182	throttle	6

Indianapolis 500 (cont)

Place	Driver	Car	Laps	Time/reason for retiring	Grid
19	Edmunds	McKay	170	spun	27
20	Tolan	Greenman-Casale	138	clutch	31
21	Herman	Dunn Engineering	111	accident	30
22	Agabashian	Bowes Seal Fast	107	fuel leak	4
23	Sachs	Schmidt	105	fuel pump	2
24	Magill	Dayton Steel Foundry	101	accident	18
25	E Johnson	Chapman	93	wheel bearing	20
26	Cheesbourg	Seal Line	81	fuel leak	23
27	Keller	Bardahl	75	accident	8
28	Daywalt	Helse	53	accident	29
29	Elisian	McNamara	51	timing gear	7
30	Ward	Wolcott Fuel Injection	27	supercharger	24
31	Ruttman	John Zink	13	engine	3
32	E Russo	Sclavi-Amos	0	accident	26
33	George	Travelon Trailer	0	accident	9

Fastest Lap: J Rathmann, 1m 02.75s. 143.43 mph/230.8 kph

French Grand Prix: Rouen, 7 July 1957

77 laps of 4.07 mile/6.54 km circuit

Place	Driver	Car	Laps	Time/reason for retiring	Grid
1	Fangio	Maserati	77	3h 07m 46.4s	1
2	Musso	Lancia-Ferrari	77	3h 08m 37.2s	3
3	Collins	Lancia-Ferrari	77	3h 09m 52.4s	5
4	Hawthorn	Lancia-Ferrari	76		7
5	Behra	Maserati	70		2
6	Schell	Maserati	70		4
7	M McDowell/ J Brabham	Cooper-Climax	68		15
	Lewis-Evans	Vanwall	30	steering	10
	Menditeguy	Maserati	30	engine	9
	Salvadori	Vanwall	25	valve	6
	MacKay-Fraser	BRM	24	transmission	12
	Trintignant	Lancia-Ferrari	23	magneto	8
	Gould	Maserati	4	rear axle	14
	J Brabham	Cooper-Climax	4	accident	13
	Flockhart	BRM	2	accident	11

Fastest Lap: Musso, 2m 22.4s. 102.77 mph/165.39 kph

British Grand Prix: Aintree, 20 July 1957

90 laps of 3 mile/4.83 km circuit

Place	Driver	Car	Laps	Time/reason for retiring	Grid
1	Brooks/Moss	Vanwall	90	3h 06m 37.8s	3
2	Musso	Lancia-Ferrari	90	3h 07m 03.4s	10
3	Hawthorn	Lancia-Ferrari	90	3h 07m 20.6s	5
4	Trintignant/Collins*	Lancia-Ferrari	88		9
5	Salvadori	Cooper-Climax	85		14
6	Gerard	Cooper-Bristol	82		17
7	Lewis-Evans	Vanwall	82		6
8	J Brabham	Cooper-Climax	74	clutch	13
9	Bueb	Maserati	71		18
	Behra	Maserati	68	clutch	2
	Collins	Lancia-Ferrari	52	radiator	8
	Moss/Brooks	Vanwall	50	engine	1
	Fangio	Maserati	48	engine	4
	Fairman	BRM	47	engine	15
	Leston	BRM	44	engine	12
	Schell	Maserati	38	water pump	7
	Menditeguy	Maserati	34	transmission	11
	Bonnier	Maserati	17	transmission	16

Fastest Lap: Moss, 1m 59.2s. 90.6 mph/145.81 kph
* Collins only drove 3 laps, and did not receive points.

German Grand Prix: Nürburgring, 4 August 1957

22 laps of 14.17 mile/22.81 km circuit

Place	Driver	Car	Laps	Time/reason for retiring	Grid
1	Fangio	Maserati	22	3h 30m 38.3s	1
2	Hawthorn	Lancia-Ferrari	22	3h 30m 41.9s	2
3	Collins	Lancia-Ferrari	22	3h 31m 13.9s	4
4	Musso	Lancia-Ferrari	22	3h 34m 15.9s	8
5	Moss	Vanwall	22	3h 35m 15.8s	7
6	Behra	Maserati	22	3h 35m 16.8s	3
7	Schell	Maserati	22	3h 37m 25.8s	6
8	Gregory	Maserati	21		10
9	Brooks	Vanwall	21		5
10	Scarlatti	Maserati	21		13
11	Halford	Maserati	21		16
12	Barth	Porsche*	21		12
13	Naylor	Cooper-Climax*	20		17
14	de Beaufort	Porsche*	20		20
15	Marsh	Cooper-Climax*	17		22
	Herrmann	Maserati	14	chassis	11
	Maglioli	Porsche*	13	engine	15
	Godia	Maserati	11	steering	21

German Grand Prix (cont)

Place	Driver	Car	Laps	Time/reason for retiring	Grid
	Salvadori	Cooper-Climax*	11	suspension	14
	Lewis-Evans	Vanwall	10	gearbox	9
	J Brabham	Cooper-Climax*	6	transmission	18
	England	Cooper-Climax*	4	distributor	23
	Gibson	Cooper-Climax*	3	steering	24
	Gould	Maserati	2	rear axle	19

Fastest Lap: Fangio, 9m 17.4s. 91.54 mph/147.3 kph
* Formula 2 cars.

Pescara Grand Prix: Pescara, 18 August 1957

18 laps of 15.89 mile/25.58 km circuit

Place	Driver	Car	Laps	Time/reason for retiring	Grid
1	Moss	Vanwall	18	2h 59m 22.7s	2
2	Fangio	Maserati	18	3h 02m 36.6s	1
3	Schell	Maserati	18	3h 06m 09.5s	5
4	Gregory	Maserati	18	3h 07m 39.2s	7
5	Lewis-Evans	Vanwall	17		8
6	Scarlatti	Maserati	17		10
7	J Brabham	Cooper-Climax	15		16
	Halford	Cooper-Climax	10	transmission	14
	Godia	Maserati	10	engine	12
	Musso	Lancia-Ferrari	9	oil tank	3
	Bonnier	Maserati	7	overheating	9
	Salvadori	Cooper-Climax	3	accident, suspension	15
	Behra	Maserati	3	oil pipe	4
	Piotti	Maserati	0	engine	13
	Gould	Maserati	0	accident	11
	Brooks	Vanwall	0	engine	6

Fastest Lap: Moss, 9m 44.6s. 97.88 mph/157.52 kph

Italian Grand Prix: Monza, 8 September 1957

87 laps of 3.57 mile/5.75 km circuit

Place	Driver	Car	Laps	Time/reason for retiring	Grid
1	Moss	Vanwall	87	2h 35m 03.9s	2
2	Fangio	Maserati	87	2h 35m 45.1s	4
3	von Trips	Lancia-Ferrari	85		8
4	Gregory	Maserati	84		11
5	Scarlatti/Schell	Maserati	84		12

Italian Grand Prix (cont)

Place	Driver	Car	Laps	Time/reason for retiring	Grid
6	Hawthorn	Lancia-Ferrari	83		10
7	Brooks	Vanwall	82		3
8	Musso	Lancia-Ferrari	82		9
9	Godia	Maserati	81		15
10	Gould	Maserati	78		18
11	Simon/Volonterio	Maserati	72		16
	Collins	Lancia-Ferrari	61	valve	7
	Behra	Maserati	49	overheating	5
	Lewis-Evans	Vanwall	48	engine	1
	Halford	Maserati	46	engine	14
	Schell	Maserati	33	oil pipe	6
	Bonnier	Maserati	30	overheating	13
	Piotti	Maserati	2	engine	17

Fastest Lap: Brooks, 1m 43.7s. 124.04 mph/199.92 kph

World Championship 1957

1	Fangio	40 (46)
2	Moss	25
3	Musso	16
4	Hawthorn	13
5	Brooks	11
6	Gregory	10
7 =	Behra, Collins, Hanks, Schell	8
11	J Rathmann	7
12 =	Lewis-Evans, Trintignant	5
14 =	Bryan, Menditeguy, von Trips	4
17	P Russo	3
18 =	Linden, Salvadori	2
20 =	Gonzalez, de Portago, Scarlatti	1

1958

Although the engine formula remained the same, minimum race lengths were reduced to 300 kilometres or two hours, and the use of commercial petrol became compulsory, in place of specialized alcohol-based racing fuels. The world championship for constructors was introduced for the first time and went to Vanwall, but Ferrari's Mike Hawthorn won the driver's championship from Stirling Moss with five second places, despite the latter having won four of the ten grand prix to Hawthorn's one. Fangio, the dominant driver of the 1950s and one of the greatest of all time, competed in only two races, retiring after the French Grand Prix. Rear-engined Cooper-Climaxes, entered by the private owner Rob Walker, shocked the establishment by winning two early-season races: Moss, driving for Walker in Argentina because Vanwall had not entered, beat the Ferraris by superior race craft, and Trintignant outlasted the opposition at Monaco. Hawthorn retired with the championship, but died in a road accident in early 1959. Maria Teresa de Filippis became the first woman to drive in a world championship event.

Argentine Grand Prix: Buenos Aires, 19 January 1958

80 laps of 2.43 mile/3.91 km circuit

Place	Driver	Car	Laps	Time/reason for retiring	Grid
1	Moss	Cooper-Climax	80	2h 19m 33.7s	7
2	Musso	Ferrari	80	2h 19m 36.4s	5
3	Hawthorn	Ferrari	80	2h 19m 46.3s	2
4	Fangio	Maserati	80	2h 20m 26.7s	1
5	Behra	Maserati	78		4
6	Schell	Maserati	77		8
7	Menditeguy	Maserati	76		6
8	Godia	Maserati	75		9
9	Gould	Maserati	71		10
	Collins	Ferrari	0	rear axle	3

Fastest Lap: Fangio, 1m 41.8s. 85.96 mph/138.34 kph

Monaco Grand Prix: Monte Carlo, 18 May 1958

100 laps of 1.95 mile/3.15 km circuit

Place	Driver	Car	Laps	Time/reason for retiring	Grid
1	Trintignant	Cooper-Climax	100	2h 52m 27.9s	5
2	Musso	Ferrari	100	2h 52m 48.1s	10
3	Collins	Ferrari	100	2h 53m 06.7s	9
4	J Brabham	Cooper-Climax	97		3
5	Schell	BRM	91		12
	von Trips	Ferrari	90	engine – unclassified	11
6	Allison	Lotus-Climax	90		13
	Bonnier	Maserati	71	accident	16
	G Hill	Lotus-Climax	69	engine	15
	Salvadori	Cooper-Climax	55	gearbox	4
	Hawthorn	Ferrari	46	fuel pump	6
	Moss	Vanwall	37	engine	8
	Behra	BRM	27	brakes	2
	Scarlatti	Maserati	26	engine	14
	Brooks	Vanwall	21	spark plug	1
	Lewis-Evans	Vanwall	11	steering	7

Fastest Lap: Hawthorn, 1m 40.6s. 69.93 mph/112.55 kph

Dutch Grand Prix: Zandvoort, 26 May 1958

75 laps of 2.6 mile/4.19 km circuit

Place	Driver	Car	Laps	Time/reason for retiring	Grid
1	Moss	Vanwall	75	2h 04m 49.2s	2
2	Schell	BRM	75	2h 05m 37.1s	7
3	Behra	BRM	75	2h 06m 31.5s	4
4	Salvadori	Cooper-Climax	74		9
5	Hawthorn	Ferrari	74		6
6	Allison	Lotus-Climax	73		11
7	Musso	Ferrari	73		12
8	J Brabham	Cooper-Climax	73		5
9	Trintignant	Cooper-Climax	72		8
10	Bonnier	Maserati	71		15
11	de Beaufort	Porsche	69		17
	Scarlatti	Maserati	51	rear axle	16
	Lewis-Evans	Vanwall	45	valve	1
	G Hill	Lotus-Climax	41	gasket	13
	Collins	Ferrari	32	spun/stalled	10
	Gregory	Maserati	16	engine	14
	Brooks	Vanwall	13	rear axle	3

Fastest Lap: Moss, 1m 37.6s. 96.1 mph/154.66 kph

Indianapolis 500: Indianapolis, 30 May 1958

200 laps of 2.5 mile/4.02 km circuit

Place	Driver	Car	Laps	Time/reason for retiring	Grid
1	Bryan	Belond AP	200	3h 44m 13.8s	7
2	G Amick	Demler	200		25
3	Boyd	Bowes Seal Fast	200		8
4	Bettenhausen	Jones & Maley	200		9
5	J Rathmann	Leader Card	200		20
6	Reece	John Zink	200		3
7	Freeland	Bob Estes	200		13
8	Larson	John Zink	200		19
9	E Johnson	Bryant Heating	200		26
10	Cheesbourg	Novi	200		33
11	Keller	Bardahl	200		21
12	Parsons	Gerhardt	200		6
13	Tolan	Greenman-Casale	200		30
14	Christie	Federal Engineering	189	spun	17
15	Wilson	Sorenson	151	fire	32
16	Foyt	Dean Van Lines	148	spun	12
17	Magill	Dayton Steel Foundry	136	disqualified	31
18	P Russo	Novi Foundry	122	throttle	14
19	Templeman	McNamara	116	brakes	23
20	Ward	Wolcott	93	magneto	11
21	Garrett	Chapman	80	magneto	15
22	Sachs	Schmidt	68	transmission	18
23	Thomson	D-A Lubricants	52	steering	22
24	Weyant	Dunn Engineering	38	accident	29
25	Turner	Massaglia	21	fuel pump	10
26	Veith	Bowes Seal Fast	1	accident	4
27	D Rathmann	McNamara	0	accident	1
28	Elisian	John Zink	0	accident	2
29	O'Connor	Sumar	0	fatal accident	5
30	Goldsmith	Dayton Beach	0	accident	16
31	J Unser	McKay	0	accident	24
32	Sutton	Jim Robbins	0	accident	27
33	Bisch	Helse	0	accident	28

Fastest Lap: Bettenhausen, 1m 02.37s. 144.3 mph/232.2 kph

Belgian Grand Prix: Spa, 15 June 1958

24 laps of 8.76 mile/14.1 km circuit

Place	Driver	Car	Laps	Time/reason for retiring	Grid
1	Brooks	Vanwall	24	1h 37m 06.3s	5
2	Hawthorn	Ferrari	24	1h 37m 27.0s	1
3	Lewis-Evans	Vanwall	24	1h 40m 07.2s	11

Belgian Grand Prix (cont)

Place	Driver	Car	Laps	Time/reason for retiring	Grid
4	Allison	Lotus-Climax	24	1h 41m 21.8s	12
5	Schell	BRM	23		7
6	Gendebien	Ferrari	23		6
7	Trintignant	Maserati	23		16
8	Salvadori	Cooper-Climax	23		13
9	Bonnier	Maserati	22		14
10	de Filippis	Maserati	22		19
	Godia	Maserati	21	engine	18
	J Brabham	Cooper-Climax	16	gasket	8
	G Hill	Lotus-Climax	12	engine	15
	Musso	Ferrari	5	accident	2
	Behra	BRM	5	engine	10
	Collins	Ferrari	5	overheating	4
	Seidel	Maserati	3	engine	17
	Gregory	Maserati	0	engine	9
	Moss	Vanwall	0	valves	3

Fastest Lap: Hawthorn, 3m 58.3s. 132.36 mph/213.01 kph

French Grand Prix: Reims, 6 July 1958

50 laps of 5.16 mile/8.3 km circuit

Place	Driver	Car	Laps	Time/reason for retiring	Grid
1	Hawthorn	Ferrari	50	2h 03m 21.3s	1
2	Moss	Vanwall	50	2h 03m 45.9s	6
3	von Trips	Ferrari	50	2h 04m 21.0s	21
4	Fangio	Maserati	50	2h 05m 51.9s	8
5	Collins	Ferrari	50	2h 08m 46.2s	4
6	J Brabham	Cooper-Climax	49		12
7	P Hill	Maserati	49		13
8	Bonnier	Maserati	48		16
9	Gerini	Maserati	47		15
10	Ruttmann	Maserati	45		18
11	Behra	BRM	39	fuel pump	9
12	Schell	BRM	39	overheating	3
13	Lewis-Evans/ Brooks	Vanwall	38	engine	10
14	Salvadori	Cooper-Climax	37		14
	Godia	Maserati	28	accident	11
	Trintignant	BRM	23	oil pipe	7
	Brooks	Vanwall	15	gearbox	5
	G Hill	Lotus-Climax	11	engine	19
	Musso	Ferrari	9	fatal accident	2
	Shelby	Maserati	8	engine	17
	Allison	Lotus-Climax	6	engine	20

Fastest Lap: Hawthorn, 2m 24.9s. 128.17 mph/206.26 kph

British Grand Prix: Silverstone, 19 July 1958

75 laps of 2.93 mile/4.71 km circuit

Place	Driver	Car	Laps	Time/reason for retiring	Grid
1	Collins	Ferrari	75	2h 09m 04.2s	6
2	Hawthorn	Ferrari	75	2h 09m 28.4s	4
3	Salvadori	Cooper-Climax	75	2h 09m 54.8s	3
4	Lewis-Evans	Vanwall	75	2h 09m 55.0s	7
5	Schell	BRM	75	2h 10m 19.0s	2
6	J Brabham	Cooper-Climax	75	2h 10m 27.4s	10
7	Brooks	Vanwall	74		9
8	Trintignant	Cooper-Climax	73		12
9	Shelby	Maserati	72		15
	von Trips	Ferrari	59	engine	11
	Bonnier	Maserati	49	gearbox	13
	Gerini	Maserati	43	gearbox	18
	Burgess	Cooper-Climax	40	clutch	16
	Moss	Vanwall	25	engine	1
	Allison	Lotus-Climax	21	engine	5
	Bueb	Connaught	19	gearbox	17
	Behra	BRM	19	puncture	8
	Stacey	Lotus-Climax	19	overheating	20
	G Hill	Lotus-Climax	17	overheating	14
	Fairman	Connaught	7	engine	19

Fastest Lap: Hawthorn, 1m 40.8s. 104.54 mph/168.23 kph

German Grand Prix: Nürburgring, 3 August 1958

15 laps of 14.17 mile/22.8 km circuit

Place	Driver	Car	Laps	Time/reason for retiring	Grid
1	Brooks	Vanwall	15	2h 21m 15.0s	2
2	Salvadori	Cooper-Climax	15	2h 24m 44.7s	6
3	Trintignant	Cooper-Climax	15	2h 26m 26.2s	7
4	von Trips	Ferrari	15	2h 27m 31.3s	5
5*	†McLaren	Cooper-Climax	15	2h 27m 41.3s	12
6	†Barth	Porsche	15	2h 27m 47.4s	13
7	†Burgess	Cooper-Climax	15	2h 28m 14.3s	11
8	†Marsh	Cooper-Climax	15	2h 28m 24.9s	14
9	†P Hill	Ferrari	15	2h 29m 00.5s	10
10*	Allison	Lotus-Climax	13		24
11	†Bueb	Lotus-Climax	13		16
	Hawthorn	Ferrari	11	engine	1
	Collins	Ferrari	10	fatal accident	4
	Schell	BRM	8	brakes	8
	†Seidel	Cooper-Climax	8	suspension	17
	†G Hill	Lotus-Climax	4	oil pipe	22
	Behra	BRM	3	suspension	9

German Grand Prix (cont)

Place	Driver	Car	Laps	Time/reason for retiring	Grid
	†Goethals	Cooper-Climax	3	fuel pump	23
	Herrmann	Maserati	3	engine	20
	Moss	Vanwall	3	magneto	3
	†de Beaufort	Porsche	3	mechanical	15
	†Gibson	Cooper-Climax	2	mechanical	18
	†J Brabham	Cooper-Climax	0	accident	19
	†Naylor	Cooper-Climax	0	fuel pump	25
	Bonnier	Maserati	0	accident	21

Fastest Lap: Moss, 9m 09.2s. 92.91 mph/149.52 kph
* Allison's Lotus was 5th Formula 1 car to finish, but he did not receive points as he finished after Formula 2 cars [marked † in results].

Portuguese Grand Prix: Oporto, 14 August 1958

50 laps of 4.6 mile/7.41 km circuit

Place	Driver	Car	Laps	Time/reason for retiring	Grid
1	Moss	Vanwall	50	2h 11m 27.8s	1
2	Hawthorn	Ferrari	50	2h 16m 40.6s	2
3	Lewis-Evans	Vanwall	49		3
4	Behra	BRM	49		4
5	von Trips	Ferrari	49		6
6	Schell	BRM	49		7
7	J Brabham	Cooper-Climax	48		8
8	Trintignant	Cooper-Climax	48		9
9	Shelby	Maserati	47	brakes, accident	10
10	Salvadori	Cooper-Climax	46		11
	Brooks	Vanwall	36	accident	5
	G Hill	Lotus-Climax	25	accident	12
	Allison	Maserati	15	mechanical	13
	Bonnier	Maserati	9	illness	14
	de Filippis	Maserati	6	mechanical	15

Fastest Lap: Hawthorn, 2m 32.4s. 108.74 mph/175 kph

Italian Grand Prix: Monza, 7 September 1958

70 laps of 3.57 mile/5.75 km circuit

Place	Driver	Car	Laps	Time/reason for retiring	Grid
1	Brooks	Vanwall	70	2h 03m 47.8s	2
2	Hawthorn	Ferrari	70	2h 04m 12.0s	3
3	P Hill	Ferrari	70	2h 04m 16.1s	7
4	*Gregory/Shelby	Maserati	69		11

Italian Grand Prix (cont)

Place	Driver	Car	Laps	Time/reason for retiring	Grid
5	Salvadori	Cooper-Climax	62		14
6	G Hill	Lotus-Climax	62		12
7	Allison	Lotus-Climax	61		16
	de Filippis	Maserati	57	con rod	21
	Cabianca	Maserati	51	engine	20
	Behra	BRM	42	brakes	8
	Herrmann	Maserati	32	valve	18
	Lewis-Evans	Vanwall	30	overheating	4
	Trintignant	Cooper-Climax	24	gearbox	13
	Moss	Vanwall	17	gearbox	1
	Bonnier	BRM	14	fire	10
	Gendebien	Ferrari	4	de Dion tube	5
	Gerini	Maserati	2	mechanical	19
	Shelby	Maserati	1	mechanical	17
	Schell	BRM	0	accident	9
	von Trips	Ferrari	0	accident	6
	J Brabham	Cooper-Climax	0	accident	15

Fastest Lap: P Hill, 1m 42.9s. 125 mph/201.17 kph
* No points awarded for shared drive.

Moroccan Grand Prix: Casablanca, 19 October 1958

53 laps of 4.73 mile/7.62 km circuit

Place	Driver	Car	Laps	Time/reason for retiring	Grid
1	Moss	Vanwall	53	2h 09m 15.0s	2
2	Hawthorn	Ferrari	53	2h 10m 39.8s	1
3	P Hill	Ferrari	53	2h 10m 40.6s	5
4	Bonnier	BRM	53	2h 11m 01.8s	8
5	Schell	BRM	53	2h 11m 48.8s	10
6	Gregory	Maserati	52		13
7	Salvadori	Cooper-Climax	51		14
8	Fairman	Cooper-Climax	50		11
9	Herrmann	Maserati	50		18
10	Allison	Lotus-Climax	49		16
11	†J Brabham	Cooper-Climax	49		19
12	†McLaren	Cooper-Climax	48		21
13	Gerini	Maserati	48		17
14	†LaCaze	Cooper-Climax	48		23
15	†Guelfi	Cooper-Climax	48		25
16	G Hill	Lotus-Climax	45		12
	Lewis-Evans	Vanwall	41	fatal accident	3
	†Picard	Cooper-Climax	30	accident	24
	Brooks	Vanwall	29	engine	7
	Gendebien	Ferrari	29	accident	6
	†Bridger	Cooper-Climax	29	accident	22
	Behra	BRM	26	engine	4

Moroccan Grand Prix (cont)

Place	Driver	Car	Laps	Time/reason for retiring	Grid
	Seidel	Maserati	15	accident	20
	Flockhart	BRM	15	camshaft	15
	Trintignant	Cooper-Climax	9	engine	9

Fastest Lap: Moss, 2m 22.5s. 119.59 mph/192.46 kph
† Formula 2 car.

World Championship 1958

1	Hawthorn	42 (49)
2	Moss	41
3	Brooks	24
4	Salvadori	15
5 =	Collins, Schell	14
7 =	Musso, Trintignant	12
9	Lewis-Evans	11
10 =	Behra, P Hill, von Trips	9
13	Bryan	8
14	Fangio	7
15	G Amick	6
16 =	Bettenhausen, Boyd	4
18 =	Allison, Bonnier, J Brabham	3
21 =	McLaren, J Rathmann	2

Constructors' Championship

1	Vanwall	48 (57)
2	Ferrari	40 (57)
3	Cooper-Climax	31
4	BRM	18
5	Maserati	7
6	Lotus-Climax	3

1959

Brabham took his first world championship; Cooper won five races and BRM finally won one, maintaining British domination despite the withdrawal of Vanwall. Aston Martin also appeared with a car which, in the face of Cooper's rear-engined revolution, was outdated and overweight. The German Grand Prix was held for the second time on the very high speed Avus circuit, where Jean Behra was killed during a sports car race. Bruce McLaren became the youngest driver to win a grand prix with his victory at Sebring.

Monaco Grand Prix: Monte Carlo, 10 May 1959

100 laps of 1.95 mile/3.15 km circuit

Place	Driver	Car	Laps	Time/reason for retiring	Grid
1	J Brabham	Cooper-Climax	100	2h 55m 51.3s	3
2	Brooks	Ferrari	100	2h 56m 11.7s	4
3	Trintignant	Cooper-Climax	98		6
4	P Hill	Ferrari	97		5
5	McLaren	Cooper-Climax	96		13
6	Salvadori	Cooper-Maserati	83	transmission	8
	Moss	Cooper-Climax	81	transmission	1
	Flockhart	BRM	64	brakes	10
	Schell	BRM	48	fuel tank	9
	Bonnier	BRM	44	brakes, accident	7
	Behra	Ferrari	24	engine	2
	G Hill	Lotus-Climax	21	fire	14
	Gregory	Cooper-Climax	6	transmission	11
	†Halford	Lotus-Climax	1	accident	16
	†Allison	Ferrari	1	accident	15
	†von Trips	Porsche	1	accident	12

Fastest Lap: J Brabham, 1m 40.4s. 70.07 mph/112.77 kph
† Formula 2 cars.

1959

Indianapolis 500: Indianapolis, 30 May 1959

200 laps of 2.5 mile/4.02 km circuit

Place	Driver	Car	Laps	Time/reason for retiring	Grid
1	Ward	Leader Card	200	3h 40m 49.20s	6
2	J Rathmann	Simoniz	200		3
3	Thomson	Racing Associates	200		1
4	Bettenhausen	Hoover Motor Express	200		15
5	Goldsmith	Demler	200		16
6	Boyd	Bowes Seal Fast	200		11
7	Carter	Smokey's R-T	200		12
8	E Johnson	Bryant Heating	200		8
9	P Russo	Bardahl	200		27
10	Foyt	Dean Van Lines	200		17
11	Hartley	Drewy's	200		9
12	Veith	John Zink	200		7
13	Herman	Dunn Engineering	200		23
14	Daywalt	Federal Engineering	200		13
15	Arnold	Hall-Mar	200		21
16	McWithey	Ray Brady	200		33
17	Sachs	Schmidt	182	spun	2
18	Keller	Helse	163	engine	28
19	Flaherty	John Zink	162	accident	18
20	D Rathmann	McNamara	150	fire	4
21	Cheesbourg	Greenman-Casale	147	magneto	30
22	Freeland	Jim Robbins	136	magneto	25
23	R Crawford	Mirror Glaze	115	accident	32
24	Branson	Bob Estes	112	torsion bar	10
25	Christie	Federal Engineering	109	engine	24
26	Grim	Sumar	85	magneto	5
27	Turner	Travelon Trailer	47	fuel tank	14
28	Weyant	McKay	45	accident	29
29	Larson	Bowes Seal Fast	45	accident	19
30	Magill	Dayton Steel Foundry	45	accident	31
31	R Amick	Wheeler-Foutch	45	accident	26
32	Sutton	Wolcott	34	accident	22
33	Bryan	Belond AP	1	engine	20

Fastest Lap: Thomson, 1m 01.89s. 145.42 mph/234.03 kph

Dutch Grand Prix: Zandvoort, 31 May 1959

75 laps of 2.61 mile/4.19 km circuit

Place	Driver	Car	Laps	Time/reason for retiring	Grid
1	Bonnier	BRM	75	2h 05m 26.8s	1
2	J Brabham	Cooper-Climax	75	2h 05m 41.0s	2
3	Gregory	Cooper-Climax	75	2h 06m 49.8s	7

Dutch Grand Prix (cont)

Place	Driver	Car	Laps	Time/reason for retiring	Grid
4	Ireland	Lotus-Climax	74		9
5	Behra	Ferrari	74		4
6	P Hill	Ferrari	73		12
7	G Hill	Lotus-Climax	73		5
8	Trintignant	Cooper-Climax	73		11
9	Allison	Ferrari	71		15
10	de Beaufort	Porsche	68		14
	Moss	Cooper-Climax	62	gearbox	3
	Schell	BRM	46	engine	6
	Brooks	Ferrari	42	oil leak	8
	Shelby	Aston Martin	25	engine	10
	Salvadori	Aston Martin	3	overheating	13

Fastest Lap: Moss, 1m 36.7s. 97 mph/156.1 kph

French Grand Prix: Reims, 5 July 1959

50 laps of 5.16 mile/8.3 km circuit

Place	Driver	Car	Laps	Time/reason for retiring	Grid
1	Brooks	Ferrari	50	2h 01m 26.5s	1
2	P Hill	Ferrari	50	2h 01m 54.0s	3
3	J Brabham	Cooper-Climax	50	2h 03m 04.2s	2
4	Gendebien	Ferrari	50	2h 03m 14.0s	11
5	McLaren	Cooper-Climax	50	2h 03m 14.2s	10
6	Flockhart	BRM	50	2h 03m 32.2s	13
7	Schell	BRM	47		9
	Moss	BRM	42	disqualified: push start	4
8	Scarlatti	Maserati	41		21
9	de Beaufort	Maserati	40		20
10	d'Orey	Maserati	40		18
11	Trintignant	Cooper-Climax	36		8
	Behra	Ferrari	31	piston	5
	Salvadori	Cooper-Maserati	20	piston	16
	Gurney	Ferrari	19	radiator	12
	Ireland	Lotus-Climax	13	wheel bearing	15
	Burgess	Cooper-Maserati	13	engine	19
	Gregory	Cooper-Climax	9	heat exhaustion	7
	G Hill	Lotus-Climax	7	radiator	14
	Davis	Cooper-Maserati	6	oil pipe	17
	Bonnier	BRM	6	head gasket	6

Fastest Lap: Moss, 2m 22.8s. 130.05 mph/209.29 kph

British Grand Prix: Aintree, 18 July 1959

75 laps of 3 mile/4.83 km circuit

Place	Driver	Car	Laps	Time/reason for retiring	Grid
1	J Brabham	Cooper-Climax	75	2h 30m 11.6s	1
2	Moss	BRM	75	2h 30m 33.8s	7
3	McLaren	Cooper-Climax	75	2h 30m 34.0s	8
4	Schell	BRM	74		3
5	Trintignant	Cooper-Climax	74		4
6	Salvadori	Aston Martin	74		2
7	Gregory	Cooper-Climax	73		5
8	Stacey	Lotus-Climax	71		12
9	G Hill	Lotus-Climax	70		9
10	†Bristow	Cooper-Borgward	70		16
11	†H Taylor	Cooper-Climax	69		21
12	†Ashdown	Cooper-Climax	69		23
13	†Bueb	Cooper-Borgward	69		18
	Shelby	Aston Martin	68	magneto	6
	d'Orey	Maserati	56	accident	20
	Flockhart	BRM	53	spun/stalled	11
	Fairman	Cooper-Climax	37	gearbox	15
	Bonnier	BRM	37	throttle	10
	Burgess	Cooper-Maserati	31	gearbox	13
	Herrmann	Cooper-Maserati	20	gearbox	19
	†Piper	Lotus-Climax	19	head gasket	22
	Naylor	JBW-Maserati	17	transmission	14
	†M Taylor	Cooper-Climax	15	transmission	24
	Brooks	Vanwall	12	misfire	17

Fastest Lap: Moss/McLaren, 1m 57s. 92.31 mph/148.56 kph
† Formula 2 cars.

German Grand Prix: Berlin, 2 August 1959

60 laps (2 heats) of 5.16 mile/8.3 km circuit

Place	Driver	Car	Laps	Time/reason for retiring	Grid
1	Brooks	Ferrari	60	2h 09m 31.6s	1
2	Gurney	Ferrari	60	2h 10m 33.2s	3
3	P Hill	Ferrari	60	2h 10m 36.7s	6
4	Trintignant	Cooper-Climax	59		12
5	Bonnier	BRM	58		7
6	Burgess	Cooper-Maserati	56		15
7	Schell	BRM	49		8
	McLaren	Cooper-Climax	36	clutch	9
	Herrmann	BRM	36	accident	11
	Gregory	Cooper-Climax	23	engine	5
	J Brabham	Cooper-Climax	15	clutch	4
	G Hill	Lotus-Climax	10	oil radiator	10

German Grand Prix *(cont)*

Place	Driver	Car	Laps	Time/reason for retiring	Grid
	Ireland	Lotus-Climax	7	gearbox	13
	Allison	Ferrari	2	clutch	14
	Moss	Cooper-Climax	1	gearbox	2

Fastest Lap: Brooks, 2m 04.5s. 149.13 mph/240 kph

Portuguese Grand Prix: Monsanto, 23 August 1959

62 laps of 3.38 mile/5.44 km circuit

Place	Driver	Car	Laps	Time/reason for retiring	Grid
1	Moss	Cooper-Climax	62	2h 11m 55.1s	1
2	Gregory	Cooper-Climax	62	2h 12m 01.6s	3
3	Gurney	Ferrari	61		6
4	Trintignant	Cooper-Climax	60		4
5	Schell	BRM	59		9
6	Salvadori	Aston Martin	59		12
7	Flockhart	BRM	59		11
8	Shelby	Aston Martin	58		13
9	Brooks	Ferrari	57		10
10	Cabral	Cooper-Maserati	56		14
	McLaren	Cooper-Climax	38	transmission	8
	J Brabham	Cooper-Climax	23	accident	2
	Bonnier	BRM	10	engine	5
	P Hill	Ferrari	5	accident	7
	G Hill	Lotus-Climax	5	accident	15
	Ireland	Lotus-Climax	3	gearbox	16

Fastest Lap: Moss, 2m 05.1s. 97.3 mph/156.58 kph

Italian Grand Prix: Monza, 13 September 1959

72 laps of 3.57 mile/5.75 km circuit

Place	Driver	Car	Laps	Time/reason for retiring	Grid
1	Moss	Cooper-Climax	72	2h 04m 05.4s	1
2	P Hill	Ferrari	72	2h 04m 52.1s	5
3	J Brabham	Cooper-Climax	72	2h 05m 17.9s	3
4	Gurney	Ferrari	72	2h 05m 25.0s	4
5	Allison	Ferrari	71		8
6	Gendebien	Ferrari	70		6
7	Schell	BRM	70		7
8	Bonnier	BRM	70		11
9	Trintignant	Cooper-Climax	70		13

🏁

Italian Grand Prix (cont)

Place	Driver	Car	Laps	Time/reason for retiring	Grid
10	Shelby	Aston Martin	70		19
11	Davis	Cooper-Maserati	68		18
12	Scarlatti	Cooper-Climax	68		12
13	Flockhart	BRM	67		15
14	Burgess	Cooper-Maserati	67		16
15	Cabianca	Maserati	64		21
	Salvadori	Aston Martin	44	engine	17
	McLaren	Cooper-Climax	22	engine	9
	Fairman	Cooper-Maserati	18	piston	20
	Ireland	Lotus-Climax	14	brakes	14
	G Hill	Lotus-Climax	1	engine	10
	Brooks	Ferrari	0	piston	2

Fastest Lap: P Hill, 1m 40.4s. 128.11 mph/206.18 kph

United States Grand Prix: Sebring, 12 December 1959

42 laps of 5.2 mile/8.37 km circuit

Place	Driver	Car	Laps	Time/reason for retiring	Grid
1	McLaren	Cooper-Climax	42	2h 12m 35.7s	10
2	Trintignant	Cooper-Climax	42	2h 12m 36.3s	5
3	Brooks	Ferrari	42	2h 15m 36.6s	4
4	J Brabham	Cooper-Climax	42	2h 17m 33.0s	2
5	Ireland	Lotus-Climax	39		9
6	von Trips	Ferrari	38		6
7	Blanchard	Porsche	38		16
	Salvadori	Cooper-Maserati	23	transmission	11
	Allison	Ferrari	23	clutch	7
	Ward	Kurtis-Kraft Offy	20	clutch	18
	de Tomaso	Cooper-Osca	13	brakes	15
	P Hill	Ferrari	8	clutch	8
	d'Orey	Tec Mec Maserati	6	oil leak	17
	Schell	Cooper-Climax	5	clutch	3
	Constantine	Cooper-Climax	5	head gasket	14
	Moss	Cooper-Climax	4	gearbox	1
	Stacey	Lotus-Climax	1	clutch	12
	Said	Connaught	0	engine	13

Fastest Lap: Trintignant, 3m 05.0s. 101.19 mph/162.85 kph

World Championship 1959

1	J Brabham	31 (34)
2	Brooks	27
3	Moss	25.5
4	P Hill	20
5	Trintignant	19
6	McLaren	16.5
7	Gurney	13
8=	Bonnier, Gregory	10
10	Ward	8
11	J Rathmann	6
12=	Ireland, Schell, Thomson	5
15=	Bettenhausen, Gendebien	3
17=	Allison, Behra, Goldsmith	2

Constructors' Championship

1	Cooper-Climax	40 (53)
2	Ferrari	32 (38)
3	BRM	18
4	Lotus-Climax	5

1960

The last year of the 2.5 litre formula produced another Brabham and Cooper victory, and saw Lotus, Ferrari and BRM campaigning rear-engined cars. Lance Reventlow's Scarabs, like the Astons, were front-engined and outclassed. Moss's Rob Walker Lotus gave Colin Chapman his first grand prix win at Monaco and followed it with victory in the USA. All the other grand prix went to Cooper, except for the Italian which was boycotted by the British constructors since the Italians were using Monza's banked circuit. The points-scoring system was changed with the point for fastest lap being dropped and a point given for sixth place.

Argentine Grand Prix: Buenos Aires, 7 February 1960

80 laps of 2.43 mile/3.91 km circuit

Place	Driver	Car	Laps	Time/reason for retiring	Grid
1	McLaren	Cooper-Climax	80	2h 17m 49.5s	13
2	Allison	Ferrari	80	2h 18m 15.8s	7
3	Trintignant/Moss	Cooper-Climax	80	2h 18m 26.4s	8
4	Menditeguy	Cooper-Maserati	80	2h 18m 42.8s	12
5	von Trips	Ferrari	79		5
6	Ireland	Lotus-Climax	79		2
7	Bonnier	BRM	79		4
8	P Hill	Ferrari	77		6
9	Rodriguez Larreta	Lotus-Climax	77		15
10	Gonzalez	Ferrari	77		11
11	Bonomi	Cooper-Maserati	76		17
12	Gregory	Behra-Porsche F2	76		16
13	Munaron	Maserati	72		19
14	Estefano	Maserati	70		20
	Schell	Cooper-Climax	63	fuel pump	9
	J Brabham	Cooper-Climax	42	gearbox	10
	Moss	Cooper-Climax	40	suspension	1
	G Hill	BRM	37	overheating	3
	Stacey	Lotus-Climax	24	exhaustion	14

Argentine Grand Prix (cont)

Place	Driver	Car	Laps	Time/reason for retiring	Grid
	Chimeri	Maserati	23	exhaustion	21
	Creus	Maserati	16	exhaustion	22
	Scarlatti	Maserati	10	overheating	18

Fastest Lap: Moss, 1m 38.9s. 88.48 mph/142.39 kph
* Moss and Trintignant gained no points for shared drive.

Monaco Grand Prix: Monte Carlo, 29 May 1960

100 laps of 1.95 mile/3.15 km circuit

Place	Driver	Car	Laps	Time/reason for retiring	Grid
1	Moss	Cooper-Climax	100	2h 53m 45.5s	1
2	McLaren	Cooper-Climax	100	2h 54m 37.6s	11
3	P Hill	Ferrari	100	2h 54m 47.4s	10
4	Brooks	Cooper-Climax	99		3
5	Bonnier	BRM	83		5
6	Ginther	Ferrari	70		9
7	G Hill	BRM	66	accident	6
8	von Trips	Ferrari	61	clutch	8
9	Ireland	Lotus-Climax	56	engine	7
	Gurney	BRM	44	suspension	14
	J Brabham	Cooper-Climax	40	disqualified: push start	2
	Salvadori	Cooper-Climax	29	overheating	12
	Stacey	Lotus-Climax	23	engine mounting	13
	Surtees	Lotus-Climax	17	transmission	15
	Bristow	Cooper-Climax	17	gearbox	4
	Trintignant	Cooper-Maserati	4	gearbox	16

Fastest Lap: McLaren, 1m 36.2s. 73.13 mph/117.69 kph

Indianapolis 500: Indianapolis, 30 May 1960

200 laps of 2.5 mile/4.02 km circuit

Place	Driver	Car	Laps	Time/reason for retiring	Grid
1	J Rathmann	Ken-Paul	200	3h 36m 11.36s	2
2	Ward	Leader Card	200		3
3	Goldsmith	Demler	200		24
4	Branson	Bob Estes	200		8
5	Thomson	Adams Quarter Horse	200		17
6	E Johnson	Jim Robbins	200		7
7	Ruby	Agajanian	200		12
8	Veith	Schmidt	200		25

Indianapolis 500 (cont)

Place	Driver	Car	Laps	Time/reason for retiring	Grid
9	Tinglestad	Jim Robbins	200		28
10	Christie	Federal Engineering	200		14
11	R Amick	King O'Lawn	200		22
12	Carter	Thompson Industries	200		27
13	Homeier	Ridgewood Builders	200		31
14	Hartley	Sumar	196		24
15	Stevenson	Leader Card	196		9
16	Grim	Bill Forbes	194		21
17	Templeman	Federal Engineering	191	clutch	19
18	Hurtubuise	Travelon Trailer	185	engine	23
19	Bryan	Metal-Cal	152	fuel pump	10
20	Ruttman	John Zink	134	rear axle	6
21	Sachs	Dean Van Lines	132	magneto	1
22	Freeland	Ross-Babcock Traveler	129	magneto	11
23	Bettenhausen	Dowgard	125	engine	18
24	Weiler	Ansted-Rotary	103	accident	15
25	Foyt	Bowes Seal Fast	90	clutch	16
26	E Russo	Go-Kart	84	accident	29
27	Boyd	Bowes Seal Fast	77	engine	13
28	Force	McKay	74	brakes	20
29	McWithey	Hoover Motor Express	60	brakes	32
30	Sutton	S-R Racing Enterprises	47	engine	5
31	D Rathmann	Jim Robbins	42	brakes	4
32	Herman	Joe Hunt Magneto	34	clutch	30
33	D Wilson	Bryant Heating	11	magneto	33

Fastest Lap: J Rathmann, 1m 01.59s. 146.13 mph/235.17 kph

Dutch Grand Prix: Zandvoort, 6 June 1960

75 laps of 2.6 mile/4.19 km circuit

Place	Driver	Car	Laps	Time/reason for retiring	Grid
1	J Brabham	Cooper-Climax	75	2h 01m 47.2s	2
2	Ireland	Lotus-Climax	75	2h 02m 11.2s	3
3	G Hill	BRM	75	2h 02m 43.8s	5
4	Moss	Lotus-Climax	75	2h 02m 44.9s	1
5	von Trips	Ferrari	74		15
6	Ginther	Ferrari	74		12
7	H Taylor	Cooper-Climax	70		14
8	de Beaufort	Cooper-Climax F2	69		17
	Stacey	Lotus-Climax	57	transmission	8
	P Hill	Ferrari	54	engine	13
	Bonnier	BRM	54	engine	4

Dutch Grand Prix (cont)

Place	Driver	Car	Laps	Time/reason for retiring	Grid
	Clark	Lotus-Climax	42	transmission	11
	Trintignant	Cooper-Maserati	39	gearbox	16
	Gurney	BRM	11	brakes	6
	Bristow	Cooper-Climax	9	engine	7
	McLaren	Cooper-Climax	8	universal joint	9
	Brooks	Cooper-Climax	4	gearbox	10

Fastest Lap: Moss, 1m 33.8s. 99.99 mph/160.93 kph

Belgian Grand Prix: Spa, 19 June 1960

36 laps of 8.76 mile/14.1 km circuit

Place	Driver	Car	Laps	Time/reason for retiring	Grid
1	J Brabham	Cooper-Climax	36	2h 21m 37.3s	1
2	McLaren	Cooper-Climax	36	2h 22m 40.6s	11
3	Gendebien	Cooper-Climax	35		4
4	P Hill	Ferrari	35		3
	G Hill	BRM	35	engine – unclassified	5
5	Clark	Lotus-Climax	34		9
6	Bianchi	Cooper-Climax	28		14
	Stacey	Lotus-Climax	24	fatal accident	16
	Mairesse	Ferrari	23	transmission	12
	von Trips	Ferrari	22	transmission	10
	Bristow	Cooper-Climax	19	fatal accident	8
	Daigh	Scarab	16	engine	17
	Bonnier	BRM	14	engine	6
	Ireland	Lotus-Climax	13	accident	7
	Gurney	BRM	4	engine	13
	Brooks	Cooper-Climax	2	gearbox	2
	Reventlow	Scarab	1	engine	15

Fastest Lap: Brabham/P Hill/Ireland, 3m 51.9s. 136.01 mph/218.89 kph

French Grand Prix: Reims, 3 July 1960

50 laps of 5.16 mile/8.3 km circuit

Place	Driver	Car	Laps	Time/reason for retiring	Grid
1	J Brabham	Cooper-Climax	50	1h 57m 24.9s	1
2	Gendebien	Cooper-Climax	50	1h 58m 13.2s	11
3	McLaren	Cooper-Climax	50	1h 58m 16.8s	9
4	H Taylor	Cooper-Climax	49		13
5	Clark	Lotus-Climax	49		12

French Grand Prix (cont)

Place	Driver	Car	Laps	Time/reason for retiring	Grid
6	Flockhart	Lotus-Climax	49		8
7	Ireland	Lotus-Climax	43		4
8	Halford	Cooper-Climax	40	not running	16
9	Gregory	Cooper-Maserati	37		17
10	Burgess	Cooper-Maserati	36		20
	von Trips	Ferrari	31	transmission	6
	P Hill	Ferrari	29	transmission	2
	Bonnier	BRM	22	engine	10
	Bianchi	Cooper-Climax	18	transmission	15
	Gurney	BRM	17	engine	7
	Munaron	Cooper-Ferrari	15	transmission	19
	Mairesse	Ferrari	14	transmission	5
	Brooks	Vanwall	7	vibration	14
	Trintignant	Cooper-Maserati	0	accident	18
	G Hill	BRM	0	accident	3

Fastest Lap: Brabham, 2m 17.5s. 135.06 mph/217.35 kph

British Grand Prix: Silverstone, 16 July 1960

77 laps of 2.93 mile/4.71 km circuit

Place	Driver	Car	Laps	Time/reason for retiring	Grid
1	J Brabham	Cooper-Climax	77	2h 04m 24.6s	1
2	Surtees	Lotus-Climax	77	2h 05m 14.2s	11
3	Ireland	Lotus-Climax	77	2h 05m 54.2s	5
4	McLaren	Cooper-Climax	76		3
5	Brooks	Cooper-Climax	76		9
6	von Trips	Ferrari	75		7
7	P Hill	Ferrari	75		10
8	H Taylor	Cooper-Climax	74		16
9	Gendebien	Cooper-Climax	74		12
10	Gurney	BRM	74		6
11	Trintignant	Aston Martin	72		21
12	Piper	Lotus-Climax	72		23
13	Naylor	JBW-Maserati	72		18
14	G Hill	BRM	71	accident	2
15	Gregory	Cooper-Maserati	71		14
16	Munaron	Cooper-Ferrari	68		24
17	Clark	Lotus-Climax	68		8
	Bianchi	Cooper-Climax	60	magneto	17
	Bonnier	BRM	59	suspension	4
	Daigh	Cooper-Climax	56	overheating	19
	Burgess	Cooper-Maserati	56	engine	20
	Fairman	Cooper-Climax	44	fuel pump	15
	Salvadori	Aston Martin	44	steering	13
	Greene	Cooper-Maserati	12	overheating	22

Fastest Lap: G Hill, 1m 34.4s. 111.62 mph/179.64 kph

Portuguese Grand Prix: Oporto, 14 August 1960

55 laps of 4.6 mile/7.4 km circuit

Place	Driver	Car	Laps	Time/reason for retiring	Grid
1	J Brabham	Cooper-Climax	55	2h 19m 00.03s	3
2	McLaren	Cooper-Climax	55	2h 19m 58.00s	6
3	Clark	Lotus-Climax	55	2h 20m 53.26s	8
4	von Trips	Ferrari	55	2h 20m 58.84s	9
	Moss	Lotus-Climax	50	disqualified: pushed car against traffic	4
5	Brooks	Cooper-Climax	49		12
6	Ireland	Lotus-Climax	48		7
7	Gendebien	Cooper-Climax	46		14
	Cabral	Cooper-Maserati	37	gearbox	15
	Surtees	Lotus-Climax	36	radiator	1
	P Hill	Ferrari	29	accident	10
	Gurney	BRM	24	engine	2
	Gregory	Cooper-Maserati	21	gearbox	11
	G Hill	BRM	8	gearbox	5
	Bonnier	BRM	6	engine	13

Fastest Lap: Surtees, 2m 27.53s. 112.31 mph/180.74 kph

Italian Grand Prix: Monza, 4 September 1960

50 laps of 6.2 mile/10 km circuit

Place	Driver	Car	Laps	Time/reason for retiring	Grid
1	P Hill	Ferrari	50	2h 21m 09.2s	1
2	Ginther	Ferrari	50	2h 23m 36.8s	2
3	Mairesse	Ferrari	49		3
4	Cabianca	Cooper-Ferrari	48		4
5	*von Trips	Ferrari	48		6
6	*Herrmann	Porsche	47		10
7	*Barth	Porsche	47		12
8	*Drogo	Cooper-Climax	45		15
9	Seidel	Cooper-Climax	44		13
10	*Gamble	Behra-Porsche	41		14
	Naylor	JBW-Maserati	41	gearbox	7
	Thiele	Cooper-Maserati	32	gearbox	9
	Munaron	Cooper-Ferrari	27	oil pipe	8
	Scarlatti	Cooper-Maserati	26	throttle	5
	*V Wilson	Cooper-Climax	23	sump	16
	Owen	Cooper-Climax	1	accident	11

Fastest Lap: P Hill, 2m 43.6s. 136.73 mph/220.05 kph
* Formula 2 cars.

United States Grand Prix: Riverside, 20 November 1960

75 laps of 3.28 mile/5.27 km circuit

Place	Driver	Car	Laps	Time/reason for retiring	Grid
1	Moss	Lotus-Climax	75	2h 28m 52.2s	1
2	Ireland	Lotus-Climax	75	2h 29m 30.2s	7
3	McLaren	Cooper-Climax	75	2h 30m 14.2s	10
4	J Brabham	Cooper-Climax	74		2
5	Bonnier	BRM	74		4
6	P Hill	Cooper-Climax	74		13
7	Hall	Lotus-Climax	73		12
8	Salvadori	Cooper-Climax	73		15
9	von Trips	Cooper-Maserati	72		16
10	Daigh	Scarab	70		18
11	Lovely	Cooper-Ferrari	69		20
12	Gendebien	Cooper-Climax	69		8
13	Drake	Maserati	68		22
14	H Taylor	Cooper-Climax	68		14
15	Trintignant	Cooper-Maserati	66		19
16	Clark	Lotus-Climax	61		5
	G Hill	BRM	34	gearbox	11
	Burgess	Cooper-Maserati	29	ignition	23
	Naylor	JBW-Maserati	20	engine	17
	Gurney	BRM	18	overheating	3
	Flockhart	Cooper-Climax	11	transmission	21
	Brooks	Cooper-Climax	6	spun	9
	Surtees	Lotus-Climax	4	accident	6

Fastest Lap: Brabham, 1m 56.3s. 101.38 mph/163.15 kph

World Championship 1960

1	J Brabham	43
2	McLaren	34 (37)
3	Moss	19
4	Ireland	18
5	P Hill	16
6=	Gendebien, von Trips	10
8=	Clark, Ginther, J Rathmann	8
11	Brooks	7
12=	Allison, Surtees, Ward	6
15=	Bonnier, Goldsmith, G Hill, Mairesse	4
19=	Branson, Cabianca, Menditeguy, H Taylor	3
23	Thomson	2
24=	Bianchi, Flockhart, Herrmann, Johnson	1

Constructors' Championship

1	Cooper-Climax	48 (58)
2	Lotus-Climax	34 (37)
3	Ferrari	26 (27)
4	BRM	8
5=	Cooper-Ferrari, Cooper-Maserati	3

1961

The first year of the 1.5 litre formula was dominated by a well-prepared Ferrari team. Only Stirling Moss, in an outdated Lotus, was able to beat the Ferraris on two tracks where his skills offset the Ferrari power advantage. The contest for the championship between Ferrari's leading drivers, Phil Hill and Wolfgang von Trips, ended in tragedy when von Trips collided with Jim Clark at Monza, killing the Ferrari driver and 14 spectators. Baghetti won his only grand prix, on his championship debut. With the change of formula and the introduction of a United States Grand Prix, the Indianapolis 500 was dropped from the championship. The number of points awarded to a race winner was increased to nine.

Monaco Grand Prix: Monte Carlo, 14 May 1961

100 laps of 1.95 mile/3.15 km circuit

Place	Driver	Car	Laps	Time/reason for retiring	Grid
1	Moss	Lotus-Climax	100	2h 45m 50.1s	1
2	Ginther	Ferrari	100	2h 45m 53.7s	2
3	P Hill	Ferrari	100	2h 46m 31.4s	5
4	von Trips	Ferrari	98	not running	6
5	Gurney	Porsche	98		10
6	McLaren	Cooper-Climax	95		7
7	Trintignant	Cooper-Maserati	95		15
8	Allison	Lotus-Climax	93		14
9	Herrmann	Porsche	91		12
10	Clark	Lotus-Climax	89		3
11	Surtees	Cooper-Climax	68	fuel pump	11
12	Bonnier	Porsche	59	fuel pump	9
13	Brooks	BRM-Climax	54	engine	8
	May	Lotus-Climax	41	gearbox	13
	J Brabham	Cooper-Climax	38	engine	16
	G Hill	BRM-Climax	11	fuel pump	4

Fastest Lap: Ginther/Moss, 1m 36.3s. 73.05 mph/117.57 kph

Dutch Grand Prix: Zandvoort, 22 May 1961

75 laps of 2.6 mile/4.19 km circuit

Place	Driver	Car	Laps	Time/reason for retiring	Grid
1	von Trips	Ferrari	75	2h 01m 52.1s	2
2	P Hill	Ferrari	75	2h 01m 53.0s	1
3	Clark	Lotus-Climax	75	2h 02m 05.2s	10
4	Moss	Lotus-Climax	75	2h 02m 14.3s	4
5	Ginther	Ferrari	75	2h 02m 14.4s	3
6	J Brabham	Cooper-Climax	75	2h 03m 12.2s	7
7	Surtees	Cooper-Climax	75	2h 03m 18.8s	9
8	G Hill	BRM-Climax	75	2h 03m 21.9s	5
9	Brooks	BRM-Climax	74		8
10	Gurney	Porsche	74		6
11	Bonnier	Porsche	73		11
12	McLaren	Cooper-Climax	73		13
13	T Taylor	Lotus-Climax	73		14
14	de Beaufort	Porsche	72		15
15	Herrmann	Porsche	72		12

Fastest Lap: Clark, 1m 35.5s. 98.21 mph/158.06 kph
* A unique race: no pit stops and no retirements.

Belgian Grand Prix: Spa, 18 June 1961

30 laps of 8.76 mile/14.1 km circuit

Place	Driver	Car	Laps	Time/reason for retiring	Grid
1	P Hill	Ferrari	30	2h 03m 03.8s	1
2	von Trips	Ferrari	30	2h 03m 04.5s	2
3	Ginther	Ferrari	30	2h 03m 23.3s	5
4	Gendebien	Ferrari	30	2h 03m 49.4s	3
5	Surtees	Cooper-Climax	30	2h 04m 30.6s	4
6	Gurney	Porsche	30	2h 04m 34.8s	10
7	Bonnier	Porsche	30	2h 05m 50.9s	9
8	Moss	Lotus-Climax	30	2h 06m 59.4s	8
9	Lewis	Cooper-Climax	29		13
10	Gregory	Cooper-Climax	29		12
11	de Beaufort	Porsche	28		14
12	Clark	Lotus-Climax	24		16
13	Brooks	BRM-Climax	24		7
	G Hill	BRM-Climax	23	oil leak	6
	Trintignant	Cooper-Maserati	22	transmission	20
	Bandini	Cooper-Maserati	19	oil pressure	17
	J Brabham	Cooper-Climax	11	engine	11
	Bianchi	Lotus-Climax	9	oil pipe	21
	Ireland	Lotus-Climax	9	engine	18
	McLaren	Cooper-Climax	8	fuel system	15
	Mairesse	Lotus-Climax	7	engine	19

Fastest Lap: Ginther, 3m 59.8s. 131.53 mph/211.68 kph

French Grand Prix: Reims, 2 July 1961

52 laps of 5.16 mile/8.3 km circuit

Place	Driver	Car	Laps	Time/reason for retiring	Grid
1	Baghetti	Ferrari	52	2h 14m 17.5s	12
2	Gurney	Porsche	52	2h 14m 17.6s	9
3	Clark	Lotus-Climax	52	2h 15m 18.6s	5
4	Ireland	Lotus-Climax	52	2h 15m 27.8s	10
5	McLaren	Cooper-Climax	52	2h 15m 59.3s	8
6	G Hill	BRM-Climax	52	2h 15m 59.4s	6
7	Bonnier	Porsche	52	2h 17m 32.9s	13
8	Salvadori	Cooper-Climax	51		15
9	P Hill	Ferrari	50		1
10	H Taylor	Lotus-Climax	49		25
11	May	Lotus-Climax	48		22
12	Gregory	Cooper-Climax	43		16
13	Trintignant	Cooper-Maserati	42		23
14	Burgess	Lotus-Climax	42		24
	Ginther	Ferrari	40	oil pressure	3
	Moss	Lotus-Climax	30	suspension	4
	Mairesse	Lotus-Climax	25	fuel system	20
	Scarlatti	de Tomaso-Osca	24	engine	26
	de Beaufort	Porsche	22	engine	17
	Bianchi	Lotus-Climax	21	clutch	19
	von Trips	Ferrari	17	engine	2
	J Brabham	Cooper-Climax	13	oil pressure	14
	Collomb	Cooper-Climax	6	engine	21
	Brooks	BRM-Climax	3	overheating	11
	Surtees	Cooper-Climax	3	suspension	7
	Lewis	Cooper-Climax	3	overheating	18

Fastest Lap: P Hill, 2m 27.1s. 126.25 mph/203.18 kph

British Grand Prix: Aintree, 15 July 1961

75 laps of 3 mile/4.83 km circuit

Place	Driver	Car	Laps	Time/reason for retiring	Grid
1	von Trips	Ferrari	75	2h 40m 53.6s	4
2	P Hill	Ferrari	75	2h 41m 39.6s	1
3	Ginther	Ferrari	75	2h 41m 40.4s	2
4	J Brabham	Cooper-Climax	75	2h 42m 02.2s	9
5	Bonnier	Porsche	75	2h 42m 09.8s	3
6	Salvadori	Cooper-Climax	75	2h 42m 19.8s	13
7	Gurney	Porsche	74		12
8	McLaren	Cooper-Climax	74		14
9	Brooks	BRM-Climax	73		6
10	Ireland	Lotus-Climax	72		7
11	Gregory	Cooper-Climax	71		16

British Grand Prix (cont)

Place	Driver	Car	Laps	Time/reason for retiring	Grid
12	Bandini	Cooper-Maserati	71		21
13	Maggs	Lotus-Climax	69		24
14	Burgess	Lotus-Climax	69		25
15	Greene	Gilby-Climax	69		23
16	de Beaufort	Porsche	69		18
17	Clark	Lotus-Climax	62	oil leak	8
18	Seidel	Lotus-Climax	58		22
	Fairman/Moss	Ferguson-Climax	56	disqualified: push start	20
	Bianchi	Lotus-Climax	45	gearbox	30
	Moss	Lotus-Climax	44	brakes	5
	G Hill	BRM-Climax	43	engine	11
	Baghetti	Ferrari	27	spun	19
	Marsh	Lotus-Climax	25	engine	27
	Surtees	Cooper-Climax	23	transmission	10
	T Parnell	Lotus-Climax	12	clutch	29
	Lewis	Cooper-Climax	7	handling	15
	Ashmore	Lotus-Climax	7	engine	26
	H Taylor	Lotus-Climax	5	accident	17
	Natili	Cooper-Maserati	0	engine	28

Fastest Lap: Brooks, 1m 57.8s. 91.68 mph/147.5 kph

German Grand Prix: Nürburgring, 6 August 1961

15 laps of 14.17 mile/22.81 km circuit

Place	Driver	Car	Laps	Time/reason for retiring	Grid
1	Moss	Lotus-Climax	15	2h 18m 12.4s	3
2	von Trips	Ferrari	15	2h 18m 33.8s	5
3	P Hill	Ferrari	15	2h 18m 34.9s	1
4	Clark	Lotus-Climax	15	2h 19m 29.5s	8
5	Surtees	Cooper-Climax	15	2h 20m 05.5s	10
6	McLaren	Cooper-Climax	15	2h 20m 53.8s	12
7	Gurney	Porsche	15	2h 21m 35.0s	7
8	Ginther	Ferrari	15	2h 23m 35.5s	14
9	Lewis	Cooper-Climax	15	2h 23m 36.1s	18
10	Salvadori	Cooper-Climax	15	2h 30m 23.9s	15
11	Maggs	Lotus-Climax	14		22
12	Burgess	Cooper-Climax	14		24
13	Herrmann	Porsche	14		11
14	de Beaufort	Porsche	14		17
15	Marsh	Lotus-Climax	13		20
16	Mairesse	Ferrari	13	accident	13
17	Ashmore	Lotus-Climax	13		25
18	Trintignant	Cooper-Maserati	12		21
	Collomb	Cooper-Climax	11	engine	26
	Bandini	Cooper-Maserati	9	engine	19

German Grand Prix (cont)

Place	Driver	Car	Laps	Time/reason for retiring	Grid
	Brooks	BRM-Climax	6	engine	9
	Bonnier	Porsche	4	engine	4
	Seidel	Lotus-Climax	2	steering	23
	Ireland	Lotus-Climax	1	fire	16
	G Hill	BRM-Climax	1	accident	6
	J Brabham	Cooper-Climax	0	accident	2

Fastest Lap: P Hill, 8m 57.8s. 94.88 mph/152.69 kph

Italian Grand Prix: Monza, 10 September 1961

43 laps of 6.21 mile/10 km circuit

Place	Driver	Car	Laps	Time/reason for retiring	Grid
1	P Hill	Ferrari	43	2h 03m 13.0s	4
2	Gurney	Porsche	43	2h 03m 44.2s	12
3	McLaren	Cooper-Climax	43	2h 05m 41.4s	14
4	Lewis	Cooper-Climax	43	2h 05m 53.4s	16
5	Brooks	BRM-Climax	43	2h 05m 53.4s	13
6	Salvadori	Cooper-Climax	42		18
7	de Beaufort	Porsche	41		15
8	Bandini	Cooper-Maserati	41		21
9	Trintignant	Cooper-Maserati	41		22
10	T Parnell	Lotus-Climax	40		27
11	H Taylor	Lotus-Climax	39		23
12	Pirocchi	Cooper-Maserati	38		29
	Moss	Lotus-Climax	36	wheel	11
	Ginther	Ferrari	23	engine	3
	Starraba	Lotus-Maserati	19	engine	30
	Bonnier	Porsche	14	suspension	8
	Vaccarella	de Tomaso-Conrero	13	engine	20
	Baghetti	Ferrari	13	engine	6
	R Rodriguez	Ferrari	13	engine	2
	Gregory	Lotus-Climax	11	suspension	17
	G Hill	BRM-Climax	10	engine	5
	J Brabham	Cooper-Climax	8	engine	10
	Naylor	JBW-Climax	6	engine	21
	Fairman	Cooper-Climax	5	engine	26
	Ireland	Lotus-Climax	4	chassis	9
	Surtees	Cooper-Climax	2	accident	19
	Seidel	Lotus-Climax	1	engine	28
	Bussinello	de Tomaso-Osca	1	engine	24
	Lippi	de Tomaso-Osca	1	engine	32
	Clark	Lotus-Climax	1	accident	7
	von Trips	Ferrari	1	fatal accident	1
	Ashmore	Lotus-Climax	0	accident	25

Fastest Lap: Baghetti, 2m 48.4s. 132.83 mph/213.78 kph

United States Grand Prix: Watkins Glen, 8 October 1961

100 laps of 2.3 mile/3.7 km circuit

Place	Driver	Car	Laps	Time/reason for retiring	Grid
1	Ireland	Lotus-Climax	100	2h 13m 45.8s	8
2	Gurney	Porsche	100	2h 13m 50.1s	7
3	Brooks	BRM-Climax	100	2h 14m 34.8s	6
4	McLaren	Cooper-Climax	100	2h 14m 43.8s	4
5	G Hill	BRM-Climax	99		2
6	Bonnier	Porsche	98		10
7	Salvadori	Cooper-Climax	96	engine	12
8	Clark	Lotus-Climax	96		5
9	Penske	Cooper-Climax	96		16
10	Ryan	Lotus-Climax	95		13
11	Sharp	Cooper-Climax	93		17
12	Gendebien/Gregory	Lotus-Climax	92		15
	Ruby	Lotus-Climax	75	magneto	19
	Hall	Lotus-Climax	75	fuel leak	18
	Moss	Lotus-Climax	58	engine	3
	J Brabham	Cooper-Climax	57	engine	1
	Gregory	Lotus-Climax	23	gearbox	11
	Hansgen	Cooper-Climax	14	accident	14
	Surtees	Cooper-Climax	0	engine	9

Fastest Lap: Brabham, 1m 18.2s. 105.88 mph/170.4 kph

World Championship 1961

1	P Hill	34 (38)
2	von Trips	33
3 =	Gurney, Moss	21
5	Ginther	16
6	Ireland	12
7 =	Clark, McLaren	11
9	Baghetti	9
10	Brooks	6
11 =	Brabham, Surtees	4
13 =	Bonnier, Gendebien, G Hill, Lewis	3
17	Salvadori	2

Constructors' Championship

1	Ferrari	40 (52)
2	Lotus-Climax	32
3	Porsche	22 (23)
4	Cooper-Climax	14 (18)
5	BRM-Climax	7

1962

Ferrari were completely eclipsed in 1962, partly as a result of internal upheavals, partly because the British team had made great progress. BRM finally came good with Graham Hill taking the championship relatively easily. Dan Gurney gave Porsche their only grand prix win at Rouen, and Cooper won their last race until 1966. Lola made the first of their sporadic forays into grand prix racing, and Jack Brabham emerged as a constructor, scoring his first points in his own car. Stirling Moss, one of the great drivers, crashed heavily before the championship season began and never raced in grand prix again. He remained the most successful English driver in terms of wins until 1991 when Nigel Mansell overtook him, after competing in many more races. Ricardo Rodriguez became the youngest driver to score championship points with his fourth place in Belgium.

Dutch Grand Prix: Zandvoort, 20 May 1962

80 laps of 2.61 mile/4.19 km circuit

Place	Driver	Car	Laps	Time/reason for retiring	Grid
1	G Hill	BRM	80	2h 11m 02.1s	2
2	T Taylor	Lotus-Climax	80	2h 11m 29.3s	10
3	P Hill	Ferrari	80	2h 12m 23.2s	9
4	Baghetti	Ferrari	79		12
5	Maggs	Cooper-Climax	78		15
6	de Beaufort	Porsche	76		14
7	Bonnier	Porsche	75		13
8	R Rodriguez	Ferrari	73	spun	11
9	Ginther	BRM	71	accident	7
10	Lewis	Cooper-Climax	70		19
11	Clark	Lotus-Climax	70		3
12	Ireland	Lotus-Climax	61	spun	6
13	Gregory	Lotus-Climax	54	gearbox	16
14	Seidel	Emeryson-Climax	52		20
	Gurney	Porsche	47	gearbox	8
	McLaren	Cooper-Climax	21	gearbox	5
	Salvadori	Lola-Climax	11	withdrawn	17
	Surtees	Lola-Climax	8	suspension	1
	J Brabham	Lotus-Climax	3	accident	4
	Pon	Porsche	2	spun	18

Fastest Lap: McLaren, 1m 34.4s. 99.36 mph/159.9 kph

Monaco Grand Prix: Monte Carlo, 3 June 1962

100 laps of 1.95 mile/3.15 km circuit

Place	Driver	Car	Laps	Time/reason for retiring	Grid
1	McLaren	Cooper-Climax	100	2h 46m 29.7s	3
2	P Hill	Ferrari	100	2h 46m 31.0s	9
3	Bandini	Ferrari	100	2h 47m 53.8s	10
4	Surtees	Lola-Climax	99		11
5	Bonnier	Porsche	93		15
6	G Hill	BRM	92	engine	2
	Mairesse	Ferrari	90		4
	J Brabham	Lotus-Climax	77	suspension	6
	Ireland	Lotus-Climax	63	fuel pump	8
	Clark	Lotus-Climax	55	clutch	1
	Salvadori	Lola-Climax	44	suspension	12
	Maggs	Cooper-Climax	43	gearbox	16
	T Taylor	Lotus-Climax	24	oil	14
	Ginther	BRM	0	accident	13
	Gurney	Porsche	0	accident	5
	Trintignant	Lotus-Climax	0	accident	7

Fastest Lap: Clark, 1m 35.5s. 73.67 mph/118.55 kph

Belgian Grand Prix: Spa, 17 June 1962

32 laps of 8.76 mile/14.1 km circuit

Place	Driver	Car	Laps	Time/reason for retiring	Grid
1	Clark	Lotus-Climax	32	2h 07m 32.3s	12
2	G Hill	BRM	32	2h 08m 16.4s	1
3	P Hill	Ferrari	32	2h 09m 38.8s	4
4	R Rodriguez	Ferrari	32	2h 09m 38.9s	7
5	Surtees	Lola-Climax	31		11
6	J Brabham	Lotus-Climax	30		15
7	de Beaufort	Porsche	30		13
8	Trintignant	Lotus-Climax	30		16
9	Bianchi	Lotus-Climax	29		18
10	Siffert	Lotus-Climax	29		17
11	T Taylor	Lotus-Climax	25	accident	3
12	Mairesse	Ferrari	25	accident	6
13	Ginther	BRM	22	transmission	9
14	Maggs	Cooper-Climax	21	gearbox	10
15	McLaren	Cooper-Climax	19	oil	2
16	Campbell-Jones	Lotus-Climax	16		19
	Gregory	Lotus-BRM	12	withdrawn	8
	Ireland	Lotus-Climax	8	suspension	5
	Baghetti	Ferrari	3	ignition	14

Fastest Lap: Clark, 3m 55.6s. 133.87 mph/215.45 kph

French Grand Prix: Rouen, 8 July 1962

54 laps of 4.07 mile/6.54 km circuit

Place	Driver	Car	Laps	Time/reason for retiring	Grid
1	Gurney	Porsche	54	2h 07m 35.5s	6
2	Maggs	Cooper-Climax	53		11
3	Ginther	BRM	52		10
4	McLaren	Cooper-Climax	51		3
5	Surtees	Lola-Climax	51		5
6	de Beaufort	Porsche	51		17
7	Trintignant	Lotus-Climax	50		13
8	T Taylor	Lotus-Climax	48		12
9	G Hill	BRM	44		2
	Bonnier	Porsche	42	gearbox	9
	Clark	Lotus-Climax	33	suspension	1
	Lewis	Cooper-Climax	27	brakes	16
	Salvadori	Lola-Climax	20	oil pressure	14
	Gregory	Lotus-BRM	14	ignition	7
	J Brabham	Lotus-Climax	10	suspension	4
	Siffert	Lotus-BRM	5	clutch	15
	Ireland	Lotus-Climax	1	wheel	8

Fastest Lap: G Hill, 2m 16.9s. 106.9 mph/172.03 kph

British Grand Prix: Aintree, 21 July 1962

75 laps of 3 mile/4.83 km circuit

Place	Driver	Car	Laps	Time/reason for retiring	Grid
1	Clark	Lotus-Climax	75	2h 26m 20.8s	1
2	Surtees	Lola-Climax	75	2h 27m 10.0s	2
3	McLaren	Cooper-Climax	75	2h 28m 05.6s	4
4	G Hill	BRM	75	2h 28m 17.6s	5
5	J Brabham	Lotus-Climax	74		9
6	Maggs	Cooper-Climax	74		13
7	Gregory	Lotus-Climax	74		14
8	T Taylor	Lotus-Climax	74		10
9	Gurney	Porsche	73		6
10	Lewis	Cooper-Climax	72		15
11	Settember	Emeryson-Climax	71		19
12	Burgess	Cooper-Climax	71		16
13	Ginther	BRM	70		8
14	de Beaufort	Porsche	69		17
15	Chamberlain	Lotus-Climax	64		20
16	Ireland	Lotus-Climax	61		3
	P Hill	Ferrari	46	ignition	12
	Salvadori	Lola-Climax	34	ignition	11

British Grand Prix (cont)

Place	Driver	Car	Laps	Time/reason for retiring	Grid
	Bonnier	Porsche	26	crownwheel and pinion	7
	Seidel	Lotus-BRM	10	brakes	21
	Shelly	Lotus-Climax	5	overheating	18

Fastest Lap: Clark, 1m 55s. 93.91 mph/151.14 kph

German Grand Prix: Nürburgring, 5 August 1962

15 laps of 14.17 mile/22.81 km circuit

Place	Driver	Car	Laps	Time/reason for retiring	Grid
1	G Hill	BRM	15	2h 38m 45.3s	2
2	Surtees	Lola-Climax	15	2h 38m 47.8s	4
3	Gurney	Porsche	15	2h 38m 49.7s	1
4	Clark	Lotus-Climax	15	2h 39m 27.4s	3
5	McLaren	Cooper-Climax	15	2h 40m 04.9s	5
6	R Rodriguez	Ferrari	15	2h 40m 09.1s	10
7	Bonnier	Porsche	15	2h 43m 22.6s	6
8	Ginther	BRM	15	2h 43m 45.4s	7
9	Maggs	Cooper-Climax	15	2h 43m 52.1s	23
10	Baghetti	Ferrari	15	2h 47m 00.0s	13
11	Burgess	Cooper-Climax	15	2h 47m 00.6s	16
12	Siffert	Lotus-Climax	15	2h 47m 03.8s	17
13	de Beaufort	Porsche	15	2h 47m 57.1s	8
14	Walter	Porsche	14		14
15	Vaccarella	Porsche	14		15
16	Bianchi	ENB-Maserati	14		25
	Lewis	Cooper-Climax	10		21
	J Brabham	Brabham-Climax	8	throttle	24
	P Hill	Ferrari	8	shock absorbers	12
	Greene	Gilby-BRM	7	suspension	19
	Trintignant	Lotus-Climax	3	gearbox	11
	Bandini	Ferrari	3	accident	18
	Salvadori	Lola-Climax	3	gearbox	9
	Schiller	Lotus-BRM	3	oil	20
	Collomb	Cooper-Climax	2	gearbox	22
	T Taylor	Lotus-Climax	0	accident	26

Fastest Lap: G Hill, 10m 12.2s. 83.35 mph/134.13 kph

Italian Grand Prix: Monza, 16 September 1962

43 laps of 3.57 mile/5.75 km circuit

Place	Driver	Car	Laps	Time/reason for retiring	Grid
1	G Hill	BRM	86	2h 29m 08.4s	2
2	Ginther	BRM	86	2h 29m 38.2s	3
3	McLaren	Cooper-Climax	86	2h 30m 06.2s	4
4	Mairesse	Ferrari	86	2h 30m 06.6s	10
5	Baghetti	Ferrari	86	2h 30m 39.7s	18
6	Bonnier	Porsche	85		9
7	Maggs	Cooper-Climax	85		12
8	Bandini	Ferrari	84		17
9	Vaccarella	Lotus-Climax	84		14
10	de Beaufort	Porsche	81		20
11	P Hill	Ferrari	81		15
12	Gregory	Lotus-BRM	77		6
	Gurney	Porsche	66		7
	R Rodriguez	Ferrari	63	engine	11
	Ireland	Lotus-Climax	45	suspension	5
	Surtees	Lola-Climax	42	engine	8
	Salvadori	Lola-Climax	41	engine	13
	T Taylor	Lotus-Climax	25	transmission	16
	Settember	Emeryson-Climax	18	overheating	21
	Trintignant	Lotus-Climax	17	electrical	19
	Clark	Lotus-Climax	12	transmission	1

Fastest Lap: G Hill, 1m 42.3s. 125.73 mph/202.35 kph

United States Grand Prix: Watkins Glen, 7 October 1962

100 laps of 2.3 mile/3.7 km circuit

Place	Driver	Car	Laps	Time/reason for retiring	Grid
1	Clark	Lotus-Climax	100	2h 07m 13.0s	1
2	G Hill	BRM	100	2h 07m 22.2s	3
3	McLaren	Cooper-Climax	99		6
4	J Brabham	Brabham-Climax	99		5
5	Gurney	Porsche	99		4
6	Gregory	Lotus-BRM	99		7
7	Maggs	Cooper-Climax	97		10
8	Ireland	Lotus-Climax	96		15
9	Penske	Lotus-Climax	96		12
10	Schroeder	Lotus-Climax	93		16
11	Sharp	Cooper-Climax	91		14
12	T Taylor	Lotus-Climax	85		8
13	Bonnier	Porsche	79		9
	Ginther	BRM	34	engine	2
	Trintignant	Lotus-Climax	31	brakes	17

United States Grand Prix (cont)

Place	Driver	Car	Laps	Time/reason for retiring	Grid
	Mayer	Cooper-Climax	30	engine	11
	Surtees	Lola-Climax	18	oil	18
	de Beaufort	Porsche	8	accident	13

Fastest Lap: Clark, 1m 15s. 110.4 mph/177. 67 kph

South African Grand Prix: East London, 29 December 1962

82 laps of 2.44 mile/3.92 km circuit.

Place	Driver	Car	Laps	Time/reason for retiring	Grid
1	G Hill	BRM	82	2h 08m 03.3s	2
2	McLaren	Cooper-Climax	82	2h 08m 53.1s	8
3	Maggs	Cooper-Climax	82	2h 08m 53.6s	6
4	J Brabham	Brabham-Climax	82	2h 08m 57.1s	3
5	Ireland	Lotus-Climax	81		4
6	Lederle	Lotus-Climax	78		10
7	Ginther	BRM	78		7
8	Love	Cooper-Climax	78		12
9	Johnstone	BRM	76		17
10	Pieterse	Lotus-Climax	71		13
11	de Beaufort	Porsche	70		16
	Serrurier	LDS-Alfa	62	radiator	14
	Clark	Lotus-Climax	61	oil	1
	Salvadori	Lola-Climax	56	fuel tank	11
	Harris	Cooper-Alfa	31	engine	15
	Surtees	Lola-Climax	26	engine	5
	T Taylor	Lotus-Climax	11	transmission	9

Fastest Lap: Clark, 1m 31s. 96.35 mph/155.06 kph

World Championship 1962

1	G Hill	42 (52)
2	Clark	30
3	McLaren	27 (32)
4	Surtees	19
5	Gurney	15
6	P Hill	14
7	Maggs	13
8	Ginther	10
9	J Brabham	9
10	T Taylor	6
11	Baghetti	5
12=	Bandini, R Rodriguez	4
14=	Bonnier, Mairesse	3
16=	de Beaufort, Ireland	2
18=	Gregory, Lederle	1

Constructors' Championship

1	BRM	42 (56)
2	Lotus-Climax	36 (38)
3	Cooper-Climax	29 (41)
4	Lola-Climax	19
5=	Porsche	18 (19)
	Ferrari	18
7	Brabham-Climax	6
8	Lotus-BRM	1

1963

Jim Clark won his first championship with seven wins to two by Graham Hill and one by John Surtees in a revised Ferrari. Clark's total of wins in a season was beaten by Ayrton Senna in 1988, but Clark won 70% of the races in the championship, whereas Senna won only 50%. The ATS venture, founded by ex-Ferrari workers, a complete disaster which ruined Phil Hill's grand prix career, was unrelated to the late 1970s German operation which was marginally more successful.

Monaco Grand Prix: Monte Carlo, 26 May 1963

100 laps of 1.95 mile/3.15 km circuit

Place	Driver	Car	Laps	Time/reason for retiring	Grid
1	G Hill	BRM	100	2h 41m 49.7s	2
2	Ginther	BRM	100	2h 41m 54.3s	4
3	McLaren	Cooper-Climax	100	2h 42m 02.5s	8
4	Surtees	Ferrari	100	2h 42m 03.8s	3
5	Maggs	Cooper-Climax	98		10
6	T Taylor	Lotus-Climax	98		9
7	Bonnier	Cooper-Climax	94		11
8	Clark	Lotus-Climax	78	gearbox	1
9	J Brabham	Lotus-Climax	77		15
	Ireland	Lotus-BRM	40	accident	5
	Mairesse	Ferrari	37	transmission	7
	Trintignant	Lola-Climax	34	engine	14
	Gurney	Brabham-Climax	25	crownwheel and pinion	6
	Hall	Lotus-BRM	20	gearbox	13
	Siffert	Lotus-BRM	3	engine	12

Fastest Lap: Surtees, 1m 34.5s. 74.45 mph/119.81 kph

Belgian Grand Prix: Spa, 9 June 1963

32 laps of 8.76 mile/14.1 km circuit

Place	Driver	Car	Laps	Time/reason for retiring	Grid
1	Clark	Lotus-Climax	32	2h 27m 47.6s	8
2	McLaren	Cooper-Climax	32	2h 32m 41.6s	5
3	Gurney	Brabham-Climax	31		2
4	Ginther	BRM	31		9
5	Bonnier	Cooper-Climax	30		13
6	de Beaufort	Porsche	30		18
	Maggs	Cooper-Climax	27	spun	4
	Settember	Scirocco-BRM	25	spun	19
	Surtees	Ferrari	18	engine	10
	Bianchi	Lola-Climax	17	spun	16
	G Hill	BRM	17	gearbox	1
	Hall	Lotus-BRM	16	spun	12
	Siffert	Lotus-BRM	16	spun	14
	P Hill	ATS	13	transmission	17
	J Brabham	Brabham-Climax	11	electrical	6
	Amon	Lola-Climax	9	oil	15
	Ireland	BRP-BRM	8	gearbox	7
	Baghetti	ATS	7	gearbox	20
	Mairesse	Ferrari	6	engine	3
	T Taylor	Lotus-Climax	4	oil	11

Fastest Lap: Clark, 3m 58.1s. 132.47 mph/213.19 kph

Dutch Grand Prix: Zandvoort, 23 June 1963

80 laps of 2.61 mile/4.19 km circuit

Place	Driver	Car	Laps	Time/reason for retiring	Grid
1	Clark	Lotus-Climax	80	2h 08m 13.07s	1
2	Gurney	Brabham-Climax	79		14
3	Surtees	Ferrari	79		5
4	Ireland	BRP-BRM	79		7
5	Ginther	BRM	79		6
6	Scarfiotti	Ferrari	78		11
7	Siffert	Lotus-BRM	77		17
8	Hall	Lotus-BRM	77		18
9	de Beaufort	Porsche	75		19
10	G Hill	BRM	69	engine	2
11	J Brabham	Brabham-Climax	67	chassis	4
12	T Taylor	Lotus-Climax	66		10
13	Bonnier	Cooper-Climax	56		8
	Amon	Lola-Climax	28	water pump	12
	Baghetti	ATS	17	ignition	15
	P Hill	ATS	15	wheel	13

Dutch Grand Prix (cont)

Place	Driver	Car	Laps	Time/reason for retiring	Grid
	Maggs	Cooper-Climax	13	overheating	9
	McLaren	Cooper-Climax	6	gearbox	3
	Mitter	Porsche	1	clutch	16

Fastest Lap: Clark, 1m 33.7s. 100.1 mph/161.1 kph

French Grand Prix: Reims, 30 June 1963

53 laps of 5.16 mile/8.3 km circuit

Place	Driver	Car	Laps	Time/reason for retiring	Grid
1	Clark	Lotus-Climax	53	2h 10m 54.3s	1
2	Maggs	Cooper-Climax	53	2h 11m 59.2s	8
3	G Hill	BRM	53	2h 13m 08.2s	2
4	J Brabham	Brabham-Climax	53	2h 13m 09.5s	5
5	Gurney	Brabham-Climax	53	2h 13m 27.7s	3
6	Siffert	Lotus-BRM	52		10
7	Amon	Lola-Climax	51		15
8	Trintignant	Lotus-Climax	50		14
9	Ireland	BRP-BRM	49		9
10	Bandini	BRM	45		19
11	Hall	Lotus-BRM	45		16
12	McLaren	Cooper-Climax	42	electrical	6
13	T Taylor	Lotus-Climax	41	crownwheel and pinion	7
14	P Hill	Lotus-BRM	34		13
15	Bonnier	Cooper-Climax	32		11
	Gregory	Lotus-BRM	30	gearbox	17
	Surtees	Ferrari	12	fuel pump	4
	Settember	Scirocco-BRM	5	wheel	18
	Ginther	BRM	4	radiator	12

Fastest Lap: Clark, 2m 21.6s. 131.15 mph/211.06 kph
* G Hill was push started, incurring a 1 minute penalty from the organisers, and was awarded no championship points for his third place.

British Grand Prix: Silverstone, 20 July 1963

82 laps of 2.93 mile/4.71 km circuit

Place	Driver	Car	Laps	Time/reason for retiring	Grid
1	Clark	Lotus-Climax	82	2h 14m 09.6s	1
2	Surtees	Ferrari	82	2h 14m 35.4s	5
3	G Hill	BRM	82	2h 14m 47.2s	3
4	Ginther	BRM	81		9
5	Bandini	BRM	81		8
6	Hall	Lotus-BRM	80		13

British Grand Prix (cont)

Place	Driver	Car	Laps	Time/reason for retiring	Grid
7	Amon	Lola-Climax	80		14
8	Hailwood	Lotus-Climax	78		17
9	Maggs	Cooper-Climax	78		7
10	de Beaufort	Porsche	76		21
11	Gregory	Lotus-BRM	75		22
12	Anderson	Lola-Climax	75		16
13	Campbell-Jones	Lola-Climax	74		23
	Siffert	Lotus-BRM	66	gearbox	15
	Bonnier	Cooper-Climax	65	oil	12
	Gurney	Brabham-Climax	59	engine	2
	Raby	Gilby-BRM	59	gearbox	19
	Burgess	Scirocco-BRM	36	ignition	20
	J Brabham	Brabham-Climax	27	engine	4
	Ireland	BRP-BRM	26	disqualified: push start	11
	T Taylor	Lotus-Climax	23	disqualified: push start	10
	Settember	Scirocco-BRM	20	ignition	18
	McLaren	Cooper-Climax	7	engine	6

Fastest Lap: Surtees, 1m 36.0s. 109.76 mph/176.65 kph

German Grand Prix: Nürburgring, 4 August 1963

15 laps of 14.17 mile/22.81 km circuit

Place	Driver	Car	Laps	Time/reason for retiring	Grid
1	Surtees	Ferrari	15	2h 13m 06.8s	2
2	Clark	Lotus-Climax	15	2h 14m 24.3s	1
3	Ginther	BRM	15	2h 15m 51.7s	6
4	Mitter	Porsche	15	2h 21m 18.3s	15
5	Hall	Lotus-BRM	14		16
6	Bonnier	Cooper-Climax	14		12
7	J Brabham	Brabham-Climax	14		8
8	T Taylor	Lotus-Climax	14		18
9	Siffert	Lotus-BRM	10	transmission	9
10	Collomb	Lotus-Climax	10		21
	de Beaufort	Porsche	9	lost wheel	17
	Maggs	Cooper-Climax	7	engine	10
	Gurney	Brabham-Climax	6	gearbox	13
	Cabral	Cooper-Climax	6	gearbox	20
	Burgess	Scirocco-BRM	5	steering	19
	Settember	Scirocco-BRM	5	accident	22
	McLaren	Cooper-Climax	3	accident	5
	Amon	Lola-Climax	2	accident	14
	G Hill	BRM	2	gearbox	4
	Mairesse	Ferrari	1	accident	7
	Ireland	Lotus-BRM	0	accident	11
	Bandini	BRM	0	accident	3

Fastest Lap: Surtees, 8m 47.0s. 96.82 mph/155.82 kph

Italian Grand Prix: Monza, 8 September 1963

86 laps of 3.57 mile/5.75 km circuit

Place	Driver	Car	Laps	Time/reason for retiring	Grid
1	Clark	Lotus-Climax	86	2h 24m 19.6s	3
2	Ginther	BRM	86	2h 25m 54.6s	4
3	McLaren	Cooper-Climax	85		8
4	Ireland	BRP-BRM	84	engine	10
5	J Brabham	Brabham-Climax	84		7
6	Maggs	Cooper-Climax	84		13
7	Bonnier	Cooper-Climax	84		11
8	Hall	Lotus-BRM	84		16
9	Trintignant	BRM	83		19
10	Hailwood	Lola-Climax	82		17
11	P Hill	ATS	79		14
12	Anderson	Lola-Climax	79		18
13	Spence	Lotus-Climax	73	oil	9
14	Gurney	Brabham-Climax	64	fuel feed	5
15	Baghetti	ATS	63		20
	G Hill	BRM	59	clutch	2
	Siffert	Lotus-BRM	40	oil	15
	Bandini	Ferrari	37	gearbox	6
	Gregory	Lotus-BRM	26	engine	12
	Surtees	Ferrari	16	engine	1

Fastest Lap: Clark, 1m 38.9s. 130.05 mph/209.3 kph

United States Grand Prix: Watkins Glen, 6 October 1963

110 laps of 2.3 mile/3.7 km circuit

Place	Driver	Car	Laps	Time/reason for retiring	Grid
1	G Hill	BRM	110	2h 19m 22.1s	1
2	Ginther	BRM	110	2h 19m 54.6s	4
3	Clark	Lotus-Climax	109		2
4	J Brabham	Brabham-Climax	108		5
5	Bandini	Ferrari	106		9
6	de Beaufort	Porsche	99		19
7	Broeker	Stebro-Ford	88		21
8	Bonnier	Cooper-Climax	85		12
	Surtees	Ferrari	82	engine	3
	Hall	Lotus-BRM	76		16
	McLaren	Cooper-Climax	74	fuel feed	11
	Siffert	Lotus-BRM	56	gearbox	14
	Ward	Lotus-BRM	44	gearbox	17
	Maggs	Cooper-Climax	44	engine	10
	Gurney	Brabham-Climax	42	chassis/fuel	6
	P Rodriguez	Lotus-Climax	36	engine	13
	T Taylor	Lotus-Climax	24	ignition	7

United States Grand Prix (cont)

Place	Driver	Car	Laps	Time/reason for retiring	Grid
	Gregory	Lola-Climax	14	overheating	8
	Sharp	Lotus-BRM	6	tappet	18
	P Hill	ATS	4	oil	15
	Baghetti	ATS	0	oil	20

Fastest Lap: Clark, 1m 14.5s. 111.14 mph/178.86 kph

Mexican Grand Prix: Mexico City, 27 October 1963

65 laps of 3.11 mile/5 km circuit

Place	Driver	Car	Laps	Time/reason for retiring	Grid
1	Clark	Lotus-Climax	65	2h 09m 52.1s	1
2	J Brabham	Brabham-Climax	65	2h 11m 33.2s	10
3	Ginther	BRM	65	2h 11m 46.8s	5
4	G Hill	BRM	64		3
5	Bonnier	Cooper-Climax	62		8
6	Gurney	Brabham-Climax	62		4
7	Sharp	Lotus-BRM	61		16
8	Hall	Lotus-BRM	61		15
9	Siffert	Lotus-BRM	59		9
10	de Beaufort	Porsche	58		18
	Solana	BRM	57	engine	11
	P Hill	ATS	39	suspension	17
	Bandini	Ferrari	35	engine	7
	McLaren	Cooper-Climax	29	engine	6
	P Rodriguez	Lotus-Climax	25	suspension	20
	Gregory	Lola-Climax	25	suspension	14
	T Taylor	Lotus-Climax	18	engine	12
	Surtees	Ferrari	18	disqualified: push start	2
	Baghetti	ATS	10	fuel system	21
	Amon	Lotus-BRM	8	engine	19
	Maggs	Cooper-Climax	7	engine	13

Fastest Lap: Clark, 1m 58.1s. 94.71 mph/152.41 kph

South African Grand Prix: East London, 28 December 1963

85 laps of 2.44 mile/3.92 km circuit.

Place	Driver	Car	Laps	Time/reason for retiring	Grid
1	Clark	Lotus-Climax	85	2h 10m 36.9s	1
2	Gurney	Brabham-Climax	85	2h 11m 43.7s	3
3	G Hill	BRM	84		6

South African Grand Prix (cont)

Place	Driver	Car	Laps	Time/reason for retiring	Grid
4	McLaren	Cooper-Climax	84		9
5	Bandini	Ferrari	84		5
6	Bonnier	Cooper-Climax	83		11
7	Maggs	Cooper-Climax	82		10
8	T Taylor	Lotus-Climax	81		8
9	Love	Cooper-Climax	80		13
10	de Beaufort	Porsche	79		20
11	Serrurier	LDS-Alfa	78		18
12	Blokdyk	Cooper-Maserati	77		19
13	J Brabham	Brabham-Climax	71	spun	2
14	Niemann	Lotus-Ford	66		15
	de Klerk	Alfa Special	53	gearbox	16
	Prophet	Brabham-Ford	48	oil	14
	Ginther	BRM	43	transmission	7
	Surtees	Ferrari	43	engine	4
	Pieterse	Lotus-Climax	3	engine	12
	Tingle	LDS-Alfa	2	transmission	17

Fastest Lap: Gurney, 1m 29.1s. 98.41 mph/158.37 kph

World Championship 1963

1	Clark	54 (73)
2	G Hill	29
3	Ginther	29 (34)
4	Surtees	22
5	Gurney	19
6	McLaren	17
7	Brabham	14
8	Maggs	9
9 =	Bandini, Bonnier, Ireland	6
12 =	Hall, Mitter	3
14	de Beaufort	2
15 =	Scarfiotti, Siffert, T Taylor	1

Constructors' Championship

1	Lotus-Climax	54 (74)
2	BRM	36 (45)
3	Brabham-Climax	28 (30)
4	Ferrari	26
5	Cooper-Climax	25 (26)
6	BRP-BRM	6
7	Porsche	5
8	Lotus-BRM	4

1964

The championship, fiercely contested by Clark, Surtees and Graham Hill, was decided at the Mexican Grand Prix when Hill was delayed after a collision with Bandini's Ferrari. Clark was forced to stop with an oil leak on the last lap, and Ferrari signalled Bandini to let Surtees through into the second place which gave him the championship by one point from Hill. Honda made a low-key debut in grand prix racing with the American driver Ronnie Bucknum, and Maurice Trintignant retired at the age of 47 after one of the longest world championship careers.

Monaco Grand Prix: Monte Carlo, 10 May 1964

100 laps of 1.95 mile/3.15 km circuit

Place	Driver	Car	Laps	Time/reason for retiring	Grid
1	G Hill	BRM	100	2h 41m 19.5s	3
2	Ginther	BRM	99		8
3	Arundell	Lotus-Climax	97		6
4	Clark	Lotus-Climax	96	engine	1
5	Bonnier	Cooper-Climax	96		11
6	Hailwood	Lotus-BRM	96		15
7	Anderson	Brabham-Climax	86		12
8	Siffert	Lotus-BRM	78		16
	P Hill	Cooper-Climax	70	suspension	9
	Bandini	Ferrari	67	gearbox	7
	Gurney	Brabham-Climax	61	gearbox	5
	Trintignant	BRM	53	exhaustion	13
	J Brabham	Brabham-Climax	29	fuel injection	2
	McLaren	Cooper-Climax	17	oil	10
	Surtees	Ferrari	14	gearbox	4
	T Taylor	BRP-BRM	7	fuel leak	14

Fastest Lap: G Hill, 1m 33.9s. 74.92 mph/120.58 kph

1964

Dutch Grand Prix: Zandvoort, 24 May 1964

80 laps of 2.61 mile/4.19 km circuit

Place	Driver	Car	Laps	Time/reason for retiring	Grid
1	Clark	Lotus-Climax	80	2h 07m 35.4s	2
2	Surtees	Ferrari	80	2h 08m 29.0s	4
3	Arundell	Lotus-Climax	79		6
4	G Hill	BRM	79		3
5	Amon	Lotus-BRM	79		13
6	Anderson	Brabham-Climax	78		11
7	McLaren	Cooper-Climax	78		5
8	P Hill	Cooper-Climax	76		9
9	Bonnier	Brabham-BRM	76		12
10	Baghetti	BRM	74		15
11	Ginther	BRM	64		8
12	Hailwood	Lotus-BRM	57	crownwheel and pinion	14
13	Siffert	Brabham-BRM	55		17
	J Brabham	Brabham-Climax	44	ignition	7
	Bandini	Ferrari	25	fuel injection	10
	Gurney	Brabham-Climax	23	steering wheel	1
	de Beaufort	Porsche	8	engine	16

Fastest Lap: Clark, 1m 32.8s. 101.07 mph/162.66 kph

Belgian Grand Prix: Spa, 14 June 1964

32 laps of 8.76 mile/14.1 km circuit

Place	Driver	Car	Laps	Time/reason for retiring	Grid
1	Clark	Lotus-Climax	32	2h 06m 40.5s	6
2	McLaren	Cooper-Climax	32	2h 06m 43.9s	7
3	J Brabham	Brabham-Climax	32	2h 07m 28.6s	3
4	Ginther	BRM	32	2h 08m 39.1s	8
5	G Hill	BRM	31	fuel	2
6	Gurney	Brabham-Climax	31	fuel	1
7	T Taylor	BRP-BRM	31		12
8	Baghetti	BRM	31		17
9	Arundell	Lotus-Climax	28		4
10	Ireland	BRP-BRM	28		16
	Revson	Lotus-BRM	27	disqualified: push start	10
	Siffert	Brabham-BRM	13	engine	13
	P Hill	Cooper-Climax	13	engine	15
	Bandini	Ferrari	11	engine	9
	A Pilette	Scirocco-Climax	10	engine	18
	Bonnier	Brabham-BRM	7	driver ill	14
	Amon	Lotus-BRM	3	engine	11
	Surtees	Ferrari	3	engine	5

Fastest Lap: Gurney, 3m 49.2s. 137.61 mph/221.47 kph

French Grand Prix: Rouen, 28 June 1964

57 laps of 4.07 mile/6.54 km circuit

Place	Driver	Car	Laps	Time/reason for retiring	Grid
1	Gurney	Brabham-Climax	57	2h 07m 49.1s	2
2	G Hill	BRM	57	2h 08m 13.2s	6
3	J Brabham	Brabham-Climax	57	2h 08m 14.0s	5
4	Arundell	Lotus-Climax	57	2h 08m 59.7s	4
5	Ginther	BRM	57	2h 10m 01.2s	9
6	McLaren	Cooper-Climax	56		7
7	P Hill	Cooper-Climax	56		10
8	Hailwood	Lotus-BRM	56		13
9	Bandini	Ferrari	55		8
10	Amon	Lotus-BRM	53		14
11	Trintignant	BRM	52		16
12	Anderson	Brabham-Climax	50		15
	Ireland	BRP-BRM	31	spun	11
	Clark	Lotus-Climax	31	engine	1
	Surtees	Ferrari	6	engine	3
	T Taylor	BRP-BRM	6	brakes	12
	Siffert	Brabham-BRM	4	engine	17

Fastest Lap: Brabham, 2m 11.4s. 111.37 mph/179.23 kph

British Grand Prix: Brands Hatch, 11 July 1964

80 laps of 2.65 mile/4.27 km circuit

Place	Driver	Car	Laps	Time/reason for retiring	Grid
1	Clark	Lotus-Climax	80	2h 15m 07.0s	1
2	G Hill	BRM	80	2h 15m 09.8s	2
3	Surtees	Ferrari	80	2h 16m 27.6s	5
4	J Brabham	Brabham-Climax	79		4
5	Bandini	Ferrari	78		8
6	P Hill	Cooper-Climax	78		15
7	Anderson	Brabham-Climax	78		7
8	Ginther	BRM	77		14
9	Spence	Lotus-Climax	77		13
10	Ireland	BRP-BRM	77		10
11	Siffert	Brabham-BRM	76		16
12	Baghetti	BRM	76		21
13	Gurney	Brabham-Climax	75		3
14	J Taylor	Cooper-Ford	56		20
	Bonnier	Brabham-BRM	46	brakes	9
	Revson	Lotus-BRM	43	engine	22
	Raby	Brabham-BRM	37	wheel	17
	Maggs	BRM	37	gearbox	23
	T Taylor	Lotus-BRM	22	driver ill	18
	Hailwood	Lotus-BRM	16	oil	12

British Grand Prix (cont)

Place	Driver	Car	Laps	Time/reason for retiring	Grid
	Amon	Lotus-BRM	9	clutch	11
	McLaren	Cooper-Climax	6	gearbox	6
	Gardner	Brabham-Ford	0	accident	19

Fastest Lap: Clark, 1m 38.8s. 96.56 mph/155.4 kph

German Grand Prix: Nürburgring, 2 August 1964

15 laps of 14.17 mile/22.81 km circuit

Place	Driver	Car	Laps	Time/reason for retiring	Grid
1	Surtees	Ferrari	15	2h 12m 04.8s	1
2	G Hill	BRM	15	2h 13m 20.4s	5
3	Bandini	Ferrari	15	2h 16m 57.6s	4
4	Siffert	Brabham-BRM	15	2h 17m 27.9s	10
5	Trintignant	BRM	14	engine	14
6	Maggs	BRM	14		16
7	Ginther	BRM	14		11
8	Spence	Lotus-Climax	14		17
9	Mitter	Lotus-Climax	14		19
10	Gurney	Brabham-Climax	14		3
	Amon	Lotus-BRM	12	suspension	9
	J Brabham	Brabham-Climax	11	crownwheel and pinion	6
	Bucknum	Honda	11	spun	22
	Revson	Lotus-BRM	10	accident	18
	Clark	Lotus-Climax	7	engine	2
	McLaren	Cooper-Climax	4	engine	7
	Anderson	Brabham-Climax	4	suspension	15
	Barth	Cooper-Climax	3	clutch	20
	Baghetti	BRM	2	throttle	21
	P Hill	Cooper-Climax	1	engine	8
	Hailwood	Lotus-BRM	0	engine	13
	Bonnier	Brabham-BRM	0	ignition	12

Fastest Lap: Surtees, 8m 39.0s. 98.31 mph/158.22 kph
* de Beaufort fatally injured in practice.

Austrian Grand Prix: Zeltweg, 23 August 1964

105 laps of 1.99 mile/3.2 km circuit

Place	Driver	Car	Laps	Time/reason for retiring	Grid
1	Bandini	Ferrari	105	2h 06m 18.2s	7
2	Ginther	BRM	105	2h 06m 24.4s	5
3	Anderson	Brabham-Climax	102		14

Austrian Grand Prix (cont)

Place	Driver	Car	Laps	Time/reason for retiring	Grid
4	Maggs	BRM	102		19
5	Ireland	BRP-BRM	102		11
6	Bonnier	Brabham-Climax	101		10
7	Baghetti	BRM	96		15
8	Hailwood	Lotus-BRM	95		18
9	J Brabham	Brabham-Climax	76		6
	Rindt	Brabham-BRM	58	steering	13
	P Hill	Cooper-Climax	58	accident	20
	Gurney	Brabham-Climax	47	suspension	4
	McLaren	Cooper-Climax	43	engine	9
	Spence	Lotus-Climax	41	transmission	8
	Clark	Lotus-Climax	40	transmission	3
	T Taylor	BRP-BRM	21	suspension	16
	Siffert	Brabham-BRM	18	spun	12
	Surtees	Ferrari	8	suspension	2
	Amon	Lotus-Climax	7	engine	17
	G Hill	BRM	5	distributor	1

Fastest Lap: Gurney, 1m 10.56s. 101.57 mph/163.46 kph

Italian Grand Prix: Monza, 6 September 1964

78 laps of 3.57 mile/5.75 km circuit

Place	Driver	Car	Laps	Time/reason for retiring	Grid
1	Surtees	Ferrari	78	2h 10m 51.8s	1
2	McLaren	Cooper-Climax	78	2h 11m 57.8s	5
3	Bandini	Ferrari	77		7
4	Ginther	BRM	77		9
5	Ireland	BRP-BRM	77		13
6	Spence	Lotus-Climax	77		8
7	Siffert	Brabham-BRM	77		6
8	Baghetti	BRM	77		15
9	Scarfiotti	Ferrari	77		16
10	Gurney	Brabham-Climax	75		2
11	Anderson	Brabham-Climax	75		14
12	Bonnier	Brabham-Climax	74		12
13	Revson	Lotus-BRM	72		18
	J Brabham	Brabham-Climax	59	engine	11
	Clark	Lotus-Climax	27	engine	4
	Cabral	ATS	24	engine	19
	Trintignant	BRM	21	engine	20
	Bucknum	Honda	12	brakes	10
	Hailwood	Lotus-BRM	4	engine	17
	G Hill	BRM	0	clutch	3

Fastest Lap: Surtees, 1m 38.8s. 130.19 mph/209.51 kph

United States Grand Prix: Watkins Glen, 4 October 1964

110 laps of 2.3 mile/3.7 km circuit

Place	Driver	Car	Laps	Time/reason for retiring	Grid
1	G Hill	BRM	110	2h 16m 38.0s	4
2	Surtees	Ferrari	110	2h 17m 08.5s	2
3	Siffert	Brabham-BRM	109		12
4	Ginther	BRM	107		13
5	Hansgen	Lotus-Climax	107		17
6	T Taylor	BRP-BRM	106		15
7	Spence/Clark	Lotus-Climax	102		6
8	Hailwood	Lotus-BRM	101		16
9	Gurney	Brabham-Climax	69	oil	3
10	Sharp	Brabham-BRM	65		18
	Bandini	Ferrari	58	engine	8
	Clark/Spence	Lotus-Climax	54	fuel injection	1
	Bucknum	Honda	50	overheating	14
	Amon	Lotus-BRM	47	engine	11
	Bonnier	Brabham-Climax	37	wheel	9
	McLaren	Cooper-Climax	26	engine	5
	J Brabham	Brabham-Climax	14	engine	7
	P Hill	Cooper-Climax	4	ignition	19
	Ireland	BRP-BRM	2	gear lever	10

Fastest Lap: Clark, 1m 12.7s. 113.89 mph/183.29 kph
* When his own car gave trouble, Clark took over Spence's in order to try to finish ahead of his championship rivals Surtees and G Hill, thereby denying them points, although he could not score himself in a shared drive.

Mexican Grand Prix: Mexico City, 25 October 1964

65 laps of 3.11 mile/5 km circuit

Place	Driver	Car	Laps	Time/reason for retiring	Grid
1	Gurney	Brabham-Climax	65	2h 09m 50.32s	2
2	Surtees	Ferrari	65	2h 10m 59.26s	4
3	Bandini	Ferrari	65	2h 10m 59.95s	3
4	Spence	Lotus-Climax	65	2h 11m 12.18s	5
5	Clark	Lotus-Climax	64	engine	1
6	P Rodriguez	Ferrari	64		9
7	McLaren	Cooper-Climax	64		10
8	Ginther	BRM	64		11
9	P Hill	Cooper-Climax	63	engine	15
10	Solana	Lotus-Climax	63		14
11	G Hill	BRM	63		6
12	Ireland	BRP-BRM	61		16
13	Sharp	Brabham-BRM	60		19
	Amon	Lotus-BRM	45	gearbox	12
	J Brabham	Brabham-Climax	44	engine	7

Mexican Grand Prix (cont)

Place	Driver	Car	Laps	Time/reason for retiring	Grid
	Hailwood	Lotus-BRM	11	overheating	17
	Siffert	Brabham-BRM	10	fuel pump	13
	Bonnier	Brabham-Climax	9	suspension	8
	T Taylor	BRP-BRM	5	overheating	18

Fastest Lap: Clark, 1m 58.37s. 94.49 mph/152.07 kph

World Championship 1964

1	Surtees	40
2	G Hill	39 (41)
3	Clark	32
4 =	Bandini, Ginther	23
6	Gurney	19
7	McLaren	13
8 =	Arundell, Brabham	11
10	Siffert	7
11	Anderson	5
12 =	Ireland, Maggs, Spence	4
15	Bonnier	3
16 =	Amon, Hansgen, Trintignant	2
19 =	Hailwood, P Hill, P Rodriguez, T Taylor	1

Constructors' Championship

1	Ferrari	45 (49)
2	BRM	42 (51)
3	Lotus-Climax	37 (40)
4	Brabham-Climax	30
5	Cooper-Climax	16
6	Brabham-BRM	7
7	BRP-BRM	5
8	Lotus-BRM	3

Clark's second championship included six wins interrupted only by non-starting at Monaco while he was away winning Indianapolis. Jackie Stewart finished third in the championship on his debut, and Richie Ginther won his only, and Honda's first, grand prix in the final race of the 1.5 litre formula.

South African Grand Prix: East London, 1 January 1965

85 laps of 2.44 mile/3.92 km circuit

Place	Driver	Car	Laps	Time/reason for retiring	Grid
1	Clark	Lotus-Climax	85	2h 06m 46.0s	1
2	Surtees	Ferrari	85	2h 07m 15.0s	2
3	G Hill	BRM	85	2h 07m 17.8s	5
4	Spence	Lotus-Climax	85	2h 07m 40.4s	4
5	McLaren	Cooper-Climax	84		8
6	Stewart	BRM	83		11
7	Siffert	Brabham-BRM	83		14
8	J Brabham	Brabham-Climax	81		3
9	Hawkins	Brabham-Ford	81		16
10	de Klerk	Alfa Special	79		17
11	Maggs	Lotus-BRM	77		13
12	Gardner	Brabham-BRM	75		15
13	Tingle	LDS-Alfa	73		20
14	Prophet	Brabham-Ford	71		19
15	Bandini	Ferrari	66	electrical	6
16	Anderson	Brabham-Climax	50		12
	Bonnier	Brabham-Climax	42	transmission	7
	Rindt	Cooper-Climax	39	electrical	10
	Love	Cooper-Climax	20	transmission	18
	Gurney	Brabham-Climax	11	ignition	9

Fastest Lap: Clark, 1m 27.6s. 100.1 mph/161.09 kph

Monaco Grand Prix: Monte Carlo, 30 May 1965

100 laps of 1.95 mile/3.15 km circuit

Place	Driver	Car	Laps	Time/reason for retiring	Grid
1	G Hill	BRM	100	2h 37m 39.6s	1
2	Bandini	Ferrari	100	2h 38m 43.6s	4
3	Stewart	BRM	100	2h 39m 21.5s	3
4	Surtees	Ferrari	99	out of fuel	5
5	McLaren	Cooper-Climax	98		7
6	Siffert	Brabham-BRM	98		10
7	Bonnier	Brabham-Climax	97		13
8	Hulme	Brabham-Climax	92		8
9	Anderson	Brabham-Climax	85		9
	Hawkins	Lotus-Climax	79	accident	14
	Attwood	Lotus-BRM	43	accident	6
	J Brabham	Brabham-Climax	42	engine	2
	Bucknum	Honda	32	gearbox	15
	Gardner	Brabham-BRM	28	engine	11
	Hailwood	Lotus-BRM	11	gearbox	12
	Ginther	Honda	0	transmission	16

Fastest Lap: G Hill, 1m 31.7s. 76.72 mph/123.47 kph

Belgian Grand Prix: Spa, 13 June 1965

32 laps of 8.76 mile/14.1 km circuit

Place	Driver	Car	Laps	Time/reason for retiring	Grid
1	Clark	Lotus-Climax	32	2h 23m 34.8s	2
2	Stewart	BRM	32	2h 24m 19.6s	3
3	McLaren	Cooper-Climax	31		9
4	J Brabham	Brabham-Climax	31		10
5	G Hill	BRM	31		1
6	Ginther	Honda	31		4
7	Spence	Lotus-Climax	31		12
8	Siffert	Brabham-BRM	31		8
9	Bandini	Ferrari	30		15
10	Gurney	Brabham-Climax	30		5
11	Rindt	Cooper-Climax	29		14
12	Bianchi	BRM	29		17
13	Ireland	Lotus-BRM	27		16
	Attwood	Lotus-BRM	26	spun	13
	Gregory	BRM	12	fuel pump	19
	Bucknum	Honda	9	engine	11
	Bonnier	Brabham-Climax	8	ignition	7
	Surtees	Ferrari	5	ignition	6
	Gardner	Brabham-BRM	2	ignition	18

Fastest Lap: Clark, 4m 12.9s. 124.72 mph/200.71 kph

French Grand Prix: Clermont-Ferrand, 27 June 1965

40 laps of 5.01 mile/8.06 km circuit

Place	Driver	Car	Laps	Time/reason for retiring	Grid
1	Clark	Lotus-Climax	40	2h 14m 38.4s	1
2	Stewart	BRM	40	2h 15m 04.7s	2
3	Surtees	Ferrari	40	2h 17m 11.9s	4
4	Hulme	Brabham-Climax	40	2h 17m 31.5s	6
5	G Hill	BRM	39		13
6	Siffert	Brabham-BRM	39		14
7	Spence	Lotus-Climax	39		10
	Bandini	Ferrari	36	spun	3
	Anderson	Brabham-Climax	30	spun	15
	McLaren	Cooper-Climax	23	suspension	9
	Bonnier	Brabham-Climax	21	ignition	11
	Amon	Lotus-BRM	20	fuel system	8
	Ireland	Lotus-BRM	18	gearbox	17
	Gurney	Brabham-Climax	16	engine	5
	Ginther	Honda	9	ignition	7
	Bucknum	Honda	4	engine	16
	Rindt	Cooper-Climax	3	accident	12

Fastest Lap: Clark, 3m 18.9s. 90.59 mph/145.79 kph

British Grand Prix: Silverstone, 10 July 1965

80 laps of 2.93 mile/4.71 km circuit

Place	Driver	Car	Laps	Time/reason for retiring	Grid
1	Clark	Lotus-Climax	80	2h 05m 25.4s	1
2	G Hill	BRM	80	2h 05m 28.6s	2
3	Surtees	Ferrari	80	2h 05m 53.0s	5
4	Spence	Lotus-Climax	80	2h 06m 05.0s	6
5	Stewart	BRM	80	2h 06m 40.0s	4
6	Gurney	Brabham-Climax	79		7
7	Bonnier	Brabham-Climax	79		13
8	Gardner	Brabham-BRM	78		12
9	Siffert	Brabham-BRM	78		17
10	McLaren	Cooper-Climax	77		10
11	Raby	Brabham-BRM	73		19
12	Gregory	BRM	70		18
13	Attwood	Lotus-BRM	63		15
	Rindt	Cooper-Climax	62		11
	Ireland	Lotus-BRM	41	engine	14
	Rhodes	Cooper-Climax	38	ignition	20
	Anderson	Brabham-Climax	33	gearbox	16

British Grand Prix (cont)

Place	Driver	Car	Laps	Time/reason for retiring	Grid
	Hulme	Brabham-Climax	29	alternator belt	9
	Ginther	Honda	26	ignition	3
	Bandini	Ferrari	2	engine	8

Fastest Lap: G Hill, 1m 32.2s. 114.29 mph/183.93 kph

Dutch Grand Prix: Zandvoort, 18 July 1965

80 laps of 2.61 mile/4.19 km circuit

Place	Driver	Car	Laps	Time/reason for retiring	Grid
1	Clark	Lotus-Climax	80	2h 03m 59.1s	2
2	Stewart	BRM	80	2h 04m 07.1s	6
3	Gurney	Brabham-Climax	80	2h 04m 12.1s	5
4	G Hill	BRM	80	2h 04m 44.2s	1
5	Hulme	Brabham-Climax	79		7
6	Ginther	Honda	79		3
7	Surtees	Ferrari	79		4
8	Spence	Lotus-Climax	79		8
9	Bandini	Ferrari	79		12
10	Ireland	Lotus-BRM	78		13
11	Gardner	Brabham-BRM	77		11
12	Attwood	Lotus-BRM	77		17
13	Siffert	Brabham-BRM	55		10
	Rindt	Cooper-Climax	48	oil pressure	14
	McLaren	Cooper-Climax	36	crownwheel and pinion	9
	Bonnier	Brabham-Climax	16	ignition	15
	Anderson	Brabham-Climax	11	overheating	16

Fastest Lap: Clark, 1m 30.6s. 103.53 mph/166.61 kph

German Grand Prix: Nürburgring, 1 August 1965

15 laps of 14.17 mile/22.81 km circuit

Place	Driver	Car	Laps	Time/reason for retiring	Grid
1	Clark	Lotus-Climax	15	2h 07m 52.4s	1
2	G Hill	BRM	15	2h 08m 08.3s	3
3	Gurney	Brabham-Climax	15	2h 08m 13.8s	5
4	Rindt	Cooper-Climax	15	2h 11m 22.0s	8
5	J Brabham	Brabham-Climax	15	2h 12m 33.6s	14
6	Bandini	Ferrari	15	2h 13m 01.0s	7
7	Bonnier	Brabham-Climax	15	2h 13m 50.9s	9

German Grand Prix (cont)

Place	Driver	Car	Laps	Time/reason for retiring	Grid
8	Gregory	BRM	14		18
	Surtees	Ferrari	11	gearbox	4
	Siffert	Brabham-BRM	9	engine	11
	Attwood	Lotus-BRM	8	water pipe	16
	Mitter	Lotus-Climax	8	water pipe	12
	Spence	Lotus-Climax	8	driveshaft	6
	McLaren	Cooper-Climax	7	gearbox	10
	Hulme	Brabham-Climax	5	fuel	13
	Amon	Lotus-BRM	3	ignition	15
	Hawkins	Lotus-Climax	3	oil	19
	Stewart	BRM	2	suspension	2
	Gardner	Brabham-BRM	0	gearbox	17

Fastest Lap: Clark, 8m 24.1s. 101.22 mph/162.9 kph

Italian Grand Prix: Monza, 12 September 1965

76 laps of 3.57 mile/5.75 km circuit

Place	Driver	Car	Laps	Time/reason for retiring	Grid
1	Stewart	BRM	76	2h 04m 52.8s	3
2	G Hill	BRM	76	2h 04m 56.1s	4
3	Gurney	Brabham-Climax	76	2h 05m 09.3s	9
4	Bandini	Ferrari	76	2h 05m 09.3s	5
5	McLaren	Cooper-Climax	75		11
6	Attwood	Lotus-BRM	75		13
7	Bonnier	Brabham-Climax	74		14
8	Rindt	Cooper-Climax	74		7
9	Ireland	Lotus-BRM	74		16
	Clark	Lotus-Climax	63	fuel pump	1
	Spence	Lotus-Climax	62	ignition	8
	Vaccarella	Ferrari	58		15
	Bussinello	BRM	58		21
	Ginther	Honda	56		17
	Hulme	Brabham-Climax	46	suspension	12
	Gardner	Brabham-BRM	45	engine	18
	Siffert	Brabham-BRM	43	gearbox	10
	Geki	Lotus-Climax	37	crownwheel and pinion	20
	Surtees	Ferrari	34	clutch	2
	Bucknum	Honda	27	engine	6
	Gregory	BRM	22	gearbox	23
	Baghetti	Brabham-Climax	12	engine	19
	Bassi	BRM	8	engine	22

Fastest Lap: Clark, 1m 36.4s. 133.43 mph/214.73 kph

United States Grand Prix: Watkins Glen, 3 October 1965

110 laps of 2.3 mile/3.7 km circuit

Place	Driver	Car	Laps	Time/reason for retiring	Grid
1	G Hill	BRM	110	2h 20m 36.1s	1
2	Gurney	Brabham-Climax	110	2h 20m 48.6s	8
3	J Brabham	Brabham-Climax	110	2h 21m 33.6s	7
4	Bandini	Ferrari	109		5
5	P Rodriguez	Ferrari	109		15
6	Rindt	Cooper-Climax	108		13
7	Ginther	Honda	108		3
8	Bonnier	Brabham-Climax	107		10
9	Bondurant	Ferrari	106		14
10	Attwood	Lotus-BRM	101		16
11	Siffert	Brabham-BRM	99		11
12	Solana	Lotus-Climax	95		17
13	Bucknum	Honda	92		12
	Stewart	BRM	12	suspension	6
	McLaren	Cooper-Climax	11	oil	9
	Clark	Lotus-Climax	11	engine	2
	Ireland	Lotus-BRM	9	driver ill	18
	Spence	Lotus-Climax	9	engine	4

Fastest Lap: G Hill, 1m 11.9s. 115.16 mph/185.33 kph

Mexican Grand Prix: Mexico City, 24 October 1965

65 laps of 3.1 mile/5 km circuit

Place	Driver	Car	Laps	Time/reason for retiring	Grid
1	Ginther	Honda	65	2h 08m 32.1s	3
2	Gurney	Brabham-Climax	65	2h 08m 35s	2
3	Spence	Lotus-Climax	65	2h 09m 32.3s	6
4	Siffert	Brabham-BRM	65	2h 10m 26.5s	11
5	Bucknum	Honda	64		10
6	Attwood	Lotus-BRM	64		16
7	P Rodriguez	Ferrari	62		13
8	Bandini	Ferrari	62		7
	G Hill	BRM	56	engine	5
	Solana	Lotus-Climax	55	ignition	9
	Bonnier	Brabham-Climax	43	suspension	12
	Rindt	Cooper-Climax	39	ignition	15
	J Brabham	Brabham-Climax	38	oil	4
	Stewart	BRM	35	clutch	8
	Bondurant	Lotus-BRM	29	suspension	17
	McLaren	Cooper-Climax	25	gearbox	14
	Clark	Lotus-Climax	8	engine	1

Fastest Lap: Gurney, 1m 55.84s. 96.55 mph/155.39 kph

World Championship 1965

1	Clark	54
2	G Hill	40 (45)
3	J Stewart	33 (34)
4	Gurney	25
5	Surtees	17
6	Bandini	13
7	Ginther	11
8=	McLaren, Spence	10
10	Brabham	9
11=	Hulme, Siffert	5
13	Rindt	4
14=	Attwood, Bucknum, P Rodriguez	2

Constructors' Championship

1	Lotus-Climax	54 (58)
2	BRM	45 (61)
3	Brabham-Climax	27 (31)
4	Ferrari	26 (27)
5	Cooper-Climax	14
6	Honda	11
7	Brabham-BRM	5
8	Lotus-BRM	2

1966

The new formula adopted for 1966 specified 3 litre engines and the British constructors were forced to look elsewhere after Climax's withdrawal from racing. Ferrari appeared to be as well prepared as in 1961, but Surtees left the team after a dispute at Le Mans, joining Cooper; Jack Brabham took his third championship, this time in a car of his own manufacture. Bruce McLaren and Dan Gurney emulated Brabham by building their own cars, though with little initial success. BRM and Lotus used 2 litre engines for much of the season. BRM's new H16 engine was largely unsuccessful, though Clark used one in his Lotus to win the US Grand Prix.

Monaco Grand Prix: Monte Carlo, 22 May 1966

100 laps of 1.95 mile/3.15 km circuit

Place	Driver	Car	Laps	Time/reason for retiring	Grid
1	Stewart	BRM	100	2h 33m 10.5s	3
2	Bandini	Ferrari	100	2h 33m 50.7s	5
3	G Hill	BRM	99		4
4	Bondurant	BRM	95		16
	Ginther	Cooper-Maserati	80	driveshaft	9
	Ligier	Cooper-Maserati	75	running	15
	Bonnier	Cooper-Maserati	73	running	14
	Clark	Lotus-Climax	60	suspension	1
	Rindt	Cooper-Maserati	56	engine	7
	Siffert	Brabham-BRM	35	clutch	13
	Spence	Lotus-BRM	34	suspension	12
	J Brabham	Brabham-Repco	17	gearbox	11
	Surtees	Ferrari	16	transmission	2
	Hulme	Brabham-Climax	15	driveshaft	6
	McLaren	McLaren-Ford	9	oil	10
	Anderson	Brabham-Climax	3	engine	8

Fastest Lap: Bandini, 1m 29.8s. 78.34 mph/126.08 kph
* Under new regulations cars completing less than 90% of race distance were not classified.

Belgian Grand Prix: Spa, 12 June 1966

28 laps of 8.76 mile/14.1 km circuit

Place	Driver	Car	Laps	Time/reason for retiring	Grid
1	Surtees	Ferrari	28	2h 09m 11.3s	1
2	Rindt	Cooper-Maserati	28	2h 09m 53.4s	2
3	Bandini	Ferrari	27		5
4	J Brabham	Brabham-Repco	26		4
5	Ginther	Cooper-Maserati	25		8
6	Ligier	Cooper-Maserati	24	running	12
7	Gurney	Eagle-Climax	23	running	15
	Bondurant	BRM	0	accident	11
	Bonnier	Cooper-Maserati	0	accident	6
	Clark	Lotus-Climax	0	accident	10
	G Hill	BRM	0	accident	9
	Hulme	Brabham-Climax	0	accident	13
	Siffert	Cooper-Maserati	0	accident	14
	Spence	Lotus-BRM	0	accident	7
	Stewart	BRM	0	accident	3

Fastest Lap: Surtees, 4m 18.7s. 121.92 mph/196.21 kph
* Under new regulations cars completing less than 90% of race distance were not classified.

French Grand Prix: Reims, 3 July 1966

48 laps of 5.16 mile/8.3 km circuit

Place	Driver	Car	Laps	Time/reason for retiring	Grid
1	J Brabham	Brabham-Repco	48	1h 48m 31.3s	4
2	Parkes	Ferrari	48	1h 48m 40.8s	3
3	Hulme	Brabham-Repco	46		9
4	Rindt	Cooper-Maserati	46		5
5	Gurney	Eagle-Climax	45		14
6	J Taylor	Brabham-BRM	45		15
7	Anderson	Brabham-Climax	44		12
8	Amon	Cooper-Maserati	44		7
9	Ligier	Cooper-Maserati	42		11
	P Rodriguez	Lotus-Climax	40	oil	13
	Bandini	Ferrari	37	still running	1
	Bonnier	Brabham-Climax	32	still running	17
	G Hill	BRM	13	engine	8
	Siffert	Cooper-Maserati	10	fuel sytem	6
	Spence	Lotus-BRM	8	clutch	10
	Surtees	Cooper-Maserati	5	fuel sytem	2
	Arundell	Lotus-BRM	3	gearbox	16

Fastest Lap: Bandini, 2m 11.3s. 141.44 mph/227.62 kph

British Grand Prix: Brands Hatch, 16 July 1966

80 laps of 2.65 mile/4.27 km circuit

Place	Driver	Car	Laps	Time/reason for retiring	Grid
1	J Brabham	Brabham-Repco	80	2h 13m 13.4s	1
2	Hulme	Brabham-Repco	80	2h 13m 23.0s	2
3	G Hill	BRM	79		4
4	Clark	Lotus-Climax	79		5
5	Rindt	Cooper-Maserati	79		7
6	McLaren	McLaren-Serenissima	78		13
7	Irwin	Brabham-Climax	78		12
8	J Taylor	Brabham-BRM	76		16
9	Bondurant	BRM	76		14
10	Ligier	Cooper-Maserati	75		17
11	Lawrence	Cooper-Ferrari	73		19
	Siffert	Cooper-Maserati	70		11
	Anderson	Brabham-Climax	70		10
	Surtees	Cooper-Maserati	66	transmission	6
	Bonnier	Brabham-Climax	42	clutch	15
	Arundell	Lotus-BRM	31	gearbox	20
	Stewart	BRM	16	engine	8
	Spence	Lotus-BRM	14	oil	9
	Gurney	Eagle-Climax	8	engine	3
	T Taylor	Shannon-Climax	0	engine	18

Fastest Lap: Brabham, 1m 37.0s. 98.35 mph/158.28 kph

Dutch Grand Prix: Zandvoort, 24 July 1966

90 laps of 2.61 mile/4.19 km circuit

Place	Driver	Car	Laps	Time/reason for retiring	Grid
1	J Brabham	Brabham-Repco	90	2h 20m 32.5s	1
2	G Hill	BRM	89		7
3	Clark	Lotus-Climax	88		3
4	Stewart	BRM	88		8
5	Spence	Lotus-BRM	87		12
6	Bandini	Ferrari	87		9
7	Bonnier	Cooper-Maserati	84		13
8	J Taylor	Brabham-BRM	84		17
9	Ligier	Cooper-Maserati	84		16
	Siffert	Cooper-Maserati	79	engine	11
	Anderson	Brabham-Climax	72	suspension	14
	Surtees	Cooper-Maserati	43	electrical	10
	Hulme	Brabham-Repco	36	ignition	2
	Arundell	Lotus-BRM	27	ignition	15

Dutch Grand Prix (cont)

Place	Driver	Car	Laps	Time/reason for retiring	Grid
	Gurney	Eagle-Climax	26	oil	4
	Parkes	Ferrari	10	accident	5
	Rindt	Cooper-Maserati	2	accident	6

Fastest Lap: Hulme, 1m 30.6s. 103.53 mph/166.61 kph

German Grand Prix: Nürburgring, 2 August 1966

15 laps of 14.17 mile/22.81 km circuit

Place	Driver	Car	Laps	Time/reason for retiring	Grid
1	J Brabham	Brabham-Repco	15	2h 27m 03.0s	5
2	Surtees	Cooper-Maserati	15	2h 27m 47.4s	2
3	Rindt	Cooper-Maserati	15	2h 29m 35.6s	9
4	G Hill	BRM	15	2h 33m 44.4s	10
5	Stewart	BRM	15	2h 35m 31.9s	3
6	Bandini	Ferrari	15	2h 37m 59.4s	6
7	Gurney	Eagle-Climax	15		8
8	*Beltoise	Matra-Ford	14		18
9	*Hahne	Matra-BRM	14		27
10	*J Schlesser	Matra-Ford	14		19
11	*Herrmann	Brabham-Ford	14		22
12	Arundell	Lotus-BRM	14		17
	Spence	Lotus-BRM	12	alternator	13
	Clark	Lotus-Climax	11	accident	1
	Lawrence	Cooper-Ferrari	10	suspension	26
	Scarfiotti	Ferrari	9	electrical	4
	Parkes	Ferrari	9	accident	7
	Hulme	Brabham-Repco	8	ignition	15
	*P Rodriguez	Lotus-Ford	7	engine	20
	Bonnier	Cooper-Maserati	3	clutch	12
	*Courage	Lotus-Ford	3	accident	23
	*Rees	Brabham-Ford	3	engine	24
	*Ahrens	Brabham-Ford	2	gearbox	21
	Anderson	Brabham-Climax	2	transmission	14
	Bondurant	BRM	2	engine	11
	*Ickx	Matra-Ford	0	accident	16
	J Taylor	Brabham-BRM	0	fatal accident	25

Fastest Lap: Surtees, 8m 49.0s. 96.45 mph/155.23 kph
* Formula 2 cars.

Italian Grand Prix: Monza, 4 September 1966

68 laps of 3.57 mile/5.75 km circuit

Place	Driver	Car	Laps	Time/reason for retiring	Grid
1	Scarfiotti	Ferrari	68	1h 47m 14.8s	2
2	Parkes	Ferrari	68	1h 47m 20.6s	1
3	Hulme	Brabham-Repco	68	1h 47m 20.6s	10
4	Rindt	Cooper-Maserati	67		8
5	Spence	Lotus-BRM	67		14
6	Anderson	Brabham-Climax	66		15
7	Bondurant	BRM	65		18
8	Arundell	Lotus-BRM	63		13
9	Geki	Lotus-Climax	63		20
	Baghetti	Ferrari	59	running	16
	Clark	Lotus-BRM	58	gearbox	3
	Siffert	Cooper-Maserati	46	engine	17
	Bandini	Ferrari	33	ignition	5
	Surtees	Cooper-Maserati	31	fuel	4
	Ginther	Honda	16	accident	7
	Gurney	Eagle-Weslake	7	engine	19
	J Brabham	Brabham-Repco	7	oil	6
	Stewart	BRM	5	fuel	9
	Bonnier	Cooper-Maserati	3	throttle	12
	G Hill	BRM	0	engine	11

Fastest Lap: Scarfiotti, 1m 32.4s. 139.2 mph/224.03 kph

United States Grand Prix: Watkins Glen, 2 October 1966

108 laps of 2.3 mile/3.7 km circuit

Place	Driver	Car	Laps	Time/reason for retiring	Grid
1	Clark	Lotus-BRM	108	2h 09m 40.1s	2
2	Rindt	Cooper-Maserati	107		9
3	Surtees	Cooper-Maserati	107		4
4	Siffert	Cooper-Maserati	105		13
5	McLaren	McLaren-Ford	105		11
6	Arundell	Lotus-Climax	101		19
	Ireland	BRM	96	alternator	17
	Ginther	Honda	81		8
	Spence	Lotus-BRM	74	ignition	12
	Bucknum	Honda	58	engine	18
	Bonnier	Cooper-Maserati	57		15
	J Brabham	Brabham-Repco	55	engine	1
	Stewart	BRM	53	engine	6
	G Hill	BRM	52	crownwheel and pinion	5
	Bandini	Ferrari	34	engine	3
	Hulme	Brabham-Repco	18	oil	7

United States Grand Prix (cont)

Place	Driver	Car	Laps	Time/reason for retiring	Grid
	Gurney	Eagle-Weslake	13	clutch	14
	P Rodriguez	Lotus-BRM	13	starter	10
	Bondurant	Eagle-Climax	5	disqualified	16

Fastest Lap: Surtees, 1m 09.7s. 118.85 mph/191.26 kph

Mexican Grand Prix: Mexico City, 25 October 1966

65 laps of 3.11 mile/5 km circuit

Place	Driver	Car	Laps	Time/reason for retiring	Grid
1	Surtees	Cooper-Maserati	65	2h 06m 35.4s	1
2	J Brabham	Brabham-Repco	65	2h 06m 43.22s	4
3	Hulme	Brabham-Repco	64		6
4	Ginther	Honda	64		3
5	Gurney	Eagle-Climax	64		9
6	Bonnier	Cooper-Maserati	63		12
7	Arundell	Lotus-BRM	61		17
8	Bucknum	Honda	60		13
	P Rodriguez	Lotus-Climax	48	crownwheel and pinion	8
	McLaren	McLaren-Ford	39	engine	14
	Siffert	Cooper-Maserati	32	suspension	11
	Rindt	Cooper-Maserati	31	suspension	5
	Ireland	BRM	27	transmission	16
	Stewart	BRM	25	oil	10
	Bondurant	Eagle-Weslake	23	fuel feed	18
	G Hill	BRM	17	engine	7
	Solana	Cooper-Maserati	8	overheating	15
	Clark	Lotus-BRM	8	gearbox	2

Fastest Lap: Ginther, 1m 53.75s. 98.33 mph/158.24 kph

World Championship 1966

1	J Brabham	42 (45)
2	Surtees	28
3	Rindt	22 (24)
4	Hulme	18
5	G Hill	17
6	Clark	16
7	Stewart	14
8 =	Bandini, Parkes	12
10	Scarfiotti	9
11	Ginther	5
12 =	Gurney, Spence	4
14 =	Bondurant, McLaren, Siffert	3
17 =	Anderson, Arundell, Bonnier, J Taylor	1

Constructors' Championship

1	Brabham-Repco	42 (49)
2	Ferrari	31 (32)
3	Cooper-Maserati	30 (35)
4	BRM	22
5	Lotus-BRM	13
6	Lotus-Climax	8
7	Eagle-Climax	4
8	Honda	3
9	McLaren-Ford	2
10 =	Brabham-BRM, Brabham-Climax, McLaren-Serenissima	1

1967

At the Dutch Grand Prix, Lotus unveiled the new Cosworth-built Ford-sponsored engine which was to be one of the outstanding racing engines of all time, winning 155 grand prix, Le Mans and Indianapolis. Although Jim Clark won four races, Denny Hulme took the title by virtue of his greater consistency. At Monza Clark pitted to replace a tyre, made up a lap to retake the lead, only to run out of fuel on the last lap; a drive that confirmed his status as one of the all-time greats. Dan Gurney's Eagle won its only victory, and Pedro Rodriguez gave Cooper their last win in a dramatic South African Grand Prix in which local driver John Love came close to victory in his outdated Cooper-Climax.

South African Grand Prix: Kyalami, 2 January 1967

80 laps of 2.54 mile/4.09 km circuit

Place	Driver	Car	Laps	Time/reason for retiring	Grid
1	P Rodriguez	Cooper-Maserati	80	2h 05m 45.9s	4
2	Love	Cooper-Climax	80	2h 06m 12.3s	5
3	Surtees	Honda	79		6
4	Hulme	Brabham-Repco	78		2
5	Anderson	Brabham-Climax	78		10
6	J Brabham	Brabham-Repco	76		1
	Charlton	Brabham-Climax	67		8
	Botha	Brabham-Climax	60		17
	Tingle	LDS-Climax	56	accident	14
	Courage	Lotus-BRM	51	fuel system	18
	Gurney	Eagle-Climax	44	suspension	11
	Siffert	Cooper-Maserati	41	engine	16
	Rindt	Cooper-Maserati	38	engine	7
	Spence	BRM	31	oil	13
	Bonnier	Cooper-Maserati	30	engine	12
	Clark	Lotus-BRM	22	engine	3
	G Hill	Lotus-BRM	6	accident	15
	Stewart	BRM	2	engine	9

Fastest Lap: Hulme, 1m 29.9s. 101.873 mph/163.95 kph

Monaco Grand Prix: Monte Carlo, 7 May 1967

100 laps of 1.95 mile/3.15 km circuit

Place	Driver	Car	Laps	Time/reason for retiring	Grid
1	Hulme	Brabham-Repco	100	2h 34m 34.3s	4
2	G Hill	Lotus-BRM	99		8
3	Amon	Ferrari	98		14
4	McLaren	McLaren-BRM	97		10
5	P Rodriguez	Cooper-Maserati	96		16
6	Spence	BRM	96		12
	Bandini	Ferrari	81	fatal accident	2
	Courage	BRM	64	spun	13
	Clark	Lotus-Climax	42	suspension	5
	Surtees	Honda	32	engine	3
	Siffert	Cooper-Maserati	31	engine	9
	Rindt	Cooper-Maserati	14	gearbox	15
	Stewart	BRM	14	crownwheel and pinion	6
	Gurney	Eagle-Weslake	4	fuel system	7
	Servoz-Gavin	Matra-Ford F2	1	fuel system	11
	J Brabham	Brabham-Repco	0	engine	1

Fastest Lap: Clark, 1m 29.5s. 78.61 mph/126.5 kph

Dutch Grand Prix: Zandvoort, 4 June 1967

90 laps of 2.61 mile/4.19 km circuit

Place	Driver	Car	Laps	Time/reason for retiring	Grid
1	Clark	Lotus-Ford	90	2h 14m 45.1s	8
2	J Brabham	Brabham-Repco	90	2h 15m 08.7s	3
3	Hulme	Brabham-Repco	90	2h 15m 10.8s	7
4	Amon	Ferrari	90	2h 15m 12.4s	9
5	Parkes	Ferrari	89		10
6	Scarfiotti	Ferrari	89		15
7	Irwin	Lotus-BRM	88		13
8	Spence	BRM	87		12
9	Anderson	Brabham-Climax	86		17
10	Siffert	Cooper-Maserati	83		16
	Surtees	Honda	72	throttle	6
	Stewart	BRM	50	brakes	11
	Rindt	Cooper-Maserati	40	suspension	4
	P Rodriguez	Cooper-Maserati	39	gearbox	5
	G Hill	Lotus-Ford	10	engine	1
	Gurney	Eagle-Weslake	8	fuel system	2
	McLaren	McLaren-BRM	1	accident	14

Fastest Lap: Clark, 1m 28.08s. 106.49 mph/171.38 kph

Belgian Grand Prix: Spa, 18 June 1967

28 laps of 8.76 mile/14.1 km circuit

Place	Driver	Car	Laps	Time/reason for retiring	Grid
1	Gurney	Eagle-Weslake	28	1h 40m 49.4s	2
2	Stewart	BRM	28	1h 41m 52.4s	6
3	Amon	Ferrari	28	1h 42m 29.4s	5
4	Rindt	Cooper-Maserati	28	1h 43m 03.3s	4
5	Spence	BRM	27		11
6	Clark	Lotus-Ford	27		1
7	Siffert	Cooper-Maserati	27		16
8	Anderson	Brabham-Climax	26		17
9	P Rodriguez	Cooper-Maserati	25	engine	13
10	Ligier	Cooper-Maserati	25		18
	Scarfiotti	Ferrari	24		9
	J Brabham	Brabham-Repco	14	engine	7
	Hulme	Brabham-Repco	13	engine	14
	Bonnier	Cooper-Maserati	9	engine	12
	G Hill	Lotus-Ford	2	clutch	3
	Irwin	BRM	0	engine	15
	Surtees	Honda	0	engine	10
	Parkes	Ferrari	0	accident	8

Fastest Lap: Gurney, 3m 31.9s. 148.85 mph/239.55 kph

French Grand Prix: Le Mans, 2 July 1967

80 laps of 2.75 mile/4.42 km circuit

Place	Driver	Car	Laps	Time/reason for retiring	Grid
1	J Brabham	Brabham-Repco	80	2h 13m 21.3s	2
2	Hulme	Brabham-Repco	80	2h 14m 10.8s	6
3	Stewart	BRM	79		10
4	Siffert	Cooper-Maserati	77		11
5	Irwin	BRM	76	engine	9
6	P Rodriguez	Cooper-Maserati	76		13
	Ligier	Cooper-Maserati	68		15
	Amon	Ferrari	47	throttle	7
	Gurney	Eagle-Weslake	40	fuel system	3
	Rindt	Cooper-Maserati	33	engine	8
	McLaren	Eagle-Weslake	25	ignition	5
	Clark	Lotus-Ford	22	crownwheel and pinion	4
	Anderson	Brabham-Climax	16	ignition	14
	G Hill	Lotus-Ford	13	crownwheel and pinion	1
	Spence	BRM	9	transmission	12

Fastest Lap: G Hill, 1m 36.7s. 102.29 mph/164.62 kph

British Grand Prix: Silverstone, 15 July 1967

80 laps of 2.93 mile/4.71 km circuit

Place	Driver	Car	Laps	Time/reason for retiring	Grid
1	Clark	Lotus-Ford	80	1h 59m 25.6s	1
2	Hulme	Brabham-Repco	80	1h 59m 38.4s	4
3	Amon	Ferrari	80	1h 59m 42.2s	6
4	J Brabham	Brabham-Repco	80	1h 59m 47.4s	3
5	P Rodriguez	Cooper-Maserati	79		9
6	Surtees	Honda	78		7
7	Irwin	BRM	77		13
8	Hobbs	BRM	77		14
9	Rees	Cooper-Maserati	76		15
10	Ligier	Brabham-Repco	76		20
	Anderson	Brabham-Climax	67	engine	16
	G Hill	Lotus-Ford	64	engine	2
	Spence	BRM	43	ignition	11
	Gurney	Eagle-Weslake	33	clutch	5
	Moser	Cooper-ATS	28	oil	19
	Rindt	Cooper-Maserati	26	engine	8
	Stewart	BRM	19	transmission	12
	McLaren	Eagle-Weslake	13	engine	10
	Siffert	Cooper-Maserati	9	engine	17
	Bonnier	Cooper-Maserati	0	engine	18

Fastest Lap: Hulme, 1m 27s. 121.12 mph/194.92 kph

German Grand Prix: Nürburgring, 6 August 1967

15 laps of 14.19 mile/22.84 km circuit

Place	Driver	Car	Laps	Time/reason for retiring	Grid
1	Hulme	Brabham-Repco	15	2h 05m 55.7s	2
2	J Brabham	Brabham-Repco	15	2h 06m 34.2s	7
3	Amon	Ferrari	15	2h 06m 34.7s	8
4	Surtees	Honda	15	2h 08m 21.4s	6
5	Bonnier	Cooper-Maserati	15	2h 14m 37.8s	16
6	Ligier	Brabham-Repco	14		17
7	Irwin	BRM	13		15
8	P Rodriguez	Cooper-Maserati	13		10
	Gurney	Eagle-Weslake	12	transmission	4
	Siffert	Cooper-Maserati	11	fuel system	12
	G Hill	Lotus-Ford	7	suspension	13
	Hahne	Lola-BMW	6	suspension	14
	Stewart	BRM	5	crownwheel and pinion	3
	Rindt	Cooper-Maserati	4	steering	9
	McLaren	Eagle-Weslake	3	oil	5
	Clark	Lotus-Ford	3	suspension	1
	Spence	BRM	2	crownwheel and pinion	11

German Grand Prix (cont)

Place	Driver	Car	Laps	Time/reason for retiring	Grid

Fastest Lap: Gurney, 8m 15.1s. 103.17 mph/166.04 kph

* On this occasion the concurrent F2 class started from a separate grid. The result was:

1	Oliver	Lotus-Ford	15	2h 12m 04.9s	2
2	Rees	Brabham-Ford	15	2h 14m 43.6s	3
3	Hobbs	Lola-BMW	13		5
4	Hart	Protos-Ford	12		8
	Ickx	Matra-Ford	11	suspension	1
	Ahrens	Protos-Ford	4	radiator	6
	J Schlesser	Matra-Ford	2	clutch	4
	Mitter	Brabham-Ford	0	engine	7

On the road the finishing order after Surtees was Oliver, Bonnier, Rees, Ligier, Irwin, Hobbs, Rodriguez, Hart, Siffert.

Canadian Grand Prix: Mosport, 27 August 1967

90 laps of 2.46 mile/3.96 km circuit

Place	Driver	Car	Laps	Time/reason for retiring	Grid
1	J Brabham	Brabham-Repco	90	2h 40m 40.0s	7
2	Hulme	Brabham-Repco	90	2h 41m 41.9s	3
3	Gurney	Eagle-Weslake	89		5
4	G Hill	Lotus-Ford	88		2
5	Spence	BRM	87		10
6	Amon	Ferrari	87		4
7	McLaren	McLaren-BRM	86		6
8	Bonnier	Cooper-Maserati	85		14
9	Hobbs	BRM	85		12
10	Attwood	Cooper-Maserati	84		13
11	Fisher	Lotus-BRM	81		17
	Clark	Lotus-Ford	68	ignition	1
	Wietzes	Lotus-Ford	68	ignition	16
	Stewart	BRM	64	throttle	9
	Pease	Eagle-Climax	47	still running	15
	Irwin	BRM	17	spun	11
	Rindt	Cooper-Maserati	3	ignition	8

Fastest Lap: Clark, 1m 23.1s. 106.54 mph/171.47 kph

Italian Grand Prix: Monza, 10 September 1967

68 laps of 3.57 mile/5.75 km circuit

Place	Driver	Car	Laps	Time/reason for retiring	Grid
1	Surtees	Honda	68	1h 43m 45s	9
2	J Brabham	Brabham-Repco	68	1h 43m 45.2s	2
3	Clark	Lotus-Ford	68	1h 44m 08.1s	1
4	Rindt	Cooper-Maserati	68	1h 44m 41.6s	11
5	Spence	BRM	67		12
6	Ickx	Cooper-Maserati	66		14
7	Amon	Ferrari	64		4
	G Hill	Lotus-Ford	58	engine	8
	Baghetti	Lotus-Ford	50	engine	17
	Siffert	Cooper-Maserati	50	accident	13
	McLaren	McLaren-BRM	46	engine	3
	Bonnier	Cooper-Maserati	46	overheating	15
	Stewart	BRM	45	engine	7
	Hulme	Brabham-Repco	30	overheating	6
	Ligier	Brabham-Repco	26	engine	18
	Irwin	BRM	16	fuel system	16
	Scarfiotti	Eagle-Weslake	5	engine	10
	Gurney	Eagle-Weslake	4	engine	5

Fastest Lap: Clark, 1m 28.5s. 145.34 mph/233.9 kph

United States Grand Prix: Watkins Glen, 1 October 1967

108 laps of 2.3 mile/3.7 km circuit

Place	Driver	Car	Laps	Time/reason for retiring	Grid
1	Clark	Lotus-Ford	108	2h 03m 13.2s	2
2	G Hill	Lotus-Ford	108	2h 03m 19.5s	1
3	Hulme	Brabham-Repco	107		6
4	Siffert	Cooper-Maserati	106		12
5	J Brabham	Brabham-Repco	104		5
6	Bonnier	Cooper-Maserati	101		15
7	Beltoise	Matra-Ford F2	101		18
	Surtees	Honda	96	alternator	11
	Amon	Ferrari	95	engine	4
	Stewart	BRM	72	fuel system	10
	Ickx	Cooper-Maserati	45	overheating	16
	Ligier	Brabham-Repco	43	engine	17
	Irwin	BRM	41	engine	14
	Spence	BRM	35	engine	13
	Rindt	Cooper-Maserati	33	engine	8
	Gurney	Eagle-Weslake	24	suspension	3
	McLaren	McLaren-BRM	16	water pipe	9
	Solana	Lotus-Ford	7	ignition	7

Fastest Lap: G Hill, 1m 06.0s. 125.46 mph/201.9 kph

Mexican Grand Prix: Mexico City, 22 October 1967

65 laps of 3.11 mile/5 km circuit

Place	Driver	Car	Laps	Time/reason for retiring	Grid
1	Clark	Lotus-Ford	65	1h 59m 28.7s	1
2	J Brabham	Brabham-Repco	65	2h 00m 54.06s	5
3	Hulme	Brabham-Repco	64		6
4	Surtees	Honda	64		7
5	Spence	BRM	63		11
6	P Rodriguez	Cooper-Maserati	63		13
7	Beltoise	Matra-Ford F2	63		14
8	Williams	Ferrari	63		16
9	Amon	Ferrari	62		2
10	Bonnier	Cooper-Maserati	61		17
11	Ligier	Brabham-Repco	61		18
12	Siffert	Cooper-Maserati	59	engine	10
	McLaren	McLaren-BRM	44	oil	8
	Irwin	BRM	32	oil	15
	Stewart	BRM	23	engine	12
	G Hill	Lotus-Ford	17	transmission	4
	Solana	Lotus-Ford	12	suspension	9
	Gurney	Eagle-Weslake	3	radiator	3

Fastest Lap: Clark, 1m 48.13s. 104.44 mph/166.47 kph

World Championship 1967

1	Hulme	51
2	J Brabham	46 (48)
3	Clark	41
4 =	Amon, Surtees	20
6 =	G Hill, P Rodriguez	15
8	Gurney	13
9	Stewart	10
10	Spence	9
11 =	Love, Rindt, Siffert	6
14 =	Bonnier, McLaren	3
16 =	Anderson, Irwin, Parkes	2
19 =	Ickx, Ligier, Scarfiotti	1

Constructors' Championship

1	Brabham-Repco	63 (67)
2	Lotus-Ford	44
3	Cooper-Maserati	28
4 =	Ferrari, Honda	20
6	BRM	17
7	Eagle-Weslake	13
8 =	Cooper-Climax, Lotus-BRM	6
10	McLaren-BRM	3
11	Brabham-Climax	2

1968

Jim Clark, the best driver of his era, passed Fangio's total of wins in South Africa but was killed in a Formula 2 race at Hockenheim on 7 April. Graham Hill and Lotus recovered to take the championship, and the Ford Cosworth engine powered all but one of the race winners. Bruce McLaren joined Brabham and Gurney as a successful driver-constructor, and Jo Siffert won a popular victory in Rob Walker's Lotus at Brands Hatch.

South African Grand Prix: Kyalami, 1 January 1968

80 laps of 2.55 mile/4.1 km circuit

Place	Driver	Car	Laps	Time/reason for retiring	Grid
1	Clark	Lotus-Ford	80	1h 53m 56.6s	1
2	G Hill	Lotus-Ford	80	1h 54m 21.9s	2
3	Rindt	Brabham-Repco	80	1h 54m 27.0s	4
4	Amon	Ferrari	78		8
5	Hulme	McLaren-BRM	78		9
6	Beltoise	Matra-Ford F2	77		18
7	Siffert	Cooper-Maserati	77		16
8	Surtees	Honda	75		6
9	Love	Brabham-Repco	75		17
	Pretorius	Brabham-Climax	70		23
	Gurney	Eagle-Weslake	57	oil	12
	Ickx	Ferrari	51	oil	11
	Bonnier	Cooper-Maserati	46	overheating	19
	Stewart	Matra-Ford	43	engine	3
	Tingle	LDS-Repco	34	overheating	22
	van Rooyen	Cooper-Climax	21	engine	20
	P Rodriguez	BRM	19	fuel	10
	J Brabham	Brabham-Repco	16	engine	5
	de Adamich	Ferrari	13	accident	7
	Spence	BRM	7	fuel	13
	Redman	Cooper-Maserati	4	oil	21
	Charlton	Brabham-Repco	3	crownwheel and pinion	14
	Scarfiotti	Cooper-Maserati	2	water pipe	15

Fastest Lap: Clark, 1m 23.7s. 109.68 mph/176.52 kph

Spanish Grand Prix: Jarama, 12 May 1968

90 laps of 2.12 mile/3.4 km circuit

Place	Driver	Car	Laps	Time/reason for retiring	Grid
1	G Hill	Lotus-Ford	90	2h 15m 20.1s	6
2	Hulme	McLaren-Ford	90	2h 15m 36.0s	3
3	Redman	Cooper-BRM	89		13
4	Scarfiotti	Cooper-BRM	89		12
5	Beltoise	Matra-Ford	81		5
	McLaren	McLaren-Ford	77	oil	4
	Surtees	Honda	74	gearbox	7
	Siffert	Lotus-Ford	62	transmission	10
	Amon	Ferrari	57	fuel system	1
	Courage	BRM	52	fuel system	11
	P Rodriguez	BRM	27	accident	2
	Ickx	Ferrari	13	ignition	8
	Rindt	Brabham-Repco	10	oil	9

Fastest Lap: Beltoise, 1m 28.3s. 86.24 mph/138.8 kph

Monaco Grand Prix: Monte Carlo, 26 May 1968

80 laps of 1.95 mile/3.15 km circuit

Place	Driver	Car	Laps	Time/reason for retiring	Grid
1	G Hill	Lotus-Ford	80	2h 00m 32.3s	1
2	Attwood	BRM	80	2h 00m 34.5s	6
3	Bianchi	Cooper-BRM	76		14
4	Scarfiotti	Cooper-BRM	76		15
5	Hulme	McLaren-Ford	73		10
	Surtees	Honda	16	gearbox	4
	P Rodriguez	BRM	16	accident	9
	Courage	BRM	11	chassis	11
	Beltoise	Matra	11	accident	8
	Siffert	Lotus-Ford	11	crownwheel and pinion	3
	Gurney	Eagle-Weslake	9	engine	16
	Rindt	Brabham-Repco	8	accident	5
	J Brabham	Brabham-Repco	7	suspension	12
	Servoz-Gavin	Matra-Ford	3	transmission	2
	Oliver	Lotus-Ford	0	accident	13
	McLaren	McLaren-Ford	0	accident	7

Fastest Lap: Attwood, 1m 28.1s. 78.85 mph/128.51 kph

Belgian Grand Prix: Spa, 9 June 1968

28 laps of 8.76 mile/14.1 km circuit

Place	Driver	Car	Laps	Time/reason for retiring	Grid
1	McLaren	McLaren-Ford	28	1h 40m 02.1s	6
2	P Rodriguez	BRM	28	1h 40m 14.2s	8
3	Ickx	Ferrari	28	1h 40m 41.7s	3
4	Stewart	Matra-Ford	27		2
5	Oliver	Lotus-Ford	26	transmission	15
6	Bianchi	Cooper-BRM	26		12
7	Siffert	Lotus-Ford	25	engine	9
8	Beltoise	Matra	25		13
	Courage	BRM	21	engine	7
	Hulme	McLaren-Ford	17	transmission	5
	Surtees	Honda	10	suspension	4
	Amon	Ferrari	7	radiator	1
	Redman	Cooper-BRM	6	accident	10
	Rindt	Brabham-Repco	5	engine	17
	J Brabham	Brabham-Repco	5	throttle	18
	Attwood	BRM	5	water pipe	11
	G Hill	Lotus-Ford	5	transmission	14
	Bonnier	McLaren-BRM	0	wheel	16

Fastest Lap: Surtees, 3m 30.5s. 149.84 mph/241.14 kph

Dutch Grand Prix: Zandvoort, 23 June 1968

90 laps of 2.61 mile/4.19 km circuit

Place	Driver	Car	Laps	Time/reason for retiring	Grid
1	Stewart	Matra-Ford	90	2h 46m 11.3s	5
2	Beltoise	Matra	90	2h 47m 45.2s	16
3	P Rodriguez	BRM	89		11
4	Ickx	Ferrari	88		6
5	Moser	Brabham-Repco	87		17
6	Amon	Ferrari	85		1
7	Attwood	BRM	85		15
8	Bonnier	McLaren-BRM	82		19
9	G Hill	Lotus-Ford	81	spun	3
	Oliver	Lotus-Ford	80		10
	Gurney	Eagle-Weslake	63	throttle	12
	Siffert	Lotus-Ford	55	gearbox	13
	Courage	BRM	51	spun	14
	Surtees	Honda	50	alternator	9
	Rindt	Brabham-Repco	39	ignition	2
	J Brabham	Brabham-Repco	22	spun	4

Dutch Grand Prix (cont)

Place	Driver	Car	Laps	Time/reason for retiring	Grid
	McLaren	McLaren-Ford	19	accident	8
	Hulme	McLaren-Ford	10	engine	7
	Bianchi	Cooper-BRM	9	accident	18

Fastest Lap: Beltoise, 1m 45.91s. 88.56 mph/142.52 kph

French Grand Prix: Rouen, 7 July 1968

60 laps of 4.07 mile/6.54 km circuit

Place	Driver	Car	Laps	Time/reason for retiring	Grid
1	Ickx	Ferrari	60	2h 25m 40.9s	3
2	Surtees	Honda	60	2h 27m 39.5s	7
3	Stewart	Matra-Ford	59		2
4	Elford	Cooper-BRM	58		17
5	Hulme	McLaren-Ford	58		4
6	Courage	BRM	57		14
7	Attwood	BRM	57		12
8	McLaren	McLaren-Ford	56		6
9	Beltoise	Matra	56		8
10	Amon	Ferrari	55		5
11	Siffert	Lotus-Ford	54		11
	P Rodriguez	BRM	53		10
	Rindt	Brabham-Repco	45	fuel tank	1
	J Brabham	Brabham-Repco	15	fuel system	13
	Servoz-Gavin	Cooper-BRM	14	accident	15
	G Hill	Lotus-Ford	14	transmission	9
	J Schlesser	Honda	2	fatal accident	16

Fastest Lap: P Rodriguez, 2m 11.5s. 111.29 mph/179.1 kph

British Grand Prix: Brands Hatch, 20 July 1968

80 laps of 2.65 mile/4.27 km circuit

Place	Driver	Car	Laps	Time/reason for retiring	Grid
1	Siffert	Lotus-Ford	80	2h 01m 20.3s	4
2	Amon	Ferrari	80	2h 01m 24.7s	3
3	Ickx	Ferrari	79		12
4	Hulme	McLaren-Ford	79		11
5	Surtees	Honda	78		9
6	Stewart	Matra-Ford	78		7
7	McLaren	McLaren-Ford	77		10
8	Courage	BRM	72		16

British Grand Prix (cont)

Place	Driver	Car	Laps	Time/reason for retiring	Grid
	Rindt	Brabham-Repco	55	fuel	5
	P Rodriguez	BRM	52	engine	13
	Moser	Brabham-Repco	52	running	19
	Oliver	Lotus-Ford	43	transmission	2
	Widdows	Cooper-BRM	34	ignition	18
	Elford	Cooper-BRM	26	engine	17
	G Hill	Lotus-Ford	26	transmission	1
	Beltoise	Matra	11	engine	14
	Attwood	BRM	10	radiator	15
	Gurney	Eagle-Weslake	8	fuel system	6
	Bonnier	McLaren-BRM	7	engine	20
	J Brabham	Brabham-Repco	0	engine	8

Fastest Lap: Siffert, 1m 29.7s. 106.35 mph/171.16 kph

German Grand Prix: Nürburgring, 4 August 1968

14 laps of 14.19 mile/22.84 km circuit

Place	Driver	Car	Laps	Time/reason for retiring	Grid
1	Stewart	Matra-Ford	14	2h 19m 03.2s	6
2	G Hill	Lotus-Ford	14	2h 23m 06.4s	4
3	Rindt	Brabham-Repco	14	2h 23m 12.6s	3
4	Ickx	Ferrari	14	2h 24m 58.4s	1
5	J Brabham	Brabham-Repco	14	2h 25m 24.3s	15
6	P Rodriguez	BRM	14	2h 25m 28.2s	14
7	Hulme	McLaren-Ford	14	2h 25m 34.2s	11
8	Courage	BRM	14	2h 26m 59.6s	8
9	Gurney	Eagle-Weslake	14	2h 27m 16.9s	10
10	Hahne	Lola-BMW	14	2h 29m 14.6s	18
11	Oliver	Lotus-Ford	13		13
12	Ahrens	Brabham-Repco	13		17
13	McLaren	McLaren-Ford	13		16
14	Attwood	BRM	13		20
	Amon	Ferrari	11	accident	2
	Beltoise	Matra	8	accident	12
	Bianchi	Cooper-BRM	6	fuel	19
	Siffert	Lotus-Ford	6	ignition	9
	Surtees	Honda	3	ignition	7
	Elford	Cooper-BRM	0	accident	5

Fastest Lap: Stewart, 9m 36.0s. 88.68 mph/142.72 kph

Italian Grand Prix: Monza, 8 September 1968

68 laps of 3.57 mile/5.75 km circuit

Place	Driver	Car	Laps	Time/reason for retiring	Grid
1	Hulme	McLaren-Ford	68	1h 40m 14.8s	7
2	Servoz-Gavin	Matra-Ford	68	1h 41m 43.2s	13
3	Ickx	Ferrari	68	1h 41m 43.4s	4
4	Courage	BRM	67		17
5	Beltoise	Matra	66		18
6	Bonnier	McLaren-BRM	64		19
	Siffert	Lotus-Ford	58	suspension	9
	J Brabham	Brabham-Repco	56	oil	16
	Hobbs	Honda	42	engine	14
	Stewart	Matra-Ford	42	engine	6
	Oliver	Lotus-Ford	38	transmission	11
	McLaren	McLaren-Ford	34	oil	2
	Rindt	Brabham-Repco	33	engine	10
	P Rodriguez	BRM	22	engine	15
	Gurney	Eagle-Weslake	19	engine	12
	G Hill	Lotus-Ford	10	wheel	5
	Surtees	Honda	8	accident	1
	Amon	Ferrari	8	accident	3
	Bell	Ferrari	4	fuel system	8
	Elford	Cooper-BRM	2	accident	20

Fastest Lap: Oliver, 1m 26.5s. 148.7 mph/239.31 kph

Canadian Grand Prix: St Jovite, 22 September 1968

90 laps of 2.65 mile/4.27km circuit

Place	Driver	Car	Laps	Time/reason for retiring	Grid
1	Hulme	McLaren-Ford	90	2h 27m 11.2s	6
2	McLaren	McLaren-Ford	89		8
3	P Rodriguez	BRM	88		12
4	G Hill	Lotus-Ford	86		5
5	Elford	Cooper-BRM	86		16
6	Stewart	Matra-Ford	83		11
	Beltoise	Matra	77	gearbox	15
	Amon	Ferrari	72	transmission	2
	Servoz-Gavin	Matra-Ford	71	accident	13
	Bianchi	Cooper-BRM	56	running	18
	Pescarolo	Matra	54	oil	19
	Rindt	Brabham-Repco	39	engine	1
	Oliver	Lotus-Ford	32	transmission	9
	J Brabham	Brabham-Repco	31	exhaust	10
	Siffert	Lotus-Ford	29	oil	3
	Gurney	McLaren-Ford	29	radiator	4
	Courage	BRM	22	gearbox	14

Canadian Grand Prix (cont)

Place	Driver	Car	Laps	Time/reason for retiring	Grid
	Brack	Lotus-Ford	18	transmission	20
	Surtees	Honda	10	gearbox	7
	Bonnier	McLaren-BRM	0	fuel system	17

Fastest Lap: Siffert, 1m 35.1s. 100.32 mph/161.44 kph

United States Grand Prix: Watkins Glen, 6 October 1968

108 laps of 2.3 mile/3.7 km circuit

Place	Driver	Car	Laps	Time/reason for retiring	Grid
1	Stewart	Matra-Ford	108	1h 59m 20.3s	2
2	G Hill	Lotus-Ford	108	1h 59m 45s	3
3	Surtees	Honda	107		9
4	Gurney	McLaren-Ford	107		7
5	Siffert	Lotus-Ford	105		12
6	McLaren	McLaren-Ford	103		10
	Courage	BRM	93	fuel	14
	Hulme	McLaren-Ford	92	accident	5
	Bianchi	Cooper-BRM	88	clutch	19
	J Brabham	Brabham-Repco	77	engine	8
	Rindt	Brabham-Repco	73	engine	6
	Elford	Cooper-BRM	71	engine	16
	P Rodriguez	BRM	66	suspension	11
	Bonnier	McLaren-BRM	62	engine	17
	Amon	Ferrari	59	water pump	4
	Beltoise	Matra	44	transmission	13
	B Unser	BRM	35	engine	18
	Andretti	Lotus-Ford	32	clutch	1
	Bell	Ferrari	14	engine	15

Fastest Lap: Stewart, 1m 05.2s. 126.96 mph/204.31 kph

Mexican Grand Prix: Mexico City, 3 November 1968

65 laps of 3.1 mile/5 km circuit

Place	Driver	Car	Laps	Time/reason for retiring	Grid
1	G Hill	Lotus-Ford	65	1h 56m 44s	3
2	McLaren	McLaren-Ford	65	1h 58m 03.3s	9
3	Oliver	Lotus-Ford	65	1h 58m 24.6s	14
4	P Rodriguez	BRM	65	1h 58m 25.0s	12
5	Bonnier	Honda	64		18
6	Siffert	Lotus-Ford	64		1
7	Stewart	Matra-Ford	64		7

Mexican Grand Prix (cont)

Place	Driver	Car	Laps	Time/reason for retiring	Grid
8	Elford	Cooper-BRM	63		17
9	Pescarolo	Matra	62		20
	J Brabham	Brabham-Repco	59	oil	8
	Servoz-Gavin	Matra-Ford	57	ignition	16
	Gurney	McLaren-Ford	28	suspension	5
	Courage	BRM	25	engine	19
	Bianchi	Cooper-BRM	21	engine	21
	Surtees	Honda	17	overheating	6
	Amon	Ferrari	16	transmission	2
	Solana	Lotus-Ford	14	driver	11
	Beltoise	Matra	10	suspension	13
	Hulme	McLaren-Ford	10	suspension	4
	Ickx	Ferrari	3	ignition	15
	Rindt	Brabham-Repco	2	ignition	10

Fastest Lap: Siffert, 1m 44.2s. 107.31 mph/172.7 kph

World Championship 1968

1	G Hill	48
2	Stewart	36
3	Hulme	33
4	Ickx	27
5	McLaren	22
6	P Rodriguez	18
7 =	Siffert, Surtees	12
9	Beltoise	11
10	Amon	10
11	Clark	9
12	Rindt	8
13 =	Attwood, Oliver, Servoz-Gavin, Scarfiotti	6
17 =	Bianchi, Elford	5
19 =	Courage, Redman	4
21 =	Bonnier, Gurney	3
23 =	Brabham, Moser	2

Constructors' Championship

1	Lotus-Ford	62
2	McLaren-Ford	49
3	Matra-Ford	45
4	Ferrari	32
5	BRM	28
6 =	Cooper-BRM, Honda	14
8	Brabham-Repco	10
9	Matra	8
10	McLaren-BRM	3

1969

The Ford Cosworth swept all before it in 1969 as Jackie Stewart took his first title. Lotus, Matra and McLaren experimented unsuccessfully with four wheel drive. Frank Williams made his debut as the entrant of Piers Courage's Brabham. Cooper, Eagle and Honda withdrew from grand prix racing.

South African Grand Prix: Kyalami, 2 January 1969

80 laps of 2.55 mile/4.1 km circuit

Place	Driver	Car	Laps	Time/reason for retiring	Grid
1	Stewart	Matra-Ford	80	1h 50m 39.1s	4
2	G Hill	Lotus-Ford	80	1h 50m 57.9s	7
3	Hulme	McLaren-Ford	80	1h 51m 10.9s	3
4	Siffert	Lotus-Ford	80	1h 51m 28.3s	12
5	McLaren	McLaren-Ford	79		8
6	Beltoise	Matra-Ford	78		11
7	Oliver	BRM	77		14
8	Tingle	Brabham-Repco	73		17
	de Klerk	Brabham-Repco	67		16
	Rindt	Lotus-Ford	43	fuel system	2
	Surtees	BRM	39	engine	18
	P Rodriguez	BRM	37	water	15
	Amon	Ferrari	33	engine	5
	J Brabham	Brabham-Ford	31	handling	1
	Andretti	Lotus-Ford	31	gearbox	6
	Love	Lotus-Ford	30	ignition	10
	Ickx	Brabham-Ford	19	ignition	13
	van Rooyen	McLaren-Ford	11	brakes	9

Fastest Lap: Stewart, 1m 21.6s. 112.5 mph/181.05 kph

Spanish Grand Prix: Montjuich Park, 4 May 1969

90 laps of 2.36 mile/3.79 km circuit

Place	Driver	Car	Laps	Time/reason for retiring	Grid
1	Stewart	Matra-Ford	90	2h 16m 54.0s	4
2	McLaren	McLaren-Ford	88		13
3	Beltoise	Matra-Ford	87		12
4	Hulme	McLaren-Ford	87		8
5	Surtees	BRM	84		9
6	Ickx	Brabham-Ford	83	suspension	7
	P Rodriguez	BRM	72	engine	14
	Amon	Ferrari	56	engine	2
	J Brabham	Brabham-Ford	51	engine	5
	Siffert	Lotus-Ford	30	engine	6
	Rindt	Lotus-Ford	19	accident	1
	Courage	Brabham-Ford	18	engine	11
	G Hill	Lotus-Ford	8	accident	3
	Oliver	BRM	0	oil	10

Fastest Lap: Rindt, 1m 28.3s. 96.02 mph/154.54 kph

Monaco Grand Prix: Monte Carlo, 18 May 1969

80 laps of 1.95 mile/3.15 km circuit

Place	Driver	Car	Laps	Time/reason for retiring	Grid
1	G Hill	Lotus-Ford	80	1h 56m 59.4s	4
2	Courage	Brabham-Ford	80	1h 57m 16.7s	9
3	Siffert	Lotus-Ford	80	1h 57m 34s	5
4	Attwood	Lotus-Ford	80	1h 57m 52.3s	10
5	McLaren	McLaren-Ford	79		11
6	Hulme	McLaren-Ford	78		12
7	Elford	Cooper-Maserati	74		16
	Ickx	Brabham-Ford	48	suspension	7
	Stewart	Matra-Ford	22	transmission	1
	Beltoise	Matra-Ford	20	transmission	3
	Amon	Ferrari	16	transmission	2
	Moser	Brabham-Ford	15	transmission	15
	P Rodriguez	BRM	15	engine	14
	Surtees	BRM	9	gearbox/accident	6
	J Brabham	Brabham-Ford	9	accident	8
	Oliver	BRM	0	accident	13

Fastest Lap: Stewart, 1m 25.1s. 82.67 mph/133.04 kph

Dutch Grand Prix: Zandvoort, 21 June 1969

90 laps of 2.61 mile/4.19 km circuit

Place	Driver	Car	Laps	Time/reason for retiring	Grid
1	Stewart	Matra-Ford	90	2h 06m 42.1s	2
2	Siffert	Lotus-Ford	90	2h 07m 06.6s	10
3	Amon	Ferrari	90	2h 07m 12.6s	4
4	Hulme	McLaren-Ford	90	2h 07m 19.3s	7
5	Ickx	Brabham-Ford	90	2h 07m 19.8s	5
6	J Brabham	Brabham-Ford	90	2h 07m 52.9s	8
7	G Hill	Lotus-Ford	88		3
8	Beltoise	Matra-Ford	87		11
9	Surtees	BRM	87		12
10	Elford	McLaren-Ford	84		15
	Moser	Brabham-Ford	54	steering	14
	McLaren	McLaren-Ford	24	suspension	6
	Rindt	Lotus-Ford	16	transmission	1
	Courage	Brabham-Ford	12	clutch	9
	Oliver	BRM	9	gearbox	13

Fastest Lap: Stewart, 1m 22.94s. 113.09 mph/182 kph

French Grand Prix: Clermont-Ferrand, 6 July 1969

38 laps of 5.01 mile/8.06 km circuit

Place	Driver	Car	Laps	Time/reason for retiring	Grid
1	Stewart	Matra-Ford	38	1h 56m 47.4s	1
2	Beltoise	Matra-Ford	38	1h 57m 44.5s	5
3	Ickx	Brabham-Ford	38	1h 57m 44.7s	4
4	McLaren	McLaren-Ford	37		7
5	Elford	McLaren-Ford	37		10
6	G Hill	Lotus-Ford	37		8
7	Moser	Brabham-Ford	36		13
8	Hulme	McLaren-Ford	35		2
9	Siffert	Lotus-Ford	34		9
	Amon	Ferrari	30	engine	6
	Rindt	Lotus-Ford	22	illness	3
	Courage	Brabham-Ford	21	bodywork	11
	Miles	Lotus-Ford	1	fuel system	12

Fastest Lap: Stewart, 3m 02.7s. 98.6 mph/158.72 kph

British Grand Prix: Silverstone, 19 July 1969

84 laps of 2.93 mile/4.71 km circuit

Place	Driver	Car	Laps	Time/reason for retiring	Grid
1	Stewart	Matra-Ford	84	1h 55m 55.6s	2
2	Ickx	Brabham-Ford	83		4
3	McLaren	McLaren-Ford	83		7
4	Rindt	Lotus-Ford	83		1
5	Courage	Brabham-Ford	83		10
6	Elford	McLaren-Ford	82		11
7	G Hill	Lotus-Ford	82		12
8	Siffert	Lotus-Ford	81		9
9	Beltoise	Matra-Ford	78		17
10	Miles	Lotus-Ford	75		14
	P Rodriguez	Ferrari	61	engine	8
	Amon	Ferrari	45	gearbox	5
	Hulme	McLaren-Ford	27	ignition	3
	Oliver	BRM	19	transmission	13
	Bonnier	Lotus-Ford	6	engine	16
	Bell	McLaren-Ford	5	suspension	15
	Surtees	BRM	1	suspension	6

Fastest Lap: Stewart, 1m 21.3s. 129.6 mph/208.6 kph

German Grand Prix: Nürburgring, 3 August 1969

14 laps of 14.19 mile/22.84 km circuit

Place	Driver	Car	Laps	Time/reason for retiring	Grid
1	Ickx	Brabham-Ford	14	1h 49m 55.4s	1
2	Stewart	Matra-Ford	14	1h 50m 53.1s	2
3	McLaren	McLaren-Ford	14	1h 53m 17s	8
4	G Hill	Lotus-Ford	14	1h 53m 54.2s	9
5	Siffert	Lotus-Ford	12	suspension	4
6	Beltoise	Matra-Ford	12	suspension	10
	Hulme	McLaren-Ford	11	transmission	5
	Oliver	BRM	11	sump	12
	Rindt	Lotus-Ford	10	ignition	3
	Bonnier	Lotus-Ford	4	fuel	13
	Courage	Brabham-Ford	1	accident	7
	Elford	McLaren-Ford	0	accident	6
	Andretti	Lotus-Ford	0	accident	11

Fastest Lap: Ickx, 7m 43.8s. 110.13 mph/177.24 kph

* Mitter killed in practice accident; on this occasion the concurrent F2 class started from a separate grid; all F2 finishers were ahead of Siffert and Beltoise. The result was:

1	Pescarolo	Matra-Ford	14	1h 58m 06.45s	3
2	Attwood	Brabham-Ford	13		6

German Grand Prix (cont)

Place	Driver	Car	Laps	Time/reason for retiring	Grid
3	Ahrens	Brabham-Ford	13		5
4	Stommelen	Lotus-Ford	13		7
5	Westbury	Brabham-Ford	13		4
6	Perrot	Brabham-Ford	13		8
	Cevert	Tecno-Ford	9	crownwheel and pinion	2
	Servoz-Gavin	Matra-Ford	6	engine	1

Fastest Lap: Servoz-Gavin, 8m 12.4s. 103.74 mph/166.95 kph

Italian Grand Prix: Monza, 7 September 1969

68 laps of 3.57 mile/5.75 km circuit

Place	Driver	Car	Laps	Time/reason for retiring	Grid
1	Stewart	Matra-Ford	68	1h 39m 11.26s	3
2	Rindt	Lotus-Ford	68	1h 39m 11.34s	1
3	Beltoise	Matra-Ford	68	1h 39m 11.43s	6
4	McLaren	McLaren-Ford	68	1h 39m 11.45s	5
5	Courage	Brabham-Ford	68	1h 39m 44.7s	4
6	P Rodriguez	Ferrari	66		12
7	Hulme	McLaren-Ford	66		2
8	Siffert	Lotus-Ford	64	engine	8
9	G Hill	Lotus-Ford	63	transmission	9
10	Ickx	Brabham-Ford	61	fuel	15
	Surtees	BRM	60		10
	Oliver	BRM	48	oil	11
	Moser	Brabham-Ford	9	fuel	13
	J Brabham	Brabham-Ford	6	oil	7
	Miles	Lotus-Ford	3	engine	14

Fastest Lap: Beltoise, 1m 25.2s. 150.97 mph/242.96 kph

Canadian Grand Prix: Mosport Park, 20 September 1969

90 laps of 2.46 mile/3.96 km circuit

Place	Driver	Car	Laps	Time/reason for retiring	Grid
1	Ickx	Brabham-Ford	90	1h 59m 25.7s	1
2	J Brabham	Brabham-Ford	90	2h 00m 11.9s	6
3	Rindt	Lotus-Ford	90	2h 00m 17.7s	3
4	Beltoise	Matra-Ford	89		2
5	McLaren	McLaren-Ford	87		9
6	Servoz-Gavin	Matra-Ford	84		15
7	Lovely	Lotus-Ford	81		16
8	Brack	BRM	80		18
	G Hill	Lotus-Ford	42	engine	7

Canadian Grand Prix (cont)

Place	Driver	Car	Laps	Time/reason for retiring	Grid
	Siffert	Lotus-Ford	40	transmission	8
	Miles	Lotus-Ford	40	gearbox	11
	P Rodriguez	Ferrari	37	oil	13
	Stewart	Matra-Ford	32	accident	4
	Pease	Eagle-Climax	22	disqualified: too slow	17
	Surtees	BRM	15	engine	14
	Courage	Brabham-Ford	13	fuel	10
	Cordts	Brabham-Climax	10	oil	19
	Hulme	McLaren-Ford	9	distributor	5
	Oliver	BRM	2	engine	12
	Moser	Brabham-Ford	0	accident	20

Fastest Lap: Ickx/Brabham, 1m 18.1s. 113.35 mph/182.41 kph

United States Grand Prix: Watkins Glen, 5 October 1969

108 laps of 2.3 mile/3.7 km circuit

Place	Driver	Car	Laps	Time/reason for retiring	Grid
1	Rindt	Lotus-Ford	108	1h 57m 56.8s	1
2	Courage	Brabham-Ford	108	1h 58m 43.8s	8
3	Surtees	BRM	106		10
4	J Brabham	Brabham-Ford	106		9
5	P Rodriguez	Ferrari	101		11
6	Moser	Brabham-Ford	98		16
	Servoz-Gavin	Matra-Ford	92		14
	G Hill	Lotus-Ford	90	accident	4
	Ickx	Brabham-Ford	77	engine	7
	Eaton	BRM	76	engine	17
	Beltoise	Matra-Ford	72	engine	6
	Hulme	McLaren-Ford	52	gearbox	2
	Stewart	Matra-Ford	35	engine	3
	Lovely	Lotus-Ford	25	transmission	15
	Oliver	BRM	23	engine	13
	Andretti	Lotus-Ford	3	suspension	12
	Siffert	Lotus-Ford	3	fuel system	5

Fastest Lap: Rindt, 1m 04.3s. 128.7 mph/207.11 kph

Mexican Grand Prix: Mexico City, 19 October 1969

65 laps of 3.11 mile/5 km circuit

Place	Driver	Car	Laps	Time/reason for retiring	Grid
1	Hulme	McLaren-Ford	65	1h 54m 08.8s	4
2	Ickx	Brabham-Ford	65	1h 54m 11.4s	2
3	J Brabham	Brabham-Ford	65	1h 54m 47.3s	1

Mexican Grand Prix (cont)

Place	Driver	Car	Laps	Time/reason for retiring	Grid
4	Stewart	Matra-Ford	65	1h 54m 55.8s	3
5	Beltoise	Matra-Ford	65	1h 55m 47.3s	7
6	Oliver	BRM	63		11
7	P Rodriguez	Ferrari	63		14
8	Servoz-Gavin	Matra-Ford	63		13
9	Lovely	Lotus-Ford	62		15
10	Courage	Brabham-Ford	61		8
11	Moser	Brabham-Ford	60	fuel	12
	Surtees	BRM	53	gearbox	9
	Rindt	Lotus-Ford	21	suspension	6
	Eaton	BRM	6	gearbox	16
	Siffert	Lotus-Ford	4	accident	5
	Miles	Lotus-Ford	3	fuel system	10

Fastest Lap: Ickx, 1m 43.05s. 108.54 mph/146.67 kph

World Championship 1969

1	Stewart	63
2	Ickx	37
3	McLaren	26
4	Rindt	22
5	Beltoise	21
6	Hulme	20
7	G Hill	19
8	Courage	16
9	Siffert	15
10	J Brabham	14
11	Surtees	6
12	Amon	4
13=	Attwood, Elford, Rodriguez	3
16=	Moser, Oliver, Servoz-Gavin	1

Constructors' Championship

1	Matra-Ford	66
2	Brabham-Ford	49 (51)
3	Lotus-Ford	47
4	McLaren-Ford	38 (40)
5=	BRM, Ferrari	7

1970

The year was marred by the deaths of Piers Courage in the Dutch Grand Prix, Bruce McLaren in a testing accident, and Jochen Rindt after a practice crash at Monza. Rindt took the world championship posthumously. The Ford Cosworth was challenged by Ferrari, who took four wins, and BRM, who achieved one. New constructor March ran a works team for Amon and Siffert, while Ken Tyrrell ran cars for his drivers Stewart and Servoz-Gavin (replaced by Cevert after his retirement), and there were other cars for Peterson and Andretti. Tyrrell was also working on his own car which Stewart raced in Canada. Surtees made his debut as a constructor.

South African Grand Prix: Kyalami, 7 March 1970

80 laps of 2.55 mile/4.1 km circuit

Place	Driver	Car	Laps	Time/reason for retiring	Grid
1	J Brabham	Brabham-Ford	80	1h 49m 34.6s	3
2	Hulme	McLaren-Ford	80	1h 49m 42.7s	6
3	Stewart	March-Ford	80	1h 49m 51.7s	1
4	Beltoise	Matra	80	1h 50m 47.7s	8
5	Miles	Lotus-Ford	79		14
6	G Hill	Lotus-Ford	79		19
7	Pescarolo	Matra	78		18
8	Love	Lotus-Ford	78		22
9	P Rodriguez	BRM	76		16
10	Siffert	March-Ford	75		9
11	de Klerk	Brabham-Ford	75		21
	Charlton	Lotus-Ford	73	ignition	13
	Rindt	Lotus-Ford	72	engine	4
	Surtees	McLaren-Ford	60	engine	7
	Ickx	Ferrari	59	engine	5
	Eaton	BRM	58	engine	23
	Servoz-Gavin	March-Ford	57	engine	17
	Courage	De Tomaso-Ford	38	accident	20
	McLaren	McLaren-Ford	38	engine	10
	Andretti	March-Ford	25	overheating	11
	Stommelen	Brabham-Ford	22	engine	15
	Oliver	BRM	21	gearbox	12
	Amon	March-Ford	13	overheating	2

Fastest Lap: Surtees/Brabham, 1m 20.8s. 113.61 mph/182.84 kph

Spanish Grand Prix: Jarama, 19 April 1970

90 laps of 2.12 mile/3.4 km circuit

Place	Driver	Car	Laps	Time/reason for retiring	Grid
1	Stewart	March-Ford	90	2h 10m 58.2s	3
2	McLaren	McLaren-Ford	89		11
3	Andretti	March-Ford	89		15
4	G Hill	Lotus-Ford	89		14
5	Servoz-Gavin	March-Ford	88		13
	Surtees	McLaren-Ford	75	gearbox	12
	J Brabham	Brabham-Ford	60	engine	1
	Stommelen	Brabham-Ford	42	engine	16
	Pescarolo	Matra	33	engine	9
	Beltoise	Matra	31	engine	4
	Amon	March-Ford	9	engine	6
	Hulme	McLaren-Ford	9	ignition	2
	Rindt	Lotus-Ford	9	ignition	8
	Rodriguez	BRM	3	withdrawn	5
	Ickx	Ferrari	0	accident	7
	Oliver	BRM	0	accident	10

Fastest Lap: Brabham, 1m 24.3s. 90.34 mph/145.38 kph

Monaco Grand Prix: Monte Carlo, 10 May 1970

80 laps of 1.95 mile/3.15 km circuit

Place	Driver	Car	Laps	Time/reason for retiring	Grid
1	Rindt	Lotus-Ford	80	1h 54m 36.6s	8
2	J Brabham	Brabham-Ford	80	1h 54m 59.7s	4
3	Pescarolo	Matra	80	1h 55m 28.0s	7
4	Hulme	McLaren-Ford	80	1h 56m 04.9s	3
5	G Hill	Lotus-Ford	79		16
6	Rodriguez	BRM	78		15
7	Peterson	March-Ford	78		12
8	Siffert	March-Ford	76	fuel injection	11
	Amon	March-Ford	60	suspension	2
	Courage	De Tomaso-Ford	58		9
	Stewart	March-Ford	57	engine	1
	Oliver	BRM	42	engine	14
	Beltoise	Matra	21	crownwheel and pinion	6
	McLaren	McLaren-Ford	19	suspension	10
	Surtees	McLaren-Ford	14	oil pressure	13
	Ickx	Ferrari	11	transmission	5

Fastest Lap: Rindt, 1m 23.2s. 84.56 mph/136.08 kph

Belgian Grand Prix: Spa, 7 June 1970

28 laps of 8.76 mile/14.1 km circuit

Place	Driver	Car	Laps	Time/reason for retiring	Grid
1	Rodriguez	BRM	28	1h 38m 09.9s	6
2	Amon	March-Ford	28	1h 38m 11s	3
3	Beltoise	Matra	28	1h 39m 53.6s	11
4	Giunti	Ferrari	28	1h 40m 48.4s	8
5	Stommelen	Brabham-Ford	28	1h 41m 41.7s	7
6	Pescarolo	Matra	27	battery	17
7	Siffert	March-Ford	26	fuel pressure	10
8	Ickx	Ferrari	26		4
	Peterson	March-Ford	20		9
	G Hill	Lotus-Ford	19	engine	16
	J Brabham	Brabham-Ford	18	clutch	5
	Stewart	March-Ford	13	engine	1
	Miles	Lotus-Ford	12	gearbox	13
	Rindt	Lotus-Ford	10	engine	2
	Oliver	BRM	6	engine	14
	Courage	De Tomaso-Ford	3	oil pressure	12
	Bell	Brabham-Ford	0	gearbox	15

Fastest Lap: Amon, 3m 27.4s. 152.08 mph/244.74 kph

Dutch Grand Prix: Zandvoort, 21 June 1970

80 laps of 2.61 mile/4.19 km circuit

Place	Driver	Car	Laps	Time/reason for retiring	Grid
1	Rindt	Lotus-Ford	80	1h 50m 43.4s	1
2	Stewart	March-Ford	80	1h 51m 13.4s	2
3	Ickx	Ferrari	79		3
4	Regazzoni	Ferrari	79		6
5	Beltoise	Matra	79		10
6	Surtees	McLaren-Ford	79		14
7	Miles	Lotus-Ford	78		8
8	Pescarolo	Matra	78		13
9	Peterson	March-Ford	78		16
10	Rodriguez	BRM	77		7
11	J Brabham	Brabham-Ford	76		12
	G Hill	Lotus-Ford	71		20
	Cevert	March-Ford	31	engine	15
	Eaton	BRM	26	oil tank	18
	Oliver	BRM	23	engine	5
	Courage	De Tomaso-Ford	22	fatal accident	9
	Siffert	March-Ford	22	engine	17

Dutch Grand Prix (cont)

Place	Driver	Car	Laps	Time/reason for retiring	Grid
	Gethin	McLaren-Ford	18	accident	11
	Gurney	McLaren-Ford	2	engine	19
	Amon	March-Ford	1	clutch	4

Fastest Lap: Ickx, 1m 19.23s. 118.38 mph/190.52 kph

French Grand Prix: Clermont-Ferrand, 5 July 1970

38 laps of 5.01 mile/8.06 km circuit

Place	Driver	Car	Laps	Time/reason for retiring	Grid
1	Rindt	Lotus-Ford	38	1h 55m 57s	6
2	Amon	March-Ford	38	1h 56m 04.6s	3
3	J Brabham	Brabham-Ford	38	1h 56m 41.8s	5
4	Hulme	McLaren-Ford	38	1h 56m 42.7s	7
5	Pescarolo	Matra	38	1h 57m 16.4s	8
6	Gurney	McLaren-Ford	38	1h 57m 16.7s	17
7	Stommelen	Brabham-Ford	38	1h 58m 17.2s	14
8	Miles	Lotus-Ford	38	1h 58m 44.2s	18
9	Stewart	March-Ford	38	1h 59m 06.6s	4
10	G Hill	Lotus-Ford	37		20
11	Cevert	March-Ford	37		13
12	Eaton	BRM	36		19
13	Beltoise	Matra	35	fuel system	2
14	Giunti	Ferrari	35		11
	de Adamich	McLaren-Alfa	29		15
	Siffert	March-Ford	23	accident	16
	Peterson	March-Ford	17	crownwheel and pinion	9
	Ickx	Ferrari	16	engine	1
	Rodriguez	BRM	6	gearbox	10
	Oliver	BRM	5	engine	12

Fastest Lap: Brabham, 3m 00.75s. 99.69 mph/160.43 kph

British Grand Prix: Brands Hatch, 18 July 1970

80 laps of 2.65 mile/4.27 km circuit

Place	Driver	Car	Laps	Time/reason for retiring	Grid
1	Rindt	Lotus-Ford	80	1h 57m 02s	1
2	J Brabham	Brabham-Ford	80	1h 57m 34.9s	2
3	Hulme	McLaren-Ford	80	1h 57m 54.6s	5
4	Regazzoni	Ferrari	80	1h 57m 56.8s	6
5	Amon	March-Ford	79		17
6	G Hill	Lotus-Ford	79		21

British Grand Prix (cont)

Place	Driver	Car	Laps	Time/reason for retiring	Grid
7	Cevert	March-Ford	79		14
8	E Fittipaldi	Lotus-Ford	78		20
9	Peterson	March-Ford	72		13
	Lovely	Lotus-Ford	69		22
	Gurney	McLaren-Ford	60	oil pressure	11
	Rodriguez	BRM	58	accident	15
	Oliver	BRM	54	engine	4
	Stewart	March-Ford	52	clutch	8
	Surtees	Surtees-Ford	51	oil pressure	18
	Pescarolo	Matra	41	accident	12
	Beltoise	Matra	24	wheel	10
	Andretti	March-Ford	21	suspension	9
	Siffert	March-Ford	19	suspension	19
	Miles	Lotus-Ford	15	engine	7
	Eaton	BRM	10	oil pressure	16
	Ickx	Ferrari	6	transmission	3

Fastest Lap: Brabham, 1m 25.9s. 111.06 mph/178.73 kph

German Grand Prix: Hockenheim, 2 August 1970

50 laps of 4.22 mile/6.79 km circuit

Place	Driver	Car	Laps	Time/reason for retiring	Grid
1	Rindt	Lotus-Ford	50	1h 42m 00.3s	2
2	Ickx	Ferrari	50	1h 42m 01s	1
3	Hulme	McLaren-Ford	50	1h 43m 22.1s	16
4	E Fittipaldi	Lotus-Ford	50	1h 43m 55.4s	13
5	Stommelen	Brabham-Ford	49		11
6	Pescarolo	Matra	49		5
7	Cevert	March-Ford	49		14
8	Siffert	March-Ford	47	engine	4
9	Surtees	Surtees-Ford	46	engine	15
	G Hill	Lotus-Ford	37	engine	20
	Amon	March-Ford	34	engine	6
	Regazzoni	Ferrari	30	engine	3
	Miles	Lotus-Ford	24	engine	10
	Stewart	March-Ford	20	engine	7
	Andretti	March-Ford	15	gearbox	9
	Peterson	March-Ford	11	engine	19
	Rodriguez	BRM	7	ignition	8
	Oliver	BRM	5	engine	18
	J Brabham	Brabham-Ford	4	oil	12
	Beltoise	Matra	4	suspension	21
	Gethin	McLaren-Ford	3	throttle	17

Fastest Lap: Ickx, 2m 00.5s. 126.03 mph/202.83 kph

Austrian Grand Prix: Österreichring, 16 August 1970

60 laps of 3.67 mile/5.91 km circuit

Place	Driver	Car	Laps	Time/reason for retiring	Grid
1	Ickx	Ferrari	60	1h 42m 17.3s	3
2	Regazzoni	Ferrari	60	1h 42m 17.9s	2
3	Stommelen	Brabham-Ford	60	1h 43m 45.2s	17
4	Rodriguez	BRM	59		22
5	Oliver	BRM	59		14
6	Beltoise	Matra	59		7
7	Giunti	Ferrari	59		5
8	Amon	March-Ford	59		6
9	Siffert	March-Ford	59		20
10	Gethin	McLaren-Ford	59		21
11	Eaton	BRM	58		23
12	de Adamich	McLaren-Alfa	57		15
13	J Brabham	Brabham-Ford	56		8
14	Pescarolo	Matra	56		13
15	E Fittipaldi	Lotus-Ford	55		16
	Hulme	McLaren-Ford	30	engine	11
	Surtees	Surtees-Ford	27	engine	12
	Schenken	De Tomaso-Ford	25	engine	19
	Rindt	Lotus-Ford	21	engine	1
	Moser	Bellasi-Ford	13	radiator	24
	Andretti	March-Ford	13	accident	18
	Stewart	March-Ford	7	fuel pipe	4
	Miles	Lotus-Ford	4	brakes	10
	Cevert	March-Ford	0	engine	9

Fastest Lap: Ickx/Regazzoni, 1m 40.4s. 131.7 mph/211.95 kph

Italian Grand Prix: Monza, 6 September 1970

68 laps of 3.57 mile/5.75 km circuit

Place	Driver	Car	Laps	Time/reason for retiring	Grid
1	Regazzoni	Ferrari	68	1h 39m 06.9s	3
2	Stewart	March-Ford	68	1h 39m 12.6s	4
3	Beltoise	Matra	68	1h 39m 12.7s	14
4	Hulme	McLaren-Ford	68	1h 39m 13.0s	9
5	Stommelen	Brabham-Ford	68	1h 39m 13.3s	17
6	Cevert	March-Ford	68	1h 40m 10.3s	11
7	Amon	March-Ford	67		18
8	de Adamich	McLaren-Alfa	61		12
	Gethin	McLaren-Ford	60		16
	Oliver	BRM	36	engine	6
	Peterson	March-Ford	35	engine	13
	J Brabham	Brabham-Ford	31	accident	8
	Ickx	Ferrari	25	clutch	1

Italian Grand Prix (cont)

Place	Driver	Car	Laps	Time/reason for retiring	Grid
	Eaton	BRM	21	overheating	20
	Schenken	De Tomaso-Ford	17	engine	19
	Pescarolo	Matra	14	engine	15
	Giunti	Ferrari	14	fuel system	5
	Rodriguez	BRM	12	engine	2
	Siffert	March-Ford	3	engine	7
	Surtees	Surtees-Ford	0	electrics	10

Fastest Lap: Regazzoni, 1m 25.2s. 150.97 mph/242.96 kph
* Rindt killed in practice crash.

Canadian Grand Prix: St Jovite, 20 September 1970

90 laps of 2.65 mile/4.27 km circuit

Place	Driver	Car	Laps	Time/reason for retiring	Grid
1	Ickx	Ferrari	90	2h 21m 18.4s	2
2	Regazzoni	Ferrari	90	2h 21m 33.2s	3
3	Amon	March-Ford	90	2h 22m 16.3s	6
4	Rodriguez	BRM	89		7
5	Surtees	Surtees-Ford	89		5
6	Gethin	McLaren-Ford	88		11
7	Pescarolo	Matra	87		8
8	Beltoise	Matra	85		13
9	Cevert	March-Ford	85		4
10	Eaton	BRM	85		9
	Schenken	De Tomaso-Ford	79		17
	G Hill	Lotus-Ford	77		20
	de Adamich	McLaren-Alfa	68	oil pressure	12
	Peterson	March-Ford	65	running	16
	Hulme	McLaren-Ford	58	flywheel	15
	J Brabham	Brabham-Ford	56	oil leak	19
	Oliver	BRM	52	running	10
	Stewart	Tyrrell-Ford	31	stub axle	1
	Stommelen	Brabham-Ford	22	steering	18
	Siffert	March-Ford	21	engine	14

Fastest Lap: Regazzoni, 1m 32.2s. 103.47 mph/166.51 kph

United States Grand Prix: Watkins Glen, 4 October 1970

108 laps of 2.3 mile/3.7 km circuit

Place	Driver	Car	Laps	Time/reason for retiring	Grid
1	E Fittipaldi	Lotus-Ford	108	1h 57m 32.8s	3
2	P Rodriguez	BRM	108	1h 58m 09.2s	4
3	Wissell	Lotus-Ford	108	1h 58m 18s	9
4	Ickx	Ferrari	107		1
5	Amon	March-Ford	107		5
6	Bell	Surtees-Ford	107		13
7	Hulme	McLaren-Ford	106		11
8	Pescarolo	Matra	105		12
9	Siffert	March-Ford	105		23
10	J Brabham	Brabham-Ford	105		16
11	Peterson	March-Ford	104		15
12	Stommelen	Brabham-Ford	104		19
13	Regazzoni	Ferrari	101		6
14	Gethin	McLaren-Ford	100		21
	Stewart	Tyrrell-Ford	82	oil leak	2
	G Hill	Lotus-Ford	72	clutch	10
	Cevert	March-Ford	62	lost wheel	17
	Schenken	De Tomaso-Ford	61	suspension	20
	Bonnier	McLaren-Ford	50	water pipe	24
	Beltoise	Matra	27	handling	18
	Hutchinson	Brabham-Ford	21	fuel tank	22
	Oliver	BRM	14	engine	7
	Eaton	BRM	10	engine	14
	Surtees	Surtees-Ford	6	flywheel	8

Fastest Lap: Ickx, 1m 02.74s. 131.97 mph/212.39 kph

Mexican Grand Prix: Mexico City, 25 October 1970

65 laps of 3.11 mile/5 km circuit

Place	Driver	Car	Laps	Time/reason for retiring	Grid
1	Ickx	Ferrari	65	1h 53m 28.4s	3
2	Regazzoni	Ferrari	65	1h 54m 13.8s	1
3	Hulme	McLaren-Ford	65	1h 54m 14.3s	14
4	Amon	March-Ford	65	1h 54m 15.4s	5
5	Beltoise	Matra	65	1h 54m 18.5s	6
6	P Rodriguez	BRM	65	1h 54m 53.1s	7
7	Oliver	BRM	64		13
8	Surtees	Surtees-Ford	64		15
9	Pescarolo	Matra	61		11
	Wissell	Lotus-Ford	56		12
	J Brabham	Brabham-Ford	52	engine	4
	Stewart	Tyrrell-Ford	33	suspension	2
	Gethin	McLaren-Ford	27	engine	10

Mexican Grand Prix (cont)

Place	Driver	Car	Laps	Time/reason for retiring	Grid
	Stommelen	Brabham-Ford	15	fuel system	17
	Cevert	March-Ford	8	engine	9
	G Hill	Lotus-Ford	4	overheating	8
	Siffert	March-Ford	3	engine	16
	E Fittipaldi	Lotus-Ford	1	engine	18

Fastest Lap: Ickx, 1m 43.1s. 108.47 mph/174.57 kph

World Championship 1970

1	Rindt	45
2	Ickx	40
3	Regazzoni	33
4	Hulme	27
5 =	J Brabham, Stewart	25
7 =	Amon, P Rodriguez	23
9	Beltoise	16
10	E Fittipaldi	12
11	Stommelen	10
12	Pescarolo	8
13	G Hill	7
14	McLaren	6
15 =	Andretti, Wissell	4
17 =	Giunti, Surtees	3
19 =	Miles, Oliver, Servoz-Gavin	2
22 =	Bell, Cevert, Gethin, Gurney	1

Constructors' Championship

1	Lotus-Ford	59
2	Ferrari	52 (55)
3	March-Ford	48
4 =	Brabham-Ford, McLaren-Ford	35
6 =	BRM, Matra	23
8	Surtees-Ford	3

Although Jackie Stewart took his second championship, and Tyrrell's first, he was the only Ford Cosworth winner. Ferrari and BRM each achieved two twins, with Peter Gethin's Monza victory the fastest, as well as one of the closest, of all time. Lotus experimented with a gas turbine powered car in several races without much success.

South African Grand Prix: Kyalami, 6 March 1971

79 laps of 2.55 mile/4.1 km circuit

Place	Driver	Car	Laps	Time/reason for retiring	Grid
1	Andretti	Ferrari	79	1h 47m 35.5s	4
2	Stewart	Tyrrell-Ford	79	1h 47m 56.4s	1
3	Regazzoni	Ferrari	79	1h 48m 06.9s	3
4	Wissell	Lotus-Ford	79	1h 48m 44.9s	14
5	Amon	Matra	78		2
6	Hulme	McLaren-Ford	78		7
7	Redman	Surtees-Ford	78		17
8	Ickx	Ferrari	78		8
9	G Hill	Brabham-Ford	77		19
10	Peterson	March-Ford	77		13
11	Pescarolo	March-Ford	77		18
12	Stommelen	Surtees-Ford	77		15
13	de Adamich	March-Alfa	73		22
	E Fittipaldi	Lotus-Ford	57	engine	5
	Surtees	Surtees-Ford	55	gearbox	6
	Cevert	Tyrrell-Ford	45	accident	9
	Ganley	BRM	41	illness	24
	P Rodriguez	BRM	32	overheating	10
	Siffert	BRM	30	overheating	16
	Charlton	Brabham-Ford	30	engine	12
	Love	March-Ford	29	gearbox	21
	Pretorius	Brabham-Ford	21	engine	20
	Gethin	McLaren-Ford	6	fuel leak	11
	Bonnier	McLaren-Ford	4	suspension	23
	Soler-Roig	March-Ford	4	engine	25

Fastest Lap: Andretti, 1m 20.3s. 114.33 mph/184 kph

Spanish Grand Prix: Montjuich Park, 18 April 1971

75 laps of 2.36 mile/3.79 km circuit

Place	Driver	Car	Laps	Time/reason for retiring	Grid
1	Stewart	Tyrrell-Ford	75	1h 49m 03.4s	4
2	Ickx	Ferrari	75	1h 49m 06.8s	1
3	Amon	Matra	75	1h 50m 01.5s	3
4	P Rodriguez	BRM	75	1h 50m 21.3s	5
5	Hulme	McLaren-Ford	75	1h 50m 30.4s	9
6	Beltoise	Matra	74		6
7	Cevert	Tyrrell-Ford	74		12
8	Gethin	McLaren-Ford	73		7
9	Schenken	Brabham-Ford	72		21
10	Ganley	BRM	71		17
11	Surtees	Surtees-Ford	67		22
	Wissell	Lotus-Ford	58		16
	E Fittipaldi	Lotus-Ford	53	suspension	14
	Pescarolo	March-Ford	53	engine and wing	11
	Andretti	Ferrari	50	engine	8
	Soler-Roig	March-Ford	46	fuel pipe	20
	de Adamich	March-Alfa	26	transmission	18
	Peterson	March-Ford	24	ignition	13
	Regazzoni	Ferrari	12	engine	2
	Stommelen	Surtees-Ford	8	fuel pressure	19
	Siffert	BRM	5	gearbox	10
	G Hill	Brabham-Ford	4	steering	15

Fastest Lap: Ickx, 1m 25.1s. 99.64 mph/160.36 kph

Monaco Grand Prix: Monte Carlo, 23 May 1971

80 laps of 1.95 mile/3.15 km circuit

Place	Driver	Car	Laps	Time/reason for retiring	Grid
1	Stewart	Tyrrell-Ford	80	1h 52m 21.3s	1
2	Peterson	March-Ford	80	1h 52m 46.9s	8
3	Ickx	Ferrari	80	1h 53m 14.6s	2
4	Hulme	McLaren-Ford	80	1h 53m 28s	6
5	E Fittipaldi	Lotus-Ford	79		17
6	Stommelen	Surtees-Ford	79		16
7	Surtees	Surtees-Ford	79		10
8	Pescarolo	March-Ford	77		13
9	P Rodriguez	BRM	76		5
10	Schenken	Brabham-Ford	76		18
	Siffert	BRM	58	oil pipe	3
	Beltoise	Matra	47	crownwheel and pinion	7
	Amon	Matra	45	crownwheel and pinion	4
	Regazzoni	Ferrari	24	accident	11
	Gethin	McLaren-Ford	22	accident	14

Monaco Grand Prix (cont)

Place	Driver	Car	Laps	Time/reason for retiring	Grid
	Wissell	Lotus-Ford	21	suspension	12
	Cevert	Tyrrell-Ford	5	accident	15
	G Hill	Brabham-Ford	1	accident	9

Fastest Lap: Stewart, 1m 22.2s. 85.59 mph/137.74 kph

Dutch Grand Prix: Zandvoort, 20 June 1971

70 laps of 2.61 mile/4.19 km circuit

Place	Driver	Car	Laps	Time/reason for retiring	Grid
1	Ickx	Ferrari	70	1h 56m 20.1s	1
2	P Rodriguez	BRM	70	1h 56m 28.1s	2
3	Regazzoni	Ferrari	69		4
4	Peterson	March-Ford	68		13
5	Surtees	Surtees-Ford	68		7
6	Siffert	BRM	68		8
7	Ganley	BRM	66		9
8	van Lennep	Surtees-Ford	65		21
9	Beltoise	Matra	65		11
10	G Hill	Brabham-Ford	65		16
11	Stewart	Tyrrell-Ford	65		3
12	Hulme	McLaren-Ford	63		14
	Pescarolo	March-Ford	62		15
	S Barber	March-Ford	60		24
	Gethin	McLaren-Ford	60		23
	Soler-Roig	March-Ford	57	engine	17
	Schenken	Brabham-Ford	38	suspension	19
	Cevert	Tyrrell-Ford	29	accident	12
	Stommelen	Surtees-Ford	18	disqualified: push start	10
	Wissell	Lotus-Ford	16	disqualified: reversed into pits	6
	Nanni	March-Alfa	7	accident	20
	D Walker	Lotus Turbine	5	accident	22
	Andretti	Ferrari	4	fuel system	18
	Amon	Matra	1	accident	5

Fastest Lap: Ickx, 1m 34.95s. 98.78 mph/158.98 kph

French Grand Prix: Paul Ricard, 4 July 1971

55 laps of 3.61 mile/5.8 km circuit

Place	Driver	Car	Laps	Time/reason for retiring	Grid
1	Stewart	Tyrrell-Ford	55	1h 46m 41.7s	1
2	Cevert	Tyrrell-Ford	55	1h 47m 09.8s	7
3	E Fittipaldi	Lotus-Ford	55	1h 47m 15.8s	17

French Grand Prix (cont)

Place	Driver	Car	Laps	Time/reason for retiring	Grid
4	Siffert	BRM	55	1h 47m 18.9s	6
5	Amon	Matra	55	1h 47m 22.8s	9
6	Wissell	Lotus-Ford	55	1h 47m 57.7s	15
7	Beltoise	Matra	55	1h 47m 58.6s	8
8	Surtees	Surtees-Ford	55	1h 48m 06.6s	13
9	Gethin	McLaren-Ford	54		19
10	Ganley	BRM	54		16
11	Stommelen	Surtees-Ford	53		10
12	Schenken	Brabham-Ford	50	oil pressure	14
13	Mazet	March-Ford	50		23
	Max	March-Ford	46		22
	Pescarolo	March-Ford	44	gearbox	18
	G Hill	Brabham-Ford	34	oil pipe	4
	de Adamich	March-Alfa	31	engine	20
	P Rodriguez	BRM	27	ignition	5
	Regazzoni	Ferrari	20	accident	2
	Peterson	March-Alfa	19	engine	12
	Hulme	McLaren-Ford	15	ignition	11
	Ickx	Ferrari	4	engine	3
	Soler-Roig	March-Ford	3	fuel pump	21

Fastest Lap: Stewart, 1m 44.1s. 113.92 mph/183.33 kph

British Grand Prix: Silverstone, 17 July 1971

68 laps of 2.93 mile/4.71 km circuit

Place	Driver	Car	Laps	Time/reason for retiring	Grid
1	Stewart	Tyrrell-Ford	68	1h 31m 31.5s	2
2	Peterson	March-Ford	68	1h 32m 07.6s	5
3	E Fittipaldi	Lotus-Ford	68	1h 32m 22s	4
4	Pescarolo	March-Ford	67		17
5	Stommelen	Surtees-Ford	67		12
6	Surtees	Surtees-Ford	67		18
7	Beltoise	Matra	66		15
8	Ganley	BRM	66		11
9	Siffert	BRM	66		3
10	Cevert	Tyrrell-Ford	65		10
11	Nanni	March-Ford	65		21
12	Schenken	Brabham-Ford	63	transmission	7
	Wissell	Lotus Turbine	57		19
	de Adamich	March-Alfa	56		24
	Gethin	McLaren-Ford	53	engine	14
	Ickx	Ferrari	51	engine	6
	Regazzoni	Ferrari	48	oil pressure	1
	Amon	Matra	35	engine	9
	Hulme	McLaren-Ford	32	engine	8

British Grand Prix (cont)

Place	Driver	Car	Laps	Time/reason for retiring	Grid
	Bell	Surtees-Ford	23	suspension	23
	Beuttler	March-Ford	21	oil pressure	20
	Charlton	Lotus-Ford	1	engine	13
	Oliver	McLaren-Ford	0	accident	22
	G Hill	Brabham-Ford	0	accident	16

Fastest Lap: Stewart, 1m 19.9s. 131.88 mph/212.24 kph

German Grand Prix: Nürburgring, 1 August 1971

12 laps of 14.19 mile/22.84 km circuit

Place	Driver	Car	Laps	Time/reason for retiring	Grid
1	Stewart	Tyrrell-Ford	12	1h 29m 15.7s	1
2	Cevert	Tyrrell-Ford	12	1h 29m 45.8s	5
3	Regazzoni	Ferrari	12	1h 29m 52.8s	4
4	Andretti	Ferrari	12	1h 31m 20.7s	11
5	Peterson	March-Ford	12	1h 31m 44.8s	7
6	Schenken	Brabham-Ford	12	1h 32m 12.3s	9
7	Surtees	Surtees-Ford	12	1h 32m 34.7s	15
8	Wissell	Lotus-Ford	12	1h 35m 47.4s	17
9	G Hill	Brabham-Ford	12	1h 35m 52.7s	13
10	Stommelen	Surtees-Ford	11		12
11	Elford	BRM	11		18
12	Nanni	March-Alfa	10		21
	E Fittipaldi	Lotus-Ford	8	oil leak	8
	Siffert	BRM	6	suspension	3
	Amon	Matra	6	accident	16
	Gethin	McLaren-Ford	5	accident	19
	Pescarolo	March-Ford	5	suspension	10
	Beuttler	March-Ford	3	disqualified: wrong way into pits	22
	Hulme	McLaren-Ford	3	fuel leak	6
	de Adamich	March-Alfa	2	fuel injection	20
	Ganley	BRM	2	engine	14
	Ickx	Ferrari	1	accident	2

Fastest Lap: Cevert, 7m 20.1s. 116.07 mph/186.79 kph

Austrian Grand Prix: Österreichring, 15 August 1971

54 laps of 3.67 mile/5.91 km circuit

Place	Driver	Car	Laps	Time/reason for retiring	Grid
1	Siffert	BRM	54	1h 30m 23.9s	1
2	E Fittipaldi	Lotus-Ford	54	1h 30m 28.0s	5
3	Schenken	Brabham-Ford	54	1h 30m 43.7s	7

Austrian Grand Prix (cont)

Place	Driver	Car	Laps	Time/reason for retiring	Grid
4	Wissell	Lotus-Ford	54	1h 30m 55.8s	10
5	G Hill	Brabham-Ford	54	1h 31m 12.3s	8
6	Pescarolo	March-Ford	54	1h 31m 48.4s	13
7	Stommelen	Surtees-Ford	54	1h 32m 01.3s	12
8	Peterson	March-Ford	53		11
9	Oliver	McLaren-Ford	53		21
10	Gethin	BRM	52		16
11	Marko	BRM	52		17
12	Nanni	March-Alfa	51		15
	Beuttler	March-Ford	47		19
	Cevert	Tyrrell-Ford	42	engine	3
	Stewart	Tyrrell-Ford	35	stub axle	2
	Ickx	Ferrari	31	engine	6
	Lauda	March-Ford	19	handling	20
	Surtees	Surtees-Ford	12	engine	18
	Regazzoni	Ferrari	8	engine	4
	Ganley	BRM	5	ignition	14
	Hulme	McLaren-Ford	4	engine	9

Fastest Lap: Siffert, 1m 38.47s. 134.28 mph/216.1 kph

Italian Grand Prix: Monza, 5 September 1971

55 laps of 3.57 mile/5.75 km circuit

Place	Driver	Car	Laps	Time/reason for retiring	Grid
1	Gethin	BRM	55	1h 18m 12.60s	11
2	Peterson	March-Ford	55	1h 18m 12.61s	6
3	Cevert	Tyrrell-Ford	55	1h 18m 12.69s	5
4	Hailwood	Surtees-Ford	55	1h 18m 12.78s	17
5	Ganley	BRM	55	1h 18m 13.21s	4
6	Amon	Matra	55	1h 18m 44.96s	1
7	Oliver	McLaren-Ford	55	1h 19m 37.43s	13
8	E Fittipaldi	Lotus Turbine	54		18
9	Siffert	BRM	53		3
10	Bonnier	McLaren-Ford	51		21
	G Hill	Brabham-Ford	47	gearbox	14
	Jarier	March-Ford	47	running	23
	Beuttler	March-Ford	41	engine	16
	Pescarolo	March-Ford	40	suspension	10
	de Adamich	March-Alfa	33	engine	20
	Regazzoni	Ferrari	17	engine	8
	Ickx	Ferrari	15	engine	2
	Stewart	Tyrrell-Ford	15	engine	7
	Nanni	March-Alfa	11	electrical	19
	Moser	Bellasi-Ford	5	suspension	22

Italian Grand Prix (cont)

Place	Driver	Car	Laps	Time/reason for retiring	Grid
	Schenken	Brabham-Ford	5	suspension	9
	Marko	BRM	3	engine	12
	Surtees	Surtees-Ford	3	engine	15

Fastest Lap: Pescarolo, 1m 23.8s. 153.49 mph/247.02 kph

Canadian Grand Prix: Mosport, 19 September 1971

64 laps of 2.46 mile/3.96 km circuit

Place	Driver	Car	Laps	Time/reason for retiring	Grid
1	Stewart	Tyrrell-Ford	64	1h 55m 12.9s	1
2	Peterson	March-Ford	64	1h 55m 51.2s	6
3	Donohue	McLaren-Ford	64	1h 56m 47.8s	8
4	Hulme	McLaren-Ford	63		9
5	Wissell	Lotus-Ford	63		7
6	Cevert	Tyrrell-Ford	62		3
7	E Fittipaldi	Lotus-Ford	62		4
8	Ickx	Ferrari	62		11
9	Siffert	BRM	61		2
10	Amon	Matra	61		5
11	Surtees	Surtees-Ford	60		13
12	Marko	BRM	60		18
13	Andretti	Ferrari	60		12
14	Gethin	BRM	59		15
15	Eaton	BRM	59		20
16	Nanni	March-Ford	57		19
	Beuttler	March-Ford	56		21
	Lovely	Lotus-Ford	55		24
	Stommelen	Surtees-Ford	26	overheating	22
	Beltoise	Matra	15	accident	10
	S Barber	March-Ford	13	oil pressure	23
	Regazzoni	Ferrari	7	accident	17
	G Hill	Brabham-Ford	2	accident	14
	Schenken	Brabham-Ford	0	ignition	16

Fastest Lap: Hulme, 1m 43.5s. 85.52 mph/137.64 kph

United States Grand Prix: Watkins Glen, 3 October 1971

59 laps of 3.38 mile/5.44 km circuit

Place	Driver	Car	Laps	Time/reason for retiring	Grid
1	Cevert	Tyrrell-Ford	59	1h 43m 52s	5
2	Siffert	BRM	59	1h 44m 32.1s	6
3	Peterson	March-Ford	59	1h 44m 36.1s	11

United States Grand Prix (cont)

Place	Driver	Car	Laps	Time/reason for retiring	Grid
4	Ganley	BRM	59	1h 44m 48.7s	12
5	Stewart	Tyrrell-Ford	59	1h 44m 52s	1
6	Regazzoni	Ferrari	59	1h 45m 08.4s	4
7	G Hill	Brabham-Ford	58		18
8	Beltoise	Matra	58		10
9	Gethin	BRM	58		21
10	Hobbs	McLaren-Ford	58		22
11	de Adamich	March-Alfa	57		26
12	Amon	Matra	57		8
13	Marko	BRM	57		16
14	Cannon	BRM	56		24
15	Hailwood	Surtees-Ford	54	accident	14
16	Bonnier	McLaren-Ford	54	out of fuel	28
17	Surtees	Surtees-Ford	54		13
	S Barber	March-Ford	52		25
	E Fittipaldi	Lotus-Ford	49		2
	Lovely	Lotus-Ford	49		29
	Ickx	Ferrari	48	electrical	7
	Hulme	McLaren-Ford	47	accident	3
	Schenken	Brabham-Ford	40	engine	15
	Craft	Brabham-Ford	29	suspension	27
	Pescarolo	March-Ford	22	engine	20
	Posey	Surtees-Ford	14	engine	17
	Nanni	March-Ford	10	radiator and steering	23
	Wissell	Lotus-Ford	5	accident	9
	Revson	Tyrrell-Ford	0	clutch	19

Fastest Lap: Ickx, 1m 43.47s. 117.5 mph/189.09 kph

World Championship 1971

1	Stewart	62
2	Peterson	33
3	Cevert	26
4 =	Ickx, Siffert	19
6	E Fittipaldi	16
7	Regazzoni	13
8	Andretti	12
9 =	Amon, Hulme, Gethin, P Rodriguez, Wissell	9
14 =	Ganley, Schenken	5
16 =	Donohue, Pescarolo	4
18 =	Hailwood, Stommelen, Surtees	3
21	G Hill	2
22	Beltoise	1

Constructors' Championship

1	Tyrrell-Ford	73
2	BRM	36
3 =	March-Ford	33 (34)
	Ferrari	33
5	Lotus-Ford	21
6	McLaren-Ford	10
7	Matra	9
8	Surtees-Ford	8
9	Brabham-Ford	5

1972

Emerson Fittipaldi became the youngest world champion. Beltoise won his only, and BRM's last, grand prix, at Monaco in the rain. Stewart missed the Belgian Grand Prix with a stomach ulcer. The successful Formula 2 constructor Tecno entered grand prix racing with little success. As well as his customer Marches, Frank Williams also ran the first Williams car, the Len Bailey-designed Politoys, at Brands Hatch.

Argentine Grand Prix: Buenos Aires, 23 January 1972

95 laps of 2.08 mile/3.35 km circuit

Place	Driver	Car	Laps	Time/reason for retiring	Grid
1	Stewart	Tyrrell-Ford	95	1h 57m 58.8s	2
2	Hulme	McLaren-Ford	95	1h 58m 24.8s	4
3	Ickx	Ferrari	95	1h 58m 58.2s	8
4	Regazzoni	Ferrari	95	1h 59m 05.5s	6
5	Schenken	Surtees-Ford	95	1h 59m 07.9s	11
6	Peterson	March-Ford	94		10
7	Reutemann	Brabham-Ford	93		1
8	Pescarolo	March-Ford	93		14
9	Ganley	BRM	93		12
10	Marko	BRM	93		18
11	Lauda	March-Ford	93		21
	E Fittipaldi	Lotus-Ford	59	suspension	5
	Cevert	Tyrrell-Ford	59	gearbox	7
	Wissell	BRM	58	water hose	16
	Revson	McLaren-Ford	49	engine	3
	Andretti	Ferrari	20	engine	9
	G Hill	Brabham-Ford	11	fuel pump	15
	de Adamich	Surtees-Ford	10	metering unit	13
	D Walker	Lotus-Ford	8	disqualified: illegal repairs	19
	Gethin	BRM	1	oil pipe	17
	Soler-Roig	BRM	1	accident	20

Fastest Lap: Stewart, 1m 13.66s. 101.58 mph/163.48 kph

South African Grand Prix: Kyalami, 4 March 1972

79 laps of 2.55 mile/4.1 km circuit

Place	Driver	Car	Laps	Time/reason for retiring	Grid
1	Hulme	McLaren-Ford	79	1h 45m 49.1s	5
2	E Fittipaldi	Lotus-Ford	79	1h 46m 03.2s	3
3	Revson	McLaren-Ford	79	1h 46m 14.9s	12
4	Andretti	Ferrari	79	1h 46m 27.6s	6
5	Peterson	March-Ford	79	1h 46m 38.1s	9
6	G Hill	Brabham-Ford	78		14
7	Lauda	March-Ford	78		21
8	Ickx	Ferrari	78		7
9	Cevert	Tyrrell-Ford	78		8
10	D Walker	Lotus-Ford	78		19
11	Pescarolo	March-Ford	77		22
12	Regazzoni	Ferrari	77		2
13	Stommelen	March-Ford	77		25
14	Marko	BRM	76		23
15	Amon	Matra	76		13
16	Love	Surtees-Ford	73	accident	26
17	Pace	March-Ford	73		24
	Ganley	BRM	70		16
	de Adamich	Surtees-Ford	69		20
	Gethin	BRM	65		18
	Beltoise	BRM	60	engine	11
	Stewart	Tyrrell-Ford	44	gearbox	1
	Hailwood	Surtees-Ford	28	suspension	4
	Reutemann	Brabham-Ford	27	fuel line	15
	Schenken	Surtees-Ford	8	engine	10
	Charlton	Lotus-Ford	1	fuel pump	17

Fastest Lap: Hailwood, 1m 18.9s. 116.35 mph/187.25 kph

Spanish Grand Prix: Jarama, 1 May 1972

90 laps of 2.12 mile/3.4 km circuit

Place	Driver	Car	Laps	Time/reason for retiring	Grid
1	E Fittipaldi	Lotus-Ford	90	2h 03m 41.2s	3
2	Ickx	Ferrari	90	2h 04m 00.2s	1
3	Regazzoni	Ferrari	89		8
4	de Adamich	Surtees-Ford	89		13
5	Revson	McLaren-Ford	89		11
6	Pace	March-Ford	89		16
7	W Fittipaldi	Brabham-Ford	88		14
8	Schenken	Surtees-Ford	88		18
9	D Walker	Lotus-Ford	87	out of fuel	24
10	G Hill	Brabham-Ford	86		23
11	Pescarolo	March-Ford	86		19
	Stewart	Tyrrell-Ford	69	accident	4

Spanish Grand Prix (cont)

Place	Driver	Car	Laps	Time/reason for retiring	Grid
	Amon	Matra	65	gearbox	6
	Gethin	BRM	65	engine	21
	Cevert	Tyrrell-Ford	64	ignition	12
	Hulme	McLaren-Ford	47	gearbox	2
	Ganley	BRM	37	engine	20
	Wissell	BRM	24	accident	10
	Andretti	Ferrari	23	engine	5
	Hailwood	Surtees-Ford	19	electrical	15
	Peterson	March-Ford	15	fuel leak	9
	Stommelen	March-Ford	15	accident	17
	Beltoise	BRM	8	gearbox	7
	Lauda	March-Ford	6	differential	25
	Soler-Roig	BRM	6	accident	22

Fastest Lap: Ickx, 1m 21.01s. 94 mph/151.28 kph

Monaco Grand Prix: Monte Carlo, 14 May 1972

80 laps of 1.95 mile/3.15 km circuit

Place	Driver	Car	Laps	Time/reason for retiring	Grid
1	Beltoise	BRM	80	2h 26m 54.7s	4
2	Ickx	Ferrari	80	2h 27m 32.9s	2
3	E Fittipaldi	Lotus-Ford	79		1
4	Stewart	Tyrrell-Ford	78		8
5	Redman	McLaren-Ford	77		10
6	Amon	Matra	77		6
7	de Adamich	Surtees-Ford	77		18
8	Marko	BRM	77		17
9	W Fittipaldi	Brabham-Ford	77		21
10	Stommelen	March-Ford	77		25
11	Peterson	March-Ford	76		15
12	G Hill	Brabham-Ford	76		19
13	Beuttler	March-Ford	76		23
14	D Walker	Lotus-Ford	75		14
15	Hulme	McLaren-Ford	74		7
16	Lauda	March-Ford	74		22
17	Pace	March-Ford	72		24
	Cevert	Tyrrell-Ford	70		12
	Pescarolo	March-Ford	58	accident	9
	Regazzoni	Ferrari	51	accident	3
	Hailwood	Surtees-Ford	48	accident	11
	Ganley	BRM	47	accident	20
	Schenken	Surtees-Ford	31	accident	13
	Gethin	BRM	27	accident	5
	Wissell	BRM	16	engine	16

Fastest Lap: Beltoise, 1m 40s. 70.35 mph/113.22 kph

Belgian Grand Prix: Nivelles, 4 June 1972

85 laps of 2.31 mile/3.72 km circuit

Place	Driver	Car	Laps	Time/reason for retiring	Grid
1	E Fittipaldi	Lotus-Ford	85	1h 44m 06.7s	1
2	Cevert	Tyrrell-Ford	85	1h 44m 33.3s	5
3	Hulme	McLaren-Ford	85	1h 45m 04.8s	3
4	Hailwood	Surtees-Ford	85	1h 45m 18.7s	8
5	Pace	March-Ford	84		11
6	Amon	Matra	84		13
7	Revson	McLaren-Ford	83		7
8	Ganley	BRM	83		15
9	Peterson	March-Ford	83		14
10	Marko	BRM	83		23
11	Stommelen	March-Ford	83		20
12	Lauda	March-Ford	82		25
13	Reutemann	Brabham-Ford	81		9
14	D Walker	Lotus-Ford	79		12
	G Hill	Brabham-Ford	72	suspension	16
	Pescarolo	March-Ford	59	running	19
	Regazzoni	Ferrari	57	accident	2
	de Adamich	Surtees-Ford	55	engine	10
	Nanni	Tecno	53	accident	24
	Ickx	Ferrari	46	fuel injection	4
	Beuttler	March-Ford	31	transmission	22
	W Fittipaldi	Brabham-Ford	27	gearbox	18
	Gethin	BRM	26	fuel pump	17
	Beltoise	BRM	14	overheating	6
	Schenken	Surtees-Ford	10	overheating	21

Fastest Lap: Amon, 1m 12.12s. 115.06 mph/185.89 kph

French Grand Prix: Clermont-Ferrand, 2 July 1972

38 laps of 5.01 mile/8.06 km circuit

Place	Driver	Car	Laps	Time/reason for retiring	Grid
1	Stewart	Tyrrell-Ford	38	1h 52m 21.5s	3
2	E Fittipaldi	Lotus-Ford	38	1h 52m 49.2s	8
3	Amon	Matra	38	1h 52m 53.4s	1
4	Cevert	Tyrrell-Ford	38	1h 53m 10.8s	7
5	Peterson	March-Ford	38	1h 53m 18.3s	9
6	Hailwood	Surtees-Ford	38	1h 53m 57.6s	10
7	Hulme	McLaren-Ford	38	1h 54m 09.6s	2
8	W Fittipaldi	Brabham-Ford	38	1h 54m 46.6s	14
9	Redman	McLaren-Ford	38	1h 55m 17s	13
10	G Hill	Brabham-Ford	38	1h 55m 21s	20
11	Ickx	Ferrari	37		4
12	Reutemann	Brabham-Ford	37		17

French Grand Prix (cont)

Place	Driver	Car	Laps	Time/reason for retiring	Grid
13	Nanni	Ferrari	37		19
14	de Adamich	Surtees-Ford	37		12
15	Beltoise	BRM	37		24
16	Stommelen	March-Ford	37		15
17	Schenken	Surtees-Ford	36		5
18	D Walker	Lotus-Ford	34	gearbox	22
	Beuttler	March-Ford	33	out of fuel	23
	Depailler	Tyrrell-Ford	33	running	16
	Wissell	BRM	24	gear linkage	18
	Pace	March-Ford	18	engine	11
	Marko	BRM	8	injury	6
	Lauda	March-Ford	3	transmission	21

Fastest Lap: Amon, 2m 53.9s. 103.61 mph/166.75 kph

British Grand Prix: Brands Hatch, 15 July 1972

76 laps of 2.65 mile/4.27 km circuit

Place	Driver	Car	Laps	Time/reason for retiring	Grid
1	E Fittipaldi	Lotus-Ford	76	1h 47m 50.2s	2
2	Stewart	Tyrrell-Ford	76	1h 47m 54.3s	4
3	Revson	McLaren-Ford	76	1h 49m 02.7s	3
4	Amon	Matra	75		17
5	Hulme	McLaren-Ford	75		11
6	Merzario	Ferrari	75		9
7	Peterson	March-Ford	74	accident	8
8	Reutemann	Brabham-Ford	73		10
9	Lauda	March-Ford	73		19
10	Stommelen	March-Ford	71		25
11	Beltoise	BRM	70		6
12	W Fittipaldi	Brabham-Ford	69	suspension	22
13	Beuttler	March-Ford	69		23
	Schenken	Surtees-Ford	63	suspension	5
	Cevert	Tyrrell-Ford	60	accident	12
	D Walker	Lotus-Ford	58	suspension	15
	Ickx	Ferrari	48	oil pressure	1
	G Hill	Brabham-Ford	47	accident	21
	Pace	March-Ford	39	differential	13
	Oliver	BRM	36	suspension	14
	Hailwood	Surtees-Ford	30	gearbox	7
	Charlton	Lotus-Ford	21	gearbox	24
	Nanni	Tecno	9	accident	18
	Pescarolo	Williams-Ford	7	accident	26
	Gethin	BRM	5	engine	16
	de Adamich	Surtees-Ford	3	accident	20

Fastest Lap: Stewart, 1m 24s. 113.57 mph/182.78 kph

German Grand Prix: Nürburgring, 30 July 1972

14 laps of 14.19 mile/22.84 km circuit

Place	Driver	Car	Laps	Time/reason for retiring	Grid
1	Ickx	Ferrari	14	1h 42m 12.3s	1
2	Regazzoni	Ferrari	14	1h 43m 00.6s	7
3	Peterson	March-Ford	14	1h 43m 19s	4
4	Ganley	BRM	14	1h 44m 32.5s	18
5	Redman	McLaren-Ford	14	1h 44m 48s	19
6	G Hill	Brabham-Ford	14	1h 45m 11.9s	15
7	W Fittipaldi	Brabham-Ford	14	1h 45m 12.4s	21
8	Beuttler	March-Ford	14	1h 47m 23s	27
9	Beltoise	BRM	14	1h 47m 32.5s	13
10	Cevert	Tyrrell-Ford	14	1h 47m 56s	5
11	Stewart	Tyrrell-Ford	13	accident	2
12	Merzario	Ferrari	13		22
13	de Adamich	Surtees-Ford	13		20
14	Schenken	Surtees-Ford	13		12
15	Amon	Matra	13		8
	Pace	March-Ford	11		11
	Pescarolo	March-Ford	10	accident	9
	E Fittipaldi	Lotus-Ford	10	gearbox	3
	Hulme	McLaren-Ford	8	engine	10
	Hailwood	Surtees-Ford	8	suspension	16
	Reutemann	Brabham-Ford	6	crownwheel and pinion	6
	Stommelen	March-Ford	5	electrical	14
	D Walker	Lotus-Ford	5	oil tank	23
	Bell	Tecno	4	engine	25
	Charlton	Lotus-Ford	3	illness	26
	Lauda	March-Ford	3	oil tank	24
	Wissell	BRM	3	engine	17

Fastest Lap: Ickx, 7m 13.6s. 117.81 mph/189.59 kph

Austrian Grand Prix: Österreichring, 13 August 1972

54 laps of 3.67 mile/5.91 km circuit

Place	Driver	Car	Laps	Time/reason for retiring	Grid
1	E Fittipaldi	Lotus-Ford	54	1h 29m 16.7s	1
2	Hulme	McLaren-Ford	54	1h 29m 17.8s	7
3	Revson	McLaren-Ford	54	1h 29m 53.2s	4
4	Hailwood	Surtees-Ford	54	1h 30m 01.4s	12
5	Amon	Matra	54	1h 30m 02.3s	6
6	Ganley	BRM	54	1h 30m 17.9s	10
7	Stewart	Tyrrell-Ford	54	1h 30m 25.8s	3
8	Beltoise	BRM	54	1h 30m 38.1s	21
9	Cevert	Tyrrell-Ford	53		20
10	Lauda	March-Ford	53		22

Austrian Grand Prix (cont)

Place	Driver	Car	Laps	Time/reason for retiring	Grid
11	Schenken	Surtees-Ford	52		8
12	Peterson	March-Ford	52		11
13	Gethin	BRM	51		16
14	de Adamich	Surtees-Ford	51		13
15	Stommelen	March-Ford	48		17
	Pace	March-Ford	46		18
	Nanni	Tecno	45		23
	G Hill	Brabham-Ford	35	metering unit	14
	W Fittipaldi	Brabham-Ford	30	brake pipe	15
	Beuttler	March-Ford	23	metering unit	24
	Migault	Connew-Ford	22	suspension	25
	Ickx	Ferrari	19	fuel pressure	9
	Reutemann	Brabham-Ford	13	metering unit	5
	Regazzoni	Ferrari	12	fuel pressure	2
	D Walker	Lotus-Ford	6	engine	19

Fastest Lap: Hulme, 1m 38.32s. 134.48 mph/216.43 kph

Italian Grand Prix: Monza, 10 September 1972

55 laps of 3.59 mile/5.78 km circuit

Place	Driver	Car	Laps	Time/reason for retiring	Grid
1	E Fittipaldi	Lotus-Ford	55	1h 29m 58.4s	6
2	Hailwood	Surtees-Ford	55	1h 30m 12.9s	9
3	Hulme	McLaren-Ford	55	1h 30m 22.2s	5
4	Revson	McLaren-Ford	55	1h 30m 34.1s	8
5	G Hill	Brabham-Ford	55	1h 31m 04s	13
6	Gethin	BRM	55	1h 31m 20.3s	12
7	Andretti	Ferrari	54		7
8	Beltoise	BRM	54		16
9	Peterson	March-Ford	54		24
10	Beuttler	March-Ford	54		25
11	Ganley	BRM	52		17
12	Wissell	BRM	51		10
13	Lauda	March-Ford	50		20
	Ickx	Ferrari	45	electrical	1
	Amon	Matra	37	brakes	2
	de Adamich	Surtees-Ford	32	brakes	21
	Schenken	Surtees-Ford	20	suspension	22
	Surtees	Surtees-Ford	19	fuel vaporization	19
	W Fittipaldi	Brabham-Ford	19	suspension	15
	Regazzoni	Ferrari	16	accident	4
	Pace	March-Ford	15	accident	18
	Reutemann	Brabham-Ford	14	suspension	11

Italian Grand Prix (cont)

Place	Driver	Car	Laps	Time/reason for retiring	Grid
	Cevert	Tyrrell-Ford	13	engine	14
	Nanni	Tecno	6	engine	23
	Stewart	Tyrrell-Ford	0	clutch	3

Fastest Lap: Ickx, 1m 36.6s. 134.15 mph/215.89 kph

Canadian Grand Prix: Mosport, 24 September 1972

80 laps of 2.46 mile/3.96 km circuit

Place	Driver	Car	Laps	Time/reason for retiring	Grid
1	Stewart	Tyrrell-Ford	80	1h 43m 16.9s	5
2	Revson	McLaren-Ford	80	1h 44m 05.1s	1
3	Hulme	McLaren-Ford	80	1h 44m 11.5s	2
4	Reutemann	Brabham-Ford	80	1h 44m 17.6s	9
5	Regazzoni	Ferrari	80	1h 44m 23.9s	7
6	Amon	Matra	79		10
7	Schenken	Surtees-Ford	79		13
8	G Hill	Brabham-Ford	79		17
9	Pace	March-Ford	78	fuel pressure	18
10	Ganley	BRM	78		14
11	E Fittipaldi	Lotus-Ford	78		4
12	Ickx	Ferrari	76		8
13	Pescarolo	March-Ford	73		21
	Wissell	Lotus-Ford	64	fuel line	16
	Beuttler	March-Ford	59		24
	Peterson	March-Ford	54	disqualified: pushed car against traffic	3
	Cevert	Tyrrell-Ford	50	gearbox	6
	Gethin	BRM	25	suspension	12
	S Barber	March-Ford	24	still running	22
	Beltoise	BRM	20	oil cooler	20
	Brack	BRM	20	accident	23
	W Fittipaldi	Brabham-Ford	4	gearbox	11
	de Adamich	Surtees-Ford	1	gearbox	15
	Lauda	March-Ford	0	disqualified: push start	19

Fastest Lap: Stewart, 1m 15.7s. 116.93 mph/188.18 kph

United States Grand Prix: Watkins Glen, 8 October 1972

59 laps of 3.38 mile/5.44 km circuit

Place	Driver	Car	Laps	Time/reason for retiring	Grid
1	Stewart	Tyrrell-Ford	59	1h 41m 45.4s	1
2	Cevert	Tyrrell-Ford	59	1h 42m 17.6s	4
3	Hulme	McLaren-Ford	59	1h 42m 22.9s	3

United States Grand Prix (cont)

Place	Driver	Car	Laps	Time/reason for retiring	Grid
4	Peterson	March-Ford	59	1h 43m 07.9s	24
5	Ickx	Ferrari	59	1h 43m 08.5s	11
6	Andretti	Ferrari	58		9
7	Depailler	Tyrrell-Ford	58		10
8	Regazzoni	Ferrari	58		6
9	J Scheckter	McLaren-Ford	58		7
10	Wissell	Lotus-Ford	57		15
11	G Hill	Brabham-Ford	57		26
12	Posey	Surtees-Ford	57		22
13	Beuttler	March-Ford	57		20
14	Pescarolo	March-Ford	57		21
15	Amon	Matra	57		31
16	S Barber	March-Ford	57		19
17	Hailwood	Surtees-Ford	56	accident	13
18	Revson	McLaren-Ford	54	ignition	2
	Lauda	March-Ford	49	running	24
	Pace	March-Ford	48	fuel system	14
	Gethin	BRM	47	engine	27
	Ganley	BRM	44	engine	16
	D Walker	Lotus-Ford	44	engine	29
	W Fittipaldi	Brabham-Ford	43	engine	12
	Beltoise	BRM	40	ignition	17
	Redman	BRM	34	engine	23
	Reutemann	Brabham-Ford	31	engine	5
	de Adamich	Surtees-Ford	25	suspension	18
	Schenken	Surtees-Ford	22	suspension	30
	E Fittipaldi	Lotus-Ford	17	suspension	8
	Bell	Tecno	8	overheating	28

Fastest Lap: Stewart, 1m 41.64s. 119.61 mph/192.5 kph

World Championship 1972

1	E Fittipaldi	61
2	Stewart	45
3	Hulme	39
4	Ickx	27
5	Revson	23
6=	Cevert, Regazzoni	15
8	Hailwood	13
9=	Amon, Peterson	12
11	Beltoise	9
12=	Andretti, Ganley, G Hill, Redman	4
16=	de Adamich, Pace, Reutemann	3
19	Schenken	2
20=	Gethin, Merzario	1

Constructors' Championship

1	Lotus-Ford	61
2	Tyrrell-Ford	51
3	McLaren-Ford	47 (49)
4	Ferrari	33
5	Surtees-Ford	18
6	March-Ford	15
7	BRM	14
8	Matra	12
9	Brabham-Ford	7

1973

Jackie Stewart retired as world champion for the third time, having established a new record number of wins (27). His main competition came from Emerson Fittipaldi and Peterson whose total of seven victories carried Lotus to the constructors' championship. Once again the Ford Cosworth engine was unbeaten. Shadow and Ensign made their debuts. Tecno staggered on until the Austrian Grand Prix, and the 1973 Williams was called an Iso.

Argentine Grand Prix: Buenos Aires, 28 January 1973

96 laps of 2.08 mile/3.35 km circuit.

Place	Driver	Car	Laps	Time/reason for retiring	Grid
1	E Fittipaldi	Lotus-Ford	96	1h 56m 18.2s	2
2	Cevert	Tyrrell-Ford	96	1h 56m 22.9s	6
3	Stewart	Tyrrell-Ford	96	1h 56m 51.4s	4
4	Ickx	Ferrari	96	1h 57m 00.8s	3
5	Hulme	McLaren-Ford	95		8
6	W Fittipaldi	Brabham-Ford	95		12
7	Regazzoni	BRM	93		1
8	Revson	McLaren-Ford	92		11
9	Merzario	Ferrari	92		14
10	Beuttler	March-Ford	90	suspension	18
	Jarier	March-Ford	84	gearbox	17
	Beltoise	BRM	79	engine	7
	Ganley	Williams-Ford	79	running	19
	Peterson	Lotus-Ford	67	oil pressure	5
	Lauda	BRM	66	oil pressure	13
	Reutemann	Brabham-Ford	16	gearbox	9
	Pace	Surtees-Ford	10	suspension	15
	Hailwood	Surtees-Ford	10	transmission	10
	Nanni	Williams-Ford	0	engine	16

Fastest Lap: E Fittipaldi, 1m 11.22s. 105.08 mph/169.11 kph

Brazilian Grand Prix: Interlagos, 11 February 1973

· 40 laps of 4.95 mile/7.96 km circuit

Place	Driver	Car	Laps	Time/reason for retiring	Grid
1	E Fittipaldi	Lotus-Ford	40	1h 43m 55.6s	2
2	Stewart	Tyrrell-Ford	40	1h 44m 09.1s	8
3	Hulme	McLaren-Ford	40	1h 45m 42s	5
4	Merzario	Ferrari	39		17
5	Ickx	Ferrari	39		3
6	Regazzoni	BRM	39		4
7	Ganley	Williams-Ford	39		16
8	Lauda	BRM	38		13
9	Nanni	Williams-Ford	38		18
10	Cevert	Tyrrell-Ford	38		9
11	Reutemann	Brabham-Ford	38		7
12	Bueno	Surtees-Ford	36		20
	Beltoise	BRM	23	electrical	10
	Beuttler	March-Ford	17	overheating	19
	Pace	Surtees-Ford	8	suspension	6
	Hailwood	Surtees-Ford	6	gearbox	14
	Jarier	March-Ford	5	gearbox	15
	Peterson	Lotus-Ford	5	wheel	1
	W Fittipaldi	Brabham-Ford	5	overheating	11
	Revson	McLaren-Ford	2	gearbox	12

Fastest Lap: E Fittipaldi/Hulme, 2m 35s. 114.88 mph/184.88 kph

South African Grand Prix: Kyalami, 3 March 1973

79 laps of 2.55 mile/4.1 km circuit

Place	Driver	Car	Laps	Time/reason for retiring	Grid
1	Stewart	Tyrrell-Ford	79	1h 43m 11.1s	16
2	Revson	McLaren-Ford	79	1h 43m 35.6s	6
3	E Fittipaldi	Lotus-Ford	79	1h 43m 36.1s	2
4	Merzario	Ferrari	78		15
5	Hulme	McLaren-Ford	77		1
6	Follmer	Shadow-Ford	77		21
7	Reutemann	Brabham-Ford	77		8
8	de Adamich	Surtees-Ford	77		20
9	J Scheckter	McLaren-Ford	75	engine	3
10	Ganley	Williams-Ford	73		19
11	Peterson	Lotus-Ford	73		4
	Pace	Surtees-Ford	69	accident	9
	Keizan	Tyrrell-Ford	67		22
	Jarier	March-Ford	66		18
	Cevert	Tyrrell-Ford	66		25
	Beuttler	March-Ford	65		23
	W Fittipaldi	Brabham-Ford	52	gearbox	17
	Pretorius	Williams-Ford	35	overheating	24

South African Grand Prix (cont)

Place	Driver	Car	Laps	Time/reason for retiring	Grid
	Lauda	BRM	26	engine	10
	Oliver	Shadow-Ford	14	engine	14
	Beltoise	BRM	4	clutch	7
	Charlton	Lotus-Ford	3	accident	13
	Ickx	Ferrari	2	accident	11
	Regazzoni	BRM	2	accident	5
	Hailwood	Surtees-Ford	2	accident	12

Fastest Lap: E Fittipaldi, 1m 17.1s. 119.07 mph/191.63 kph

Spanish Grand Prix: Montjuich Park, 29 April 1973

75 laps of 2.36 mile/3.79 km circuit

Place	Driver	Car	Laps	Time/reason for retiring	Grid
1	E Fittipaldi	Lotus-Ford	75	1h 48m 18.7s	7
2	Cevert	Tyrrell-Ford	75	1h 49m 01.4s	3
3	Follmer	Shadow-Ford	75	1h 49m 31.8s	14
4	Revson	McLaren-Ford	74		5
5	Beltoise	BRM	74		10
6	Hulme	McLaren-Ford	74		2
7	Beuttler	March-Ford	74		19
8	Pescarolo	March-Ford	73		18
9	Regazzoni	BRM	69		8
10	W Fittipaldi	Brabham-Ford	69		12
11	Nanni	Williams-Ford	69		20
12	Ickx	Ferrari	69		6
	Reutemann	Brabham-Ford	65	transmission	15
	Ganley	Williams-Ford	62	fuel system	21
	Peterson	Lotus-Ford	56	gearbox	1
	Stewart	Tyrrell-Ford	46	brakes	4
	Lauda	BRM	27	tyres	11
	G Hill	Shadow-Ford	26	brakes	22
	Hailwood	Surtees-Ford	24	oil pipe	9
	Oliver	Shadow-Ford	23	engine	13
	de Adamich	Brabham-Ford	17	lost wheel	17
	Pace	Surtees-Ford	13	transmission	16

Fastest Lap: Peterson, 1m 23.8s. 101.19 mph/162.84 kph

Belgian Grand Prix: Zolder, 20 May 1973

70 laps of 2.62 mile/4.22 km circuit

Place	Driver	Car	Laps	Time/reason for retiring	Grid
1	Stewart	Tyrrell-Ford	70	1h 42m 13.4s	6
2	Cevert	Tyrrell-Ford	70	1h 42m 45.3s	4
3	E Fittipaldi	Lotus-Ford	70	1h 44m 16.2s	9

Belgian Grand Prix (cont)

Place	Driver	Car	Laps	Time/reason for retiring	Grid
4	de Adamich	Brabham-Ford	69		18
5	Lauda	BRM	69		14
6	Amon	Tecno	67		15
7	Hulme	McLaren-Ford	67		2
8	Pace	Surtees-Ford	66		8
9	G Hill	Shadow-Ford	65		23
10	Regazzoni	BRM	63	accident	12
11	Beuttler	March-Ford	63	accident	20
	Jarier	March-Ford	60	accident	16
	Beltoise	BRM	56	engine	5
	W Fittipaldi	Brabham-Ford	45	engine	19
	Peterson	Lotus-Ford	42	accident	1
	Revson	McLaren-Ford	33	accident	10
	Ganley	Williams-Ford	16	accident	21
	Reutemann	Brabham-Ford	13	accident	7
	Follmer	Shadow-Ford	13	throttle	11
	Oliver	Shadow-Ford	11	accident	22
	Nanni	Williams-Ford	6	engine	17
	Ickx	Ferrari	6	oil pump	3
	Hailwood	Surtees-Ford	4	accident	13

Fastest Lap: Cevert, 1m 25.42s. 110.51 mph/177.85 kph

Monaco Grand Prix: Monte Carlo, 3 June 1973

78 laps of 2.04 mile/3.28 km circuit

Place	Driver	Car	Laps	Time/reason for retiring	Grid
1	Stewart	Tyrrell-Ford	78	1h 57m 44.3s	1
2	E Fittipaldi	Lotus-Ford	78	1h 57m 45.6s	5
3	Peterson	Lotus-Ford	77		2
4	Cevert	Tyrrell-Ford	77		4
5	Revson	McLaren-Ford	76		15
6	Hulme	McLaren-Ford	76		3
7	de Adamich	Brabham-Ford	75		25
8	Hailwood	Surtees-Ford	75		13
9	Hunt	March-Ford	73	engine	18
10	Oliver	Shadow-Ford	72		22
11	W Fittipaldi	Brabham-Ford	71	fuel system	9
	Jarier	March-Ford	67	gearbox	14
	G Hill	Shadow-Ford	61	suspension	24
	Merzario	Ferrari	58	oil pressure	16
	Reutemann	Brabham-Ford	46	gearbox	19
	Ickx	Ferrari	44	transmission	7
	Ganley	Williams-Ford	40	transmission	10
	Beltoise	BRM	39	accident	11
	Purley	March-Ford	31	fuel system	23

Monaco Grand Prix (cont)

Place	Driver	Car	Laps	Time/reason for retiring	Grid
	Pace	Surtees-Ford	30	transmission	17
	Nanni	Williams-Ford	30	transmission	21
	Lauda	BRM	24	gearbox	6
	Amon	Tecno	22	overheating	12
	Regazzoni	BRM	15	brakes	8
	Beuttler	March-Ford	3	engine	20

Fastest Lap: E Fittipaldi, 1m 28.1s. 83.23 mph/133.95 kph

Swedish Grand Prix: Anderstorp, 17 June 1973

80 laps of 2.5 mile/4.02 km circuit

Place	Driver	Car	Laps	Time/reason for retiring	Grid
1	Hulme	McLaren-Ford	80	1h 56m 46.1s	6
2	Peterson	Lotus-Ford	80	1h 56m 50.1s	1
3	Cevert	Tyrrell-Ford	80	1h 57m 00.7s	2
4	Reutemann	Brabham-Ford	80	1h 57m 04.1s	5
5	Stewart	Tyrrell-Ford	80	1h 57m 12.1s	3
6	Ickx	Ferrari	79		8
7	Revson	McLaren-Ford	79		7
8	Beuttler	March-Ford	78		20
9	Regazzoni	BRM	77		12
10	Pace	Surtees-Ford	77		15
11	Ganley	Williams-Ford	77		11
12	E Fittipaldi	Lotus-Ford	76	gearbox	4
13	Lauda	BRM	75		14
14	Follmer	Shadow-Ford	74		18
	Beltoise	BRM	57	engine	9
	Oliver	Shadow-Ford	50	suspension	16
	Hailwood	Surtees-Ford	41	tyres	10
	Jarier	March-Ford	38	throttle	19
	G Hill	Shadow-Ford	16	ignition	17
	W Fittipaldi	Brabham-Ford	0	accident	13

Fastest Lap: Hulme, 1m 26.15s. 104.33 mph/167.91 kph

French Grand Prix: Paul Ricard, 1 July 1973

54 laps of 3.61 mile/5.81 km circuit

Place	Driver	Car	Laps	Time/reason for retiring	Grid
1	Peterson	Lotus-Ford	54	1h 41m 36.5s	5
2	Cevert	Tyrrell-Ford	54	1h 42m 17.4s	4
3	Reutemann	Brabham-Ford	54	1h 42m 23.0s	8

French Grand Prix (cont)

Place	Driver	Car	Laps	Time/reason for retiring	Grid
4	Stewart	Tyrrell-Ford	54	1h 42m 23.5s	1
5	Ickx	Ferrari	54	1h 42m 25.4s	12
6	Hunt	March-Ford	54	1h 42m 59.1s	14
7	Merzario	Ferrari	54	1h 43m 05.7s	10
8	Hulme	McLaren-Ford	54	1h 43m 06.1s	6
9	Lauda	BRM	54	1h 43m 22.3s	17
10	G Hill	Shadow-Ford	53		16
11	Beltoise	BRM	53		15
12	Regazzoni	BRM	53		9
13	Pace	Surtees-Ford	51		18
14	Ganley	Williams-Ford	51		24
15	von Opel	Ensign-Ford	51		25
16	W Fittipaldi	Brabham-Ford	50	throttle	19
	J Scheckter	McLaren-Ford	42	accident	2
	E Fittipaldi	Lotus-Ford	41	accident	3
	Hailwood	Surtees-Ford	29	oil leak	11
	de Adamich	Brabham-Ford	27	transmission	13
	Wissell	March-Ford	19	overheating	22
	Follmer	Shadow-Ford	16	fuel pressure	20
	Pescarolo	March-Ford	15	overheating	23
	Jarier	March-Ford	7	transmission	7
	Oliver	Shadow-Ford	0	clutch	21

Fastest Lap: Hulme, 1m 51s. 117.1 mph/188.45 kph

British Grand Prix: Silverstone, 14 July 1973

67 laps of 2.93 mile/4.71 km circuit

Place	Driver	Car	Laps	Time/reason for retiring	Grid
1	Revson	McLaren-Ford	67	1h 29m 18.5s	3
2	Peterson	Lotus-Ford	67	1h 29m 21.3s	1
3	Hulme	McLaren-Ford	67	1h 29m 21.5s	2
4	Hunt	March-Ford	67	1h 29m 21.9s	11
5	Cevert	Tyrrell-Ford	67	1h 29m 55.1s	7
6	Reutemann	Brabham-Ford	67	1h 30m 03.2s	8
7	Regazzoni	BRM	67	1h 30m 30.2s	10
8	Ickx	Ferrari	67	1h 30m 35.9s	18
9	Ganley	Williams-Ford	66		17
10	Stewart	Tyrrell-Ford	66		4
11	Beuttler	March-Ford	65		23
12	Lauda	BRM	63		9
13	von Opel	Ensign-Ford	61		20
	W Fittipaldi	Brabham-Ford	44	oil pipe	13
	E Fittipaldi	Lotus-Ford	36	transmission	5
	Watson	Brabham-Ford	36	fuel system	22
	G Hill	Shadow-Ford	24	suspension	26

British Grand Prix (cont)

Place	Driver	Car	Laps	Time/reason for retiring	Grid
	Amon	Tecno	6	fuel pressure	28
	McRae	Williams-Ford	0	throttle	27

* The original race was stopped after a multiple accident at the end of lap 1; the following did not restart:

	Beltoise	BRM	0	accident	16
	de Adamich	Brabham-Ford	0	accident	19
	Follmer	Shadow-Ford	0	accident	24
	Hailwood	Surtees-Ford	0	accident	12
	Mass	Surtees-Ford	0	accident	14
	Pace	Surtees-Ford	0	accident	15
	J Scheckter	McLaren-Ford	0	accident	6
	Williamson	March-Ford	0	accident	21
	Oliver	Shadow-Ford	0	accident at start	25

Fastest Lap: Hunt, 1m 18.6s. 134.06 mph/215.75 kph

Dutch Grand Prix: Zandvoort, 29 July 1973

72 laps of 2.63 mile/4.23 km circuit

Place	Driver	Car	Laps	Time/reason for retiring	Grid
1	Stewart	Tyrrell-Ford	72	1h 39m 12.5s	2
2	Cevert	Tyrrell-Ford	72	1h 39m 28.3s	3
3	Hunt	March-Ford	72	1h 40m 15.5s	7
4	Revson	McLaren-Ford	72	1h 40m 21.6s	6
5	Beltoise	BRM	72	1h 40m 25.8s	9
6	van Lennep	Williams-Ford	70		19
7	Pace	Surtees-Ford	69		8
8	Regazzoni	BRM	68		12
9	Ganley	Williams-Ford	68		14
10	Follmer	Shadow-Ford	67		21
11	Peterson	Lotus-Ford	66	gearbox	1
	G Hill	Shadow-Ford	56		16
	Hailwood	Surtees-Ford	52	electrical	23
	Lauda	BRM	51	fuel pump	11
	Hulme	McLaren-Ford	31	engine	4
	W Fittipaldi	Brabham-Ford	27	accident	13
	Amon	Tecno	22	fuel pressure	18
	Reutemann	Brabham-Ford	9	tyre	5
	Purley	March-Ford	8	stopped to help Williamson	20
	Williamson	March-Ford	7	fatal accident	17
	Beuttler	March-Ford	2	electrical	22
	E Fittipaldi	Lotus-Ford	2	unwell	15
	Oliver	Shadow-Ford	1	accident	10

Fastest Lap: Peterson, 1m 20.31s. 117.71 mph/189.44 kph

German Grand Prix: Nürburgring, 5 August 1973

14 laps of 14.19 mile/22.84 km circuit

Place	Driver	Car	Laps	Time/reason for retiring	Grid
1	Stewart	Tyrrell-Ford	14	1h 42m 03s	1
2	Cevert	Tyrrell-Ford	14	1h 42m 04.6s	3
3	Ickx	McLaren-Ford	14	1h 42m 44.2s	4
4	Pace	Surtees-Ford	14	1h 42m 56.8s	11
5	W Fittipaldi	Brabham-Ford	14	1h 43m 22.9s	13
6	E Fittipaldi	Lotus-Ford	14	1h 43m 27.3s	14
7	Mass	Surtees-Ford	14	1h 43m 28.2s	15
8	Oliver	Shadow-Ford	14	1h 43m 28.7s	17
9	Revson	McLaren-Ford	14	1h 44m 14.8s	7
10	Pescarolo	March-Ford	14	1h 44m 25.5s	12
11	Stommelen	Brabham-Ford	14	1h 45m 41.7s	16
12	Hulme	McLaren-Ford	14	1h 45m 41.7s	8
13	G Hill	Shadow-Ford	14	1h 45m 52s	20
14	Hailwood	Surtees-Ford	13		18
15	Purley	March-Ford	13		22
16	Beuttler	March-Ford	13		19
	Reutemann	Brabham-Ford	7	engine	6
	Regazzoni	BRM	7	engine	10
	Follmer	Shadow-Ford	5	accident	21
	Beltoise	BRM	4	gearbox	9
	Lauda	BRM	1	accident	5
	Peterson	Lotus-Ford	0	ignition	2

Fastest Lap: Pace, 7m 11.4s. 118.41 mph/190.56 kph

Austrian Grand Prix: Österreichring, 19 August 1973

54 laps of 3.67 mile/5.91 km circuit

Place	Driver	Car	Laps	Time/reason for retiring	Grid
1	Peterson	Lotus-Ford	54	1h 28m 48.8s	2
2	Stewart	Tyrrell-Ford	54	1h 28m 57.8s	7
3	Pace	Surtees-Ford	54	1h 29m 35.4s	8
4	Reutemann	Brabham-Ford	54	1h 29m 36.7s	5
5	Beltoise	BRM	54	1h 30m 10.4s	13
6	Regazzoni	BRM	54	1h 30m 27.2s	14
7	Merzario	Ferrari	53		6
8	Hulme	McLaren-Ford	53		3
9	van Lennep	Williams-Ford	52		23
10	Hailwood	Surtees-Ford	49		15
11	E Fittipaldi	Lotus-Ford	48	fuel pipe	1
	Ganley	Williams-Ford	44		21
	Jarier	March-Ford	37	engine	12
	von Opel	Ensign-Ford	34	fuel pressure	19
	W Fittipaldi	Brabham-Ford	31	fuel system	16

Austrian Grand Prix (cont)

Place	Driver	Car	Laps	Time/reason for retiring	Grid
	G Hill	Shadow-Ford	28	suspension	22
	Follmer	Shadow-Ford	23	crownwheel and pinion	20
	Stommelen	Brabham-Ford	21	wheel bearing	17
	Oliver	Shadow-Ford	9	fuel leak	18
	Cevert	Tyrrell-Ford	6	suspension	10
	Hunt	March-Ford	3	fuel system	9
	Beuttler	March-Ford	0	oil cooler	11
	Revson	McLaren-Ford	0	clutch	4

Fastest Lap: Pace, 1m 37.3s. 135.91 mph/218.72 kph

Italian Grand Prix: Monza, 9 September 1973

55 laps of 3.59 mile/5.78 km circuit

Place	Driver	Car	Laps	Time/reason for retiring	Grid
1	Peterson	Lotus-Ford	55	1h 29m 17.0s	1
2	E Fittipaldi	Lotus-Ford	55	1h 29m 17.8s	4
3	Revson	McLaren-Ford	55	1h 29m 45.8s	2
4	Stewart	Tyrrell-Ford	55	1h 29m 50.2s	6
5	Cevert	Tyrrell-Ford	55	1h 30m 03.2s	11
6	Reutemann	Brabham-Ford	55	1h 30m 16.8s	10
7	Hailwood	Surtees-Ford	55	1h 30m 45.7s	8
8	Ickx	Ferrari	54		14
9	Purley	March-Ford	54		24
10	Follmer	Shadow-Ford	54		21
11	Oliver	Shadow-Ford	54		19
12	Stommelen	Brabham-Ford	54		9
13	Beltoise	BRM	54		13
14	G Hill	Shadow-Ford	54		22
15	Hulme	McLaren-Ford	53		3
	Ganley	Williams-Ford	44		20
	Beuttler	March-Ford	34	gearbox	12
	Lauda	BRM	33	accident	15
	Regazzoni	BRM	30	ignition	18
	Pace	Surtees-Ford	17	tyre	5
	van Lennep	Williams-Ford	13	overheating	23
	von Opel	Ensign-Ford	9	overheating	17
	W Fittipaldi	Brabham-Ford	5	brakes	16
	Merzario	Ferrari	1	suspension	7

Fastest Lap: Stewart, 1m 35.3s. 135.55 mph/218.15 kph

Canadian Grand Prix: Mosport, 23 September 1973

80 laps of 2.46 mile/3.96 km circuit

Place	Driver	Car	Laps	Time/reason for retiring	Grid
1	Revson	McLaren-Ford	80	1h 59m 04.1s	2
2	E Fittipaldi	Lotus-Ford	80	1h 59m 36.8s	5
3	Oliver	Shadow-Ford	80	1h 59m 38.6s	14
4	Beltoise	BRM	80	1h 59m 40.6s	16
5	Stewart	Tyrrell-Ford	79		9
6	Ganley	Williams-Ford	79		22
7	Hunt	March-Ford	78		15
8	Reutemann	Brabham-Ford	78		4
9	Hailwood	Surtees-Ford	78		12
10	Amon	Tyrrell-Ford	77		11
11	W Fittipaldi	Brabham-Ford	77		10
12	Stommelen	Brabham-Ford	76		18
13	Hulme	McLaren-Ford	75		7
14	Schenken	Williams-Ford	75		24
15	Merzario	Ferrari	75		20
16	G Hill	Shadow-Ford	73		17
17	Follmer	Shadow-Ford	73		13
18	Pace	Surtees-Ford	72	wheel	19
	Jarier	March-Ford	71		23
	von Opel	Ensign-Ford	68		26
	Lauda	BRM	62	transmission	8
	J Scheckter	McLaren-Ford	32	accident	3
	Cevert	Tyrrell-Ford	32	accident	6
	Beuttler	March-Ford	20	engine	21
	Peterson	Lotus-Ford	16	suspension	1
	Gethin	BRM	5	oil pump	25

Fastest Lap: E Fittipaldi, 1m 15.5s. 117.26 mph/188.71 kph

United States Grand Prix: Watkins Glen, 7 October 1973

55 laps of 3.38 mile/5.44 km circuit

Place	Driver	Car	Laps	Time/reason for retiring	Grid
1	Peterson	Lotus-Ford	55	1h 41m 15.8s	1
2	Hunt	March-Ford	55	1h 41m 16.5s	4
3	Reutemann	Brabham-Ford	55	1h 41m 38.7s	2
4	Hulme	McLaren-Ford	55	1h 42m 06.0s	7
5	Revson	McLaren-Ford	55	1h 42m 36.2s	6
6	E Fittipaldi	Lotus-Ford	55	1h 43m 03.7s	3
7	Ickx	Williams-Ford	54		21
8	Regazzoni	BRM	54		13
9	Beltoise	BRM	54		12
10	Beuttler	March-Ford	54		24
11	Jarier	March-Ford	53	accident	15

United States Grand Prix (cont)

Place	Driver	Car	Laps	Time/reason for retiring	Grid
12	Ganley	Williams-Ford	53		17
13	G Hill	Shadow-Ford	53		16
14	Follmer	Shadow-Ford	53		18
15	Oliver	Shadow-Ford	51		20
16	Merzario	Ferrari	51		10
	W Fittipaldi	Brabham-Ford	48		23
	J Scheckter	McLaren-Ford	39	suspension	9
	Mass	Surtees-Ford	35	engine	14
	Lauda	BRM	35	fuel pump	19
	Hailwood	Surtees-Ford	34	suspension	5
	Pace	Surtees-Ford	32	suspension	8
	Watson	Brabham-Ford	7	engine	22
	Redman	Shadow-Ford	5	disqualified: push start	11
	von Opel	Ensign-Ford	0	throttle slides	25

Fastest Lap: Hunt, 1m 41.65s. 119.6 mph/192.47 kph
* Cevert killed in practice crash; Stewart withdrew from race.

World Championship 1973

1	Stewart	71
2	E Fittipaldi	55
3	Peterson	52
4	Cevert	47
5	Revson	38
6	Hulme	26
7	Reutemann	16
8	Hunt	14
9	Ickx	12
10	Beltoise	9
11	Pace	7
12	Merzario	6
13	Follmer	5
14	Oliver	4
15 =	de Adamich, W Fittipaldi	3
17 =	Lauda, Regazzoni	2
19 =	Amon, Ganley, van Lennep	1

Constructors' Championship

1	Lotus-Ford	92 (96)
2	Tyrrell-Ford	82 (86)
3	McLaren-Ford	58
4	Brabham-Ford	22
5	March-Ford	14
6 =	BRM, Ferrari	12
8	Shadow-Ford	9
9	Surtees-Ford	7
10	Williams-Ford	2
11	Tecno	1

1974

Emerson Fittipaldi and Regazzoni went into the last race level on points, but Regazzoni dropped down the field with handling problems, so that Fittipaldi's fourth place gave him the championship. Fittipaldi, Peterson and Reutemann each won three races, Scheckter and Lauda two each, Regazzoni and Hulme, who retired at the end of the season, one each. Graham Hill ran a new team of Lolas, the larger-than-life Hesketh team entered its own car after running James Hunt in a March, and Americans Roger Penske and Parnelli Jones entered their own cars late in the season. Chris Amon's own car, like the Token and the Trojan, was not a success.

Argentine Grand Prix: Buenos Aires, 13 January 1974

53 laps of 3.71 mile/5.97 km circuit

Place	Driver	Car	Laps	Time/reason for retiring	Grid
1	Hulme	McLaren-Ford	53	1h 41m 02s	10
2	Lauda	Ferrari	53	1h 41m 11.3s	8
3	Regazzoni	Ferrari	53	1h 41m 22.4s	2
4	Hailwood	McLaren-Ford	53	1h 41m 33.8s	9
5	Beltoise	BRM	53	1h 41m 53.9s	14
6	Depailler	Tyrrell-Ford	53	1h 42m 54.5s	15
7	Reutemann	Brabham-Ford	52	out of fuel	6
8	Ganley	March-Ford	52	out of fuel	19
9	Pescarolo	BRM	52		21
10	E Fittipaldi	McLaren-Ford	52		3
11	Edwards	Lola-Ford	51		25
12	Watson	Brabham-Ford	49		20
13	Peterson	Lotus-Ford	48		1
	G Hill	Lola-Ford	45	overheating	17
	Robarts	Brabham-Ford	35	gearbox	22
	Ickx	Lotus-Ford	35	transmission	7
	Stuck	March-Ford	31	clutch	23
	Migault	BRM	31	engine	24
	J Scheckter	Tyrrell-Ford	25	overheating	12
	Pace	Surtees-Ford	21	engine	11
	Merzario	Williams-Ford	19	engine	13
	Hunt	March-Ford	11	overheating	5
	Mass	Surtees-Ford	10	engine	18
	Revson	Shadow-Ford	1	accident	4
	Jarier	Shadow-Ford	0	accident	16

Fastest Lap: Regazzoni, 1m 52.1s. 119.09 mph/191.66 kph

Brazilian Grand Prix: Interlagos, 27 January 1974

32 laps of 4.95 mile/7.96 km circuit

Place	Driver	Car	Laps	Time/reason for retiring	Grid
1	E Fittipaldi	McLaren-Ford	32	1h 24m 37.1s	1
2	Regazzoni	Ferrari	32	1h 24m 50.6s	8
3	Ickx	Lotus-Ford	31		5
4	Pace	Surtees-Ford	31		12
5	Hailwood	McLaren-Ford	31		7
6	Peterson	Lotus-Ford	31		4
7	Reutemann	Brabham-Ford	31		2
8	Depailler	Tyrrell-Ford	31		16
9	Hunt	March-Ford	31		18
10	Beltoise	BRM	31		17
11	G Hill	Lola-Ford	31		21
12	Hulme	McLaren-Ford	31		11
13	J Scheckter	Tyrrell-Ford	31		14
14	Pescarolo	BRM	30		22
15	Robarts	Brabham-Ford	30		24
16	Migault	BRM	30		23
17	Mass	Surtees-Ford	30		10
	Watson	Brabham-Ford	27	clutch	15
	Stuck	March-Ford	24	transmission	13
	Jarier	Shadow-Ford	22	brakes	19
	Merzario	Williams-Ford	20	throttle	9
	Revson	Shadow-Ford	11	overheating	6
	Ganley	March-Ford	9	engine	20
	Edwards	Lola-Ford	3	wing	25
	Lauda	Ferrari	3	engine	3

Fastest Lap: Regazzoni, 2m 36.1s. 114.1 mph/186.63 kph
* Stopped early because of rain.

South African Grand Prix: Kyalami, 30 March 1974

78 laps of 2.55 mile/4.1 km circuit

Place	Driver	Car	Laps	Time/reason for retiring	Grid
1	Reutemann	Brabham-Ford	78	1h 42m 40.96s	4
2	Beltoise	BRM	78	1h 43m 14.9s	11
3	Hailwood	McLaren-Ford	78	1h 43m 32.1s	12
4	Depailler	Tyrrell-Ford	78	1h 43m 25.2s	15
5	Stuck	March-Ford	78	1h 43m 27.2s	7
6	Merzario	Williams-Ford	78	1h 43m 37s	3
7	E Fittipaldi	McLaren-Ford	78	1h 43m 49.4s	5
8	J Scheckter	Tyrrell-Ford	78	1h 43m 51.5s	8
9	Hulme	McLaren-Ford	77		9
10	Brambilla	March-Ford	77		19
11	Pace	Surtees-Ford	77		2

South African Grand Prix (cont)

Place	Driver	Car	Laps	Time/reason for retiring	Grid
12	G Hill	Lola-Ford	77		18
13	I Scheckter	Lotus-Ford	76		22
14	Keizan	Tyrrell-Ford	76		24
15	Migault	BRM	75		25
16	Lauda	Ferrari	74	engine	1
17	Robarts	Brabham-Ford	74		23
18	Pescarolo	BRM	72		21
19	Charlton	McLaren-Ford	71		20
	Regazzoni	Ferrari	65	oil pressure	6
	Watson	Brabham-Ford	54	fuel pipe	13
	Ickx	Lotus-Ford	31	withdrew	10
	Hunt	Hesketh-Ford	13	transmission	14
	Mass	Surtees-Ford	11	withdrew	17
	Driver	Lotus-Ford	6	clutch	26
	Peterson	Lotus-Ford	2	accident	16
	Belso	Williams-Ford	0	clutch	27

Fastest Lap: Reutemann, 1m 18.2s. 117.46 mph/189.03 kph
* Revson was killed in pre-race testing.

Spanish Grand Prix: Jarama, 28 April 1974

84 laps of 2.12 mile/3.4 km circuit

Place	Driver	Car	Laps	Time/reason for retiring	Grid
1	Lauda	Ferrari	84	2h 00m 29.6s	1
2	Regazzoni	Ferrari	84	2h 01m 05.2s	3
3	E Fittipaldi	McLaren-Ford	83		4
4	Stuck	March-Ford	82		13
5	J Scheckter	Tyrrell-Ford	82		9
6	Hulme	McLaren-Ford	82		8
7	Redman	Shadow-Ford	81		21
8	Depailler	Tyrrell-Ford	81		16
9	Hailwood	McLaren-Ford	81		17
10	Hunt	Hesketh-Ford	81		10
11	Watson	Brabham-Ford	80		15
12	Pescarolo	BRM	80		20
13	Pace	Surtees-Ford	78		14
14	Schenken	Trojan-Ford	76	not running	25
	Jarier	Shadow-Ford	73		12
	G Hill	Lola-Ford	43	engine	19
	Merzario	Williams-Ford	37	accident	7
	Mass	Surtees-Ford	35	gearbox	18
	Migault	BRM	27	engine	22
	Ickx	Lotus-Ford	26	brakes	5
	Peterson	Lotus-Ford	23	engine	2

Spanish Grand Prix (cont)

Place	Driver	Car	Laps	Time/reason for retiring	Grid
	Amon	Amon-Ford	22	brakes	23
	von Opel	Brabham-Ford	14	oil	24
	Reutemann	Brabham-Ford	12	accident	6
	Beltoise	BRM	2	engine	11

Fastest Lap: Lauda, 1m 20.83s. 94.21 mph/151.62 kph

Belgian Grand Prix: Nivelles, 12 May 1974

85 laps of 2.31 mile/3.72 km circuit

Place	Driver	Car	Laps	Time/reason for retiring	Grid
1	E Fittipaldi	McLaren-Ford	85	1h 44m 20.6s	4
2	Lauda	Ferrari	85	1h 44m 20.9s	3
3	J Scheckter	Tyrrell-Ford	85	1h 45m 06.2s	2
4	Regazzoni	Ferrari	85	1h 45m 12.6s	1
5	Beltoise	BRM	85	1h 45m 28.6s	7
6	Hulme	McLaren-Ford	85	1h 45m 31.1s	12
7	Hailwood	McLaren-Ford	84		13
8	G Hill	Lola-Ford	83		29
9	Brambilla	March-Ford	83		31
10	Schenken	Trojan-Ford	83		23
11	Watson	Brabham-Ford	83		19
12	Edwards	Lola-Ford	82		21
13	Jarier	Shadow-Ford	82		17
14	van Lennep	Williams-Ford	82		30
15	Schuppan	Ensign-Ford	82		14
16	Migault	BRM	82		25
17	T Pilette	Brabham-Ford	81		27
18	Redman	Shadow-Ford	80	engine	18
	Ickx	Lotus-Ford	72	overheating	16
	Pryce	Token-Ford	66	suspension	20
	Reutemann	Brabham-Ford	62	fuel system	24
	Peterson	Lotus-Ford	56	fuel leak	5
	Larrousse	Brabham-Ford	53	tyres	28
	Mass	Surtees-Ford	53	suspension	26
	Depailler	Tyrrell-Ford	53	brakes	11
	Pace	Surtees-Ford	50	wheel	8
	von Opel	Brabham-Ford	49	oil pressure	22
	Hunt	Hesketh-Ford	45	suspension	9
	Merzario	Williams-Ford	29	transmission	6
	Pescarolo	BRM	12	accident	15
	Stuck	March-Ford	6	clutch	10

Fastest Lap: Hulme, 1m 11.31s. 116.82 mph/188 kph

Monaco Grand Prix: Monte Carlo, 26 May 1974

78 laps of 2.04 mile/3.28 km circuit

Place	Driver	Car	Laps	Time/reason for retiring	Grid
1	Peterson	Lotus-Ford	78	1h 58m 03.7s	3
2	J Scheckter	Tyrrell-Ford	78	1h 58m 32.5s	5
3	Jarier	Shadow-Ford	78	1h 58m 52.6s	6
4	Regazzoni	Ferrari	78	1h 59m 06.8s	2
5	E Fittipaldi	McLaren-Ford	77		13
6	Watson	Brabham-Ford	77		21
7	G Hill	Lola-Ford	76		19
8	Edwards	Lola-Ford	75		24
9	Depailler	Tyrrell-Ford	74		4
	Pescarolo	BRM	62	gearbox	25
	Ickx	Lotus-Ford	34	engine	18
	Lauda	Ferrari	32	ignition	1
	Hunt	Hesketh-Ford	27	transmission	7
	Hailwood	McLaren-Ford	11	accident	10
	Reutemann	Brabham-Ford	5	accident	8
	Migault	BRM	4	accident	20
	Schuppan	Ensign-Ford	4	accident	23
	Stuck	March-Ford	3	accident	9
	Brambilla	March-Ford	0	accident	15
	Beltoise	BRM	0	accident	11
	Schenken	Trojan-Ford	0	accident	22
	Pace	Surtees-Ford	0	accident	17
	Redman	Shadow-Ford	0	accident	16
	Merzario	Williams-Ford	0	accident	14
	Hulme	McLaren-Ford	0	accident	12

Fastest Lap: Peterson, 1m 27.9s. 83.42 mph/134.25 kph

Swedish Grand Prix: Anderstorp, 9 June 1974

80 laps of 2.5 mile/4.02 km circuit

Place	Driver	Car	Laps	Time/reason for retiring	Grid
1	J Scheckter	Tyrrell-Ford	80	1h 58m 31.4s	2
2	Depailler	Tyrrell-Ford	80	1h 58m 31.8s	1
3	Hunt	Hesketh-Ford	80	1h 58m 34.7s	6
4	E Fittipaldi	McLaren-Ford	80	1h 59m 24.9s	9
5	Jarier	Shadow-Ford	80	1h 59m 47.8s	8
6	G Hill	Lola-Ford	79		15
7	Edwards	Lola-Ford	79		18
8	Belso	Williams-Ford	79		21
9	von Opel	Brabham-Ford	79		20
10	Brambilla	March-Ford	79	engine	17
11	Watson	Brabham-Ford	77		14
	Lauda	Ferrari	69	suspension	3
	Wissell	March-Ford	59	suspension	16

Swedish Grand Prix (cont)

Place	Driver	Car	Laps	Time/reason for retiring	Grid
	Hulme	McLaren-Ford	56	suspension	12
	Mass	Surtees-Ford	53	suspension	22
	Reutemann	Brabham-Ford	29	oil leak	10
	Ickx	Lotus-Ford	27	oil pressure	7
	Regazzoni	Ferrari	23	gearbox	4
	Pace	Surtees-Ford	14	handling	24
	Kinnunen	Surtees-Ford	8	engine	25
	Peterson	Lotus-Ford	8	transmission	5
	Hailwood	McLaren-Ford	5	fuel leak	11
	Beltoise	BRM	2	engine	13
	Roos	Shadow-Ford	1	gearbox	23
	Pescarolo	BRM	0	fire	19

Fastest Lap: Depailler, 1m 27.26s. 103 mph/165.76 kph

Dutch Grand Prix: Zandvoort, 23 June 1974

75 laps of 2.63 mile/4.23 km circuit

Place	Driver	Car	Laps	Time/reason for retiring	Grid
1	Lauda	Ferrari	75	1h 43m 00.4s	1
2	Regazzoni	Ferrari	75	1h 43m 08.6s	2
3	E Fittipaldi	McLaren-Ford	75	1h 43m 30.6s	3
4	Hailwood	McLaren-Ford	75	1h 43m 31.6s	4
5	J Scheckter	Tyrrell-Ford	75	1h 43m 34.6s	5
6	Depailler	Tyrrell-Ford	75	1h 43m 51.9s	8
7	Watson	Brabham-Ford	75	1h 44m 14.3s	13
8	Peterson	Lotus-Ford	73		10
9	von Opel	Brabham-Ford	73		23
10	Brambilla	March-Ford	72		15
11	Ickx	Lotus-Ford	71		18
12	Reutemann	Brabham-Ford	71		12
	Schuppan	Ensign-Ford	68	disqualified	17
	Hulme	McLaren-Ford	65	ignition	9
	Migault	BRM	59	gearbox	25
	Merzario	Williams-Ford	54	gearbox	21
	Edwards	Lola-Ford	36	fuel system	14
	Jarier	Shadow-Ford	27	clutch	7
	Beltoise	BRM	18	gearbox	16
	G Hill	Lola-Ford	16	clutch	19
	Pescarolo	BRM	14	withdrew	24
	Mass	Surtees-Ford	8	oil system	20
	Hunt	Hesketh-Ford	1	accident	6
	Stuck	March-Ford	0	accident	22
	Pryce	Shadow-Ford	0	accident	11

Fastest Lap: Peterson, 1m 21.44s. 116.08 mph/186.8 kph
* Schuppan (Ensign-Ford), first reserve, started illegally from 26th place on the grid and completed the race before he was disqualified.

French Grand Prix: Dijon, 7 July 1974

80 laps of 2.04 mile/3.29 km circuit

Place	Driver	Car	Laps	Time/reason for retiring	Grid
1	Peterson	Lotus-Ford	80	1h 21m 55.0s	2
2	Lauda	Ferrari	80	1h 22m 15.4s	1
3	Regazzoni	Ferrari	80	1h 22m 22.9s	4
4	J Scheckter	Tyrrell-Ford	80	1h 22m 23.1s	7
5	Ickx	Lotus-Ford	80	1h 22m 32.6s	13
6	Hulme	McLaren-Ford	80	1h 22m 33.2s	11
7	Hailwood	McLaren-Ford	79		6
8	Depailler	Tyrrell-Ford	79		9
9	Merzario	Williams-Ford	79		15
10	Beltoise	BRM	79		17
11	Brambilla	March-Ford	79		16
12	Jarier	Shadow-Ford	79		12
13	G Hill	Lola-Ford	78		21
14	Migault	BRM	78		22
15	Edwards	Lola-Ford	77		20
16	Watson	Brabham-Ford	76		14
	E Fittipaldi	McLaren-Ford	27	engine	5
	Reutemann	Brabham-Ford	24	handling	8
	Mass	Surtees-Ford	4	clutch	18
	Pescarolo	BRM	0	clutch	19
	Pryce	Shadow-Ford	0	accident	3
	Hunt	Hesketh-Ford	0	accident	10

Fastest Lap: Scheckter, 1m 00.0s. 122.62 mph/197.34 kph

British Grand Prix: Brands Hatch, 20 July 1974

75 laps of 2.65 mile/4.27 km circuit

Place	Driver	Car	Laps	Time/reason for retiring	Grid
1	J Scheckter	Tyrrell-Ford	75	1h 43m 02.2s	3
2	E Fittipaldi	McLaren-Ford	75	1h 43m 17.5s	8
3	Ickx	Lotus-Ford	75	1h 44m 03.7s	12
4	Regazzoni	Ferrari	75	1h 44m 09.4s	7
5	Lauda	Ferrari	74		1
6	Reutemann	Brabham-Ford	74		4
7	Hulme	McLaren-Ford	74		19
8	Pryce	Shadow-Ford	74		5
9	Pace	Brabham-Ford	74		20
10	Peterson	Lotus-Ford	73		2
11	Watson	Brabham-Ford	73		13
12	Beltoise	BRM	72		23
13	G Hill	Lola-Ford	69		22
14	Mass	Surtees-Ford	68		17
	Pescarolo	BRM	64	engine	24

British Grand Prix (cont)

Place	Driver	Car	Laps	Time/reason for retiring	Grid
	Migault	BRM	63	running	14
	Hailwood	McLaren-Ford	57	spun	11
	Jarier	Shadow-Ford	45	suspension	16
	Stuck	March-Ford	36	accident	9
	Depailler	Tyrrell-Ford	35	engine	10
	Merzario	Williams-Ford	25	engine	15
	Brambilla	March-Ford	17	fuel pressure	18
	Schenken	Trojan-Ford	6	suspension	25
	Hunt	Hesketh-Ford	2	suspension	6
	Gethin	Lola-Ford	0	driver discomfort	21

Fastest Lap: Lauda, 1m 21.1s. 117.63 mph/189.31 kph
* Lauda, unable to leave pits because of blocked pit road after late wheel change and initially classified ninth, awarded fifth place after appeal.

German Grand Prix: Nürburgring, 4 August 1974

14 laps of 14.19 mile/22.84 km circuit

Place	Driver	Car	Laps	Time/reason for retiring	Grid
1	Regazzoni	Ferrari	14	1h 41m 35s	2
2	J Scheckter	Tyrrell-Ford	14	1h 42m 25.7s	4
3	Reutemann	Brabham-Ford	14	1h 42m 58.3s	6
4	Peterson	Lotus-Ford	14	1h 42m 59.2s	8
5	Ickx	Lotus-Ford	14	1h 43m 00s	9
6	Pryce	Shadow-Ford	14	1h 43m 53.1s	11
7	Stuck	March-Ford	14	1h 44m 33.7s	20
8	Jarier	Shadow-Ford	14	1h 45m 00.9s	18
9	G Hill	Lola-Ford	14	1h 45m 01.4s	19
10	Pescarolo	BRM	14	1h 45m 52.7s	24
11	Bell	Surtees-Ford	14	1h 46m 52.7s	25
12	Pace	Brabham-Ford	14	1h 48m 01.3s	17
13	Brambilla	March-Ford	14	1h 50m 18.1s	23
14	Ashley	Token-Ford	13		26
15	Hailwood	McLaren-Ford	12	accident	12
	Hunt	Hesketh-Ford	11	gearbox	13
	Mass	Surtees-Ford	10	engine	10
	Depailler	Tyrrell-Ford	5	suspension	5
	Merzario	Williams-Ford	5	throttle	16
	Beltoise	BRM	4	transmission	15
	Schuppan	Ensign-Ford	4	gearbox	22
	E Fittipaldi	McLaren-Ford	2	suspension	3
	Laffite	Williams-Ford	2	suspension	21
	Watson	Brabham-Ford	1	suspension	14
	Lauda	Ferrari	0	accident	1
	Hulme	McLaren-Ford	0	accident	7

Fastest Lap: Scheckter, 7m 11.1s. 118.49 mph/190.69 kph

Austrian Grand Prix: Österreichring, 18 August 1974

54 laps of 3.67 mile/5.91 km circuit

Place	Driver	Car	Laps	Time/reason for retiring	Grid
1	Reutemann	Brabham-Ford	54	1h 28m 44.7s	2
2	Hulme	McLaren-Ford	54	1h 29m 27.6s	10
3	Hunt	Hesketh-Ford	54	1h 29m 46.3s	7
4	Watson	Brabham-Ford	54	1h 29m 54.1s	11
5	Regazzoni	Ferrari	54	1h 29m 57.8s	8
6	Brambilla	March-Ford	54	1h 29m 58.5s	20
7	Hobbs	McLaren-Ford	53		17
8	Jarier	Shadow-Ford	52		23
9	Quester	Surtees-Ford	51		25
10	Schenken	Trojan-Ford	50		19
11	Stuck	March-Ford	48	suspension	15
12	G Hill	Lola-Ford	48		21
	Ashley	Token-Ford	46		24
	Peterson	Lotus-Ford	45	transmission	6
	Ickx	Lotus-Ford	43	accident	22
	Depailler	Tyrrell-Ford	42	accident	14
	Pace	Brabham-Ford	41	fuel leak	4
	E Fittipaldi	McLaren-Ford	37	engine	3
	Laffite	Williams-Ford	37	running	12
	Merzario	Williams-Ford	24	fuel pressure	9
	Pryce	Shadow-Ford	22	spun	16
	Beltoise	BRM	21	engine	18
	Lauda	Ferrari	16	engine	1
	Stommelen	Lola-Ford	14	accident	13
	J Scheckter	Tyrrell-Ford	8	engine	5

Fastest Lap: Regazzoni, 1m 37.22s. 136 mph/218.88 kph

Italian Grand Prix: Monza, 8 September 1974

52 laps of 3.59 mile/5.78 km circuit

Place	Driver	Car	Laps	Time/reason for retiring	Grid
1	Peterson	Lotus-Ford	52	1h 22m 56.6s	7
2	E Fittipaldi	McLaren-Ford	52	1h 22m 57.4s	6
3	J Scheckter	Tyrrell-Ford	52	1h 23m 21.3s	12
4	Merzario	Williams-Ford	52	1h 24m 24.3s	15
5	Pace	Brabham-Ford	51		3
6	Hulme	McLaren-Ford	51		19
7	Watson	Brabham-Ford	51		4
8	G Hill	Lola-Ford	51		21
9	Hobbs	McLaren-Ford	51		23
10	Pryce	Shadow-Ford	50		22
11	Depailler	Tyrrell-Ford	50		10
	Regazzoni	Ferrari	40	engine	5
	Lauda	Ferrari	31	engine	1

Italian Grand Prix (cont)

Place	Driver	Car	Laps	Time/reason for retiring	Grid
	Ickx	Lotus-Ford	30	throttle	16
	Stommelen	Lola-Ford	24	suspension	14
	Laffite	Williams-Ford	21	engine	17
	Jarier	Shadow-Ford	19	engine	9
	Brambilla	March-Ford	16	accident	13
	Schenken	Trojan-Ford	14	gearbox	20
	Reutemann	Brabham-Ford	11	gearbox	2
	Stuck	March-Ford	10	engine	18
	Pescarolo	BRM	3	engine	25
	Hunt	Hesketh-Ford	2	engine	8
	Migault	BRM	0	gearbox	24
	Beltoise	BRM	0	electrical	11

Fastest Lap: Pace, 1m 34.2s. 137.26 mph/220.89 kph

Canadian Grand Prix: Mosport Park, 22 September 1974

80 laps of 2.46 mile/3.96 km circuit

Place	Driver	Car	Laps	Time/reason for retiring	Grid
1	E Fittipaldi	McLaren-Ford	80	1h 40m 26.1s	1
2	Regazzoni	Ferrari	80	1h 40m 39.2s	6
3	Peterson	Lotus-Ford	80	1h 40m 40.6s	10
4	Hunt	Hesketh-Ford	80	1h 40m 41.8s	8
5	Depailler	Tyrrell-Ford	80	1h 41m 21.5s	7
6	Hulme	McLaren-Ford	79		14
7	Andretti	Parnelli-Ford	79		16
8	Pace	Brabham-Ford	79		9
9	Reutemann	Brabham-Ford	79		4
10	Koinigg	Surtees-Ford	78		22
11	Stommelen	Lola-Ford	78		11
12	Donohue	Penske-Ford	78		24
13	Ickx	Lotus-Ford	78		21
14	G Hill	Lola-Ford	77		20
15	Laffite	Williams-Ford	74		18
16	Mass	Surtees-Ford	72		12
	Amon	BRM	70		25
	Lauda	Ferrari	67	accident	2
	Pryce	Shadow-Ford	65	engine	13
	Watson	Brabham-Ford	61	suspension	15
	Beltoise	BRM	60	running	17
	J Scheckter	Tyrrell-Ford	48	brakes	3
	Jarier	Shadow-Ford	46	transmission	5
	Merzario	Williams-Ford	40	handling	19
	Wietzes	Brabham-Ford	33	engine	26
	Stuck	March-Ford	12	fuel pressure	23

Fastest Lap: Lauda, 1m 13.66s. 120.18 mph/193.41 kph

United States Grand Prix: Watkins Glen, 6 October 1974

59 laps of 3.38 mile/5.44 km circuit

Place	Driver	Car	Laps	Time/reason for retiring	Grid
1	Reutemann	Brabham-Ford	59	1h 40m 21.4s	1
2	Pace	Brabham-Ford	59	1h 40m 32.2s	4
3	Hunt	Hesketh-Ford	59	1h 41m 31.8s	2
4	E Fittipaldi	McLaren-Ford	59	1h 41m 39.2s	8
5	Watson	Brabham-Ford	59	1h 41m 47.2s	7
6	Depailler	Tyrrell-Ford	59	1h 41m 49s	13
7	Mass	Surtees-Ford	59	1h 41m 51.5s	20
8	G Hill	Lola-Ford	58		24
9	Amon	BRM	57		12
10	Jarier	Shadow-Ford	57		10
11	Regazzoni	Ferrari	55		9
12	Stommelen	Lola-Ford	54		21
	Peterson	Lotus-Ford	52	fuel line	19
	Wilds	Ensign-Ford	50		22
	Pryce	Shadow-Ford	47		18
	J Scheckter	Tyrrell-Ford	44	fuel	6
	Merzario	Williams-Ford	43	electrical	15
	Lauda	Ferrari	38	suspension	5
	Laffite	Williams-Ford	31	wheel	11
	Donohue	Penske-Ford	27	suspension	14
	Dolhem	Surtees-Ford	25	withdrew	26
	Brambilla	March-Ford	21	fuel system	25
	Koinigg	Surtees-Ford	9	fatal accident	23
	Ickx	Lotus-Ford	7	suspension	16
	Hulme	McLaren-Ford	4	engine	17
	Andretti	Parnelli-Ford	3	disqualified	3

Fastest Lap: Pace, 1m 40.61s. 120.84 mph/194.47 kph

* Dolhem, first reserve, started when Andretti was unable to start on the grid; Andretti subsequently started with help from his mechanics outside the pits and was therefore disqualified. Grid positions given here include Andretti. Schenken, Lotus-Ford, second reserve, started illegally and was also disqualified.

World Championship 1974

1	E Fittipaldi	55
2	Regazzoni	52
3	J Scheckter	45
4	Lauda	38
5	Peterson	35
6	Reutemann	32
7	Hulme	20
8	Hunt	15
9	Depailler	14
10 =	Hailwood, Ickx	12
12	Pace	11
13	Beltoise	10
14 =	Jarier, Watson	6
16	Stuck	5
17	Merzario	4
18 =	Brambilla, G Hill, Pryce	1

Constructors' Championship

1	McLaren-Ford	73 (75)
2	Ferrari	65
3	Tyrrell-Ford	52
4	Lotus-Ford	42
5	Brabham-Ford	35
6	Hesketh-Ford	15
7	BRM	10
8	Shadow-Ford	7
9	March-Ford	6
10	Williams-Ford	4
11	Surtees-Ford	3
12	Lola-Ford	1

1975

Niki Lauda won the championship comfortably for Ferrari. Jochen Mass and Vittorio Brambilla won their only grand prix in rain-shortened races for which half points were awarded. Lella Lombardi became the first woman to score in the championship with her half point for sixth in Spain. In November Graham Hill, Tony Brise and four other members of Hill's team were killed when Hill's plane crashed in fog. Graham Hill remains the only driver to have won the world championship, the Indianapolis 500 and Le Mans, a true indication of his versatility, skill and tenacity. His 176 grand prix starts remained a record until overtaken by Riccardo Patrese in 1990.

Argentine Grand Prix: Buenos Aires, 12 January 1975

53 laps of 3.71 mile/5.97 km circuit

Place	Driver	Car	Laps	Time/reason for retiring	Grid
1	E Fittipaldi	McLaren-Ford	53	1h 39m 26.29s	5
2	Hunt	Hesketh-Ford	53	1h 39m 32.20s	6
3	Reutemann	Brabham-Ford	53	1h 39m 43.35s	3
4	Regazzoni	Ferrari	53	1h 40m 02.08s	7
5	Depailler	Tyrell-Ford	53	1h 40m 20.54s	8
6	Lauda	Ferrari	53	1h 40m 45.94s	4
7	Donohue	Penske-Ford	52		18
8	Ickx	Lotus-Ford	52		18
9	Brambilla	March-Ford	52		12
10	G Hill	Lola-Ford	52		21
11	J Scheckter	Tyrell-Ford	52		9
12	Pryce	Shadow-Ford	51	transmission	14
13	Stommelen	Lola-Ford	51		19
14	Mass	McLaren-Ford	50		13
	Pace	Brabham-Ford	46	engine	2
	Merzario	Williams-Ford	44		20
	Andretti	Parnelli-Ford	27	drive-shaft	10
	Wilds	BRM	24	oil pump	22
	Peterson	Lotus-Ford	15	brakes	11
	Laffite	Williams-Ford	15	gearbox	17
	W Fittipaldi	Fittipaldi-Ford	12	accident	23
	Watson	Surtees-Ford	6	disqualified: illegal repairs	15

Fastest Lap: Hunt, 1m 50.91s, 120.372 mph/193.72 kph
* Jarier, Shadow-Ford, in pole position, broke down on warming up lap.

Brazilian Grand Prix: Interlagos, 26 January 1975

40 laps of 4.95 mile/7.96 km circuit

Place	Driver	Car	Laps	Time/reason for retiring	Grid
1	Pace	Brabham-Ford	40	1h 44m 41.17s	6
2	E Fittipaldi	McLaren-Ford	40	1h 44m 46.96s	2
3	Mass	McLaren-Ford	40	1h 45m 17.83s	10
4	Regazzoni	Ferrari	40	1h 45m 24.45s	5
5	Lauda	Ferrari	40	1h 45m 43.05s	4
6	Hunt	Hesketh-Ford	40	1h 45m 46.29s	7
7	Andretti	Parnelli-Ford	40	1h 45m 47.98s	18
8	Reutemann	Brabham-Ford	40	1h 46m 20.79s	3
9	Ickx	Lotus-Ford	40	1h 46m 33.01s	12
10	Watson	Surtees-Ford	40	1h 47m 10.77s	13
11	Laffite	Williams-Ford	39		19
12	G Hill	Lola-Ford	39		20
13	W Fittipaldi	Fittipaldi-Ford	39		21
14	Stommelen	Lola-Ford	39		23
15	Peterson	Lotus-Ford	38		16
	Jarier	Shadow-Ford	32	fuel system	1
	Depailler	Tyrell-Ford	31	accident	9
	Pryce	Shadow-Ford	31	accident	14
	Merzario	Williams-Ford	24	fuel system	11
	Wilds	BRM	22	electrical	22
	Donohue	Penske-Ford	22	handling	15
	J Scheckter	Tyrrell-Ford	18	oil tank	8
	Brambilla	March-Ford	1	engine	17

Fastest Lap: Jarier, 2m 34.16s. 115.503 mph/185.884 kph

South African Grand Prix: Kyalami, 1 March 1975

78 laps of 2.55 mile/4.1 km circuit

Place	Driver	Car	Laps	Time/reason for retiring	Grid
1	J Scheckter	Tyrell-Ford	78	1h 43m 16.90s	3
2	Reutemann	Brabham-Ford	78	1h 43m 20.64s	2
3	Depailler	Tyrell-Ford	78	1h 43m 33.82s	5
4	Pace	Brabham-Ford	78	1h 43m 34.21s	1
5	Lauda	Ferrari	78	1h 43m 45.54s	4
6	Mass	McLaren-Ford	78	1h 44m 20.24s	16
7	Stommelen	Lola-Ford	78	1h 44m 29.81s	14
8	Donohue	Penske-Ford	77		18
9	Pryce	Shadow-Ford	77		19
10	Peterson	Lotus-Ford	77		8
11	Tunmer	Lotus-Ford	76		25
12	Ickx	Lotus-Ford	76		21
13	Keizan	Lotus-Ford	76		22
14	Charlton	McLaren-Ford	76		20

South African Grand Prix (cont)

Place	Driver	Car	Laps	Time/reason for retiring	Grid
15	Evans	BRM	76		24
16	Regazzoni	Ferrari	71	throttle	9
17	Andretti	Parnelli-Ford	70	drive-shaft	6
	Laffite	Williams-Ford	69	running	23
	E Fittipaldi	McLaren-Ford	65	running	11
	I Scheckter	Tyrrell-Ford	55	accident	17
	Hunt	Hesketh-Ford	53	fuel	12
	Jarier	Shadow-Ford	37	engine	13
	Lombardi	March-Ford	23	engine	26
	Merzario	Williams-Ford	22	engine	15
	Watson	Surtees-Ford	19	clutch	10
	Brambilla	March-Ford	16	oil leak	7

Fastest Lap: Pace, 1m 17.20s. 118.912 mph/191.378 kph

Spanish Grand Prix: Montjuich, 27 April 1975

29 laps of 2.36 mile/3.79 km circuit

Place	Driver	Car	Laps	Time/reason for retiring	Grid
1	Mass	McLaren-Ford	29	42m 53.7s	11
2	Ickx	Lotus-Ford	29	42m 54.8s	16
3	Reutemann	Brabham-Ford	28	42m 37.5s	15
4	Jarier	Shadow-Ford	28	43m 44.8s	10
5	Brambilla	March-Ford	28		5
6	Lombardi	March-Ford	27		24
7	Brise	Williams-Ford	27		18
8	Watson	Surtees-Ford	26		6
	Stommelen	Hill-Ford	25	accident	9
	Pace	Brabham-Ford	25	accident	14
	Regazzoni	Ferrari	25	running	2
	Peterson	Lotus-Ford	23	accident	12
	Pryce	Shadow-Ford	23	accident	8
	Wunderink	Ensign-Ford	20	drive-shaft	19
	Migault	Hill-Ford	18	running	22
	Andretti	Parnelli-Ford	16	accident	4
	Evans	BRM	7	fuel system	23
	Hunt	Hesketh-Ford	6	accident	3
	J Scheckter	Tyrrell-Ford	3	engine	13
	Donohue	Penske-Ford	3	accident	17
	Jones	Hesketh-Ford	3	accident	20
	Depailler	Tyrrell-Ford	1	accident	7
	Merzario	Williams-Ford	1	withdrew	25
	W Fittipaldi	Fittipaldi-Ford	1	withdrew	21
	Lauda	Ferrari	0	accident	1

Fastest Lap: Andretti, 1m 25.1s. 99.641 mph/160.356 kph
* Race stopped after Stommelen's crash which killed 5 spectators; half points awarded.
Merzario and W Fittipaldi withdrew in protest against the poor fitting of guard rails.

Monaco Grand Prix: Monte Carlo, 11 May 1975

75 laps of 2.04 mile/3.28 km circuit

Place	Driver	Car	Laps	Time/reason for retiring	Grid
1	Lauda	Ferrari	75	2h 1m 21.31s	1
2	E Fittipaldi	McLaren-Ford	75	2h 1m 24.09s	9
3	Pace	Brabham-Ford	75	2h 1m 39.12s	8
4	Peterson	Lotus-Ford	75	2h 1m 59.76s	4
5	Depailler	Tyrell-Ford	75	2h 2m 2.17s	12
6	Mass	McLaren-Ford	75	2h 2m 3.38s	15
7	J Scheckter	Tyrell-Ford	74		7
8	Ickx	Lotus-Ford	74		14
9	Reutemann	Brabham-Ford	73		10
	Donohue	Penske-Ford	66	accident	16
	Hunt	Hesketh-Ford	63	accident	11
	Jones	Hesketh-Ford	61	lost wheel	18
	Brambilla	March-Ford	48	accident	5
	Pryce	Shadow-Ford	39	accident	2
	Watson	Surtees-Ford	36	spun	17
	Regazzoni	Ferrari	36	accident	6
	Andretti	Parnelli-Ford	9	fire	13
	Jarier	Shadow-Ford	0	accident	3

Fastest Lap: Depailler, 1m 28.67s. 82.696 mph/133.087 kph

Belgian Grand Prix: Zolder, 25 May 1975

70 laps of 2.65 mile/4.26 km circuit

Place	Driver	Car	Laps	Time/reason for retiring	Grid
1	Lauda	Ferrari	70	1h 43m 53.98s	1
2	J Scheckter	Tyrell-Ford	70	1h 44m 13.20s	9
3	Reutemann	Brabham-Ford	70	1h 44m 35.80s	6
4	Depailler	Tyrell-Ford	70	1h 44m 54.06s	12
5	Regazzoni	Ferrari	70	1h 44m 57.84s	4
6	Pryce	Shadow-Ford	70	1h 45m 22.43s	5
7	E Fittipaldi	McLaren-Ford	69		8
8	Pace	Brabham-Ford	69		2
9	Evans	BRM	68		20
10	Watson	Surtees-Ford	68		18
11	Donohue	Penske-Ford	67		21
12	W Fittipaldi	Fittipaldi-Ford	67		24
	Migault	Hill-Ford	57	suspension	22
	Brambilla	March-Ford	54	brakes	3
	Ickx	Lotus-Ford	52	brakes	16
	Peterson	Lotus-Ford	36	accident	14
	Lombardi	March-Ford	18	engine	23
	Laffite	Williams-Ford	18	gearbox	17
	Brise	Hill-Ford	17	engine	7

Belgian Grand Prix (cont)

Place	Driver	Car	Laps	Time/reason for retiring	Grid
	Hunt	Hesketh-Ford	15	gear linkage	11
	Jarier	Shadow-Ford	13	spun	10
	Merzario	Williams-Ford	2	clutch	19
	Jones	Hesketh-Ford	1	accident	13
	Mass	McLaren-Ford	0	accident	15

Fastest Lap: Regazzoni, 1m 26.76s. 109.887 mph/176.846 kph

Swedish Grand Prix: Anderstorp, 8 June 1975

80 laps of 2.5 mile/4.02 km circuit

Place	Driver	Car	Laps	Time/reason for retiring	Grid
1	Lauda	Ferrari	80	1h 59m 18.319s	5
2	Reutemann	Brabham-Ford	80	1h 59m 24.607s	4
3	Regazzoni	Ferrari	80	1h 59m 47.414s	12
4	Andretti	Parnelli-Ford	80	2h 0m 2.699s	15
5	Donohue	Penske-Ford	80	2h 0m 49.082s	16
6	Brise	Hill-Ford	79		17
7	J Scheckter	Tyrrell-Ford	79		8
8	E Fittipaldi	McLaren-Ford	79		11
9	Peterson	Lotus-Ford	79		9
10	Palm	Hesketh-Ford	78	out of fuel	21
11	Jones	Hesketh-Ford	79		19
12	Depailler	Tyrrell-Ford	78		2
13	Evans	BRM	78		23
14	Magee	Williams-Ford	78		22
15	Ickx	Lotus-Ford	77		18
16	Watson	Surtees-Ford	77		10
17	W Fittipaldi	Fittipaldi-Ford	74		25
	Pryce	Shadow-Ford	53	spun	7
	I Scheckter	Williams-Ford	49	accident	20
	Schuppan	Hill-Ford	47	drive-shaft	26
	Pace	Brabham-Ford	41	accident	6
	Jarier	Shadow-Ford	38	engine	3
	Brambilla	March-Ford	36	transmission	1
	Mass	McLaren-Ford	34	water leak	14
	Hunt	Hesketh-Ford	21	brake fluid	13
	Lombardi	March-Ford	10	fuel system	24

Fastest Lap: Lauda, 1m 28.267s. 101.827 mph/163.875 kph

Dutch Grand Prix: Zandvoort, 22 June 1975

75 laps of 2.63 mile/4.23 km circuit

Place	Driver	Car	Laps	Time/reason for retiring	Grid
1	Hunt	Hesketh-Ford	75	1h 46m 57.40s	3
2	Lauda	Ferrari	75	1h 46m 58.46s	1
3	Regazzoni	Ferrari	75	1h 47m 52.46s	2
4	Reutemann	Brabham-Ford	74		5
5	Pace	Brabham-Ford	74		9
6	Pryce	Shadow-Ford	74		12
7	Brise	Hill-Ford	74		7
8	Donohue	Penske-Ford	74		18
9	Depailler	Tyrrell-Ford	73		13
10	van Lennep	Ensign-Ford	71		22
11	W Fittipaldi	Fittipaldi-Ford	71		24
12	I Scheckter	Williams-Ford	70		19
13	Jones	Hill-Ford	70		17
14	Lombardi	March-Ford	70		23
15	Peterson	Lotus-Ford	69	out of fuel	16
16	J Scheckter	Tyrrell-Ford	67	engine	4
	Laffite	Williams-Ford	65	engine	15
	Mass	McLaren-Ford	61	accident	8
	Jarier	Shadow-Ford	44	accident	10
	Watson	Surtees-Ford	43	vibration	14
	E Fittipaldi	McLaren-Ford	40	engine	6
	Evans	BRM	23	crownwheel and pinion	20
	Ickx	Lotus-Ford	6	engine	21
	Brambilla	March-Ford	0	accident	11

Fastest Lap: Lauda, 1m 21.54. 115.934 mph/ 186.578 kph

French Grand Prix: Paul Ricard, 6 July 1975

54 laps of 3.61 mile/5.81 km circuit

Place	Driver	Car	Laps	Time/reason for retiring	Grid
1	Lauda	Ferrari	54	1h 40m 18.84s	1
2	Hunt	Hesketh-Ford	54	1h 40m 20.43s	3
3	Mass	McLaren-Ford	54	1h 40m 21.15s	7
4	E Fittipaldi	McLaren-Ford	54	1h 40m 58.61s	10
5	Andretti	Parnelli-Ford	54	1h 41m 20.92s	15
6	Depailler	Tyrrell-Ford	54	1h 41m 26.24s	13
7	Brise	Hill-Ford	54	1h 41m 28.45s	12
8	Jarier	Shadow-Ford	54	1h 41m 38.62s	4
9	J Scheckter	Tyrrell-Ford	54	1h 41m 50.52s	2
10	Peterson	Lotus-Ford	54	1h 41m 54.86s	17
11	Laffite	Williams-Ford	54	1h 41m 55.61s	16
12	Jabouille	Tyrrell-Ford	54	1h 41m 55.97s	21
13	Watson	Surtees-Ford	53		14

French Grand Prix (cont)

Place	Driver	Car	Laps	Time/reason for retiring	Grid
14	Reutemann	Brabham-Ford	53		11
15	van Lennep	Ensign-Ford	53		22
16	Jones	Hill-Ford	53		20
17	Evans	BRM	52		24
18	Lombardi	March-Ford	50		25
	Pace	Brabham-Ford	26	drive-shaft	5
	Ickx	Lotus-Ford	17	brakes	19
	W Fittipaldi	Fittipaldi-Ford	14	engine	23
	Donohue	Penske-Ford	6	drive-shaft	18
	Brambilla	March-Ford	6	suspension	8
	Regazzoni	Ferrari	6	engine	9
	Pryce	Shadow-Ford	2	transmission	2

Fastest Lap: Mass, 1m 50.6s. 117.51 mph/189.11 kph

British Grand Prix: Silverstone, 19 July 1975

56 laps of 2.93 mile/4.72 km circuit

Place	Driver	Car	Laps	Time/reason for retiring	Grid
1	E Fittipaldi	McLaren-Ford	56	1h 22m 5.0s	7
2	Pace	Brabham-Ford	55	accident	2
3	J Scheckter	Tyrrell-Ford	55	accident	6
4	Hunt	Hesketh-Ford	55	accident	9
5	Donohue	March-Ford	55	accident	15
6	Brambilla	March-Ford	55		5
7	Mass	McLaren-Ford	55	accident	10
8	Lauda	Ferrari	54		3
9	Depailler	Tyrrell-Ford	54	accident	17
10	Jones	Hill-Ford	54		20
11	Watson	Surtees-Ford	54	accident	18
12	Andretti	Parnelli-Ford	54		12
13	Regazzoni	Ferrari	54		4
14	Jarier	Shadow-Ford	53	accident	11
15	Brise	Hill-Ford	53	accident	13
16	Henton	Lotus-Ford	53	accident	21
17	Nicholson	Lyncar-Ford	51	accident	26
18	Morgan	Surtees-Ford	50	accident	23
19	W Fittipaldi	Fittipaldi-Ford	50	accident	24
	H-J Stuck	March-Ford	45	accident	14
	Crawford	Lotus-Ford	28	accident	25
	Pryce	Shadow-Ford	20	accident	1
	Lombardi	March-Ford	18	engine	22
	Peterson	Lotus-Ford	7	engine	16
	Laffite	Williams-Ford	5	gearbox	19
	Reutemann	Brabham-Ford	4	engine	8

Fastest Lap: Regazzoni, 1m 20.9s. 130.472 mph/209.97 kph
* Race stopped early due to hail storm.

German Grand Prix: Nürburgring, 3 August 1975

14 laps of 14.19 mile/22.84 km circuit

Place	Driver	Car	Laps	Time/reason for retiring	Grid
1	Reutemann	Brabham-Ford	14	1h 41m 14.1s	10
2	Laffite	Williams-Ford	14	1h 42m 51.8s	15
3	Lauda	Ferrari	14	1h 43m 37.4s	1
4	Pryce	Shadow-Ford	14	1h 44m 45.5s	16
5	Jones	Hill-Ford	14	1h 45m 04.4s	20
6	van Lennep	Ensign-Ford	14	1h 46m 19.6s	23
7	Lombardi	March-Ford	14	1h 48m 44.5s	24
8	Ertl	Hesketh-Ford	14	1h 48m 55.0s	22
9	Depailler	Tyrrell-Ford	13		4
10	Andretti	Parnelli-Ford	12	out of fuel	13
	Hunt	Hesketh-Ford	10	transmission	9
	Regazzoni	Ferrari	9	engine	5
	Brise	Hill-Ford	9	accident	17
	J Scheckter	Tyrrell-Ford	7	accident	3
	Jarier	Shadow-Ford	7	tyre	12
	Pace	Brabham-Ford	5	suspension	2
	W Fittipaldi	Fittipaldi-Ford	4	engine	21
	E Fittipaldi	McLaren-Ford	3	suspension	8
	H-J Stuck	March-Ford	3	engine	7
	Brambilla	March-Ford	3	suspension	11
	Watson	Lotus-Ford	2	suspension	14
	Peterson	Lotus-Ford	1	clutch	18
	Donohue	March-Ford	1	puncture	19
	Mass	McLaren-Ford	0	accident	6

Fastest Lap: Regazzoni, 7m 6.4s. 119.794 mph/192.79 kph

Austrian Grand Prix: Österreichring, 17 August 1975

29 laps of 3.67 mile/5.911 km circuit

Place	Driver	Car	Laps	Time/reason for retiring	Grid
1	Brambilla	March-Ford	29	57m 56.69s	8
2	Hunt	Hesketh-Ford	29	58m 23.72s	12
3	Pryce	Shadow-Ford	29	58m 31.54s	15
4	Mass	McLaren-Ford	29	59m 09.35s	9
5	Peterson	Lotus-Ford	29	59m 20.02s	13
6	Lauda	Ferrari	29	59m 26.97s	1
7	Regazzoni	Ferrari	29	59m 35.76s	5
8	J Scheckter	Tyrrell-Ford	28		10
9	E Fittipaldi	McLaren-Ford	28		3
10	Watson	Surtees-Ford	28		18
11	Depailler	Tyrrell-Ford	28		7
12	Amon	Ensign-Ford	28		21
13	Lunger	Hesketh-Ford	28		17

Austrian Grand Prix (cont)

Place	Driver	Car	Laps	Time/reason for retiring	Grid
14	Reutemann	Brabham-Ford	28		11
15	Brise	Hill-Ford	28		16
16	Stommelen	Hill-Ford	27		23
17	Lombardi	March-Ford	26		20
	Wunderink	Ensign-Ford	25		25
	Ertl	Hesketh-Ford	23	electrical	24
	Laffite	Williams-Ford	21	handling	12
	Pace	Brabham-Ford	17	engine	6
	Vonlanthen	Williams-Ford	14	engine	26
	H-J Stuck	March-Ford	10	accident	4
	Jarier	Shadow-Matra	10	fuel system	14
	Evans	BRM	2	engine	22
	Andretti	Parnelli-Ford	1	spun	19

Fastest Lap: Brambilla, 1m 53.90s. 116.099 mph/186.627 kph

* Race stopped early due to rain. Half points awarded. Donohue died after practice crash.

Italian Grand Prix: Monza, 7 September 1975

52 laps of 3.59 mile/5.78 km circuit

Place	Driver	Car	Laps	Time/reason for retiring	Grid
1	Regazzoni	Ferrari	52	1h 22m 42.6s	2
2	E Fittipaldi	McLaren-Ford	52	1h 22m 59.2s	3
3	Lauda	Ferrari	52	1h 23m 05.8s	1
4	Reutemann	Brabham-Ford	52	1h 23m 37.7s	7
5	Hunt	Hesketh-Ford	52	1h 23m 39.7s	8
5	Pryce	Shadow-Ford	52	1h 23m 58.5s	14
7	Depailler	Tyrrell-Ford	51		12
8	J Scheckter	Tyrrell-Ford	51		4
9	Ertl	Hesketh-Ford	51		17
10	Lunger	Hesketh-Ford	50		21
11	Merzario	Fittipaldi-Ford	48		26
12	Amon	Ensign-Ford	48		19
13	Crawford	Lotus-Ford	46		25
14	Zorzi	Williams-Ford	46		22
	Jarier	Shadow-Matra	32	fuel pump	13
	Lombardi	March-Ford	21	accident	24
	H-J Stuck	March-Ford	15	accident	16
	Laffite	Williams-Ford	7	gearbox	18
	Pace	Brabham-Ford	6	throttle linkage	10
	Stommelen	Hill-Ford	3	accident	23
	Mass	McLaren-Ford	2	accident	5
	Brambilla	March-Ford	1	clutch	9
	Andretti	Parnelli-Ford	1	accident	15

Italian Grand Prix (cont)

Place	Driver	Car	Laps	Time/reason for retiring	Grid
	Brise	Hill-Ford	1	accident	6
	Peterson	Lotus-Ford	1	engine	11
	Evans	BRM	0	electrical	20

Fastest Lap: Regazzoni, 1m 33.1s. 138.877 mph/223.501 kph

United States Grand Prix: Watkins Glen, 5 October 1975

59 laps of 3.38 mile/5.44 km circuit

Place	Driver	Car	Laps	Time/reason for retiring	Grid
1	Lauda	Ferrari	59	1h 42m 58.175s	1
2	E Fittipaldi	McLaren-Ford	59	1h 43m 03.118s	2
3	Mass	McLaren-Ford	59	1h 43m 45.812s	9
4	Hunt	Hesketh-Ford	59	1h 43m 47.650s	15
5	Peterson	Lotus-Ford	59	1h 43m 48.161s	14
6	J Scheckter	Tyrrell-Ford	59	1h 43m 48.496s	10
7	Brambilla	March-Ford	59	1h 44m 42.206s	6
8	H-J Stuck	March-Ford	58		13
9	Watson	Penske-Ford	57		12
10	W Fittipaldi	Fittipaldi-Ford	55		22
	Pryce	Shadow-Ford	52		7
	Henton	Lotus-Ford	49		19
	Lunger	Hesketh-Ford	46	accident	18
	Wunderink	Ensign-Ford	41	gearbox	21
	Regazzoni	Ferrari	28	withdrawn	11
	Jarier	Shadow-Ford	19	wheel bearing	4
	Reutemann	Brabham-Ford	9	engine	3
	Andretti	Parnelli-Ford	9	suspension	5
	Brise	Hill-Ford	5	accident	17
	Leclère	Tyrrell-Ford	5	engine	20
	Depailler	Tyrrell-Ford	2	accident	8
	Pace	Brabham-Ford	2	accident	16

Fastest Lap: Fittipaldi, 1m 43.374s. 117.604 mph/189.265 kph

World Championship 1975

1	Lauda	64.5
2	E Fittipaldi	45
3	Reutemann	37
4	Hunt	33
5	Regazzoni	25
6	Pace	24
7=	Mass, J Scheckter	20
9	Depailler	12
10	Pryce	8
11	Brambilla	6.5
12=	Laffite, Peterson	6
14	Andretti	5
15	Donohue	4
16	Ickx	3
17	Jones	2
18	Jarier	1.5
19=	Brise, van Lennep	1
21	Lombardi	0.5

Constructors' Championship 1975

1	Ferrari	72.5
2	Brabham-Ford	54 (56)
3	McLaren-Ford	53
4	Hesketh-Ford	33
5	Tyrrell-Ford	25
6	Shadow-Ford	9.5
7	Lotus-Ford	9
8	March-Ford	6.5
9	Williams-Ford	6
10	Parnelli-Ford	5
11	Hill-Ford	3
12	Penske-Ford	2
13	Ensign-Ford	1

1976

In an extraordinarily political season the world championship went to James Hunt by one point from Niki Lauda, although Ferrari took the constructors' title. Controversy began in Spain where Hunt was initially disqualified from first place, giving the race to Lauda, only for the decision to be overturned on appeal months later. The six wheeled Tyrrell confounded the sceptics by winning in Sweden, with Lauda third and Hunt fifth. Hunt won in France and, it seemed, in Britain. But the race had been restarted after a first lap accident and Hunt was eventually disqualified after an appeal from Ferrari, giving the race to Lauda. Lauda then crashed heavily in Germany and appeared likely to die from his injuries. Hunt won the race and finished fourth to Watson's Penske (the team's only win) in Austria. Miraculously Lauda returned to finish fourth in Italy, where Hunt, Mass and Watson were relegated to the back of the grid for alleged infringements of the regulations. Hunt won in Canada and in the USA but Lauda took third to lead Hunt by three points going into the final race. In appalling weather Andretti won, Lauda gave up because of the hazardous conditions, and Hunt eventually finished third to take the title. Chris Amon, probably the best driver never to win a championship race, drove his last grand prix in Germany. The 1976 Wolf-Williams cars were originally Heskeths, and Williams had left the team by September. The Boro-Ford was a renamed Ensign-Ford.

Brazilian Grand Prix: Interlagos, 25 January 1976

40 laps of 4.95 mile/7.96 km circuit

Place	Driver	Car	Laps	Time/reason for retiring	Grid
1	Lauda	Ferrari	40	1h 45m 16.78s	2
2	Depailler	Tyrrell-Ford	40	1h 45m 38.25s	9
3	Pryce	Shadow-Ford	40	1h 45m 40.62s	12
4	H-J Stuck	March-Ford	40	1h 46m 44.95s	14
5	J Scheckter	Tyrrell-Ford	40	1h 47m 13.24s	13
6	Mass	McLaren-Ford	40	1h 47m 15.05s	6

Brazilian Grand Prix (cont)

Place	Driver	Car	Laps	Time/reason for retiring	Grid
7	Regazzoni	Ferrari	40	1h 47m 32.02s	4
8	Ickx	Williams-Ford	39		19
9	Zorzi	Williams-Ford	39		17
10	Pace	Brabham-Alfa	39		10
11	Hoffman	Fittipaldi-Ford	39		20
12	Reutemann	Brabham-Alfa	37	out of fuel	15
13	E Fittipaldi	Fittipaldi-Ford	37		5
14	Lombardi	March-Ford	36		22
	Jarier	Shadow-Ford	33	accident	3
	Hunt	McLaren-Ford	32	accident	1
	Brambilla	March-Ford	15	oil leak	7
	Laffite	Ligier-Matra	14	gear linkage	11
	Peterson	Lotus-Ford	10	accident	18
	Andretti	Lotus-Ford	6	accident	16
	Watson	Penske-Ford	2	fire	8
	Ashley	BRM	2	oil pump	21

Fastest Lap: Jarier, 2m 35.07s. 114.831 mph/184.803 kph

South African Grand Prix: Kyalami, 6 March 1976

78 laps of 2.55 mile/4.1 km circuit

Place	Driver	Car	Laps	Time/reason for retiring	Grid
1	Lauda	Ferrari	78	1h 42m 18.4s	1
2	Hunt	McLaren-Ford	78	1h 42m 19.7s	2
3	Mass	McLaren-Ford	78	1h 43m 04.3s	4
4	J Scheckter	Tyrrell-Ford	78	1h 43m 26.8s	12
5	Watson	Penske-Ford	77		3
6	Andretti	Parnelli-Ford	77		13
7	Pryce	Shadow-Ford	77		7
8	Brambilla	March-Ford	77		5
9	Depailler	Tyrrell-Ford	77		6
10	Evans	Lotus-Ford	77		23
11	Lunger	Surtees-Ford	77		20
12	H-J Stuck	March-Ford	76		17
13	Leclère	Williams-Ford	76		22
14	Amon	Ensign-Ford	76		18
15	Ertl	Hesketh-Ford	74		24
16	Ickx	Williams-Ford	73		19
17	E Fittipaldi	Fittipaldi-Ford	70	engine	21
	Regazzoni	Ferrari	52	engine	9
	Laffite	Ligier-Matra	49	engine	8
	Jarier	Shadow-Ford	28	radiator	15
	Pace	Brabham-Alfa	22	engine	14
	Nilsson	Lotus-Ford	18	clutch	25

South African Grand Prix (cont)

Place	Driver	Car	Laps	Time/reason for retiring	Grid
	Reutemann	Brabham-Alfa	16	engine	11
	Peterson	March-Ford	15	accident	10
	I Scheckter	Tyrrell-Ford	0	accident	16

Fastest Lap: Lauda, 1m 17.97s. 117.74 mph/189.5 kph

United States Grand Prix West: Long Beach, 28 March 1976

80 laps of 2.02 mile/3.25 km circuit

Place	Driver	Car	Laps	Time/reason for retiring	Grid
1	Regazzoni	Ferrari	80	1h 53m 18.5s	1
2	Lauda	Ferrari	80	1h 54m 00.9s	4
3	Depailler	Tyrrell-Ford	80	1h 54m 08.4s	2
4	Laffite	Ligier-Matra	80	1h 54m 31.3s	12
5	Mass	McLaren-Ford	80	1h 54m 40.8s	14
6	E Fittipaldi	Fittipaldi-Ford	79		16
7	Jarier	Shadow-Ford	79		7
8	Amon	Ensign-Ford	78		17
9	Pace	Brabham-Alfa	77		13
10	Peterson	March-Ford	77		6
	Jones	Surtees-Ford	70		19
	Watson	Penske-Ford	69		9
	J Scheckter	Tyrrell-Ford	34	suspension	11
	Pryce	Shadow-Ford	32	drive-shaft	5
	Andretti	Parnelli-Ford	15	water leak	15
	Hunt	McLaren-Ford	3	accident	3
	H-J Stuck	March-Ford	2	accident	18
	Nilsson	Lotus-Ford	0	accident	20
	Reutemann	Brabham-Alfa	0	accident	10
	Brambilla	March-Ford	0	accident	8

Fastest Lap: Regazzoni, 1m 23.08s. 87.53 mph/140.87 kph

Spanish Grand Prix: Jarama, 2 May 1976

75 laps of 2.12 mile/3.4 km circuit

Place	Driver	Car	Laps	Time/reason for retiring	Grid
1	*Hunt	McLaren-Ford	75	1h 42m 20.43s	1
2	Lauda	Ferrari	75	1h 42m 51.40s	2
3	Nilsson	Lotus-Ford	75	1h 43m 08.45s	7
4	Reutemann	Brabham-Alfa	74		12
5	Amon	Ensign-Ford	74		10

Spanish Grand Prix (cont)

Place	Driver	Car	Laps	Time/reason for retiring	Grid
6	Pace	Brabham-Alfa	74		11
7	Ickx	Williams-Ford	74		21
8	Pryce	Shadow-Ford	74		22
9	Jones	Surtees-Ford	74		20
10	Leclère	Williams-Ford	73		23
11	Regazzoni	Ferrari	72		5
12	*Laffite	Ligier-Matra	72		8
13	Perkins	Boro-Ford	72		24
	Mass	McLaren-Ford	65	engine	4
	Jarier	Shadow-Ford	61	electrics	15
	J Scheckter	Tyrrell-Ford	53	engine	14
	Watson	Penske-Ford	51	engine	13
	Merzario	March-Ford	36	gear linkage	18
	Andretti	Lotus-Ford	34	gearbox	9
	Depailler	Tyrrell-Ford	25	accident	3
	Brambilla	March-Ford	21	accident	6
	H-J Stuck	March-Ford	16	gearbox	17
	Peterson	March-Ford	11	transmission	16
	E Fittipaldi	Fittipaldi-Ford	3	gear linkage	19

Fastest Lap: Mass, 1m 20.93. 94.096 mph/151.433 kph
* Originally disqualified but reinstated on appeal.

Belgian Grand Prix: Zolder, 16 May 1976

70 laps of 2.65 mile/4.26 km circuit

Place	Driver	Car	Laps	Time/reason for retiring	Grid
1	Lauda	Ferrari	70	1h 42m 53.23s	1
2	Regazzoni	Ferrari	70	1h 42m 56.69s	2
3	Laffite	Ligier-Matra	70	1h 43m 28.61s	6
4	J Scheckter	Tyrrell-Ford	70	1h 44m 24.31s	7
5	Jones	Surtees-Ford	69		16
6	Mass	McLaren-Ford	69		18
7	Watson	Penske-Ford	69		17
8	Perkins	Boro-Ford	69		20
9	Jarier	Shadow-Ford	69		14
10	Pryce	Shadow-Ford	68		13
11	Leclère	Williams-Ford	68		25
12	Kessel	Brabham-Ford	63		23
	Lunger	Surtees-Ford	62	electrical	26
	Pace	Brabham-Alfa	58	electrical	9
	Amon	Ensign-Ford	51	lost wheel	8
	Hunt	McLaren-Ford	35	transmission	3
	H-J Stuck	March-Ford	33	suspension	15
	Ertl	Hesketh-Ford	31	engine	24
	Depailler	Tyrrell-Ford	29	engine	4
	Andretti	Lotus-Ford	28	drive-shaft	11

Belgian Grand Prix (cont)

Place	Driver	Car	Laps	Time/reason for retiring	Grid
	Neve	Brabham-Ford	24	drive-shaft	19
	Merzario	March-Ford	21	engine	21
	Reutemann	Brabham-Alfa	17	engine	12
	Peterson	March-Ford	16	accident	10
	Nilsson	Lotus-Ford	7	accident	22
	Brambilla	March-Ford	6	drive-shaft	5

Fastest Lap: Lauda, 1m 25.98s. 110.88 mph/178.45 kph

Monaco Grand Prix: Monte Carlo, 30 May 1976

78 laps of 2.06 mile/3.31 km circuit

Place	Driver	Car	Laps	Time/reason for retiring	Grid
1	Lauda	Ferrari	78	1h 59m 51.47s	1
2	J Scheckter	Tyrrell-Ford	78	2h 00m 02.60s	5
3	Depailler	Tyrrell-Ford	78	2h 00m 56.31s	4
4	H-J Stuck	March-Ford	77		6
5	Mass	McLaren-Ford	77		11
6	E Fittipaldi	Fittipaldi-Ford	77		7
7	Pryce	Shadow-Ford	77		15
8	Jarier	Shadow-Ford	76		10
9	Pace	Brabham-Alfa	76		13
10	Watson	Penske-Ford	76		17
11	Leclère	Williams-Ford	76		18
12	Laffite	Ligier-Matra	75	accident	8
13	Amon	Ensign-Ford	74		12
	Regazzoni	Ferrari	73	accident	2
	Nilsson	Lotus-Ford	39	engine	16
	Peterson	March-Ford	26	accident	3
	Hunt	McLaren-Ford	24	engine	14
	Brambilla	March-Ford	9	suspension	9
	Jones	Surtees-Ford	1	accident	19
	Reutemann	Brabham-Alfa	0	accident	20

Fastest Lap: Regazzoni, 1m 30.28s. 82.06 mph/132.07 kph

Swedish Grand Prix: Anderstorp, 13 June 1976

72 laps of 2.5 mile/4.02 km circuit

Place	Driver	Car	Laps	Time/reason for retiring	Grid
1	J Scheckter	Tyrrell-Ford	72	1h 46m 53.73s	1
2	Depailler	Tyrrell-Ford	72	1h 47m 13.5s	4
3	Lauda	Terrari	72	1h 47m 27.6s	5

Swedish Grand Prix (cont)

Place	Driver	Car	Laps	Time/reason for retiring	Grid
4	Laffite	Ligier-Matra	72	1h 47m 49.55s	7
5	Hunt	McLaren-Ford	72	1h 47m 53.21s	8
6	Regazzoni	Ferrari	72	1h 47m 54.1s	11
7	Peterson	March-Ford	72	1h 47m 57.22s	9
8	Pace	Brabham-Alfa	72	1h 48m 05.34s	10
9	Pryce	Shadow-Ford	71		12
10	Brambilla	March-Ford	71		15
11	Mass	McLaren-Ford	71		13
12	Jarier	Shadow-Ford	71		14
13	Jones	Surtees-Ford	71		18
14	Merzario	March-Ford	70	engine	19
15	Lunger	Surtees-Ford	70		24
	Ertl	Hesketh-Ford	54	spun	23
	H-J Stuck	March-Ford	52	engine	20
	Andretti	Lotus-Ford	45	engine	2
	Amon	Ensign-Ford	38	accident	3
	Leclère	Williams-Ford	20	engine	25
	Perkins	Boro-Ford	18	engine	22
	E Fittipaldi	Fittipaldi-Ford	10	handling	21
	Kessel	Brabham-Ford	5	accident	26
	Nilsson	Lotus-Ford	2	accident	6
	Reutemann	Brabham-Alfa	2	engine	16
	Watson	Penske-Ford	0	accident	17

Fastest Lap: Andretti, 1m 28s. 102.14 mph/164.37 kph

French Grand Prix: Paul Ricard, 4 July 1976

54 laps of 3.61 mile/5.81 km circuit

Place	Driver	Car	Laps	Time/reason for retiring	Grid
1	Hunt	McLaren-Ford	54	1h 40m 58.60s	1
2	Depailler	Tyrrell-Ford	54	1h 41m 11.30s	3
3	*Watson	Penske-Ford	54	1h 41m 22.15s	8
4	Pace	Brabham-Alfa	54	1h 41m 23.42s	5
5	Andretti	Lotus-Ford	54	1h 41m 42.52s	7
6	J Scheckter	Tyrrell-Ford	54	1h 41m 53.67s	9
7	H-J Stuck	March-Ford	54	1h 42m 20.15s	17
8	Pryce	Shadow-Ford	54	1h 42m 29.27s	16
9	Merzario	March-Ford	54	1h 42m 52.17s	20
10	Ickx	Williams-Ford	53		19
11	Reutemann	Brabham-Alfa	53		10
12	Jarier	Shadow-Ford	53		15
13	Leclère	Williams-Ford	53		22
14	Laffite	Ligier-Matra	53		13
15	Mass	McLaren-Ford	53		14
16	Lunger	Surtees-Ford	53		23
17	Edwards	Hesketh-Ford	53		25

French Grand Prix (cont)

Place	Driver	Car	Laps	Time/reason for retiring	Grid
18	Neve	Ensign-Ford	53		26
19	Peterson	March-Ford	51	fuel system	6
	Jones	Surtees-Ford	44	suspension	18
	Brambilla	March-Ford	28	engine	11
	E Fittipaldi	Fittipaldi-Ford	21	engine	21
	Pescarolo	Surtees-Ford	19	suspension	24
	Regazzoni	Ferrari	17	engine	4
	Lauda	Ferrari	8	engine	2
	Nilsson	Lotus-Ford	8	transmission	12
	Ertl	Hesketh-Ford	4	drive-shaft (illegal start)	[27]

Fastest Lap: Lauda, 1m 51.0s. 117.086 mph/188.432 kph
* Originally disqualified but reinstated on appeal.

British Grand Prix: Brands Hatch, 18 July 1976

76 laps of 2.61 mile/4.21 km circuit

Place	Driver	Car	Laps	Time/reason for retiring	Grid
*	Hunt	McLaren-Ford	76	disqualified	2
1	Lauda	Ferrari	76	1h 44m 19.66s	1
2	J Scheckter	Tyrrell-Ford	76	1h 44m 35.84s	8
3	Watson	Penske-Ford	75		11
4	Pryce	Shadow-Ford	75		20
5	Jones	Surtees-Ford	75		19
6	E Fittipaldi	Fittipaldi-Ford	74		21
7	Ertl	Hesketh-Ford	73		23
8	Pace	Brabham-Alfa	73		16
9	Jarier	Shadow-Ford	70		24
	Nilsson	Lotus-Ford	67	engine	14
	Peterson	March-Ford	60	engine	7
	Lunger	Surtees-Ford	55	gearbox	18
	Depailler	Tyrrell-Ford	47	engine	5
	Reutemann	Brabham-Alfa	46	engine	15
	Merzario	March-Ford	39	engine	9
*	Regazzoni	Ferrari	36	engine	4
*	Laffite	Ligier-Matra	31	suspension	13
	Evans	Brabham-Ford	24	gearbox	22
	Brambilla	March-Ford	22	suspension	10
	Pescarolo	Surtees-Ford	16	engine	26
	Amon	Ensign-Ford	8	engine	6
	Andretti	Lotus-Ford	4	engine	3
	Mass	McLaren-Ford	1	clutch	12
	H-J Stuck	March-Ford	0	accident	17
	Edwards	Hesketh-Ford	0	accident	25

Fastest Lap: Lauda, 1m 19.91s. 117.74 mph/189.491 kph
* Race stopped after first-lap crash; Hunt, Laffite and Regazzoni disqualified for technical infringements.

German Grand Prix: Nürburgring, 1 August 1976

14 laps of 14.19 mile/22.84 km circuit

Place	Driver	Car	Laps	Time/reason for retiring	Grid
1	Hunt	McLaren-Ford	14	1h 41m 42.7s	1
2	J Scheckter	Tyrrell-Ford	14	1h 42m 10.4s	8
3	Mass	McLaren-Ford	14	1h 42m 35.1s	9
4	Pace	Brabham-Alfa	14	1h 42m 36.9s	7
5	Nilsson	Lotus-Ford	14	1h 43m 40.0s	16
6	Stommelen	Brabham-Alfa	14	1h 44m 13.0s	15
7	Watson	Penske-Ford	14	1h 44m 16.6s	19
8	Pryce	Shadow-Ford	14	1h 44m 30.9s	18
9	Regazzoni	Ferrari	14	1h 45m 28.7s	5
10	Jones	Surtees-Ford	14	1h 45m 30.0s	14
11	Jarier	Shadow-Ford	14	1h 46m 34.4s	23
12	Andretti	Lotus-Ford	14	1h 46m 40.8s	12
13	E Fittipaldi	Fittipaldi-Ford	14	1h 47m 07.9s	20
14	Pesenti-Rossi	Tyrrell-Ford	13		26
15	Edwards	Hesketh-Ford	13		25
	Merzario	Williams-Ford	3	brakes	21
	Brambilla	March-Ford	1	accident	13
	Depailler	Tyrrell-Ford	0	accident	3
	Reutemann	Brabham-Alfa	0	engine	10
	Peterson	March-Ford	0	accident	11

* Race restarted after Lauda crashed; the following did not take part in the restarted race:

	Lauda	Ferrari	1	accident	2
	Lunger	Surtees-Ford	1	accident	24
	Ertl	Hesketh-Ford	1	accident	22
	H-J Stuck	March-Ford	1	clutch	4
	Laffite	Ligier-Matra	1	gearbox	6
	Amon	Ensign-Ford	1	withdrew	17

Fastest Lap: Scheckter, 7m 10.8s. 118.57 mph/190.82 kph

Austrian Grand Prix: Österreichring, 15 August 1976

54 laps of 3.67 mile/5.91 km circuit

Place	Driver	Car	Laps	Time/reason for retiring	Grid
1	Watson	Penske-Ford	54	1h 30m 07.86s	2
2	Laffite	Ligier-Matra	54	1h 30m 18.65s	5
3	Nilsson	Lotus-Ford	54	1h 30m 19.84s	4
4	Hunt	McLaren-Ford	54	1h 30m 20.30s	1
5	Andretti	Ford	54	1h 30m 29.35s	9
6	Peterson	March-Ford	54	1h 30m 42.20s	3
7	Mass	McLaren-Ford	54	1h 31m 07.31s	12
8	Ertl	Hesketh-Ford	53		20

Austrian Grand Prix (cont)

Place	Driver	Car	Laps	Time/reason for retiring	Grid
9	Pescarolo	Surtees-Ford	52		22
10	Lunger	Surtees-Ford	51	accident	16
11	Pesenti-Rossi	Tyrrell-Ford	51		23
12	Lombardi	Brabham-Ford	50		24
	Binder	Ensign-Ford	47	throttle	19
	Kessel	Brabham-Ford	44		25
	Brambilla	March-Ford	43	accident	7
	E Fittipaldi	Fittipaldi-Ford	43	accident	17
	Jarier	Shadow-Ford	40	fuel pump	18
	Pace	Brabham-Alfa	40	accident	8
	Jones	Surtees-Ford	40	accident	15
	H-J Stuck	March-Ford	26	fuel pressure	11
	Depailler	Tyrrell-Ford	24	suspension	13
	Merzario	Williams-Ford	17	accident	21
	Pryce	Shadow-Ford	14	brakes	6
	J Scheckter	Tyrrell-Ford	14	accident	10
	Reutemann	Brabham-Alfa	0	clutch	14

Fastest Lap: Hunt, 1m 35.91s. 137.83 mph/221.813 kph

Dutch Grand Prix: Zandvoort, 29 August 1976

75 laps of 2.63 mile/4.23 km circuit

Place	Driver	Car	Laps	Time/reason for retiring	Grid
1	Hunt	McLaren-Ford	75	1h 44m 52.09s	2
2	Regazzoni	Ferrari	75	1h 44m 53.01s	5
3	Andretti	Lotus-Ford	75	1h 44m 54.18s	6
4	Pryce	Shadow-Ford	75	1h 44m 59.03s	3
5	J Scheckter	Tyrrell-Ford	75	1h 45m 14.55s	8
6	Brambilla	March-Ford	75	1h 45m 37.12s	7
7	Depailler	Tyrrell-Ford	75	1h 45m 48.37s	14
8	Jones	Surtees-Ford	74		16
9	Mass	McLaren-Ford	74		15
10	Jarier	Shadow-Ford	74		20
11	Pescarolo	Surtees-Ford	74		22
12	Stommelen	Hesketh-Ford	72		25
	Ickx	Ensign-Ford	66	electrical	11
	Hayje	Penske-Ford	63	drive-shaft	21
	Pace	Brabham-Alfa	53	oil leak	9
	Laffite	Ligier-Matra	53	engine	10
	Peterson	March-Ford	52	engine	1
	Ertl	Hesketh-Ford	49	spun	24
	Watson	Penske-Ford	47	gearbox	4
	Perkins	Boro-Ford	44	accident	19
	E Fittipaldi	Fittipaldi-Ford	40	electrical	17
	Reutemann	Brabham-Alfa	11	clutch	12

Dutch Grand Prix (cont)

Place	Driver	Car	Laps	Time/reason for retiring	Grid
	Nilsson	Lotus-Ford	10	accident	13
	Andersson	Surtees-Ford	9	engine	26
	H-J Stuck	March-Ford	9	engine	18
	Merzario	Williams-Ford	5	accident	23

Fastest Lap: Regazzoni, 1m 22.59s. 114.46 mph/184.2 kph

Italian Grand Prix: Monza, 12 September 1976

52 laps of 3.6 mile/5.8 km circuit

Place	Driver	Car	Laps	Time/reason for retiring	Grid
1	Peterson	March-Ford	52	1h 30m 35.6s	8
2	Regazzoni	Ferrari	52	1h 30m 37.9s	9
3	Laffite	Ligier-Matra	52	1h 30m 38.6s	1
4	Lauda	Ferrari	52	1h 30m 55.0s	5
5	J Scheckter	Tyrrell-Ford	52	1h 30m 55.1s	2
6	Depailler	Tyrrell-Ford	52	1h 31m 11.3s	4
7	Brambilla	March-Ford	52	1h 31m 19.5s	16
8	Pryce	Shadow-Ford	52	1h 31m 28.5s	15
9	Reutemann	Ferrari	52	1h 31m 33.1s	7
10	Ickx	Ensign-Ford	52	1h 31m 48.0s	10
11	Watson	Penske-Ford	52	1h 32m 17.8s	26
12	Jones	Surtees-Ford	51		18
13	Nilsson	Lotus-Ford	51		12
14	Lunger	Surtees-Ford	50		23
15	E Fittipaldi	Fittipaldi-Ford	50		20
16	Ertl	Hesketh-Ford	49	drive-shaft	19
17	Pescarolo	Surtees-Ford	49		22
18	Pesenti-Rossi	Tyrrell-Ford	49		21
19	Jarier	Shadow-Ford	47		17
	Stommelen	Brabham-Alfa	41	engine	11
	H-J Stuck	March-Ford	23	accident	6
	Andretti	Lotus-Ford	23	accident	14
	Hunt	McLaren-Ford	11	spun	24
	Perkins	Boro-Ford	8	engine	13
	Pace	Brabham-Alfa	4	engine	3
	Mass	McLaren-Ford	2	engine	25

Fastest Lap: Peterson, 1m 41.3s. 128.077 mph/206.120 kph

Canadian Grand Prix: Mosport, 3 October 1976

80 laps of 2.46 mile/3.96 km circuit

Place	Driver	Car	Laps	Time/reason for retiring	Grid
1	Hunt	McLaren-Ford	80	1h 40m 09.626s	1
2	Depailler	Tyrrell-Ford	80	1h 40m 15.957s	4
3	Andretti	Lotus-Ford	80	1h 40m 19.992s	5
4	J Scheckter	Tyrrell-Ford	80	1h 40m 29.371s	7
5	Mass	McLaren-Ford	80	1h 40m 51.437s	11
6	Regazzoni	Ferrari	80	1h 40m 55.882s	12
7	Pace	Brabham-Alfa	80	1h 40m 56.098s	10
8	Lauda	Ferrari	80	1h 41m 22.583s	6
9	Peterson	March-Ford	79		2
10	Watson	Penske-Ford	79		14
11	Pryce	Shadow-Ford	79		13
12	Nilsson	Lotus-Ford	79		15
13	Ickx	Ensign-Ford	79		16
14	Brambilla	March-Ford	79		3
15	Lunger	Surtees-Ford	78		22
16	Jones	Surtees-Ford	78		20
17	Perkins	Brabham-Alfa	78		19
18	Jarier	Shadow-Ford	77		18
19	Pescarolo	Surtees-Ford	77		21
20	Edwards	Hesketh-Ford	75		27
	Laffite	Ligier-Matra	43	engine	9
	E Fittipaldi	Fittipaldi-Ford	41	exhaust	17
	H-J Stuck	March-Ford	36	handling	8
	Merzario	Williams-Ford	11	spun	24

Fastest Lap: Depailler, 1m 13.817s. 119.924 mph/192.998 kph

United States Grand Prix: Watkins Glen, 10 October 1976

59 laps of 3.39 mile/5.44 km circuit

Place	Driver	Car	Laps	Time/reason for retiring	Grid
1	Hunt	McLaren-Ford	59	1h 42m 40.741s	1
2	J Scheckter	Tyrrell-Ford	59	1h 42m 48.771s	2
3	Lauda	Ferrari	59	1h 43m 43.065s	5
4	Mass	McLaren-Ford	59	1h 43m 43.199s	17
5	H-J Stuck	March-Ford	59	1h 43m 48.719s	6
6	Watson	Penske-Ford	59	1h 43m 48.931s	8
7	Regazzoni	Ferrari	58		14
8	Jones	Surtees-Ford	58		18
9	E Fittipaldi	Fittipaldi-Ford	57		15
10	Jarier	Shadow-Ford	57		16
11	Lunger	Surtees-Ford	57		24
12	Ribeiro	Hesketh-Ford	57		22
13	Ertl	Hesketh-Ford	54		21

United States Grand Prix (cont)

Place	Driver	Car	Laps	Time/reason for retiring	Grid
14	Warwick Brown	Williams-Ford	54		23
	Pescarolo	Surtees-Ford	48		26
	Pryce	Shadow-Ford	45	engine	9
	Laffite	Ligier-Matra	34	tyre	12
	Brambilla	March-Ford	34	tyre	4
	Pace	Brabham-Alfa	31	accident	10
	Perkins	Brabham-Alfa	30	suspension	13
	Andretti	Lotus-Ford	23	suspension	11
	Ickx	Ensign-Ford	14	accident	19
	Nilsson	Lotus-Ford	13	engine	20
	Peterson	March-Ford	12	suspension	3
	Merzario	Williams-Ford	9	spun	25
	Depailler	Tyrrell-Ford	7	fuel line	7

Fastest Lap: Hunt, 1m 42.851s, 118.202 mph/190.227 kph

Japanese Grand Prix: Fuji, 24 October 1976

73 laps of 2.71 mile/4.36 km circuit

Place	Driver	Car	Laps	Time/reason for retiring	Grid
1	Andretti	Lotus-Ford	73	1h 43m 58.86s	1
2	Depailler	Tyrrell-Ford	72	1h 43m 59.14s	13
3	Hunt	McLaren-Ford	72	1h 44m 00.06s	2
4	Jones	Surtees-Ford	72	1h 44m 12.07s	20
5	Regazzoni	Ferrari	72	1h 44m 18.76s	7
6	Nilsson	Lotus-Ford	72	1h 44m 18.92s	16
7	Laffite	Ligier-Matra	72		11
8	Ertl	Hesketh-Ford	72		22
9	Takahara	Surtees-Ford	70		24
10	Jarier	Shadow-Ford	69		15
11	Hasemi	Kojima-Ford	66		10
	J Scheckter	Tyrrell-Ford	58	overheating	5
	Binder	Williams-Ford	49	wheel bearing	25
	Pryce	Shadow-Ford	46	engine	14
	Brambilla	March-Ford	38	engine	8
	H-J Stuck	March-Ford	37	electrical	18
	Mass	McLaren-Ford	35	accident	12
	Watson	Penske-Ford	33	engine	4
	Hoshino	Tyrrell-Ford	27	tyres	21
	Merzario	Williams-Ford	23	gearbox	19
	E Fittipaldi	Fittipaldi-Ford	9	withdrew	23
	Pace	Brabham-Alfa	7	withdrew	6
	Lauda	Ferrari	2	withdrew	3
	Perkins	Brabham-Alfa	1	withdrew	17
	Peterson	March-Ford	0	engine	9

Fastest Lap: Hasemi, 1m 18.23s. 124.643 mph/200.593 kph

World Championship 1976

1	Hunt	69
2	Lauda	68
3	J Scheckter	49
4	Depailler	39
5	Regazzoni	31
6	Andretti	22
7 =	Laffite, Watson	20
9	Mass	19
10	Nilsson	11
11 =	Peterson, Pryce	10
13	Stuck	8
14 =	Jones, Pace	7
16 =	E Fittipaldi, Reutemann	3
18	Amon	2
19 =	Brambilla, Stommelen	1

Constructors' Championship

1	Ferrari	83
2	McLaren-Ford	74
3	Tyrrell-Ford	71
4	Lotus-Ford	29
5 =	Ligier-Matra, Penske-Ford	20
7	March-Ford	19
8	Shadow-Ford	10
9	Brabham-Alfa	9
10	Surtees-Ford	7
11	Fittipaldi-Ford	3
12	Ensign-Ford	2
13	Parnelli-Ford	1

1977

Lauda took his second championship, though Andretti won more races. Jody Scheckter's Wolf won first time out, Shadow took their only victory, and Gunnar Nilsson achieved the only win of a career tragically cut short by cancer. Renault entered grand prix racing with a turbocharged car which was initially not very successful. The German ATS team took over the Penske cars and the South African Grand Prix was the last race a BRM ever qualified to start.

Argentine Grand Prix: Buenos Aires, 9 January 1977

53 laps of 3.71 mile/5.97 km circuit

Place	Driver	Car	Laps	Time/reason for retiring	Grid
1	J Scheckter	Wolf-Ford	53	1h 40m 11.19s	10
2	Pace	Brabham-Alfa	53	1h 40m 54.43s	6
3	Reutemann	Ferrari	53	1h 40m 57.21s	7
4	E Fittipaldi	Fittipaldi-Ford	53	1h 41m 06.67s	15
5	Andretti	Lotus-Ford	51	wheel bearing	8
6	Regazzoni	Ensign-Ford	51		11
7	Brambilla	Surtees-Ford	48	fuel system	12
	I Scheckter	March-Ford	45	battery	16
	Pryce	Shadow-Ford	45		9
	Watson	Brabham-Alfa	41	handling	2
	Ribeiro	March-Ford	39	gear lever	19
	Laffite	Ligier-Matra	37		14
	Depailler	Tyrrell-Ford	32	overheating	3
	Hunt	McLaren-Ford	31	suspension	1
	Mass	McLaren-Ford	28	engine	5
	Peterson	Tyrrell-Ford	28	spun	13
	Hoffman	Fittipaldi-Ford	22	engine	18
	Lauda	Ferrari	20	fuel system	4
	Binder	Surtees-Ford	18	nose	17
	Zorzi	Shadow-Ford	2	gearbox	20

Fastest Lap: Hunt, 1m 51.06s. 120.209 mph/193.459 kph

Brazilian Grand Prix: Interlagos, 23 January 1977

40 laps of 4.95 mile/7.96 km circuit

Place	Driver	Car	Laps	Time/reason for retiring	Grid
1	Reutemann	Ferrari	40	1h 45m 07.72s	2
2	Hunt	McLaren-Ford	40	1h 45m 18.43s	1
3	Lauda	Ferrari	40	1h 46m 55.23s	13
4	E Fittipaldi	Fittipaldi-Ford	39		16
5	Nilsson	Lotus-Ford	39		10
6	Zorzi	Shadow-Ford	39		18
7	Hoffman	Fittipaldi-Ford	38		19
	Pryce	Shadow-Ford	33	engine	12
	Pace	Brabham-Alfa	33	accident	5
	Binder	Surtees-Ford	32	suspension	20
	Watson	Brabham-Alfa	30	accident	7
	Laffite	Ligier-Matra	26	accident	14
	Depailler	Tyrrell-Ford	23	accident	6
	Andretti	Lotus-Ford	19	electrical	3
	Ribeiro	March-Ford	16	engine	21
	Mass	McLaren-Ford	12	accident	4
	Regazzoni	Ensign-Ford	12	accident	9
	Peterson	Tyrrell-Ford	12	accident	8
	J Scheckter	Wolf-Ford	11	engine	15
	Brambilla	Surtees-Ford	11	accident	11
	I Scheckter	March-Ford	1	transmission	17
	Perkins	BRM	1	engine	22

Fastest Lap: Hunt, 2m 34.55s. 115.217 mph/185.425 kph

South African Grand Prix: Kyalami, 5 March 1977

78 laps of 2.55 mile/4.1 km circuit

Place	Driver	Car	Laps	Time/reason for retiring	Grid
1	Lauda	Ferrari	78	1h 42m 21.6s	3
2	J Scheckter	Wolf-Ford	78	1h 42m 26.8s	5
3	Depailler	Tyrrell-Ford	78	1h 42m 27.3s	4
4	Hunt	McLaren-Ford	78	1h 42m 31.1s	1
5	Mass	McLaren-Ford	78	1h 42m 41.5s	13
6	Watson	Brabham-Alfa	78	1h 42m 41.8s	11
7	Brambilla	Surtees-Ford	78	1h 42m 45.2s	14
8	Reutemann	Ferrari	78	1h 42m 48.3s	8
9	Regazzoni	Ensign-Ford	78	1h 43m 07.8s	16
10	E Fittipaldi	Fittipaldi-Ford	78	1h 43m 33.3s	9
11	Binder	Surtees-Ford	77		19
12	Nilsson	Lotus-Ford	77		10
13	Pace	Brabham-Alfa	76		2
14	Lunger	March-Ford	76		23
15	Perkins	BRM	73		22

South African Grand Prix (cont)

Place	Driver	Car	Laps	Time/reason for retiring	Grid
	Ribeiro	March-Ford	66	engine	17
	H-J Stuck	March-Ford	55	engine	18
	Andretti	Lotus-Ford	43	suspension	6
	Hayje	March-Ford	33	gearbox	21
	Pryce	Shadow-Ford	22	fatal accident	15
	Laffite	Ligier-Matra	22	accident	12
	Zorzi	Shadow-Ford	21	engine	20
	Peterson	Tyrrell-Ford	5	fuel pressure	7

Fastest Lap: Watson, 1m 17.63s. 118.253 mph/190.310 kph

United States Grand Prix West: Long Beach, 3 April 1977

80 laps of 2.02 mile/3.25 km circuit

Place	Driver	Car	Laps	Time/reason for retiring	Grid
1	Andretti	Lotus-Ford	80	1h 51m 35.470s	2
2	Lauda	Ferrari	80	1h 51m 36.243s	1
3	J Scheckter	Wolf-Ford	80	1h 51m 40.327s	3
4	Depailler	Tyrrell-Ford	80	1h 52m 49.957s	12
5	E Fittipaldi	Fittipaldi-Ford	80	1h 52m 56.378s	7
6	Jarier	Penske-Ford	79		9
7	Hunt	McLaren-Ford	79		8
8	Nilsson	Lotus-Ford	79		16
9	Laffite	Ligier-Matra	78	electrical	5
10	Henton	March-Ford	77		18
11	Binder	Surtees-Ford	77		19
	Peterson	Tyrrell-Ford	62	fuel line	10
	Regazzoni	Ensign-Ford	57	gearbox	13
	H-J Stuck	Brabham-Alfa	53	brakes	17
	Jones	Shadow-Ford	40	gearbox	14
	Mass	McLaren-Ford	39	vibration	15
	Watson	Brabham-Alfa	33	disqualified: push start	6
	Zorzi	Shadow-Ford	27	gearbox	20
	Ribeiro	March-Ford	15	gearbox	22
	Reutemann	Ferrari	5	accident	4
	Lunger	March-Ford	4	accident	21
	Brambilla	Surtees-Ford	0	accident	11

Fastest Lap: Lauda, 1m 22.753s. 87.876 mph/141.422 kph

Spanish Grand Prix: Jarama, 8 May 1977

75 laps of 2.12 mile/3.4 km circuit

Place	Driver	Car	Laps	Time/reason for retiring	Grid
1	Andretti	Lotus-Ford	75	1h 42m 52.22s	1
2	Reutemann	Ferrari	75	1h 43m 08.07s	3
3	J Scheckter	Wolf-Ford	75	1h 43m 16.73s	4
4	Mass	McLaren-Ford	75	1h 43m 17.09s	8
5	Nilsson	Lotus-Ford	75	1h 43m 58.05s	11
6	H-J Stuck	Brabham-Alfa	74		12
7	Laffite	Ligier-Matra	74		2
8	Peterson	Tyrrell-Ford	74		14
9	Binder	Surtees-Ford	73		19
10	Lunger	March-Ford	72		24
11	I Scheckter	March-Ford	72		16
12	Neve	March-Ford	71		21
13	Villota	McLaren-Ford	70		22
14	E Fittipaldi	Fittipaldi-Ford	70		18
	Watson	Brabham-Alfa	64	fuel system	5
	Jones	Shadow-Ford	56	accident	13
	Keegan	Hesketh-Ford	32	accident	15
	Ertl	Hesketh-Ford	29	radiator	17
	Zorzi	Shadow-Ford	25	engine	23
	Merzario	March-Ford	16	suspension	20
	Depailler	Tyrrell-Ford	12	engine	9
	Hunt	McLaren-Ford	10	engine	6
	Regazzoni	Ensign-Ford	9	accident	7
	Brambilla	Surtees-Ford	9	accident	10

Fastest Lap: Laffite, 1m 20.81s. 94.236 mph/151.659 kph

Monaco Grand Prix: Monte Carlo, 22 May 1977

76 laps of 2.06 mile/3.31 km circuit

Place	Driver	Car	Laps	Time/reason for retiring	Grid
1	J Scheckter	Wolf-Ford	76	1h 57m 52.77s	2
2	Lauda	Ferrari	76	1h 57m 53.66s	6
3	Reutemann	Ferrari	76	1h 58m 25.57s	3
4	Mass	McLaren-Ford	76	1h 58m 27.37s	9
5	Andretti	Lotus-Ford	76	1h 58m 28.32s	10
6	Jones	Shadow-Ford	76	1h 58m 29.38s	11
7	Laffite	Ligier-Matra	76	1h 58m 57.21s	16
8	Brambilla	Surtees-Ford	76	1h 59m 01.41s	14
9	Patrese	Shadow-Ford	75		15
10	Ickx	Ensign-Ford	75		17
11	Jarier	Penske-Ford	74		12
12	Keegan	Hesketh-Ford	73		20
	Nilsson	Lotus-Ford	51	gearbox	13

Monaco Grand Prix (cont)

Place	Driver	Car	Laps	Time/reason for retiring	Grid
	Watson	Brabham-Alfa	48	gearbox	1
	Depailler	Tyrrell-Ford	46	gearbox	8
	Binder	Surtees-Ford	41	fuel injection	19
	E Fittipaldi	Fittipaldi-Ford	37	engine	18
	Hunt	McLaren-Ford	25	engine	7
	H-J Stuck	Brabham-Alfa	19	fire	5
	Peterson	Tyrrell-Ford	10	brakes	4

Fastest Lap: Scheckter, 1m 31.07s. 81.352 mph/130.923 kph

Belgian Grand Prix: Zolder, 5 June 1977

70 laps of 2.65 mile/4.26 km circuit

Place	Driver	Car	Laps	Time/reason for retiring	Grid
1	Nilsson	Lotus-Ford	70	1h 55m 05.71s	3
2	Lauda	Ferrari	70	1h 55m 19.90s	11
3	Peterson	Tyrrell-Ford	70	1h 55m 25.66s	8
4	Brambilla	Surtees-Ford	70	1h 55m 30.69s	12
5	Jones	Shadow-Ford	70	1h 56m 21.18s	17
6	H-J Stuck	Brabham-Alfa	69		18
7	Hunt	McLaren-Ford	69		9
8	Depailler	Tyrrell-Ford	69		5
9	Ertl	Hesketh-Ford	69		24
10	Neve	March-Ford	68		23
11	Jarier	Penske-Ford	68		25
12	Perkins	Surtees-Ford	67		22
13	Purley	Lec-Ford	67		22
14	Merzario	March-Ford	65		14
15	Hayje	March-Ford	63		26
	J Scheckter	Wolf-Ford	62	engine	4
	Mass	McLaren-Ford	39	accident	6
	Laffite	Ligier-Matra	32	engine	10
	Regazzoni	Ensign-Ford	29	engine	13
	Keegan	Hesketh-Ford	14	accident	19
	Reutemann	Ferrari	14	accident	17
	Patrese	Shadow-Ford	12	accident	15
	I Scheckter	March-Ford	8	accident	21
	E Fittipaldi	Fittipaldi-Ford	2	electrical	16
	Andretti	Lotus-Ford	0	accident	2
	Watson	Brabham-Alfa	0	accident	1

Fastest Lap: Nilsson, 1m 27.36s. 109.132 mph/175.632 kph

Swedish Grand Prix: Anderstorp, 19 June 1977

72 laps of 2.5 mile/4.02 km circuit

Place	Driver	Car	Laps	Time/reason for retiring	Grid
1	Laffite	Ligier-Matra	72	1h 46m 55.520s	8
2	Mass	McLaren-Ford	72	1h 47m 03.969s	9
3	Reutemann	Ferrari	72	1h 47m 09.889s	12
4	Depailler	Tyrrell-Ford	72	1h 47m 11.828s	6
5	Watson	Brabham-Alfa	72	1h 47m 14.255s	2
6	Andretti	Lotus-Ford	72	1h 47m 20.797s	1
7	Regazzoni	Ensign-Ford	72	1h 47m 26.786s	14
8	Jarier	Penske-Ford	72	1h 48m 00.087s	17
9	Oliver	Shadow-Ford	72	1h 48m 17.999s	16
10	H-J Stuck	Brabham-Alfa	71		5
11	Lunger	McLaren-Ford	71		22
12	Hunt	McLaren-Ford	71		3
13	Keegan	Hesketh-Ford	71		24
14	Purley	Lec-Ford	70		19
15	Neve	March-Ford	69		20
16	Ertl	Hesketh-Ford	68		23
17	Jones	Shadow-Ford	67		11
18	E Fittipaldi	Fittipaldi-Ford	66		18
19	Nilsson	Lotus-Ford	64	wheel bearing	7
	I Scheckter	March-Ford	61	drive-shaft	21
	Brambilla	Surtees-Ford	52	fuel pressure	13
	Lauda	Ferrari	47	handling	15
	J Scheckter	Wolf-Ford	29	accident	4
	Peterson	Tyrrell-Ford	7	ignition	10

Fastest Lap: Andretti, 1m 27.607s. 102.594 mph/165.110 kph

French Grand Prix: Dijon, 3 July 1977

80 laps of 2.36 mile/3.8 km circuit

Place	Driver	Car	Laps	Time/reason for retiring	Grid
1	Andretti	Lotus-Ford	80	1h 39m 40.13s	1
2	Watson	Brabham-Alfa	80	1h 39m 41.68s	4
3	Hunt	McLaren-Ford	80	1h 40m 14.00s	2
4	Nilsson	Lotus-Ford	80	1h 40m 51.21s	3
5	Lauda	Ferrari	80	1h 40m 54.58s	9
6	Reutemann	Ferrari	79		6
7	Regazzoni	Ensign-Ford	79		15
8	Laffite	Ligier-Matra	78		5
9	Mass	McLaren-Ford	78		7
10	Keegan	Hesketh-Ford	78		14
11	E Fittipaldi	Fittipaldi-Ford	77		22
12	Peterson	Tyrrell-Ford	77		17
13	Brambilla	Surtees-Ford	77		11

French Grand Prix (cont)

Place	Driver	Car	Laps	Time/reason for retiring	Grid
	I Scheckter	March-Ford	69		20
	J Scheckter	Wolf-Ford	66	accident	8
	H-J Stuck	Brabham-Alfa	64	accident	13
	Jones	Shadow-Ford	60	drive-shaft	10
	Merzario	March-Ford	27	gearbox	18
	Depailler	Tyrell-Ford	21	accident	12
	Patrese	Shadow-Ford	6	engine	15
	Purley	Lec-Ford	5	accident	21
	Jarier	Penske-Ford	4	accident	19

Fastest Lap: Andretti, 1m 13.75s. 115.259 mph/185.492 kph

British Grand Prix: Silverstone, 16 July 1977

68 laps of 2.93 mile/4.72 km circuit

Place	Driver	Car	Laps	Time/reason for retiring	Grid
1	Hunt	McLaren-Ford	68	1h 31m 46.06s	1
2	Lauda	Ferrari	68	1h 32m 04.37s	3
3	Nilsson	Lotus-Ford	68	1h 32m 05.63s	5
4	Mass	McLaren-Ford	68	1h 32m 33.82s	4
5	H-J Stuck	Brabham-Alfa	68	1h 32m 57.79s	7
6	Laffite	Ligier-Matra	67		15
7	Jones	Shadow-Ford	67		12
8	Brambilla	Surtees-Ford	67		8
8	Jarier	Penske-Ford	67		20
10	Neve	March-Ford	66		26
11	G Villeneuve	McLaren-Ford	66		9
12	Schuppan	Surtees-Ford	66		23
13	Lunger	McLaren-Ford	64		19
14	Andretti	Lotus-Ford	62	engine	6
15	Reutemann	Ferrari	62		14
	Watson	Brabham-Alfa	60	engine	2
	J Scheckter	Wolf-Ford	59	engine	4
	E Fittipaldi	Fittipaldi-Ford	42	engine	22
	Merzario	March-Ford	28	drive-shaft	17
	Patrese	Shadow-Ford	20	fuel pressure	25
	Depailler	Tyrrell-Ford	16	accident	18
	Jabouille	Renault	16	turbocharger	21
	I Scheckter	March-Ford	6	accident	24
	Tambay	Ensign-Ford	3	electrical	16
	Peterson	Tyrrell-Ford	3	engine	10
	Keegan	Hesketh-Ford	0	accident	13

Fastest Lap: Hunt, 1m 19.60s. 132.603 mph/213.403 kph

German Grand Prix: Hockenheim, 31 July 1977

47 laps of 4.22 mile/6.79 km circuit

Place	Driver	Car	Laps	Time/reason for retiring	Grid
1	Lauda	Ferrari	47	1h 31m 48.62s	3
2	J Scheckter	Wolf-Ford	47	1h 32m 02.95s	1
3	H-J Stuck	Brabham-Alfa	47	1h 32m 09.52s	5
4	Reutemann	Ferrari	47	1h 32m 48.89s	8
5	Brambilla	Surtees-Ford	47	1h 33m 15.99s	10
6	Tambay	Ensign-Ford	47	1h 33m 18.43s	11
7	Schuppan	Surtees-Ford	46		19
8	Ribeiro	March-Ford	46		20
9	Peterson	Tyrrell-Ford	42	engine	14
10	Patrese	Shadow-Ford	42	lost wheel	16
	Keegan	Hesketh-Ford	40	accident	23
	Andretti	Lotus-Ford	34	engine	7
	Hunt	McLaren-Ford	32	fuel pump	4
	Nilsson	Lotus-Ford	31	engine	9
	Mass	McLaren-Ford	26	gearbox	13
	Depailler	Tyrrell-Ford	22	engine	15
	Laffite	Ligier-Matra	21	engine	6
	Rebaque	Hesketh-Ford	20	battery	24
	Lunger	McLaren-Ford	14	accident	21
	I Scheckter	March-Ford	9	clutch	18
	Watson	Brabham-Alfa	8	engine	2
	Jarier	Penske-Ford	5	accident	12
	Jones	Shadow-Ford	0	accident	17
	Regazzoni	Ensign-Ford	0	accident	22

Fastest Lap: Lauda, 1m 55.99s. 130.930 mph/210.711 kph

Austrian Grand Prix: Österreichring, 14 August 1977

54 laps of 3.69 mile/5.94 km circuit

Place	Driver	Car	Laps	Time/reason for retiring	Grid
1	Jones	Shadow-Ford	54	1h 37m 16.49s	14
2	Lauda	Ferrari	54	1h 37m 36.62s	1
3	H-J Stuck	Brabham-Alfa	54	1h 37m 50.99s	4
4	Reutemann	Ferrari	54	1h 37m 51.24s	5
5	Peterson	Tyrrell-Ford	54	1h 38m 18.58s	15
6	Mass	McLaren-Ford	53		9
7	Keegan	Hesketh-Ford	53		20
8	Watson	Brabham-Alfa	53		12
9	Neve	March-Ford	53		22
10	Lunger	McLaren-Ford	53		17
11	E Fittipaldi	Fittipaldi-Ford	53		23
12	Binder	Penske-Ford	53		19
13	Depailler	Tyrrell-Ford	53		10

Austrian Grand Prix (cont)

Place	Driver	Car	Laps	Time/reason for retiring	Grid
14	Jarier	Penske-Ford	52		18
15	Brambilla	Surtees-Ford	52		13
16	Schuppan	Surtees-Ford	52		25
17	Villota	McLaren-Ford	50	accident	26
	J Scheckter	Wolf-Ford	45	spun	8
	Hunt	McLaren-Ford	43	engine	2
	Tambay	Ensign-Ford	41	engine	7
	Nilsson	Lotus-Ford	38	engine	16
	Merzario	Shadow-Ford	29	gear-change	21
	Laffite	Ligier-Matra	21	oil leak	6
	Andretti	Lotus-Ford	11	engine	3
	I Scheckter	March-Ford	2	accident	24
	Regazzoni	Ensign-Ford	0	accident	11

Fastest Lap: Watson, 1m 40.96s. 131.663 mph/211.892 kph

Dutch Grand Prix: Zandvoort, 28 August 1977

75 laps of 2.63 mile/4.23 km circuit

Place	Driver	Car	Laps	Time/reason for retiring	Grid
1	Lauda	Ferrari	75	1h 41m 45.93s	4
2	Laffite	Ligier-Matra	75	1h 41m 47.82s	2
3	J Scheckter	Wolf-Ford	74		15
4	E Fittipaldi	Fittipaldi-Ford	74		17
5	Tambay	Ensign-Ford	73	out of fuel	12
6	Reutemann	Ferrari	73		6
7	H-J Stuck	Brabham-Alfa	73		19
8	Binder	Penske-Ford	73		18
9	Lunger	McLaren-Ford	73		20
10	I Scheckter	March-Ford	73		25
11	Ribeiro	March-Ford	72		24
12	Brambilla	Surtees-Ford	67	accident	22
13	Patrese	Shadow-Ford	67		16
	Henton	Ensign-Ford	52	disqualified: push start	23
	Jabouille	Renault	39	suspension	10
	Nilsson	Lotus-Ford	34	accident	5
	Jones	Shadow-Ford	32	engine	13
	Depailler	Tyrrell-Ford	31	engine	11
	Peterson	Tyrrell-Ford	18	ignition	7
	Regazzoni	Ensign-Ford	17	throttle	9
	Andretti	Lotus-Ford	14	engine	1
	Keegan	Hesketh-Ford	8	accident	26
	Hunt	McLaren-Ford	5	accident	3
	Jarier	Penske-Ford	4	engine	21
	Watson	Brabham-Alfa	2	engine	8
	Mass	McLaren-Ford	0	accident	14

Fastest Lap: Lauda, 1m 19.99s. 118.181 mph/190.194 kph

Italian Grand Prix: Monza, 11 September 1977

52 laps of 3.6 mile/5.8 km circuit

Place	Driver	Car	Laps	Time/reason for retiring	Grid
1	Andretti	Lotus-Ford	52	1h 27m 50.30s	4
2	Lauda	Ferrari	52	1h 28m 07.26s	5
3	Jones	Shadow-Ford	52	1h 28m 13.93s	16
4	Mass	McLaren-Ford	52	1h 28m 18.78s	9
5	Regazzoni	Ensign-Ford	52	1h 28m 21.41s	7
6	Peterson	Tyrrell-Ford	52	1h 29m 09.52s	12
7	Neve	March-Ford	50		24
8	Laffite	Ligier-Matra	50		8
9	Keegan	Hesketh-Ford	48		23
	I Scheckter	March-Ford	41	transmission	17
	Reutemann	Ferrari	39	accident	2
	Giacomelli	McLaren-Ford	38	engine	15
	Patrese	Shadow-Ford	38	accident	6
	H-J Stuck	Brabham-Alfa	31	engine	11
	Hunt	McLaren-Ford	26	spun	1
	Depailler	Tyrrell-Ford	24	engine	13
	J Scheckter	Wolf-Ford	23	engine	3
	Jabouille	Renault	23	engine	20
	Jarier	Penske-Ford	19	engine	18
	Brambilla	Surtees-Ford	5	radiator	10
	Tambay	Ensign-Ford	9	engine	21
	Lunger	McLaren-Ford	4	engine	22
	Nilsson	Lotus-Ford	4	suspension	19
	Watson	Brabham-Alfa	3	accident	14

Fastest Lap: Andretti, 1m 39.1s. 130.920 mph/210.696 kph

United States Grand Prix: Watkins Glen, 2 October 1977

59 laps of 3.38 mile/5.44 km circuit

Place	Driver	Car	Laps	Time/reason for retiring	Grid
1	Hunt	McLaren-Ford	59	1h 58m 23.267s	1
2	Andretti	Lotus-Ford	59	1h 58m 25.293s	4
3	J Scheckter	Wolf-Ford	59	1h 59m 42.146s	9
4	Lauda	Ferrari	59	2h 00m 03.882s	7
5	Regazzoni	Ensign-Ford	59	2h 00m 11.405s	19
6	Reutemann	Ferrari	58		6
7	Laffite	Ligier-Matra	58		10
8	Keegan	Hesketh-Ford	58		20
9	Jarier	Shadow-Ford	58		16
10	Lunger	McLaren-Ford	57		17
11	Binder	Surtees-Ford	57		25
12	Watson	Brabham-Alfa	57		3
13	E Fittipaldi	Fittipaldi-Ford	57		18

United States Grand Prix (cont)

Place	Driver	Car	Laps	Time/reason for retiring	Grid
14	Depailler	Tyrrell-Ford	56		8
15	Ribeiro	March-Ford	56		23
16	Peterson	Tyrrell-Ford	56		5
17	Ashley	Hesketh-Ford	55		22
18	Neve	March-Ford	55		24
19	Brambilla	Surtees-Ford	54		11
	Jabouille	Renault	30	alternator	14
	Nilsson	Lotus-Ford	17	accident	12
	H-J Stuck	Brabham-Alfa	14	accident	2
	I Scheckter	March-Ford	10	accident	21
	Mass	McLaren-Ford	8	fuel pump	15
	Ongais	Penske-Ford	6	accident	26
	Jones	Shadow-Ford	3	accident	13

Fastest Lap: Peterson, 1m 51.854s. 108.688 mph/174.916 kph

Canadian Grand Prix: Mosport, 9 October 1977

80 laps of 2.5 mile/3.96 km circuit

Place	Driver	Car	Laps	Time/reason for retiring	Grid
1	J Scheckter	Wolf-Ford	80	1h 40m 00.00s	9
2	Depailler	Tyrrell-Ford	80	1h 40m 06.77s	6
3	Mass	McLaren-Ford	80	1h 40m 15.76s	5
4	Jones	Shadow-Ford	80	1h 40m 46.69s	7
5	Tambay	Ensign-Ford	80	1h 41m 03.26s	16
6	Brambilla	Surtees-Ford	78	accident	15
7	Ongais	Penske-Ford	78		22
8	Ribeiro	March-Ford	78		23
9	Andretti	Lotus-Ford	77	engine	1
10	Patrese	Shadow-Ford	76	accident	8
11	Lunger	McLaren-Ford	76	engine	20
12	G Villeneuve	Ferrari	76	drive-shaft	17
	Hunt	McLaren-Ford	61	accident	2
	Neve	March-Ford	56	engine	21
	Peterson	Tyrrell-Ford	34	fuel leak	3
	Keegan	Hesketh-Ford	32	accident	25
	Binder	Surtees-Ford	31	accident	24
	E Fittipaldi	Fittipaldi-Ford	29	engine	19
	I Scheckter	March-Ford	29	engine	18
	Reutemann	Ferrari	20	fuel pressure	12
	H-J Stuck	Brabham-Alfa	19	engine	13
	Nilsson	Lotus-Ford	17	accident	4
	Laffite	Ligier-Matra	12	drive-shaft	11
	Watson	Brabham-Alfa	1	accident	10
	Regazzoni	Ensign-Ford	0	accident	14

Fastest Lap: Andretti, 1m 13.299s. 130.771 mph/194.362kph

Japanese Grand Prix: Fuji, 23 October 1977

73 laps of 2.71 mile/4.36 km circuit

Place	Driver	Car	Laps	Time/reason for retiring	Grid
1	Hunt	McLaren-Ford	73	1h 31m 51.68s	2
2	Reutemann	Ferrari	73	1h 32m 54.13s	7
3	Depailler	Tyrrell-Ford	73	1h 32m 58.07s	15
4	Jones	Shadow-Ford	73	1h 32m 58.29s	12
5	Laffite	Ligier-Matra	72	out of fuel	5
6	Patrese	Shadow-Ford	72		13
7	H-J Stuck	Brabham-Alfa	72		4
8	Brambilla	Surtees-Ford	71		9
9	Takahashi	Tyrrell-Ford	71		22
10	J Scheckter	Wolf-Ford	71		6
11	Hosino	Kojima-Ford	71		11
12	Ribeiro	March-Ford	69		23
	Nilsson	Lotus-Ford	63	gearbox	14
	Regazzoni	Ensign-Ford	43	engine	10
	Watson	Brabham-Alfa	29	gearbox	3
	Mass	McLaren-Ford	28	engine	8
	Tambay	Ensign-Ford	14	engine	16
	Peterson	Tyrrell-Ford	5	accident	18
	G Villeneuve	Ferrari	5	accident	20
	Jarier	Ligier-Matra	3	engine	17
	Binder	Surtees-Ford	1	accident	21
	Takahara	Kojima-Ford	1	accident	19
	Andretti	Lotus-Ford	1	accident	1

Fastest Lap: Scheckter, 1m 14.3s. 131.235 mph/211.203 kph

World Championship 1977

1	Lauda	72
2	J Scheckter	55
3	Andretti	47
4	Reutemann	42
5	Hunt	40
6	Mass	25
7	Jones	22
8 =	Depailler, Nilsson	20
10	Laffite	18
11	Stuck	12
12	E Fittipaldi	11
13	Watson	9
14	Peterson	7
15	Brambilla, Pace	6
17 =	Regazzoni, Tambay	5
19 =	Jarier, Patrese, Zorzi	1

Constructors' Championship

1	Ferrari	95 (97]
2	Lotus-Ford	62
3	McLaren-Ford	60
4	Wolf-Ford	55
5 =	Brabham-Alfa, Tyrrell-Ford	27
7	Shadow-Ford	23
8	Ligier-Matra	18
9	Fittipaldi-Ford	11
10	Ensign-Ford	10
11	Surtees-Ford	6
12	Penske-Ford	1

1978

Mario Andretti took the championship comfortably from his team mate
Peterson, who died after a crash at Monza. Lauda won in Sweden with a car
equipped with a large rear-mounted fan which increased road holding; the
win stood but the car was banned from further races on 'safety' grounds.
Surtees withdrew at the end of the season.

Argentine Grand Prix: Buenos Aires, 15 January 1978

52 laps of 3.71 mile/5.97 km circuit

Place	Driver	Car	Laps	Time/reason for retiring	Grid
1	Andretti	Lotus-Ford	52	1h 37m 04.47s	1
2	Lauda	Brabham-Alfa	52	1h 37m 17.68s	5
3	Depailler	Tyrrell-Ford	52	1h 37m 18.11s	10
4	Hunt	McLaren-Ford	52	1h 37m 20.52s	6
5	Peterson	Lotus-Ford	52	1h 38m 19.32s	3
6	Tambay	McLaren-Ford	52	1h 38m 24.37s	9
7	Reutemann	Ferrari	52	1h 38m 27.07s	2
8	G Villeneuve	Ferrari	52	1h 38m 43.35s	7
9	E Fittipaldi	Fittipaldi-Ford	52	1h 38m 45.07s	17
10	J Scheckter	Wolf-Ford	52	1h 38m 47.97s	15
11	Mass	ATS-Ford	52	1h 38m 53.54s	13
12	Jarier	ATS-Ford	51		11
13	Lunger	McLaren-Ford	51		24
14	Pironi	Tyrrell-Ford	51		23
15	Regazzoni	Shadow-Ford	51		16
16	Laffite	Ligier-Matra	50	engine	8
17	H-J Stuck	Shadow-Ford	50		18
18	Brambilla	Surtees-Ford	50		12
	Watson	Brabham-Alfa	41	engine	4
	Jones	Williams-Ford	36	fuel	14
	Ongais	Ensign-Ford	35	rotor arm	21
	Leoni	Ensign-Ford	28	engine	22
	Merzario	Merzario-Ford	9	differential	20
	Keegan	Surtees-Ford	4	overheating	19

Fastest Lap: Hunt, 1m 50.58s. 120.731 mph/194.298 kph

Brazilian Grand Prix: Rio de Janeiro, 29 January 1978

63 laps of 3.13 mile/5.03 km circuit

Place	Driver	Car	Laps	Time/reason for retiring	Grid
1	Reutemann	Ferrari	63	1h 49m 59.86s	4
2	E Fittipaldi	Fittipaldi-Ford	63	1h 50m 48.99s	7
3	Lauda	Brabham-Alfa	63	1h 50m 56.88s	10
4	Andretti	Lotus-Ford	63	1h 51m 32.98s	3
5	Regazzoni	Shadow-Ford	62		15
6	Pironi	Tyrrell-Ford	62		17
7	Mass	ATS-Ford	62		18
8	Watson	Brabham-Alfa	61		19
9	Laffite	Ligier-Matra	61		14
10	Patrese	Arrows-Ford	59		16
11	Jones	Williams-Ford	58		8
	Rebaque	Lotus-Ford	40	driver	20
	G Villeneuve	Ferrari	35	accident	6
	Tambay	McLaren-Ford	34	accident	5
	H-J Stuck	Shadow-Ford	25	fuel pump	9
	Hunt	McLaren-Ford	25	accident	2
	J Scheckter	Wolf-Ford	16	suspension	12
	Peterson	Lotus-Ford	15	suspension	1
	Ongais	Ensign-Ford	13	brakes	21
	Lunger	McLaren-Ford	11	overheating	13
	Depailler	Tyrrell-Ford	8	accident	11
	Keegan	Surtees-Ford	5	accident	22

Fastest Lap: Reutemann, 1m 43.07s. 109.188 mph/175.721 kph

South African Grand Prix: Kyalami, 4 March 1978

78 laps of 2.55 mile/4.1 km circuit

Place	Driver	Car	Laps	Time/reason for retiring	Grid
1	Peterson	Lotus-Ford	78	1h 42m 15.767s	12
2	Depailler	Tyrrell-Ford	78	1h 42m 16.233s	11
3	Watson	Brabham-Alfa	78	1h 42m 20.209s	10
4	Jones	Williams-Ford	78	1h 42m 54.753s	18
5	Laffite	Ligier-Matra	78	1h 43m 24.985s	13
6	Pironi	Tyrrell-Ford	77		14
7	Andretti	Lotus-Ford	77		2
8	Jarier	ATS-Ford	77		17
9	Stommelen	Arrows-Ford	77		22
10	Rebaque	Lotus-Ford	77		21
11	Lunger	McLaren-Ford	76		20
12	Brambilla	Surtees-Ford	76		19
	Patrese	Arrows-Ford	63	engine	7
	J Scheckter	Wolf-Ford	59	accident	5
	Tambay	McLaren-Ford	56	accident	4

South African Grand Prix (cont)

Place	Driver	Car	Laps	Time/reason for retiring	Grid
	Reutemann	Ferrari	55	accident	9
	G Villeneuve	Ferrari	55	oil leak	8
	Keegan	Surtees-Ford	52	engine	23
	Lauda	Brabham-Alfa	52	engine	1
	Mass	ATS-Ford	43	engine	15
	Merzario	Merzario-Ford	39	suspension	26
	Jabouille	Renault	38	engine	6
	Rosberg	Theodore-Ford	14	clutch	24
	E Fittipaldi	Fittipaldi-Ford	8	transmission	16
	Cheever	Hesketh-Ford	8	engine	25
	Hunt	McLaren-Ford	5	engine	3

Fastest Lap: Andretti, 1m 17.09s. 119.082 mph/191.650 kph

United States Grand Prix West: Long Beach, 2 April 1978

80.5 laps of 2.02 mile/3.25 km circuit

Place	Driver	Car	Laps	Time/reason for retiring	Grid
1	Reutemann	Ferrari	80	1h 52m 01.301s	1
2	Andretti	Lotus-Ford	80	1h 52m 12.362s	4
3	Depailler	Tyrrell-Ford	80	1h 52m 30.252s	12
4	Peterson	Lotus-Ford	80	1h 52m 46.904s	6
5	Laffite	Ligier-Matra	80	1h 53m 24.185s	14
6	Patrese	Arrows-Ford	79		9
7	Jones	Williams-Ford	79		8
8	E Fittipaldi	Fittipaldi-Ford	79		15
9	Stommelen	Arrows-Ford	79		18
10	Regazzoni	Shadow-Ford	79		20
11	Jarier	ATS-Ford	75		19
12	Tambay	McLaren-Ford	74	accident	11
	J Scheckter	Wolf-Ford	59	accident	10
	Brambilla	Surtees-Ford	50	crownwheel and pinion	17
	Jabouille	Renault	43	turbocharger	13
	G Villeneuve	Ferrari	38	accident	2
	Lauda	Brabham-Alfa	27	ignition	3
	Pironi	Tyrrell-Ford	25	gearbox	22
	Merzario	Merzario-Ford	17	gearbox	21
	Mass	ATS-Ford	11	brakes	16
	Watson	Brabham-Alfa	9	oil tank	5
	Hunt	McLaren-Ford	5	accident	7

Fastest Lap: Jones, 1m 22.215s. 88.415 mph/142.348 kph
* Start and finish lines in different places. All finishers completed 0.5 of a lap extra.

1978

Monaco Grand Prix: Monte Carlo, 7 May 1978

75 laps of 2.06 mile/3.31 km circuit

Place	Driver	Car	Laps	Time/reason for retiring	Grid
1	Depailler	Tyrrell-Ford	75	1h 55m 14.66s	5
2	Lauda	Brabham-Alfa	75	1h 55m 37.11s	3
3	J Scheckter	Wolf-Ford	75	1h 55m 46.95s	9
4	Watson	Brabham-Alfa	75	1h 55m 48.19s	2
5	Pironi	Tyrrell-Ford	75	1h 56m 27.72s	13
6	Patrese	Arrows-Ford	75	1h 56m 23.42s	14
7	Tambay	McLaren-Ford	74		11
8	Reutemann	Ferrari	74		1
9	E Fittipaldi	Fittipaldi-Ford	74		20
10	Jabouille	Renault	71		12
11	Andretti	Lotus-Ford	69		4
	G Villeneuve	Ferrari	62	accident	8
	Peterson	Lotus-Ford	56	gearbox	7
	Hunt	McLaren-Ford	43	anti-roll bar	6
	Stommelen	Arrows-Ford	38	driver	19
	Jones	Williams-Ford	29	oil leak	10
	Ickx	Ensign-Ford	27	brakes	16
	H-J Stuck	Shadow-Ford	24	steering	17
	Laffite	Ligier-Matra	13	gearbox	15
	Keegan	Surtees-Ford	8	crownwheel and pinion	18

Fastest Lap: Lauda, 1m 28.65s. 83.573 mph/134.497 kph

Belgian Grand Prix: Zolder, 21 May 1978

70 laps of 2.65 mile/4.26 km circuit

Place	Driver	Car	Laps	Time/reason for retiring	Grid
1	Andretti	Lotus-Ford	70	1h 39m 52.02s	1
2	Peterson	Lotus-Ford	70	1h 40m 01.92s	7
3	Reutemann	Ferrari	70	1h 40m 16.36s	2
4	G Villeneuve	Ferrari	70	1h 40m 39.06s	4
5	Laffite	Ligier-Matra	69	accident	14
6	Pironi	Tyrrell-Ford	69		23
7	Lunger	McLaren-Ford	69		24
8	Giacomelli	McLaren-Ford	69		21
9	Arnoux	Martini-Ford	68		19
10	Jones	Williams-Ford	68		11
11	Mass	ATS-Ford	68		16
12	Ickx	Ensign-Ford	64		22
13	Brambilla	Surtees-Ford	63	engine	12
	H-J Stuck	Shadow-Ford	56	spun	20
	Jabouille	Renault	56	running	10
	J Scheckter	Wolf-Ford	53	accident	5
	Depailler	Tyrrell-Ford	51	gearbox	13

Belgian Grand Prix (cont)

Place	Driver	Car	Laps	Time/reason for retiring	Grid
	Regazzoni	Shadow-Ford	40	differential	18
	Patrese	Arrows-Ford	31	suspension	8
	Stommelen	Arrows-Ford	26	accident	17
	Watson	Brabham-Alfa	18	accident	9
	E Fittipaldi	Fittipaldi-Ford	0	accident	15
	Hunt	McLaren-Ford	0	accident	6
	Lauda	Brabham-Alfa	0	accident	3

Fastest Lap: Peterson, 1m 23.13s. 144.685 mph/184.569 kph

Spanish Grand Prix: Jarama, 4 June 1978

75 laps of 2.12 mile/3.4 km circuit

Place	Driver	Car	Laps	Time/reason for retiring	Grid
1	Andretti	Lotus-Ford	75	1h 41m 47.06s	1
2	Peterson	Lotus-Ford	75	1h 42m 06.62s	2
3	Laffite	Ligier-Matre	75	1h 42m 24.30s	10
4	J Scheckter	Wolf-Ford	75	1h 42m 47.12s	9
5	Watson	Brabham-Alfa	75	1h 42m 52.98s	7
6	Hunt	McLaren-Ford	74		4
7	Brambilla	Surtees-Ford	74		16
8	Jones	Williams-Ford	74		18
9	Mass	ATS-Ford	74		17
10	G Villeneuve	Ferrari	74		5
11	Keegan	Surtees-Ford	73		23
12	Pironi	Tyrrell-Ford	71		13
13	Jabouille	Renault	71		11
14	Stommelen	Arrows-Ford	71		19
15	Regazzoni	Shadow-Ford	67	fuel system	22
	Ickx	Ensign-Ford	64	engine	21
	E Fittipaldi	Fittipaldi-Ford	62	throttle	15
	Reutemann	Ferrari	57	accident	3
	Lauda	Brabham-Alfa	56	engine	6
	Depailler	Tyrrell-Ford	51	engine	12
	H-J Stuck	Shadow-Ford	45	suspension	24
	Rebaque	Lotus-Ford	21	exhaust	20
	Patrese	Arrows-Ford	21	engine	8
	Tambay	McLaren-Ford	16	spun	14

Fastest Lap: Andretti, 1m 20.06s. 95.119 mph/153.080 kph

Swedish Grand Prix: Anderstorp, 17 June 1978

70 laps of 2.51 mile/4.03 km circuit

Place	Driver	Car	Laps	Time/reason for retiring	Grid
1	Lauda	Brabham-Alfa	70	1h 41m 00.606s	3
2	Patrese	Arrows-Ford	70	1h 41m 34.625s	5
3	Peterson	Lotus-Ford	70	1h 41m 34.711s	4
4	Tambay	McLaren-Ford	69		15
5	Regazzoni	Shadow-Ford	69		16
6	E Fittipaldi	Fittipaldi-Ford	69		13
7	Laffite	Ligier-Matra	69		11
8	Hunt	McLaren-Ford	69		14
9	G Villeneuve	Ferrari	69		7
10	Reutemann	Ferrari	69		8
11	H-J Stuck	Shadow-Ford	68		20
12	Rebaque	Lotus-Ford	68		21
13	Mass	ATS-Ford	68		19
14	Stommelen	Arrows-Ford	67		24
15	Rosberg	ATS-Ford	63		23
	Merzario	Merzario-Ford	62	running	22
	Andretti	Lotus-Ford	46	engine	1
	Jones	Williams-Ford	46	wheel bearing	9
	Depailler	Tyrrell-Ford	42	suspension	12
	Jabouille	Renault	28	engine	10
	Watson	Brabham-Alfa	19	throttle	2
	J Scheckter	Wolf-Ford	16	overheating	6
	Pironi	Tyrrell-Ford	8	accident	17
	Brambilla	Surtees-Ford	7	accident	18

Fastest Lap: Lauda, 1m 24.836s, 106.288 mph/171.055 kph

French Grand Prix: Paul Ricard, 2 July 1978

54 laps of 3.61 mile/5.81 km circuit

Place	Driver	Car	Laps	Time/reason for retiring	Grid
1	Andretti	Lotus-Ford	54	1h 38m 51.92s	2
2	Peterson	Lotus-Ford	54	1h 38m 54.85s	5
3	Hunt	McLaren-Ford	54	1h 39m 11.72s	4
4	Watson	Brabham-Alfa	54	1h 39m 28.80s	1
5	Jones	Williams-Ford	54	1h 39m 33.73s	14
6	J Scheckter	Wolf-Ford	54	1h 39m 46.45s	7
7	Laffite	Ligier-Matra	54	1h 39m 46.66s	10
8	Patrese	Arrows-Ford	54	1h 40m 16.80s	12
9	Tambay	McLaren-Ford	54	1h 40m 18.98s	6
10	Pironi	Tyrrell-Ford	54	1h 40m 21.90s	16
11	H-J Stuck	Shadow-Ford	53		20
12	G Villeneuve	Ferrari	53		9
13	Mass	ATS-Ford	53		25
14	Arnoux	Martini-Ford	53		18

French Grand Prix (cont)

Place	Driver	Car	Laps	Time/reason for retiring	Grid
15	Stommelen	Arrows-Ford	53		21
16	Rosberg	ATS-Ford	52		26
17	Brambilla	Surtees-Ford	52		19
18	Reutemann	Ferrari	49		8
	Lunger	McLaren-Ford	45	engine	24
	E Fittipaldi	Fittipaldi-Ford	43	suspension	15
	Keegan	Surtees-Ford	40	engine	23
	Giacomelli	McLaren-Ford	28	engine	22
	Depailler	Tyrrell-Ford	10	engine	13
	Lauda	Brabham-Alfa	10	engine	3
	Regazzoni	Shadow-Ford	4	electrical	17
	Jabouille	Renault	1	engine	11

Fastest Lap: Reutemann, 1m 48.56s. 119.718 mph/192.668 kph

British Grand Prix: Brands Hatch, 16 July 1978

76 laps of 2.61 mile/4.21 km circuit

Place	Driver	Car	Laps	Time/reason for retiring	Grid
1	Reutemann	Ferrari	76	1h 42m 12.39s	8
2	Lauda	Brabham-Alfa	76	1h 42m 13.62s	4
3	Watson	Brabham-Alfa	76	1h 42m 49.64s	9
4	Depailler	Tyrrell-Ford	76	1h 43m 25.66s	10
5	H-J Stuck	Shadow-Ford	75		18
6	Tambay	McLaren-Ford	75		20
7	Giacomelli	McLaren-Ford	75		16
8	Lunger	McLaren-Ford	75		24
9	Brambilla	Surtees-Ford	75		25
10	Laffite	Ligier-Matra	73		7
	Mass	ATS-Ford	66		26
	Rosberg	ATS-Ford	59	suspension	22
	Regazzoni	Shadow-Ford	49	gearbox	17
	Jabouille	Renault	46	engine	12
	Patrese	Arrows-Ford	40	suspension	5
	Pironi	Tyrrell-Ford	40	gearbox	19
	J Scheckter	Wolf-Ford	36	gearbox	3
	E Fittipaldi	Fittipaldi-Ford	32	engine	11
	Merzario	Merzario-Ford	32	fuel pump	23
	Daly	Ensign-Ford	30	lost wheel	15
	Andretti	Lotus-Ford	28	engine	2
	Jones	Williams-Ford	26	drive-shaft	6
	G Villeneuve	Ferrari	19	drive-shaft	13
	Rebaque	Lotus-Ford	15	gearbox	21
	Hunt	McLaren-Ford	7	accident	14
	Peterson	Lotus-Ford	6	fuel leak	1

Fastest Lap: Lauda, 1m 18.60s. 119.707 mph/192.649 kph

German Grand Prix: Hockenheim, 30 July 1978

45 laps of 4.22 mile/6.79 km circuit

Place	Driver	Car	Laps	Time/reason for retiring	Grid
1	Andretti	Lotus-Ford	45	1h 28m 00.90s	1
2	J Scheckter	Wolf-Ford	45	1h 28m 16.25s	4
3	Laffite	Ligier-Matra	45	1h 28m 28.91s	7
4	E Fittipaldi	Fittipaldi-Ford	45	1h 28m 37.78s	10
5	Pironi	Tyrrell-Ford	45	1h 28m 58.16s	16
6	Rebaque	Lotus-Ford	45	1h 29m 38.76s	18
7	Watson	Brabham-Alfa	45	1h 29m 40.43s	5
8	G Villeneuve	Ferrari	45	1h 29m 57.77s	15
9	Patrese	Arrows-Ford	44		14
10	Rosberg	Wolf-Ford	42		19
	Stommelen	Arrows-Ford	42	disqualified: wrong way into pits	17
11	Ertl	Ensign-Ford	41	engine	23
	Peterson	Lotus-Ford	36	gearbox	2
	Hunt	McLaren-Ford	34	disqualified: wrong way into pits	8
	Jones	Williams-Ford	31	fuel	6
	Piquet	Ensign-Ford	31	engine	21
	Brambilla	Surtees-Ford	24	fuel	20
	Tambay	McLaren-Ford	16	puncture	11
	Reutemann	Ferrari	14	fuel	12
	Lauda	Brabham-Alfa	11	engine	3
	Jabouille	Renault	5	engine	9
	H-J Stuck	Shadow-Ford	1	accident	24
	Mass	ATS-Ford	1	accident	22
	Depailler	Tyrrell-Ford	0	accident	13

Fastest Lap: Peterson, 1m 55.62s. 131.35 mph/211.39 kph

Austrian Grand Prix: Österreichring, 13 August 1978

54 laps of 3.69 mile/5.94 km circuit

Place	Driver	Car	Laps	Time/reason for retiring	Grid
1	Peterson	Lotus-Ford	54	1h 41m 21.57s	1
2	Depailler	Tyrrell-Ford	54	1h 42m 09.01s	13
3	G Villeneuve	Ferrari	54	1h 43m 01.33s	11
4	E Fittipaldi	Fittipaldi-Ford	53		6
5	Laffite	Ligier-Matra	53		5
6	Brambilla	Surtees-Ford	53		21
7	Watson	Brabham-Alfa	53		10
8	Lunger	McLaren-Ford	52		17
9	Arnoux	Martini-Ford	52		26
	Rosberg	Wolf-Ford	47		25
	Regazzoni	Shadow-Ford	47		22
	Daly	Ensign-Ford	43	disqualified: push start	19
	Tambay	McLaren-Ford	40	accident	14

Austrian Grand Prix (cont)

Place	Driver	Car	Laps	Time/reason for retiring	Grid
	H-J Stuck	Shadow-Ford	33	accident	23
	Jabouille	Renault	31	gearbox	3
	Lauda	Brabham-Alfa	28	accident	12
	Reutemann	Ferrari	27	disqualified: push start	4
	Pironi	Tyrrell-Ford	20	accident	9
	Hunt	McLaren-Ford	8	accident	8
	Jones	Williams-Ford	7	accident	15
	Ertl	Ensign-Ford	6	accident	24
	Patrese	Arrows-Ford	6	accident	16
	J Scheckter	Wolf-Ford	3	accident	7
	Rebaque	Lotus-Ford	1	clutch	18
	Piquet	McLaren-Ford	2	accident	20
	Andretti	Lotus-Ford	0	accident	2

Fastest Lap: Peterson, 1m 43.12s. 128.91 mph/207.45 kph

Dutch Grand Prix: Zandvoort, 27 August 1978

75 laps of 2.63 mile/4.23 km circuit

Place	Driver	Car	Laps	Time/reason for retiring	Grid
1	Andretti	Lotus-Ford	75	1h 41m 04.23s	1
2	Peterson	Lotus-Ford	75	1h 41m 04.55s	2
3	Lauda	Brabham-Alfa	75	1h 41m 16.44s	3
4	Watson	Brabham-Alfa	75	1h 41m 25.15s	8
5	E Fittipaldi	Fittipaldi-Ford	75	1h 41m 25.73s	10
6	G Villeneuve	Ferrari	75	1h 41m 50.18s	5
7	Reutemann	Ferrari	75	1h 42m 04.73s	4
8	Laffite	Ligier-Matra	74		6
9	Tambay	McLaren-Ford	74		14
10	Hunt	McLaren-Ford	74		7
11	Rebaque	Lotus-Ford	74		20
12	J Scheckter	Wolf-Ford	73		15
	Giacomelli	McLaren-Ford	60	spun	19
	H-J Stuck	Shadow-Ford	56	differential	18
	Arnoux	Martini-Ford	40	wing	23
	Merzario	Merzario-Ford	40	engine	26
	Brambilla	Surtees-Ford	37	disqualified: push start	22
	Jabouille	Renault	35	engine	9
	Lunger	McLaren-Ford	35	engine	21
	Rosberg	Wolf-Ford	21	throttle	24
	Jones	Williams-Ford	17	throttle cable	11
	Piquet	McLaren-Ford	16	drive-shaft	25
	Depailler	Tyrrell-Ford	13	engine	12
	Daly	Ensign-Ford	10	drive-shaft	16
	Patrese	Arrows-Ford	0	accident	13
	Pironi	Tyrrell-Ford	0	accident	17

Fastest Lap: Lauda, 1m 19.57s. 118.81 mph/191.2 kph

1978

Italian Grand Prix: Monza, 10 September 1978

40 laps of 3.6 mile/5.8 km circuit

Place	Driver	Car	Laps	Time/reason for retiring	Grid
1	Lauda	Brabham-Alfa	40	1h 07m 04.53s	4
2	Watson	Brabham-Alfa	40	1h 07m 06.02s	7
3	Reutemann	Ferrari	40	1h 07m 25.01s	11
4	Laffite	Ligier-Matra	40	1h 07m 42.07s	8
5	Tambay	McLaren-Ford	40	1h 07m 44.93s	19
6	*Andretti	Lotus-Ford	40	1h 07m 50.87s	1
7	*G Villeneuve	Ferrari	40	1h 07m 53.02s	2
8	E Fittipaldi	Fittipaldi-Ford	40	1h 07m 59.78s	13
9	Piquet	McLaren-Ford	40	1h 08m 11.37s	24
10	Daly	Ensign-Ford	40	1h 08m 13.65s	18
11	Depailler	Tyrrell-Ford	40	1h 08m 21.11s	16
12	J Scheckter	Wolf-Ford	39		9
13	Jones	Williams-Ford	39		6
14	Giacomelli	McLaren-Ford	39		20
	Regazzoni	Shadow-Ford	33		15
	Patrese	Arrows-Ford	29	engine	12
	Hunt	McLaren-Ford	19	distributor	10
	Merzario	Merzario-Ford	14	engine	22
	Jabouille	Renault	6	engine	3
	Brambilla	Surtees-Ford	0	accident	23
	Lunger	McLaren-Ford	0	accident	21
	Peterson	Lotus-Ford	0	fatal accident	5
	Pironi	Tyrrell-Ford	0	accident	14
	H-J Stuck	Shadow-Ford	0	accident	17

Fastest Lap: Andretti, 1m 38.23s. 132.08 mph/212.56 kph
* Penalised 1 minute for jumping start.

United States Grand Prix: Watkins Glen, 1 October 1978

59 laps of 3.38 mile/5.44 km circuit

Place	Driver	Car	Laps	Time/reason for retiring	Grid
1	Reutemann	Ferrari	59	1h 40m 48.800s	2
2	Jones	Williams-Ford	59	1h 41m 08.539s	3
3	J Scheckter	Wolf-Ford	59	1h 41m 34.501s	11
4	Jabouille	Renault	59	1h 42m 13.807s	9
5	E Fittipaldi	Fittipaldi-Ford	59	1h 42m 16.889s	13
6	Tambay	McLaren-Ford	59	1h 42m 30.010s	18
7	Hunt	McLaren-Ford	58		6
8	Daly	Ensign-Ford	58		19
9	Arnoux	Surtees-Ford	58		21
10	Pironi	Tyrrell-Ford	58		16
11	Laffite	Ligier-Matra	58		10
12	Rahal	Wolf-Ford	58		20

United States Grand Prix (cont)

Place	Driver	Car	Laps	Time/reason for retiring	Grid
13	Lunger	Ensign-Ford	58		24
14	Regazzoni	Shadow-Ford	56		17
15	Jarier	Lotus-Ford	55	out of fuel	8
16	Stommelen	Arrows-Ford	54		22
	Merzario	Merzario-Ford	46	gearbox	26
	Bleekemolen	ATS-Ford	43	oil pump	25
	Lauda	Brabham-Alfa	28	engine	5
	Andretti	Lotus-Ford	27	engine	1
	Watson	Brabham-Alfa	25	engine	7
	Depailler	Tyrrell-Ford	23	wheel	12
	G Villeneuve	Ferrari	22	engine	4
	Rosberg	ATS-Ford	21	gear linkage	15
	H-J Stuck	Shadow-Ford	1	fuel pump	14
	Rebaque	Lotus-Ford	0	clutch	23

Fastest Lap: Jarier, 1m 39.557s. 122.113 mph/196.521 kph

Canadian Grand Prix: Montreal, 8 October 1978

70 laps of 2.8 mile/4.5 km circuit

Place	Driver	Car	Laps	Time/reason for retiring	Grid
1	G Villeneuve	Ferrari	70	1h 57m 49.196s	3
2	J Scheckter	Wolf-Ford	70	1h 58m 02.568s	2
3	Reutemann	Ferrari	70	1h 58m 08.604s	11
4	Patrese	Arrows-Ford	70	1h 58m 13.863s	12
5	Depailler	Tyrrell-Ford	70	1h 58m 17.754s	13
6	Daly	Ensign-Ford	70	1h 58m 43.672s	15
7	Pironi	Tyrrell-Ford	70	1h 59m 10.446s	18
8	Tambay	McLaren-Ford	70	1h 59m 15.756s	17
9	Jones	Williams-Ford	70	1h 59m 18.138s	5
10	Andretti	Lotus-Ford	69		9
11	Piquet	Brabham-Alfa	69		14
12	Jabouille	Renault	65		22
	Rosberg	ATS-Ford	58		21
	Laffite	Ligier-Matra	52	transmission	10
	Hunt	McLaren-Ford	51	accident	19
	Jarier	Lotus-Ford	49	cooler	1
	Arnoux	Surtees-Ford	37	engine	16
	Rahal	Wolf-Ford	16	fuel system	20
	Watson	Brabham-Alfa	8	accident	4
	Lauda	Brabham-Alfa	5	accident	7
	H-J Stuck	Shadow-Ford	1	accident	8
	E Fittipaldi	Fittipaldi-Ford	0	accident	6

Fastest Lap: Jones, 1m 38.072s. 102.635 mph/165.174 kph

World Championship 1978

1	Andretti	64
2	Peterson	51
3	Reutemann	48
4	Lauda	44
5	Depailler	34
6	Watson	25
7	J Scheckter	24
8	Laffite	19
9 =	E Fittipaldi, G Villeneuve	17
11 =	Jones, Patrese	11
13 =	Hunt, Tambay	8
15	Pironi	7
16	Regazzoni	4
17	Jabouille	3
18	H-J Stuck	2
19 =	Brambilla, Daly, Rebaque	1

Constructors' Championship

1	Lotus-Ford	86
2	Ferrari	58
3	Brabham-Alfa	53
4	Tyrrell-Ford	38
5	Wolf-Ford	24
6	Ligier-Matra	19
7	Fittipaldi-Ford	17
8	McLaren-Ford	15
9 =	Arrows-Ford, Williams-Ford	11
11	Shadow-Ford	6
12	Renault	3
13 =	Surtees-Ford, Ensign-Ford	1

1979

Renault's perseverance with the turbocharged concept paid off with
Jabouille's win in France, but Jody Scheckter's speed and reliability took
him to the championship in front of his team mate Gilles Villeneuve. Alan
Jones dominated the second half of the season with four wins in eight races.
Alfa Romeo reappeared at the Belgian Grand Prix, James Hunt retired after
the Monaco Grand Prix, and Niki Lauda during practice for the Canadian
Grand Prix. The constructors' championship scoring system was changed to
include all cars from a constructor finishing in the first six of a race.

Argentine Grand Prix: Buenos Aires, 21 January 1979

53 laps of 3.71 mile/5.97 km circuit

Place	Driver	Car	Laps	Time/reason for retiring	Grid
1	Laffite	Ligier-Ford	53	1h 36m 03.21s	1
2	Reutemann	Lotus-Ford	53	1h 36m 18.15s	3
3	Watson	McLaren-Ford	53	1h 37m 32.02s	6
4	Depailler	Ligier-Ford	53	1h 37m 44.93s	2
5	Andretti	Lotus-Ford	52		7
6	E Fittipaldi	Fittipaldi-Ford	52		11
7	de Angelis	Shadow-Ford	52		15
8	Mass	Arrows-Ford	51		13
9	Jones	Williams-Ford	51		14
10	Regazzoni	Williams-Ford	51		16
11	Daly	Ensign-Ford	51		23
	G Villeneuve	Ferrari	48	engine	10
	Rebaque	Lotus-Ford	46	suspension	18
	Lammers	Shadow-Ford	42	broken cv joint	20
	Hunt	Wolf-Ford	41	electrics	17
	Jarier	Tyrrell-Ford	15	engine	4
	Jabouille	Renault	15	engine	12
	Lauda	Brabham-Alfa	8	fuel pressure	22
	Arnoux	Renault	6	engine	24
	J Scheckter	Ferrari	0	accident	5
	Pironi	Tyrrell-Ford	0	accident	8
	Tambay	McLaren-Ford	0	accident	9
	Piquet	Brabham-Alfa	0	accident	19
	Merzario	Merzario-Ford	0	accident	21

Fastest Lap: Laffite, 1m 46.91s. 124.88 mph/200.97 kph

Brazilian Grand Prix: Interlagos, 4 February 1979

40 laps of 4.89 mile/7.87 km circuit

Place	Driver	Car	Laps	Time/reason for retiring	Grid
1	Laffite	Ligier-Ford	40	1h 40m 09.64s	1
2	Depailler	Ligier-Ford	40	1h 40m 14.92s	2
3	Reutemann	Lotus-Ford	40	1h 40m 53.78s	3
4	Pironi	Tyrrell-Ford	40	1h 41m 35.52s	8
5	G Villeneuve	Ferrari	39		5
6	J Scheckter	Ferrari	39		6
7	Mass	Arrows-Ford	39		18
8	Watson	McLaren-Ford	39		14
9	Patrese	Arrows-Ford	39		15
10	Jabouille	Renault	39		7
11	E Fittipaldi	Fittipaldi-Ford	39		9
12	de Angelis	Shadow-Ford	39		19
13	Daly	Ensign-Ford	39		22
14	Lammers	Shadow-Ford	39		20
15	Regazzoni	Williams-Ford	38		16
	Jones	Williams-Ford	33	fuel pressure	13
	H-J Stuck	ATS-Ford	31	steering wheel	23
	Arnoux	Renault	28	spun	11
	Tambay	McLaren-Ford	7	accident	17
	Hunt	Wolf-Ford	7	steering rack	10
	Piquet	Brabham-Alfa	5	accident	21
	Lauda	Brabham-Alfa	5	gear linkage	12
	Andretti	Lotus-Ford	2	misfire	4

Fastest Lap: Laffite, 2m 28.76s. 118.4 mph/190.55 kph

South African Grand Prix: Kyalami, 3 March 1979

78 laps of 2.55 mile/4.1 km circuit

Place	Driver	Car	Laps	Time/reason for retiring	Grid
1	G Villeneuve	Ferrari	78	1h 41m 49.96s	3
2	J Scheckter	Ferrari	78	1h 41m 53.38s	2
3	Jarier	Tyrrell-Ford	78	1h 42m 12.07s	9
4	Andretti	Lotus-Ford	78	1h 42m 17.84s	8
5	Reutemann	Lotus-Ford	78	1h 42m 56.93s	11
6	Lauda	Brabham-Alfa	77		4
7	Piquet	Brabham-Alfa	77		12
8	Hunt	Wolf-Ford	77		13
9	Regazzoni	Williams-Ford	76		22
10	Tambay	McLaren-Ford	75		17
11	Patrese	Arrows-Ford	75		16
12	Mass	Arrows-Ford	74		20
13	E Fittipaldi	Fittipaldi-Ford	74		18
	Rebaque	Lotus-Ford	71	engine	23

South African Grand Prix (cont)

Place	Driver	Car	Laps	Time/reason for retiring	Grid
	Arnoux	Renault	67	puncture	10
	Jones	Williams-Ford	63	suspension	19
	Watson	McLaren-Ford	61	ignition	14
	H-J Stuck	ATS-Ford	57	accident	24
	Jabouille	Renault	47	engine	1
	Laffite	Ligier-Ford	45	accident	6
	Pironi	Tyrrell-Ford	25	throttle	7
	de Angelis	Shadow-Ford	16	accident	15
	Depailler	Ligier-Ford	4	accident	5
	Lammers	Shadow-Ford	2	accident	21

Fastest Lap: Villeneuve, 1m 14.412s. 123.369 mph/198.54 kph

United States Grand Prix West: Long Beach, 8 April 1979

80.5 laps of 2.02 mile/3.25 km circuit

Place	Driver	Car	Laps	Time/reason for retiring	Grid
1	G Villeneuve	Ferrari	80	1h 50m 25.40s	1
2	J Scheckter	Ferrari	80	1h 50m 54.78s	3
3	Jones	Williams-Ford	80	1h 51m 25.09s	10
4	Andretti	Lotus-Ford	80	1h 51m 29.73s	6
5	Depailler	Ligier-Ford	80	1h 51m 48.92s	4
6	Jarier	Tyrrell-Ford	79		7
7	de Angelis	Shadow-Ford	78		20
8	Piquet	Brabham-Alfa	78		12
9	Mass	Arrows-Ford	78		13
	Pironi	Tyrrell-Ford	72	disqualified: push start	17
	Rebaque	Lotus-Ford	71	accident	23
	Daly	Ensign-Ford	69	accident	24
	Watson	McLaren-Ford	62	injection	18
	H-J Stuck	ATS-Ford	49	disqualified: push start	21
	Regazzoni	Williams-Ford	48	engine	15
	Lammers	Shadow-Ford	47	suspension	14
	Patrese	Arrows-Ford	40	brakes	9
	Reutemann	Lotus-Ford	21	drive-shaft	2
	E Fittipaldi	Fittipaldi-Ford	19	drive-shaft	16
	Merzario	Merzario-Ford	13	engine	22
	Laffite	Ligier-Ford	8	brakes	5
	Hunt	Wolf-Ford	0	drive-shaft	8
	Lauda	Brabham-Alfa	0	accident	11
	Tambay	McLaren-Ford	0	accident	19

Fastest Lap: Villeneuve, 1m 21.2s. 89.56 mph/144.28 kph
* Start and finish lines in different places. All finishers completed 0.5 of a lap extra.

Spanish Grand Prix: Jarama, 29 April 1979

75 laps of 2.12 mile/3.4 km circuit

Place	Driver	Car	Laps	Time/reason for retiring	Grid
1	Depailler	Ligier-Ford	75	1h 39m 11.84s	2
2	Reutemann	Lotus-Ford	75	1h 39m 32.78s	8
3	Andretti	Lotus-Ford	75	1h 39m 39.15s	4
4	J Scheckter	Ferrari	75	1h 39m 40.52s	5
5	Jarier	Tyrrell-Ford	75	1h 39m 42.23s	12
6	Pironi	Tyrrell-Ford	75	1h 40m 00.27s	10
7	G Villeneuve	Ferrari	75	1h 40m 04.15s	3
8	Mass	Arrows-Ford	75	1h 40m 26.68s	17
9	Arnoux	Renault	74		11
10	Patrese	Arrows-Ford	74		16
11	E Fittipaldi	Fittipaldi-Ford	74		19
12	Lammers	Shadow-Ford	73		24
13	Tambay	McLaren-Ford	72		20
14	H-J Stuck	ATS-Ford	69		21
	Lauda	Brabham-Alfa	63	water leak	6
	Rebaque	Lotus-Ford	58	engine	23
	Jones	Williams-Ford	54	gear selection	13
	de Angelis	Shadow-Ford	52	engine	22
	Regazzoni	Williams-Ford	32	engine	14
	Hunt	Wolf-Ford	26	brakes	15
	Watson	McLaren-Ford	21	engine	18
	Jabouille	Renault	21	turbo	9
	Laffite	Ligier-Ford	15	engine	1
	Piquet	Brabham-Alfa	15	fuel metering	7

Fastest Lap: Villeneuve, 1m 16.44s. 99.61 mph/160.3 kph

Belgian Grand Prix: Zolder, 13 May 1979

70 laps of 2.65 mile/4.26 km circuit

Place	Driver	Car	Laps	Time/reason for retiring	Grid
1	J Scheckter	Ferrari	70	1h 39m 59.53s	7
2	Laffite	Ligier-Ford	70	1h 40m 14.89s	1
3	Pironi	Tyrrell-Ford	70	1h 40m 34.70s	12
4	Reutemann	Lotus-Ford	70	1h 40m 46.02s	10
5	Patrese	Arrows-Ford	70	1h 41m 03.84s	16
6	Watson	McLaren-Ford	70	1h 41m 05.38s	19
7	G Villeneuve	Ferrari	69		6
8	H-J Stuck	ATS-Ford	69		20
9	E Fittipaldi	Fittipaldi-Ford	68		23
10	Lammers	Shadow-Ford	68		21
11	Jarier	Tyrrell-Ford	67		11
	Depailler	Ligier-Ford	46	accident	2
	Hunt	Wolf-Ford	40	accident	9

Belgian Grand Prix (cont)

Place	Driver	Car	Laps	Time/reason for retiring	Grid
	Jones	Williams-Ford	39	electrical	4
	Andretti	Lotus-Ford	27	brakes	5
	Piquet	Brabham-Alfa	23	engine	3
	Lauda	Brabham-Alfa	23	engine	13
	Arnoux	Renault	22	turbocharger	18
	Giacomelli	Alfa Romeo	21	accident	14
	de Angelis	Shadow-Ford	21	accident	24
	Mass	Arrows-Ford	17	spun	22
	Rebaque	Lotus-Ford	13	drive-shaft	15
	Jabouille	Renault	13	turbocharger	17
	Regazzoni	Williams-Ford	1	accident	8

Fastest Lap: Villeneuve, 1m 23.09s. 114.74 mph/184.66 kph

Monaco Grand Prix: Monte Carlo, 27 May 1979

76 laps of 2.06 mile/3.31 km circuit

Place	Driver	Car	Laps	Time/reason for retiring	Grid
1	J Scheckter	Ferrari	76	1h 55m 22.48s	1
2	Regazzoni	Williams-Ford	76	1h 55m 22.92s	16
3	Reutemann	Lotus-Ford	76	1h 55m 31.05s	11
4	Watson	McLaren-Ford	76	1h 56m 03.79s	14
5	Depailler	Ligier-Ford	74	engine	3
6	Mass	Arrows-Ford	69		8
7	Piquet	Brabham-Alfa	68	transmission	18
8	Jabouille	Renault	68		20
	Laffite	Ligier-Ford	55	gearbox	5
	G Villeneuve	Ferrari	54	transmission	2
	Jones	Williams-Ford	43	accident	9
	Jarier	Tyrrell-Ford	34	suspension	6
	H-J Stuck	ATS-Ford	30	wheel	12
	Lauda	Brabham-Alfa	21	accident	4
	Pironi	Tyrrell-Ford	21	accident	7
	Andretti	Lotus-Ford	21	suspension	13
	E Fittipaldi	Fittipaldi-Ford	17	engine	17
	Arnoux	Renault	8	accident	19
	Hunt	Wolf-Ford	4	transmission	10
	Patrese	Arrows-Ford	4	suspension	15

Fastest Lap: Depailler, 1m 28.82s. 83.41 mph/134.24 kph

1979

French Grand Prix: Dijon, 1 July 1979

80 laps of 2.36 mile/3.8 km circuit

Place	Driver	Car	Laps	Time/reason for retiring	Grid
1	Jabouille	Renault	80	1h 35m 20.42s	1
2	G Villeneuve	Ferrari	80	1h 35m 35.01s	3
3	Arnoux	Renault	80	1h 35m 35.25s	2
4	Jones	Williams-Ford	80	1h 35m 57.03s	7
5	Jarier	Tyrrell-Ford	80	1h 36m 24.93s	10
6	Regazzoni	Williams Ford	80	1h 36m 25.93s	9
7	J Scheckter	Ferrari	79		5
8	Laffite	Ligier-Ford	79		8
9	Rosberg	Wolf-Ford	79		16
10	Tambay	McLaren-Ford	78		20
11	Watson	McLaren-Ford	78		15
12	Rebaque	Lotus-Ford	78		23
13	Reutemann	Lotus-Ford	77	accident	13
14	Patrese	Arrows-Ford	77		19
15	Mass	Arrows-Ford	75		22
16	de Angelis	Shadow-Ford	75		24
17	Giacomelli	Alfa Romeo	75		17
18	Lammers	Shadow-Ford	73		21
	Pironi	Tyrrell-Ford	71	suspension	11
	E Fittipaldi	Fittipaldi-Ford	53	oil	18
	Piquet	Brabham-Alfa	52	accident	4
	Andretti	Lotus-Ford	51	brakes	12
	Ickx	Ligier-Ford	45	engine	14
	Lauda	Brabham-Alfa	23	spun	6

Fastest Lap: Arnoux, 1m 09.16s. 122.9 mph/197.8 kph

British Grand Prix: Silverstone, 14 July 1979

68 laps of 2.93 mile/4.72 km circuit

Place	Driver	Car	Laps	Time/reason for retiring	Grid
1	Regazzoni	Williams-Ford	68	1h 26m 11.17s	4
2	Arnoux	Renault	68	1h 26m 35.45s	5
3	Jarier	Tyrrell-Ford	67		16
4	Watson	McLaren-Ford	67		7
5	J Scheckter	Ferrari	67		11
6	Ickx	Liger-Ford	67		17
7	Tambay	McLaren-Ford	66	out of fuel	18
8	Reutemann	Lotus-Ford	66		8
9	Rebaque	Lotus-Ford	66		24
10	Pironi	Tyrrell-Ford	66		15
11	Lammers	Shadow-Ford	65		21
12	de Angelis	Shadow-Ford	65	includes jump start penalty	12

British Grand Prix (cont)

Place	Driver	Car	Laps	Time/reason for retiring	Grid
13	Gaillard	Ensign-Ford	65		23
14	G Villeneuve	Ferrari	63	fuel vaporization	13
	Mass	Arrows-Ford	36	gearbox	20
	Patrese	Arrows-Ford	45	gearbox	19
	Rosberg	Wolf-Ford	44	fuel system	14
	Laffite	Ligier-Ford	44	engine	10
	Jones	Williams-Ford	38	water pump	1
	E Fittipaldi	Fittipaldi-Ford	25	engine	22
	Jabouille	Renault	21	engine	2
	Lauda	Brabham-Alfa	12	brakes	6
	Andretti	Lotus-Ford	3	wheel	9
	Piquet	Brabham-Alfa	1	spun	3

Fastest Lap: Regazzoni, 1m 14.40s. 141.87 mph/228.32 kph

German Grand Prix: Hockenheim, 29 July 1979

45 laps of 4.22 mile/6.79 km circuit

Place	Driver	Car	Laps	Time/reason for retiring	Grid
1	Jones	Williams-Ford	45	1h 24m 48.83s	2
2	Regazzoni	Williams-Ford	45	1h 24m 51.74s	6
3	Laffite	Ligier-Ford	45	1h 25m 07.22s	3
4	J Scheckter	Ferrari	45	1h 25m 20.03s	5
5	Watson	McLaren-Ford	45	1h 26m 26.63s	12
6	Mass	Arrows-Ford	44		18
7	Lees	Tyrrell-Ford	44		16
8	G Villeneuve	Ferrari	44		9
9	Pironi	Tyrrell-Ford	44		8
10	Lammers	Shadow-Ford	44		20
11	de Angelis	Shadow-Ford	43		21
12	Piquet	Brabham-Alfa	42	engine	4
	Patrese	Arrows-Ford	34	puncture	19
	Tambay	McLaren-Ford	30	suspension	15
	Rosberg	Wolf-Ford	29	engine	17
	Lauda	Brabham-Alfa	27	engine	7
	Ickx	Ligier-Ford	24	puncture	14
	Rebaque	Lotus-Ford	22	handling	24
	Andretti	Lotus-Ford	16	cv joint	11
	Arnoux	Renault	9	puncture	10
	Jabouille	Renault	7	spun	1
	E Fittipaldi	Fittipaldi-Ford	4	electrical	22
	Reutemann	Lotus-Ford	1	accident	13
	H-J Stuck	ATS-Ford	0	suspension	23

Fastest Lap: Villeneuve, 1m 51.89s. 135.7 mph/218.4 kph

1979

Austrian Grand Prix: Österreichring, 12 August 1979

54 laps of 3.69 mile/5.94 km circuit

Place	Driver	Car	Laps	Time/reason for retiring	Grid
1	Jones	Williams-Ford	54	1h 27m 38.01s	2
2	G Villeneuve	Ferrari	54	1h 28m 14.06s	5
3	Laffite	Ligier-Ford	54	1h 28m 24.78s	8
4	J Scheckter	Ferrari	54	1h 28m 25.22s	9
5	Regazzoni	Williams-Ford	54	1h 28m 26.93s	6
6	Arnoux	Renault	53		1
7	Pironi	Tyrrell-Ford	53		10
8	Daly	Tyrrell-Ford	53		11
9	Watson	McLaren-Ford	53		16
10	Tambay	McLaren-Ford	53		14
	Lauda	Brabham-Alfa	45	oil	4
	Gaillard	Ensign-Ford	42	suspension	24
	de Angelis	Shadow-Ford	34	engine	22
	Patrese	Arrows-Ford	34	suspension	13
	Piquet	Brabham-Alfa	32	engine	7
	H-J Stuck	ATS-Ford	28	engine	18
	Ickx	Ligier-Ford	26	engine	21
	Reutemann	Lotus-Ford	22	handling	17
	Jabouille	Renault	16	transmission	3
	E Fittipaldi	Fittipaldi-Ford	15	brakes	19
	Rosberg	Wolf-Ford	15	electrical	12
	Lammers	Shadow-Ford	3	accident	23
	Mass	Arrows-Ford	1	engine	20
	Andretti	Lotus-Ford	0	clutch	15

Fastest Lap: Arnoux, 1m 35.77s. 138.8 mph/223.38 kph

Dutch Grand Prix: Zandvoort, 26 August 1979

75 laps of 2.63 mile/4.23 km circuit

Place	Driver	Car	Laps	Time/reason for retiring	Grid
1	Jones	Williams-Ford	75	1h 41m 19.775s	2
2	J Scheckter	Ferrari	75	1h 41m 41.558s	5
3	Laffite	Ligier-Ford	75	1h 42m 23.028s	7
4	Piquet	Brabham-Alfa	74		11
5	Ickx	Ligier-Ford	74		20
6	Mass	Arrows-Ford	73		18
7	Rebaque	Lotus-Ford	73		24
	Pironi	Tyrrell-Ford	51	suspension	10
	G Villeneuve	Ferrari	49	suspension	6
	de Angelis	Shadow-Ford	40	drive-shaft	22
	Rosberg	Wolf-Ford	33	engine	8
	Jabouille	Renault	26	clutch	4
	Watson	McLaren-Ford	22	engine	12

Dutch Grand Prix (cont)

Place	Driver	Car	Laps	Time/reason for retiring	Grid
	Jarier	Tyrrell-Ford	20	spun	16
	H-J Stuck	ATS-Ford	19	drive-shaft	15
	Lammers	Shadow-Ford	12	gearbox	23
	Andretti	Lotus-Ford	9	suspension	17
	Patrese	Arrows-Ford	7	accident	19
	Tambay	McLaren-Ford	6	engine	14
	Lauda	Brabham-Alfa	4	withdrew	9
	E Fittipaldi	Fittipaldi-Ford	2	electrical	21
	Reutemann	Lotus-Ford	1	accident	13
	Arnoux	Renault	1	accident	1
	Regazzoni	Williams-Ford	0	accident	3

Fastest Lap: Villeneuve, 1m 19.44s. 119 mph/191.5 kph

Italian Grand Prix: Monza, 9 September 1979

50 laps of 3.6 mile/5.8 km circuit

Place	Driver	Car	Laps	Time/reason for retiring	Grid
1	J Scheckter	Ferrari	50	1h 22m 00.22s	3
2	G Villeneuve	Ferrari	50	1h 22m 00.68s	5
3	Regazzoni	Williams-Ford	50	1h 22m 05.00s	6
4	Lauda	Brabham-Alfa	50	1h 22m 54.62s	9
5	Andretti	Lotus-Ford	50	1h 22m 59.92s	10
6	Jarier	Tyrrell-Ford	50	1h 23m 01.77s	16
7	Reutemann	Lotus-Ford	50	1h 23m 24.36s	13
8	E Fittipaldi	Fittipaldi-Ford	49		20
9	Jones	Williams-Ford	49		4
10	Pironi	Tyrrell-Ford	49		12
11	H-J Stuck	ATS-Ford	49		15
12	Brambilla	Alfa Romeo	49		22
13	Patrese	Arrows-Ford	47		17
14	Jabouille	Renault	45	engine	1
	Laffite	Ligier-Ford	41	engine	7
	Rosberg	Wolf-Ford	41	engine	23
	Ickx	Ligier-Ford	40	engine	11
	de Angelis	Shadow-Ford	33	clutch	24
	Giacomelli	Alfa Romeo	28	spun	18
	Watson	McLaren-Ford	13	accident	19
	Arnoux	Renault	13	misfire	2
	Tambay	McLaren-Ford	3	engine	14
	Mass	Arrows-Ford	3	suspension	21
	Piquet	Brabham-Alfa	1	accident	8

Fastest Lap: Regazzoni, 1m 35.60s. 135.71 mph/218.4 kph

Canadian Grand Prix: Montreal, 30 September 1979

72 laps of 2.74 mile/4.41 km circuit

Place	Driver	Car	Laps	Time/reason for retiring	Grid
1	Jones	Williams-Ford	72	1h 52m 06.892s	1
2	G Villeneuve	Ferrari	72	1h 52m 07.972s	2
3	Regazzoni	Williams-Ford	72	1h 53m 20.548s	3
4	J Scheckter	Ferrari	71		9
5	Pironi	Tyrrell-Ford	71		6
6	Watson	McLaren-Ford	70		17
7	Zunino	Brabham-Ford	68		19
8	E Fittipaldi	Fittipaldi-Ford	67		15
9	Lammers	Shadow-Ford	67		21
10	Andretti	Lotus-Ford	66	out of fuel	10
	Piquet	Brabham-Ford	61	gearbox	4
	Brambilla	Alfa Romeo	52	fuel metering	18
	Ickx	Ligier-Ford	47	gearbox	16
	Jarier	Tyrrell-Ford	33	engine	13
	Daly	Tyrrell-Ford	28	engine	24
	Rebaque	Rebaque-Ford	26	engine	22
	de Angelis	Shadow-Ford	24	rotor arm	23
	Jabouille	Renault	24	brakes	7
	Reutemann	Lotus-Ford	23	suspension	11
	Patrese	Arrows-Ford	20	spun	14
	Tambay	McLaren-Ford	19	engine	20
	Arnoux	Renault	14	accident	8
	H-J Stuck	ATS-Ford	14	accident	12
	Laffite	Ligier-Ford	10	engine	5

Fastest Lap: 1m 31.272s. 108.08 mph/173.92 kph

United States Grand Prix East: Watkins Glen, 7 October 1979

59 laps of 3.38 mile/5.44 km circuit

Place	Driver	Car	Laps	Time/reason for retiring	Grid
1	G Villeneuve	Ferrari	59	1h 52m 17.734s	3
2	Arnoux	Renault	59	1h 53m 06.521s	7
3	Pironi	Tyrrell-Ford	59	2h 53m 10.933s	10
4	de Angelis	Shadow-Ford	59	1h 53m 48.246s	20
5	H-J Stuck	ATS-Ford	59	1h 53m 58.993s	14
6	Watson	McLaren-Ford	58		13
7	E Fittipaldi	Fittipaldi-Ford	54		23
	Piquet	Brabham-Ford	53	drive-shaft	2
	Daly	Tyrrell-Ford	52	accident	15
	J Scheckter	Ferrari	48	tyre	16
	Patrese	Arrows-Ford	44	suspension	19
	Jones	Williams-Ford	36	lost wheel	1

United States Grand Prix (cont)

Place	Driver	Car	Laps	Time/reason for retiring	Grid
	Surer	Ensign-Ford	32	engine	21
	Regazzoni	Williams-Ford	29	accident	5
	Zunino	Brabham-Ford	25	accident	9
	Jabouille	Renault	24	camshaft	8
	Tambay	McLaren-Ford	20	engine	22
	Rosberg	Wolf-Ford	20	accident	12
	Jarier	Tyrrell-Ford	18	accident	11
	Andretti	Lotus-Ford	16	gearbox	17
	Reutemann	Lotus-Ford	6	accident	6
	Laffite	Ligier-Ford	3	accident	4
	Ickx	Ligier-Ford	2	accident	24
	Giacomelli	Alfa Romeo	0	accident	18

Fastest Lap: Piquet, 1m 40.054s. 121.25 mph/195.13 kph

World Championship 1979

1	J Scheckter	51 (60)
2	G Villeneuve	47 (53)
3	Jones	40 (43)
4	Laffite	36
5	Regazzoni	29 (32)
6 =	Depailler	20 (22)
	Reutemann	20 (25)
8	Arnoux	17
9	Watson	15
10 =	Andretti, Jarier, Pironi	14
13	Jabouille	9
14	Lauda	4
15 =	de Angelis, Ickx, Mass, Piquet	3
19 =	Patrese, H-J Stuck	2
21	E Fittipaldi	1

Constructors' Championship

1	Ferrari	113
2	Williams-Ford	75
3	Ligier-Ford	61
4	Lotus-Ford	39
5	Tyrrell-Ford	28
6	Renault	26
7	McLaren-Ford	15
8	Brabham-Alfa	7
9	Arrows-Ford	5
10	Shadow-Ford	3
11	ATS-Ford	2
12	Fittipaldi-Ford	1

1980

Alan Jones continued his 1979 late season domination to take the title for Williams in 1980. Political difficulties between the teams and the authorities meant that the Spanish Grand Prix, won by Jones, was not counted as part of the championship. Patrick Depailler was killed in a testing accident at Hockenheim.

Argentine Grand Prix: Buenos Aires, 13 January 1980

53 laps of 3.71 mile/5.97 km circuit

Place	Driver	Car	Laps	Time/reason for retiring	Grid
1	Jones	Williams-Ford	53	1h 43m 24.38s	1
2	Piquet	Brabham-Ford	53	1h 43m 48.97s	4
3	Rosberg	Fittipaldi-Ford	53	1h 44m 43.02s	13
4	Daly	Tyrrell-Ford	53	1h 44m 47.86s	22
5	Giacomelli	Alfa Romeo	52		20
6	Prost	McLaren-Ford	52		12
7	Zunino	Brabham-Ford	51		16
	Regazzoni	Ensign-Ford	44	running	15
	E Fittipaldi	Fittipaldi-Ford	37	running	24
	Depailler	Alfa Romeo	46	engine	23
	J Scheckter	Ferrari	45	engine	11
	G Villeneuve	Ferrari	36	accident	8
	Laffite	Liger-Ford	30	engine	2
	Surer	ATS-Ford	27	fire	21
	Patrese	Arrows-Ford	27	engine	7
	Mass	Arrows-Ford	20	gearbox	14
	Andretti	Lotus-Ford	20	fuel	6
	Reutemann	Williams-Ford	12	engine	10
	de Angelis	Lotus-Ford	7	suspension	5
	Watson	McLaren-Ford	5	gearbox	17
	Jabouille	Renault	3	clutch	9
	Arnoux	Renault	2	suspenson	19
	Pironi	Ligier-Ford	1	engine	3
	Jarier	Tyrrell-Ford	1	accident	18

Fastest Lap: Jones, 1m 50.45s. 120.873 mph/194.527 kph.

Brazilian Grand Prix: Interlagos, 27 January 1980

40 laps of 4.89 mile/7.87 km circuit

Place	Driver	Car	Laps	Time/reason for retiring	Grid
1	Arnoux	Renault	40	1h 40m 01.33s	6
2	de Angelis	Lotus-Ford	40	1h 40m 23.19s	7
3	Jones	Williams-Ford	40	1h 41m 07.44s	10
4	Pironi	Ligier-Ford	40	1h 41m 41.46s	2
5	Prost	McLaren-Ford	40	1h 42m 26.74s	13
6	Patrese	Arrows-Ford	39		14
7	Surer	ATS-Ford	39		20
8	Zunino	Brabham-Ford	39		18
9	Rosberg	Fittipaldi-Ford	39		15
10	Mass	Arrow-Ford	39		16
11	Watson	McLaren-Ford	39		23
12	Jarier	Tyrrell-Ford	39		22
13	Giacomelli	Alfa Romeo	39		17
14	Daly	Tyrrell-Ford	38		24
15	E Fittipaldi	Fittipaldi-Ford	38		19
16	G Villeneuve	Ferrari	36	throttle	3
	Depailler	Alfa Romeo	33	electrical	21
	Jabouille	Renault	25	turbo	1
	Piquet	Brabham-Ford	14	accident	9
	Regazzoni	Ensign-Ford	13	handling	12
	Laffite	Ligier-Ford	13	electrical	5
	J Scheckter	Ferrari	10	engine	8
	Reutemann	Williams-Ford	1	drive-shaft	4
	Andretti	Lotus-Ford	1	spun	11

Fastest Lap: Arnoux, 2m 27.31s. 119.565 mph/192.421 kph

South African Grand Prix: Kyalami, 1 March 1980

78 laps of 2.55 mile/4.1 km circuit

Place	Driver	Car	Laps	Time/reason for retiring	Grid
1	Arnoux	Renault	78	1h 36m 52.54s	2
2	Laffite	Ligier-Ford	78	1h 37m 26.61s	4
3	Pironi	Ligier-Ford	78	1h 37m 45.03s	5
4	Piquet	Brabham-Ford	78	1h 37m 53.56s	3
5	Reutemann	Williams-Ford	77		6
6	Mass	Arrows-Ford	77		19
7	Jarier	Tyrrell-Ford	77		13
8	E Fittipaldi	Fittipaldi-Ford	77		18
9	Regazzoni	Ensign-Ford	77		20
10	Zunino	Brabham-Ford	77		17
11	Watson	McLaren-Ford	76		21
12	Andretti	Lotus-Ford	76		15
13	Lees	Shadow-Ford	70	accident	24

South African Grand Prix (cont)

Place	Driver	Car	Laps	Time/reason for retiring	Grid
	Giacomelli	Alfa Romeo	69	engine	12
	Jabouille	Renault	61	puncture	1
	Daly	Tyrrell-Ford	61	puncture	16
	Rosberg	Fittipaldi-Ford	58	accident	23
	Depailler	Alfa Romeo	53	running	7
	Jones	Williams-Ford	34	gearbox	8
	G Villeneuve	Ferrari	31	transmission	10
	J Scheckter	Ferrari	14	engine	9
	Patrese	Arrows-Ford	10	accident	11
	Cheever	Osella-Ford	8	accident	22
	de Angelis	Lotus-Ford	1	accident	14

Fastest Lap: Arnoux, 1m 13.15s. 125.49 mph/201.96 kph

United States Grand Prix West: Long Beach, 30 March 1980

80.5 laps of 2.02 mile/3.25 km circuit

Place	Driver	Car	Laps	Time/reason for retiring	Grid
1	Piquet	Brabham-Ford	80	1h 50m 18.550s	1
2	Patrese	Arrows-Ford	80	1h 51m 07.762s	8
3	E Fittipaldi	Fittipaldi-Ford	80	1h 51m 37.113s	24
4	Watson	McLaren-Ford	79		21
5	J Scheckter	Ferrari	79		16
6	Pironi	Ligier-Ford	79		9
7	Mass	Arrows-Ford	79		17
8	Daly	Tyrrell-Ford	79		14
9	Arnoux	Renault	78		2
10	Jabouille	Renault	71		11
	Rosberg	Fittipaldi-Ford	58	engine	22
	Regazzoni	Ensign-Ford	50	accident	23
	Giacomelli	Alfa Romeo	49	accident	6
	Jones	Williams-Ford	47	accident	5
	G Villeneuve	Ferrari	46	drive-shaft	10
	Depailler	Alfa Romeo	40	suspension	3
	Laffite	Ligier-Ford	36	tyre	13
	Cheever	Osella-Ford	11	drive-shaft	19
	Reutemann	Williams-Ford	3	drive-shaft	7
	Jarier	Tyrrell-Ford	3	accident	12
	de Angelis	Lotus Ford	3	accident	20
	Zunino	Brabham-Ford	0	accident	18
	Andretti	Lotus-Ford	0	accident	15
	Lammers	ATS-Ford	0	drive-shaft	4

Fastest Lap: Piquet, 1m 19.830s. 91.094 mph/146.328 kph
* Start and finish lines in different places. All finishers completed 0.5 of a lap extra.

1980

Belgian Grand Prix: Zolder, 4 May 1980

72 laps of 2.65 mile/4.26 km circuit

Place	Driver	Car	Laps	Time/reason for retiring	Grid
1	Pironi	Ligier-Ford	72	1h 38m 46.51s	2
2	Jones	Williams-Ford	72	1h 39m 33.88s	1
3	Reutemann	Williams-Ford	72	1h 40m 10.63s	4
4	Arnoux	Renault	71		6
5	Jarier	Tyrrell-Ford	71		9
6	G Villeneuve	Ferrari	71		12
7	Rosberg	Fittipaldi-Ford	71		21
8	J Scheckter	Ferrari	70		14
9	Daly	Tyrrell-Ford	70		11
10	de Angelis	Lotus-Ford	69	accident	8
11	Laffite	Ligier-Ford	68		3
	Lammers	ATS-Ford	64	engine	15
	Watson	McLaren-Ford	61	running	20
	Patrese	Arrows-Ford	58	accident	16
	Andretti	Lotus-Ford	41	gear linkage	17
	Depailler	Alfa Romeo	38	exhaust	10
	Piquet	Brabham-Ford	32	accident	7
	Prost	McLaren-Ford	29	transmission	19
	E Fittipaldi	Fittipaldi-Ford	16	electrical	24
	Needell	Ensign-Ford	12	engine	23
	Giacomelli	Alfa Romeo	11	suspension	18
	Zunino	Brabham/Ford	5	clutch	22
	Jabouille	Renault	1	clutch	5
	Mass	Arrows-Ford	1	accident	13

Fastest Lap: Laffite, 1m 20.88s. 117.876 mph/189.703 kph

Monaco Grand Prix: Monte Carlo, 18 May 1980

76 laps of 2.06 mile/3.31 km circuit

Place	Driver	Car	Laps	Time/reason for retiring	Grid
1	Reutemann	Williams-Ford	76	1h 55m 34.365s	2
2	Laffite	Ligier-Ford	76	1h 56m 47.994s	5
3	Piquet	Brabham-Ford	76	1h 56m 52.091s	4
4	Mass	Arrows-Ford	75		15
5	G Villeneuve	Ferrari	75		6
6	E Fittipaldi	Fittipaldi-Ford	74		18
7	Andretti	Lotus-Ford	73		19
8	Patrese	Arrows-Ford	73		11
9	de Angelis	Lotus-Ford	68	accident	14
	Lammers	ATS-Ford	64		13
	Pironi	Ligier-Ford	54	accident	1
	Arnoux	Renault	53	accident	20
	Depailler	Alfa Romeo	50	engine	7

Monaco Grand Prix (cont)

Place	Driver	Car	Laps	Time/reason for retiring	Grid
	J Scheckter	Ferrari	27	handling	17
	Jabouille	Renault	25	gearbox	16
	Jones	Williams-Ford	24	differential	3
	Jarier	Tyrrell-Ford	0	accident	9
	Giacomelli	Alfa Romeo	0	accident	8
	Prost	McLaren-Ford	0	accident	10
	Daly	Tyrrell-Ford	0	accident	12

Fastest Lap: Patrese, 1m 26.058s. 86.089 mph/138.548 kph

French Grand Prix: Paul Ricard, 29 June 1980

54 laps of 3.61 mile/5.81 km circuit

Place	Driver	Car	Laps	Time/reason for retiring	Grid
1	Jones	Williams-Ford	54	1h 32m 43.42s	4
2	Pironi	Ligier-Ford	54	1h 32m 47.94s	3
3	Laffite	Ligier-Ford	54	1h 33m 13.68s	1
4	Piquet	Brabham-Ford	54	1h 33m 58.30s	8
5	Arnoux	Renault	54	1h 33m 59.57s	2
6	Reutemann	Williams-Ford	54	1h 34m 00.16s	5
7	Watson	McLaren-Ford	53		13
8	G Villeneuve	Ferrari	53		17
9	Patrese	Arrows-Ford	53		18
10	Mass	Arrows-Ford	53		15
11	Daly	Tyrrell-Ford	52		20
12	J Scheckter	Ferrari	52		19
13	E Fittipaldi	Fittipaldi-Ford	50		24
14	Jarier	Tyrrell-Ford	50		16
	Cheever	Osella-Ford	43	engine	21
	Surer	ATS-Ford	26	gearbox	11
	Depailler	Alfa Romeo	25	handling	10
	Andretti	Lotus-Ford	18	gearbox	12
	Rosberg	Fittipaldi-Ford	8	accident	23
	Giacomelli	Alfa Romeo	8	handling	9
	Prost	McLaren-Ford	6	transmission	7
	de Angelis	Lotus-Ford	3	clutch	14
	Zunino	Brabham-Ford	0	clutch	22
	Jabouille	Renault	0	transmission	6

Fastest Lap: Jones, 1m 41.45s. 128.108 mph/206.171 kph

British Grand Prix: Brands Hatch, 13 July 1980

76 laps of 2.61 mile/4.21 km circuit

Place	Driver	Car	Laps	Time/reason for retiring	Grid
1	Jones	Williams-Ford	76	1h 34m 49.228s	3
2	Piquet	Brabham-Ford	76	1h 35m 00.235s	5
3	Reutemann	Williams-Ford	76	1h 35m 02.513s	4
4	Daly	Tyrrell-Ford	75		10
5	Jarier	Tyrrell-Ford	75		11
6	Prost	McLaren-Ford	75		7
7	Rebaque	Brabham-Ford	74		17
8	Watson	McLaren-Ford	74		12
9	Patrese	Arrows-Ford	73		21
10	J Scheckter	Ferrari	73		23
11	Keegan	Williams-Ford	73		18
12	E Fittipaldi	Fittipaldi-Ford	72		22
13	Mass	Arrows-Ford	69		24
	Arnoux	Renault	67	running	16
	Pironi	Ligier-Ford	63	wheel	1
	Surer	ATS-Ford	59	engine	15
	Andretti	Lotus-Ford	57	gearbox	9
	Giacomelli	Alfa Romeo	42	accident	6
	G Villeneuve	Ferrari	35	engine	19
	Laffite	Ligier-Ford	30	accident	2
	Depailler	Alfa Romeo	27	engine	8
	Cheever	Osella-Ford	17	suspension	20
	de Angelis	Lotus-Ford	16	suspension	14
	Jabouille	Renault	6	engine	13

Fastest Lap: Pironi, 1m 12.368s. 130.015 mph/209.239 kph

German Grand Prix: Hockenheim, 10 August 1980

45 laps of 4.22 mile/6.79 km circuit

Place	Driver	Car	Laps	Time/reason for retiring	Grid
1	Laffite	Ligier-Ford	45	1h 22m 59.73s	5
2	Reutemann	Williams-Ford	45	1h 23m 02.92s	4
3	Jones	Williams-Ford	45	1h 23m 43.26s	1
4	Piquet	Brabham-Ford	45	1h 23m 44.21s	6
5	Giacomelli	Alfa Romeo	45	1h 24m 16.22s	19
6	G Villeneuve	Ferrari	45	1h 24m 28.45s	16
7	Andretti	Lotus-Ford	45	1h 24m 32.74s	9
8	Mass	Arrows-Ford	45	1h 24m 47.48s	17
9	Patrese	Arrows-Ford	44		10
10	Daly	Tyrrell-Ford	44		22
11	Prost	McLaren-Ford	44		14
12	Surer	ATS-Ford	44		13
13	J Scheckter	Ferrari	44		21

German Grand Prix (cont)

Place	Driver	Car	Laps	Time/reason for retiring	Grid
14	Lammers	Ensign-Ford	44		24
15	Jarier	Tyrrell-Ford	44		23
16	de Angelis	Lotus-Ford	43	wheel bearing	11
	Watson	McLaren-Ford	39	engine	20
	Jabouille	Renault	27	engine	2
	Arnoux	Renault	26	engine	3
	Cheever	Osella-Ford	23	gearbox	18
	Pironi	Ligier-Ford	18	drive-shaft	7
	E Fittipaldi	Fittipaldi-Ford	18	broken skirt	12
	Rosberg	Fittipaldi-Ford	8	wheel bearing	8
	Rebaque	Brabham-Ford	4	gearbox	15

Fastest Lap: Jones, 1m 48.49s. 139.960 mph/225.245 kph

Austrian Grand Prix: Österreichring, 17 August 1980

54 laps of 3.69 mile/5.94 km circuit

Place	Driver	Car	Laps	Time/reason for retiring	Grid
1	Jabouille	Renault	54	1h 26m 15.73s	2
2	Jones	Williams-Ford	54	1h 26m 16.55s	3
3	Reutemann	Williams-Ford	54	1h 26m 35.09s	4
4	Laffite	Ligier-Ford	54	1h 26m 57.75s	5
5	Piquet	Brabham-Ford	54	1h 27m 18.54s	7
6	de Angelis	Lotus-Ford	54	1h 27m 30.70s	9
7	Prost	McLaren-Ford	54	1h 27m 49.14s	12
8	G Villeneuve	Ferrari	53		15
9	Arnoux	Renault	53		1
10	Rebaque	Brabham-Ford	53		14
11	E Fittipaldi	Fittipaldi-Ford	53		23
12	Surer	ATS-Ford	53		16
13	J Scheckter	Ferrari	53		22
14	Patrese	Arrows-Ford	53		18
15	Keegan	Williams-Ford	52		20
16	Rosberg	Fittipaldi-Ford	52		11
	Mansell	Lotus-Ford	40	engine	24
	Watson	McLaren-Ford	34	engine	21
	Giacomelli	Alfa Romeo	28	suspension	8
	Jarier	Tyrrell-Ford	25	engine	13
	Pironi	Ligier-Ford	25	handling	6
	Cheever	Osella-Ford	23	wheel bearing	19
	Daly	Tyrrell-Ford	12	brakes	10
	Andretti	Lotus-Ford	6	engine	17

Fastest Lap: Arnoux, 1m 32.53s. 143.659 mph/231.197 kph

Dutch Grand Prix: Zandvoort, 31 August 1980

72 laps of 2.64 mile/4.25 km circuit

Place	Driver	Car	Laps	Time/reason for retiring	Grid
1	Piquet	Brabham-Ford	72	1h 38m 13.83s	5
2	Arnoux	Renault	72	1h 38m 26.76s	1
3	Laffite	Ligier-Ford	72	1h 38m 27.26s	6
4	Reutemann	Williams-Ford	72	1h 38m 29.12s	3
5	Jarier	Tyrrell-Ford	72	1h 39m 13.85s	17
6	Prost	McLaren-Ford	72	1h 39m 36.45s	18
7	G Villeneuve	Ferrari	71		7
8	Andretti	Lotus-Ford	70	out of fuel	10
9	J Scheckter	Ferrari	70		12
10	Surer	ATS-Ford	69		20
11	Jones	Williams-Ford	69		4
	Daly	Tyrrell-Ford	60	brakes	23
	Giacomelli	Alfa Romeo	58	damaged skirt	8
	Cheever	Osella-Ford	38	engine	19
	Patrese	Arrows-Ford	29	engine	14
	Jabouille	Renault	23	handling	2
	Lees	Ensign-Ford	21	accident	24
	Brambilla	Alfa Romeo	21	accident	22
	Watson	McLaren-Ford	18	engine	9
	E Fittipaldi	Fittipaldi-Ford	16	brakes	21
	Mansell	Lotus-Ford	15	brakes	16
	Pironi	Ligier-Ford	2	accident	15
	de Angelis	Lotus-Ford	2	accident	11
	Rebaque	Brabham-Ford	1	gearbox	13

Fastest Lap: Arnoux, 1m 19.35s. 119.867 mph/192.907 kph

Italian Grand Prix: Imola, 14 September 1980

60 laps of 3.11 mile/5 km circuit

Place	Driver	Car	Laps	Time/reason for retiring	Grid
1	Piquet	Brabham-Ford	60	1h 38m 07.52s	5
2	Jones	Williams-Ford	60	1h 38m 36.45s	6
3	Reutemann	Williams-Ford	60	1h 39m 21.19s	3
4	de Angelis	Lotus-Ford	59		18
5	Rosberg	Fittipaldi-Ford	59		11
6	Pironi	Ligier-Ford	59		13
7	Prost	McLaren-Ford	59		24
8	J Scheckter	Ferrari	59		16
9	Laffite	Ligier-Ford	59		20
10	Arnoux	Renault	58		1
11	Keegan	Williams-Ford	58		21
12	Cheever	Osella-Ford	57		17
13	Jarier	Tyrrell-Ford	54	brakes	12

Italian Grand Prix (cont)

Place	Driver	Car	Laps	Time/reason for retiring	Grid
	Jabouille	Renault	53	gearbox	2
	Surer	ATS-Ford	45	engine	23
	Andretti	Lotus-Ford	40	engine	10
	Patrese	Arrows-Ford	38	engine	7
	Daly	Tyrrell-Ford	33	accident	22
	Watson	McLaren-Ford	20	brakes	14
	Rebaque	Brabham-Ford	18	suspension	9
	E Fittipaldi	Fittipaldi-Ford	17	accident	15
	G Villeneuve	Ferrari	5	accident	8
	Giacomelli	Alfa Romeo	5	accident	4
	Brambilla	Alfa Romeo	4	accident	19

Fastest Lap: Jones, 1m 36.098s. 116.399 mph/187.326 kph

Canadian Grand Prix: Montreal, 28 September 1980

70 laps of 2.74 mile/4.41 km circuit

Place	Driver	Car	Laps	Time/reason for retiring	Grid
1	Jones	Williams-Ford	70	1h 46m 45.53s	2
2	Reutemann	Williams-Ford	70	1h 47m 01.07s	5
3	Pironi	Ligier-Ford	70	1h 47m 04.60s	3
4	Watson	McLaren-Ford	70	1h 47m 16.51s	7
5	G Villeneuve	Ferrari	70	1h 47m 40.76s	22
6	Rebaque	Brabham-Ford	69		10
7	Jarier	Tyrrell-Ford	69		15
8	Laffite	Ligier-Ford	68	out of fuel	9
9	Rosberg	Fittipaldi-Ford	68		6
10	de Angelis	Lotus-Ford	68		17
11	Mass	Arrows-Ford	67		21
12	Lammers	Ensign-Ford	66		19
	Prost	McLaren-Ford	41	accident	12
	Arnoux	Renault	39	brakes	23
	Jabouille	Renault	25	accident	13
	Piquet	Brabham-Ford	23	engine	1
	Andretti	Lotus-Ford	11	engine	18
	de Cesaris	Alfa Romeo	8	engine	8
	Cheever	Osella-Ford	8	fuel pressure	14
	E Fittipaldi	Fittipaldi-Ford	8	gearbox	16
	Giacomelli	Alfa Romeo	7	damaged skirt	4
	Patrese	Arrows-Ford	6	accident	11
	Daly	Tyrell-Ford	0	accident at first start	20
	Thackwell	Tyrell-Ford	0	accident at first start	24

Fastest Lap: Pironi, 1m 28.769s. 113.397 mph/182.496 kph

United States Grand Prix: Watkins Glen, 5 October 1980

59 laps of 3.38 mile/5.44 km circuit

Place	Driver	Car	Laps	Time/reason for retiring	Grid
1	Jones	Williams-Ford	59	1h 34m 36.05s	5
2	Reutemann	Williams-Ford	59	1h 34m 40.26s	3
3	Pironi	Ligier-Ford	59	1h 34m 48.62s	7
4	de Angelis	Lotus-Ford	59	1h 35m 05.74s	4
5	Laffite	Ligier Ford	58		12
6	Andretti	Lotus-Ford	58		11
7	Arnoux	Renault	58		6
8	Surer	ATS-Ford	57		16
9	Keegan	Williams-Ford	57		14
10	Rosberg	Fittipaldi-Ford	57		13
11	J Scheckter	Ferrari	56		22
	Watson	McLaren-Ford	50	running	9
	G Villeneuve	Ferrari	49	accident	17
	Jarier	Tyrrell-Ford	40	running	21
	Mass	Arrows-Ford	36	drive-shaft	23
	Giacomelli	Alfa Romeo	31	electrical	1
	Piquet	Brabham-Ford	25	spun	2
	Cheever	Osella-Ford	21	suspension	15
	Rebaque	Brabham-Ford	20	engine	8
	Patrese	Arrows-Ford	16	accident	19
	Lammers	Ensign-Ford	16	steering	24
	E Fittipaldi	Fittipaldi-Ford	15	suspension	18
	Daly	Tyrrell-Ford	3	accident	20
	de Cesaris	Alfa Romeo	2	accident	10

Fastest Lap: Jones, 1m 34.068s. 129.238 mph/207.989 kph

World Championship 1980

1	Jones	67 (71)
2	Piquet	54
3	Reutemann	42 (49)
4	Laffite	34
5	Pironi	32
6	Arnoux	29
7	de Angelis	13
8	Jabouille	9
9	Patrese	7
10 =	Daly, Jarier, Rosberg, G Villeneuve, Watson	6
15 =	E Fittipaldi, Prost	5
17 =	Giacomelli, Mass	4
19	J Scheckter	2
20 =	Andretti, Rebaque	1

Constructors' Championship

1	Williams-Ford	120
2	Ligier-Ford	66
3	Brabham-Ford	55
4	Renault	38
5	Lotus-Ford	14
6	Tyrrell-Ford	12
7=	Arrows-Ford, Fittipaldi-Ford, McLaren-Ford	11
10	Ferrari	8
11	Alfa Romeo	4

1981

In a closely fought season Piquet took the championship from Reutemann by one point. Renault was joined in the turbocharged camp by Ferrari and the Toleman Team, which used a Brian Hart engine, while Brabham experimented with a BMW turbo which did not race until 1982. The South African Grand Prix, won by Reutemann, was excluded from the championship as a result of continuing squabbles between teams and the authorities.

United States Grand Prix West: Long Beach, 15 March 1981

80.5 laps of 2.02 mile/3.25 km circuit

Place	Driver	Car	Laps	Time/reason for retiring	Grid
1	Jones	Williams-Ford	80	1h 50m 41.33s	2
2	Reutemann	Williams-Ford	80	1h 50m 50.52s	3
3	Piquet	Brabham-Ford	80	1h 51m 16.25s	4
4	Andretti	Alfa Romeo	80	1h 51m 30.64s	6
5	Cheever	Tyrrell-Ford	80	1h 51m 48.03s	8
6	Tambay	Theodore-Ford	79		17
7	Serra	Fittipaldi-Ford	78		18
8	Arnoux	Renault	77		20
	Surer	Ensign-Ford	70	electrical	19
	Pironi	Ferrari	67	engine	11
	Jarier	Ligier-Matra	64	fuel pump	10
	Rebaque	Brabham-Ford	49	accident	15
	Laffite	Ligier-Matra	41	accident	12
	Giacomelli	Alfa Romeo	41	accident	9
	Lammers	ATS-Ford	41	accident	21
	Rosberg	Fittipaldi-Ford	41	distributor	16
	Patrese	Arrows-Ford	33	fuel filter	1
	Gabbiani	Osella-Ford	26	accident	24
	Mansell	Lotus-Ford	25	accident	7

United States Grand Prix (cont)

Place	Driver	Car	Laps	Time/reason for retiring	Grid
	G Villeneuve	Ferrari	17	drive-shaft	5
	Watson	McLaren-Ford	16	engine	23
	de Angelis	Lotus-Ford	13	accident	13
	Prost	Renault	0	accident	14
	de Cesaris	McLaren-Ford	0	accident	22

Fastest Lap: Jones, 1m 20.901s. 89.887 mph/144.659 kph
* Start and finish lines in different places. All finishers completed 0.5 of a lap extra.

Brazilian Grand Prix: Rio de Janeiro, 29 March 1981

62 laps of 3.13 mile/5.03 km circuit

Place	Driver	Car	Laps	Time/reason for retiring	Grid
1	Reutemann	Williams-Ford	62	2h 00m 23.66s	2
2	Jones	Williams-Ford	62	2h 00m 28.10s	3
3	Patrese	Arrows-Ford	62	2h 01m 26.74s	4
4	Surer	Ensign-Ford	62	2h 01m 40.69s	18
5	de Angelis	Lotus-Ford	62	2h 01m 50.08s	10
6	Laffite	Ligier-Matra	62	2h 01m 50.49s	16
7	Jarier	Ligier-Matra	62	2h 01m 53.91s	23
8	Watson	McLaren-Ford	61		15
9	Rosberg	Fittipaldi-Ford	61		12
10	Tambay	Theodore-Ford	61		19
11	Mansell	Lotus-Ford	61		13
12	Piquet	Brabham-Ford	60		1
13	Zunino	Tyrrell-Ford	57		24
	Cheever	Tyrrell-Ford	49	running	14
	Giacomelli	Alfa Romeo	40	electrical	6
	G Villeneuve	Ferrari	25	turbo	7
	Rebaque	Brabham-Ford	22	suspension	11
	Stohr	Arrows-Ford	20	accident	21
	Prost	Renault	20	accident	5
	Pironi	Ferrari	19	accident	17
	de Cesaris	McLaren-Ford	9	electrical	20
	Serra	Fittipaldi-Ford	0	accident	22
	Arnoux	Renault	0	accident	8
	Andretti	Alfa Romeo	0	accident	9

Fastest Lap: Surer, 1m 54.302s. 98.458 mph/158.453 kph

1981

Argentine Grand Prix: Buenos Aires, 12 April 1981

53 laps of 3.71 mile/5.97 km circuit

Place	Driver	Car	Laps	Time/reason for retiring	Grid
1	Piquet	Brabham-Ford	53	1h 34m 32.74s	1
2	Reutemann	Williams-Ford	53	1h 34m 59.35s	4
3	Prost	Renault	53	1h 35m 22.72s	2
4	Jones	Williams-Ford	53	1h 35m 40.62s	3
5	Arnoux	Renault	53	1h 36m 04.59s	5
6	de Angelis	Lotus-Ford	52		10
7	Patrese	Arrows-Ford	52		9
8	Andretti	Alfa Romeo	52		17
9	Stohr	Arrows-Ford	52		19
10	Giacomelli	Alfa Romeo	51	out of fuel	22
11	de Cesaris	McLaren-Ford	51		18
12	Lammers	ATS-Ford	51		23
13	Zunino	Tyrrell-Ford	51	penalised one lap	24
	G Villeneuve	Ferrari	40	drive-shaft	7
	Tambay	Theodore-Ford	36	engine	14
	Watson	McLaren-Ford	36	crownwheel and pinion	11
	Rebaque	Brabham-Ford	32	distributor	6
	Serra	Fittipaldi-Ford	28	gearbox	20
	Laffite	Ligier-Matra	19	handling	21
	Surer	Ensign-Ford	14	engine	16
	Rosberg	Fittipaldi-Ford	4	fuel pump	8
	Mansell	Lotus-Ford	3	engine	15
	Pironi	Ferrari	3	engine	12
	Cheever	Tyrrell-Ford	1	clutch	13

Fastest Lap: Piquet, 1m 45.287s. 126.800 mph/204.066 kph

San Marino Grand Prix: Imola, 3 May 1981

60 laps of 3.13 mile/5.04 km circuit

Place	Driver	Car	Laps	Time/reason for retiring	Grid
1	Piquet	Brabham-Ford	60	1h 51m 23.97s	5
2	Patrese	Arrows-Ford	60	1h 51m 28.55s	9
3	Reutemann	Williams-Ford	60	1h 51m 30.31s	2
4	Rebaque	Brabham-Ford	60	1h 51m 46.86s	13
5	Pironi	Ferrari	60	1h 51m 49.84s	6
6	de Cesaris	McLaren-Ford	60	1h 52m 30.58s	14
7	G Villeneuve	Ferrari	60	1h 53m 05.94s	1
8	Arnoux	Renault	59		3
9	Surer	Ensign-Ford	59		21
10	Watson	McLaren-Ford	58		7
11	Tambay	Theodore-Ford	58		16
12	Jones	Williams-Ford	58		8
13	Borgudd	ATS-Ford	57		24
	Jabouille	Ligier-Matra	45	running	18
	Salazar	March-Ford	38	oil pressure	23
	Alboreto	Tyrrell-Ford	31	accident	17
	Gabbiani	Osella-Ford	31	accident	20
	Giacomelli	Alfa Romeo	28	accident	11
	Cheever	Tyrrell-Ford	28	accident	19
	Andretti	Alfa Romeo	26	gearbox	12
	Rosberg	Fittipaldi-Ford	14	engine	15
	Laffite	Ligier-Matra	7	accident	10
	Prost	Renault	3	gearbox	4
	Guerra	Osella-Ford	0	accident	22

Fastest Lap: Villeneuve, 1m 48.064s. 104.328 mph/167.9 kph

Belgian Grand Prix: Zolder, 17 May 1981

54 laps of 2.65 mile/4.26 km circuit

Place	Driver	Car	Laps	Time/reason for retiring	Grid
1	Reutemann	Williams-Ford	54	1h 16m 31.61s	1
2	Laffite	Ligier-Matra	54	1h 17m 07.67s	9
3	Mansell	Lotus-Ford	54	1h 17m 15.30s	10
4	G Villeneuve	Ferrari	54	1h 17m 19.25s	7
5	de Angelis	Lotus-Ford	54	1h 17m 20.81s	14

Belgian Grand Prix (cont)

Place	Driver	Car	Laps	Time/reason for retiring	Grid
6	Cheever	Tyrrell-Ford	54	1h 17m 24.12s	8
7	Watson	McLaren-Ford	54	1h 17m 33.27s	5
8	Pironi	Ferrari	54	1h 18m 03.65s	3
9	Giacomelli	Alfa Romeo	54	1h 18m 07.19s	17
10	Andretti	Alfa Romeo	53		18
11	Surer	Ensign-Ford	52		15
12	Alboreto	Tyrrell-Ford	52		19
13	Ghinzani	Osella-Ford	50		24
	Rebaque	Brabham-Ford	39	accident	21
	Jabouille	Ligier-Matra	35	transmission	16
	Serra	Fittipaldi-Ford	29	engine	20
	Gabbiani	Osella-Ford	22	engine	22
	Jones	Williams-Ford	19	accident	6
	de Cesaris	McLaren-Ford	11	gearbox	23
	Piquet	Brabham-Ford	10	accident	2
	Rosberg	Fittipaldi-Ford	10	gear-lever	11
	Prost	Renault	2	clutch	12
	Stohr	Arrows-Ford	0	accident	13
	Patrese	Arrows-Ford	0	accident	4

Fastest Lap: Reutemann, 1m 23.30s. 114.45 mph/184.19 kph

Monaco Grand Prix: Monte Carlo, 31 May 1981

76 laps of 2.06 mile/3.31 km circuit

Place	Driver	Car	Laps	Time/reason for retiring	Grid
1	G Villeneuve	Ferrari	76	1h 54m 23.38s	2
2	Jones	Williams-Ford	76	1h 55m 03.29s	7
3	Laffite	Ligier-Matra	76	1h 55m 52.62s	8
4	Pironi	Ferrari	75		17
5	Cheever	Tyrrell-Ford	74		15
6	Surer	Ensign-Ford	74		19
7	Tambay	Theodore-Ford	72		16
	Piquet	Brabham-Ford	53	accident	1
	Watson	McLaren-Ford	53	engine	10
	Alboreto	Tyrrell-Ford	50	spun	20
	Giacomelli	Alfa Romeo	50	accident	18
	Prost	Renault	45	engine	9

Monaco Grand Prix (cont)

Place	Driver	Car	Laps	Time/reason for retiring	Grid
	Reutemann	Williams-Ford	34	gearbox	4
	Arnoux	Renault	32	accident	13
	de Angelis	Lotus-Ford	32	engine	6
	Patrese	Arrows-Ford	29	gearbox	5
	Mansell	Lotus-Ford	16	suspension	3
	Stohr	Arrows-Ford	15	electrical	14
	de Cesaris	McLaren-Ford	0	accident	11
	Andretti	Alfa Romeo	0	accident	12

Fastest Lap: Jones, 1m 27.470s. 84.699 mph/136.311 kph

Spanish Grand Prix: Jarama, 21 June 1981

80 laps of 2.06 mile/3.31 km circuit

Place	Driver	Car	Laps	Time/reason for retiring	Grid
1	G Villeneuve	Ferrari	80	1h 46m 35.01s	7
2	Laffite	Ligier-Matra	80	1h 46m 35.23s	1
3	Watson	McLaren-Ford	80	1h 46m 35.59s	4
4	Reutemann	Williams-Ford	80	1h 46m 36.02s	3
5	de Angelis	Lotus-Ford	80	1h 46m 36.25s	10
6	Mansell	Lotus-Ford	80	1h 47m 03.59s	11
7	Jones	Williams-Ford	80	1h 47m 31.59s	2
8	Andretti	Alfa Romeo	80	1h 47m 35.81s	8
9	Arnoux	Renault	80	1h 47m 42.09s	17
10	Giacomelli	Alfa Romeo	80	1h 47m 48.66s	6
11	Serra	Fittipaldi-Ford	79		21
12	Rosberg	Fittipaldi-Ford	78		15
13	Tambay	Theodore-Ford	78		16
14	Salazar	Ensign-Ford	77		24
15	Pironi	Ferrari	76		13
16	Daly	March-Ford	75		22
	Cheever	Tyrrell-Ford	61	running	20
	Jabouille	Ligier-Matra	52	brakes	19
	Rebaque	Brabham-Ford	46	gearbox	18
	Piquet	Brabham-Ford	43	accident	9
	Stohr	Arrows-Ford	43	engine	23
	Prost	Renault	28	accident	5
	Patrese	Arrows-Ford	21	engine	12
	de Cesaris	McLaren-Ford	9	accident	14

Fastest Lap: Jones, 1m 17.818s. 95.207 mph/153.22 kph

1981

French Grand Prix: Dijon, 5 July 1981

80 laps of 2.36 mile/3.8 km circuit

Place	Driver	Car	Laps	Time/reason for retiring	Grid
1	Prost	Renault	80	1h 35m 48.13s	3
2	Watson	McLaren-Ford	80	1h 35m 50.42s	2
3	Piquet	Brabham-Ford	80	1h 36m 12.35s	4
4	Arnoux	Renault	80	1h 36m 30.43s	1
5	Pironi	Ferrari	79		14
6	de Angelis	Lotus-Ford	79		8
7	Mansell	Lotus-Ford	79		13
8	Andretti	Alfa Romeo	79		10
9	Rebaque	Brabham-Ford	78		15
10	Reutemann	Williams-Ford	78		7
11	de Cesaris	McLaren-Ford	78		5
12	Surer	Theodore-Ford	78		21
13	Cheever	Tyrrell-Ford	77		19
14	Patrese	Arrows-Ford	77		18
15	Giacomelli	Alfa Romeo	77		12
16	Alboreto	Tyrrell-Ford	77		23
17	Jones	Williams-Ford	76		9
	Laffite	Ligier-Matra	57	suspension	6
	Daly	March-Ford	55	engine	20
	Villeneuve	Ferrari	41	electrical	11
	Tambay	Theodore-Ford	30	wheel bearing	16
	Rosberg	Fittipaldi-Ford	11	suspension	17
	Salazar	Ensign-Ford	6	suspension	22

Fastest Lap: Prost, 1m 09.14s. 122.944 mph/197.859 kph

British Grand Prix: Silverstone, 18 July 1981

68 laps of 2.93 mile/4.72 km circuit

Place	Driver	Car	Laps	Time/reason for retiring	Grid
1	Watson	McLaren-Ford	68	1h 26m 54.80s	5
2	Reutemann	Williams-Ford	68	1h 27m 35.45s	9
3	Laffite	Ligier-Matra	67		14
4	Cheever	Tyrrell-Ford	67		23
5	Rebaque	Brabham-Ford	67		13
6	Borgudd	ATS-Ford	67		21
7	Daly	March-Ford	66		17

British Grand Prix (cont)

Place	Driver	Car	Laps	Time/reason for retiring	Grid
8	Jarier	Osella-Ford	65		20
9	Arnoux	Renault	64	engine	1
10	Patrese	Arrows-Ford	64	engine	10
11	Surer	Theodore-Ford	61	fuel	24
	Andretti	Alfa Romeo	59	throttle	11
	Rosberg	Fittipaldi-Ford	56	suspension	16
	de Angelis	Lotus-Ford	25	black flagged, retired	22
	Prost	Renault	17	engine	2
	Tambay	Ligier-Matra	15	ignition	15
	Pironi	Ferrari	13	engine	4
	Piquet	Brabham-Ford	11	accident	3
	Giacomelli	Alfa Romeo	5	gearbox	12
	G Villeneuve	Ferrari	4	accident	8
	Jones	Williams-Ford	3	accident	7
	de Cesaris	McLaren-Ford	3	accident	6
	Alboreto	Tyrrell-Ford	0	clutch	19
	Stohr	Arrows-Ford	0	accident	18

Fastest Lap: Arnoux, 1m 15.067s. 140.61 mph/226.289 kph

German Grand Prix: Hockenheim, 2 August 1981

45 laps of 4.22 mile/6.79 km circuit

Place	Driver	Car	Laps	Time/reason for retiring	Grid
1	Piquet	Brabham-Ford	45	1h 25m 55.60s	6
2	Prost	Renault	45	1h 26m 07.12s	1
3	Laffite	Ligier-Matra	45	1h 27m 00.20s	7
4	Rebaque	Brabham-Ford	45	1h 27m 35.29s	16
5	Cheever	Tyrrell-Ford	45	1h 27m 46.12s	18
6	Watson	McLaren-Ford	44		9
7	de Angelis	Lotus-Ford	44		14
8	Jarier	Osella-Ford	44		17
9	Andretti	Alfa Romeo	44		12
10	G Villeneuve	Ferrari	44		8
11	Jones	Williams-Ford	44		4
12	Stohr	Arrows-Ford	44		24
13	Arnoux	Renault	44		2
14	Surer	Theodore-Ford	43		22
15	Giacomelli	Alfa Romeo	43		19

German Grand Prix (cont)

Place	Driver	Car	Laps	Time/reason for retiring	Grid
	Salazar	Ensign-Ford	39	running	23
	Borgudd	ATS-Ford	35	engine	20
	Reutemann	Williams-Ford	27	engine	3
	Patrese	Arrows-Ford	27	engine	13
	Tambay	Ligier-Matra	27	wheel	11
	Daly	March-Ford	15	steering	21
	Mansell	Lotus-Ford	12	fuel leak	15
	de Cesaris	McLaren-Ford	4	spun	10
	Pironi	Ferrari	1	engine	5

Fastest Lap: Jones, 1m 52.42s. 135.068 mph/217.371 kph

Austrian Grand Prix: Österreichring, 16 August 1981

53 laps of 3.69 mile/5.94 km circuit

Place	Driver	Car	Laps	Time/reason for retiring	Grid
1	Laffite	Ligier-Matra	53	1h 27m 36.47s	4
2	Arnoux	Renault	53	1h 27m 41.64s	1
3	Piquet	Brabham-Ford	53	1h 27m 43.81s	7
4	Jones	Williams-Ford	53	1h 27m 48.51s	6
5	Reutemann	Williams-Ford	53	1h 28m 08.32s	5
6	Watson	McLaren-Ford	53	1h 29m 07.61s	12
7	de Angelis	Lotus-Ford	52		9
8	de Cesaris	McLaren-Ford	52		18
9	Pironi	Ferrari	52		8
10	Jarier	Osella-Ford	51		14
11	Daly	March-Ford	47		19
	Andretti	Alfa Romeo	46	engine	13
	Borgudd	ATS-Ford	44	brakes	21
	Patrese	Arrows-Ford	43	engine	10
	Salazar	Ensign-Ford	43	engine	20
	Alboreto	Tyrrell-Ford	40	engine	22
	Giacomelli	Alfa Romeo	35	engine	16
	Rebaque	Brabham-Ford	31	clutch	15
	Stohr	Arrows-Ford	27	spun	24
	Prost	Renault	26	suspension	2
	Tambay	Ligier-Matra	26	engine	17
	Mansell	Lotus-Ford	23	engine	11
	G Villeneuve	Ferrari	11	accident	3
	Surer	Theodore-Ford	0	distributor	23

Fastest Lap: Laffite, 1m 37.62s. 136.168 mph/219.142 kph

Dutch Grand Prix: Zandvoort, 30 August 1981

72 laps of 2.64 mile/4.25 km circuit

Place	Driver	Car	Laps	Time/reason for retiring	Grid
1	Prost	Renault	72	1h 40m 22.43s	1
2	Piquet	Brabham-Ford	72	1h 40m 30.67s	3
3	Jones	Williams-Ford	72	1h 40m 57.93s	4
4	Rebaque	Brabham-Ford	71		14
5	de Angelis	Lotus-Ford	71		9
6	Salazar	Ensign-Ford	70		23
7	Stohr	Arrows-Ford	69		20
8	Surer	Theodore-Ford	69		19
9	Alboreto	Tyrrell-Ford	68	engine	24
10	Borgudd	ATS-Ford	68		22
	Andretti	Alfa Romeo	62	accident	7
	Watson	McLaren-Ford	50	electrical	8
	Cheever	Tyrrell-Ford	46	accident	21
	Jarier	Osella-Ford	29	gearbox	17
	Arnoux	Renault	21	accident	2
	Giacomelli	Alfa Romeo	19	accident	13
	Laffite	Ligier-Matra	18	accident	6
	Reutemann	Williams-Ford	18	accident	5
	Patrese	Arrows-Ford	16	suspension	10
	Daly	March-Ford	5	suspension	18
	Pironi	Ferrari	4	accident	12
	Mansell	Lotus-Ford	1	electrical	16
	Tambay	Ligier-Matra	0	accident	11
	G Villeneuve	Ferrari	0	accident	15

Fastest Lap: Jones, 1m 21.83s. 116.234 mph/187.061 kph

Italian Grand Prix: Monza, 13 September 1981

52 laps of 3.6 mile/5.8 km circuit

Place	Driver	Car	Laps	Time/reason for retiring	Grid
1	Prost	Renault	52	1h 26m 33.897s	3
2	Jones	Williams-Ford	52	1h 26m 56.072s	5
3	Reutemann	Williams-Ford	52	1h 27m 24.484s	2
4	de Angelis	Lotus-Ford	52	1h 28m 06.799s	11
5	Pironi	Ferrari	52	1h 28m 08.419s	8
6	Piquet	Brabham-Ford	51	engine	6
7	de Cesaris	McLaren-Ford	51	accident	16
8	Giacomelli	Alfa Romeo	50		10
9	Jarier	Osella-Ford	50		18
10	Henton	Toleman-Hart	49		23
	Andretti	Alfa Romeo	41	engine	13
	Daly	March-Ford	37	gearbox	19
	Tambay	Ligier-Matra	22	puncture	15
	Mansell	Lotus-Ford	21	handling	12
	Watson	McLaren-Ford	19	accident	7
	Patrese	Arrows-Ford	19	gearbox	20
	Alboreto	Tyrrell-Ford	16	accident	22
	Salazar	Ensign-Ford	13	tyre	24
	Arnoux	Renault	12	accident	1
	Cheever	Tyrrell-Ford	11	spun	17
	Laffite	Ligier-Matra	11	puncture	4
	Borgudd	ATS-Ford	10	spun	21
	G Villeneuve	Ferrari	6	turbo	9
	Rebaque	Brabham-Ford	0	electrical	14

Fastest Lap: Reutemann, 1m 37.528s. 133.030 mph/214.092 kph

Canadian Grand Prix: Montreal, 27 September 1981

63 laps of 2.74 mile/4.41 km circuit

Place	Driver	Car	Laps	Time/reason for retiring	Grid
1	Laffite	Ligier-Matra	63	2h 01m 25.205s	10
2	Watson	McLaren-Ford	63	2h 01m 31.438s	9
3	G Villeneuve	Ferrari	63	2h 03m 15.480s	11
4	Giacomelli	Alfa Romeo	62		15
5	Piquet	Brabham-Ford	62		1

Canadian Grand Prix (cont)

Place	Driver	Car	Laps	Time/reason for retiring	Grid
6	de Angelis	Lotus-Ford	62		7
7	Andretti	Alfa Romeo	62		16
8	Daly	March-Ford	61		20
9	Surer	Theodore-Ford	61		19
10	Reutemann	Williams-Ford	60		2
11	Alboreto	Tyrrell-Ford	59		22
12	Cheever	Tyrrell-Ford	56	engine	14
	de Cesaris	McLaren-Ford	51	spun	13
	Prost	Renault	48	accident	4
	Mansell	Lotus-Ford	45	accident	5
	Borgudd	ATS-Ford	39	spun	21
	Rebaque	Brabham-Ford	35	spun	6
	Jarier	Osella-Ford	26	accident	23
	Pironi	Ferrari	24	engine	12
	Jones	Williams-Ford	24	handling	3
	Salazar	Ensign-Ford	8	spun	24
	Tambay	Ligier-Matra	6	spun	17
	Patrese	Arrows-Ford	6	spun	18
	Arnoux	Renault	0	accident	8

Fastest Lap: Watson, 1m 49.475s. 90.11 mph/145.019 kph

United States Grand Prix: Las Vegas, 17 October 1981

75 laps of 2.27 mile/3.65 km circuit

Place	Driver	Car	Laps	Time/reason for retiring	Grid
1	Jones	Williams-Ford	75	1h 44m 09.077s	2
2	Prost	Renault	75	1h 44m 29.125s	5
3	Giacomelli	Alfa Romeo	75	1h 44m 29 505s	8
4	Mansell	Lotus-Ford	75	1h 44m 56.550s	9
5	Piquet	Brabham-Ford	75	1h 45m 25.515s	4
6	Laffite	Ligier-Matra	75	1h 45m 27 252s	12
7	Watson	McLaren-Ford	75	1h 45m 27.574s	6
8	Reutemann	Williams-Ford	74		1
9	Pironi	Ferrari	73		18
10	Rosberg	Fittipaldi-Ford	73		20
11	Patrese	Arrows-Ford	71		11

United States Grand Prix (cont)

Place	Driver	Car	Laps	Time/reason for retiring	Grid
12	de Cesaris	McLaren-Ford	69		14
13	Alboreto	Tyrrell-Ford	67		17
	Salazar	Ensign-Ford	61		24
	Warwick	Toleman-Hart	43	gearbox	22
	Andretti	Alfa Romeo	29	suspension	10
	G Villeneuve	Ferrari	22	disqualified: illegal start	3
	Rebaque	Brabham-Ford	20	spun	16
	Surer	Theodore-Ford	19	suspension	23
	Cheever	Tyrrell-Ford	10	engine	19
	Arnoux	Renault	10	electrical	13
	Tambay	Ligier-Matra	2	accident	7
	de Angelis	Lotus-Ford	2	water leak	15
	Jarier	Osella-Ford	0	transmission	21

Fastest Lap: Pironi, 1m 20.156s. 101.861 mph/163.929 kph

World Championship 1981

1	Piquet	50
2	Reutemann	49
3	Jones	46
4	Laffite	44
5	Prost	43
6	Watson	27
7	G Villeneuve	25
8	de Angelis	14
9 =	Arnoux, Rebaque	11
11 =	Cheever, Patrese	10
13	Pironi	9
14	Mansell	8
15	Giacomelli	7
16	Surer	4
17	Andretti	3
18 =	Borgudd, de Cesaris, Salazar, Tambay	1

Constructors' Championship

1	Williams-Ford	95
2	Brabham-Ford	61
3	Renault	54
4	Ligier-Matra	44
5	Ferrari	34
6	McLaren-Ford	28
7	Lotus-Ford	22
8 =	Alfa Romeo, Arrows-Ford, Tyrrell-Ford	10
11	Ensign-Ford	5
12 =	ATS-Ford, Theodore-Ford	1

1982

Eleven different drivers won races and the championship went to Keke Rosberg, who won only one race but profited from a consistent finishing record and the inconsistency of others. Lauda emerged from retirement to win two races. The Ferrari challenge was vitiated by the death of Villeneuve and the accident which ended Pironi's career, although the team took the constructors' title. Brabham won races with both the BMW turbo and the normally aspirated Ford Cosworth.

South African Grand Prix: Kyalami, 23 January 1982

77 laps of 2.55 mile/4.1 km circuit

Place	Driver	Car	Laps	Time/reason for retiring	Grid
1	Prost	Renault	77	1h 32m 08.40s	5
2	Reutemann	Williams-Ford	77	1h 32m 23.35s	8
3	Arnoux	Renault	77	1h 32m 36.30s	1
4	Lauda	McLaren-Ford	77	1h 32m 40.51s	13
5	Rosberg	Williams-Ford	77	1h 32m 54.54s	7
6	Watson	McLaren-Ford	77	1h 32m 59.39s	9
7	Alboreto	Tyrrell-Ford	76		10
8	de Angelis	Lotus-Ford	76		15
9	Salazar	ATS-Ford	75		12
10	Winkelhock	ATS-Ford	75		20
11	Giacomelli	Alfa Romeo	74		19
12	Mass	March-Ford	74		22
13	de Cesaris	Alfa Romeo	73		16
14	Daly	Theodore-Ford	73		24
15	Boesel	March-Ford	72		21
16	Borgudd	Tyrrell-Ford	72		23
17	Serra	Fittipaldi-Ford	72		25
18	Pironi	Ferrari	71		6
	Laffite	Ligier-Matra	54	fuel system	11
	Warwick	Toleman-Hart	43	accident	14
	Patrese	Brabham-BMW	18	turbo	4
	Cheever	Ligier-Matra	11	fuel system	17
	G Villeneuve	Ferrari	6	turbo	3
	Piquet	Brabham-BMW	3	accident	2
	Mansell	Lotus-Ford	0	electrical	18
	Jarier	Osella-Ford	0	accident	26

Fastest Lap: Prost, 1m 08.28s. 134.46 mph/216.39 kph

Brazilian Grand Prix: Rio de Janeiro, 21 March 1982

63 laps of 3.13 mile/5.03 km circuit

Place	Driver	Car	Laps	Time/reason for retiring	Grid
	Piquet	Brabham-Ford	63	disqualified: under weight	7
	Rosberg	Williams-Ford	63	disqualified: under weight	3
1	Prost	Renault	63	1h 44m 33.13s	1
2	Watson	McLaren-Ford	63	1h 44m 36.12s	12
3	Mansell	Lotus-Ford	63	1h 45m 10.00s	14
4	Alboreto	Tyrrell-Ford	63	1h 45m 23.90s	13
5	Winkelhock	ATS-Ford	62		15
6	Pironi	Ferrari	62		8
7	Borgudd	Tyrrell-Ford	61		21
8	Mass	March-Ford	61		22
9	Jarier	Osella-Ford	60		23
10	Baldi	Arrows-Ford	59		19
	Salazar	ATS-Ford	38	engine	18
	Serra	Fittipaldi-Ford	36	accident	25
	Patrese	Brabham-Ford	33	driver	9
	G Villeneuve	Ferrari	29	spun	2
	Lauda	McLaren-Ford	22	accident	5
	Arnoux	Renault	21	accident	4
	Reutemann	Williams-Ford	21	accident	6
	de Angelis	Lotus-Ford	21	accident	11
	Cheever	Ligier-Matra	19	water	26
	Giacomelli	Alfa Romeo	16	engine	16
	Laffite	Ligier-Matra	15	engine	24
	de Cesaris	Alfa Romeo	14	undertray	10
	Daly	Theodore-Ford	12	spun	20
	Boesel	March-Ford	11	accident	17

Fastest Lap: Prost, 1m 37.02s. 116 mph/186.69 kph

United States Grand Prix: Long Beach, 4 April 1982

75.5 laps of 2.13 mile/3.43 km circuit

Place	Driver	Car	Laps	Time/reason for retiring	Grid
1	Lauda	McLaren-Ford	75	1h 58m 25.32s	2
2	Rosberg	Williams-Ford	75	1h 58m 39.98s	8
	G Villeneuve	Ferrari	75	disqualified: illegal wing	7
3	Patrese	Brabham-Ford	75	1h 59m 44.46s	18
4	Alboreto	Tyrrell-Ford	75	1h 59m 46.27s	12
5	de Angelis	Lotus-Ford	74		16
6	Watson	McLaren-Ford	74		11
7	Mansell	Lotus-Ford	73		17
8	Mass	March-Ford	73		21
9	Boesel	March-Ford	70		23
10	Borgudd	Tyrrell-Ford	68		24

United States Grand Prix (cont)

Place	Driver	Car	Laps	Time/reason for retiring	Grid
	Cheever	Ligier-Matra	58	gearbox	13
	de Cesaris	Alfa Romeo	33	accident	1
	Henton	Arrows-Ford	32	accident	20
	Guerrero	Ensign-Ford	27	accident	19
	Laffite	Ligier-Matra	26	spun	15
	Jarier	Osella-Ford	26	transmission	10
	Piquet	Brabham-Ford	25	accident	6
	Daly	Theodore-Ford	22	accident	22
	Andretti	Williams-Ford	19	accident	14
	Prost	Renault	10	accident	4
	Pironi	Ferrari	6	accident	9
	Arnoux	Renault	5	accident	3
	Giacomelli	Alfa Romeo	5	accident	5
	Salazar	ATS-Ford	3	accident	26
	Winkelhock	ATS-Ford	1	accident	25

Fastest Lap: Lauda, 1m 30.83s. 84.42 mph/135.86 kph
* Start and finish lines in different places. All finishers completed 0.5 of a lap extra.

San Marino Grand Prix: Imola, 25 April 1981

60 laps of 3.13 mile/5.04 km circuit

Place	Driver	Car	Laps	Time/reason for retiring	Grid
1	Pironi	Ferrari	60	1h 36m 38.89s	4
2	G Villeneuve	Ferrari	60	1h 36m 39.25s	3
3	Alboreto	Tyrrell-Ford	60	1h 37m 46.57s	5
4	Jarier	Osella-Ford	59		8
5	Salazar	ATS-Ford	57		13
	Winkelhock	ATS-Ford	54	disqualified: under weight	11
	T Fabi	Toleman-Hart	52	running	9
	Arnoux	Renault	44	engine	1
	Giacomelli	Alfa Romeo	24	engine	6
	Paletti	Osella-Ford	7	suspension	12
	Prost	Renault	6	engine	2
	de Cesaris	Alfa Romeo	4	fuel system	7
	Henton	Tyrrell-Ford	0	transmission	10

Fastest Lap: Pironi, 1m 35.04s. 119.63 mph/190.92 kph
* Race boycotted by other teams.

Belgian Grand Prix: Zolder, 9 May 1982

70 laps of 2.65 mile/4.26 km circuit

Place	Driver	Car	Laps	Time/reason for retiring	Grid
1	Watson	McLaren-Ford	70	1h 35m 42.00s	10
2	Rosberg	Williams-Ford	70	1h 35m 49.26s	3
	Lauda	McLaren-Ford	70	disqualified: under weight	4
3	Cheever	Ligier-Matra	69		14
4	de Angelis	Lotus-Ford	68		11
5	Piquet	Brabham-BMW	67		8
6	Serra	Fittipaldi-Ford	67		23
7	Surer	Arrows-Ford	66		22
8	Boesel	March-Ford	66		24
9	Laffite	Ligier-Matra	66		17
	Daly	Williams-Ford	60	accident	13
	Mass	March-Ford	60	engine	25
	Prost	Renault	59	spun	1
	Patrese	Brabham-BMW	52	accident	9
	Baldi	Arrows-Ford	51	throttle	26
	Jarier	Osella-Ford	37	wing	16
	de Cesaris	Alfa Romeo	34	gearbox	6
	Henton	Tyrrell-Ford	33	engine	20
	Alboreto	Tyrrell-Ford	29	engine	5
	Warwick	Toleman-Hart	29	transmission	19
	T Fabi	Toleman-Hart	13	brakes	21
	Mansell	Lotus-Ford	9	gearbox	7
	Arnoux	Renault	7	turbo	2
	Winkelhock	ATS-Ford	0	clutch	12
	Salazar	ATS-Ford	0	accident	18
	Giacomelli	Alfa Romeo	0	accident	15

Fastest Lap: Watson, 1m 20.21s. 118.86 mph/191.28 kph
* Gilles Villeneuve killed in practice.

Monaco Grand Prix: Monte Carlo, 23 May 1982

76 laps of 2.06 mile/3.31 km circuit

Place	Driver	Car	Laps	Time/reason for retiring	Grid
1	Patrese	Brabham-Ford	76	1h 54m 11.26s	2
2	Pironi	Ferrari	75	electrical	5
3	de Cesaris	Alfa Romeo	75	out of fuel	7
4	Mansell	Lotus-Ford	75		11
5	de Angelis	Lotus-Ford	75		15
6	Daly	Williams-Ford	74	accident	8
7	Prost	Renault	73	accident	4
8	Henton	Tyrrell-Ford	72		17
9	Surer	Arrows-Ford	70		19

Monaco Grand Prix (cont)

Place	Driver	Car	Laps	Time/reason for retiring	Grid
10	Alboreto	Tyrrell-Ford	69	suspension	9
	Rosberg	Williams-Ford	64	accident	6
	Lauda	McLaren-Ford	56	engine	12
	Piquet	Brabham-BMW	49	gearbox	13
	Watson	McLaren-Ford	35	electrical	10
	Winkelhock	ATS-Ford	31	transmission	14
	Laffite	Ligier-Matra	29	driver	18
	Cheever	Ligier-Matra	27	engine	16
	Salazar	ATS-Ford	22	fire extinguisher	20
	Arnoux	Renault	14	spun	1
	Giacomelli	Alfa Romeo	4	transmission	3

Fastest Lap: Patrese, 1m 26.35s. 85.8 mph/138.07 kph

United States Grand Prix East: Detroit, 6 June 1982

62 laps of 2.49 mile/4.01 km circuit

Place	Driver	Car	Laps	Time/reason for retiring	Grid
1	Watson	McLaren-Ford	62	1h 58m 41.04s	17
2	Cheever	Ligier-Matra	62	1h 58m 56.77s	9
3	Pironi	Ferrari	62	1h 59m 09.12s	4
4	Rosberg	Williams-Ford	62	1h 59m 53.02s	3
5	Daly	Williams-Ford	62	2h 00m 04.80s	12
6	Laffite	Ligier-Matra	61		13
7	Mass	March-Ford	61		18
8	Surer	Arrows-Ford	61		19
9	Henton	Tyrrell-Ford	60		20
10	Arnoux	Renault	59		15
11	Serra	Fittipaldi-Ford	59		25
12	Prost	Renault	54		1
	Mansell	Lotus-Ford	44	engine	7
	Lauda	McLaren-Ford	40	accident	10
	Alboreto	Tyrrell-Ford	40	accident	16
	Giacomelli	Alfa Romeo	30	accident	6
	de Angelis	Lotus-Ford	17	gearbox	8
	Salazar	ATS-Ford	13	accident	24
	Guerrero	Ensign-Ford	6	accident	11
	Patrese	Brabham-Ford	6	accident	14
	de Cesaris	Alfa Romeo	2	transmission	2
	Jarier	Osella-Ford	2	engine	22
	Winkelhock	ATS-Ford	1	accident	5
	Boesel	March-Ford	0	accident	21
	Baldi	Arrows-Ford	0	accident	23

Fastest Lap: Prost, 1m 50.44s. 81.27 mph/130.8 kph

Canadian Grand Prix: Montreal, 13 June 1982

70 laps of 2.74 mile/4.41 km circuit

Place	Driver	Car	Laps	Time/reason for retiring	Grid
1	Piquet	Brabham-BMW	70	1h 46m 39.58s	4
2	Patrese	Brabham-Ford	70	1h 46m 53.38s	8
3	Watson	McLaren-Ford	70	1h 47m 41.41s	6
4	de Angelis	Lotus-Ford	69		10
5	Surer	Arrows-Ford	69		16
6	de Cesaris	Alfa Romeo	68	out of fuel	9
7	Daly	Williams-Ford	68	out of fuel	13
8	Baldi	Arrows-Ford	68		17
9	Pironi	Ferrari	67		1
10	Cheever	Ligier-Matra	66	out of fuel	12
11	Mass	March-Ford	66		22
	Henton	Tyrrell-Ford	59		26
	Rosberg	Williams-Ford	52	gearbox	7
	Boesel	March-Ford	47	engine	21
	Alboreto	Tyrrell-Ford	41	gearbox	15
	Prost	Renault	30	engine	3
	Arnoux	Renault	28	spun	2
	Salazar	ATS-Ford	20	engine	24
	Lauda	McLaren-Ford	17	clutch	11
	Laffite	Ligier-Matra	8	fuel system	19
	Guerrero	Ensign-Ford	2	clutch	20
	Giacomelli	Alfa Romeo	1	accident	5
	Mansell	Lotus-Ford	1	accident	14
	Lees	Theodore-Ford	0	accident	25
	Jarier	Osella-Ford	0	withdrawn	18
	Paletti	Osella-Ford	0	fatal accident	23

Fastest Lap: Pironi, 1m 28.32s. 111.69 mph/179.75 kph

Dutch Grand Prix: Zandvoort, 3 July 1982

72 laps of 2.64 mile/4.25 km circuit

Place	Driver	Car	Laps	Time/reason for retiring	Grid
1	Pironi	Ferrari	72	1h 38m 03.25s	4
2	Piquet	Brabham-BMW	72	1h 38m 24.90s	3
3	Rosberg	Williams-Ford	72	1h 38m 25.62s	7
4	Lauda	McLaren-Ford	71		5
5	Daly	Williams-Ford	71		12
6	Baldi	Arrows-Ford	71		16
7	Alboreto	Tyrrell-Ford	71		14
8	Tambay	Ferrari	71		6
9	Watson	McLaren-Ford	71		11
10	Surer	Arrows-Ford	71		17
11	Giacomelli	Alfa Romeo	70		8

Dutch Grand Prix (cont)

Place	Driver	Car	Laps	Time/reason for retiring	Grid
12	Winkelhock	ATS-Ford	70		18
13	Salazar	ATS-Ford	70		25
14	Jarier	Osella-Ford	69		23
15	Patrese	Brabham-BMW	69		10
	Mass	March-Ford	60	engine	24
	Lammers	Theodore-Ford	41	engine	26
	de Angelis	Lotus-Ford	40	handling	15
	de Cesaris	Alfa Romeo	35	electrical	9
	Prost	Renault	33	engine	2
	Arnoux	Renault	21	accident	1
	Henton	Tyrrell-Ford	21	throttle	20
	Boesel	March-Ford	21	engine	22
	Serra	Fittipaldi-Ford	18	fuel system	19
	Warwick	Toleman-Hart	15	oil leak	13
	Laffite	Ligier-Matra	5	handling	21

Fastest Lap: Warwick, 1m 19.78s. 119.22 mph/191.87 kph

British Grand Prix: Brands Hatch, 18 July 1982

76 laps of 2.61 mile/4.21 km circuit

Place	Driver	Car	Laps	Time/reason for retiring	Grid
1	Lauda	McLaren-Ford	76	1h 35m 33.81s	5
2	Pironi	Ferrari	76	1h 35m 59.54s	4
3	Tambay	Ferrari	76	1h 36m 12.25s	13
4	de Angelis	Lotus-Ford	76	1h 36m 15.05s	7
5	Daly	Williams-Ford	76	1h 36m 15.24s	10
6	Prost	Renault	76	1h 36m 15.45s	8
7	Giacomelli	Alfa Romeo	75		14
8	Henton	Tyrrell-Ford	75		17
9	Baldi	Arrows-Ford	74		26
10	Mass	March-Ford	73		25
	de Cesaris	Alfa Romeo	66	electrical	11
	Cheever	Ligier-Matra	60	engine	24
	Surer	Arrows-Ford	59	mechanical	22
	Rosberg	Williams-Ford	50	fuel pressure	1
	Alboreto	Tyrrell-Ford	44	running	9
	Laffite	Ligier-Matra	41	gearbox	20
	Warwick	Toleman-Hart	40	transmission	16
	Mansell	Lotus-Ford	29	handling	23
	Piquet	Brabham-BMW	9	fuel system	3
	Guerrero	Ensign-Ford	3	engine	19
	Jarier	Osella-Ford	2	accident	18
	Serra	Fittipaldi-Ford	2	accident	21
	Watson	McLaren-Ford	2	spun	12

British Grand Prix (cont)

Place	Driver	Car	Laps	Time/reason for retiring	Grid
	T Fabi	Toleman-Hart	0	accident	15
	Arnoux	Renault	0	accident	6
	Patrese	Brabham-BMW	0	accident	2

Fastest Lap: Henton, 1m 13.03s. 128.86 mph/207.35 kph

French Grand Prix: Paul Ricard, 25 July 1982

54 laps of 3.61 mile/5.81 km circuit

Place	Driver	Car	Laps	Time/reason for retiring	Grid
1	Arnoux	Renault	54	1h 33m 33.22s	1
2	Prost	Renault	54	1h 33m 50.53s	2
3	Pironi	Ferrari	54	1h 34m 15.35s	3
4	Tambay	Ferrari	54	1h 34m 49.46s	5
5	Rosberg	Williams-Ford	54	1h 35m 04.21s	10
6	Alboreto	Tyrrell-Ford	54	1h 35m 05.56s	15
7	Daly	Williams-Ford	53		11
8	Lauda	McLaren-Ford	53		9
9	Giacomelli	Alfa Romeo	53		8
10	Henton	Tyrrell-Ford	53		23
11	Winkelhock	ATS-Ford	52		18
12	Lees	Lotus-Ford	52		24
13	Surer	Arrows-Ford	52		20
14	Laffite	Ligier-Matra	51		16
15	Warwick	Toleman-Hart	50		14
16	Cheever	Ligier-Matra	49		19
	de Cesaris	Alfa Romeo	25	accident	7
	Piquet	Brabham-BMW	23	engine	6
	de Angelis	Lotus-Ford	17	fuel pressure	13
	Watson	McLaren-Ford	13	electrical	12
	Mass	March-Ford	10	accident	26
	Baldi	Arrows-Ford	10	accident	25
	Patrese	Brabham-BMW	9	engine	4
	Salazar	ATS-Ford	2	accident	22
	T Fabi	Toleman-Hart	0	oil pressure	21
	Jarier	Osella-Ford	0	transmission	17

Fastest Lap: Patrese, 1m 40.08s. 129.87 mph/209 kph

German Grand Prix: Hockenheim, 8 August 1982

45 laps of 4.22 mile/6.8 km circuit

Place	Driver	Car	Laps	Time/reason for retiring	Grid
1	Tambay	Ferrari	45	1h 27m 25.18s	5
2	Arnoux	Renault	45	1h 27m 41.56s	3
3	Rosberg	Williams-Ford	44		9
4	Alboreto	Tyrrell-Ford	44		7
5	Giacomelli	Alfa Romeo	44		11
6	Surer	Arrows-Ford	44		26
7	Henton	Tyrrell-Ford	44		17
8	Guerrero	Ensign-Ford	44		21
9	Mansell	Lotus-Ford	43		18
10	Warwick	Toleman-Hart	43		14
11	Serra	Fittipaldi-Ford	43		25
	Watson	McLaren-Ford	36	suspension	10
	Laffite	Ligier-Matra	36	handling	15
	Daly	Williams-Ford	25	engine	19
	Boesel	March-Ford	22	tyre	24
	de Angelis	Lotus-Ford	21	driver ill	13
	Piquet	Brabham-BMW	18	accident	4
	Salazar	ATS-Ford	17	accident	22
	Prost	Renault	14	electrical	2
	Patrese	Brabham-BMW	13	engine	6
	de Cesaris	Alfa Romeo	9	accident	8
	Cheever	Ligier-Matra	8	handling	12
	Baldi	Arrows-Ford	6	engine	23
	Jarier	Osella-Ford	3	suspension	20
	Winkelhock	ATS-Ford	3	transmission	16

Fastest Lap: Piquet, 1m 54.04s. 133.33 mph/214.58 kph
* Pironi crashed after setting fastest practice time; pole position left vacant.

Austrian Grand Prix: Österreichring, 15 August 1982

53 laps of 3.69 mile/5.94 km circuit

Place	Driver	Car	Laps	Time/reason for retiring	Grid
1	de Angelis	Lotus-Ford	53	1h 25m 02.12s	7
2	Rosberg	Williams-Ford	53	1h 25m 02.34s	6
3	Laffite	Ligier-Matra	52		14
4	Tambay	Ferrari	52		4
5	Lauda	McLaren-Ford	52		10
6	Baldi	Arrows-Ford	52		23
7	Serra	Fittipaldi-Ford	51		20
8	Prost	Renault	48	fuel injection	3
	Watson	McLaren-Ford	44	engine	18
	Henton	Tyrrell-Ford	32	engine	19
	Piquet	Brabham-BMW	31	engine	1
	Byrne	Theodore-Ford	28	spun	26

Austrian Grand Prix (cont)

Place	Driver	Car	Laps	Time/reason for retiring	Grid
	Surer	Arrows-Ford	28	engine	21
	Patrese	Brabham-BMW	27	engine	2
	Cheever	Ligier-Matra	22	engine	22
	Mansell	Lotus-Ford	17	engine	12
	Arnoux	Renault	16	engine	5
	Winkelhock	ATS-Ford	15	engine	25
	Warwick	Toleman-Hart	7	suspension	15
	T Fabi	Toleman-Hart	7	transmission	17
	Guerrero	Ensign-Ford	6	transmission	16
	Alboreto	Tyrrell-Ford	1	accident	8
	Keegan	March-Ford	1	accident	24
	de Cesaris	Alfa Romeo	0	accident	11
	Daly	Williams-Ford	0	accident	9
	Giacomelli	Alfa Romeo	0	accident	13

Fastest Lap: Piquet, 1m 33.7s. 141.86 mph/228.3 kph

Swiss Grand Prix: Dijon, 29 August 1982

80 laps of 2.36 mile/3.8 km circuit

Place	Driver	Car	Laps	Time/reason for retiring	Grid
1	Rosberg	Williams-Ford	80	1h 32m 41.09s	8
2	Prost	Renault	80	1h 32m 45.53s	1
3	Lauda	McLaren-Ford	80	1h 33m 41.43s	4
4	Piquet	Brabham-BMW	79		6
5	Patrese	Brabham-BMW	79		3
6	de Angelis	Lotus-Ford	79		14
7	Alboreto	Tyrrell-Ford	79		11
8	Mansell	Lotus-Ford	79		25
9	Daly	Williams-Ford	79		7
10	de Cesaris	Alfa Romeo	78		5
11	Henton	Tyrrell-Ford	78		17
12	Giacomelli	Alfa Romeo	78		9
13	Watson	McLaren-Ford	77		10
14	Salazar	ATS-Ford	77		24
15	Surer	Arrows-Ford	76		13
	Arnoux	Renault	75	fuel injection	2
	Cheever	Ligier-Matra	70	running	15
	Winkelhock	ATS-Ford	55	engine	19
	Jarier	Osella-Ford	44	engine	16
	Laffite	Ligier-Matra	33	handling	12
	T Fabi	Toleman-Hart	31	overheating	22
	Boesel	March-Ford	31	clutch	23
	Keegan	March-Ford	25	spun	21
	Warwick	Toleman-Hart	24	engine	20
	Guerrero	Ensign-Ford	4	engine	18

Fastest Lap: Prost, 1m 07.48s. 125.97 mph/202.74 kph

1982

Italian Grand Prix: Monza, 12 September 1982

52 laps of 3.6 mile/5.8 km circuit

Place	Driver	Car	Laps	Time/reason for retiring	Grid
1	Arnoux	Renault	52	1h 22m 25.73s	6
2	Tambay	Ferrari	52	1h 22m 39.80s	3
3	Andretti	Ferrari	52	1h 23m 14.19s	1
4	Watson	McLaren-Ford	52	1h 23m 53.58s	12
5	Alboreto	Tyrrell-Ford	51		11
6	Cheever	Ligier-Matra	51		14
7	Mansell	Lotus-Ford	51		23
8	Rosberg	Williams-Ford	50		7
9	Salazar	ATS-Ford	50		25
10	de Cesaris	Alfa Romeo	50		9
11	Serra	Fittipaldi-Ford	49		26
12	Baldi	Arrows-Ford	49		24
	Guerrero	Ensign-Ford	40	running	18
	de Angelis	Lotus-Ford	33	throttle	17
	Giacomelli	Alfa Romeo	32	handling	8
	Surer	Arrows-Ford	28	ignition	19
	Prost	Renault	27	fuel injection	5
	Lauda	McLaren-Ford	21	handling	10
	Jarier	Osella-Ford	10	lost wheel	15
	Piquet	Brabham-BMW	7	clutch	2
	Patrese	Brabham-BMW	6	clutch	4
	Laffite	Ligier-Matra	5	gearbox	21
	T Fabi	Toleman-Hart	2	engine	22
	Daly	Williams-Ford	0	accident	13
	Warwick	Toleman-Hart	0	accident	16
	Henton	Tyrrell-Ford	0	accident	20

Fastest Lap: Arnoux, 1m 33.62s. 138.59 mph/223.03 kph

United States Grand Prix: Las Vegas, 25 September 1982

75 laps of 2.27 mile/3.65 km circuit

Place	Driver	Car	Laps	Time/reason for retiring	Grid
1	Alboreto	Tyrrell-Ford	75	1h 41m 56.89s	3
2	Watson	McLaren-Ford	75	1h 42m 24.18s	8
3	Cheever	Ligier-Matra	75	1h 42m 53.34s	4
4	Prost	Renault	75	1h 43m 05.54s	1
5	Rosberg	Williams-Ford	75	1h 43m 08.26s	6
6	Daly	Williams-Ford	74		13
7	Surer	Arrows-Ford	74		15
8	Henton	Tyrrell-Ford	74		17
9	de Cesaris	Alfa Romeo	73		16
10	Giacomelli	Alfa Romeo	73		14
11	Baldi	Arrows-Ford	73		21

United States Grand Prix (cont)

Place	Driver	Car	Laps	Time/reason for retiring	Grid
12	Keegan	March-Ford	73		23
13	Boesel	March-Ford	69		22
	Winkelhock	ATS-Ford	62	running	20
	Lauda	McLaren-Ford	53	engine	12
	Byrne	Theodore-Ford	39	spun	24
	Warwick	Toleman-Hart	32	ignition	9
	de Angelis	Lotus-Ford	28	engine	18
	Andretti	Ferrari	26	suspension	7
	Piquet	Brabham-BMW	26	engine	11
	Arnoux	Renault	20	engine	2
	Patrese	Brabham-BMW	17	clutch	5
	Mansell	Lotus-Ford	8	accident	19
	Laffite	Ligier-Matra	5	engine	10

Fastest Lap: Alboreto, 1m 19.64s. 102.52 mph/164.99 kph

World Championship 1982

1	Rosberg	44
2 =	Pironi, Watson	39
4	Prost	34
5	Lauda	30
6	Arnoux	28
7 =	Alboreto, Tambay	25
9	de Angelis	23
10	Patrese	21
11	Piquet	20
12	Cheever	15
13	Daly	8
14	Mansell	7
15 =	Reutemann, G Villeneuve	6
17 =	de Cesaris, Laffite	5
19	Andretti	4
20	Jarier, Surer	3
22 =	Baldi, Giacomelli, Salazar, Winkelhock	2
26	Serra	1

Constructors' Championship

1	Ferrari	74
2	McLaren-Ford	69
3	Renault	62
4	Williams-Ford	58
5	Lotus-Ford	30
6	Tyrrell-Ford	25
7	Brabham-BMW	22
8	Ligier-Matra	20
9	Brabham-Ford	19
10	Alfa Romeo	7
11	Arrows-Ford	5
12	ATS-Ford	4
13	Osella-Ford	3
14	Fittipaldi-Ford	1

1983

Piquet took the championship, driving a turbocharged Brabham-BMW, although Arnoux and Prost were in contention until the last race. Ferrari won the constructors' championship with their turbo car. Other teams also turned to turbo power: McLaren used a TAG-financed Porsche-built engine; Lotus did a deal with Renault; ATS obtained BMWs; Toleman used Brian Hart's engine; Spirit debuted the Honda which Williams used later in the season, and Alfa raced their turbo for the first time. Alboreto's win in Detroit was the 155th and last for the Ford Cosworth which made its debut in 1967.

Brazilian Grand Prix: Rio de Janeiro, 13 March 1983

63 laps of 3.13 mile/5.03 km circuit

Place	Driver	Car	Laps	Time/reason for retiring	Grid
1	Piquet	Brabham-BMW	63	1h 48m 27.73s	4
	Rosberg	Williams-Ford	63	disqualified: push start	1
3	Lauda	McLaren-Ford	63	1h 49m 19.61s	9
4	Laffite	Williams-Ford	63	1h 49m 41.70s	18
5	Tambay	Ferrari	63	1h 49m 45.85s	3
6	Surer	Arrows-Ford	63	1h 49m 45.94s	20
7	Prost	Renault	62		2
8	Warwick	Toleman-Hart	62		5
9	Serra	Arrows-Ford	62		23
10	Arnoux	Ferrari	62		6
11	Sullivan	Tyrrell-Ford	62		21
12	Mansell	Lotus-Ford	61		22
	de Angelis	Lotus-Ford	60	disqualified: changed car before start	13
14	Cecotto	Theodore-Ford	60		19
15	Salazar	RAM-Ford	59		26
16	Winkelhock	ATS-BMW	59		25
	Guerrero	Theodore-Ford	53		14
	Cheever	Renault	41	turbo	8
	Watson	McLaren-Ford	34	engine	16
	Boesel	Ligier-Ford	25	electrical	17
	Baldi	Alfa Romeo	23	accident	10

Brazilian Grand Prix (cont)

Place	Driver	Car	Laps	Time/reason for retiring	Grid
	Jarier	Ligier-Ford	22	suspension	12
	Patrese	Brabham-BMW	19	exhaust	7
	C Fabi	Osella-Ford	17	engine	24
	Giacomelli	Toleman-Hart	16	spun	15
	Alboreto	Tyrrell-Ford	7	accident	11

Fastest Lap: Piquet, 1m 39.83s, 112.73 mph/181.43 kph

United States Grand Prix West: Long Beach, 27 March 1983

75 laps of 2.04 mile/3.28 km circuit

Place	Driver	Car	Laps	Time/reason for retiring	Grid
1	Watson	McLaren-Ford	75	1h 53m 34.9s	22
2	Lauda	McLaren-Ford	75	1h 54m 02.9s	23
3	Arnoux	Ferrari	75	1h 54m 48.5s	2
4	Laffite	Williams-Ford	74		4
5	Surer	Arrows-Ford	74		16
6	Cecotto	Theodore-Ford	74		17
7	Boesel	Ligier-Ford	73		26
8	Sullivan	Tyrrell-Ford	73		9
9	Alboreto	Tyrrell-Ford	73		7
10	Patrese	Brabham-BMW	72	distributor	11
11	Prost	Renault	72		8
12	Mansell	Lotus-Ford	72		13
	Cheever	Renault	67	gearbox	15
	Jones	Arrows-Ford	58	driver	12
	Piquet	Brabham-BMW	51	throttle	20
	de Cesaris	Alfa Romeo	48	gearbox	19
	de Angelis	Lotus-Renault	29	tyres	5
	Guerrero	Theodore-Ford	27	gearbox	18
	Jarier	Ligier-Ford	26	accident	10
	Giacomelli	Toleman-Hart	26	battery	14
	Baldi	Alfa Romeo	26	accident	21
	Tambay	Ferrari	25	accident	1
	Rosberg	Williams-Ford	25	accident	3
	Salazar	RAM-Ford	25	gearbox	25
	Warwick	Toleman-Hart	11	tyre	6
	Winkelhock	ATS-BMW	3	accident	24

Fastest Lap: Lauda, 1m 28.33s. 82.94 mph/133.48 kph

French Grand Prix: Paul Ricard, 17 April 1983

54 laps of 3.61 mile/5.81 km circuit

Place	Driver	Car	Laps	Time/reason for retiring	Grid
1	Prost	Renault	54	1h 34m 13.9s	1
2	Piquet	Brabham-BMW	54	1h 34m 43.6s	6
3	Cheever	Renault	54	1h 34m 54.2s	2
4	Tambay	Ferrari	54	1h 35m 20.8s	11
5	Rosberg	Williams-Ford	53		16
6	Laffite	Williams-Ford	53		19
7	Arnoux	Ferrari	53		4
8	Alboreto	Tyrrell-Ford	53		15
9	Jarier	Ligier-Ford	53		20
10	Surer	Arrows-Ford	53		21
11	Cecotto	Theodore-Ford	52		17
12	de Cesaris	Alfa Romeo	50		7
13	Giacomelli	Toleman-Hart	49	gearbox	13
	Boesel	Ligier-Ford	47	engine	25
	C Fabi	Osella-Ford	36	engine	23
	Winkelhock	ATS-BMW	36	engine	10
	Lauda	McLaren-Ford	29	wheel bearing	12
	Baldi	Alfa Romeo	28	accident	8
	Serra	Arrows-Ford	26	gearbox	26
	Guerrero	Theodore-Ford	23	engine	22
	Sullivan	Tyrrell-Ford	21	clutch	24
	de Angelis	Lotus-Renault	20	electrical	5
	Patrese	Brabham-BMW	19	overheating	3
	Warwick	Toleman-Hart	14	engine	9
	Mansell	Lotus-Ford	6	driver	18
	Watson	McLaren-Ford	3	throttle	14

Fastest Lap: Prost, 1m 42.7s. 126.56 mph/203.67 kph

San Marino Grand Prix: Imola, 1 May 1983

60 laps of 3.13 mile/5.04 km circuit

Place	Driver	Car	Laps	Time/reason for retiring	Grid
1	Tambay	Ferrari	60	1h 37m 52.5s	3
2	Prost	Renault	60	1h 38m 41.2s	4
3	Arnoux	Ferrari	59		1
4	Rosberg	Williams-Ford	59		11
5	Watson	McLaren-Ford	59		24
6	Surer	Arrows-Ford	59		12
7	Laffite	Williams-Ford	59		16
8	Serra	Arrows-Ford	58		20
9	Boesel	Ligier-Ford	58		25
10	Baldi	Alfa Romeo	57	engine	10
11	Winkelhock	ATS-BMW	57		7

🏁

San Marino Grand Prix (cont)

Place	Driver	Car	Laps	Time/reason for retiring	Grid
12	Mansell	Lotus-Ford	56	accident	15
	Patrese	Brabham-BMW	54	accident	5
	de Cesaris	Alfa Romeo	46	distributor	8
	de Angelis	Lotus-Renault	44	handling	9
	Piquet	Brabham-BMW	42	engine	2
	Jarier	Ligier-Ford	40	radiator	19
	Sullivan	Tyrrell-Ford	37	accident	22
	Warwick	Toleman-Hart	27	accident	14
	C Fabi	Osella-Ford	20	accident	26
	Giacomelli	Toleman-Hart	21	suspension	17
	Lauda	McLaren-Ford	11	accident	18
	Cecotto	Theodore-Ford	11	.accident	23
	Alboreto	Tyrrell-Ford	10	accident	13
	Guerrero	Theodore-Ford	3	accident	21
	Cheever	Renault	2	turbo	6

Fastest Lap: Patrese, 1m 34.44s. 119.38 mph/192.13 kph

Monaco Grand Prix: Monte Carlo, 15 May 1983

76 laps of 2.06 mile/3.31 km circuit

Place	Driver	Car	Laps	Time/reason for retiring	Grid
1	Rosberg	Williams-Ford	76	1h 56m 38.1s	5
2	Piquet	Brabham-BMW	76	1h 56m 56.6s	6
3	Prost	Renault	76	1h 57m 09.5s	1
4	Tambay	Ferrari	76	1h 57m 42.4s	4
5	Sullivan	Tyrrell-Ford	74		20
6	Baldi	Alfa Romeo	74		13
7	Serra	Arrows-Ford	74		15
	Patrese	Brabham-BMW	64	electrical	17
	Laffite	Williams-Ford	54	gearbox	8
	Warwick	Toleman-Hart	50	accident	10
	de Angelis	Lotus-Renault	50	drive-shaft	19
	Surer	Arrows-Ford	49	accident	12
	Jarier	Ligier-Ford	33	suspension	9
	Cheever	Renault	30	engine	3
	de Cesaris	Alfa Romeo	14	gearbox	7
	Arnoux	Ferrari	6	accident	2
	Boesel	Ligier-Ford	3	accident	18
	Winkelhock	ATS-BMW	3	accident	16
	Alboreto	Tyrrell-Ford	0	accident	11
	Mansell	Lotus-Ford	0	accident	14

Fastest Lap: Piquet, 1m 27.3s. 84.88 mph/136.6 kph

Belgian Grand Prix: Spa, 22 May 1983

40 laps of 4.32 mile/6.95 km circuit

Place	Driver	Car	Laps	Time/reason for retiring	Grid
1	Prost	Renault	40	1h 27m 11.5s	1
2	Tambay	Ferrari	40	1h 27m 34.7s	2
3	Cheever	Renault	40	1h 27m 51.4s	8
4	Piquet	Brabham-BMW	40	1h 27m 53.8s	4
5	Rosberg	Williams-Ford	40	1h 28m 02.0s	9
6	Laffite	Williams-Ford	40	1h 28m 44.6s	11
7	Warwick	Toleman-Hart	40	1h 29m 10.0s	22
8	Giacomelli	Toleman-Hart	40	1h 29m 49.8s	16
9	de Angelis	Lotus-Renault	39		13
10	Cecotto	Theodore-Ford	39		25
11	Surer	Arrows-Ford	39		10
12	Sullivan	Tyrrell-Ford	39		23
13	Boesel	Ligier-Ford	39		26
14	Alboreto	Tyrrell-Ford	38		17
	Lauda	McLaren-Ford	33	engine	15
	Mansell	Lotus-Ford	30	gearbox	19
	de Cesaris	Alfa Romeo	25	engine	3
	Guerrero	Theodore-Ford	23	engine	14
	Arnoux	Ferrari	22	engine	5
	C Fabi	Osella-Ford	19	suspension	24
	Winkelhock	ATS-BMW	18	wheel	7
	Watson	McLaren-Ford	8	accident	20
	Jarier	Ligier-Ford	8	accident	21
	Boutsen	Arrows-Ford	4	suspension	18
	Baldi	Alfa Romeo	3	throttle	12
	Patrese	Brabham-BMW	0	engine	6

Fastest Lap: de Cesaris, 2m 07.5s. 121.92 mph/196.22 kph

United States Grand Prix: Detroit, 5 June 1983

60 laps of 2.5 mile/4.02 km circuit

Place	Driver	Car	Laps	Time/reason for retiring	Grid
1	Alboreto	Tyrrell-Ford	60	1h 50m 53.7s	6
2	Rosberg	Williams-Ford	60	1h 51m 01.4s	12
3	Watson	McLaren-Ford	60	1h 51m 03.0s	21
4	Piquet	Brabham-BMW	60	1h 52m 05.9s	2
5	Laffite	Williams-Ford	60	1h 52m 26.3s	20
6	Mansell	Lotus-Ford	59		14
7	Boutsen	Arrows-Ford	59		10
8	Prost	Renault	59		13
9	Giacomelli	Toleman-Hart	59		17
10	Boesel	Ligier-Ford	58		23
11	Surer	Arrows-Ford	58		5

United States Grand Prix (cont)

Place	Driver	Car	Laps	Time/reason for retiring	Grid
12	Baldi	Alfa Romeo	56		25
	Lauda	McLaren-Ford	49	shock absorber	18
	Guerrero	Theodore-Ford	38	running	11
	Cecotto	Theodore-Ford	34	gearbox	26
	de Cesaris	Alfa Romeo	33	turbo	8
	Arnoux	Ferrari	31	electrical	1
	Sullivan	Tyrrell-Ford	30	electrical	16
	Jarier	Ligier-Ford	29	wheel	19
	Winkelhock	ATS-BMW	26	accident	22
	Warwick	Toleman-Hart	25	engine	9
	Patrese	Brabham-BMW	24	brakes	15
	de Angelis	Lotus-Renault	5	transmission	4
	Cheever	Renault	4	distributor	7
	Ghinzani	Osella-Alfa	4	overheating	24
	Tambay	Ferrari	0	stalled	3

Fastest Lap: Watson, 1m 47.67s. 83.59 mph/134.53 kph

Canadian Grand Prix: Montreal, 12 June 1983

70 laps of 2.74 mile/4.41 km circuit

Place	Driver	Car	Laps	Time/reason for retiring	Grid
1	Arnoux	Ferrari	70	1h 48m 31.8s	1
2	Cheever	Renault	70	1h 49m 13.9s	6
3	Tambay	Ferrari	70	1h 49m 24.5s	4
4	Rosberg	Williams-Ford	70	1h 49m 48.9s	9
5	Prost	Renault	69		2
6	Watson	McLaren-Ford	69		20
7	Boutsen	Arrows-Ford	69		15
8	Alboreto	Tyrrell-Ford	68		17
	Sullivan	Tyrrell-Ford	68	disqualified: under weight	22
9	Winkelhock	ATS-BMW	67		7
10	Baldi	Alfa Romeo	67		26
	Patrese	Brabham-BMW	57	gearbox	5
	Warwick	Toleman-Hart	47		12
	Giacomelli	Toleman-Hart	43		10
	Mansell	Lotus-Ford	43	handling	18
	de Cesaris	Alfa Romeo	43	engine	8
	Laffite	Williams-Ford	38	gearbox	13
	Boesel	Ligier-Ford	32	wheel	24
	Guerrero	Theodore-Ford	27	engine	21
	C Fabi	Osella-Ford	27	engine	25
	Cecotto	Theodore-Ford	18	crownwheel and pinion	23
	Piquet	Brabham-BMW	16	throttle	3
	Lauda	McLaren-Ford	11	spun	19

Canadian Grand Prix (cont)

Place	Driver	Car	Laps	Time/reason for retiring	Grid
	de Angelis	Lotus-Renault	2	throttle	11
	Jarier	Ligier-Ford	1	gearbox	16
	Surer	Arrows-Ford	1	transmission	14

Fastest Lap: Tambay, 1m 30.85s. 108.58 mph/174.75 kph

British Grand Prix: Silverstone, 16 July 1983

67 laps of 2.93 mile/4.72 km circuit

Place	Driver	Car	Laps	Time/reason for retiring	Grid
1	Prost	Renault	67	1h 24m 39.8s	3
2	Piquet	Brabham-BMW	67	1h 24m 58.9s	6
3	Tambay	Ferrari	67	1h 25m 06.0s	2
4	Mansell	Lotus-Renault	67	1h 25m 18.7s	18
5	Arnoux	Ferrari	67	1h 25m 38.7s	1
6	Lauda	McLaren-Ford	66		15
7	Baldi	Alfa Romeo	66		11
8	de Cesaris	Alfa Romeo	66		9
9	Watson	McLaren-Ford	66		24
10	Jarier	Ligier-Ford	65		25
11	Rosberg	Williams-Ford	65		13
12	Laffite	Williams-Ford	65		20
13	Alboreto	Tyrrell-Ford	65		16
14	Sullivan	Tyrrell-Ford	65		23
15	Boutsen	Arrows-Ford	65		17
16	Guerrero	Theodore-Ford	64		21
17	Surer	Arrows-Ford	64		19
	Winkelhock	ATS-BMW	49	overheating	8
	Boesel	Ligier-Ford	48	suspension	22
	Ghinzani	Osella-Alfa	46	fuel pressure	26
	Warwick	Toleman-Hart	27	gearbox	10
	Patrese	Brabham-BMW	9	turbo	5
	Johansson	Spirit-Honda	5	fuel pump	14
	Cheever	Renault	3	engine	7
	Giacomelli	Toleman-Hart	3	turbo	12
	de Angelis	Lotus-Renault	1	distributor	4

Fastest Lap: Prost, 1m 14.21s. 142.23 mph/228.9 kph

German Grand Prix: Hockenheim, 7 August 1983

45 laps of 4.22 mile/6.8 km circuit

Place	Driver	Car	Laps	Time/reason for retiring	Grid
1	Arnoux	Ferrari	45	1h 27m 10.3s	2
2	de Cesaris	Alfa Romeo	45	1h 28m 20.9s	3
3	Patrese	Brabham-BMW	45	1h 28m 54.4s	8
4	Prost	Renault	45	1h 29m 11.1s	5
	Lauda	McLaren-Ford	44	disqualified: reversed in pits	18
5	Watson	McLaren-Ford	44		23
6	Laffite	Williams-Ford	44		15
7	Surer	Arrows-Ford	44		20
8	Jarier	Ligier-Ford	44		19
9	Boutsen	Arrows-Ford	44		14
10	Rosberg	Williams-Ford	44		12
11	Cecotto	Theodore-Ford	44		22
12	Sullivan	Tyrrell-Ford	43		21
13	Piquet	Brabham-BMW	42	fire	4
	Cheever	Renault	38	fuel injection	6
	Ghinzani	Osella-Alfa	34	engine	26
	Boesel	Ligier-Ford	27	engine	25
	Baldi	Alfa Romeo	24	engine	7
	Giacomelli	Toleman-Hart	19	turbo	10
	Warwick	Toleman-Hart	17	engine	9
	Johansson	Spirit-Honda	11	engine	13
	Tambay	Ferrari	11	engine	1
	de Angelis	Lotus-Renault	10	overheating	11
	Alboreto	Tyrrell-Ford	4	fuel pump	16
	Mansell	Lotus-Renault	1	engine	17
	Guerrero	Theodore-Ford	0	engine	24

Fastest Lap: Arnoux, 1m 53.94s. 133.44 mph/214.76 kph

Austrian Grand Prix: Österreichring, 14 August 1983

53 laps of 3.69 mile/5.94 km circuit

Place	Driver	Car	Laps	Time/reason for retiring	Grid
1	Prost	Renault	53	1h 24m 32.8s	5
2	Arnoux	Ferrari	53	1h 24m 39.6s	2
3	Piquet	Brabham-BMW	53	1h 25m 00.4s	4
4	Cheever	Renault	53	1h 25m 01.1s	8
5	Mansell	Lotus-Renault	52		3
6	Lauda	McLaren-Ford	51		14
7	Jarier	Ligier-Ford	51		20
8	Rosberg	Williams-Ford	51		15
9	Watson	McLaren-Ford	51		17
10	C Fabi	Osella-Alfa	50		26
11	Ghinzani	Osella-Alfa	49		25
12	Johansson	Spirit-Honda	48		16

Austrian Grand Prix (cont)

Place	Driver	Car	Laps	Time/reason for retiring	Grid
13	Boutsen	Arrows-Ford	48		19
	Winkelhock	ATS-BMW	33	overheating	13
	de Cesaris	Alfa Romeo	31	out of fuel	11
	Tambay	Ferrari	30	engine	1
	Patrese	Brabham-BMW	29	overheating	6
	Guerrero	Theodore-Ford	25	gearbox	21
	Laffite	Williams-Ford	21	handling	24
	Baldi	Alfa Romeo	13	engine	9
	Alboreto	Tyrrell-Ford	8	accident	18
	Warwick	Toleman-Hart	2	turbo	10
	Giacomelli	Toleman-Hart	1	accident	7
	Sullivan	Tyrrell-Ford	0	accident	23
	Surer	Arrows-Ford	0	accident	22
	de Angelis	Lotus-Renault	0	accident	12

Fastest Lap: Prost, 1m 33.96s. 141.46 mph/227.66 kph

Dutch Grand Prix: Zandvoort, 28 August 1983

72 laps of 2.64 mile/4.25 km circuit

Place	Driver	Car	Laps	Time/reason for retiring	Grid
1	Arnoux	Ferrari	72	1h 38m 42s	10
2	Tambay	Ferrari	72	1h 39m 02.8s	2
3	Watson	McLaren-Ford	72	1h 39m 25.7s	15
4	Warwick	Toleman-Hart	72	1h 39m 58.8s	7
5	Baldi	Alfa Romeo	72	1h 40m 06.2s	12
6	Alboreto	Tyrrell-Ford	71		18
7	Johansson	Spirit-Honda	70		16
8	Surer	Arrows-Ford	70		14
9	Patrese	Brabham-BMW	70		6
10	Boesel	Ligier-Ford	70		24
11	C Fabi	Osella-Alfa	68	engine	25
12	Guerrero	Theodore-Ford	68		20
13	Giacomelli	Toleman-Hart	68		13
14	Boutsen	Arrows-Ford	68	engine	21
	Rosberg	Williams-Ford	53	misfire	23
	Winkelhock	ATS-BMW	50	disqualified: overtook on parade lap	9
	Piquet	Brabham-BMW	41	accident	1
	Prost	Renault	41	accident	4
	Cheever	Renault	39	turbo	11
	Laffite	Williams-Ford	37	tyres	17
	Mansell	Lotus-Renault	26	spun	5
	Lauda	McLaren-TAG	25	brakes	19
	Sullivan	Tyrrell-Ford	20	engine	26
	de Angelis	Lotus-Renault	12	fuel metering	3
	de Cesaris	Alfa Romeo	5	engine	8
	Jarier	Ligier-Ford	3	suspension	22

Fastest Lap: Arnoux, 1m 19.86s. 119.1 mph/191.67 kph

Italian Grand Prix: Monza, 11 September 1983

52 laps of 3.6 mile/5.8 km circuit

Place	Driver	Car	Laps	Time/reason for retiring	Grid
1	Piquet	Brabham-BMW	52	1h 23m 10.9s	4
2	Arnoux	Ferrari	52	1h 23m 21.1s	3
3	Cheever	Renault	52	1h 23m 29.5s	7
4	Tambay	Ferrari	52	1h 23m 39.9s	2
5	de Angelis	Lotus-Renault	52	1h 24m 04.6s	8
6	Warwick	Toleman-Hart	52	1h 24m 24.3s	12
7	Giacomelli	Toleman-Hart	52	1h 24m 44.8s	14
8	Mansell	Lotus-Renault	52	1h 24m 46.9s	11
9	Jarier	Ligier-Ford	51		19
10	Surer	Arrows-Ford	51		20
11	* Rosberg	Williams-Ford	51		16
12	Cecotto	Theodore-Ford	50		26
13	Guerrero	Theodore-Ford	50		21
	C Fabi	Osella-Alfa	46	oil system	25
	Sullivan	Tyrrell-Ford	44	fuel pump	22
	Boutsen	Arrows-Ford	42	engine	18
	Winkelhock	ATS-BMW	35	exhaust	9
	Alboreto	Tyrrell-Ford	29	clutch	24
	Prost	Renault	26	turbo	5
	Lauda	McLaren-TAG	24	electrical	13
	Watson	McLaren-TAG	13	engine	15
	Ghinzani	Osella-Alfa	10	gearbox	23
	Baldi	Alfa Romeo	5	turbo	10
	Johansson	Spirit-Honda	4	distributor	17
	Patrese	Brabham-BMW	3	electrical	1
	de Cesaris	Alfa Romeo	2	spun	6

Fastest Lap: Piquet, 1m 34.43s. 137.39 mph/221.11 kph
* Includes 1 minute penalty.

European Grand Prix: Brands Hatch, 25 September 1983

76 laps of 2.61 mile/4.21 km circuit

Place	Driver	Car	Laps	Time/reason for retiring	Grid
1	Piquet	Brabham-BMW	76	1h 36m 45.9s	4
2	Prost	Renault	76	1h 36m 52.4s	8
3	Mansell	Lotus-Renault	76	1h 37m 16.2s	3
4	de Cesaris	Alfa Romeo	76	1h 37m 20.3s	14
5	Warwick	Toleman-Hart	76	1h 37m 30.8s	11
6	Giacomelli	Toleman-Hart	76	1h 37m 38.1s	12
7	Patrese	Brabham-BMW	76	1h 37m 58.6s	2
8	Winkelhock	ATS-BMW	75		9
9	Arnoux	Ferrari	75		5
10	Cheever	Renault	75		7

European Grand Prix (cont)

Place	Driver	Car	Laps	Time/reason for retiring	Grid
11	Boutsen	Arrows-Ford	75		18
12	Guerrero	Theodore-Ford	75		21
13	Palmer	Williams-Ford	74		25
14	Johansson	Spirit-Honda	74		19
15	Boesel	Ligier-Ford	73		23
	Tambay	Ferrari	67	accident	6
	Alboreto	Tyrrell-Ford	65	engine	26
	Ghinzani	Osella-Alfa	63	running	24
	Surer	Arrows-Ford	51	engine	17
	Rosberg	Williams-Ford	43	engine	16
	Baldi	Alfa Romeo	39	clutch	15
	Watson	McLaren-TAG	36	accident	10
	Sullivan	Tyrrell-Ford	27	fire	20
	Lauda	McLaren-TAG	26	engine	13
	de Angelis	Lotus-Renault	13	engine	1
	Jarier	Ligier-Ford	0	transmission	22

Fastest Lap: Mansell, 1m 14.34s. 126.56 mph/203.68 kph

South African Grand Prix: Kyalami, 15 October 1983

77 laps of 2.55 mile/4.1 km circuit

Place	Driver	Car	Laps	Time/reason for retiring	Grid
1	Patrese	Brabham-BMW	77	1h 33m 25.7s	3
2	de Cesaris	Alfa Romeo	77	1h 33m 35.0s	9
3	Piquet	Brabham-BMW	77	1h 33m 47.7s	2
4	Warwick	Toleman-Hart	76		13
5	Rosberg	Williams-Honda	76		6
6	Cheever	Renault	76		14
7	Sullivan	Tyrrell-Ford	75		19
8	Surer	Arrows-Ford	75		22
9	Boutsen	Arrows-Ford	74		20
10	Jarier	Ligier-Ford	73		21
11	Lauda	McLaren-TAG	71	electrical	12
12	Acheson	RAM-Ford	71		24
	Mansell	Lotus-Renault	68		7
	Boesel	Ligier-Ford	66		23
	Alboreto	Tyrrell-Ford	60	engine	18
	Tambay	Ferrari	56	turbo	1
	Giacomelli	Toleman-Hart	56	turbo	16
	Prost	Renault	35	turbo	5
	C Fabi	Osella-Alfa	28	engine	25
	de Angelis	Lotus-Renault	20	engine	11
	Watson	McLaren-TAG	18	disqualified: overtook on parade lap	15
	Arnoux	Ferrari	9	engine	4
	Baldi	Alfa Romeo	5	engine	17

South African Grand Prix (cont)

Place	Driver	Car	Laps	Time/reason for retiring	Grid
	Ghinzani	Osella-Alfa	1	engine	26
	Winkelhock	ATS-BMW	1	engine	8
	Laffite	Williams-Honda	1	accident	10

Fastest Lap: Piquet, 1m 09.95s. 131.25 mph/211.22 kph

World Championship 1983

1	Piquet	59
2	Prost	57
3	Arnoux	49
4	Tambay	40
5	Rosberg	27
6=	Cheever, Watson	22
8	de Cesaris	15
9	Patrese	13
10	Lauda	12
11	Laffite	11
12=	Alboreto, Mansell	10
14	Warwick	9
15	Surer	4
16	Baldi	3
17=	de Angelis, Sullivan	2
19=	Cecotto, Giacomelli	1

Constructors' Championship

1	Ferrari	89
2	Renault	79
3	Brabham-BMW	72
4	Williams-Ford	36
5	McLaren-Ford	34
6	Alfa Romeo	18
7	Tyrrell-Ford	12
8	Lotus-Renault	11
9	Toleman-Hart	10
10	Arrows-Ford	4
11	Williams-Honda	2
12=	Lotus-Ford, Theodore-Ford	1

1984

McLaren dominated the 1984 championship with Lauda shading out Prost by .5 of a point. Prost's victory at Monaco scored only half points since the race had to be stopped early because of rain. Tyrrell, the only runner using the Ford Cosworth, was stripped of its placings and championship points after being found guilty of using pit stops to bring cars that were racing underweight up to the specified weight. The Austrian Grand Prix was the first to be made up entirely of turbocharged cars.

Brazilian Grand Prix: Rio de Janeiro, 25 March 1984

61 laps of 3.13 mile/5.03 km circuit

Place	Driver	Car	Laps	Time/reason for retiring	Grid
1	Prost	McLaren-TAG	61	1h 42m 34.5s	4
2	Rosberg	Williams-Honda	61	1h 43m 15.0s	9
3	de Angelis	Lotus-Renault	61	1h 43m 33.6s	1
4	Cheever	Alfa Romeo	60		12
	* Brundle	Tyrrell-Ford	60		18
5	Tambay	Renault	59	out of fuel	8
6	Boutsen	Arrows-Ford	59		20
7	Surer	Arrows-Ford	59		24
8	Palmer	RAM-Hart	58		26
	Warwick	Renault	51	suspension	3
	de Cesaris	Ligier-Renault	42	gearbox	14
	Patrese	Alfa Romeo	41	gearbox	11
	Lauda	McLaren-TAG	38	electrical	6
	Mansell	Lotus-Renault	35	accident	5
	Piquet	Brabham-BMW	32	engine	7
	T Fabi	Brabham-BMW	32	turbo	15
	Arnoux	Ferrari	30	battery	10
	Ghinzani	Osella-Alfa	28	gearbox	21
	Hesnault	Ligier-Renault	25	overheating	19
	Alliot	RAM-Hart	24	battery	25
	Cecotto	Toleman-Hart	18	turbo	17
	Laffite	Williams-Honda	15	electrical	13
	Alboreto	Ferrari	14	brakes	2
	Baldi	Spirit-Hart	12	distributor	23
	* Bellof	Tyrrell-Ford	11	throttle	22
	Senna	Toleman-Hart	8	turbo	16

Fastest Lap: Prost, 1m 36.499s. 116.62 mph/187.69 kph
* Brundle finished fifth, but all Tyrrell placings in 1984 were later disqualified.

1984

South African Grand Prix: Kyalami, 7 April 1984

75 laps of 2.55 mile/4.1 km circuit

Place	Driver	Car	Laps	Time/reason for retiring	Grid
1	Lauda	McLaren-TAG	75	1h 29m 23.4s	8
2	Prost	McLaren-TAG	75	1h 30m 29.4s	5
3	Warwick	Renault	74		9
4	Patrese	Alfa Romeo	73		18
5	de Cesaris	Ligier-Renault	73		14
6	Senna	Toleman-Hart	72		13
7	de Angelis	Lotus-Renault	71		7
8	Baldi	Spirit-Hart	71		20
9	Surer	Arrows-Ford	71		23
10	Hesnault	Ligier-Renault	71		17
	Brundle	Tyrrell-Ford	71		25
11	Alboreto	Ferrari	70	ignition	10
12	Boutsen	Arrows-Ford	70		26
	Tambay	Renault	66	fuel system	4
	Laffite	Williams-Honda	60	cv joint	11
	Bellof	Tyrrell-Ford	60	wheel	24
	Winkelhock	ATS-BMW	53	battery	12
	Rosberg	Williams-Honda	51	lost wheel	2
	Mansell	Lotus-Renault	51	turbo	3
	Arnoux	Ferrari	40	fuel injection	15
	Piquet	Brabham-BMW	29	turbo	1
	Cecotto	Toleman-Hart	26	tyre	19
	Alliot	RAM-Hart	24	water leak	22
	Palmer	RAM-Hart	22	gearbox	21
	T Fabi	Brabham-BMW	18	turbo	6
	Cheever	Alfa Romeo	4	radiator	16

Fastest Lap: Tambay, 1m 08.88s. 133.28 mph/214.49 kph

Belgian Grand Prix: Zolder, 29 April 1984

70 laps of 2.65 mile/4.26 km circuit

Place	Driver	Car	Laps	Time/reason for retiring	Grid
1	Alboreto	Ferrari	70	1h 36m 32.05s	1
2	Warwick	Renault	70	1h 37m 14.43s	4
3	Arnoux	Ferrari	70	1h 37m 41.85s	2
4	Rosberg	Williams-Honda	69	out of fuel	3
5	de Angelis	Lotus-Renault	69		5
	* Bellof	Tyrrell-Ford	69		21
6	Senna	Toleman-Hart	68		19
7	Tambay	Renault	68		12
8	Surer	Arrows-Ford	68		24
9	Piquet	Brabham-BMW	66	engine	9
10	Palmer	RAM-Hart	64		26

Belgian Grand Prix (cont)

Place	Driver	Car	Laps	Time/reason for retiring	Grid
	Baldi	Spirit-Hart	53	suspension	25
	Brundle	Tyrrell-Ford	51	lost wheel	22
	T Fabi	Brabham-BMW	42	spun	18
	de Cesaris	Ligier-Renault	42	accident	13
	Winkelhock	ATS-BMW	39	exhaust	6
	Lauda	McLaren-TAG	35	water pump	14
	Cheever	Alfa Romeo	28	engine	11
	Laffite	Williams-Honda	15	electrics	15
	Hesnault	Ligier-Renault	15	radiator	23
	Boutsen	Arrows-BMW	15	misfire	17
	Ghinzani	Osella-Alfa	14	transmission	20
	Mansell	Lotus-Renault	14	clutch	10
	Prost	McLaren-TAG	5	distributor	8
	Patrese	Alfa Romeo	2	ignition	7
	Cecotto	Toleman-Hart	1	clutch	16

Fastest Lap: Arnoux, 1m 19.29s. 120.23 mph/193.5 kph
* Bellof finished sixth, but all Tyrrell placings in 1984 were later disqualified.

San Marino Grand Prix: Imola, 6 May 1984

60 laps of 3.13 mile/5.04 km circuit

Place	Driver	Car	Laps	Time/reason for retiring	Grid
1	Prost	McLaren-TAG	60	1h 36m 53.68s	2
2	Arnoux	Ferrari	60	1h 37m 07.10s	6
3	de Angelis	Lotus-Renault	59	out of fuel	11
4	Warwick	Renault	59		4
	* Bellof	Tyrrell-Ford	59		21
5	Boutsen	Arrows-Ford	59		20
6	de Cesaris	Ligier-Renault	58	out of fuel	12
7	Cheever	Alfa Romeo	58	out of fuel	8
8	Baldi	Spirit-Hart	58		24
9	Palmer	RAM-Hart	57		25
	* Brundle	Tyrrell-Ford	55	fuel feed	22
10	Alliot	RAM-Hart	53	engine	23
11	Cecotto	Toleman-Hart	52	turbo	19
	Piquet	Brabham-BMW	48	turbo	1
	T Fabi	Brabham-BMW	48	turbo	9
	Gartner	Osella-Alfa	46	engine	26
	Surer	Arrows-BMW	40	turbo	16
	Winkelhock	ATS-BMW	31	turbo	7
	Alboreto	Ferrari	23	exhaust	13
	Lauda	McLaren-TAG	15	engine	5
	Laffite	Williams-Honda	11	engine	15
	Patrese	Alfa Romeo	6	electrics	10
	Mansell	Lotus-Renault	2	spun	18

San Marino Grand Prix (cont)

Place	Driver	Car	Laps	Time/reason for retiring	Grid
	Rosberg	Williams-Honda	2	electrical	3
	Tambay	Renault	0	accident	14
	Hesnault	Ligier-Renault	0	accident	17

Fastest Lap: Piquet, 1m 33.28s. 120.87 mph/194.52 kph
* Bellof finished fifth, but all Tyrrell placings in 1984 were later disqualified.

French Grand Prix: Dijon, 20 May 1984

79 laps of 2.42 mile/3.89 km circuit

Place	Driver	Car	Laps	Time/reason for retiring	Grid
1	Lauda	McLaren-TAG	79	1h 31m 11.95s	9
2	Tambay	Renault	79	1h 31m 19.11s	1
3	Mansell	Lotus-Renault	79	1h 31m 35.92s	6
4	Arnoux	Ferrari	79	1h 31m 55.66s	11
5	de Angelis	Lotus-Renault	79	1h 32m 18.08s	2
6	Rosberg	Williams-Honda	78		4
7	Prost	McLaren-TAG	78		5
8	Laffite	Williams-Honda	78		12
9	T Fabi	Brabham-BMW	78		17
10	de Cesaris	Ligier-Renault	77		26
11	Boutsen	Arrows-BMW	77		14
	* Brundle	Tyrrell-Ford	76		23
12	Ghinzani	Osella-Alfa	74		25
13	Palmer	RAM-Hart	72		21
	Baldi	Spirit-Hart	61	engine	24
	Warwick	Renault	53	accident	7
	Surer	Arrows-Ford	51	accident	19
	Cheever	Alfa Romeo	51	engine	16
	Senna	Toleman-Hart	35	turbo	13
	Alboreto	Ferrari	33	engine	10
	Cecotto	Toleman-Hart	22	turbo	18
	Patrese	Alfa Romeo	15	engine	15
	Piquet	Brabham-BMW	11	turbo	3
	Bellof	Tyrrell-Ford	11	driver error re engine	20
	Winkelhock	ATS-BMW	5	clutch	8
	Alliot	RAM-Hart	4	electrical	22

Fastest Lap: Prost, 1m 05.26s. 133.24 mph/214.43 kph

Monaco Grand Prix: Monte Carlo, 3 June 1984

31 laps of 2.06 mile/3.31 km circuit

Place	Driver	Car	Laps	Time/reason for retiring	Grid
1	Prost	McLaren-TAG	31	1h 01m 07.74s	1
2	Senna	Toleman-Hart	31	1h 01m 15.19s	13
* Bellof		Tyrrell-Ford	31	1h 01m 28.88s	20
3	Arnoux	Ferrari	31	1h 01m 36.82s	3
4	Rosberg	Williams-Honda	31	1h 01m 42.99s	10
5	de Angelis	Lotus-Renault	31	1h 01m 52.18s	11
6	Alboreto	Ferrari	30		4
7	Ghinzani	Osella-Alfa	30		19
8	Laffite	Williams-Honda	30		16
	Patrese	Alfa Romeo	24	steering	14
	Lauda	McLaren-TAG	23	spun	8
	Winkelhock	ATS-BMW	22	spun	12
	Mansell	Lotus-Renault	15	accident	2
	Piquet	Brabham-BMW	14	electrical	9
	Hesnault	Ligier-Renault	12	electrical	17
	C Fabi	Brabham-BMW	9	spun	15
	Cecotto	Toleman-Hart	1	spun	18
	de Cesaris	Ligier-Renault	1	accident	7
	Warwick	Renault	0	accident	5
	Tambay	Renault	0	accident	6

Fastest Lap: Senna, 1m 54.33s. 64.8 mph/104.28 kph
* Race scheduled for 77 laps; stopped early because of rain; ½ points awarded. Bellof finished third, but all Tyrrell placings in 1984 were later disqualified.

Canadian Grand Prix: Montreal, 17 June 1984

70 laps of 2.74 mile/4.41 km circuit

Place	Driver	Car	Laps	Time/reason for retiring	Grid
1	Piquet	Brabham-BMW	70	1h 46m 23.75s	1
2	Lauda	McLaren-TAG	70	1h 46m 26.36s	8
3	Prost	McLaren-TAG	70	1h 47m 51.78s	2
4	de Angelis	Lotus-Renault	69		3
5	Arnoux	Ferrari	68		5
6	Mansell	Lotus-Renault	68		7
7	Senna	Toleman-Hart	68		9
8	Winkelhock	ATS-BMW	68		12
9	Cecotto	Toleman-Hart	68		20
* Brundle		Tyrrell-Ford	68		21
10	Alliot	RAM-Hart	65		26
11	Cheever	Alfa Romeo	63	out of fuel	11
	Surer	Arrows-Ford	59	engine	23
	Warwick	Renault	57	underbody	4
	Rothengatter	Spirit-Hart	56	running	24

Canadian Grand Prix (cont)

Place	Driver	Car	Laps	Time/reason for retiring	Grid
	Bellof	Tyrrell-Ford	52	drive-shaft	22
	de Cesaris	Ligier-Renault	40	brakes	10
	C Fabi	Brabham-BMW	39	turbo	16
	Boutsen	Arrows-BMW	38	engine	18
	Patrese	Alfa Romeo	37	accident	14
	Rosberg	Williams-Honda	32	fuel system	15
	Laffite	Williams-Honda	31	turbo	17
	Thackwell	RAM-Hart	29	turbo	25
	Ghinzani	Osella-Alfa	11	gearbox	19
	Alboreto	Ferrari	10	engine	6
	Hesnault	Ligier-Renault	7	turbo	13

Fastest Lap: Piquet, 1m 28.76s. 111.69 mph/178.86 kph

United States Grand Prix: Detroit, 24 June 1984

63 laps of 2.5 mile/4.02 km circuit

Place	Driver	Car	Laps	Time/reason for retiring	Grid
1	Piquet	Brabham-BMW	63	1h 55m 41.84s	1
	* Brundle	Tyrrell-Ford	63	1h 55m 42.68s	11
2	de Angelis	Lotus-Renault	63	1h 56m 14.48s	5
3	T Fabi	Brabham-BMW	63	1h 57m 08.37s	23
4	Prost	McLaren-TAG	63	1h 57m 37.10s	2
5	Laffite	Williams-Honda	62		19
	Alboreto	Ferrari	49	engine	4
	Rosberg	Williams-Honda	47	exhaust	21
	Warwick	Renault	40	gearbox	6
	Bellof	Tyrrell-Ford	33	accident	16
	Tambay	Renault	33	transmission	9
	Alliot	RAM-Hart	33	brakes	20
	Lauda	McLaren-TAG	33	electrical	10
	Mansell	Lotus-Renault	27	gearbox	3
	Boutsen	Arrows-BMW	27	engine	13
	de Cesaris	Ligier-Renault	24	overheating	12
	Cecotto	Toleman-Hart	23	clutch	17
	Cheever	Alfa Romeo	21	engine	8
	Senna	Toleman-Hart	21	accident	7
	Patrese	Alfa Romeo	20	spun	25
	Hesnault	Ligier-Renault	3	accident	18
	Ghinzani	Osella-Alfa	3	accident	26
	Arnoux	Ferrari	2	accident	15
	Palmer	RAM-Hart	2	tyre	24
	Winkelhock	ATS-BMW	0	accident	14
	Surer	Arrows-Ford	0	accident	22

Fastest Lap: Warwick, 1m 46.22s. 84.73 mph/136.36 kph
* Brundle finished second, but all Tyrrell placings in 1984 were later disqualified.

United States Grand Prix: Dallas, 8 July 1984

67 laps of 2.42 mile/3.9 km circuit

Place	Driver	Car	Laps	Time/reason for retiring	Grid
1	Rosberg	Williams-Honda	67	2h 01m 22.62s	8
2	Arnoux	Ferrari	67	2h 01m 45.08s	4
3	de Angelis	Lotus-Renault	66		2
4	Laffite	Williams-Honda	65		24
5	Ghinzani	Osella-Alfa	65		18
6	Mansell	Lotus-Renault	64	gearbox	1
7	C Fabi	Brabham-BMW	64		11
8	Winkelhock	ATS-BMW	64		13
	Lauda	McLaren-TAG	60	accident	5
	Prost	McLaren-TAG	56	accident	7
	Boutsen	Arrows-BMW	55	accident	20
	Alboreto	Ferrari	54	accident	9
	Surer	Arrows-BMW	54	accident	22
	Senna	Toleman-Hart	47	drive-shaft	6
	Palmer	RAM-Hart	46	electrical	25
	Piquet	Brabham-BMW	45	accident	12
	Tambay	Renault	25	accident	10
	Cecotto	Toleman-Hart	25	accident	15
	de Cesaris	Ligier-Renault	15	accident	16
	Rothengatter	Spirit-Hart	15	fuel leak	23
	Patrese	Alfa Romeo	12	accident	21
	Warwick	Renault	10	spun	3
	Bellof	Tyrrell-Ford	9	accident	17
	Cheever	Alfa Romeo	8	accident	14
	Hesnault	Ligier-Renault	0	accident	19

Fastest Lap: Lauda, 1m 45.35s. 82.83 mph/133.3 kph

British Grand Prix: Brands Hatch, 22 July 1984

71 laps of 2.61 mile/4.21 km circuit

Place	Driver	Car	Laps	Time/reason for retiring	Grid
1	Lauda	McLaren-TAG	71	1h 29m 28.53s	3
2	Warwick	Renault	71	1h 30m 10.66s	6
3	Senna	Toleman-Hart	71	1h 30m 31.86s	7
4	de Angelis	Lotus-Renault	70		4
5	Alboreto	Ferrari	70		9
6	Arnoux	Ferrari	70		13
7	Piquet	Brabham-BMW	70		1
8	Tambay	Renault	69	turbo	10
9	Ghinzani	Osella-Alfa	68		21
10	de Cesaris	Ligier-Renault	68		19
	Bellof	Tyrrell-Ford	68		26

British Grand Prix (cont)

Place	Driver	Car	Laps	Time/reason for retiring	Grid
11	Surer	Arrows-BMW	67		15
12	Patrese	Alfa Romeo	66		17
13	Rothengatter	Spirit-Hart	62		22
	Hesnault	Ligier-Renault	43	electrical	20
	Prost	McLaren-TAG	37	gearbox	2
	Mansell	Lotus-Renault	24	gearbox	8
	Boutsen	Arrows-BMW	24	electrical	12
	Laffite	Williams-Honda	14	water pump	16
	Palmer	RAM-Hart	10	steering	23
	T Fabi	Brabham-BMW	9	electrical	14
	Winkelhock	ATS-BMW	8	spun	11
	Rosberg	Williams-Honda	5	turbo	5
	Cheever	Alfa Romeo	1	accident	18
	Johansson	Tyrrell-Ford	1	accident	25
	Alliot	RAM-Hart	0	accident	24
	Gartner	Osella-Alfa	0	accident	26

Fastest Lap: Lauda, 1m 13.19s. 128.52 mph/206.84 kph

German Grand Prix: Hockenheim, 5 August 1984

44 laps of 4.22 mile/6.8 km circuit

Place	Driver	Car	Laps	Time/reason for retiring	Grid
1	Prost	McLaren-TAG	44	1h 24m 43.21s	1
2	Lauda	McLaren-TAG	44	1h 24m 46.36s	7
3	Warwick	Renault	44	1h 25m 19.63s	3
4	Mansell	Lotus-Renault	44	1h 25m 34.87s	16
5	Tambay	Renault	44	1h 25m 55.16s	4
6	Arnoux	Ferrari	43		10
7	de Cesaris	Ligier-Renault	43		11
8	Hesnault	Ligier-Renault	43		17
	Johansson	Tyrrell-Ford	42		26
9	Rothengatter	Spirit-Hart	40		24
	Winkelhock	ATS-BMW	31	turbo	13
	Cheever	Alfa Romeo	29	engine	18
	T Fabi	Brabham-BMW	28	turbo	8
	Piquet	Brabham-BMW	23	gearbox	5
	Patrese	Alfa Romeo	16	metering unit	20
	Ghinzani	Osella-Alfa	14	electrical	21
	Gartner	Osella-Alfa	13	turbo	23
	Alboreto	Ferrari	13	engine	6
	Palmer	RAM-Hart	11	turbo	25
	Rosberg	Williams-Honda	10	electrical	19
	Laffite	Williams-Honda	10	engine	12
	Boutsen	Arrows-BMW	8	oil pressure	15
	de Angelis	Lotus-Renault	8	turbo	2

German Grand Prix (cont)

Place	Driver	Car	Laps	Time/reason for retiring	Grid
	Alliot	RAM-Hart	7	overheating	22
	Senna	Toleman-Hart	4	accident	9
	Surer	Arrows-BMW	1	turbo	14

Fastest Lap: Prost, 1m 53.54s. 133.92 mph/215.52 kph

Austrian Grand Prix: Österreichring, 19 August 1984

51 laps of 3.69 mile/5.94 km circuit

Place	Driver	Car	Laps	Time/reason for retiring	Grid
1	Lauda	McLaren-TAG	51	1h 21m 12.85s	4
2	Piquet	Brabham-BMW	51	1h 21m 36.38s	1
3	Alboreto	Ferrari	51	1h 22m 01.85s	12
4	T Fabi	Brabham-BMW	51	1h 22m 09.16s	7
5	Boutsen	Arrows-BMW	50		16
6	Surer	Arrows-BMW	50		18
7	Arnoux	Ferrari	50		14
8	Hesnault	Ligier-Renault	49		20
9	Palmer	RAM-Hart	49		23
10	Patrese	Alfa Romeo	48	out of fuel	13
11	Alliot	RAM-Hart	48		24
12	Berger	ATS-BMW	48	gearbox	19
	Tambay	Renault	42	engine	5
	Senna	Toleman-Hart	35	oil pressure	10
	Mansell	Lotus-Renault	32	engine	8
	Prost	McLaren-TAG	28	spun	2
	de Angelis	Lotus-Renault	28	engine	3
	Rothengatter	Spirit-Hart	23	running	25
	Cheever	Alfa Romeo	18	engine	15
	Warwick	Renault	17	engine	6
	de Cesaris	Ligier-Renault	15	fuel injection	17
	Rosberg	Williams-Honda	15	handling	9
	Laffite	Williams-Honda	12	engine	11
	Gartner	Osella-Alfa	6	engine	21
	Ghinzani	Osella-Alfa	4	gearbox	22

Fastest Lap: Lauda, 1m 32.88s. 143.11 mph/230.31 kph

Dutch Grand Prix: Zandvoort, 26 August 1984

71 laps of 2.64 mile/4.25 km circuit

Place	Driver	Car	Laps	Time/reason for retiring	Grid
1	Prost	McLaren-TAG	71	1h 37m 21.47s	1
2	Lauda	McLaren-TAG	71	1h 37m 31.75s	6
3	Mansell	Lotus-Renault	71	1h 38m 41.01s	12
4	de Angelis	Lotus-Renault	70		3
5	T Fabi	Brabham-BMW	70		10
6	Tambay	Renault	70		5
7	Hesnault	Ligier-Renault	69		20
	Johansson	Tyrrell-Ford	69		25
	Bellof	Tyrrell-Ford	69		24
8	Rosberg	Williams-Honda	68	out of fuel	7
9	Palmer	RAM-Hart	67		22
10	Alliot	RAM-Hart	67		26
11	Arnoux	Ferrari	66	electrical	15
12	Gartner	Osella-Alfa	66		23
13	Cheever	Alfa Romeo	65	out of fuel	17
	Boutsen	Arrows-BMW	59	accident	11
	Rothengatter	Spirit-Hart	53	throttle	27
	Patrese	Alfa Romeo	51	engine	18
	de Cesaris	Ligier-Renault	31	engine	14
	Laffite	Williams-Honda	23	engine	8
	Warwick	Renault	23	spun	4
	Winkelhock	ATS-BMW	22	spun	16
	Senna	Toleman-Hart	19	engine	13
	Surer	Arrows-BMW	17	wheel	19
	Piquet	Brabham-BMW	10	oil pressure	2
	Ghinzani	Osella-Alfa	8	fuel pump	21
	Alboreto	Ferrari	7	engine	9

Fastest Lap: Arnoux, 1m 19.47s. 119.69 mph/192.63 kph

Italian Grand Prix: Monza, 9 September 1984

51 laps of 3.6 mile/5.8 km circuit

Place	Driver	Car	Laps	Time/reason for retiring	Grid
1	Lauda	McLaren-TAG	51	1h 20m 29.07s	4
2	Alboreto	Ferrari	51	1h 20m 53.31s	11
3	Patrese	Alfa Romeo	50		9
4	Johansson	Toleman-Hart	49		17
5	Gartner	Osella-Alfa	49		23
6	Berger	ATS-BMW	49		20
7	Ghinzani	Osella-Alfa	48	out of fuel	21
8	Rothengatter	Spirit-Hart	48		24
9	Cheever	Alfa Romeo	45	out of fuel	10
10	Boutsen	Arrows-BMW	45		19

Italian Grand Prix (cont)

Place	Driver	Car	Laps	Time/reason for retiring	Grid
	Tambay	Renault	43	throttle	8
	T Fabi	Brabham-BMW	43	engine	5
	Surer	Arrows-BMW	43	engine	15
	Warwick	Renault	31	oil pressure	12
	Palmer	RAM-Hart	20	oil pressure	25
	Piquet	Brabham-BMW	15	engine	1
	de Angelis	Lotus-Renault	14	gearbox	3
	Mansell	Lotus-Renault	13	spun	7
	Laffite	Williams-Honda	10	turbo	13
	Rosberg	Williams-Honda	8	engine	6
	de Cesaris	Ligier-Renault	7	engine	16
	Hesnault	Ligier-Renault	7	spun	18
	Alliot	RAM-Hart	6	electrical	22
	Arnoux	Ferrari	5	gearbox	14
	Prost	McLaren-TAG	4	engine	2

Fastest Lap: Lauda, 1m 31.91s. 141.16 mph/227.17 kph
* Gartner and Berger (fifth and sixth) ineligible to score points.

European Grand Prix: Nürburgring, 7 October 1984

67 laps of 2.82 mile/4.54 km circuit

Place	Driver	Car	Laps	Time/reason for retiring	Grid
1	Prost	McLaren-TAG	67	1h 35m 13.28s	2
2	Alboreto	Ferrari	67	1h 35m 37.19s	5
3	Piquet	Brabham-BMW	67	1h 35m 38.21s	1
4	Lauda	McLaren-TAG	67	1h 35m 56.37s	15
5	Arnoux	Ferrari	67	1h 36m 14.71s	6
6	Patrese	Alfa Romeo	66		9
7	de Cesaris	Ligier-Renault	65		17
8	Baldi	Spirit-Hart	65		24
9	Boutsen	Arrows-BMW	64	electrical	11
10	Hesnault	Ligier-Renault	64		19
11	Warwick	Renault	61	overheating	7
12	Gartner	Osella-Alfa	60	fuel system	22
	T Fabi	Brabham-BMW	57	gearbox	10
	Mansell	Lotus-Renault	51	engine	8
	Tambay	Renault	47	fuel system	3
	Cheever	Alfa Romeo	37	fuel pump	13
	Alliot	RAM-Hart	37	turbo	25
	Palmer	RAM-Hart	35	turbo	21
	Laffite	Williams-Honda	27	engine	14
	de Angelis	Lotus-Renault	25	turbo	23
	Johansson	Toleman-Hart	17	overheating	26
	Rosberg	Williams-Honda	0	accident	4
	Berger	ATS-BMW	0	accident	18

European Grand Prix (cont)

Place	Driver	Car	Laps	Time/reason for retiring	Grid
	Surer	Arrows-BMW	0	accident	16
	Ghinzani	Osella-Alfa	0	accident	20
	Senna	Toleman-Hart	0	accident	12

Fastest Lap: Piquet/Alboreto, 1m 23.15s. 122.2 mph/196.66 kph

Portuguese Grand Prix: Estoril, 21 October 1984

70 laps of 2.7 mile/4.35 km circuit

Place	Driver	Car	Laps	Time/reason for retiring	Grid
1	Prost	McLaren-TAG	70	1h 41m 11.75s	2
2	Lauda	McLaren-TAG	70	1h 41m 25.18s	11
3	Senna	Toleman-Hart	70	1h 41m 31.79s	3
4	Alboreto	Ferrari	70	1h 41m 32.07s	8
5	de Angelis	Lotus-Renault	70	1h 42m 43.92s	5
6	Piquet	Brabham-BMW	69		1
7	Tambay	Renault	69		7
8	Patrese	Alfa Romeo	69		12
9	Arnoux	Ferrari	69		17
10	Winkelhock	Brabham-BMW	69		19
11	Johansson	Toleman-Hart	69		10
12	de Cesaris	Ligier-Renault	69		20
13	Berger	ATS-BMW	68		23
14	Laffite	Williams-Honda	67		15
15	Baldi	Spirit-Hart	66		25
16	Gartner	Osella-Alfa	65	out of fuel	24
17	Cheever	Alfa Romeo	64		14
	Ghinzani	Osella-Alfa	60	engine	22
	Mansell	Lotus-Renault	52	spun	6
	Warwick	Renault	51	gearbox	9
	Streiff	Renault	48	drive-shaft	13
	Rosberg	Williams-Honda	39	engine	4
	Hesnault	Ligier-Renault	31	electrical	21
	Boutsen	Arrows-BMW	24	drive-shaft	18
	Palmer	RAM-Hart	19	gearbox	26
	Surer	Arrows-BMW	8	electrical	16
	Alliot	RAM-Hart	2	engine	27

Fastest Lap: Lauda, 1m 23s. 117.24 mph/188.68 kph

World Championship 1984

1	Lauda	72
2	Prost	71.5
3	de Angelis	34
4	Alboreto	30.5
5	Piquet	29
6	Arnoux	27
7	Warwick	23
8	Rosberg	20.5
9	Senna	13
10	Mansell	13
11	Tambay	11
12	T Fabi	9
13	Patrese	8
14 =	Boutsen, Laffite	5
16 =	Cheever, de Cesaris, Johansson	3
19	Ghinzani	2
20	Surer	1

Constructors' Championship

1	McLaren-TAG	143.5
2	Ferrari	57.5
3	Lotus-Renault	47
4	Brabham-BMW	38
5	Renault	34
6	Williams-Honda	25.5
7	Toleman-Hart	16
8	Alfa Romeo	11
9	Arrows-Ford	6
10	Ligier-Renault	3
11	Osella-Alfa Romeo	2

* Brundle (8), Bellof (5), Tyrrell-Ford (13) had scored points before the team's disqualification.

1985

Prost took the championship comfortably. Tyrrell made the switch to turbos. At the instigation of the French government, Renault and Ligier did not go to South Africa in view of its apartheid policies. Lauda retired again at the end of the season. Toleman, in difficulties over the supply of tyres, bought out Spirit's tyre contract with the help of Benetton, initiating the process which was to lead to the team being renamed Benetton in 1986.

Brazilian Grand Prix: Rio de Janeiro, 7 April 1985

61 laps of 3.13 mile/5.03 km circuit

Place	Driver	Car	Laps	Time/reason for retiring	Grid
1	Prost	McLaren-TAG	61	1h 41m 26.1s	6
2	Alboreto	Ferrari	61	1h 41m 29.4s	1
3	de Angelis	Lotus-Renault	60		3
4	Arnoux	Ferrari	59		7
5	Tambay	Renault	59		11
6	Laffite	Ligier-Renault	59		15
7	Johansson	Tyrrell-Ford	58		23
8	Brundle	Tyrrell-Ford	58		21
9	Alliot	RAM-Hart	58		20
10	Warwick	Renault	57		10
11	Boutsen	Arrows-BMW	57		12
12	Ghinzani	Osella-Alfa	57		22
13	Winkelhock	RAM-Hart	57		16
	Berger	Arrows-BMW	51	suspension	19
	Senna	Lotus-Renault	48	electrical	4
	Cheever	Alfa Romeo	42	engine	18
	Martini	Minardi-Ford	41	engine	25
	Lauda	McLaren-TAG	27	fuel system	9
	de Cesaris	Ligier-Renault	26	accident	13
	Patrese	Alfa Romeo	20	puncture	14
	Rosberg	Williams-Honda	10	turbo	2
	Hesnault	Brabham-BMW	9	accident	17
	Mansell	Williams-Honda	8	exhaust	5
	Baldi	Spirit-Hart	7	turbo	24
	Piquet	Brabham-BMW	2	transmission	8

Fastest Lap: Prost, 1m 36.7s. 116.38 mph/187.29 kph

Portuguese Grand Prix: Estoril, 21 April 1985

67 laps of 2.7 mile/4.35 km circuit

Place	Driver	Car	Laps	Time/reason for retiring	Grid
1	Senna	Lotus-Renault	67	2h 00m 28s	1
2	Alboreto	Ferrari	67	2h 01m 31s	5
3	Tambay	Renault	66		12
4	de Angelis	Lotus-Renault	66		4
5	Mansell	Williams-Honda	65		9
6	Bellof	Tyrrell-Ford	65		21
7	Warwick	Renault	65		6
8	Johansson	Ferrari	62		11
9	Ghinzani	Osella-Alfa	61		26
	Winkelhock	RAM-Hart	50		15
	Lauda	McLaren-TAG	49	engine	7
	Cheever	Alfa Romeo	36	engine	14
	Prost	Mclaren-TAG	30	spun	2
	de Cesaris	Ligier-Renault	29	handling	8
	Boutsen	Arrows-BMW	28	engine	16
	Piquet	Brabham-BMW	28	handling	10
	Brundle	Tyrrell-Ford	20	gear	22
	Baldi	Spirit-Hart	19	spun	24
	Rosberg	Williams-Honda	16	spun	3
	Laffite	Ligier-Renault	15	handling	18
	Berger	Arrows-BMW	12	spun	17
	Martini	Minardi-Ford	12	spun	25
	Patrese	Alfa Romeo	4	spun	13
	Alliot	RAM-Hart	3	spun	20
	Hesnault	Brabham-BMW	3	electrical	19
	Palmer	Zakspeed	2	suspension	23

Fastest Lap: Senna, 1m 44.12s. 93.4 mph/150.4 kph

San Marino Grand Prix: Imola, 5 May 1985

60 laps of 3.13 mile/5.04 km circuit

Place	Driver	Car	Laps	Time/reason for retiring	Grid
	Prost	McLaren-TAG	60	disqualified – underweight	6
1	de Angelis	Lotus-Renault	60	1h 34m 35.96s	3
2	Boutsen	Arrows-BMW	59		5
3	Tambay	Renault	59		11
4	Lauda	McLaren-TAG	59		8
5	Mansell	Williams-Honda	58		7
6	Johansson	Ferrari	57	out of fuel	15
7	Senna	Lotus-Renault	57	out of fuel	1
8	Piquet	Brabham-BMW	57		9
9	Brundle	Tyrrell-Ford	56		24
10	Warwick	Renault	56		14

San Marino Grand Prix (cont)

Place	Driver	Car	Laps	Time/reason for retiring	Grid
	Cheever	Alfa Romeo	50	engine	12
	Ghinzani	Osella-Alfa	46	running	21
	Alboreto	Ferrari	29	electrical	4
	Winkelhock	RAM-Hart	27	engine	22
	Alliot	RAM-Hart	24	engine	20
	Rosberg	Williams-Honda	23	throttle	2
	Laffite	Ligier-Renault	22	turbo	16
	Martini	Minardi-MM	14	turbo	18
	de Cesaris	Ligier-Renault	11	spun	13
	Baldi	Spirit-Hart	9	electrical	25
	Hesnault	Brabham-BMW	5	engine	19
	Bellof	Tyrrell-Ford	5	engine	23
	Berger	Arrows-BMW	4	electrical	10
	Patrese	Alfa Romeo	4	engine	17

Fastest Lap: Alboreto, 1m 30.96s. 123.95 mph/199.47 kph

Monaco Grand Prix: Monte Carlo, 19 May 1985

78 laps of 2.06 mile/3.31 km circuit

Place	Driver	Car	Laps	Time/reason for retiring	Grid
1	Prost	McLaren-TAG	78	1h 51m 58.03s	5
2	Alboreto	Ferrari	78	1h 52m 05.6s	3
3	de Angelis	Lotus-Renault	78	1h 53m 25.2s	9
4	de Cesaris	Ligier-Renault	77		8
5	Warwick	Renault	77		10
6	Laffite	Ligier-Renault	77		16
7	Mansell	Williams-Honda	77		2
8	Rosberg	Williams-Honda	76		7
9	Boutsen	Arrows-BMW	76		6
10	Brundle	Tyrrell-Ford	74		18
11	Palmer	Zakspeed	74		19
	Lauda	McLaren-TAG	17	spun	14
	Patrese	Alfa Romeo	16	accident	12
	Piquet	Brabham-BMW	16	accident	13
	T Fabi	Toleman-Hart	16	turbo	20
	Senna	Lotus-Renault	13	engine	1
	Cheever	Alfa Romeo	10	alternator	4
	Johansson	Ferrari	1	accident	15
	Tambay	Renault	0	accident	17
	Berger	Arrows-BMW	0	accident	11

Fastest Lap: Alboreto, 1m 22.64s. 89.65 mph/144.28 kph

Canadian Grand Prix: Montreal, 16 June 1985

70 laps of 2.74 mile/4.41 km circuit

Place	Driver	Car	Laps	Time/reason for retiring	Grid
1	Alboreto	Ferrari	70	1h 46m 01.8s	3
2	Johansson	Ferrari	70	1h 46m 03.8s	4
3	Prost	McLaren-TAG	70	1h 46m 06.2s	5
4	Rosberg	Williams-Honda	70	1h 46m 29.6s	8
5	de Angelis	Lotus-Renault	70	1h 46m 45.2s	1
6	Mansell	Williams-Honda	70	1h 47m 19.7s	16
7	Tambay	Renault	69		10
8	Laffite	Ligier-Renault	69		19
9	Boutsen	Arrows-BMW	68		7
10	Patrese	Alfa Romeo	68		13
11	Bellof	Tyrrell-Ford	68		23
12	Brundle	Tyrrell-Ford	68		24
13	Berger	Arrows-BMW	67		12
14	de Cesaris	Ligier-Renault	67		15
15	Surer	Brabham-BMW	67		20
16	Senna	Lotus-Renault	65		2
17	Cheever	Alfa Romeo	64		11
	Martini	Minardi-MM	57	accident	25
	Lauda	McLaren-TAG	37	engine	17
	Ghinzani	Osella-Alfa	35	engine	22
	Alliot	RAM-Hart	28	accident	21
	Warwick	Renault	25	accident	6
	Winkelhock	RAM-Hart	5	accident	14
	T Fabi	Toleman-Hart	3	turbo	18
	Piquet	Brabham-BMW	0	transmission	9

Fastest Lap: Senna, 1m 27.45s. 112.81 mph/181.55 kph

United States Grand Prix: Detroit, 23 June 1985

63 laps of 2.5 mile/4.02 km circuit

Place	Driver	Car	Laps	Time/reason for retiring	Grid
1	Rosberg	Williams-Honda	63	1h 55m 39.9s	5
2	Johansson	Ferrari	63	1h 56m 37.4s	9
3	Alboreto	Ferrari	63	1h 56m 43.0s	3
4	Bellof	Tyrrell-Ford	63	1h 56m 46.1s	19
5	de Angelis	Lotus-Renault	63	1h 57m 06.8s	8
6	Piquet	Brabham-BMW	62		10
7	Boutsen	Arrows-BMW	62		21
8	Surer	Brabham-BMW	62		11
9	Cheever	Alfa Romeo	61		7
10	de Cesaris	Ligier-Renault	61		17
11	Berger	Arrows-BMW	60		24
12	Laffite	Ligier-Renault	58		16

United States Grand Prix (cont)

Place	Driver	Car	Laps	Time/reason for retiring	Grid
	Senna	Lotus-Renault	51	accident	1
	Brundle	Tyrrell-Ford	30	accident	18
	Alliot	RAM-Hart	27	accident	23
	Mansell	Williams-Honda	26	accident	2
	Prost	McLaren-TAG	19	brakes	4
	Patrese	Alfa Romeo	19	electrical	14
	Warwick	Renault	18	transmission	6
	Tambay	Renault	15	accident	15
	Martini	Minardi-MM	11	engine	25
	Lauda	McLaren-TAG	10	brakes	12
	T Fabi	Toleman-Hart	4	clutch	13
	Winkelhock	RAM-Hart	3	turbo	20
	Ghinzani	Osella-Alfa	0	accident	22

Fastest Lap: Senna, 1m 45.61s. 85.22 mph/137.14 kph

French Grand Prix: Paul Ricard, 7 July 1985

53 laps of 3.61 mile/5.81 km circuit

Place	Driver	Car	Laps	Time/reason for retiring	Grid
1	Piquet	Brabham-BMW	53	1h 31m 46.3s	5
2	Rosberg	Williams-Honda	53	1h 31m 52.9s	1
3	Prost	McLaren-TAG	53	1h 31m 55.6s	4
4	Johansson	Ferrari	53	1h 32m 39.8s	15
5	de Angelis	Lotus-Renault	53	1h 32m 40.0s	7
6	Tambay	Renault	53	1h 33m 01.4s	9
7	Warwick	Renault	53	1h 33m 30.5s	10
8	Surer	Brabham-BMW	52		13
9	Boutsen	Arrows-BMW	52		11
10	Cheever	Alfa Romeo	52		17
11	Patrese	Alfa Romeo	52		16
12	Winkelhock	RAM-Hart	50		19
13	Bellof	Tyrrell-Ford	50		25
14	T Fabi	Toleman-Hart	49	fuel pressure	18
15	Ghinzani	Osella-Alfa	49		23
	Brundle	Tyrrell-Renault	32	gearbox	20
	Lauda	McLaren-TAG	30	gearbox	6
	Senna	Lotus-Renault	26	engine	2
	Berger	Arrows-BMW	20	accident	8
	Martini	Minardi-MM	19	accident	24
	Alliot	RAM-Hart	8	fuel pressure	22
	Palmer	Zakspeed	6	engine	21
	Alboreto	Ferrari	5	turbo	3
	de Cesaris	Ligier-Renault	4	drive-shaft	12
	Laffite	Ligier-Renault	2	turbo	14

Fastest Lap: Rosberg, 1m 39.91s. 130.08 mph/209.3 kph

British Grand Prix: Silverstone, 21 July 1985

65 laps of 2.93 mile/4.72 km circuit

Place	Driver	Car	Laps	Time/reason for retiring	Grid
1	Prost	McLaren-TAG	65	1h 18m 10.44s	3
2	Alboreto	Ferrari	64		6
3	Laffite	Ligier-Renault	64		16
4	Piquet	Brabham-BMW	64		2
5	Warwick	Renault	64		12
6	Surer	Brabham-BMW	63		15
7	Brundle	Tyrrell-Renault	63		20
8	Berger	Arrows-BMW	63		17
9	Patrese	Alfa Romeo	62		14
10	Senna	Lotus-Renault	60	fuel injection	4
11	Bellof	Tyrrell-Ford	59		26
	Lauda	McLaren-TAG	57	electrical	10
	Boutsen	Arrows-BMW	57	spun	19
	de Cesaris	Ligier-Renault	41	clutch	7
	Martini	Minardi-MM	38	transmission	23
	de Angelis	Lotus-Renault	37		8
	Winkelhock	RAM-Hart	28	turbo	18
	Rosberg	Williams-Honda	21	exhaust	1
	Mansell	Williams-Honda	17	clutch	5
	Cheever	Alfa-Romeo	17	turbo	22
	Palmer	Zakspeed	6		24
	T Fabi	Toleman-Hart	4	crownwheel and pinion	9
	Johansson	Ferrari	1	accident	11
	Tambay	Renault	0	spun	13
	Alliot	RAM-Hart	0	accident	21
	Ghinzani	Osella-Alfa	0	accident	25

Fastest Lap: Prost, 1m 09.89s. 151.04 mph/243.07 kph

German Grand Prix: Nürburgring, 4 August 1985

67 laps of 2.82 mile/4.54 km circuit

Place	Driver	Car	Laps	Time/reason for retiring	Grid
1	Alboreto	Ferrari	67	1h 35m 31.3s	8
2	Prost	McLaren-TAG	67	1h 35m 43.0s	3
3	Laffite	Ligier-Renault	67	1h 36m 22.5s	13
4	Boutsen	Arrows-BMW	67	1h 36m 26.6s	15
5	Lauda	McLaren-TAG	67	1h 36m 45.3s	12
6	Mansell	Williams-Honda	67	1h 36m 48.2s	10
7	Berger	Arrows-BMW	66		17
8	Bellof	Tyrrell-Renault	66		19
9	Johansson	Ferrari	66		2
10	Brundle	Tyrrell-Renault	63		26
11	Martini	Minardi-MM	62	engine	27

German Grand Prix (cont)

Place	Driver	Car	Laps	Time/reason for retiring	Grid
12	Rosberg	Williams-Honda	61	brakes	4
	Cheever	Alfa Romeo	45	turbo	18
	de Angelis	Lotus-Renault	40	engine	7
	Rothengatter	Osella-Alfa	32	gearbox	25
	T Fabi	Toleman-Hart	29	clutch	1
	Senna	Lotus-Renault	27	cv joint	5
	Warwick	Renault	25	ignition	20
	Piquet	Brabham-BMW	23	turbo	6
	Tambay	Renault	19	spun	16
	Surer	Brabham-BMW	12	engine	11
	Winkelhock	RAM-Hart	8	engine	22
	Patrese	Alfa Romeo	8	gearbox	9
	Hesnault	Renault	8	clutch	23
	Alliot	RAM-Hart	8	oil pressure	21
	Palmer	Zakspeed	7	alternator belt	24
	de Cesaris	Ligier-Renault	0	steering	14

Fastest Lap: Lauda, 1m 22.81s. 122.7 mph/197.46 kph

Austrian Grand Prix: Österreichring, 18 August 1985

52 laps of 3.69 mile/5.94 km circuit

Place	Driver	Car	Laps	Time/reason for retiring	Grid
1	Prost	McLaren-TAG	52	1h 20m 12.6s	1
2	Senna	Lotus-Renault	52	1h 20m 42.6s	14
3	Alboreto	Ferrari	52	1h 20m 47.0s	9
4	Johansson	Ferrari	52	1h 20m 51.7s	12
5	de Angelis	Lotus-Renault	52	1h 21m 34.7s	7
6	Surer	Brabham-BMW	51		11
7	Bellof	Tyrrell-Renault	49	out of fuel	22
8	Boutsen	Arrows-BMW	49		16
9	Rothengatter	Osella-Alfa	48		24
10	Tambay	Renault	46	engine	8
	Laffite	Ligier-Renault	43	accident	15
	Martini	Minardi-MM	40	suspension	26
	Lauda	McLaren-TAG	39	engine	3
	Berger	Arrows-BMW	32	turbo	17
	T Fabi	Toleman-Hart	31	electrical	6
	Warwick	Renault	29	engine	13
	Acheson	RAM-Hart	28	engine	23
	Piquet	Brabham-BMW	26	exhaust	5
	Mansell	Williams-Honda	25	engine	2
	Patrese	Alfa Romeo	25	engine	10
	Palmer	Zakspeed	17	engine	25
	Alliot	RAM-Hart	16	turbo	21
	de Cesaris	Ligier-Renault	13	accident	18

Austrian Grand Prix (cont)

Place	Driver	Car	Laps	Time/reason for retiring	Grid
	Cheever	Alfa Romeo	6	turbo	20
	Rosberg	Williams-Honda	4	engine	4
	Ghinzani	Toleman-Hart	0	engine	19

Fastest Lap: Prost, 1m 29.24s. 148.94 mph/239.7 kph

Dutch Grand Prix: Zandvoort, 25 August 1985

70 laps of 2.64 mile/4.25 km circuit

Place	Driver	Car	Laps	Time/reason for retiring	Grid
1	Lauda	McLaren-TAG	70	1h 32m 29.263s	10
2	Prost	McLaren-TAG	70	1h 32m 29.495s	3
3	Senna	Lotus-Renault	70	1h 33m 17.854s	4
4	Alboreto	Ferrari	70	1h 33m 18.1s	16
5	de Angelis	Lotus-Renault	69		11
6	Mansell	Williams-Honda	69		7
7	Brundle	Tyrrell-Renault	69		21
8	Piquet	Brabham-BMW	69		1
9	Berger	Arrows-BMW	68		14
10	Surer	Brabham-BMW	65	exhaust	9
	Rothengatter	Osella-Alfa	46	running	26
	Boutsen	Arrows-BMW	44	suspension	8
	Alliot	RAM-Hart	42	engine	25
	Bellof	Tyrell-Renault	39	engine	2
	Warwick	Renault	37	gearbox	12
	de Cesaris	Ligier-Renault	35	turbo	18
	Tambay	Renault	32	transmission	6
	Rosberg	Williams-Honda	20	engine	2
	T Fabi	Toleman-Hart	18	wheel	5
	Laffite	Ligier-Renault	17	electrics	13
	Palmer	Zakspeed	13	oil pressure	23
	Ghinzani	Toleman-Hart	12	engine	15
	Johansson	Ferrari	9	engine	17
	Martini	Minardi-MM	1	accident	24
	Cheever	Alfa Romeo	1	turbo	20
	Patrese	Alfa Romeo	1	turbo	19

Fastest Lap: Prost, 1m 16.54s. 124.27 mph/200 kph

Italian Grand Prix: Monza, 8 September 1985

51 laps of 3.6 mile/5.81 km circuit

Place	Driver	Car	Laps	Time/reason for retiring	Grid
1	Prost	McLaren-TAG	51	1h 17m 59.5s	5
2	Piquet	Brabham-BMW	51	1h 18m 51.1s	4
3	Senna	Lotus-Renault	51	1h 18m 59.8s	1
4	Surer	Brabham-BMW	51	1h 19m 00.1s	9
5	Johansson	Ferrari	50		10
6	de Angelis	Lotus-Renault	50		6
7	Tambay	Renault	50		8
8	Brundle	Tyrrell-Renault	50		18
9	Boutsen	Arrows-BMW	50		14
10	Streiff	Ligier-Renault	49		19
11	Mansell	Williams-Honda	47	engine	3
12	T Fabi	Toleman-Hart	47		15
13	Alboreto	Ferrari	45	engine	7
	Rosberg	Williams-Honda	44	engine	2
	Laffite	Ligier-Renault	40	engine	20
	Lauda	McLaren-TAG	33	transmission	16
	Patrese	Alfa Romeo	31	exhaust	13
	Rothengatter	Osella-Alfa	26	engine	22
	Alliot	RAM-Hart	19	turbo	26
	Berger	Arrows-BMW	13	engine	11
	Warwick	Renault	9	transmission	12
	Jones	Lola-Hart	6	distributor	25
	Cheever	Alfa Romeo	3	engine	17
	Acheson	RAM-Hart	2	clutch	24
	Martini	Minardi-MM	0	fuel pump	23
	Ghinzani	Toleman-Hart	0	stalled	21

Fastest Lap: Mansell, 1m 28.28s. 146.96 mph/236.51 kph

Belgian Grand Prix: Spa, 15 September 1985

43 laps of 4.32 mile/6.95 km circuit

Place	Driver	Car	Laps	Time/reason for retiring	Grid
1	Senna	Lotus-Renault	43	1h 34m 19.9s	2
2	Mansell	Williams-Honda	43	1h 34m 48.3s	7
3	Prost	McLaren-TAG	43	1h 35m 15.0s	1
4	Rosberg	Williams-Honda	43	1h 35m 35.2s	10
5	Piquet	Brabham-BMW	42		3
6	Warwick	Renault	42		14
7	Berger	Arrows-BMW	42		8
8	Surer	Brabham-BMW	42		12
9	Streiff	Ligier-Renault	42		18
10	Boutsen	Arrows-BMW	40		6
11	Laffite	Ligier-Renault	38	accident	17
12	Martini	Minardi-MM	38		24

Belgian Grand Prix (cont)

Place	Driver	Car	Laps	Time/reason for retiring	Grid
13	Brundle	Tyrrell-Renault	38		21
	Rothengatter	Osella-Alfa	37		23
	Patrese	Alfa Romeo	31	engine	15
	Cheever	Alfa Romeo	26	gearbox	19
	Tambay	Renault	24	gearbox	13
	T Fabi	Toleman-Hart	23	throttle	11
	de Angelis	Lotus-Renault	19	turbo	9
	Danner	Zakspeed	16	gearbox	22
	Alliot	RAM-Hart	10	accident	20
	Johansson	Ferrari	7	engine	5
	Ghinzani	Toleman-Hart	7	accident	16
	Alboreto	Ferrari	3	clutch	4

Fastest Lap: Prost, 2m 01.73s. 127.53 mph/205.24 kph

European Grand Prix: Brands Hatch, 6 October 1985

75 laps of 2.61 mile/4.21 km circuit

Place	Driver	Car	Laps	Time/reason for retiring	Grid
1	Mansell	Williams-Honda	75	1h 32m 58.1s	3
2	Senna	Lotus-Renault	75	1h 33m 19.5s	1
3	Rosberg	Williams-Honda	75	1h 33m 56.6s	4
4	Prost	McLaren-TAG	75	1h 34m 04.2s	6
5	de Angelis	Lotus-Renault	74		9
6	Boutsen	Arrows-BMW	73		12
7	Watson	McLaren-TAG	73		21
8	Streiff	Ligier-Renault	73		5
9	Patrese	Alfa Romeo	73		11
10	Berger	Arrows-BMW	73		19
11	Cheever	Alfa Romeo	73		18
12	Tambay	Renault	72		17
	Surer	Brabham-BMW	62	turbo	7
	Johansson	Ferrari	59	electrical	13
	Laffite	Ligier-Renault	58	engine	10
	Danner	Zakspeed	50	engine	25
	Capelli	Tyrrell-Renault	44	accident	24
	Brundle	Tyrrell-Renault	40	water pipe	16
	T Fabi	Toleman-Hart	33	engine	20
	Alliot	RAM-Hart	31	engine	23
	Ghinzani	Toleman-Hart	16	engine	14
	Jones	Lola-Hart	13	radiator	22
	Alboreto	Ferrari	13	turbo	15
	Piquet	Brabham-BMW	6	accident	2
	Warwick	Renault	4	fuel injection	8
	Martini	Minardi-MM	3	accident	26

Fastest Lap: Laffite, 1m 11.53s. 131.57 mph/211.73 kph

South African Grand Prix: Kyalami, 19 October 1985

75 laps of 2.56 mile/4.1 km circuit

Place	Driver	Car	Laps	Time/reason for retiring	Grid
1	Mansell	Williams-Honda	75	1h 28m 22.9s	1
2	Rosberg	Williams-Honda	75	1h 28m 30.4s	3
3	Prost	McLaren-TAG	75	1h 30m 14.7s	9
4	Johansson	Ferrari	74		16
5	Berger	Arrows-BMW	74		11
6	Boutsen	Arrows-BMW	74		10
7	Brundle	Tyrrell-Renault	73		17
	de Angelis	Lotus-Renault	52	engine	6
	Martini	Minardi-MM	45	radiator	19
	Lauda	McLaren-TAG	37	turbo	8
	Streiff	Tyrrell-Renault	16	accident	18
	Senna	Lotus-Renault	8	engine	4
	Alboreto	Ferrari	8	turbo	15
	Piquet	Brabham-BMW	6	engine	2
	Ghinzani	Toleman-Hart	4	engine	13
	T Fabi	Toleman-Hart	3	engine	7
	Surer	Brabham-BMW	3	engine	5
	Rothengatter	Osella-Alfa	1	electrical	20
	Cheever	Alfa Romeo	0	accident	14
	Patrese	Alfa Romeo	0	accident	12

Fastest Lap: Rosberg, 1m 08.15s. 134.710 mph/216.8 kph

Australian Grand Prix: Adelaide, 3 November 1985

82 laps of 2.35 mile/3.78 km circuit

Place	Driver	Car	Laps	Time/reason for retiring	Grid
1	Rosberg	Williams-Honda	82	2h 00m 40.1s	3
2	Laffite	Ligier-Renault	82	2h 01m 26.6s	20
3	Streiff	Ligier-Renault	82	2h 02m 09.0s	18
4	Capelli	Tyrrell-Renault	81		22
5	Johansson	Ferrari	81		15
6	Berger	Arrows-BMW	81		7
7	Rothengatter	Osella-Alfa	78		25
8	Martini	Minardi-MM	78		23
	Senna	Lotus-Renault	62	engine	1
	Alboreto	Ferrari	61	gearbox	5
	Lauda	McLaren-TAG	57	accident	16
	Warwick	Renault	57	transmission	12
	Brundle	Tyrrell-Renault	49	running	17
	Surer	Brabham-BMW	42	engine	6
	Patrese	Alfa Romeo	42	exhaust	14
	T Fabi	Toleman-Hart	40	engine	24
	Boutsen	Arrows-BMW	37	oil leak	11

Australian Grand Prix (cont)

Place	Driver	Car	Laps	Time/reason for retiring	Grid
	Ghinzani	Toleman-Hart	28	clutch	21
	Prost	McLaren-TAG	26	engine	4
	Tambay	Renault	20	transmission	8
	Jones	Lola-Hart	20	electrical	19
	de Angelis	Lotus-Renault	17	disqualified: illegal start	10
	Piquet	Brabham-BMW	14	electrical fire	9
	Cheever	Alfa Romeo	5	engine	13
	Mansell	Williams-Honda	1	transmission	2

Fastest Lap: Rosberg, 1m 23.7s. 100.9 mph/162.38 kph

World Championship 1985

1	Prost	73 (76)
2	Alboreto	53
3	Rosberg	40
4	Senna	38
5	de Angelis	33
6	Mansell	31
7	Johansson	26
8	Piquet	21
9	Laffite	16
10	Lauda	14
11	Boutsen	11
12	Tambay	11
13=	Surer, Warwick	5
15=	Bellof, Streiff	4
17=	Arnoux, Berger, Capelli, de Cesaris	3

Constructors' Championship

1	McLaren-TAG	90
2	Ferrari	82
3=	Lotus-Renault, Williams-Honda	71
5	Brabham-BMW	26
6	Ligier-Renault	23
7	Renault	16
8	Arrows-BMW	14
9	Tyrrell-Ford	4
10	Tyrrell-Renault	3

1986

Normally-aspirated cars were banned for 1986. Prost took the champion-ship, albeit with fewer wins, after a spectacular tyre failure eliminated Mansell in the later stages of the Australian Grand Prix. Piquet was also in contention until the last race. Benetton (formerly Toleman) took their first win. At Brands Hatch Laffite equalled Graham Hill's record number of grand prix starts, but suffered injuries which ended his grand prix career in the same race. Elio de Angelis was killed in testing at Paul Ricard. Keke Rosberg retired from grand prix racing at the end of the season.

Brazilian Grand Prix: Rio de Janeiro, 23 March 1986

61 laps of 3.13 mile/5.03 km circuit

Place	Driver	Car	Laps	Time/reason for retiring	Grid
1	Piquet	Williams-Honda	61	1h 39m 32.58s	2
2	Senna	Lotus-Renault	61	1h 40m 07.41s	1
3	Laffite	Ligier-Renault	61	1h 40m 32.34s	5
4	Arnoux	Ligier-Renault	61	1h 41m 01.01s	4
5	Brundle	Tyrrell-Renault	60		17
6	Berger	Benetton-BMW	59		16
7	Streiff	Tyrrell-Renault	59		18
8	de Angelis	Brabham-BMW	58		14
9	Dumfries	Lotus-Renault	58		11
10	T Fabi	Benetton-BMW	56		12
	Boutsen	Arrows-BMW	37	exhaust	15
	Alboreto	Ferrari	35	fuel pump	6
	Prost	McLaren-TAG	30	engine	9
	Danner	Osella-Alfa	29	engine	24
	Johansson	Ferrari	26	brakes	8
	Tambay	Lola-Hart	24	alternator	13
	Patrese	Brabham-BMW	21	water pipe	10
	Palmer	Zakspeed	20	airbox	21
	Surer	Arrows-BMW	19	overheating	20
	Nannini	Minardi-MM	18	oil leak	25
	de Cesaris	Minardi-MM	16	gearbox	22
	Ghinzani	Osella-Alfa	16	engine	23
	Rosberg	McLaren-TAG	6	engine	7
	Jones	Lola-Hart	5	rotor arm	19
	Mansell	Williams-Honda	0	accident	3

Fastest Lap: Piquet, 1m 33.55s. 120.31 mph/193.61 kph

Spanish Grand Prix: Jerez, 13 April 1986

72 laps of 2.62 mile/4.22 km circuit

Place	Driver	Car	Laps	Time/reason for retiring	Grid
1	Senna	Lotus-Renault	72	1h 48m 47.735s	1
2	Mansell	Williams-Honda	72	1h 48m 47.749s	3
3	Prost	McLaren-TAG	72	1h 49m 09.290s	4
4	Rosberg	McLaren-TAG	71		5
5	T Fabi	Benetton-BMW	71		9
6	Berger	Benetton-BMW	71		7
7	Boutsen	Arrows-BMW	68		19
8	Tambay	Lola-Hart	66		18
	Dumfries	Lotus-Renault	52	gearbox	10
	Brundle	Tyrrell-Renault	41	oil system	12
	Laffite	Ligier-Renault	40	transmission	8
	Piquet	Williams-Honda	39	overheating	2
	Surer	Arrows-BMW	39	fuel leak	22
	de Angelis	Brabham-BMW	29	gearbox	15
	Arnoux	Ligier-Renault	29	transmission	6
	Alboreto	Ferrari	22	wheel	13
	Streiff	Tyrrell-Renault	22	oil system	20
	Danner	Osella-Alfa	14	engine	23
	Johansson	Ferrari	11	brakes	11
	Ghinzani	Osella-Alfa	10	engine	21
	Patrese	Brabham-BMW	8	gearbox	14
	de Cesaris	Minardi-MM	1	transmission	24
	Palmer	Zakspeed	0	accident	16
	Jones	Lola-Hart	0	accident	17
	Nannini	Minardi-MM	0	transmission	25

Fastest Lap: Mansell, 1m 27.18s. 108.23 mph/174.19 kph

San Marino Grand Prix: Imola, 27 April 1986

60 laps of 3.13 miles/5.04 km circuit

Place	Driver	Car	Laps	Time/reason for retiring	Grid
1	Prost	McLaren-TAG	60	1h 32m 28.41s	4
2	Piquet	Williams-Honda	60	1h 32m 36.05s	2
3	Berger	Benetton-BMW	59		9
4	Johansson	Ferrari	59		7
5	Rosberg	McLaren-TAG	58	out of fuel	6
6	Patrese	Brabham-BMW	58	out of fuel	16
7	Boutsen	Arrows-BMW	58		12
8	Brundle	Tyrrell-Renault	58		13
9	Surer	Arrows-BMW	57	out of fuel	15
10	Alboreto	Ferrari	56	turbo	5
	Ghinzani	Osella-Alfa	52	fuel	26
	Arnoux	Ligier-Renault	46	wheel	8

San Marino Grand Prix (cont)

Place	Driver	Car	Laps	Time/reason for retiring	Grid
	Streiff	Tyrrell-Renault	41	transmission	22
	T Fabi	Benetton-BMW	39	engine	10
	Palmer	Zakspeed	38	brakes	20
	Danner	Osella-Alfa	31	turbo	25
	Jones	Lola-Ford	28	overheating	21
	de Cesaris	Minardi-MM	20	engine	23
	de Angelis	Brabham-BMW	19	engine	19
	Laffite	Ligier-Renault	14	turbo	14
	Senna	Lotus-Renault	11	wheel	1
	Mansell	Williams-Honda	8	engine	3
	Dumfries	Lotus-Renault	8	wheel	17
	Rothengatter	Zakspeed	7	turbo	24
	Tambay	Lola-Hart	5	engine	11
	Nannini	Minardi-MM	0	accident	18

Fastest Lap: Piquet, 1m 28.67s. 127.15 mph/204.63 kph

Monaco Grand Prix: Monte Carlo, 11 May 1986

78 laps of 2.07 mile/3.33 km circuit

Place	Driver	Car	Laps	Time/reason for retiring	Grid
1	Prost	McLaren-TAG	78	1h 55m 41.06s	1
2	Rosberg	McLaren-TAG	78	1h 56m 06.08s	9
3	Senna	Lotus-Renault	78	1h 56m 34.71s	3
4	Mansell	Williams-Honda	78	1h 56m 52.46s	2
5	Arnoux	Ligier-Renault	77		12
6	Laffite	Ligier-Renault	77		7
7	Piquet	Williams-Honda	77		11
8	Boutsen	Arrows-BMW	75		14
9	Surer	Arrows-BMW	75		17
10	Johansson	Ferrari	75		15
11	Streiff	Tyrrell-Renault	74		13
12	Palmer	Zakspeed	74		19
	Brundle	Tyrrell-Renault	67	accident	10
	Tambay	Lola-Ford	67	accident	8
	Berger	Benetton-BMW	42	transmission	5
	Alboreto	Ferrari	38	turbo	4
	Patrese	Brabham-BMW	38	engine	6
	de Angelis	Brabham-BMW	31	intercooler	20
	T Fabi	Benetton-BMW	17	brakes	16
	Jones	Lola-Ford	2	spun	18

Fastest Lap: Prost, 1m 26.62s. 85.96 mph/138.24 kph

Belgian Grand Prix: Spa, 25 May 1986

43 laps of 4.31 mile/6.94 km circuit

Place	Driver	Car	Laps	Time/reason for retiring	Grid
1	Mansell	Williams-Honda	43	1h 27m 57.93s	5
2	Senna	Lotus-Renault	43	1h 28m 17.75s	4
3	Johansson	Ferrari	43	1h 28m 24.52s	11
4	Alboreto	Ferrari	43	1h 28m 27.56s	9
5	Laffite	Ligier-Renault	43	1h 29m 08.62s	17
6	Prost	McLaren-TAG	43	1h 30m 15.70s	3
7	T Fabi	Benetton-BMW	42		6
8	Patrese	Brabham-BMW	42		15
9	Surer	Arrows-BMW	41	fuel pump	21
10	Berger	Benetton-BMW	41		2
11	Jones	Lola-Ford	40	out of fuel	16
12	Streiff	Tyrrell-Renault	40		18
	Palmer	Zakspeed	37	electrical	20
	de Cesaris	Minardi-MM	35	out of fuel	19
	Brundle	Tyrrell-Renault	25	gearbox	12
	Rothengatter	Zakspeed	25	electrical	23
	Nannini	Minardi-MM	24	gearbox	22
	Arnoux	Ligier-Renault	23	engine	7
	Piquet	Williams-Honda	16	turbo	1
	Boutsen	Arrows-BMW	7	electrical	14
	Dumfries	Lotus-Renault	7	accident	13
	Rosberg	McLaren-TAG	6	engine	8
	Ghinzani	Osella-Alfa	3	engine	24
	Danner	Osella-Alfa	2	engine	25
	Tambay	Lola-Ford	0	accident	10

Fastest Lap: Prost, 1m 59.28s. 130.15 mph/209.45 kph

Canadian Grand Prix: Montreal, 15 June 1986

69 laps of 2.74 mile/4.41 km circuit

Place	Driver	Car	Laps	Time/reason for retiring	Grid
1	Mansell	Williams-Honda	69	1h 42m 26.42s	1
2	Prost	McLaren-TAG	69	1h 42m 47.07s	4
3	Piquet	Williams-Honda	69	1h 43m 02.68s	3
4	Rosberg	McLaren-TAG	69	1h 44m 02.09s	6
5	Senna	Lotus-Renault	68		2
6	Arnoux	Ligier-Renault	68		5
7	Laffite	Ligier-Renault	68		8
8	Alboreto	Ferrari	68		11
9	Brundle	Tyrrell-Renault	67		18
10	Jones	Lola-Ford	66		13
11	Streiff	Tyrrell-Renault	65		16

Canadian Grand Prix (cont)

Place	Driver	Car	Laps	Time/reason for retiring	Grid
12	Rothengatter	Zakspeed	63		23
	Patrese	Brabham-BMW	44	turbo	9
	Ghinzani	Osella-Alfa	43	gearbox	22
	de Cesaris	Minardi-MM	40	gearbox	20
	Boutsen	Arrows-BMW	38	electrical	12
	Berger	Benetton-BMW	34	throttle	7
	Johansson	Ferrari	29	accident	17
	Dumfries	Lotus-Renault	28	accident	15
	Palmer	Zakspeed	24	engine	21
	Warwick	Brabham-BMW	20	engine	10
	Nannini	Minardi-MM	17	turbo	19
	T Fabi	Benetton-BMW	13	battery	14
	Danner	Osella-Alfa	6	turbo	24

Fastest Lap: Piquet, 1m 25.44s. 115.46 mph/185.81 kph

United States Grand Prix: Detroit, 22 June 1986

63 laps of 2.5 mile/4.02 km circuit

Place	Driver	Car	Laps	Time/reason for retiring	Grid
1	Senna	Lotus-Renault	63	1h 51m 12.85s	1
2	Laffite	Ligier-Renault	63	1h 51m 43.86s	6
3	Prost	McLaren-TAG	63	1h 51m 44.67s	7
4	Alboreto	Ferrari	63	1h 52m 43.78s	11
5	Mansell	Williams-Honda	62		2
6	Patrese	Brabham-BMW	62		8
7	Dumfries	Lotus-Renault	61		14
8	Palmer	Zakspeed	61		20
9	Streiff	Tyrrell-Renault	61		18
10	Warwick	Brabham-BMW	60		15
	Danner	Arrows-BMW	51	fuel pump	19
	Arnoux	Ligier-Renault	46	accident	4
	Boutsen	Arrows-BMW	44	accident	13
	de Cesaris	Minardi-MM	43	differential	23
	Piquet	Williams-Honda	41	accident	3
	Johansson	Ferrari	40	electrical	5
	T Fabi	Benetton-BMW	38	clutch	17
	Cheever	Lola-Ford	37	transmission	10
	Jones	Lola-Ford	33	transmission	21
	Berg	Osella-Alfa	28	electrical	25
	Brundle	Tyrrell-Renault	15	electrical	16
	Ghinzani	Osella-Alfa	14	turbo	22
	Rosberg	McLaren-TAG	12	gearbox	9
	Berger	Benetton-BMW	8	ignition	12
	Nannini	Minardi-MM	3	turbo	24

Fastest Lap: Piquet, 1m 41.23s. 88.9 mph/143.1 kph

French Grand Prix: Paul Ricard, 6 July 1986

80 laps of 2.37 mile/3.81 km circuit

Place	Driver	Car	Laps	Time/reason for retiring	Grid
1	Mansell	Williams-Honda	80	1h 37m 19.27s	2
2	Prost	McLaren-TAG	80	1h 37m 36.40s	5
3	Piquet	Williams-Honda	80	1h 37m 56.82s	3
4	Rosberg	McLaren-TAG	80	1h 38m 08.00s	7
5	Arnoux	Ligier-Renault	79		4
6	Laffite	Ligier-Renault	79		11
7	Patrese	Brabham-BMW	78		16
8	Alboreto	Ferrari	78		6
9	Warwick	Brabham-BMW	77		14
10	Brundle	Tyrrell-Renault	77		15
11	Danner	Arrows-BMW	76		18
	Boutsen	Arrows-BMW	67		21
	Tambay	Lola-Ford	64	brake	13
	Dumfries	Lotus-Renault	56	engine	12
	Palmer	Zakspeed	46	engine	22
	Streiff	Tyrrell-Renault	43	fuel injection	17
	Rothengatter	Zakspeed	32	accident	24
	Berg	Osella-Alfa	25	turbo	26
	Berger	Benetton-BMW	22	accident	8
	T Fabi	Benetton-BMW	7	engine	9
	Johansson	Ferrari	5	throttle	10
	Senna	Lotus-Renault	3	accident	1
	Ghinzani	Osella-Alfa	3	accident	25
	Nannini	Minardi-MM	3	accident	19
	de Cesaris	Minardi-MM	3	turbo	23
	Jones	Lola-Ford	2	accident	20

Fastest Lap: Mansell, 1m 09.99s. 121.86 mph/196.12 kph

British Grand Prix: Brands Hatch, 13 July 1986

75 laps of 2.61 mile/4.21 km

Place	Driver	Car	Laps	Time/reason for retiring	Grid
1	Mansell	Williams-Honda	75	1h 30m 38.5s	2
2	Piquet	Williams-Honda	75	1h 30m 44.1s	1
3	Prost	McLaren-TAG	74		6
4	Arnoux	Ligier-Renault	73		8
5	Brundle	Tyrrell-Renault	72		11
6	Streiff	Tyrrell-Renault	72		16
7	Dumfries	Lotus-Renault	72		10
8	Warwick	Brabham-BMW	72		9
9	Palmer	Zakspeed	69		22
	Boutsen	Arrows-BMW	62		13
	Tambay	Lola-Ford	60	gearbox	17

British Grand Prix (cont)

Place	Driver	Car	Laps	Time/reason for retiring	Grid
	Alboreto	Ferrari	51	turbo	12
	Nannini	Minardi-MM	50	cv joint	20
	T Fabi	Benetton-BMW	45	fuel line	7
	Patrese	Brabham-BMW	39	engine	15
	Senna	Lotus-Renault	27	gearbox	3
	Rothengatter	Zakspeed	24	engine	25
	de Cesaris	Minardi-MM	23	alternator	21
	Berger	Benetton-BMW	22	electrical	4
	Jones	Lola-Ford	22	throttle	14
	Johansson	Ferrari	20	radiator	18
	Rosberg	McLaren-TAG	7	gearbox	5
	Danner	Arrows-BMW	0	eliminated at first start	23
	Ghinzani	Osella-Alfa	0	eliminated at first start	24
	Berg	Osella-Alfa	0	eliminated at first start	26
	Laffite	Ligier-Renault	0	eliminated at first start	19

Fastest Lap: Mansell, 1m 09.59s. 131.57 mph/211.74 kph
* Race restarted after first lap crash.

German Grand Prix: Hockenheim, 27 July 1986

44 laps of 4.22 mile/6.8 km circuit

Place	Driver	Car	Laps	Time/reason for retiring	Grid
1	Piquet	Williams-Honda	44	1h 22m 08.26s	5
2	Senna	Lotus-Renault	44	1h 22m 23.70s	3
3	Mansell	Williams-Honda	44	1h 22m 52.84s	6
4	Arnoux	Ligier-Renault	44	1h 23m 23.44s	8
5	Rosberg	McLaren-TAG	43	out of fuel	1
6	Prost	McLaren-TAG	43	out of fuel	2
7	Warwick	Brabham-BMW	43		20
8	Tambay	Lola-Ford	43		13
9	Jones	Lola-Ford	42		19
10	Berger	Benetton-BMW	42		4
11	Johansson	Ferrari	41	rear wing	11
12	Berg	Osella-Alfa	40		26
	Danner	Arrows-BMW	38	turbo	17
	Rothengatter	Zakspeed	38	gearbox	24
	Palmer	Zakspeed	37	engine	16
	Brundle	Tyrrell-Renault	34	engine	15
	Patrese	Brabham-BMW	22	spark plug	7
	de Cesaris	Minardi-MM	20	gearbox	23
	Nannini	Minardi-MM	19	overheating	22
	Dumfries	Lotus-Renault	17	radiator	12
	Boutsen	Arrows-BMW	13	turbo	21
	Alliot	Ligier-Renault	11	engine	14
	Ghinzani	Osella-Alfa	10	turbo	25

German Grand Prix (cont)

Place	Driver	Car	Laps	Time/reason for retiring	Grid
	Streiff	Tyrrell-Renault	7	engine	18
	Alboreto	Ferrari	6	transmission	10
	T Fabi	Benetton-BMW	0	accident	9

Fastest Lap: Berger, 1m 46.6s. 142.63 mph/229.53 kph

Hungarian Grand Prix: Hungaroring, 10 August 1986

76 laps of 2.49 mile/4.01 km circuit

Place	Driver	Car	Laps	Time/reason for retiring	Grid
1	Piquet	Williams-Honda	76	2h 00m 34.51s	2
2	Senna	Lotus-Renault	76	2h 00m 52.20s	1
3	Mansell	Williams-Honda	75		4
4	Johansson	Ferrari	75		7
5	Dumfries	Lotus-Renault	74		8
6	Brundle	Tyrrell-Renault	74		16
7	Tambay	Lola-Ford	74		6
8	Streiff	Tyrrell-Renault	74	.	18
9	Alliot	Ligier-Renault	73		12
10	Palmer	Zakspeed	70		24
	Arnoux	Ligier-Renault	48	engine	9
	Jones	Lola-Ford	46	transmission	10
	Berger	Benetton-BMW	44	transmission	11
	Boutsen	Arrows-BMW	40	metering unit	22
	Rosberg	McLaren-TAG	34	suspension	5
	T Fabi	Benetton-BMW	32	transmission	13
	Nannini	Minardi-MM	30	engine	17
	Alboreto	Ferrari	29	accident	15
	Warwick	Brabham-BMW	28	accident	19
	Prost	McLaren-TAG	23	accident	3
	Ghinzani	Osella-Alfa	15	suspension	23
	Danner	Arrows-BMW	7	suspension	21
	Patrese	Brabham-BMW	5	accident	14
	de Cesaris	Minardi-MM	5	engine	20
	Rothengatter	Zakspeed	2	accident	25
	Berg	Osella-Alfa	1	turbo	26

Fastest Lap: Piquet, 1m 31s. 98.67 mph/158.79 kph

1986

Austrian Grand Prix: Österreichring, 17 August 1986

52 laps of 3.7 mile/5.9 km circuit

Place	Driver	Car	Laps	Time/reason for retiring	Grid
1	Prost	McLaren-TAG	52	1h 21m 22.5s	5
2	Alboreto	Ferrari	51		9
3	Johansson	Ferrari	50		13
4	Jones	Lola-Ford	50		15
5	Tambay	Lola-Ford	50		12
6	Danner	Arrows-BMW	49		21
7	Berger	Benetton-BMW	49		2
8	Rothengatter	Zakspeed	48	out of fuel	23
9	Rosberg	McLaren-TAG	47	electrical	3
10	Arnoux	Ligier-Renault	47		11
11	Ghinzani	Osella-Alfa	46		24
	Mansell	Williams-Honda	32	cv joint	6
	Piquet	Williams-Honda	29	overheating	7
	Boutsen	Arrows-BMW	25	turbo	17
	T Fabi	Benetton-BMW	17	engine	1
	Alliot	Ligier-Renault	16	engine	10
	Nannini	Minardi-MM	13	suspension	18
	de Cesaris	Minardi-MM	13	drive-shaft	22
	Senna	Lotus-Renault	13	misfire	8
	Brundle	Tyrrell-Renault	12	engine	16
	Streiff	Tyrrell-Renault	10	engine	19
	Dumfries	Lotus-Renault	9	engine	14
	Palmer	Zakspeed	8	engine	20
	Berg	Osella-Alfa	6	electrical	25
	Patrese	Brabham-BMW	2	engine	4

Fastest Lap: Berger, 1m 29.44s. 148.61 mph/239.16 kph

Italian Grand Prix: Monza, 7 September 1986

51 laps of 3.6 mile/5.8 km circuit

Place	Driver	Car	Laps	Time/reason for retiring	Grid
1	Piquet	Williams-Honda	51	1h 17m 42.9s	6
2	Mansell	Williams-Honda	51	1h 17m 52.7s	3
3	Johansson	Ferrari	51	1h 18m 05.8s	12
4	Rosberg	McLaren-TAG	51	1h 18m 36.7s	8
5	Berger	Benetton-BMW	50	out of fuel	4
6	Jones	Lola-Ford	49		18
7	Boutsen	Arrows-BMW	49		13
8	Danner	Arrows-BMW	49		16
9	Streiff	Tyrrell-Renault	49		23
10	Brundle	Tyrrell-Renault	49		20
11	Caffi	Osella-Alfa	45		27
	T Fabi	Benetton-BMW	44	tyre	1

Italian Grand Prix (cont)

Place	Driver	Car	Laps	Time/reason for retiring	Grid
	Alboreto	Ferrari	33	engine	9
	de Cesaris	Minardi-MM	33	engine	21
	Capelli	AGS-MM	31	tyre	25
	Arnoux	Ligier-Renault	30	gearbox	11
	Prost	McLaren-TAG	27	engine	2
	Palmer	Zakspeed	27	alternator	22
	Alliot	Ligier-Renault	22	engine	14
	Dumfries	Lotus-Renault	18	gearbox	17
	Warwick	Brabham-BMW	16	brakes	7
	Nannini	Minardi-MM	15	alternator belt	19
	Ghinzani	Osella-Alfa	12	accident	26
	Tambay	Lola-Ford	2	accident	15
	Patrese	Brabham-BMW	2	accident	10
	Rothengatter	Zakspeed	1	electrical	24
	Senna	Lotus-Renault	0	clutch	5

Fastest Lap: T Fabi, 1m 28.1s. 147.27 mph/237 kph

Portuguese Grand Prix: Estoril, 21 September 1986

70 laps of 2.7 mile/4.35 km circuit

Place	Driver	Car	Laps	Time/reason for retiring	Grid
1	Mansell	Williams-Honda	70	1h 37m 21.9s	2
2	Prost	McLaren-TAG	70	1h 37m 40.7s	3
3	Piquet	Williams-Honda	70	1h 38m 11.2s	6
4	Senna	Lotus-Renault	69	out of fuel	1
5	Alboreto	Ferrari	69		13
6	Johansson	Ferrari	69		8
7	Arnoux	Ligier-Renault	69		10
8	T Fabi	Benetton-BMW	68	out of fuel	5
9	Dumfries	Lotus-Renault	68		15
10	Boutsen	Arrows-BMW	67		21
11	Danner	Arrows-BMW	67		22
12	Palmer	Zakspeed	67		20
13	Berg	Osella-Alfa	63		27
	Patrese	Brabham-BMW	62	engine	9
	Tambay	Lola-Ford	62	running	14
	Nannini	Minardi-MM	60	gearbox	18
	Berger	Benetton-BMW	44	accident	4
	de Cesaris	Minardi-MM	43	suspension	16
	Rosberg	McLaren-TAG	41	engine	7
	Warwick	Brabham-BMW	41	engine	12
	Alliot	Ligier-Renault	39	engine	11
	Streiff	Tyrrell-Renault	28	engine	23
	Brundle	Tyrrell-Renault	18	engine	19
	Jones	Lola-Ford	10	spun	17

Portuguese Grand Prix (cont)

Place	Driver	Car	Laps	Time/reason for retiring	Grid
	Rothengatter	Zakspeed	9	crownwheel and pinion	26
	Ghinzani	Osella-Alfa	8	engine	24
	Capelli	AGS-MM	6	gearbox	25

Fastest Lap: Mansell, 1m 20.94s. 120.22 mph/193.47 kph

Mexican Grand Prix: Mexico City, 12 October 1986

68 laps of 2.75 mile/4.42 km circuit

Place	Driver	Car	Laps	Time/reason for retiring	Grid
1	Berger	Benetton-BMW	68	1h 33m 18.7s	4
2	Prost	McLaren-TAG	68	1h 33m 44.1s	6
3	Senna	Lotus-Renault	68	1h 34m 11.2s	1
4	Piquet	Williams-Honda	67		2
5	Mansell	Williams-Honda	67		3
6	Alliot	Ligier-Renault	67		10
7	Boutsen	Arrows-BMW	66		21
8	de Cesaris	Minardi-MM	66		22
9	Danner	Arrows-BMW	66		20
10	Palmer	Zakspeed	65	out of fuel	18
11	Brundle	Tyrrell-Renault	65		16
12	Johansson	Ferrari	64	turbo	14
13	Patrese	Brabham-BMW	64	accident	5
14	Nannini	Minardi-MM	64		23
15	Arnoux	Ligier-Renault	63	engine	13
16	Berg	Osella-Alfa	61		25
	Dumfries	Lotus-Renault	53	battery	17
	Warwick	Brabham-BMW	37	engine	7
	Jones	Lola-Ford	35	gearbox	15
	Rosberg	McLaren-TAG	32	puncture	11
	Alboreto	Ferrari	10	engine	12
	Streiff	Tyrrell-Renault	8	turbo	19
	Ghinzani	Osella-Alfa	8	engine	24
	T Fabi	Benetton-BMW	4	engine	9
	Tambay	Lola-Ford	0	accident	8

Fastest Lap: Piquet, 1m 19.36s. 124.62 mph/200.55 kph

Australian Grand Prix: Adelaide, 26 October 1986

82 laps of 2.35 mile/3.78 km circuit

Place	Driver	Car	Laps	Time/reason for retiring	Grid
1	Prost	McLaren-TAG	82	1h 54m 20.39s	4
2	Piquet	Williams-Honda	82	1h 54m 24.59s	2
3	Johansson	Ferrari	81		12

Australian Grand Prix (cont)

Place	Driver	Car	Laps	Time/reason for retiring	Grid
4	Brundle	Tyrrell-Renault	81		16
5	Streiff	Tyrrell-Renault	80	out of fuel	10
6	Dumfries	Lotus-Renault	80		14
7	Arnoux	Ligier-Renault	79		5
8	Alliot	Ligier-Renault	79		8
9	Palmer	Zakspeed	77		21
10	T Fabi	Benetton-BMW	77		13
	Tambay	Lola-Ford	70		17
	Mansell	Williams-Honda	63	tyre	1
	Patrese	Brabham-BMW	63	electrical	19
	Rosberg	McLaren-TAG	62	tyre	7
	Berg	Osella-Alfa	61		26
	Warwick	Brabham-BMW	57	brakes	20
	Danner	Arrows-BMW	52	engine	24
	Boutsen	Arrows-BMW	50	throttle	22
	Senna	Lotus-Renault	43	engine	3
	Berger	Benetton-BMW	40	clutch	6
	de Cesaris	Minardi-MM	40	extinguisher	11
	Rothengatter	Zakspeed	29	suspension	23
	Jones	Lola-Ford	16	engine	15
	Nannini	Minardi-MM	10	accident	18
	Ghinzani	Osella-Alfa	2	crownwheel and pinion	25
	Alboreto	Ferrari	0	accident	9

Fastest Lap: Piquet, 1m 20.79s. 104.64 mph/168.4 kph

World Championship 1986

1	Prost	72 (74)
2	Mansell	70 (72)
3	Piquet	69
4	Senna	55
5	Johansson	23
6	Rosberg	22
7	Berger	17
8 =	Alboreto, Arnoux, Laffite	14
11	Brundle	8
12	Jones	4
13 =	Dumfries, Streiff	3
15 =	T Fabi, Patrese, Tambay	2
18 =	Alliot, Danner	1

Constructors' Championship

1	Williams-Honda	141
2	McLaren-TAG	96
3	Lotus-Renault	60
4	Ferrari	37
5	Ligier-Renault	29
6	Benetton-BMW	19
7	Tyrrell-Renault	11
8	Lola-Ford	6
9	Brabham-BMW	2
10	Arrows-BMW	1

1987

Mansell again scored more wins than the eventual champion, this time Nelson Piquet, but his challenge ended with a practice crash in Japan. Prost broke Stewart's record number of wins with his victory in Portugal, which gave him 28. The Jim Clark Cup and the Colin Chapman Trophy were awarded to the driver and the constructor of the best normally-aspirated 3.5 litre engined cars, which had been admitted to the championship as part of the gradual easing out of turbo engines. Jonathan Palmer won the drivers' award and the Tyrrell team the constructors'. The BMW engine in the Arrows was raced under the name of Megatron, who had acquired the rights to produce it.

Brazilian Grand Prix: Rio de Janeiro, 12 April 1987

61 laps of 3.13 mile/5.03 km circuit

Place	Driver	Car	Laps	Time/reason for retiring	Grid
1	Prost	McLaren-TAG	61	1h 39m 45.141s	5
2	Piquet	Williams-Honda	61	1h 40m 25.688s	2
3	Johansson	McLaren-TAG	61	1h 40m 41.899s	10
4	Berger	Ferrari	61	1h 41m 24.376s	7
5	Boutsen	Benetton-Ford	60		6
6	Mansell	Williams-Honda	60		1
7	Nakajima	Lotus-Honda	59		12
8	Alboreto	Ferrari	58	underbody	9
9	Danner	Zakspeed	58		17
10	Palmer	Tyrrell-Ford	58		18
11	Streiff	Tyrrell-Ford	57		20
12	Fabre	AGS-Ford	55		22
	Cheever	Arrows-Megatron	52	engine	14
	Senna	Lotus-Honda	50	oil	3
	Patrese	Brabham-BMW	48	electrical	11
	de Cesaris	Brabham-BMW	21	gearbox	13
	Warwick	Arrows-Megatron	20	overheating	8
	Caffi	Osella-Alfa Romeo	20	driver	21
	Nannini	Minardi-MM	17	suspension	15
	Brundle	Zakspeed	15	engine	19
	T Fabi	Benetton-Ford	9	misfire	4
	Campos	Minardi-MM	3	disqualified: illegal start	16

Fastest Lap: Piquet, 1m 33.86s. 119.9 mph/192.96 kph

1987

San Marino Grand Prix: Imola, 3 May 1987

59 laps of 3.13 mile/5.04 km circuit

Place	Driver	Car	Laps	Time/reason for retiring	Grid
1	Mansell	Williams-Honda	59	1h 31m 24.076s	2
2	Senna	Lotus-Honda	59	1h 31m 51.621s	1
3	Alboreto	Ferrari	59	1h 32m 03.220s	6
4	Johansson	McLaren-TAG	59	1h 32m 24.664s	8
5	Brundle	Zakspeed	57		14
6	Nakajima	Lotus-Honda	57		12
7	Danner	Zakspeed	57		17
8	Streiff	Tyrrell-Ford	57		20
9	Patrese	Brabham-BMW	57		7
10	Alliot	Lola-Ford	56		21
11	Warwick	Arrows-Megatron	55	out of fuel	10
12	Caffi	Osella-Alfa	54	out of fuel	19
13	Fabre	AGS-Ford	53		24
	T Fabi	Benetton-Ford	51	engine	4
	Boutsen	Benetton-Ford	48	engine	11
	Cheever	Arrows-Megatron	48	overheating	9
	Palmer	Tyrrell-Ford	48	electrical	23
	de Cesaris	Brabham-BMW	39	spun	13
	Campos	Minardi-MM	30	gearbox	16
	Tarquini	Osella-Alfa	26	electrical	25
	Nannini	Minardi-MM	25	engine	15
	Capelli	March-Ford	18	rotor arm	22
	Berger	Ferrari	16	black box	5
	Prost	McLaren-TAG	15	alternator belt	3
	Ghinzani	Ligier-Megatron	7	withdrew	18

Fastest Lap: T Fabi, 1m 29.25s. 125.44 mph/201.85 kph

Belgian Grand Prix: Spa, 17 May 1987

43 laps of 4.31 mile/6.94 km circuit

Place	Driver	Car	Laps	Time/reason for retiring	Grid
1	Prost	McLaren-TAG	43	1h 27m 03.217s	6
2	Johansson	McLaren-TAG	43	1h 27m 27.981s	10
3	de Cesaris	Brabham-BMW	42	out of fuel	13
4	Cheever	Arrows-Megatron	42		11
5	Nakajima	Lotus-Honda	42		15
6	Arnoux	Ligier-Megatron	41		16
7	Ghinzani	Ligier-Megatron	40	out of fuel	17
8	Alliot	Lola-Ford	40		22
9	Streiff	Tyrrell-Ford	39		23
10	Fabre	AGS-Ford	38	electrical	25
	T Fabi	Benetton-BMW	34	engine	9
	Brundle	Zakspeed	19	engine	18

Belgian Grand Prix (cont)

Place	Driver	Car	Laps	Time/reason for retiring	Grid
	Boutsen	Benetton-BMW	18	wheel bearing	7
	Mansell	Williams-Honda	17	underbody	1
	Capelli	March-Ford	14	oil	21
	Piquet	Williams-Honda	11	turbo	2
	Caffi	Osella-Alfa	11	engine	26
	Alboreto	Ferrari	9	transmission	5
	Danner	Zakspeed	9	brakes	20
	Warwick	Arrows-Megatron	8	water hose	12
	Patrese	Brabham-BMW	5	clutch	8
	Berger	Ferrari	2	engine	4
	Nannini	Minardi-MM	1	engine	14
	Senna	Lotus-Honda	0	accident	3
	Campos	Minardi-MM	0	gearbox	19
	Palmer	Tyrrell-Ford	0	accident at first start	24

Fastest Lap: Prost, 1m 57.15s. 132.51 mph/213.26 kph

Monaco Grand Prix: Monte Carlo, 30 May 1987

78 laps of 2.07 mile/3.33 km circuit

Place	Driver	Car	Laps	Time/reason for retiring	Grid
1	Senna	Lotus-Honda	78	1h 57m 54.085s	2
2	Piquet	Williams-Honda	78	1h 58m 27.297s	3
3	Alboreto	Ferrari	78	1h 59m 06.924s	5
4	Berger	Ferrari	77		8
5	Palmer	Tyrrell-Ford	76		15
6	Capelli	March-Ford	76		19
7	Brundle	Zakspeed	76		14
8	T Fabi	Benetton-Ford	76		12
9	Prost	McLaren-TAG	75	engine	4
10	Nakajima	Lotus-Honda	75		17
11	Arnoux	Ligier-Megatron	74		22
12	Ghinzani	Ligier-Megatron	74		20
13	Fabre	AGS-Ford	71		24
	Cheever	Arrows-Megatron	59	overheating	6
	Warwick	Arrows-Megatron	58	gear selector	11
	Johansson	McLaren-TAG	57	engine	7
	Alliot	Lola-Ford	42	engine	18
	Patrese	Brabham-BMW	41	electrical	10
	Caffi	Osella-Alfa	39	electrical	16
	de Cesaris	Brabham-BMW	38	suspension	21
	Mansell	Williams-Honda	29	exhaust	1
	Nannini	Minardi-MM	21	electrical	13
	Streiff	Tyrrell-Ford	9	accident	23
	Boutsen	Benetton-Ford	5	cv joint	9

Fastest Lap: Senna, 1m 27.69s. 84.9 mph/136.64 kph

United States Grand Prix: Detroit, 21 June 1987

63 laps of 2.5 mile/4.02 km circuit

Place	Driver	Car	Laps	Time/reason for retiring	Grid
1	Senna	Lotus-Honda	63	1h 50m 16.358s	2
2	Piquet	Williams-Honda	63	1h 50m 50.177s	3
3	Prost	McLaren-TAG	63	1h 51m 01.685s	5
4	Berger	Ferrari	63	1h 51m 18.959s	12
5	Mansell	Williams-Honda	62		1
6	Cheever	Arrows-Megatron	60	out of fuel	6
7	Johansson	McLaren-TAG	60		11
8	Danner	Zakspeed	60		16
9	Patrese	Brabham-BMW	60		9
10	Arnoux	Ligier-Megatron	60		21
11	Palmer	Tyrrell-Ford	60		13
12	Fabre	AGS-Ford	58		26
	Boutsen	Benetton-Ford	52	brake disc	4
	Ghinzani	Ligier-Megatron	51		23
	Streiff	Tyrrell-Ford	44	lost wheel	14
	Alliot	Lola-Ford	38	accident	20
	Alboreto	Ferrari	25	gearbox	7
	Nannini	Minardi-MM	22	engine	18
	Brundle	Zakspeed	16	turbo	15
	Warwick	Arrows-Megatron	12	accident	10
	Capelli	March-Ford	9	electrical	22
	T Fabi	Benetton-Ford	6	accident	8
	Caffi	Osella-Alfa	3	gearbox	19
	de Cesaris	Brabham-BMW	2	gearbox	17
	Campos	Minardi-MM	1	accident	25
	Nakajima	Lotus-Honda	0	accident	24

Fastest Lap: Senna, 1m 40.46s. 89.58 mph/144.17 kph

French Grand Prix: Paul Ricard, 5 July 1987

80 laps of 2.37 mile/3.81 km circuit

Place	Driver	Car	Laps	Time/reason for retiring	Grid
1	Mansell	Williams-Honda	80	1h 37m 03.839s	1
2	Piquet	Williams-Honda	80	1h 37m 11.550s	4
3	Prost	McLaren-TAG	80	1h 37m 59.094s	2
4	Senna	Lotus-Honda	79		3
5	T Fabi	Benetton-Ford	77	drive-shaft	7
6	Streiff	Tyrrell-Ford	76		25
7	Palmer	Tyrrell-Ford	76		24
8	Johansson	McLaren-TAG	74	alternator belt	9
9	Fabre	AGS-Ford	74		26
	Berger	Ferrari	71	suspension	6

French Grand Prix (cont)

Place	Driver	Car	Laps	Time/reason for retiring	Grid
	Nakajima	Lotus-Honda	71		16
	Alboreto	Ferrari	64	engine	8
	Warwick	Arrows-Megatron	62	turbo	10
	Alliot	Lola-Ford	57	transmission	23
	Capelli	March-Ford	52	engine	22
	Campos	Minardi-MM	52	turbo	21
	Arnoux	Ligier-Megatron	33	exhaust	13
	Boutsen	Benetton-Ford	31	engine	5
	Danner	Zakspeed	26	overheating	19
	Ghinzani	Ligier-Megatron	24	engine	17
	Nannini	Minardi-MM	23	turbo	15
	Patrese	Brabham-BMW	19	differential	12
	Brundle	Zakspeed	18	lost wheel	18
	Caffi	Osella-Alfa	11	gearbox	20
	de Cesaris	Brabham-BMW	2	oil leak/fire	11
	Cheever	Arrows-Megatron	0	master switch	14

Fastest Lap: Piquet, 1m 09.55s. 122.64 mph/197.37 kph

British Grand Prix: Silverstone, 12 July 1987

65 laps of 2.97 mile/4.78 km circuit

Place	Driver	Car	Laps	Time/reason for retiring	Grid
1	Mansell	Williams-Honda	65	1h 19m 11.780s	2
2	Piquet	Williams-Honda	65	1h 19m 13.698s	1
3	Senna	Lotus-Honda	64		3
4	Nakajima	Lotus-Honda	63		12
5	Warwick	Arrows-Megatron	63		13
6	T Fabi	Benetton-Ford	63		6
7	Boutsen	Benetton-Ford	62		5
8	Palmer	Tyrrell-Ford	60		23
9	Fabre	AGS-Ford	59		25
	Streiff	Tyrrell-Ford	57	engine	22
	Brundle	Zakspeed	54		17
	Prost	McLaren-TAG	53	clutch/engine	4
	Alboreto	Ferrari	52	suspension	7
	Cheever	Arrows-Megatron	45	overheating	14
	Campos	Minardi-MM	34	electrical	19
	Caffi	Osella-Alfa	32	turbo	20
	Danner	Zakspeed	32	gearbox	18
	Patrese	Brabham-BMW	28	metering unit	11
	Johansson	McLaren-TAG	18	engine	10
	Nannini	Minardi-MM	10	engine	15
	de Cesaris	Brabham-BMW	8	fuel pipe/fire	9
	Berger	Ferrari	7	accident	8

British Grand Prix (cont)

Place	Driver	Car	Laps	Time/reason for retiring	Grid
	Alliot	Lola-Ford	7	gearbox	21
	Arnoux	Ligier-Megatron	3	electrical	16
	Capelli	March-Ford	3	accident	24

Fastest Lap: Mansell, 1m 09.83s. 153.06 mph/246.32 kph

German Grand Prix: Hockenheim, 26 July 1987

44 laps of 4.22 mile/6.8 km circuit

Place	Driver	Car	Laps	Time/reason for retiring	Grid
1	Piquet	Williams-Honda	44	1h 21m 25.091s	4
2	Johansson	McLaren-TAG	44	1h 23m 04.682s	8
3	Senna	Lotus-Honda	43		2
4	Streiff	Tyrrell-Ford	43		22
5	Palmer	Tyrrell-Ford	43		23
6	Alliot	Lola-Ford	42		21
7	Prost	McLaren-TAG	39	alternator belt	3
	Brundle	Zakspeed	34		19
	Ghinzani	Ligier-Megatron	32	engine	17
	Campos	Minardi-MM	28	engine	18
	Boutsen	Benetton-Ford	26	engine	6
	Mansell	Williams-Honda	25	engine	1
	Nannini	Minardi-MM	25	engine	16
	Warwick	Arrows-Megatron	23	turbo	13
	Danner	Zakspeed	21	input shaft	20
	Berger	Ferrari	19	turbo	10
	T Fabi	Benetton-Ford	18	engine	9
	Caffi	Osella-Alfa	17	turbo	26
	de Cesaris	Brabham-BMW	12	engine	7
	Alboreto	Ferrari	10	turbo	5
	Fabre	AGS-Ford	10	valve	25
	Cheever	Arrows-Megatron	9	turbo	15
	Nakajima	Lotus-Honda	9	suspension	14
	Capelli	March-Ford	7	rotor arm	24
	Arnoux	Ligier-Megatron	6	electrical	12
	Patrese	Brabham-BMW	5	ignition	11

Fastest Lap: Mansell, 1m 45.72s. 143.82 mph/231.46 kph

Hungarian Grand Prix: Hungaroring, 9 August 1987

76 laps of 2.49 mile/4.01 km circuit

Place	Driver	Car	Laps	Time/reason for retiring	Grid
1	Piquet	Williams-Honda	76	1h 59m 26.793s	3
2	Senna	Lotus-Honda	76	2h 00m 04.520s	6
3	Prost	McLaren-TAG	76	2h 00m 54.249s	4
4	Boutsen	Benetton-Ford	75		7
5	Patrese	Brabham-BMW	75		10
6	Warwick	Arrows-Megatron	74		9
7	Palmer	Tyrrell-Ford	74		16
8	Cheever	Arrows-Megatron	74		11
9	Streiff	Tyrrell-Ford	74		14
10	Capelli	March-Ford	74		18
11	Nannini	Minardi-MM	73		20
12	Ghinzani	Ligier-Megatron	73		25
13	Fabre	AGS-Ford	71		26
14	Mansell	Williams-Honda	70	wheel	1
	Caffi	Osella-Alfa	64	electrical	21
	Arnoux	Ligier-Megatron	57	electrical	19
	Alliot	Lola-Ford	48	accident	15
	Brundle	Zakspeed	45	turbo	22
	Alboreto	Ferrari	43	engine	5
	de Cesaris	Brabham-BMW	43	gearbox	13
	Johansson	McLaren-TAG	14	gearbox	8
	T Fabi	Benetton-Ford	14	engine	12
	Campos	Minardi-MM	14	accident	24
	Berger	Ferrari	13	cv joint	2
	Danner	Zakspeed	3	electrical	23
	Nakajima	Lotus-Honda	1	drive-shaft	17

Fastest Lap: Piquet, 1m 30.15s. 99.6 mph/160.295 kph

Austrian Grand Prix: Österreichring, 16 August 1987

52 laps of 3.69 mile/5.94 km circuit

Place	Driver	Car	Laps	Time/reason for retiring	Grid
1	Mansell	Williams-Honda	52	1h 18m 44.898s	2
2	Piquet	Williams-Honda	52	1h 19m 40.602s	1
3	T Fabi	Benetton-Ford	51		5
4	Boutsen	Benetton-Ford	51		4
5	Senna	Lotus-Honda	50		7
6	Prost	McLaren-TAG	50		9
7	Johansson	McLaren-TAG	50		14
8	Ghinzani	Ligier-Megatron	50		18
9	Danner	Zakspeed	49		20
10	Arnoux	Ligier-Megatron	49		16
11	Capelli	March-Ford	49		23

Austrian Grand Prix (cont)

Place	Driver	Car	Laps	Time/reason for retiring	Grid
12	Alliot	Lola-Ford	49		22
13	Nakajima	Lotus-Honda	49		13
14	Brundle	Zakspeed	48		17
15	Palmer	Tyrrell-Ford	47		24
	Fabre	AGS-Ford	45		26
	Patrese	Brabham-BMW	43	engine	8
	Alboreto	Ferrari	42	exhaust	6
	de Cesaris	Brabham-BMW	35	engine	10
	Warwick	Arrows-Megatron	35	engine	11
	Cheever	Arrows-Megatron	31	tyre	12
	Berger	Ferrari	5	engine	3
	Campos	Minardi-MM	3	distributor belt	19
	Nannini	Minardi-MM	1	engine	15
	Caffi	Osella-Alfa	0	electrical	21
	Streiff	Tyrrell-Ford	0	accident	25

Fastest Lap: Mansell, 1m 28.32s. 150.5 mph/242.21 kph

Italian Grand Prix: Monza, 6 September 1987

50 laps of 3.6 mile/5.8 km circuit

Place	Driver	Car	Laps	Time/reason for retiring	Grid
1	Piquet	Williams-Honda	50	1h 14m 47.707s	1
2	Senna	Lotus-Honda	50	1h 14m 49.513s	4
3	Mansell	Williams-Honda	50	1h 15m 36.743s	2
4	Berger	Ferrari	50	1h 15m 45.686s	3
5	Boutsen	Benetton-Ford	50	1h 16m 09.026s	6
6	Johansson	McLaren-TAG	50	1h 16m 16.494s	11
7	T Fabi	Benetton-Ford	49		7
8	Ghinzani	Ligier-Megatron	48		19
9	Danner	Zakspeed	48		16
10	Arnoux	Ligier-Megatron	48		15
11	Nakajima	Lotus-Honda	47		14
12	Streiff	Tyrrell-Ford	47		24
13	Capelli	March-Lotus	47		25
14	Palmer	Tyrrell-Ford	47		22
15	Prost	McLaren-TAG	46		5
16	Nannini	Minardi-MM	45	out of fuel	18
	Brundle	Zakspeed	43	gearbox	17
	Alliot	Lola-Ford	37	accident	23
	Campos	Minardi-MM	34	fuel filter/fire	20
	Cheever	Arrows-Megatron	27	cv joint	13
	Forini	Osella-Alfa	27	turbo	26
	Caffi	Osella-Alfa	16	wheel	21
	Alboreto	Ferrari	13	turbo	8

Italian Grand Prix (cont)

Place	Driver	Car	Laps	Time/reason for retiring	Grid
	Warwick	Arrows-Megatron	9	metering unit	12
	de Cesaris	Brabham-BMW	7	suspension	10
	Patrese	Brabham-BMW	5	engine	9

Fastest Lap: Senna, 1m 26.8s. 149.48 mph/240.56 kph

Portuguese Grand Prix: Estoril, 20 September 1987

70 laps of 2.7mile/4.35 km circuit

Place	Driver	Car	Laps	Time/reason for retiring	Grid
1	Prost	McLaren-TAG	70	1h 37m 03.906s	3
2	Berger	Ferrari	70	1h 37m 24.399s	1
3	Piquet	Williams-Honda	70	1h 38m 07.201s	4
4	T Fabi	Benetton-Ford	69		10
5	Johansson	McLaren-TAG	69		8
6	Cheever	Arrows-Megatron	68		11
7	Senna	Lotus-Honda	68		5
8	Nakajima	Lotus-Honda	68		15
9	Capelli	March-Ford	67		22
10	Palmer	Tyrrell-Ford	67		24
11	Nannini	Minardi-MM	66	out of fuel	14
12	Streiff	Tyrrell-Ford	66		21
13	Warwick	Arrows-Megatron	66		12
14	Boutsen	Benetton-Ford	64		9
	de Cesaris	Brabham-BMW	54	injector pipe	13
	Alboreto	Ferrari	38	gear linkage	6
	Brundle	Zakspeed	35	gearbox	17
	Forini	Osella-Alfa	32	turbo	26
	Alliot	Lola-Ford	31	electrical	19
	Arnoux	Ligier-Megatron	29	radiator	18
	Caffi	Osella-Alfa	27	turbo	25
	Ghinzani	Ligier-Megatron	24	ignition	23
	Campos	Minardi-MM	24	accident	20
	Mansell	Williams-Honda	13	electrical	2
	Patrese	Brabham-BMW	13	engine	7
	Danner	Zakspeed	0	accident	16

Fastest Lap: Berger, 1m 19.28s. 122.74 mph/197.52 kph

1987

Spanish Grand Prix: Jerez, 27 September 1987

72 laps of 2.62 mile/4.22 km circuit

Place	Driver	Car	Laps	Time/reason for retiring	Grid
1	Mansell	Williams-Honda	72	1h 49m 12.692s	2
2	Prost	McLaren-TAG	72	1h 49m 34.917s	7
3	Johansson	McLaren-TAG	72	1h 49m 43.510s	11
4	Piquet	Williams-Honda	72	1h 49m 44.142s	1
5	Senna	Lotus-Honda	72	1h 50m 26.199s	5
6	Alliot	Lola-Ford	71		17
7	Streiff	Tyrrell-Ford	71		15
8	Cheever	Arrows-Megatron	70	out of fuel	13
9	Nakajima	Zakspeed	70		18
10	Warwick	Arrows-Megatron	70		12
11	Brundle	Zakspeed	70		20
12	Capelli	March-Ford	70		19
13	Patrese	Brabham-BMW	68		9
14	Campos	Minardi-MM	68		24
15	Alboreto	Ferrari	67	engine	4
16	Boutsen	Benetton-BMW	66	brakes	8
	Berger	Ferrari	62	engine	3
	Palmer	Tyrrell-Ford	55	accident	16
	Arnoux	Ligier-Megatron	55	engine	14
	Danner	Zakspeed	50	gearbox	22
	Nannini	Minardi-MM	45	turbo	21
	T Fabi	Benetton-BMW	40	engine	6
	de Cesaris	Brabham-BMW	26	gearbox	10
	Ghinzani	Ligier-Megatron	24	ignition	23
	Fabre	AGS-Ford	10	clutch	25
	Larini	Coloni-Ford	8	suspension	26

Fastest Lap: Berger, 1m 26.99s. 108.47 mph/174.57 kph

Mexican Grand Prix: Mexico City, 18 October 1987

63 laps of 2.75 mile/4.42 km circuit

Place	Driver	Car	Laps	Time/reason for retiring	Grid
1	Mansell	Williams-Honda	63	1h 26m 24.207s	1
2	Piquet	Williams-Honda	63	1h 26m 50.383s	3
3	Patrese	Brabham-BMW	63	1h 27m 51.086s	8
4	Cheever	Arrows-Megatron	63	1h 28m 05.559s	12
5	T Fabi	Benetton-Ford	61		6
6	Alliot	Lola-Ford	60		24
7	Palmer	Tyrrell-Ford	60		22
8	Streiff	Tyrrell-Ford	60		25
9	Dalmas	Lola-Ford	59		23
	Senna	Lotus-Honda	54	spun	7
	Capelli	March-Ford	51	engine	20

Mexican Grand Prix (cont)

Place	Driver	Car	Laps	Time/reason for retiring	Grid
	Caffi	Osella-Alfa	50	engine	26
	Ghinzani	Ligier-Megatron	43	overheating	21
	Campos	Minardi-MM	32	gear linkage	19
	Arnoux	Ligier-Megatron	29	ignition	18
	Warwick	Arrows-Megatron	26	accident	11
	de Cesaris	Brabham-BMW	22	spun	10
	Berger	Ferrari	20	engine	2
	Boutsen	Benetton-Ford	15	electrical	4
	Nannini	Minardi-MM	13	turbo	14
	Alboreto	Ferrari	12	engine	9
	Brundle	Zakspeed	3	engine	13
	Johansson	McLaren-TAG	1	accident	15
	Nakajima	Lotus-Honda	1	accident	16
	Danner	Zakspeed	1	accident	17
	Prost	McLaren-TAG	0	accident	5

Fastest Lap: Piquet, 1m 19.13s. 124.97 mph/201.13 kph

Japanese Grand Prix: Suzuka, 1 November 1987

51 laps of 3.64 mile/5.86 km circuit

Place	Driver	Car	Laps	Time/reason for retiring	Grid
1	Berger	Ferrari	51	1h 32m 58.072s	1
2	Senna	Lotus-Honda	51	1h 33m 15.456s	7
3	Johansson	McLaren-TAG	51	1h 33m 15.766s	9
4	Alboreto	Ferrari	51	1h 34m 18.513s	4
5	Boutsen	Benetton-Ford	51	1h 34m 23.648s	3
6	Nakajima	Lotus-Honda	51	1h 34m 34.551s	11
7	Prost	McLaren-TAG	50		2
8	Palmer	Tyrrell-Ford	50		19
9	Cheever	Arrows-Megatron	50		12
10	Warwick	Arrows-Megatron	50		13
11	Patrese	Brabham-BMW	49	engine	8
12	Streiff	Tyrrell-Ford	49		25
13	Ghinzani	Ligier-Megatron	48	fuel	24
14	Dalmas	Lola-Ford	47	electrical	22
15	Piquet	Williams-Honda	46	engine	5
	Arnoux	Ligier-Megatron	44	fuel	17
	Caffi	Osella-Alfa	43	fuel	23
	Moreno	AGS-Ford	38	injection	26
	Nannini	Minardi-MM	35	engine	14
	Brundle	Zakspeed	32	overheating	15
	de Cesaris	Brabham-BMW	26	engine	10
	T Fabi	Benetton-Ford	16	engine	6
	Danner	Zakspeed	13	engine	16

Japanese Grand Prix (cont)

Place	Driver	Car	Laps	Time/reason for retiring	Grid
	Capelli	March-Ford	13	accident	20
	Campos	Minardi-MM	2	engine	21
	Alliot	Lola-Ford	0	accident	18

Fastest Lap: Prost, 1m 43.84s. 126.21 mph/203.12 kph

Australian Grand Prix: Adelaide, 15 November 1987

82 laps of 2.35 mile/3.78 km circuit

Place	Driver	Car	Laps	Time/reason for retiring	Grid
1	Berger	Ferrari	82	1h 52m 56.144s	1
	Senna	Lotus-Honda	82	disqualified: illegal brake ducts	4
2	Alboreto	Ferrari	82	1h 54m 04.028s	6
3	Boutsen	Benetton-Ford	81		5
4	Palmer	Tyrrell-Ford	80		19
5	* Dalmas	Lola-Ford	79		21
6	Moreno	AGS-Ford	79		25
7	Danner	Zakspeed	79		24
8	de Cesaris	Brabham-BMW	78		10
9	Patrese	Williams-Honda	76		7
	Piquet	Williams-Honda	58	gearbox	3
	Capelli	March-Ford	58	spun	23
	Prost	McLaren-TAG	53	brakes	2
	Cheever	Arrows-Megatron	53	overheating	11
	Johansson	McLaren-TAG	48	brakes	8
	T Fabi	Benetton-Ford	46	brakes	9
	Campos	Minardi-MM	46	gearbox	26
	Alliot	Lola-Ford	45	electrical	17
	Arnoux	Ligier-Megatron	41	electrical	20
	Modena	Brabham-BMW	31	driver	15
	Ghinzani	Ligier-Megatron	26	turbo	22
	Nakajima	Lotus-Honda	22	suspension	14
	Warwick	Arrows-Megatron	19	transmission	12
	Brundle	Zakspeed	18	gear lever	16
	Streiff	Tyrrell-Ford	6	spun	18
	Nannini	Minardi-MM	0	accident	13

Fastest Lap: Berger, 1m 20.42s. 105.12 mph/169.18 kph
* Not entered for full series; ineligible for championship points.

World Championship 1987

1	Piquet	73 (76)
2	Mansell	61
3	Senna	57
4	Prost	46
5	Berger	36
6	Johansson	30
7	Alboreto	17
8	Boutsen	16
9	T Fabi	12
10	Cheever	8
11 =	Nakajima, Palmer	7
13	Patrese	6
14 =	de Cesaris, Streiff	4
16 =	Alliot, Warwick	3
18	Brundle	2
19 =	Arnoux, Capelli, Moreno	1

Constructors' Championship

1	Williams-Honda	137
2	McLaren-TAG	76
3	Lotus-Honda	64
4	Ferrari	53
5	Benetton-Ford	28
6 =	Arrows-Megatron, Tyrrell-Ford	11
8	Brabham-BMW	10
9	Lola-Ford	3
10	Zakspeed	2
11 =	AGS-Ford, Ligier-Megatron, March-Ford	1

1988

Ayrton Senna won his first championship with eight wins to Prost's seven. Although Prost had scored more points overall, only the best eleven results counted. Senna's eight victories set a new record for one season, though Jim Clark's seven in 1963 constituted 70% of the championship as opposed to Senna's 50%. McLaren completely dominated the championship, except for Gerhard Berger's sentimentally appropriate Ferrari win at Monza, just under a month after the death of Enzo Ferrari.

Brazilian Grand Prix: Rio de Janeiro, 3 April 1988

60 laps of 3.13 mile/5.03 km circuit

Place	Driver	Car	Laps	Time/reason for retiring	Grid
1	Prost	McLaren-Honda	60	1h 36m 06.9s	3
2	Berger	Ferrari	60	1h 36m 16.7s	4
3	Piquet	Lotus-Honda	60	1h 37m 15.4s	5
4	Warwick	Arrows-Megatron	60	1h 37m 20.2s	11
5	Alboreto	Ferrari	60	1h 37m 21.4s	6
6	Nakajima	Lotus-Honda	59		10
7	Boutsen	Benetton-Ford	59		7
8	Cheever	Arrows-Megatron	59		15
9	Johansson	Ligier-Judd	57		21
	de Cesaris	Rial-Ford	53	engine	14
	Palmer	Tyrrell-Ford	47	drive-shaft	22
	Sala	Minardi-Ford	46	wing	20
	Alliot	Lola-Ford	40	suspension	16
	Tarquini	Coloni-Ford	35	suspension	25
	Streiff	AGS-Ford	35	brakes	19
	Dalmas	Lola-Ford	32	engine	17
	Senna	McLaren-Honda	31	disqualified: changed car after parade lap	1
	Arnoux	Ligier-Judd	23	clutch	18
	Modena	EuroBrun-Ford	20	engine	24
	Mansell	Williams-Judd	18	overheating	2
	Nannini	Benetton-Ford	7	overheating	12
	Patrese	Williams-Judd	6	overheating	8
	Capelli	March-Judd	6	overheating	9
	Campos	Minardi-Ford	5	wing	23
	Gugelmin	March-Judd	0	transmission	13
	Larrauri	EuroBrun-Ford	0	engine	26

Fastest Lap: Berger, 1m 32.94s. 121.09 mph/194.87 kph

San Marino Grand Prix: Imola, 1 May 1988

60 laps of 3.13 mile/5.04 km circuit

Place	Driver	Car	Laps	Time/reason for retiring	Grid
1	Senna	McLaren-Honda	60	1h 32m 41.3s	1
2	Prost	McLaren-Honda	60	1h 32m 43.6s	2
3	Piquet	Lotus-Honda	59		3
4	Boutsen	Benetton-Ford	59		8
5	Berger	Ferrari	59		5
6	Nannini	Benetton-Ford	59		4
7	Cheever	Arrows-Megatron	59		7
8	Nakajima	Lotus-Honda	59		12
9	Warwick	Arrows-Megatron	58		14
10	Streiff	AGS-Ford	58		13
11	Sala	Minardi-Ford	58		18
12	Dalmas	Lola-Ford	58		19
13	Patrese	Williams-Judd	58		6
14	Palmer	Tyrrell-Ford	58		23
15	Gugelmin	March-Judd	58		20
16	Campos	Minardi-Ford	57		22
17	Alliot	Lola-Ford	57		15
18	Alboreto	Ferrari	54	engine	10
	Modena	EuroBrun-Ford	52		26
	Bailey	Tyrrell-Ford	48	gearbox	21
	Mansell	Williams-Judd	42	electrical	11
	Tarquini	Coloni-Ford	40	throttle	17
	Caffi	Dallara-Ford	18	gearbox	24
	Ghinzani	Zakspeed	16	electrical	25
	Capelli	March-Judd	2	gearbox	9
	de Cesaris	Rial-Ford	0	suspension	16

Fastest Lap: Prost, 1m 29.68s. 125.7 mph/202.3 kph

Monaco Grand Prix: Monte Carlo, 15 May 1988

78 laps of 2.07 mile/3.33 km circuit

Place	Driver	Car	Laps	Time/reason for retiring	Grid
1	Prost	McLaren-Honda	78	1h 57m 17.1s	2
2	Berger	Ferrari	78	1h 57m 37.5s	3
3	Alboreto	Ferrari	78	1h 57m 58.3s	4
4	Warwick	Arrows-Megatron	77		7
5	Palmer	Tyrrell-Ford	77		10
6	Patrese	Williams-Judd	77		8
7	Dalmas	Lola-Ford	77		21
8	Boutsen	Benetton-Ford	76		16
9	Larini	Osella-Alfa	75		25
10	Capelli	March-Judd	72		22
	Senna	McLaren-Honda	66	accident	1

Monaco Grand Prix (cont)

Place	Driver	Car	Laps	Time/reason for retiring	Grid
	Alliot	Lola-Ford	50	accident	13
	Gugelmin	March-Judd	45	fuel pump	14
	Ghinzani	Zakspeed	43	gearbox	23
	Nannini	Benetton-Ford	38	accident	6
	Sala	Minardi-Ford	36	drive-shaft	15
	Mansell	Williams-Judd	32	accident	5
	de Cesaris	Rial-Ford	28	engine	19
	Arnoux	Ligier-Judd	17	engine	20
	Larrauri	EuroBrun-Ford	14	accident	18
	Cheever	Arrows-Megatron	8	electrical	9
	Johansson	Ligier-Judd	6	engine	26
	Tarquini	Coloni-Ford	5	engine	24
	Piquet	Lotus-Honda	0	accident	11
	Caffi	Dallara-Ford	0	accident	17
	Streiff	AGS-Ford	0	throttle	12

Fastest Lap: Senna, 1m 26.32s. 86.3 mph/138.8 kph

Mexican Grand Prix: Mexico City, 29 May 1988

67 laps of 2.75 mile/4.42 km circuit

Place	Driver	Car	Laps	Time/reason for retiring	Grid
1	Prost	McLaren-Honda	67	1h 30m 15.7s	2
2	Senna	McLaren-Honda	67	1h 30m 22.8s	1
3	Berger	Ferrari	67	1h 31m 13.1s	3
4	Alboreto	Ferrari	66		5
5	Warwick	Arrows-Megatron	66		9
6	Cheever	Arrows-Megatron	66		7
7	Nannini	Benetton-Ford	65		8
8	Boutsen	Benetton-Ford	64		11
9	Dalmas	Lola-Ford	64		22
10	Johansson	Ligier-Judd	63		24
11	Sala	Minardi-Ford	63		25
12	Streiff	AGS-Ford	63		19
13	Larrauri	EuroBrun-Ford	63		26
14	Tarquini	Coloni-Ford	62		21
15	Ghinzani	Zakspeed	61		18
16	Capelli	March-Judd	61		10
	Piquet	Lotus-Honda	58	engine	4
	de Cesaris	Rial-Ford	52	transmission	12
	Nakajima	Lotus-Honda	27	turbo	6
	Mansell	Williams-Judd	20	engine	14
	Schneider	Zakspeed	16	engine	15
	Patrese	Williams-Judd	16	engine	17
	Arnoux	Ligier-Judd	13	accident	20

Mexican Grand Prix (cont)

Place	Driver	Car	Laps	Time/reason for retiring	Grid
	Caffi	Dallara-Ford	13	accident	23
	Gugelmin	March-Judd	10	engine	16
	Alliot	Lola-Ford	0	handling	13

Fastest Lap: Prost, 1m 18.61s. 125.81 mph/202.47 kph

Canadian Grand Prix: Montreal, 12 June 1988

69 laps of 2.73 mile/4.39 km circuit

Place	Driver	Car	Laps	Time/reason for retiring	Grid
1	Senna	McLaren-Honda	69	1h 39m 46.6s	1
2	Prost	McLaren-Honda	69	1h 39m 52.6s	2
3	Boutsen	Benetton-Ford	69	1h 40m 38.0s	7
4	Piquet	Lotus-Honda	68		6
5	Capelli	March-Judd	68		14
6	Palmer	Tyrrell-Ford	67		19
7	Warwick	Arrows-Megatron	67		16
8	Tarquini	Coloni-Ford	67		26
9	de Cesaris	Rial-Ford	66		12
10	Alliot	Lola-Ford	66		17
11	Nakajima	Lotus-Honda	66		13
12	Modena	EuroBrun-Ford	66		15
13	Sala	Minardi-Ford	64		21
14	Ghinzani	Zakspeed	63		22
	Gugelmin	March-Judd	54	gearbox	18
	Streiff	AGS-Ford	41	suspension	10
	Arnoux	Ligier-Judd	36	gearbox	20
	Alboreto	Ferrari	33	engine	4
	Patrese	Williams-Judd	32	engine	11
	Cheever	Arrows-Megatron	31	throttle	8
	Mansell	Williams-Judd	28	engine	9
	Johansson	Ligier-Judd	24	engine	25
	Berger	Ferrari	22	ignition	3
	Nannini	Benetton-Ford	15	ignition	5
	Larrauri	EuroBrun-Ford	8	accident	24
	Bailey	Tyrrell-Ford	0	accident	23

Fastest Lap: Senna, 1m 24.97s. 115.57 mph/185.99 kph

US Grand Prix: Detroit, 19 June 1988

63 laps of 2.5 mile/4.02 km circuit

Place	Driver	Car	Laps	Time/reason for retiring	Grid
1	Senna	McLaren-Honda	63	1h 54m 56.0s	1
2	Prost	McLaren-Honda	63	1h 55m 34.8s	4
3	Boutsen	Benetton-Ford	62		5
4	de Cesaris	Rial-Ford	62		12
5	Palmer	Tyrrell-Ford	62		17
6	Martini	Minardi-Ford	62		16
7	Dalmas	Lola-Ford	61		24
8	Caffi	Dallara-Ford	61		21
9	Bailey	Tyrrell-Ford	59	accident	22
	Sala	Minardi-Ford	54	transmission	25
	Alliot	Lola-Ford	46	gearbox	14
	Modena	EuroBrun-Ford	46	accident	19
	Alboreto	Ferrari	45	spun	3
	Arnoux	Ligier-Judd	45	engine	20
	Gugelmin	March-Judd	34	engine	13
	Patrese	Williams-Judd	26	electrical	10
	Piquet	Lotus-Honda	26	accident	8
	Larrauri	EuroBrun-Ford	26	gearbox	23
	Warwick	Arrows-Megatron	24	accident	9
	Mansell	Williams-Judd	18	electrical	6
	Streiff	AGS-Ford	15	suspension	11
	Nannini	Benetton-Ford	14	suspension	7
	Cheever	Arrows-Megatron	14	electrical	15
	Larini	Osella-Alfa	7	engine	26
	Berger	Ferrari	6	puncture	2
	Johansson	Ligier-Judd	2	engine	18

Fastest Lap: Prost, 1m 44.84s. 85.85 mph/138.16 kph

French Grand Prix: Paul Ricard, 3 July 1988

80 laps of 2.37 mile/3.81 km circuit

Place	Driver	Car	Laps	Time/reason for retiring	Grid
1	Prost	McLaren-Honda	80	1h 37m 37.3s	1
2	Senna	McLaren-Honda	80	1h 38m 09.1s	2
3	Alboreto	Ferrari	80	1h 38m 43.8s	4
4	Berger	Ferrari	79		3
5	Piquet	Lotus-Honda	79		7
6	Nannini	Benetton-Ford	79		6
7	Nakajima	Lotus-Honda	79		8
8	Gugelmin	March-Judd	79		16
9	Capelli	March-Judd	79		10
10	de Cesaris	Rial-Ford	78		12
11	Cheever	Arrows-Megatron	78		13

French Grand Prix (cont)

Place	Driver	Car	Laps	Time/reason for retiring	Grid
12	Caffi	Dallara-Ford	78		14
13	Dalmas	Lola-Ford	78		19
14	Modena	EuroBrun-Ford	77		20
15	Martini	Minardi-Ford	77		22
	Sala	Minardi-Ford	70		25
	Larrauri	EuroBrun-Ford	64	clutch	26
	Larini	Osella-Alfa	56	drive-shaft	24
	Schneider	Zakspeed	55	gearbox	21
	Mansell	Williams-Judd	48	suspension	9
	Alliot	Lola-Ford	46	electrical	18
	Palmer	Tyrrell-Ford	40	engine	23
	Patrese	Williams-Judd	35	brakes	15
	Boutsen	Benetton-Ford	28	engine	5
	Streiff	AGS-Ford	20	fuel leak	17
	Warwick	Arrows-Megatron	11	spun	11

Fastest Lap: Prost, 1m 11.74s. 119 mph/191.35 kph

British Grand Prix: Silverstone, 10 July 1988

65 laps of 2.97 mile/4.78 km circuit

Place	Driver	Car	Laps	Time/reason for retiring	Grid
1	Senna	McLaren-Honda	65	1h 33m 16.4s	3
2	Mansell	Williams-Judd	65	1h 33m 39.7s	11
3	Nannini	Benetton-Ford	65	1h 34m 07.6s	8
4	Gugelmin	March-Judd	65	1h 34m 27.8s	5
5	Piquet	Lotus-Honda	65	1h 34m 37.2s	7
6	Warwick	Arrows-Megatron	64		9
7	Cheever	Arrows-Megatron	64		13
8	Patrese	Williams-Judd	64		15
9	Berger	Ferrari	64		1
10	Nakajima	Lotus-Honda	64		10
11	Caffi	Dallara-Ford	64		21
12	Modena	EuroBrun-Ford	64		20
13	Dalmas	Lola-Ford	63		23
14	Alliot	Lola-Ford	63		22
15	Martini	Minardi-Ford	63		19
16	Bailey	Tyrrell-Ford	63		24
17	Alboreto	Ferrari	62	out of fuel	2
18	Arnoux	Ligier-Judd	62		25
19	Larini	Osella-Alfa	60	out of fuel	26
	Boutsen	Benetton-Ford	38	gearbox	12
	Capelli	March-Judd	34	alternator	6
	Prost	McLaren-Honda	24	handling	4
	Palmer	Tyrrell-Ford	14	transmission	17

British Grand Prix (cont)

Place	Driver	Car	Laps	Time/reason for retiring	Grid
	de Cesaris	Rial-Ford	9	transmission	14
	Streiff	AGS-Ford	8	accident	16
	Sala	Minardi-Ford	0	accident	18

Fastest Lap: Mansell, 1m 23.31s. 128.3 mph/206.48 kph

German Grand Prix: Hockenheim, 24 July 1988

44 laps of 4.22 mile/6.8 km circuit

Place	Driver	Car	Laps	Time/reason for retiring	Grid
1	Senna	McLaren-Honda	44	1h 32m 54.2s	1
2	Prost	McLaren-Honda	44	1h 33m 07.8s	2
3	Berger	Ferrari	44	1h 33m 46.3s	3
4	Alboreto	Ferrari	44	1h 34m 35.1s	4
5	Capelli	March-Judd	44	1h 34m 43.8s	7
6	Boutsen	Benetton-Ford	43		9
7	Warwick	Arrows-Megatron	43		12
8	Gugelmin	March-Judd	43		11
9	Nakajima	Lotus-Honda	43		8
10	Cheever	Arrows-Megatron	43		15
11	Palmer	Tyrrell-Ford	43		24
12	Schneider	Zakspeed	43		22
13	de Cesaris	Rial-Ford	42		14
14	Ghinzani	Zakspeed	42		23
15	Caffi	Dallara-Ford	42		19
16	Larrauri	EuroBrun-Ford	42		26
17	Arnoux	Ligier-Judd	41		17
18	Nannini	Benetton-Ford	40		6
19	Dalmas	Lola-Ford	39		21
	Streiff	AGS-Ford	38	accelerator	16
	Patrese	Williams-Judd	34	accident	13
	Larini	Osella-Alfa	27	fuel line	18
	Mansell	Williams-Judd	16	accident	11
	Modena	EuroBrun-Ford	15	engine	25
	Alliot	Lola-Ford	8	accident	20
	Piquet	Lotus-Honda	1	accident	5

Fastest Lap: Nannini, 2m 03.03s. 123.58 mph/198.89 kph

Hungarian Grand Prix: Hungaroring, 7 August 1988

76 laps of 2.49 mile/4 km circuit

Place	Driver	Car	Laps	Time/reason for retiring	Grid
1	Senna	McLaren-Honda	76	1h 57m 47.1s	1
2	Prost	McLaren-Honda	76	1h 57m 47.6s	7
3	Boutsen	Benetton-Ford	76	1h 58m 18.5s	3
4	Berger	Ferrari	76	1h 59m 15.8s	9
5	Gugelmin	March-Judd	75		8
6	Patrese	Williams-Judd	75		6
7	Nakajima	Lotus-Honda	73		19
8	Piquet	Lotus-Honda	73		13
9	Dalmas	Lola-Ford	73		17
10	Sala	Minardi-Ford	72		11
11	Modena	EuroBrun-Ford	72		26
12	Alliot	Lola-Ford	72		20
13	Tarquini	Coloni-Ford	71		22
	Warwick	Arrows-Megatron	65	brakes	12
	Mansell	Williams-Judd	60	driver	2
	Cheever	Arrows-Megatron	55	brakes	14
	Alboreto	Ferrari	40	engine	15
	Arnoux	Ligier-Judd	32	engine	25
	de Cesaris	Rial-Ford	28	cv joint	18
	Nannini	Benetton-Ford	24	water pipe	5
	Caffi	Dallara-Ford	22	engine	10
	Johansson	Ligier-Judd	19	throttle	24
	Martini	Minardi-Ford	8	accident	16
	Streiff	AGS-Ford	8	suspension	23
	Capelli	March-Judd	5	misfire	4
	Palmer	Tyrrell-Ford	3	engine	21

Fastest Lap: Prost, 1m 30.64s. 99.06 mph/159.43 kph

Belgian Grand Prix: Spa, 28 August 1988

43 laps of 4.31 mile/6.94 km circuit

Place	Driver	Car	Laps	Time/reason for retiring	Grid
1	Senna	McLaren-Honda	43	1h 28m 00.6s	1
2	Prost	McLaren-Honda	43	1h 28m 31.0s	2
	Boutsen	Benetton-Ford	43	disqualified: fuel illegal	6
	Nannini	Benetton-Ford	43	disqualified: fuel illegal	7
3	Capelli	March-Judd	43	1h 29m 16.3s	14
4	Piquet	Lotus-Honda	43	1h 29m 24.2s	9
5	Warwick	Arrows-Megatron	43	1h 29m 25.9s	10
6	Cheever	Arrows-Megatron	42		11
7	Brundle	Williams-Judd	42		12
8	Caffi	Dallara-Ford	42		15
9	Alliot	Lola-Ford	42		16

Belgian Grand Prix (cont)

Place	Driver	Car	Laps	Time/reason for retiring	Grid
10	Streiff	AGS-Ford	42		18
11	Johansson	Ligier-Judd	39	engine	20
12	Palmer	Tyrrell-Ford	39	throttle	21
13	Schneider	Zakspeed	38	gearbox	25
	Tarquini	Coloni-Ford	36	running	22
	Alboreto	Ferrari	35	engine	4
	Patrese	Williams-Judd	30	engine	5
	Gugelmin	March-Judd	29	accident	13
	Ghinzani	Zakspeed	25	oil line	24
	Nakajima	Lotus-Honda	21	engine	8
	Larini	Osella-Alfa	14	fuel pump	26
	Berger	Ferrari	11	engine	3
	Dalmas	Lola-Ford	9	engine	23
	de Cesaris	Rial-Ford	2	accident	19
	Arnoux	Ligier-Judd	2	accident	17

Fastest Lap: Berger, 2m 00.77s. 128.54 mph/206.87 kph

Italian Grand Prix: Monza, 11 September 1988

51 laps of 3.6 mile/5.8 km circuit

Place	Driver	Car	Laps	Time/reason for retiring	Grid
1	Berger	Ferrari	51	1h 17m 39.7s	3
2	Alboreto	Ferrari	51	1h 17m 40.3s	4
3	Cheever	Arrows-Megatron	51	1h 18m 15.2s	5
4	Warwick	Arrows-Megatron	51	1h 18m 15.9s	6
5	Capelli	March-Judd	51	1h 18m 32.3s	11
6	Boutsen	Benetton-Ford	51	1h 18m 39.6s	8
7	Patrese	Williams-Judd	51	1h 18m 54.5s	10
8	Gugelmin	March-Judd	51	1h 19m 12.3s	13
9	Nannini	Benetton-Ford	50		9
10	Senna	McLaren-Honda	49	accident	1
11	J-L Schlesser	Williams-Judd	49		22
12	Bailey	Tyrrell-Ford	49		26
13	Arnoux	Ligier-Judd	49		24
	Prost	McLaren-Honda	34	engine	2
	Alliot	Lola-Ford	32	engine	20
	Streiff	AGS-Ford	31	gearbox	23
	Schneider	Zakspeed	28	engine	15
	de Cesaris	Rial-Ford	27	handling	18
	Ghinzani	Zakspeed	25	engine	16
	Caffi	Dallara-Ford	24	electrical	21
	Dalmas	Lola-Ford	17	accident	25
	Martini	Minardi-Ford	15	engine	14
	Nakajima	Lotus-Honda	14	engine	12

Italian Grand Prix (cont)

Place	Driver	Car	Laps	Time/reason for retiring	Grid
	Sala	Minardi-Ford	12	gearbox	19
	Piquet	Lotus-Honda	11	accident	7
	Larini	Osella-Alfa	2	engine	17

Fastest Lap: Alboreto, 1m 29.07s. 145.7 mph/234.4 kph

Portuguese Grand Prix: Estoril, 25 September 1988

70 laps of 2.7 mile/4.35 km circuit

Place	Driver	Car	Laps	Time/reason for retiring	Grid
1	Prost	McLaren-Honda	70	1h 37m 41.0s	1
2	Capelli	March-Judd	70	1h 37m 50.5s	3
3	Boutsen	Benetton-Ford	70	1h 38m 25.6s	13
4	Warwick	Arrows-Megatron	70	1h 38m 48.4s	10
5	Alboreto	Ferrari	70	1h 38m 52.8s	7
6	Senna	McLaren-Honda	70	1h 38m 59.3s	2
7	Caffi	Dallara-Ford	69		17
8	Sala	Minardi-Ford	68		19
9	Streiff	AGS-Ford	68		21
10	Arnoux	Ligier-Judd	68		23
11	Tarquini	Coloni-Ford	65		26
12	Larini	Osella-Alfa	63		25
	Gugelmin	March-Judd	59	engine	5
	Mansell	Williams-Judd	54	accident	6
	Palmer	Tyrrell-Ford	53	engine	22
	Nannini	Benetton-Ford	52	vibration	9
	Berger	Ferrari	35	accident	4
	Piquet	Lotus-Honda	34	clutch	8
	Patrese	Williams-Judd	29	overheating	11
	Martini	Minardi-Ford	27	engine	14
	Dalmas	Lola-Ford	20	alternator	15
	Nakajima	Lotus-Honda	16	accident	16
	de Cesaris	Rial-Ford	11	drive-shaft	12
	Cheever	Arrows-Megatron	10	turbo	18
	Alliot	Lola-Ford	7	engine	20
	Johansson	Ligier-Judd	4	engine	24

Fastest Lap: Berger, 1m 21.96s. 118.7 mph/191.1 kph

1988

Spanish Grand Prix: Jerez, 2 October 1988

72 laps of 2.62 mile/4.22 km circuit

Place	Driver	Car	Laps	Time/reason for retiring	Grid
1	Prost	McLaren-Honda	72	1h 48m 43.9s	2
2	Mansell	Williams-Judd	72	1h 49m 10.1s	3
3	Nannini	Benetton-Ford	72	1h 49m 19.3s	5
4	Senna	McLaren-Honda	72	1h 49m 30.7s	1
5	Patrese	Williams-Judd	72	1h 49m 31.3s	7
6	Berger	Ferrari	72	1h 49m 35.7s	8
7	Gugelmin	March-Judd	72	1h 49m 39.8s	11
8	Piquet	Lotus-Honda	72	1h 50m 01.2s	9
9	Boutsen	Benetton-Ford	72	1h 50m 01.5s	4
10	Caffi	Dallara-Ford	71		18
11	Dalmas	Lola-Ford	71		16
12	Sala	Minardi-Ford	70		24
13	Modena	EuroBrun-Ford	70		26
14	Alliot	Lola-Ford	69		12
	Johansson	Ligier-Judd	62	lost wheel	21
	Cheever	Arrows-Megatron	60	handling	25
	Capelli	March-Judd	45	engine	6
	Warwick	Arrows-Megatron	41	accident	17
	de Cesaris	Rial-Ford	37	engine	23
	Streiff	AGS-Ford	16	engine	13
	Alboreto	Ferrari	15	engine	10
	Martini	Minardi-Ford	15	gearbox	20
	Nakajima	Lotus-Honda	14	spun	15
	Larini	Osella-Alfa	9	suspension	14
	Palmer	Tyrrell-Ford	4	accident	22
	Arnoux	Ligier-Judd	0	throttle	19

Fastest Lap: Prost, 1m 27.85s. 107.4 mph/172.86 kph

Japanese Grand Prix: Suzuka, 30 October 1988

51 laps of 3.64 mile/5.86 km circuit

Place	Driver	Car	Laps	Time/reason for retiring	Grid
1	Senna	McLaren-Honda	51	1h 33m 26.2s	1
2	Prost	McLaren-Honda	51	1h 33m 39.5s	2
3	Boutsen	Benetton-Ford	51	1h 34m 02.3s	10
4	Berger	Ferrari	51	1h 34m 52.9s	3
5	Nannini	Benetton-Ford	51	1h 34m 56.8s	12
6	Patrese	Williams-Judd	51	1h 35m 03.8s	11
7	Nakajima	Lotus-Honda	50		6
8	Streiff	AGS-Ford	50		18
9	Alliot	Lola-Ford	50		19
10	Gugelmin	March-Judd	50		13
11	Alboreto	Ferrari	50		9

Japanese Grand Prix (cont)

Place	Driver	Car	Laps	Time/reason for retiring	Grid
12	Palmer	Tyrrell-Ford	50		16
13	Martini	Minardi-Ford	49		17
14	Bailey	Tyrrell-Ford	49		26
15	Sala	Minardi-Ford	49		22
16	Suzuki	Lola-Ford	48		20
17	Arnoux	Ligier-Judd	48		23
	de Cesaris	Rial-Ford	35	engine	14
	Cheever	Arrows-Megatron	35	turbo	15
	Larini	Osella-Alfa	34	lost wheel	24
	Piquet	Lotus-Honda	34	driver	5
	Mansell	Williams-Judd	24	accident	8
	Caffi	Dallara-Ford	22	accident	21
	Capelli	March-Judd	19	engine	4
	Warwick	Arrows-Megatron	16	accident	7
	Schneider	Zakspeed	14	driver	25

Fastest Lap: Senna, 1m 46.33s. 123.26 mph/198.38 kph

Australian Grand Prix: Adelaide, 13 November 1988

82 laps of 2.35 mile/3.78 km circuit

Place	Driver	Car	Laps	Time/reason for retiring	Grid
1	Prost	McLaren-Honda	82	1h 53m 14.7s	2
2	Senna	McLaren-Honda	82	1h 53m 51.5s	1
3	Piquet	Lotus-Honda	82	1h 54m 02.2s	5
4	Patrese	Williams-Judd	82	1h 54m 34.8s	6
5	Boutsen	Benetton-Ford	81		10
6	Capelli	March-Judd	81		9
7	Martini	Minardi-Ford	80		14
8	de Cesaris	Rial-Ford	77	fuel	15
9	Johansson	Ligier-Judd	76	fuel	22
10	Alliot	Lola-Ford	75	electrical	24
11	Streiff	AGS-Ford	73	electrical	16
	Ghinzani	Zakspeed	69	fuel	26
	Mansell	Williams-Judd	65	accident	3
	Nannini	Benetton-Ford	63	accident	8
	Modena	EuroBrun-Ford	63	half-shaft	20
	Warwick	Arrows-Megatron	52	throttle	7
	Cheever	Arrows-Megatron	51	engine	18
	Gugelmin	March-Judd	46	accident	19
	Nakajima	Lotus-Honda	46	accident	13
	Sala	Minardi-Ford	41	electrical	21
	Caffi	Dallara-Ford	32	clutch	11
	Berger	Ferrari	25	accident	4
	Arnoux	Ligier-Judd	24	accident	23

Australian Grand Prix (cont)

Place	Driver	Car	Laps	Time/reason for retiring	Grid
	Palmer	Tyrrell-Ford	16	crownwheel and pinion	17
	Larrauri	EuroBrun-Ford	12	half-shaft	25
	Alboreto	Ferrari	0	accident	12

Fastest Lap: Prost, 1m 21.22s. 104.1 mph/167.6 kph

World Championship 1988

1	Senna	90 (94)
2	Prost	87 (105)
3	Berger	41
4	Boutsen	27
5	Alboreto	24
6	Piquet	22
7=	Capelli, Warwick	17
9=	Mansell, Nannini	12
11	Patrese	8
12	Cheever	6
13=	Gugelmin, Palmer	5
15	de Cesaris	3
16=	Martini, Nakajima	1

Constructors' Championship

1	McLaren-Honda	199
2	Ferrari	65
3	Benetton-Ford	39
4=	Arrows-Megatron, Lotus-Honda	23
6	March-Judd	22
7	Williams-Judd	20
8	Tyrrell-Ford	5
9	Rial-Ford	3
10	Minardi-Ford	1

1989

Turbocharged engines were banned for 1989. Although McLaren won ten races, the rivalry between their drivers, Senna and Prost, culminated in a controversial coming together in Japan. Prost retired, Senna eventually managed to restart, crossing the line first, but was disqualified for missing out part of the course. Prost took the championship. Patrese passed Graham Hill's record total of starts.

Brazilian Grand Prix: Rio de Janeiro, 26 March 1989

61 laps of 3.13 mile/5.03 km circuit

Place	Driver	Car	Laps	Time/reason for retiring	Grid
1	Mansell	Ferrari	61	1h 38m 58.744s	6
2	Prost	McLaren-Honda	61	1h 39m 06.553s	5
3	Gugelmin	March-Judd	61	1h 39m 08.114s	12
4	Herbert	Benetton-Ford	61	1h 39m 09.237s	10
5	Warwick	Arrows-Ford	61	1h 39m 16.610s	8
6	Nannini	Benetton-Ford	61	1h 39m 16.985s	11
7	Palmer	Tyrrell-Ford	60		18
8	Nakajima	Lotus-Judd	60		21
9	Grouillard	Ligier-Judd	60		22
10	Alboreto	Tyrrell-Ford	59		20
11	Senna	McLaren-Honda	59		1
12	Alliot	Lola-Lamborghini	58		26
13	de Cesaris	Dallara-Ford	57		15
14	Danner	Rial-Ford	56		17
	Patrese	Williams-Renault	51	alternator	2
	Cheever	Arrows-Ford	37	accident	24
	Schneider	Zakspeed-Yamaha	36	accident	25
	Brundle	Brabham-Judd	27	engine	13
	Capelli	March-Judd	22	suspension	7
	Piquet	Lotus-Judd	10	fuel pump	9
	Larini	Osella-Ford	10	disqualified: illegal start	19
	Modena	Brabham-Judd	9	cv joint	14
	Boutsen	Williams-Renault	3	engine	4
	Martini	Minardi-Ford	2	engine mount	16
	Sala	Minardi-Ford	0	accident	23
	Berger	Ferrari	0	accident	3

Fastest Lap: Patrese, 1m 32.507s. 121.66 mph/195.79 kph

San Marino Grand Prix: Imola, 23 April 1989

58 laps of 3.13 mile/5.04 km circuit

Place	Driver	Car	Laps	Time/reason for retiring	Grid
1	Senna	McLaren-Honda	58	1h 26m 51.25s	1
2	Prost	McLaren-Honda	58	1h 27m 31.47s	2
3	Nannini	Benetton-Ford	57		7
4	Boutsen	Williams-Renault	57		6
5	Warwick	Arrows-Ford	57		12
6	Palmer	Tyrrell-Ford	57		25
7	Caffi	Dallara-Ford	57		9
8	Tarquini	AGS-Ford	57		18
9	Cheever	Arrows-Ford	56		21
10	de Cesaris	Dallara-Ford	56		16
11	Herbert	Benetton-Ford	56		23
12	Larini	Osella-Ford	52		14
	Brundle	Brabham-Judd	51	engine	22
	Nakajima	Lotus-Judd	46	electrical	24
	Sala	Minardi-Ford	43	spun/stalled	15
	Gugelmin	March-Judd	39	gearbox	19
	Piquet	Lotus-Judd	29	engine	8
	Mansell	Ferrari	23	gearbox	3
	Patrese	Williams-Renault	21	engine	4
	Modena	Brabham-Judd	19	accident	17
	Martini	Minardi-Ford	6	gearbox	11
	Grouillard	Ligier-Ford	4	disqualified: illegal repairs	10
	Berger	Ferrari	3	accident	5
	Capelli	March-Judd	1	spun	13
	Alliot	Lola-Lamborghini	0	fuel feed	20
	Dalmas	Lola-Lamborghini	0	stalled	26

Fastest Lap: Prost, 1m 26.795s. 129.9 mph/209.04 kph

Monaco Grand Prix: Monte Carlo, 7 May 1989

77 laps of 2.07 mile/3.33 km circuit

Place	Driver	Car	Laps	Time/reason for retiring	Grid
1	Senna	McLaren-Honda	77	1h 53m 33.25s	1
2	Prost	McLaren-Honda	77	1h 54m 23.78s	2
3	Modena	Brabham-Judd	76		8
4	Caffi	Dallara-Ford	75		9
5	Alboreto	Tyrrell-Ford	75		12
6	Brundle	Brabham-Judd	75		4
7	Cheever	Arrows-Ford	75		20
8	Nannini	Benetton-Ford	74		15
9	Palmer	Tyrrell-Ford	74		23
10	Boutsen	Williams-Renault	74		3

Monaco Grand Prix (cont)

Place	Driver	Car	Laps	Time/reason for retiring	Grid
11	Capelli	March-Judd	73	electrical	22
12	Arnoux	Ligier-Ford	73		21
13	de Cesaris	Dallara-Ford	73		10
14	Herbert	Benetton-Ford	73		24
15	Patrese	Williams-Renault	73		7
	Sala	Minardi-Ford	48	engine	26
	Tarquini	AGS-Ford	46		13
	Moreno	Coloni-Ford	44	gearbox	25
	Alliot	Lola-Lamborghini	38	engine	17
	Gugelmin	March-Judd	36	engine	14
	Piquet	Lotus-Judd	32	accident	19
	Mansell	Ferrari	30	gearbox	5
	Raphanel	Coloni-Ford	19	gearbox	18
	Grouillard	Ligier-Ford	4	gearbox	16
	Martini	Minardi-Ford	3	clutch	11
	Warwick	Arrows-Ford	2	gearbox	6

Fastest Lap: Prost, 1m 25.501s. 87.1 mph/140.1 kph

Mexican Grand Prix: Mexico City, 28 May 1989

69 laps of 2.75 mile/4.42 km circuit

Place	Driver	Car	Laps	Time/reason for retiring	Grid
1	Senna	McLaren-Honda	69	1h 35m 21.431s	1
2	Patrese	Williams-Renault	69	1h 35m 36.991s	5
3	Alboreto	Tyrrell-Ford	69	1h 35m 52.685s	7
4	Nannini	Benetton-Ford	69	1h 36m 06.926s	13
5	Prost	McLaren-Honda	69	1h 36m 17.544s	2
6	Tarquini	AGS-Ford	68		17
7	Cheever	Arrows-Ford	68		24
8	Grouillard	Ligier-Ford	68		11
9	Brundle	Brabham-Judd	68		20
10	Modena	Brabham-Judd	68		9
11	Piquet	Lotus-Judd	68		26
12	Danner	Rial-Ford	67		23
13	Caffi	Dallara-Ford	67		19
14	Arnoux	Ligier-Ford	66		25
15	Herbert	Benetton-Ford	66		18
	Martini	Minardi-Ford	53	engine	22
	Mansell	Ferrari	43	gearbox	3
	Warwick	Arrows-Ford	35	electrical	10
	Nakajima	Lotus-Judd	35	spun	15
	Alliot	Lola-Lamborghini	28	running	16
	de Cesaris	Dallara-Ford	20	fuel pump	12
	Berger	Ferrari	16	gearbox	6
	Johansson	Onyx-Ford	16	transmission	21

Mexican Grand Prix (cont)

Place	Driver	Car	Laps	Time/reason for retiring	Grid
	Boutsen	Williams-Renault	15	electrical	8
	Palmer	Tyrrell-Ford	9	throttle linkage	14
	Capelli	March-Judd	6	gearbox	4

Fastest Lap: Mansell, 1m 20.42s. 122.97 mph/197.91 kph

United States Grand Prix: Phoenix, 4 June 1989

75 laps of 2.36 mile/3.8 km circuit

Place	Driver	Car	Laps	Time/reason for retiring	Grid
1	Prost	McLaren-Honda	75	2h 01m 33.133s	2
2	Patrese	Williams-Renault	75	2h 02m 12.829s	14
3	Cheever	Arrows-Ford	75	2h 02m 16.343s	17
4	Danner	Rial-Ford	74		26
5	Herbert	Benetton-Ford	74		25
6	Boutsen	Williams-Renault	74		16
7	Tarquini	AGS-Ford	73		24
8	de Cesaris	Dallara-Ford	70		13
9	Palmer	Tyrrell-Ford	69	fuel injection	21
	Berger	Ferrari	61	alternator	8
	Caffi	Dallara-Ford	52	accident	6
	Piquet	Lotus-Judd	52	suspension/accident	22
	Johansson	Onyx-Ford	50	suspension	19
	Sala	Minardi-Ford	46	engine	20
	Senna	McLaren-Honda	44	electrical	1
	Brundle	Brabham-Judd	43	brakes	5
	Modena	Brabham-Judd	37	brakes	7
	Mansell	Ferrari	31	gearbox	4
	Martini	Minardi-Ford	26	engine	15
	Nakajima	Lotus-Judd	24	throttle cable	23
	Capelli	March-Judd	22	gearbox	11
	Gugelmin	March-Judd	20	disqualified: added brake fluid	18
	Alboreto	Tyrrell-Ford	17	gearbox	9
	Nannini	Benetton-Ford	10	illness	3
	Warwick	Arrows-Ford	7	accident	10
	Alliot	Lola-Lamborghini	3	engine	12

Fastest Lap: Senna, 1m 33.969s. 90.41 mph/145.51 kph

Canadian Grand Prix: Montreal, 18 June 1989

69 laps of 2.73 mile/4.39 km circuit

Place	Driver	Car	Laps	Time/reason for retiring	Grid
1	Boutsen	Williams-Renault	69	2h 01m 24.073s	6
2	Patrese	Williams-Renault	69	2h 01m 54.080s	3
3	de Cesaris	Dallara-Ford	69	2h 03m 00.722s	9
4	Piquet	Lotus-Judd	69	2h 03m 05.557s	19
5	Arnoux	Ligier-Ford	68		22
6	Caffi	Dallara-Ford	67		8
7	Senna	McLaren-Honda	66		2
8	Danner	Rial-Ford	66		23
	Moreno	Coloni-Ford	57	gearbox	26
	Warwick	Arrows-Ford	40	engine	12
	Palmer	Tyrrell-Ford	35	accident	14
	Larini	Osella-Ford	33	electrical	15
	Capelli	March-Judd	28	accident	21
	Alliot	Lola-Lamborghini	26	accident	10
	Sala	Minardi-Ford	11	accident	24
	Gugelmin	March-Judd	11	electrical	17
	Berger	Ferrari	6	alternator belt	4
	Tarquini	AGS-Ford	6	accident	25
	Cheever	Arrows-Ford	3	electrical	16
	Prost	McLaren-Honda	2	suspension	1
	Alboreto	Tyrrell-Ford	0	gearbox	20
	Modena	Brabham-Judd	0	accident	7
	Martini	Minardi-Ford	0	accident	11
Disqualified:					
	Mansell	Ferrari		illegal start	5
	Nannini	Benetton-Ford		illegal start	13
	Johansson	Onyx-Ford		ignored black flag	18

Fastest Lap: Palmer, 1m 31.925s. 106.83 mph/171.92 kph

French Grand Prix: Paul Ricard, 9 July 1989

80 laps of 2.37 mile/3.81 km circuit

Place	Driver	Car	Laps	Time/reason for retiring	Grid
1	Prost	McLaren-Honda	80	1h 38m 29.411s	1
2	Mansell	Ferrari	80	1h 39m 13.428s	3
3	Patrese	Williams-Renault	80	1h 39m 36.332s	8
4	Alesi	Tyrrell-Ford	80	1h 39m 42.643s	16
5	Johansson	Onyx-Ford	79		13
6	Grouillard	Ligier-Ford	79		17
7	Cheever	Arrows-Ford	79		25
8	Piquet	Lotus-Judd	78		20
9	Pirro	Benetton-Ford	78		24
10	Palmer	Tyrrell-Ford	78		9

French Grand Prix (cont)

Place	Driver	Car	Laps	Time/reason for retiring	Grid
11	Bernard	Lola-Lamborghini	77		15
12	Donnelly	Arrows-Ford	77		14
13	Gachot	Onyx-Ford	76		11
	Gugelmin	March-Judd	71	running	10
	Modena	Brabham-Judd	67	engine	22
	Boutsen	Williams-Renault	50	gearbox	5
	Nakajima	Lotus-Judd	49	electrical	19
	Capelli	March-Judd	43	engine	12
	Nannini	Benetton-Ford	40	suspension	4
	Martini	Minardi-Ford	31	oil pressure	23
	Alliot	Lola-Lamborghini	30	engine	7
	Tarquini	AGS-Ford	30	engine	21
	Berger	Ferrari	29	gearbox	6
	Caffi	Dallara-Ford	27	clutch	26
	Arnoux	Ligier-Ford	14	engine	18
	Senna	McLaren-Honda	0	transmission	2

Fastest Lap: Gugelmin, 1m 12.09s. 118.32 mph/190.41 kph

British Grand Prix: Silverstone, 16 July 1989

64 laps of 2.97 mile/4.78 km circuit

Place	Driver	Car	Laps	Time/reason for retiring	Grid
1	Prost	McLaren-Honda	64	1h 19m 22.131s	2
2	Mansell	Ferrari	64	1h 19m 41.500s	3
3	Nannini	Benetton-Ford	64	1h 20m 10.150s	9
4	Piquet	Lotus-Judd	64	1h 20m 28.866s	10
5	Martini	Minardi-Ford	63		11
6	Sala	Minardi-Ford	63		15
7	Grouillard	Ligier-Ford	63		24
8	Nakajima	Lotus-Judd	63		16
9	Warwick	Arrows-Ford	62		19
10	Boutsen	Williams-Renault	62		7
11	Pirro	Benetton-Ford	62		26
12	Gachot	Onyx-Ford	62		21
	Gugelmin	March-Judd	54	gearbox	6
	Brundle	Brabham-Judd	49	engine	20
	Berger	Ferrari	49	gearbox	4
	Bernard	Lola-Lamborghini	46	engine	13
	Alliot	Lola-Lamborghini	39	engine	12
	Palmer	Tyrrell-Ford	32	accident	18
	Modena	Brabham-Judd	31	engine	14
	Alesi	Tyrrell-Ford	28	accident	22
	Larini	Osella-Ford	23	handling	17
	Patrese	Williams-Renault	19	accident	5
	Capelli	March-Judd	15	transmission	8

British Grand Prix (cont)

Place	Driver	Car	Laps	Time/reason for retiring	Grid
	de Cesaris	Dallara-Ford	14	engine	25
	Senna	McLaren-Honda	11	gearbox	1
	Moreno	Coloni-Ford	2	engine	23

Fastest Lap: Mansell, 1m 12.017s. 148.47 mph/238.93 kph

German Grand Prix: Hockenheim, 30 July 1989

45 laps of 4.22 mile/6.8 km circuit

Place	Driver	Car	Laps	Time/reason for retiring	Grid
1	Senna	McLaren-Honda	45	1h 21m 43.30s	1
2	Prost	McLaren-Honda	45	1h 22m 01.45s	2
3	Mansell	Ferrari	45	1h 23m 06.56s	3
4	Patrese	Williams-Renault	44		5
5	Piquet	Lotus-Judd	44		8
6	Warwick	Arrows-Ford	44		17
7	de Cesaris	Dallara-Ford	44		21
8	Brundle	Brabham-Judd	44		12
9	Martini	Minardi-Ford	44		13
10	Alesi	Tyrrell-Ford	43		10
11	Arnoux	Ligier-Ford	42		23
12	Cheever	Arrows-Ford	40		25
	Modena	Brabham-Judd	37	engine	16
	Nakajima	Lotus-Judd	36	spun	18
	Capelli	March-Judd	32	engine	22
	Gugelmin	March-Judd	28	transmission	14
	Pirro	Benetton-Ford	26	accident	9
	Alliot	Lola-Lamborghini	20	engine	15
	Palmer	Tyrrell-Ford	16	throttle cable	19
	Berger	Ferrari	13	accident	4
	Johansson	Onyx-Ford	8	wheel bearing	24
	Nannini	Benetton-Ford	6	ignition	7
	Boutsen	Williams-Renault	4	accident	6
	Caffi	Dallara-Ford	2	engine	20
	Alboreto	Lola-Lamborghini	1	electrical	26
	Grouillard	Ligier-Ford	0	transmission	11

Fastest Lap: Senna, 1m 45.9s. 143.6 mph/231.1 kph

1989

Hungarian Grand Prix: Hungaroring, 13 August 1989

77 laps of 2.47 mile/3.97 km circuit

Place	Driver	Car	Laps	Time/reason for retiring	Grid
1	Mansell	Ferrari	77	1h 49m 38.650s	12
2	Senna	McLaren-Honda	77	1h 50m 04.617s	2
3	Boutsen	Williams-Renault	77	1h 50m 17.004s	4
4	Prost	McLaren-Honda	77	1h 50m 22.827s	5
5	Cheever	Arrows-Ford	77	1h 50m 23.756s	16
6	Piquet	Lotus-Judd	77	1h 50m 50.689s	17
7	Caffi	Dallara-Ford	77	1h 51m 02.875s	3
8	Pirro	Benetton-Ford	76		25
9	Alesi	Tyrrell-Ford	76		11
10	Warwick	Arrows-Ford	76		9
11	Modena	Brabham-Judd	76		8
12	Brundle	Brabham-Judd	75		15
13	Palmer	Tyrrell-Ford	73		19
	Sala	Minardi-Ford	57	spun	23
	Berger	Ferrari	56	gearbox	6
	Patrese	Williams-Renault	54	radiator	1
	Johansson	Onyx-Ford	48	transmission	24
	Nannini	Benetton-Ford	46	gearbox	7
	Gachot	Onyx-Ford	38	transmission	21
	Nakajima	Lotus-Judd	33	accident	20
	Gugelmin	March-Judd	27	electrical	13
	Capelli	March-Judd	26	wheel	14
	Alboreto	Lola-Lamborghini	26	engine	26
	Martini	Minardi-Ford	19	wheel	10
	Ghinzani	Osella-Ford	19	electrical	22
	de Cesaris	Dallara-Ford	0	clutch	18

Fastest Lap: Mansell, 1m 22.637s. 107.41 mph/172.86 kph

Belgian Grand Prix: Spa, 27 August 1989

44 laps of 4.31 mile/6.94 km circuit

Place	Driver	Car	Laps	Time/reason for retiring	Grid
1	Senna	McLaren-Honda	44	1h 40m 54.196s	1
2	Prost	McLaren-Honda	44	1h 40m 55.500s	2
3	Mansell	Ferrari	44	1h 40m 56.020s	6
4	Boutsen	Williams-Renault	44	1h 41m 48.614s	4
5	Nannini	Benetton-Ford	44	1h 42m 03.001s	7
6	Warwick	Arrows-Ford	44	1h 42m 12.512s	10
7	Gugelmin	March-Judd	43		9
8	Johansson	Onyx-Ford	43		15
9	Martini	Minardi-Ford	43		14
10	Pirro	Benetton-Ford	43		13
11	de Cesaris	Dallara-Ford	43		18

Belgian Grand Prix (cont)

Place	Driver	Car	Laps	Time/reason for retiring	Grid
12	Capelli	March-Judd	43		19
13	Grouillard	Ligier-Ford	43		26
14	Palmer	Tyrrell-Ford	42		21
15	Sala	Minardi-Ford	41		25
16	Alliot	Lola-Lamborghini	39		11
	Cheever	Arrows-Ford	38	loose wheel	24
	Gachot	Onyx-Ford	21	wheel bearing	23
	Patrese	Williams-Renault	20	accident	5
	Alboreto	Lola-Lamborghini	19	accident	22
	Caffi	Dallara-Ford	13	spun	12
	Brundle	Brabham-Judd	12	brakes	20
	Berger	Ferrari	9	spun	3
	Modena	Brabham-Judd	9	handling	8
	Arnoux	Ligier-Ford	4	accident	17
	Herbert	Tyrrell-Ford	3	spun	16

Fastest Lap: Prost, 2m 11.571s. 117.992 mph/189.89 kph

Italian Grand Prix: Monza, 10 September 1989

53 laps of 3.6 mile/5.8 km circuit

Place	Driver	Car	Laps	Time/reason for retiring	Grid
1	Prost	McLaren-Honda	53	1h 19m 27.550s	4
2	Berger	Ferrari	53	1h 19m 34.876s	2
3	Boutsen	Williams-Renault	53	1h 19m 42.525s	6
4	Patrese	Williams-Renault	53	1h 20m 06.272s	5
5	Alesi	Tyrrell-Ford	52		10
6	Brundle	Brabham-Judd	52		12
7	Martini	Minardi-Ford	52		15
8	Sala	Minardi-Ford	51		26
9	Arnoux	Ligier-Ford	51		23
10	Nakajima	Lotus-Judd	51		19
11	Caffi	Dallara-Ford	47		20
	de Cesaris	Dallara-Ford	45	engine	17
	Senna	McLaren-Honda	44	engine	1
	Mansell	Ferrari	41	gearbox	3
	Gachot	Onyx-Ford	38	overheating	22
	Nannini	Benetton-Ford	33	brakes	8
	Capelli	March-Judd	30	engine	18
	Grouillard	Ligier-Ford	30	exhaust	21
	Piquet	Lotus-Judd	23	spun	11
	Palmer	Tyrrell-Ford	18	engine	14
	Warwick	Arrows-Ford	18	engine	16
	Larini	Osella-Ford	16	gearbox	24
	Alboreto	Lola-Lamborghini	14	engine	13

Italian Grand Prix (cont)

Place	Driver	Car	Laps	Time/reason for retiring	Grid
	Gugelmin	March-Judd	14	throttle	25
	Alliot	Lola-Lamborghini	1	throttle	7
	Pirro	Benetton-Ford	0	gearbox	9

Fastest Lap: Prost, 1m 28.107s. 147.256 mph/236.99 kph

Portuguese Grand Prix: Estoril, 24 September 1989

71 laps of 2.7 mile/4.35 km circuit

Place	Driver	Car	Laps	Time/reason for retiring	Grid
1	Berger	Ferrari	71	1h 36m 48.546s	2
2	Prost	McLaren-Honda	71	1h 37m 21.183s	4
3	Johansson	Onyx-Ford	71	1h 37m 43.871s	12
4	Nannini	Benetton-Ford	71	1h 38m 10.915s	13
5	Martini	Minardi-Ford	70		5
6	Palmer	Tyrrell-Ford	70		18
7	Nakajima	Lotus-Judd	70		25
8	Brundle	Brabham-Judd	70		10
9	Alliot	Lola-Lamborghini	70		17
10	Gugelmin	March-Judd	69		14
11	Alboreto	Lola-Lamborghini	69		21
12	Sala	Minardi-Ford	69		9
13	Arnoux	Ligier-Ford	69		23
14	Modena	Brabham-Judd	69		11
	Patrese	Williams-Renault	60	radiator	6
	Boutsen	Williams-Renault	60	radiator	8
	Senna	McLaren-Honda	48	accident	1
	Mansell	Ferrari	48	accident	3
	Warwick	Arrows-Ford	37	accident	22
	Piquet	Lotus-Judd	33	accident	20
	Caffi	Dallara-Ford	33	accident	7
	Pirro	Benetton-Ford	29	shock absorber	16
	Capelli	March-Judd	25	engine	24
	Cheever	Arrows-Ford	24	spun	26
	de Cesaris	Dallara-Ford	17	electrical	19
	Moreno	Coloni-Ford	11	electrical	15

Fastest Lap: Berger, 1m 18.986s. 123.195 mph/198.263 kph

Spanish Grand Prix: Jerez, 1 October 1989

73 laps of 2.62 mile/4.22 km circuit

Place	Driver	Car	Laps	Time/reason for retiring	Grid
1	Senna	McLaren-Honda	73	1h 47m 48.264s	1
2	Berger	Ferrari	73	1h 48m 15.315s	2
3	Prost	McLaren-Honda	73	1h 48m 42.052s	3
4	Alesi	Tyrrell-Ford	72		9
5	Patrese	Williams-Renault	72		6
6	Alliot	Lola-Lamborghini	72		5
7	de Cesaris	Dallara-Ford	72		15
8	Piquet	Lotus-Judd	71		7
9	Warwick	Arrows-Ford	71		16
10	Palmer	Tyrrell-Ford	71		13
	Cheever	Arrows-Ford	61	engine	22
	Pirro	Benetton-Ford	59	driver	10
	Caffi	Dallara-Ford	55	engine	23
	Brundle	Brabham-Judd	51	exhaust	8
	Gugelmin	March-Judd	47	accident	26
	Sala	Minardi-Ford	47	accident	20
	Boutsen	Williams-Renault	40	fuel pump	21
	Grouillard	Ligier-Ford	34	engine	24
	Martini	Minardi-Ford	27	stalled	4
	Capelli	March-Judd	23	transmission	19
	Lehto	Onyx-Ford	20	gearbox	17
	Ghinzani	Osella-Ford	17	gearbox	25
	Nannini	Benetton-Ford	14	spun	14
	Modena	Brabham-Judd	11	engine	12
	Larini	Osella-Ford	6	accident	11
	Nakajima	Lotus-Judd	0	accident	18

Fastest Lap: Senna, 1m 25.78s. 109.996 mph/177.022 kph

Japanese Grand Prix: Suzuka, 22 October 1989

53 laps of 3.64 mile/5.86 km circuit

Place	Driver	Car	Laps	Time/reason for retiring	Grid
	Senna	McLaren-Honda	53	disqualified: short cut	1
1	Nannini	Benetton-Ford	53	1h 35m 06.277s	6
2	Patrese	Williams-Renault	53	1h 35m 18.181s	5
3	Boutsen	Williams-Renault	53	1h 35m 19.723s	7
4	Piquet	Lotus-Judd	53	1h 36m 50.502s	11
5	Brundle	Brabham-Judd	52		13
6	Warwick	Arrows-Ford	52		25
7	Gugelmin	March-Judd	52		20
8	Cheever	Arrows-Ford	52		24
9	Caffi	Dallara-Ford	52		15

![checkered flag]

Japanese Grand Prix (cont)

Place	Driver	Car	Laps	Time/reason for retiring	Grid
10	de Cesaris	Dallara-Ford	51		16
	Prost	McLaren-Honda	46	accident	2
	Modena	Brabham-Judd	46	alternator	9
	Mansell	Ferrari	43	engine	4
	Nakajima	Lotus-Judd	41	engine	12
	Alesi	Tyrrell-Ford	37	gearbox	18
	Alliot	Lola-Lamborghini	36	engine	8
	Berger	Ferrari	34	transmission	3
	Pirro	Benetton-Ford	33	accident	22
	Grouillard	Ligier-Ford	31	engine	23
	Capelli	March-Judd	27	suspension	17
	Larini	Osella-Ford	21	brakes	10
	Palmer	Tyrrell-Ford	20	fuel leak	26
	Schneider	Zakspeed-Yamaha	1	drive-shaft	21
	Barilla	Minardi-Ford	0	clutch	19
	Sala	Minardi-Ford	0	accident	14

Fastest Lap: Prost, 1m 43.506s. 126.622 mph/203.779 kph

Australian Grand Prix: Adelaide, 5 November 1989

70 laps of 2.35 mile/3.78 km circuit

Place	Driver	Car	Laps	Time/reason for retiring	Grid
1	Boutsen	Williams-Renault	70	2h 00m 17.421s	5
2	Nannini	Benetton-Ford	70	2h 00m 46.079s	4
3	Patrese	Williams-Renault	70	2h 00m 55.104s	6
4	Nakajima	Lotus-Judd	70	2h 00m 59.752s	23
5	Pirro	Benetton-Ford	68		13
6	Martini	Minardi-Ford	67		3
7	Gugelmin	March-Judd	66		25
8	Modena	Brabham-Judd	64		8
	Cheever	Arrows-Ford	42	stalled	22
	Lehto	Onyx-Ford	27	engine	17
	Grouillard	Ligier-Ford	22	accident	24
	Piquet	Lotus-Judd	19	accident	18
	Ghinzani	Osella-Ford	18	accident	21
	Mansell	Ferrari	17	accident	7
	Senna	McLaren-Honda	13	accident	1
	Caffi	Dallara-Ford	13	accident	10
	Capelli	March-Judd	13	radiator	16
	de Cesaris	Dallara-Ford	12	accident	9
	Brundle	Brabham-Judd	12	accident	12
	Warwick	Arrows-Ford	7	accident	20
	Berger	Ferrari	6	accident	14
	Alliot	Lola-Lamborghini	6	accident	19
	Alesi	Tyrrell-Ford	5	spun	15

Australian Grand Prix (cont)

Place	Driver	Car	Laps	Time/reason for retiring	Grid
	Arnoux	Ligier-Ford	5	accident	26
	Prost	McLaren-Honda	2	withdrew	2
	Larini	Osella-Ford	0	stalled	11

Fastest Lap: Nakajima, 1m 38.48s. 86.482 mph/139.18 kph

World Championship 1989

1	Prost	76 (81)
2	Senna	60
3	Patrese	40
4	Mansell	38
5	Boutsen	37
6	Nannini	32
7	Berger	21
8	Piquet	12
9	Alesi	8
10	Warwick	7
11 =	Alboreto, Cheever, Johansson	6
14 =	Herbert, Martini	5
16 =	Brundle, Caffi, de Cesaris, Gugelmin, Modena	4
21 =	Danner, Nakajima	3
23 =	Arnoux, Palmer, Pirro	2
26 =	Alliot, Grouillard, Sala, Tarquini	1

Constructors' Championship

1	McLaren-Honda	141
2	Williams-Renault	77
3	Ferrari	59
4	Benetton-Ford	39
5	Tyrrell-Ford	16
6	Lotus-Judd	15
7	Arrows-Ford	13
8 =	Brabham-Judd, Dallara-Ford	8
10 =	Minardi-Ford, Onyx-Ford	6
12	March-Judd	4
13 =	Ligier-Ford, Rial-Ford	3
15 =	AGS-Ford, Lola-Lamborghini	1

1990

Senna and Prost continued their 1989 battle in different teams, but with similar results: the championship struggle ended in Japan with Prost and Senna colliding at the first corner. Senna became champion for the second time. Alessandro Nannini was severely injured in a helicopter crash, and Martin Donnelly in a practice crash in Spain. Ferrari won their hundredth grand prix in France. At Silverstone, Patrese started his 200th grand prix. March was renamed Leyton House.

United States Grand Prix: Phoenix, 11 March 1990

70 laps of 2.36 mile/3.8 km circuit

Place	Driver	Car	Laps	Time/reason for retiring	Grid
1	Senna	McLaren-Honda	72	1h 52m 32.8s	5
2	Alesi	Tyrrell-Ford	72	1h 52m 41.5s	4
3	Boutsen	Williams-Renault	72	1h 53m 26.9s	9
4	Piquet	Benetton-Ford	72	1h 53m 41.2s	6
5	Modena	Brabham-Judd	72	1h 53m 42.3s	10
6	Nakajima	Tyrrell-Ford	71		11
7	Martini	Minardi-Ford	71		2
8	Bernard	Lola-Lamborghini	71		15
9	Patrese	Williams-Renault	71		12
10	Alboreto	Arrows-Ford	70		21
11	Nannini	Benetton-Ford	70		22
12	Schneider	Arrows-Ford	70		20
13	Moreno	EuroBrun-Judd	67		16
14	Gugelmin	Leyton House-Judd	66		25
	Barilla	Minardi-Ford	54	driver	14
	Suzuki	Lola-Lamborghini	53	brakes	18
	Mansell	Ferrari	49	clutch	17
	Berger	McLaren-Honda	44	clutch	1
	Foitek	Brabham-Judd	39	accident	23
	Grouillard	Osella-Ford	39	accident	8
	de Cesaris	Dallara-Ford	25	engine	3
	Prost	Ferrari	21	gearbox	7
	Capelli	Leyton House-Judd	20	oil	26
	Warwick	Lotus-Lamborghini	6	suspension	24
	Larini	Ligier-Ford	4	throttle	13
	Donnelly	Lotus-Lamborghini	0	gearbox	19

Fastest Lap: Berger 1m 31.05s. 93.31 mph/150.14 kph

Brazilian Grand Prix: Interlagos, 25 March 1990

71 laps of 4.95 mile/7.96 km circuit

Place	Driver	Car	Laps	Time/reason for retiring	Grid
1	Prost	Ferrari	71	1h 37m 21.3s	6
2	Berger	McLaren-Honda	71	1h 37m 34.8s	2
3	Senna	McLaren-Honda	71	1h 37m 59.0s	1
4	Mansell	Ferrari	71	1h 38m 08.5s	5
5	Boutsen	Williams-Renault	70		3
6	Piquet	Benetton-Ford	70		13
7	Alesi	Tyrrell-Ford	70		7
8	Nakajima	Tyrrell-Ford	70		19
9	Martini	Minardi-Ford	69		8
10	Nannini	Benetton-Ford	68		15
11	Larini	Ligier-Ford	68		20
12	Alliot	Ligier-Ford	68		10
13	Patrese	Williams-Renault	65	oil leak	4
14	Morbidelli	Dallara-Ford	64		16
	Caffi	Arrows-Ford	49	driver	25
	Donnelly	Lotus-Lamborghini	43	spun	14
	Modena	Brabham-Judd	39	spun	12
	Barilla	Minardi-Ford	38	valve	17
	Dalmas	AGS-Ford	28	suspension	26
	Warwick	Lotus-Lamborghini	25	electrical	24
	Suzuki	Lola-Lamborghini	24	accident	18
	Alboreto	Arrows-Ford	24	suspension	23
	Foitek	Brabham-Judd	14	clutch	22
	Bernard	Lola-Lamborghini	13	gearbox	11
	Grouillard	Osella-Ford	8	accident	21
	de Cesaris	Dallara-Ford	0	accident	9

Fastest Lap: Berger 1m 19.9s. 121.09 mph/194.87 kph

San Marino Grand Prix: Imola, 13 May 1990

61 laps of 3.13 mile/5.04 km circuit

Place	Driver	Car	Laps	Time/reason for retiring	Grid
1	Patrese	Williams-Renault	61	1h 30m 55.5s	3
2	Berger	McLaren-Honda	61	1h 31m 00.6s	2
3	Nannini	Benetton-Ford	61	1h 31m 01.8s	9
4	Prost	Ferrari	61	1h 31m 48.6s	6
5	Piquet	Benetton-Ford	61	1h 31m 48.6s	8
6	Alesi	Tyrrell-Ford	60		7
7	Warwick	Lotus-Lamborghini	60		10
8	Donnelly	Lotus-Lamborghini	60		11
9	Alliot	Ligier-Ford	60		16
10	Larini	Ligier-Ford	59		20
11	Barilla	Minardi-Ford	59		26

San Marino Grand Prix (cont)

Place	Driver	Car	Laps	Time/reason for retiring	Grid
12	Lehto	Onyx-Ford	59		25
13	Bernard	Lola-Lamborghini	56	gearbox	13
	Grouillard	Osella-Ford	52	suspension	22
	Mansell	Ferrari	38	engine	5
	Foitek	Onyx-Ford	35	engine	23
	Modena	Brabham-Judd	31	brakes	14
	de Cesaris	Dallara-Ford	29	wheel	17
	Gugelmin	Leyton House-Judd	24	electrical	12
	Boutsen	Williams-Renault	17	engine	4
	Suzuki	Lola-Lamborghini	17	clutch	15
	Senna	McLaren-Honda	3	wheel	1
	Pirro	Dallara-Ford	2	electrical	21
	Capelli	Leyton House-Judd	0	accident	18
	Nakajima	Tyrrell-Ford	0	accident	19
	Moreno	EuroBrun-Judd	0	throttle	24

Fastest Lap: Nannini, 1m 27.16s. 129.36 mph/208.18 kph

Monaco Grand Prix: Monte Carlo, 27 May 1990

78 laps of 2.07 mile/3.33 km circuit

Place	Driver	Car	Laps	Time/reason for retiring	Grid
1	Senna	McLaren-Honda	78	1h 52m 46.9s	1
2	Alesi	Tyrrell-Ford	78	1h 52m 48.1s	3
3	Berger	McLaren-Honda	78	1h 52m 49.1s	5
4	Boutsen	Williams-Renault	77		6
5	Caffi	Arrows-Ford	76		22
6	Bernard	Lola-Lamborghini	76		24
7	Foitek	Onyx-Ford	72		20
	Warwick	Lotus-Lamborghini	66	brakes	13
	Mansell	Ferrari	63	battery	7
	Barilla	Minardi-Ford	52	gearbox	19
	Lehto	Onyx-Ford	52	gearbox	26
	Alliot	Ligier-Ford	47	gearbox	18
	Patrese	Williams-Renault	41	valves	4
	de Cesaris	Dallara-Ford	38	accelerator	12
	Nakajima	Tyrrell-Ford	36	spun	21
	Piquet	Benetton-Ford	33	disqualified: push start	10
	Prost	Ferrari	30	battery	2
	Nannini	Benetton-Ford	20	engine	16
	D Brabham	Brabham-Judd	16	cv joint	25
	Capelli	Leyton House-Judd	13	brakes	23
	Larini	Ligier-Ford	12	gearbox	17
	Suzuki	Lola-Lamborghini	11	electrical	15
	Martini	Minardi-Ford	7	electrical	8

Monaco Grand Prix (cont)

Place	Driver	Car	Laps	Time/reason for retiring	Grid
	Donnelly	Lotus-Lamborghini	6	cv joint	11
	Modena	Brabham-Judd	3	gearbox	14
	Pirro	Dallara-Ford	0	vapour lock	9

Fastest Lap: Senna, 1m 24.47s. 88.13 mph/141.84 kph

Canadian Grand Prix: Montreal, 10 June 1990

70 laps of 2.73 mile/4.4 km circuit

Place	Driver	Car	Laps	Time/reason for retiring	Grid
1	Senna	McLaren-Honda	70	1h 42m 56.4s	1
2	Piquet	Benetton-Ford	70	1h 43m 06.9s	5
3	Mansell	Ferrari	70	1h 43m 09.8s	7
4	Berger	McLaren-Honda	70	1h 43m 11.3s	2
5	Prost	Ferrari	70	1h 43m 12.2s	3
6	Warwick	Lotus-Lamborghini	68		11
7	Modena	Brabham-Judd	68		10
8	Caffi	Arrows-Ford	68		26
9	Bernard	Lola-Lamborghini	67		23
10	Capelli	Leyton House-Judd	67		24
11	Nakajima	Tyrrell-Ford	67		13
12	Suzuki	Lola-Lamborghini	66		18
13	Grouillard	Osella-Ford	65		15
	Donnelly	Lotus-Lamborghini	57	engine	12
	Foitek	Onyx-Ford	53	valve	21
	de Cesaris	Dallara-Ford	50	input shaft	25
	Lehto	Onyx-Ford	46	misfire	22
	Patrese	Williams-Renault	44	brakes	9
	Alliot	Ligier-Ford	34	engine	17
	Alesi	Tyrrell-Ford	26	accident	8
	Nannini	Benetton-Ford	21	accident	4
	Boutsen	Williams-Renault	19	accident	6
	Larini	Ligier-Ford	18	accident	20
	Pirro	Dallara-Ford	11	accident	19
	Alboreto	Arrows-Ford	11	accident	14
	Martini	Minardi-Ford	0	spun	16

Fastest Lap: Berger, 1m 22.08s. 119.65 mph/192.55 kph

1990

Mexican Grand Prix: Mexico City, 24 June 1990

69 laps of 2.75 mile/4.42 km circuit

Place	Driver	Car	Laps	Time/reason for retiring	Grid
1	Prost	Ferrari	69	1h 32m 35.78s	13
2	Mansell	Ferrari	69	1h 33m 01.13s	4
3	Berger	McLaren-Honda	69	1h 33m 01.31s	1
4	Nannini	Benetton-Ford	69	1h 33m 16.88s	14
5	Boutsen	Williams-Renault	69	1h 33m 22.45s	5
6	Piquet	Benetton-Ford	69	1h 33m 22.73s	8
7	Alesi	Tyrrell-Ford	69	1h 33m 24.7s	6
8	Donnelly	Lotus-Lamborghini	69	1h 33m 41.9s	12
9	Patrese	Williams-Renault	69	1h 33m 45.7s	2
10	Warwick	Lotus-Lamborghini	68		11
11	Modena	Brabham-Judd	68		10
12	Martini	Minardi-Ford	68		7
13	de Cesaris	Dallara-Ford	68		15
14	Barilla	Minardi-Ford	67		16
15	Foitek	Onyx-Ford	67		23
16	Larini	Ligier-Ford	67		24
17	Alboreto	Arrows-Ford	66		17
18	Alliot	Ligier-Ford	66		22
19	Grouillard	Osella-Ford	65		20
20	Senna	McLaren-Honda	63	puncture	3
	Lehto	Onyx-Ford	26	engine	26
	Bernard	Lola-Lamborghini	12	wheel	25
	Suzuki	Lola-Lamborghini	11	accident	19
	Nakajima	Tyrrell-Ford	11	accident	9
	D Brabham	Brabham-Judd	11	electrical	21
	Pirro	Dallara-Ford	10	engine	18

Fastest Lap: Prost, 1m 17.96s. 126.85 mph/204.15 kph

French Grand Prix: Paul Ricard, 8 July 1990

80 laps of 2.4 mile/3.8 km circuit

Place	Driver	Car	Laps	Time/reason for retiring	Grid
1	Prost	Ferrari	80	1h 33m 29.6s	4
2	Capelli	Leyton House-Judd	80	1h 33m 38.2s	7
3	Senna	McLaren-Honda	80	1h 33m 41.2s	3
4	Piquet	Benetton-Ford	80	1h 34m 10.8s	9
5	Berger	McLaren-Honda	80	1h 34m 11.8s	2
6	Patrese	Williams-Renault	80	1h 34m 38.9s	6
7	Suzuki	Lola-Lamborghini	79		14
8	Bernard	Lola-Lamborghini	79		11
9	Alliot	Ligier-Ford	79		12
10	Alboreto	Arrows-Ford	79		18
11	Warwick	Lotus-Lamborghini	79		16
12	Donnelly	Lotus-Lamborghini	79		17

French Grand Prix (cont)

Place	Driver	Car	Laps	Time/reason for retiring	Grid
13	Modena	Brabham-Judd	78		20
14	Larini	Ligier-Ford	78		19
15	D Brabham	Brabham-Judd	77		25
	de Cesaris	Dallara-Ford	77	disqualified: underweight	21
16	Nannini	Benetton-Ford	75	electrical	5
17	Dalmas	AGS-Ford	75		26
18	Mansell	Ferrari	72	engine	1
	Nakajima	Tyrrell-Ford	63	gearbox	15
	Gugelmin	Leyton House-Judd	58	fuel system	10
	Martini	Minardi-Ford	40	electrical	23
	Alesi	Tyrrell-Ford	23	drive-shaft	13
	Caffi	Arrows-Ford	22	suspension	22
	Boutsen	Williams-Renault	8	engine	8
	Pirro	Dallara-Ford	7	brakes	24

Fastest Lap: Mansell, 1m 08.01s. 125.44 mph/201.83 kph

British Grand Prix: Silverstone, 15 July 1990

64 laps of 2.97 mile/4.78 km circuit

Place	Driver	Car	Laps	Time/reason for retiring	Grid
1	Prost	Ferrari	64	1h 18m 30.9s	5
2	Boutsen	Williams-Renault	64	1h 19m 10.1s	4
3	Senna	McLaren-Honda	64	1h 19m 14.1s	2
4	Bernard	Lola-Lamborghini	64	1h 19m 46.3s	8
5	Piquet	Benetton-Ford	64	1h 19m 55.0s	11
6	Suzuki	Lola-Lamborghini	63		9
7	Caffi	Arrows-Ford	63		16
8	Alesi	Tyrrell-Ford	63		6
9	Modena	Brabham-Judd	62		19
10	Larini	Ligier-Ford	62		20
11	Pirro	Dallara-Ford	62		18
12	Barilla	Minardi-Ford	62		23
13	Alliot	Ligier-Ford	61		21
14	Berger	McLaren-Honda	60	throttle	3
	Mansell	Ferrari	55	gearbox	1
	Capelli	Leyton House-Judd	48	fuel system	10
	Donnelly	Lotus-Lamborghini	48	engine	14
	Warwick	Lotus-Lamborghini	46	engine	15
	Tarquini	AGS-Ford	41	engine	25
	Alboreto	Arrows-Ford	37	electrical	24
	Patrese	Williams-Renault	26	accident	7
	Nakajima	Tyrrell-Ford	20	electrical	12
	Nannini	Benetton-Ford	15	accident	13
	de Cesaris	Dallara-Ford	12	gearbox	22
	Martini	Minardi-Ford	31	alternator	17

Fastest Lap: Mansell, 1m 11.29s. 149.98 mph/241.38 kph

German Grand Prix: Hockenheim, 29 July 1990

45 laps of 4.23 mile/6.8 km circuit

Place	Driver	Car	Laps	Time/reason for retiring	Grid
1	Senna	McLaren-Honda	45	1h 20m 47.2s	1
2	Nannini	Benetton-Ford	45	1h 20m 53.7s	9
3	Berger	McLaren-Honda	45	1h 20m 55.7s	2
4	Prost	Ferrari	45	1h 21m 32.4s	3
5	Patrese	Williams-Honda	45	1h 21m 35.2s	5
6	Boutsen	Williams-Honda	45	1h 22m 08.7s	6
7	Capelli	Leyton House-Judd	44		10
8	Warwick	Lotus-Lamborghini	44		16
9	Caffi	Arrows-Ford	44		18
10	Larini	Ligier-Ford	43		22
11	Alesi	Tyrrell-Ford	40	cv joint	8
	Lehto	Onyx-Ford	39		25
	Bernard	Lola-Lamborghini	35	electrical	12
	Suzuki	Lola-Lamborghini	33	clutch	11
	Nakajima	Tyrrell-Ford	24	electrical	13
	Piquet	Benetton-Ford	23	engine	7
	Martini	Minardi-Ford	20	engine	15
	Foitek	Onyx-Ford	19	spun	26
	Alliot	Ligier-Ford	16	disqualified: push start	24
	Mansell	Ferrari	15	undertray	4
	Gugelmin	Leyton House-Judd	12	engine	14
	D Brabham	Brabham-Judd	12	valve	21
	Alboreto	Arrows-Ford	10	engine	19
	Donnelly	Lotus-Lamborghini	1	clutch	20
	Pirro	Dallara-Ford	0	accident	23
	Modena	Brabham-Judd	0	clutch	17

Fastest Lap: Boutsen, 1m 45.6s. 144.08 mph/231.88 kph

Hungarian Grand Prix: Hungaroring, 12 August 1990

77 laps of 2.46 mile/3.96 km circuit

Place	Driver	Car	Laps	Time/reason for retiring	Grid
1	Boutsen	Williams-Renault	77	1hr 49m 30.6s	1
2	Senna	McLaren-Honda	77	1h 49m 30.9s	4
3	Piquet	Benetton-Ford	77	1h 49m 58.5s	9
4	Patrese	Williams-Renault	77	1h 50m 02.4s	2
5	Warwick	Lotus-Lamborghini	77	1h 50m 44.8s	11
6	Bernard	Lola-Lamborghini	77	1h 50m 54.9s	12
7	Donnelly	Lotus-Lamborghini	76		18
8	Gugelmin	Leyton House-Judd	76		17
9	Caffi	Arrows-Ford	76		26
10	Pirro	Dallara-Ford	76		13
11	Larini	Ligier-Ford	76		25

Hungarian Grand Prix (cont)

Place	Driver	Car	Laps	Time/reason for retiring	Grid
12	Alboreto	Arrows-Ford	75		22
13	Tarquini	AGS-Ford	74		24
14	Alliot	Ligier-Ford	74		21
15	Barilla	Minardi-Ford	74		23
16	Berger	McLaren-Honda	72	accident	3
17	Mansell	Ferrari	71	accident	5
	Nannini	Benetton-Ford	64	accident	7
	Capelli	Leyton House-Judd	56	gearbox	16
	Suzuki	Lola-Lamborghini	37	oil filter	19
	Prost	Ferrari	36	gearbox	8
	Alesi	Tyrrell-Ford	36	accident	6
	Modena	Brabham-Judd	35	engine	20
	Martini	Minardi-Ford	35	accident	14
	de Cesaris	Dallara-Ford	22	engine	10
	Nakajima	Tyrrell-Ford	9	spun	15

Fastest Lap: Patrese, 1m 22.06s. 106.08 mph/174.08 kph

Belgian Grand Prix: Spa, 26 August 1990

44 laps of 4.31 mile/6.94 km circuit

Place	Driver	Car	Laps	Time/reason for retiring	Grid
1	Senna	McLaren-Honda	44	1h 26m 31.2s	1
2	Prost	Ferrari	44	1h 26m 35.6s	3
3	Berger	McLaren-Honda	44	1h 27m 00.5s	2
4	Nannini	Benetton-Ford	44	1h 27m 21.3s	6
5	Piquet	Benetton-Ford	44	1h 28m 01.7s	8
6	Gugelmin	Leyton House-Judd	44	1h 28m 20.9s	14
7	Capelli	Leyton House-Judd	43		12
8	Alesi	Tyrrell-Ford	43		9
9	Bernard	Lola-Lamborghini	43		15
10	Caffi	Arrows-Ford	43		19
11	Warwick	Lotus-Lamborghini	43		18
12	Donnelly	Lotus-Lamborghini	43		22
13	Alboreto	Arrows-Ford	43		26
14	Larini	Ligier-Ford	42		21
15	Martini	Minardi-Ford	42		16
16	Grouillard	Osella-Ford	42		23
17	Modena	Brabham-Judd	39	engine	13
	D Brabham	Brabham-Judd	36	electrical	24
	de Cesaris	Dallara-Ford	27	water leak	20
	Boutsen	Williams-Renault	21	transmission	4
	Mansell	Ferrari	19	handling	5
	Patrese	Williams-Renault	18	gearbox	7
	Pirro	Dallara-Ford	5	water pipe	17

Belgian Grand Prix (cont)

Place	Driver	Car	Laps	Time/reason for retiring	Grid
	Nakajima	Tyrrell-Ford	4	engine	10
	Barilla	Minardi-Ford	0	accident	25
	Suzuki	Lola-Lamborghini	0	accident	11

Fastest Lap: Prost, 1m 55.1s. 134.89 mph/217.09 kph

* Race started three times, stopped twice due to first lap accidents. Suzuki eliminated after first start, Barilla after second.

Italian Grand Prix: Monza, 9 September 1990

53 laps of 3.6 mile/5.8 km circuit

Place	Driver	Car	Laps	Time/reason for retiring	Grid
1	Senna	McLaren-Honda	53	1h 17m 57.9s	1
2	Prost	Ferrari	53	1h 18m 03.9s	2
3	Berger	McLaren-Honda	53	1h 18m 05.3s	3
4	Mansell	Ferrari	53	1h 18m 54.1s	4
5	Patrese	Williams-Renault	53	1h 19m 23.2s	7
6	Nakajima	Tyrrell-Ford	52		14
7	Piquet	Benetton-Ford	52		9
8	Nannini	Benetton-Ford	52		8
9	Caffi	Arrows-Ford	51		21
10	de Cesaris	Dallara-Ford	51		25
11	Larini	Ligier-Ford	51		26
12	Alboreto	Arrows-Ford	50	spun	22
13	Alliot	Ligier-Ford	50		20
	Dalmas	AGS-Ford	45		24
	Capelli	Leyton House-Judd	35	fuel pump	16
	Suzuki	Lola-Lamborghini	36	electrical	18
	Grouillard	Osella-Ford	27	wheel bearing	23
	Gugelmin	Leyton House-Judd	24	engine	10
	Modena	Brabham-Judd	21	valve	17
	Boutsen	Williams-Renault	18	suspension	6
	Warwick	Lotus-Lamborghini	15	clutch	12
	Pirro	Dallara-Ford	14	gearbox	19
	Donnelly	Lotus-Lamborghini	13	engine	11
	Bernard	Lola-Lamborghini	10	gearbox	13
	Martini	Minardi-Ford	7	suspension	15
	Alesi	Tyrrell-Ford	4	spun	5

Fastest Lap: Senna, 1m 26.25s. 150.42 mph/242.08 kph

Portuguese Grand Prix: Estoril, 23 September 1990

61 laps of 2.7 mile/4.35 km circuit

Place	Driver	Car	Laps	Time/reason for retiring	Grid
1	Mansell	Ferrari	61	1h 22m 11s	1
2	Senna	McLaren-Honda	61	1h 22m 13.8s	3
3	Prost	Ferrari	61	1h 22m 15.2s	2
4	Berger	McLaren-Honda	61	1h 22m 16.9s	4
5	Piquet	Benetton-Ford	61	1h 23m 08.4s	6
6	Nannini	Benetton-Ford	61	1h 23m 09.3s	9
7	Patrese	Williams-Renault	60		5
8	Alesi	Tyrrell-Ford	60		8
9	Alboreto	Arrows-Ford	60		19
10	Larini	Ligier-Ford	59		22
11	Martini	Minardi-Ford	59		16
12	Gugelmin	Leyton House-Judd	59		14
13	Caffi	Arrows-Ford	58	accident	17
14	Suzuki	Lola-Lamborghini	58	accident	11
15	Pirro	Dallara-Ford	58		13
	Alliot	Ligier-Ford	52	accident	20
	D Brabham	Brabham-Judd	52	gearbox	25
	Capelli	Leyton House-Judd	51	engine	12
	Boutsen	Williams-Renault	30	gearbox	7
	Bernard	Lola-Lamborghini	24	gearbox	10
	Modena	Brabham-Judd	21	gearbox	23
	Donnelly	Lotus-Lamborghini	14	alternator	15
	Warwick	Lotus-Lamborghini	5	throttle	21
	Dalmas	AGS-Ford	3	drive-shaft	24
	de Cesaris	Dallara-Ford	0	throttle	18

Fastest Lap: Patrese, 1m 18.31s. 124.26 mph/199.93 kph

Spanish Grand Prix: Jerez, 30 September 1990

73 laps of 2.62 mile/4.22 km circuit

Place	Driver	Car	Laps	Time/reason for retiring	Grid
1	Prost	Ferrari	73	1h 48m 01.5s	2
2	Mansell	Ferrari	73	1h 48m 23.5s	3
3	Nannini	Benetton-Ford	73	1h 48m 36.3s	9
4	Boutsen	Williams-Renault	73	1h 48m 44.8s	7
5	Patrese	Williams-Renault	73	1h 48m 58.9s	6
6	Suzuki	Lola-Lamborghini	73	1h 49m 05.2s	15
7	Larini	Ligier-Ford	72		20
8	Gugelmin	Leyton House-Judd	72		12
9	Dalmas	AGS-Ford	72		23
10	Alboreto	Arrows-Ford	71		25
	Warwick	Lotus-Lamborghini	63	gearbox	10
	Capelli	Leyton House-Judd	59	driver	19

Spanish Grand Prix (cont)

Place	Driver	Car	Laps	Time/reason for retiring	Grid
	Berger	McLaren-Honda	56	accident	5
	Senna	McLaren-Honda	53	engine	1
	Piquet	Benetton-Ford	47	alternator	8
	de Cesaris	Dallara-Ford	47	engine	17
	Grouillard	Osella-Ford	45	wheel	21
	Martini	Minardi-Ford	41	wheel	11
	Alliot	Ligier-Ford	22	spun	13
	Bernard	Lola-Lamborghini	20	clutch	18
	Nakajima	Tyrrell-Ford	13	spun	14
	Tarquini	AGS-Ford	5	accident	22
	Modena	Brabham-Judd	5	spun	24
	Pirro	Dallara-Ford	0	throttle	16
	Alesi	Tyrrell-Ford	0	spun	4

Fastest Lap: Patrese, 1m 24.51s. 111.64 mph/179.63 kph

Japanese Grand Prix: Suzuka, 21 October 1990

53 laps of 3.64 mile/5.86 km circuit

Place	Driver	Car	Laps	Time/reason for retiring	Grid
1	Piquet	Benetton-Ford	53	1h 34m 36.8s	6
2	Moreno	Benetton-Ford	53	1h 34m 44.0s	8
3	Suzuki	Lola-Lamborghini	53	1h 34m 59.3s	9
4	Patrese	Williams-Renault	53	1h 35m 13.1s	7
5	Boutsen	Williams-Renault	53	1h 35m 23.7s	5
6	Nakajima	Tyrrell-Ford	53	1h 35m 49.2s	13
7	Larini	Ligier-Ford	52		17
8	Martini	Minardi-Ford	52		10
9	Caffi	Arrows-Ford	52		23
10	Alliot	Ligier-Ford	52		20
	Warwick	Lotus-Lamborghini	38	gearbox	11
	Herbert	Lotus-Lamborghini	31	engine	14
	Alboreto	Arrows-Ford	28	engine	24
	Mansell	Ferrari	26	drive-shaft	3
	Pirro	Dallara-Ford	24	alternator	18
	Bernard	Lola-Lamborghini	24	oil leak	16
	Morbidelli	Minardi-Ford	18	spun	19
	Capelli	Leyton House-Judd	16	misfire	12
	de Cesaris	Dallara-Ford	13	spun	25
	Gugelmin	Leyton House-Judd	5	engine	15
	D Brabham	Brabham-Judd	2	suspension	22
	Berger	McLaren-Honda	1	spun	4
	Modena	Brabham-Judd	0	accident	21
	Prost	Ferrari	0	accident	2
	Senna	McLaren-Honda	0	accident	1

Fastest Lap: Patrese, 1m 44.23s. 125.74 mph/202.31 kph

Australian Grand Prix: Adelaide, 4 November 1990

81 laps of 2.35 mile/3.78 km circuit

Place	Driver	Car	Laps	Time/reason for retiring	Grid
1	Piquet	Benetton-Ford	81	1h 49m 44.6s	7
2	Mansell	Ferrari	81	1h 49m 47.7s	3
3	Prost	Ferrari	81	1h 50m 21.8s	4
4	Berger	McLaren-Honda	81	1h 50m 31.4s	2
5	Boutsen	Williams-Renault	81	1h 51m 35.7s	9
6	Patrese	Williams-Renault	80		6
7	Moreno	Benetton-Ford	80		8
8	Alesi	Tyrrell-Ford	80		5
9	Martini	Minardi-Ford	79		10
10	Larini	Ligier-Ford	79		12
11	Alliot	Ligier-Ford	78		19
12	Modena	Brabham-Judd	77		17
13	Grouillard	Osella-Ford	74		22
	Pirro	Dallara-Ford	68	engine	21
	Senna	McLaren-Honda	61	accident	1
	Tarquini	AGS-Ford	58	oil fire	26
	Herbert	Lotus-Lamborghini	57	stalled	18
	Nakajima	Tyrrell-Ford	53	spun	13
	Capelli	Leyton House-Judd	46	throttle	14
	Warwick	Lotus-Lamborghini	43	gearbox	11
	Gugelmin	Leyton House-Judd	27	brakes	16
	de Cesaris	Dallara-Ford	23	electrical	15
	Bernard	Lola-Lamborghini	21	gearbox	23
	Morbidelli	Minardi-Ford	20	gearbox	20
	D Brabham	Brabham-Judd	18	spun	25
	Suzuki	Lola-Lamborghini	6	differential	24

Fastest Lap: Mansell, 1m 18.2s. 108.12 mph/173.97 kph

World Championship 1990

1	Senna	78
2	Prost	71
3	Piquet	43
4	Berger	40
5	Mansell	37
6	Boutsen	34
7	Patrese	23
8	Nannini	21
9	Alesi	13
10 =	Capelli, Moreno, Suzuki	6
13	Bernard	5
14 =	Nakajima, Warwick	3
16 =	Caffi, Modena	2
18	Gugelmin	1

Constructors' Championship

1	McLaren-Honda	121
2	Ferrari	110
3	Benetton-Ford	71
4	Williams-Renault	57
5	Tyrrell-Ford	16
6	Lola-Lamborghini	11
7	Leyton House-Judd	7
8	Lotus-Lamborghini	3
9 =	Arrows-Ford, Brabham-Judd	2

1991

The Williams team offered effective opposition to Ayrton Senna and McLaren, but Nigel Mansell's title challenge was frustrated by last lap problems in Canada which dropped him from first to sixth, and by a botched tyre change leading to eventual disqualification in Portugal. Piquet became the second driver after Patrese to compete in 200 grand prix. Arrows became Footwork and Osella became Fondmetal, while new team Jordan came sixth in the Constructors' Championship in their first season.

United States Grand Prix: Phoenix, 10 March 1991

81 laps of 2.32 mile/3.72 km circuit

Place	Driver	Car	Laps	Time/reason for retiring	Grid
1	Senna	McLaren-Honda	81	2h 00m 47.626s	1
2	Prost	Ferrari	81	2h 01m 04.150s	2
3	Piquet	Benetton-Ford	81	2h 01m 05.204s	5
4	Modena	Tyrrell-Honda	81		11
5	Nakajima	Tyrrell-Honda	80		16
6	Suzuki	Lola-Ford	79		21
7	Larini	Lamborghini	78		17
7	Tarquini	AGS-Ford	77		22
9	Martini	Mindardi-Ferrari	75		15
10	Gachot	Jordan-Ford	75		14
11	Brundle	Brabham-Yamaha	73		12
12	Alesi	Ferrari	72		6
	Hakkinen	Lotus-Judd	60	engine	13
	Patrese	Williams-Renault	50	accident	3
	Moreno	Benetton-Ford	50	accident	8
	Alboreto	Footwork-Porsche	42	gearbox	25
	Capelli	Leyton House-Ilmor	41	gearbox	18
	Boutsen	Ligier-Lamborghini	41	electrical	20
	Berger	McLaren-Honda	37	fuel pressure	7
	Mansell	Williams-Renault	36	gearbox	4
	Gugelmin	Leyton House-Ilmor	45	gearbox	23
	Blundell	Brabham-Yamaha	35	accident	24
	Pirro	Dallara-Judd	17	gearbox	9
	Morbidelli	Minardi-Ferrari	16	gearbox	26
	Lehto	Dallara-Judd	13	clutch	10
	Bernard	Lola-Ford	5	engine	19

Fastest Lap: Alesi 1m 36.758s. 95.936 mph/154.5 kph

1991

Brazilian Grand Prix: Interlagos, 24 March 1991

71 laps of 2.69 mile/4.33 km circuit

Place	Driver	Car	Laps	Time/reason for retiring	Grid
1	Senna	McLaren-Honda	71	1h 38m 28.128s	1
2	Patrese	Williams-Renault	71	1h 38m 31.119s	2
3	Berger	McLaren-Honda	71	1h 38m 33.544s	4
4	Prost	Ferrari	71	1h 38m 47.497s	6
5	Piquet	Benetton-Ford	71	1h 38m 50.088s	7
6	Alesi	Ferrari	71	1h 38m 51.769s	5
7	Moreno	Benetton-Ford	70		14
8	Morbidelli	Minardi-Ferrari	69		20
9	Hakkinen	Lotus-Judd	68		21
10	Boutsen	Ligier-Lamborghini	68		17
11	Pirro	Dallara-Judd	68		12
12	Brundle	Brabham-Yamaha	67		25
13	Gachot	Jordan-Ford	63	fuel	10
	Mansell	Williams-Renault	59	gearbox	3
	Comas	Ligier-Lamborghini	50	engine	22
	Martini	Minardi-Ferrari	47	spun	19
	Blundell	Brabham-Yamaha	34	engine	24
	Bernard	Lola-Ford	33	clutch	11
	Lehto	Dallara-Judd	22	alternator	18
	de Cesaris	Jordan-Ford	20	accident	13
	Modena	Tyrrell-Honda	19	gear change	9
	Capelli	Leyton House-Ilmor	16	engine	15
	Nakajima	Tyrrell-Honda	12	accident	16
	Gugelmin	Leyton House-Ilmor	9	driver	8
	Tarquini	AGS Ford	0	accident	23

Fastest Lap: Mansell, 1m 20.44s. 120.28 mph/193.65 kph

San Marino Grand Prix: Imola, 28 April 1991

61 laps of 3.13 mile/5.04 km circuit

Place	Driver	Car	Laps	Time/reason for retiring	Grid
1	Senna	McLaren-Honda	61	1h 35m 14.750s	1
2	Berger	McLaren-Honda	61	1h 35m 16.425s	4
3	Lehto	Dallara-Judd	60		15
4	Martini	Minardi-Ferrari	59		8
5	Hakkinen	Lotus-Judd	58		24
6	Bailey	Lotus-Judd	58		25
7	Boutsen	Ligier-Lamborghini	58		23
8	Blundell	Brabham-Yamaha	58		22
9	Van de Poele	Lamborghini	57	engine	20
10	Comas	Ligier-Lamborghini	57		18
11	Brundle	Brabham-Yamaha	57		17

San Marino Grand Prix (cont)

Place	Driver	Car	Laps	Time/reason for retiring	Grid
12	Gugelmin	Leyton House-Ilmor	55	engine	14
13	Moreno	Benetton-Ford	54	engine	12
	Modena	Tyrrell-Honda	41	transmission	5
	de Cesaris	Jordan-Ford	37	gear linkage	10
	Gachot	Jordan-Ford	37	suspension	11
	Capelli	Leyton House-Ilmor	24	tyre	21
	Bernard	Lola-Ford	17	engine	16
	Patrese	Williams-Renault	17	engine	2
	Nakajima	Tyrrell-Honda	15	transmission	9
	Morbidelli	Minardi-Ferrari	10	gearbox	7
	Alesi	Ferrari	2	spun	6
	Suzuki	Lola-Ford	2	spun	19
	Piquet	Benetton-Ford	1	spun	13
	Mansell	Williams-Renault	0	accident	3

Fastest Lap: Berger, 1m 26.53s. 130.29 mph/209.77 kph
* Prost, 3rd on grid, spun off on warming-up lap and did not start.

Monaco Grand Prix: Monte Carlo, 12 May 1991

78 laps of 2.06 mile/3.31 km circuit

Place	Driver	Car	Laps	Time/reason for retiring	Grid
1	Senna	McLaren-Honda	78	1h 53m 02.344s	1
2	Mansell	Williams-Renault	78	1h 53m 20.682s	5
3	Alesi	Ferrari	78	1h 53m 49.789s	9
4	Moreno	Benetton-Ford	77		8
5	Prost	Ferrari	77		7
6	Pirro	Dallara-Judd	77		12
7	Boutsen	Ligier-Lamborghini	76		16
8	Gachot	Jordan-Ford	76		24
9	Bernard	Lola-Ford	76		21
10	Comas	Ligier-Lamborghini	76		23
11	Lehto	Dallara-Judd	75		13
12	Martini	Minardi-Ferrari	72		14
	Hakkinen	Lotus-Ford	64	fire	26
	Morbidelli	Minardi-Ferrari	49	gearbox	17
	Gugelmin	Leyton House-Ilmor	43	throttle	15
	Modena	Tyrrell-Honda	42	engine	2
	Patrese	Williams-Renault	42	accident	3
	Blundell	Brabham-Yamaha	41	accident	22
	Alboreto	Footwork-Porsche	39	engine	25
	Nakajima	Tyrrell-Honda	35	accident	11
	Suzuki	Lola-Ford	24	brakes	19
	de Cesaris	Jordan-Ford	21	throttle	10
	Capelli	Leyton House-Ilmor	12	brakes	18

Monaco Grand Prix (cont)

Place	Driver	Car	Laps	Time/reason for retiring	Grid
	Tarquini	AGS-Ford	9	gearbox	20
	Berger	McLaren-Honda	9	accident	6
	Piquet	Benetton-Ford	0	accident	4

Fastest Lap: Prost, 1m 24.37s, 88.24 mph/142.07 kph

Canadian Grand Prix: Montreal, 2 June 1991

69 laps of 2.75 mile/4.43 km circuit

Place	Driver	Car	Laps	Time/reason for retiring	Grid
1	Piquet	Benetton-Ford	69	1h 38m 51.490s	8
2	Modena	Tyrrell-Ford	69	1h 39m 23.322s	9
3	Patrese	Williams-Renault	69	1h 39m 33.707s	1
4	de Cesaris	Jordan-Ford	69	1h 40m 11.700s	11
5	Gachot	Jordan-Ford	69	1h 40m 13.841s	14
6	Mansell	Williams-Renault	68	gearbox	2
7	Martini	Minardi-Ferrari	68		18
8	Comas	Ligier-Lamborghini	68		26
9	Pirro	Dallara-Judd	68		10
10	Nakajima	Tyrrell-Ford	67		12
	Gugelmin	Leyton House-Ilmor	61	engine	23
	Lehto	Dallara-Judd	50	engine	17
	Johansson	Footwork-Porsche	48	brakes	25
	Capelli	Leyton House-Ilmor	42	engine	13
	Alesi	Ferrari	34	engine	7
	Bernard	Lola-Ford	29	transmission	19
	Prost	Ferrari	27	gearbox	4
	Boutsen	Ligier-Lamborghini	27	engine	16
	Senna	McLaren-Honda	25	electrical	3
	Hakkinen	Lotus-Judd	21	spun	24
	Brundle	Brabham-Yamaha	21	engine	20
	Morbidelli	Minardi-Ferrari	20	spun	15
	Moreno	Benetton-Ford	10	accident	5
	Berger	McLaren-Honda	4	electrical	6
	Suzuki	Lola-Ford	3	fire	22
	Alboreto	Footwork-Porsche	2	throttle	21

Fastest Lap: Mansell, 1m 22.39s. 120.28 mph/193.65 kph

Mexican Grand Prix: Mexico City, 16 June 1991

67 laps of 2.75 mile/4.42 km circuit

Place	Driver	Car	Laps	Time/reason for retiring	Grid
1	Patrese	Williams-Renault	67	1h 29m 23.322s	1
2	Mansell	Williams-Renault	67	1h 29m 53.541s	2
3	Senna	McLaren-Honda	67	1h 30m 49.561s	3
4	de Cesaris	Jordan-Ford	66		11
5	Moreno	Benetton-Ford	66		9
6	Bernard	Lola-Ford	66		18
7	Morbidelli	Minardi-Ferrari	66		23
8	Boutsen	Ligier-Lamborghini	65		14
9	Hakkinen	Lotus-Judd	65		24
10	Herbert	Lotus-Judd	65		25
11	Modena	Tyrrell-Honda	64		8
12	Nakajima	Tyrrell-Honda	64		13
	Blundell	Brabham-Yamaha	54	engine	12
	Gachot	Jordan-Ford	51	spun	20
	Suzuki	Lola-Ford	48	gearbox	19
	Piquet	Benetton-Ford	44	wheel-bearing	6
	Alesi	Ferrari	42	clutch	4
	Lehto	Dallara-Judd	30	engine	16
	Alboreto	Footwork-Porsche	24	oil pressure	26
	Brundle	Brabham-Yamaha	20	lost wheel	17
	Capelli	Leyton House-Ilmor	19	engine	22
	Prost	Ferrari	16	misfire	7
	Gugelmin	Leyton House-Ilmor	61	engine	21
	Grouillard	Fondmetal-Ford	13	oil leak	10
	Berger	McLaren-Honda	5	engine	5
	Martini	Minardi-Ferrari	4	accident	15

Fastest Lap: Mansell, 1m 16.79s. 128.79 mph/207.35 kph

French Grand Prix: Magny-Cours, 7 July 1991

72 laps of 2.65 mile/4.27 km circuit

Place	Driver	Car	Laps	Time/reason for retiring	Grid
1	Mansell	Williams-Renault	72	1h 38m 00.056s	4
2	Prost	Ferrari	72	1h 38m 05.059s	2
3	Senna	McLaren-Honda	72	1h 38m 34.990s	3
4	Alesi	Ferrari	72	1h 38m 35.976s	6
5	Patrese	Williams-Renault	71		1
6	de Cesaris	Jordan-Ford	71		12
7	Gugelmin	Leyton House-Ilmor	70		9
8	Piquet	Benetton-Ford	70		7
9	Martini	Minadardi-Ferrari	70		12
10	Herbert	Lotus-Judd	70		20

French Grand Prix (cont)

Place	Driver	Car	Laps	Time/reason for retiring	Grid
11	Comas	Ligier-Lamborghini	70		14
12	Boutsen	Ligier-Lamborghini	69		16
	Moreno	Benetton-Ford	63	driver	8
	Modena	Tyrrell-Honda	57	gearbox	11
	Grouillard	Fondmetal-Ford	47	oil leak	21
	Bernard	Lola-Ford	43	transmission	23
	Lehto	Dallara-Judd	39	tyre	26
	Blundell	Brabham-Yamaha	36	accident	17
	Suzuki	Lola-Ford	32	transmission	22
	Alboreto	Footwork-Porsche	31	gearbox	25
	Brundle	Brabham-Yamaha	21 ·	gearbox	24
	Nakajima	Tyrrell-Honda	12	spun	18
	Morbidelli	Minardi-Ferrari	8	accident	10
	Capelli	Leyton House-Ilmor	7	spun	15
	Berger	McLaren-Honda	6	engine	5
	Gachot	Jordan-Ford	0	accident	19

Fastest Lap: Mansell, 1m 19.17s 120.68 mph/195.1 kph

British Grand Prix: Silverstone, 14 July 1991

59 laps of 3.25 mile/5.23 km circuit

Place	Driver	Car	Laps	Time/reason for retiring	Grid
1	Mansell	Williams-Renault	59	1h 27m 35.479s	1
2	Berger	McLaren-Honda	59	1h 28m 17.772s	4
3	Prost	Ferrari	59	1h 28m 35.629s	5
4	Senna	McLaren-Honda	58	fuel pressure	2
5	Piquet	Benetton-Ford	58		8
6	Gachot	Jordan-Ford	58		17
7	Modena	Tyrrell-Honda	58		10
8	Nakajima	Tyrrell-Honda	58		15
9	Martini	Minardi-Ferrari	58		23
10 ·	Pirro	Dallara-Judd	57		18
11	Morbidelli	Minardi-Ferrari	57		20
12	Hakkinen	Lotus-Judd	57		25
13	Lehto	Dallara-Judd	· 56		11
14	Herbert	Lotus-Judd	55		24
	Blundell	Brabham-Yamaha	52	engine	12
	de Cesaris	Jordan-Ford	41	accident	13
	Alesi	Ferrari	31	accident	6
	Suzuki	Lola-Ford	29	accident	22
	Boutsen	Ligier-Lamborghini	29	engine	19
	Brundle	Brabham-Yamaha	28	throttle	14
	Alboreto	Footwork-Ford	25	gearbox	26
	Gugelmin	Leyton House-Ilmor	24	driver	9
	Moreno	Benetton-Ford	21	gearbox	7

British Grand Prix (cont)

Place	Driver	Car	Laps	Time/reason for retiring	Grid
	Bernard	Lola-Ford	21	crownwheel and pinion	21
	Capelli	Leyton House-Ilmor	16	spun	16
	Patrese	Williams-Renault	0	accident	3

Fastest Lap: Mansell, 1m 26.38s. 135.25 mph/217.75 kph

German Grand Prix: Hockenheim, 28 July 1991

45 laps of 4.22 mile/6.8 km circuit

Place	Driver	Car	Laps	Time/reason for retiring	Grid
1	Mansell	Williams-Renault	45	1h 19m 29.661s	1
2	Patrese	Williams-Renault	45	1h 19m 43.440s	4
3	Alesi	Ferrari	45	1h 19m 47.279s	6
4	Berger	McLaren-Honda	45	1h 20m 02.312s	3
5	de Cesaris	Jordan-Ford	45	1h 20m 47.198s	7
6	Gachot	Jordan-Ford	45	1h 21m 10.226s	11
7	Senna	McLaren-Honda	44	fuel	2
8	Moreno	Benetton-Ford	44		9
9	Boutsen	Ligier-Lamborghini	44		17
10	Pirro	Dallara-Judd	44		18
11	Brundle	Brabham-Yamaha	43		15
12	Blundell	Brabham-Yamaha	43		21
13	Modena	Tyrrell-Honda	41		14
	Prost	Ferrari	37	accident	5
	Capelli	Leyton House-Ilmor	36	misfire	12
	Lehto	Dallara-Judd	35	engine	20
	Piquet	Benetton-Ford	27	gearbox	8
	Nakajima	Tyrrell-Honda	26	gearbox	13
	Comas	Ligier-Lamborghini	22	engine	26
	Gugelmin	Leyton House-Ilmor	21	gearbox	16
	Hakkinen	Lotus-Judd	19	engine	23
	Suzuki	Lola-Ford	15	engine	22
	Morbidelli	Minardi-Ferrari	14	differential	19
	Martini	Minardi-Ferrari	11	engine	10
	Bernard	Lola-Ford	9	crownwheel and pinion	25
	Larini	Lamborghini	0	spun	24

Fastest Lap: Patrese, 1m 43.57s. 146.91 mph/236.52 kph

1991

Hungarian Grand Prix: Hungaroring, 11 August 1991

77 laps of 2.47 mile/3.97 km circuit

Place	Driver	Car	Laps	Time/reason for retiring	Grid
1	Senna	McLaren-Honda	77	1h 49m 12.796s	1
2	Mansell	Williams-Renault	77	1h 49m 17.395s	3
3	Patrese	Williams-Renault	77	1h 49m 28.390s	2
4	Berger	McLaren-Honda	77	1h 49m 34.652s	5
5	Alesi	Ferrari	77	1h 49m 44.185s	6
6	Capelli	Leyton House-Ilmor	76		9
7	de Cesaris	Jordan-Ford	76		17
8	Moreno	Benetton-Ford	76		15
9	Gachot	Jordan-Ford	75		16
10	Comas	Ligier-Lamborghini	75		25
11	Gugelmin	Leyton House-Ilmor	75		13
12	Modena	Tyrrell-Ford	75		8
13	Morbidelli	Minardi-Ferrari	75		23
14	Hakkinen	Lotus-Judd	74		26
15	Nakajima	Tyrrell-Honda	74		14
16	Larini	Lamborghini	74		24
17	Boutsen	Ligier-Lamborghini	71	engine	19
	Martini	Minardi-Ferrari	65	engine	18
	Blundell	Brabham-Yamaha	62	spun	20
	Brundle	Brabham-Yamaha	59	driver	10
	Lehto	Dallara-Judd	49	oil pressure	12
	Piquet	Benetton-Ford	38	gearbox	11
	Bernard	Lola-Ford	38	electrical	21
	Suzuki	Lola-Ford	38	electrical	22
	Pirro	Dallara-Judd	37	oil pressure	7
	Prost	Ferrari	28	engine	4

Fastest Lap: Gachot, 1m 21.55s. 108.85 mph/174.81 kph

Belgian Grand Prix: Spa, 25 August 1991

44 laps of 4.31 mile/6.94 km circuit

Place	Driver	Car	Laps	Time/reason for retiring	Grid
1	Senna	McLaren-Honda	44	1h 49m 12.796s	1
2	Berger	McLaren-Honda	44	1h 49m 34.652s	4
3	Piquet	Benetton-Ford	44	1h 27m 49.845s	6
4	Moreno	Benetton-Ford	44	1h 27m 54.979s	8
5	Patrese	Williams-Renault	44	1h 28m 14.856s	17
6	Blundell	Brabham-Yamaha	44	1h 28m 57.704s	13
7	Herbert	Lotus-Judd	44	1h 29m 02.268s	21
8	Pirro	Dallara-Judd	43		25
9	Brundle	Brabham-Yamaha	43		16
10	Grouillard	Fondmetal-Ford	43		23
11	Boutsen	Ligier-Lamborghini	43		18

Belgian Grand Prix (cont)

Place	Driver	Car	Laps	Time/reason for retiring	Grid
12	Martini	Minardi-Ferrari	42		9
13	de Cesaris	Jordan-Ford	41	engine	11
	Modena	Tyrrell-Honda	33	oil fire	10
	Lehto	Dallara-Judd	33	engine	14
	Alesi	Ferrari	30	engine	5
	Morbidelli	Minardi-Ferrari	29	clutch	19
	Hakkinen	Lotus-Judd	25	engine	24
	Comas	Ligier-Lamborghini	25	crankshaft	26
	Mansell	Williams-Renault	22	electrical	3
	Bernard	Lola-Ford	21	engine	20
	Capelli	Leyton House-Ilmor	13	engine	12
	Nakajima	Tyrrell-Honda	7	accident	22
	Prost	Ferrari	2	engine	2
	Gugelmin	Leyton House-Ilmor	1	engine	15
	M Schumacher	Jordan-Ford	0	clutch	7

Fastest Lap: Moreno, 1m 55.16s. 134.81 mph/217.08 kph

Italian Grand Prix: Monza, 8 September 1991

52 laps of 3.6 mile/5.8 km circuit

Place	Driver	Car	Laps	Time/reason for retiring	Grid
1	Mansell	Williams-Renault	53	1h 17m 54.319s	2
2	Senna	McLaren-Honda	53	1h 18m 10.581s	1
3	Prost	Ferrari	53	1h 18m 11.148s	5
4	Berger	McLaren-Honda	53	1h 18m 22.038s	3
5	M Schumacher	Benetton-Ford	53	1h 18m 28.782s	7
6	Piquet	Benetton-Ford	53	1h 18m 39.919s	8
7	de Cesaris	Jordan-Ford	53	1h 18m 45.455s	14
8	Capelli	Leyton House-Ilmor	53	1h 19m 09.338s	12
9	Morbidelli	Minardi-Ferrari	52		17
10	Pirro	Dallara-Judd	52		16
11	Comas	Ligier-Lamborghini	52		22
12	Blundell	Brabham-Yamaha	52		11
13	Brundle	Brabham-Yamaha	52		19
14	Hakkinen	Lotus-Judd	49		25
15	Gugelmin	Leyton House-Ilmor	49		18
16	Larini	Lamborghini	48		23
	Grouillard	Fondmetal-Ford	46	engine	14
	Lehto	Dallara-Judd	35	suspension	20
	Modena	Tyrrell-Ford	32	engine	13
	Alesi	Ferrari	29	engine	6
	Patrese	Williams-Renault	27	gearbox	4
	Nakajima	Tyrrell-Honda	24	throttle	15
	Bernard	Lola-Ford	21	engine	24

Italian Grand Prix (cont)

Place	Driver	Car	Laps	Time/reason for retiring	Grid
	Martini	Minardi-Ferrari	8	spun	10
	Moreno	Jordan-Ford	2	spun	9
	Boutsen	Ligier-Lamborghini	1	spun	21

Fastest Lap: Senna, 1m 26.06s. 150.76 mph/242.72 kph

Portuguese Grand Prix: Estoril, 22 September 1991

71 laps of 2.7 miles/4.35 km circuit

Place	Driver	Car	Laps	Time/reason for retiring	Grid
1	Patrese	Williams-Renault	71	1h 35m 42.304s	1
2	Senna	McLaren-Honda	71	1h 36m 03.245s	3
3	Alesi	Ferrari	71	1h 36m 35.858s	6
4	Martini	Minardi-Ferrari	71	1h 36m 45.802s	8
5	Piquet	Benetton-Ford	71	1h 36m 52.337s	11
6	M Schumacher	Benetton-Ford	71	1h 36m 58.886s	10
7	Gugelmin	Leyton House-Ilmor	70		7
8	de Cesaris	Jordan-Ford	70		14
9	Morbidelli	Minardi-Ferrari	70		13
10	Moreno	Jordan-Ford	70		16
11	Comas	Ligier-Lamborghini	70		23
12	Brundle	Brabham-Yamaha	69		19
13	Nakajima	Tyrrell-Honda	68		21
14	Hakkinen	Lotus-Judd	68		26
15	Alboreto	Footwork-Ford	68		24
16	Boutsen	Ligier-Lamborghini	68		20
17	Capelli	Leyton House-Ilmor	64	nose	9
	Modena	Tyrrell-Honda	56	engine	12
	Mansell	Williams-Renault	56	disqualified: illegal pit stop	4
	Suzuki	Lola-Ford	40	gearbox	25
	Prost	Ferrari	39	engine	5
	Berger	McLaren-Honda	37	engine	2
	Pirro	Dallara-Judd	18	engine	17
	Lehto	Dallara-Judd	14	gear lever	18
	Blundell	Brabham-Yamaha	12	suspension	15
	Herbert	Lotus-Judd	1	engine	22

Fastest Lap: Mansell, 1m 18.18s. 124.33 mph/200.17 kph

Spanish Grand Prix: Barcelona, 29 September 1991

65 laps of 2.95 mile/4.66 km circuit

Place	Driver	Car	Laps	Time/reason for retiring	Grid
1	Mansell	Williams-Renault	65	1h 38m 41.541s	2
2	Prost	Ferrari	65	1h 38m 52.872s	6
3	Patrese	Williams-Renault	65	1h 38m 57.450s	4
4	Alesi	Ferrari	65	1h 39m 04.313s	7
5	Senna	McLaren-Honda	65	1h 39m 43.943s	3
6	M Schumacher	Benetton-Ford	65	1h 40m 01.009s	5
7	Gugelmin	Leyton House-Ilmor	64		13
8	Lehto	Dallara-Judd	64		15
9	Zanardi	Jordan-Ford	64		20
10	Brundle	Brabham-Yamaha	63		11
11	Piquet	Benetton-Ford	63		10
12	Tarquini	Fondmetal-Ford	63		22
13	Martini	Minardi-Ferrari	63		19
14	Morbidelli	Minardi-Ferrari	62	accident	16
15	Pirro	Dallara-Judd	62		9
16	Modena	Tyrrell-Honda	62		14
17	Nakajima	Tyrrell-Honda	62		18
	Blundell	Brabham-Yamaha	49	engine	12
	Comas	Ligier-Lamborghini	36	engine	25
	Berger	McLaren-Honda	33	engine	1
	Alboreto	Footwork-Ford	23	engine	24
	de Cesaris	Jordan-Ford	22	electrical	17
	Hakkinen	Lotus-Judd	5	accident	21
	Capelli	Leyton House-Ilmor	1	accident	8
	Bernard	Lola-Ford	0	accident	23
	Boutsen	Ligier-Lamborghini	0	accident	26

Fastest Lap: Patrese, 1m 22.84s. 128.19 mph/206.39 kph

Japanese Grand Prix: Suzuka, 20 October 1991

53 laps of 3.64 mile/5.86 km circuit

Place	Driver	Car	Laps	Time/reason for retiring	Grid
1	Berger	McLaren-Honda	53	1h 32m 10.695s	1
2	Senna	McLaren-Honda	53	1h 32m 11.039s	2
3	Patrese	Williams-Renault	53	1h 33m 07.426s	5
4	Prost	Ferrari	53	1h 33m 31.456s	4
5	Brundle	Brabham-Yamaha	52		18
6	Modena	Tyrrell-Honda	52		13
7	Piquet	Benetton-Ford	52		26
8	Gugelmin	Leyton House-Ilmor	52		17
9	Boutsen	Ligier-Lamborghini	52		16
10	Caffi	Footwork-Ford	51		25

Japanese Grand Prix (cont)

Place	Driver	Car	Laps	Time/reason for retiring	Grid
11	Tarquini	Fondmetal-Ford	50		23
	Comas	Ligier-Lamborghini	41	engine	19
	Martini	Minardi-Ferrari	39	electrical	7
	M Schumacher	Benetton-Ford	34	engine	9
	Herbert	Lotus-Judd	31	engine	22
	Nakajima	Tyrrell-Honda	30	accident	14
	Suzuki	Lola-Ford	26	engine	24
	Morbidelli	Minardi-Ferrari	15	wheel bearing	8
	Mansell	Williams-Renault	9	accident	3
	Zanardi	Jordan-Ford	7	gearbox	12
	Hakkinen	Lotus-Judd	4	spun	20
	de Cesaris	Jordan-Ford	1	accident	10
	Lehto	Dallara-Judd	1	accident	11
	Pirro	Dallara-Judd	1	accident	15
	Wendlinger	Leyton House-Ilmor	1	accident	21
	Alesi	Ferrari	0	engine	6

Fastest Lap: Senna, 1m 41.532s. 129.195 mph/208.004 kph
* Piquet qualified 10 but started from the back of the grid due to repairs.

Australian Grand Prix: Adelaide, 3 November 1991

14 laps of 2.35 mile/3.78 km circuit

Place	Driver	Car	Laps	Time/reason for retiring	Grid
1	Senna	McLaren-Honda	14	24m 34.889s	1
2	Mansell	Williams-Renault	14	24m 36.158s	3
3	Berger	McLaren-Honda	14	24m 40.019s	2
4	Piquet	Benetton-Ford	14	25m 05.002s	5
5	Patrese	Williams-Renault	14	25m 25.436s	4
6	Morbidelli	Ferrari	14	25m 25.968s	8
7	Pirro	Dallara-Judd	14	25m 27.26s	13
8	de Cesaris	Jordan-Ford	14	25m 35.33s	12
9	Zanardi	Jordan-Ford	14	25m 50.466s	16
10	Modena	Tyrrell-Honda	14	25m 55.269s	9
11	Herbert	Lotus-Judd	14	25m 56.972s	21
12	Lehto	Dallara-Judd	14	26m 13.418s	11
13	Alboreto	Footwork-Ford	14	26m 14.202s	15
14	Gugelmin	Leyton House-Ilmor	13		14
15	Caffi	Footwork-Ford	13		23
16	Moreno	Minardi-Ferrari	13		18
17	Blundell	Brabham-Yamaha	13		17
18	Comas	Ligier-Lamborghini	13		22
19	Hakkinen	Lotus-Judd	13		25
20	Wendlinger	Leyton House-Ilmor	12		26
	Martini	Minardi-Ferrari	8	accident	10
	M Schumacher	Benetton-Ford	5	accident	6

Australian Grand Prix (cont)

Place	Driver	Car	Laps	Time/reason for retiring	Grid
	Alesi	Ferrari	5	accident	7
	Larini	Lamborghini	5	accident	19
	Boutsen	Ligier-Lamborghini	5	accident	20
	Nakajima	Tyrrell-Honda	4	accident	24

Fastest Lap: Gerhard Berger, 1m 41.141s. 83.602 mph/134.545 kph
* Race stopped early due to rain; half points awarded.

World Championship 1991

1	Senna	96
2	Mansell	72
3	Patrese	53
4	Berger	43
5	Prost	34
6	Piquet	26.5
7	Alesi	21
8	Modena	10
9	de Cesaris	9
10	Moreno	8
11	Martini	6
12=	Gachot, Lehto, M Schumacher	4
15=	Brundle, Hakkinen, Nakajima	2
18=	Bailey, Bernard, Blundell, Capelli, Pirro, Suzuki	1
24	Morbidelli	0.5

Constructors' Championship

1	McLaren-Honda	139
2	Williams-Renault	125
3	Ferrari	56.5
4	Benetton-Ford	38.5
5	Jordan-Ford	13
6	Tyrrell-Ford	12
7	Minardi-Ferrari	6
8	Dallara-Judd	5
9=	Lotus-Judd, Brabham-Yamaha	3
11	Lola-Ford	2
12	Leyton House-Ilmor	1

1992

In a brilliant performance Nigel Mansell established a new record total of wins in a season on his way to a richly deserved championship, but he was outflanked in murky contractual negotiations. Alain Prost, who had sat out of the 1992 season, took Mansell's place for 1993 and Mansell signed an Indycar contract. All this left a bad taste in the mouths of enthusiasts who were to be denied the opportunity of seeing Prost, Senna and Mansell compete against one another in 1993. Michael Schumacher's joy at his first win was a welcome reminder that motor racing still might have some pretensions to be called a sport. Leyton House reverted to the name March. Larrousse built their own cars, raced for this season as Venturis.

South African Grand Prix: Kyalami, 1 March 1992

72 laps of 2.66 mile/4.28 km circuit

Place	Driver	Car	Laps	Time/reason for retiring	Grid
1	Mansell	Williams-Renault	72	1h 36m 45.32s	1
2	Patrese	Williams-Renault	72	1h 37m 09.68s	4
3	Senna	McLaren-Honda	72	1h 37m 20s	2
4	M Schumacher	Benetton-Ford	72	1h 37m 33.18s	6
5	Berger	McLaren-Honda	72	1h 37m 58.95s	3
6	Herbert	Lotus-Ford	71		11
7	Comas	Ligier-Renault	71		13
8	Suzuki	Footwork-Mugen Honda	70		16
9	Hakkinen	Lotus-Ford	70		21
10	Alboreto	Footwork-Mugen Honda	70		17
11	Gugelmin	Jordan-Yamaha	70		23
12	Katayama	Larrousse-Lamborghini	68		18
13	Van de Poele	Brabham-Judd	68		26
	Grouillard	Tyrrell-Ilmor	62	clutch	12
	Boutsen	Ligier-Renault	60	engine	14
	Martini	Dallara-Ferrari	56	clutch	25
	Morbidelli	Minardi-Lamborghini	55	engine	19
	Lehto	Dallara-Ferrari	46	transmission	24
	C Fittipaldi	Minardi-Lamborghini	43	electrical	20
	de Cesaris	Tyrrell-Ilmor	41	engine	10
	Alesi	Ferrari	40	engine	5
	Capelli	Ferrari	28	engine	9
	Tarquini	Fondmetal-Ford	23	engine	15
	Wendlinger	March-Ilmor	13	overheating	7

South African Grand Prix (cont)

Place	Driver	Car	Laps	Time/reason for retiring	Grid
	Gachot	Larrousse-Lamborghini	8	suspension	22
	Brundle	Benetton-Ford	1	clutch	8

Fastest Lap: Mansell, 1m 17.58s. 123.576 mph/198.574 kph

Mexican Grand Prix: Mexico City, 22 March 1992

69 laps of 2.75 mile/4.42 km circuit

Place	Driver	Car	Laps	Time/reason for retiring	Grid
1	Mansell	Williams-Renault	69	1h 31m 53.59s	1
2	Patrese	Williams-Renault	69	1h 32m 06.56s	2
3	M Schumacher	Benetton-Ford	69	1h 32m 15.02s	3
4	Berger	McLaren-Honda	69	1h 32m 26.93s	5
5	de Cesaris	Tyrrell-Ilmor	68		11
6	Hakkinen	Lotus-Ford	68		18
7	Herbert	Lotus-Ford	68		12
8	Lehto	Dallara-Ferrari	68		7
9	Comas	Ligier-Renault	67		26
10	Boutsen	Ligier-Renault	67		22
11	Gachot	Larrousse-Lamborghini	66		13
12	Katayama	Larrousse-Lamborghini	66		24
13	Alboreto	Footwork-Mugen Honda	65		25
	Brundle	Benetton-Ford	47	overheating	4
	Tarquini	Fondmetal-Ford	45	clutch	14
	Chiesa	Fondmetal-Ford	37	spun	23
	Martini	Dallara-Ferrari	36	handling	9
	Alesi	Ferrari	31	engine	10
	Morbidelli	Minardi-Lamborghini	29	spun	21
	Modena	Jordan-Yamaha	17	gearbox	15
	Grouillard	Tyrrell-Ilmor	12	engine	16
	Senna	McLaren-Honda	11	transmission	6
	C Fittipaldi	Minardi-Lamborghini	2	spun	17
	Gugelmin	Jordan-Yamaha	0	engine	8
	Capelli	Ferrari	0	accident	20
	Wendlinger	March-Ilmor	0	accident	19

Fastest Lap: Berger, 1m 17.71s. 127.26 mph/204.761 kph

Brazilian Grand Prix: Interlagos, 5 April 1992

71 laps of 2.69 mile/4.33 km circuit

Place	Driver	Car	Laps	Time/reason for retiring	Grid
1	Mansell	Williams-Renault	71	1h 36m 51.86s	1
2	Patrese	Williams-Renault	71	1h 37m 21.19s	2

Brazilian Grand Prix (cont)

Place	Driver	Car	Laps	Time/reason for retiring	Grid
3	M Schumacher	Benetton-Ford	70		5
4	Alesi	Ferrari	70		6
5	Capelli	Ferrari	70		11
6	Alboreto	Footwork-Mugen Honda	70		14
7	Morbidelli	Minardi-Lamborghini	69		23
8	Lehto	Dallara-Ferrari	69		16
9	Katayama	Larrousse-Lamborghini	68		25
10	Hakkinen	Lotus-Ford	67		24
	Tarquini	Fondmetal-Ford	63	engine	19
	Wendlinger	March-Ilmor	56	clutch	9
	C Fittipaldi	Minardi-Lamborghini	55	gearbox	20
	Grouillard	Tyrrell-Ilmor	53	engine	17
	Comas	Ligier-Renault	43	engine	15
	Herbert	Lotus-Ford	37	accident	26
	Boutsen	Ligier-Renault	37	accident	10
	Gugelmin	Jordan-Yamaha	37	gearbox	21
	Brundle	Benetton-Ford	31	accident	7
	Martini	Dallara-Ferrari	25	clutch	8
	Gachot	Larrouse-Lamborghini	24	supension	18
	de Cesaris	Tyrrell-Ilmor	22	electrical	13
	Senna	McLaren-Honda	18	electrical	3
	Berger	McLaren-Honda	4	overheating	4
	Suzuki	Footwork-Mugen Honda	3	engine	22
	Modena	Jordan-Yamaha	1	gearbox	12

Fastest Lap: Patrese, 1m 19.49s. 121.71 mph/195.83 kph

Spanish Grand Prix: Barcelona, 3 May 1992

65 laps of 2.95 mile/4.66 km circuit

Place	Driver	Car	Laps	Time/reason for retiring	Grid
1	Mansell	Williams-Renault	65	1h 56m 10.67s	1
2	M Schumacher	Benetton-Ford	65	1h 56m 34.59s	2
3	Alesi	Ferrari	65	1h 56m 37.14s	8
4	Berger	McLaren-Honda	65	1h 57m 31.32s	
5	Alboreto	Footwork-Mugen Honda	64		16
6	Martini	Dallara-Ferrari	63		13
7	Suzuki	Footwork-Mugen Honda	63		19
8	Wendlinger	March-Ilmor	63		9
9	Senna	McLaren-Honda	62	spun	3
10	Capelli	Ferrari	62	spun	5
11	C Fittipaldi	Minardi-Lamborghini	61		22
12	Belmondo	March-Ilmor	61		23
	Lehto	Dallara-Ferrari	56	spun	12
	Tarquini	Fondmetal-Ford	56	spun	18
	Hakkinen	Lotus-Ford	56	spun	21

Spanish Grand Prix (cont)

Place	Driver	Car	Laps	Time/reason for retiring	Grid
	Comas	Ligier-Renault	55	spun	10
	Gachot	Larrousse-Lamborghini	35	engine	24
	Grouillard	Tyrrell-Ilmor	30	spun	15
	Morbidelli	Minardi-Lamborghini	26	handling	26
	Gugelmin	Jordan-Yamaha	24	spun	17
	Chiesa	Fondmetal-Ford	22	spun	20
	Patrese	Williams-Renault	20	spun	4
	Herbert	Lotus-Ford	13	spun	25
	Boutsen	Ligier-Renault	11	engine	14
	Brundle	Benetton-Ford	4	spun	6
	de Cesaris	Tyrrell-Ilmor	2	spun	11

Fastest Lap: Mansell, 1m 42.50s. 103.59 mph/166.68 kph

San Marino Grand Prix: Imola, 17 May 1992

60 laps of 3.13 mile/5.04 km circuit

Place	Driver	Car	Laps	Time/reason for retiring	Grid
1	Mansell	Williams-Renault	60	1h 28m 40.93s	1
2	Patrese	Williams-Renault	60	1h 28m 50.38s	2
3	Senna	McLaren-Honda	60	1h 29m 29.91s	3
4	Brundle	Benetton-Ford	60	1h 29m 33.93s	6
5	Alboreto	Footwork-Mugen Honda	59		9
6	Martini	Dallara-Ferrari	59		15
7	Gugelmin	Jordan-Yamaha	58		18
8	Grouillard	Tyrrell-Ilmor	58		20
9	Comas	Ligier-Renault	58		13
10	Suzuki	Footwork-Mugen Honda	58		11
11	Lehto	Dallara-Ferrari	57	overheating	16
12	Wendlinger	March-Ilmor	57		12
13	Belmondo	March-Ilmor	57		24
14	de Cesaris	Tyrrell-Ilmor	55	fuel pressure	14
	Katayama	Larrousse-Lamborghini	40	spun	17
	Alesi	Ferrari	39	accident	7
	Berger	McLaren-Honda	39	accident	4
	Gachot	Larrousse-Lamborghini	32	apun	19
	Boutsen	Ligier-Renault	29	engine	10
	Modena	Jordan-Yamaha	25	gearbox	23
	Morbidelli	Minardi-Lamborghini	24	transmission	21
	Tarquini	Fondmetal-Ford	24	overheating	22
	M Schumacher	Benetton-Ford	20	spun	5
	Capelli	Ferrari	11	spun	8
	C Fittipaldi	Minardi-Lamborghini	8	transmission	25
	Herbert	Lotus-Ford	8	gearbox	26

Fastest Lap: Patrese, 1m 26.1s. 130.94 mph/210.69 kph

1992

Monaco Grand Prix: Monte Carlo, 31 May 1992

78 laps of 2.06 mile/3.31 km circuit

Place	Driver	Car	Laps	Time/reason for retiring	Grid
1	Senna	McLaren-Honda	78	1h 50m 59.37s	3
2	Mansell	Williams-Renault	78	1h 50m 59.59s	1
3	Patrese	Williams-Renault	78	1h 51m 31.22s	2
4	M Schumacher	Benetton-Ford	78	1h 51m 38.67s	6
5	Brundle	Benetton-Ford	78	1h 52m 20.72s	7
6	Gachot	Larrousse-Lamborghini	77		15
7	Alboreto	Footwork-Mugen Honda	77		11
8	C Fittipaldi	Miniardi-Lamborghini	77		17
9	Lehto	Dallara-Ferrari	76		20
10	Comas	Ligier-Renault	76		23
11	Suzuki	Footwork-Mugen Honda	76		19
12	Boutsen	Ligier-Renault	75		22
	Capelli	Ferrari	60	accident	8
	Berger	McLaren-Honda	32	gearbox	5
	Hakkinen	Lotus-Ford	30	gearbox	14
	Alesi	Ferrari	28	electrical	4
	Gugelmin	Jordan-Yamaha	18	transmission	13
	Herbert	Lotus-Ford	17	accident	9
	Moreno	Andrea Moda-Judd	11	engine	26
	de Cesaris	Tyrrell-Ilmor	9	gearbox	10
	Tarquini	Fondmetal-Ford	9	engine	25
	Modena	Jordan-Yamaha	6	accident	21
	Grouillard	Tyrrell-Ilmor	4	transmission	24
	Wendlinger	March-Ilmor	1	gearbox	20
	Morbidelli	Minardi-Lamborghini	1	transmission	12
	Martini	Dallara-Ferrari	0	accident	18

Fastest Lap: Mansell, 1m 21.6s. 91.23 mph/146.8 kph

Canadian Grand Prix: Montreal, 14 June 1992

69 laps of 2.75 mile/4.43 km circuit

Place	Driver	Car	Laps	Time/reason for retiring	Grid
1	Berger	McLaren-Honda	69	1h 37m 08.3s	4
2	M Schumacher	Benetton-Ford	69	1h 37m 20.7s	5
3	Alesi	Ferrari	69	1h 38m 15.63s	8
4	Wendlinger	March-Ilmor	68		12
5	de Cesaris	Tyrrell-Ilmor	68		14
6	Comas	Ligier-Renault	68		22
7	Alboreto	Footwork-Mugen Honda	68		16
8	Martini	Dallara-Ferrari	68		15
9	Lehto	Dallara-Ferrari	68		23
10	Boutsen	Ligier-Renault	67		21

Canadian Grand Prix (cont)

Place	Driver	Car	Laps	Time/reason for retiring	Grid
11	Morbidelli	Minardi-Lamborghini	67		13
12	Grouillard	Tyrrell-Ilmor	67		26
13	C Fittipaldi	Minardi-Lamborghini	65	gearbox	25
14	Belmondo	March-Ilmor	64		20
	Katayama	Larrousse-Lamborghini	61	engine	11
	Brundle	Benetton-Ford	45	transmission	7
	Patrese	Williams-Renault	43	gearbox	2
	Senna	McLaren-Honda	37	electrical	1
	Modena	Jordan-Yamaha	36	transmission	17
	Hakkinen	Lotus-Ford	35	gearbox	10
	Herbert	Lotus-Ford	34	clutch	6
	Capelli	Ferrari	18	accident	9
	Mansell	Williams-Renault	14	accident	3
	Gugelmin	Jordan-Yamaha	14	transmission	24
	Gachot	Larrousse-Lamborghini	14	disqualified: push start	19
	Tarquini	Fondmetal-Ford	0	gearbox	18

Fastest Lap: Berger, 1m 22.33s. 120.37 mph/193.68 kph

French Grand Prix: Magny-Cours, 5 July 1992

69 laps of 2.65 mile/4.27 km circuit

Place	Driver	Car	Laps	Time/reason for retiring	Grid
1	Mansell	Williams-Renault	69	1h 38m 08.46s	1
2	Patrese	Williams-Renault	69	1h 38m 54.91s	2
3	Brundle	Benetton-Ford	69	1h 39m 21.04s	7
4	Hakkinen	Lotus-Ford	68		11
5	Comas	Ligier-Renault	68		10
6	Herbert	Lotus-Ford	68		12
7	Alboreto	Footwork-Mugen Honda	68		14
8	Morbidelli	Minardi-Lamborghini	68		16
9	Lehto	Dallara-Ferrari	67		17
10	Martini	Dallara-Ferrari	67		25
11	Grouillard	Tyrrell-Ilmor	67		22
	Alesi	Ferrari	61	engine	6
	de Cesaris	Tyrrell-Ilmor	51	spun	19
	Katayama	Larrousse-Lamborghini	49	engine	18
	Boutsen	Ligier-Renault	46	spun	9
	Capelli	Ferrari	38	electrical	8
	Wendlinger	March-Ilmor	33	gearbox	21
	Modena	Jordan-Yamaha	25	engine	20
	Suzuki	Footwork-Mugen Honda	20	spun	15
	M Schumacher	Benetton-Ford	17	accident	5
	Berger	McLaren-Honda	10	engine	4
	Tarquini	Fondmetal-Ford	6	throttle	23
	Gugelmin	Jordan-Yamaha	0	accident	24

French Grand Prix (cont)

Place	Driver	Car	Laps	Time/reason for retiring	Grid
	Gachot	Larrousse-Lamborghini	0	accident	13
	Chiesa	Fondmetal-Ford	0	accident	26
	Senna	McLaren-Honda	0	accident	3

Fastest Lap: Mansell, 1m 17.07s. 123.36 mph/198.49 kph

British Grand Prix: Silverstone, 12 July 1992

59 laps of 3.25 mile/5.23 km circuit

Place	Driver	Car	Laps	Time/reason for retiring	Grid
1	Mansell	Williams-Renault	59	1h 25m 42.99s	1
2	Patrese	Williams-Renault	59	1h 26m 22.09s	2
3	Brundle	Benetton-Ford	59	1h 26m 31.39s	6
4	M Schumacher	Benetton-Ford	59	1h 26m 36.26s	4
5	Berger	McLaren-Honda	59	1h 26m 38.79s	5
6	Hakkinen	Lotus-Ford	59	1h 27m 03.13s	9
7	Alboreto	Footwork-Mugen Honda	58		12
8	Comas	Ligier-Renault	58		10
9	Capelli	Ferrari	58		14
10	Boutsen	Ligier-Renault	57		13
11	Grouillard	Tyrrell-Ilmor	57		20
12	Suzuki	Footwork-Mugen Honda	57		17
13	Lehto	Dallara-Ferrari	57		19
14	Tarquini	Fondmetal-Ford	57		15
15	Martini	Dallara-Ferrari	56		22
16	D Hill	Brabham-Judd	55		26
17	Morbidelli	Minardi-Lamborghini	53	oil pressure	25
	Senna	McLaren-Honda	52	gearbox	3
	de Cesaris	Tyrrell-Ilmor	46	spun	18
	Alesi	Ferrari	43	fire extinguisher	8
	Modena	Jordan-Yamaha	43	engine	23
	Gugelmin	Jordan-Yamaha	37	engine	24
	Gachot	Larrousse-Lamborghini	32	wheel bearing	11
	Herbert	Lotus-Ford	31	gearbox	7
	Wendlinger	March-Ilmor	27	gearbox	21
	Katayama	Larrousse-Lamborghini	27	clutch	16

Fastest Lap: Mansell, 1m 22.54s. 141.63 mph/227.88 kph

German Grand Prix: Hockenheim, 26 July 1992

45 laps of 4.24 mile/6.82 km circuit

Place	Driver	Car	Laps	Time/reason for retiring	Grid
1	Mansell	Williams-Renault	45	1h 18m 22.03s	1
2	Senna	McLaren-Honda	45	1h 18m 26.53s	3
3	M Schumacher	Benetton-Ford	45	1h 18m 56.49s	6
4	Brundle	Benetton-Ford	45	1h 18m 58.99s	9
5	Alesi	Ferrari	45	1h 19m 34.64s	5
6	Comas	Ligier-Renault	45	1h 19m 58.53s	7
7	Boutsen	Ligier-Renault	45	1h 19m 59.21s	8
8	Patrese	Williams-Renault	44	spun	2
9	Alboreto	Footwork-Mugen Honda	44		17
10	Lehto	Dallara-Ferrari	44		21
11	Martini	Dallara-Ferrari	44		18
12	Morbidelli	Minardi-Lamborghini	44		26
13	Belmondo	March-Ilmor	44		22
14	Gachot	Larrousse-Lamborghini	44		25
15	Gugelmin	Jordan-Yamaha	43		23
16	Wendlinger	March-Ilmor	42		10
	Tarquini	Fondmetal-Ford	33	engine	19
	de Cesaris	Tyrrell-Ilmor	25	engine	20
	Herbert	Lotus-Ford	23	engine	11
	Capelli	Ferrari	21	engine	12
	Hakkinen	Lotus-Ford	21	engine	13
	Berger	McLaren-Honda	16	engine	4
	Grouillard	Tyrrell-Ilmor	8	engine	14
	Katayama	Larrousse-Lamborghini	8	spun	16
	Suzuki	Footwork-Mugen Honda	1	spun	15
	Zanardi	Minardi-Lamborghini	1	clutch	24

Fastest Lap: Patrese, 1m 41.59s. 150.06 mph/241.45 kph

Hungarian Grand Prix: Hungaroring, 16 August 1992

77 laps of 2.47 mile/3.97 km circuit

Place	Driver	Car	Laps	Time/reason for retiring	Grid
1	Senna	McLaren-Honda	77	1h 46m 19.22s	3
2	Mansell	Williams-Renault	77	1h 46m 59.36s	2
3	Berger	McLaren-Honda	77	1h 47m 10s	5
4	Hakkinen	Lotus-Ford	77	1h 47m 13.53s	16
5	Brundle	Benetton-Ford	77	1h 47m 16.71s	6
6	Capelli	Ferrari	76		10
7	Alboreto	Footwork-Mugen Honda	75		7
8	de Cesaris	Tyrrell-Ilmor	75		19
9	Belmondo	March-Ilmor	74		17
10	Gugelmin	Jordan-Yamaha	73		21
11	D Hill	Brabham-Judd	73		25

Hungarian Grand Prix (cont)

Place	Driver	Car	Laps	Time/reason for retiring	Grid
	M Schumacher	Benetton-Ford	63	accident	4
	Patrese	Williams-Renault	5	engine	1
	Martini	Dallara-Ferrari	40	gearbox	26
	Katayama	Larrousse-Lamborghini	35	engine	20
	Alesi	Ferrari	14	spun	9
	Gachot	Larrousse-Lamborghini	13	accident	15
	Suzuki	Footwork-Mugen Honda	13	accident	14
	Grouillard	Tyrrell-Ilmor	13	engine	22
	Wendlinger	March-Ilmor	13	accident	23
	Modena	Jordan-Yamaha	13	accident	24
	Van de Poele	Fondmetal-Ford	2	accident	18
	Tarquini	Fondmetal-Ford	0	accident	12
	Herbert	Lotus-Ford	0	accident	13
	Comas	Ligier-Renault	0	accident	8
	Boutsen	Ligier-Renault	0	accident	11

Fastest Lap; Mansell, 1m 18.31s. 113.35 mph/182.38 kph

Belgian Grand Prix: Spa, 30 August 1992

44 laps of 4.33 mile/6.97 km circuit

Place	Driver	Car	Laps	Time/reason for retiring	Grid
1	M Schumacher	Benetton-Ford	44	1h 36m 10.72s	3
2	Mansell	Williams-Renault	44	1h 36m 47.32s	1
3	Patrese	Williams-Renault	44	1h 36m 54.62s	4
4	Brundle	Benetton-Ford	44	1h 36m 56.78s	9
5	Senna	McLaren-Honda	44	1h 37m 19.09s	2
6	Hakkinen	Lotus-Ford	44	1h 37m 20.75s	8
7	Lehto	Dallara-Ferrari	44	1h 37m 48.96s	16
8	de Cesaris	Tyrrell-Ilmor	43		13
9	Suzuki	Footwork-Mugen Honda	43		25
10	Van de Poele	Fondmetal-Ford	43		15
11	Wendlinger	March-Ilmor	43		20
12	Naspetti	March-Ilmor	43		21
13	Herbert	Lotus-Ford	42	engine	10
14	Gugelmin	Jordan-Yamaha	42		24
15	Modena	Jordan-Yamaha	42		17
16	Morbidelli	Minardi-Lamborghini	42		23
17	Katayama	Larrousse-Lamborghini	42		26
18	Gachot	Larrousse-Lamborghini	40	accident	20
	Boutsen	Ligier-Renault	27	accident	7
	Capelli	Ferrari	25	engine	12
	Tarquini	Fondmetal-Ford	25	engine	11
	Alboreto	Footwork-Mugen Honda	20	gearbox	14
	Alesi	Ferrari	7	spun	5

Belgian Grand Prix (cont)

Place	Driver	Car	Laps	Time/reason for retiring	Grid
	Grouillard	Tyrrell-Ilmor	1	accident	22
	Martini	Dallara-Ferrari	0	spun	19
	Berger	McLaren-Honda	0	clutch	6

Fastest Lap: Schumacher, 1m 53.79s. 137.1 mph/220.73 kph

Italian Grand Prix: Monza, 13 September 1992

53 laps of 3.6 mile/5.8 km circuit

Place	Driver	Car	Laps	Time/reason for retiring	Grid
1	Senna	McLaren-Honda	53	1h 18m 15.35s	2
2	Brundle	Benetton-Ford	53	1h 18m 32.4s	9
3	M Schumacher	Benetton-Ford	53	1h 18m 39.72s	6
4	Berger	McLaren-Honda	53	1h 19m 40.84s	5
5	Patrese	Williams-Renault	53	1h 19m 48.51s	4
6	de Cesaris	Tyrrell-Ilmor	52		21
7	Alboreto	Footwork-Mugen Honda	52		16
8	Martini	Dallara-Ferrari	52		22
9	Katayama	Larrousse-Lamborghini	50	transmission	23
10	Wendlinger	March-Ilmor	50		17
11	Lehto	Dallara-Ferrari	47	engine	14
	Gugelmin	Jordan-Yamaha	46	transmission	26
	Mansell	Williams-Renault	46	hydraulics	1
	Boutsen	Ligier-Renault	41	electrical	8
	Comas	Ligier-Renault	35	accident	15
	Tarquini	Fondmetal-Ford	30	gearbox	20
	Grouillard	Tyrrell-Ilmor	26	engine	18
	Herbert	Lotus-Ford	18	engine	13
	Naspetti	March-Ilmor	17	spun	24
	Alesi	Ferrari	12	engine	3
	Capelli	Ferrari	12	spun	7
	Morbidelli	Minardi-Lamborghini	12	engine	12
	Gachot	Larrousse-Lamborghini	11	engine	10
	Hakkinen	Lotus-Ford	5	engine	11
	Suzuki	Footwork-Mugen Honda	2	accident	19
	Van de Poele	Fondmetal-Ford	0	clutch	25

Fastest Lap: Mansell, 1m 26.12s. 150.66 mph/242.56 kph

Portuguese Grand Prix: Estoril, 27 September 1992

71 laps of 2.7 mile/4.35 km circuit

Place	Driver	Car	Laps	Time/reason for retiring	Grid
1	Mansell	Williams-Renault	71	1h 34m 46.66s	1
2	Berger	McLaren-Honda	71	1h 35m 24.19s	4
3	Senna	McLaren-Honda	70		3
4	Brundle	Benetton-Ford	70		6
5	Hakkinen	Lotus-Ford	70		7
6	Alboreto	Footwork-Mugen Honda	70		8
7	M Schumacher	Benetton-Ford	69		5*
8	Boutsen	Ligier-Renault	69		11
9	de Cesaris	Tyrrell-Ilmor	69		12
10	Suzuki	Footwork-Mugen Honda	68		17*
11	Naspetti	March-Ilmor	68		23
12	C Fittipaldi	Minardi-Lamborghini	68		26
13	Modena	Jordan-Yamaha	68		24
14	Morbidelli	Minardi-Lamborghini	68		18
	Lehto	Dallara-Ferrari	51	chassis	19
	Wendlinger	March-Ilmor	48	gearbox	22
	Comas	Ligier-Renault	47	engine	14
	Katayama	Larrousse-Lamborghini	46	accident	25
	Patrese	Williams-Renault	43	accident	2
	Martini	Dallara-Ferrari	43	tyre	21
	Capelli	Ferrari	34	engine	16
	Grouillard	Tyrrell-Ilmor	27	gearbox	15
	Gachot	Larrousse-Lamborghini	25	fuel pressure	13
	Gugelmin	Jordan-Yamaha	19	electrical	20
	Alesi	Ferrari	12	spun	10
	Herbert	Lotus-Ford	2	accident	9

Fastest Lap: Mansell, 1m 18.18s. 124.33 mph/200.17 kph
*Suzuki started from pit lane, Schumacher from the back of the grid.

Japanese Grand Prix: Suzuka, 25 October 1992

53 laps of 3.64 mile/5.86 km circuit

Place	Driver	Car	Laps	Time/reason for retiring	Grid
1	Patrese	Williams-Renault	53	1h 33m 09.55s	2
2	Berger	McLaren-Honda	53	1h 33m 23.28s	4
3	Brundle	Benetton-Ford	53	1h 34m 25.06s	13
4	de Cesaris	Tyrrell-Ilmor	52		9
5	Alesi	Ferrari	52		15
6	C Fittipaldi	Minardi-Lamborghini	52		12
7	Modena	Jordan-Yamaha	52		17
8	Suzuki	Footwork-Mugen Honda	52		16
9	Lehto	Dallara-Ferrari	52		22
10	Martini	Dallara-Ferrari	52		19

Japanese Grand Prix (cont)

Place	Driver	Car	Laps	Time/reason for retiring	Grid
11	Katayama	Larrousse-Lamborghini	52		20
12	Larini	Ferrari	52		11
13	Naspetti	March-Ilmor	51		26
14	Morbidelli	Minardi-Lamborghini	51		14
15	Alboreto	Footwork-Mugen Honda	51		24
	Mansell	Williams-Renault	44	engine	1
	Hakkinen	Lotus-Ford	4	engine	7
	Gachot	Larrousse-Lamborghini	39	accident	18
	Comas	Ligier-Renault	36	oil pressure	8
	Lammers	March-Ilmor	27	gearbox	23
	Gugelmin	Jordan-Yamaha	22	accident	25
	Herbert	Lotus-Ford	15	transmission	6
	M Schumacher	Benetton-Ford	13	gearbox	5
	Grouillard	Tyrrell-Ilmor	6	accident	21
	Boutsen	Ligier-Renault	3	gearbox	10
	Senna	McLaren-Honda	2	engine	3

Fastest Lap: Mansell, 1m 40.65s. 130.33 mph/209.83 kph

Australian Grand Prix: Adelaide, 8 November 1992

81 laps of 2.35 mile/3.78 km circuit

Place	Driver	Car	Laps	Time/reason for retiring	Grid
1	Berger	McLaren-Honda	81	1h 46m 54.79s	4
2	M Schumacher	Benetton-Ford	81	1h 46m 55.53s	5
3	Brundle	Benetton-Ford	81	1h 47m 48.94s	8
4	Alesi	Ferrari	80		6
5	Boutsen	Ligier-Renault	80		22
6	Modena	Jordan-Yamaha	80		15
7	Hakkinen	Lotus-Ford	80		10
8	Suzuki	Footwork-Mugen Honda	79		18
9	C Fittipaldi	Minardi-Lamborghini	79		17
10	Morbidelli	Minardi-Lamborghini	79		16
11	Larini	Ferrari	79		19
12	Lammers	March-Ilmor	78		25
13	Herbert	Lotus-Ford	77		12
	Lehto	Dallara-Ferrari	70	transmission	24
	Naspetti	March-Ilmor	55	gearbox	23
	Gachot	Larrousse-Lamborghini	51	fuel pressure	21
	Patrese	Williams-Renault	50	electrical	3
	Katayama	Larrousse-Lamborghini	35	differential	26
	de Cesaris	Tyrrell-Ilmor	29	fire	7
	Mansell	Williams-Renault	18	accident	1
	Senna	McLaren-Honda	18	accident	2
	Gugelmin	Jordan-Yamaha	7	accident	20
	Comas	Ligier-Renault	4	engine	9

Australian Grand Prix (cont)

Place	Driver	Car	Laps	Time/reason for retiring	Grid
	Alboreto	Footwork-Mugen Honda	0	accident	11
	Grouillard	Tyrrell-Ilmor	0	accident	13
	Martini	Dallara-Ferrari	0	accident	14

Fastest Lap: Schumacher, 1m 16.08s. 111.14 mph/178.83 kph

World Championship 1992

1	Mansell	108
2	Patrese	56
3	M Schumacher	53
4	Senna	50
5	Berger	49
6	Brundle	38
7	Alesi	18
8	Hakkinen	11
9	de Cesaris	8
10	Alboreto	6
11	Comas	4
12=	Capelli, Wendlinger	3
14=	Boutsen, Herbert, Martini	2
17=	C Fittipaldi, Gachot, Modena	1

Constuctors' Championship

1	Williams-Renault	164
2	McLaren-Honda	99
3	Benetton-Ford	91
4	Ferrari	21
5	Lotus-Ford	13
6	Tyrrell-Ilmor	8
7=	Footwork-Mugen, Ligier-Renault	6
9	March-Ilmor	3
10	Dallara-Ferrari	2
11=	Jordan-Yamaha, Minardi-Lamborghini, Larrousse-Lamborghini	1

1993

Alain Prost duly completed his fourth world championship and retired for good. Mansell, the reigning world champion, proved a point in American exile by winning the Indycar series. Michael Andretti, son of Mario, made an unsuccessful attempt at grand prix racing, spoiled by changes in regulations that reduced testing time and by attempting to commute from America. Damon Hill, son of Graham, justified his elevation from Williams test driver with three wins. The successful Sauber sports car team, backed by Mercedes, made its debut in grand prix racing. March withdrew from Formula One. James Hunt died from a heart attack.

South African Grand Prix: Kyalami, 14 March 1993

72 laps of 2.65 mile/4.26 km circuit

Place	Driver	Car	Laps	Time/reason for retiring	Grid
1	Prost	Williams-Renault	72	1h 38m 45.08s	1
2	Senna	McLaren-Ford	72	1h 40m 04.91s	2
3	Blundell	Ligier-Renault	71		8
4	C Fittipaldi	Minardi-Ford	71		13
5	Lehto	Sauber-Ilmor	70		6
6	Berger	Ferrari	69	engine	15
7	Warwick	Footwork-Mugen Honda	69	spun	22
	Brundle	Ligier-Renault	57	spun	12
	Alboreto	Lola-Ferrari	55	engine	25
	Comas	Larrousse-Lamborghini	51	engine	19
	Patrese	Benetton-Ford	46	spun	7
	M Schumacher	Benetton-Ford	39	accident	3
	Herbert	Lotus-Ford	38	fuel pressure	17
	Wendlinger	Sauber-Ilmor	33	electrical	10
	Barrichello	Jordan-Hart	31	gearbox	14
	Alesi	Ferrari	30	hydraulics	5
	Alliot	Larrousse-Lamborghini	27	spun	11
	Barbazza	Minardi-Ford	21	accident	24
	A Suzuki	Footwork-Mugen Honda	21	accident	20
	Badoer	Lola-Ferrari	20	gearbox	26
	D Hill	Williams-Renault	16	accident	4

South African Grand Prix (cont)

Place	Driver	Car	Laps	Time/reason for retiring	Grid
	Zanardi	Lotus-Ford	16	accident	16
	Andretti	McLaren-Ford	4	accident	9
	Capelli	Jordan-Hart	2	accident	18
	Katayama	Tyrrell-Yamaha	1	transmission	21
	de Cesaris	Tyrrell-Yamaha	0	transmission	23

Fastest Lap: Prost, 1m 19.49s. 119.91mph/192.97kph

Brazilian Grand Prix: Interlagos, 28 March, 1993

71 laps of 2.69 mile/4.33 km circuit

Place	Driver	Car	Laps	Time/reason for retiring	Grid
1.	Senna	McLaren-Ford	71	1h 51m 15.5s	3
2	D Hill	Williams-Renault	71	1h 51m 32.1s	2
3	M Schumacher	Benetton-Ford	71	1h 52m 00.9s	4
4	Herbert	Lotus-Ford	71	1h 52m 02.0s	12
5	Blundell	Ligier-Renault	71	1h 52m 07.6s	10
6	Zanardi	Lotus-Ford	70		15
7	Alliot	Larrousse-Lamborghini	70		11
8	Alesi	Ferrari	70		9
9	Warwick	Footwork-Mugen Honda	69		18
10	Comas	Larrousse-Lamborghini	69		17
11	Alboreto	Lola-Ferrari	68		25
12	Badoer	Lola-Ferrari	68		21
	Wendlinger	Sauber-Ilmor	61	engine	8
	Lehto	Sauber-Ilmor	52	electrical	7
	de Cesaris	Tyrrell-Yamaha	48	electrical	23
	Prost	Williams-Renault	29	accident	1
	C Fittipaldi	Minardi-Ford	28	accident	20
	A Suzuki	Footwork-Mugen Honda	27	accident	19
	Katayama	Tyrrell-Yamaha	26	accident	22
	Barrichello	Jordan-Hart	13	gearbox	14
	Patrese	Benetton-Ford	3	suspension	6
	Brundle	Ligier-Renault	0	accident	16
	Barbazza	Minardi-Ford	0	accident	24
	Andretti	McLaren-Ford	0	accident	5
	Berger	Ferrari	0	accident	13

Fastest Lap: Prost, 1m 15.67s, 125.92mph/202.65kph

European Grand Prix: Donington Park, 11 April, 1993

76 laps of 2.5 mile/4.02 km circuit

Place	Driver	Car	Laps	Time/Reason for retiring	Grid
1	Senna	McLaren-Ford	76	1h 50m 46.6s	4
2	D Hill	Williams-Renault	76	1h 52m 09.8s	2
3	Prost	Williams-Renault	75		1
4	Herbert	Lotus-Ford	75		11
5	Patrese	Benetton-Ford	74		10
6	Barbazza	Minardi-Ford	74		20
7	C Fittipaldi	Minardi-Ford	73		16
8	Zanardi	Lotus-Ford	72		13
9	Comas	Larrousse-Lamborghini	72		17
10	Barrichello	Jordan-Hart	70	fuel pressure	12
11	Alboreto	Lola-Ferrari	70		24
	Warwick	Footwork-Mugen Honda	66	gearbox	14
	Boutsen	Jordan-Hart	61	throttle	19
	de Cesaris	Tyrrell-Yamaha	55	gearbox	25
	Alesi	Ferrari	36	suspension	9
	A Suzuki	Footwork-Mugen Honda	29	gearbox	23
	Alliot	Larrousse-Lamborghini	27	accident	15
	M Schumacher	Benetton-Ford	22	accident	3
	Blundell	Ligier-Renault	20	accident	21
	Berger	Ferrari	19	suspension	8
	Lehto	Sauber-Ilmor	13	handling	7
	Katayama	Tyrrell-Yamaha	11	clutch	18
	Brundle	Ligier-Renault	7	accident	22
	Andretti	McLaren-Ford	0	accident	6
	Wendlinger	Sauber-Ilmor	0	accident	5

Fastest Lap: Senna, 1m 18.03s, 115.33mph/185.61kph

San Marino Grand Prix: Imola, 25 April, 1993

61 laps of 3.13 mile/5.04 km circuit

Place	Driver	Car	Laps	Time/Reason for retiring	Grid
1	Prost	Williams-Renault	61	1h 33m 20.4s	1
2	M Schumacher	Benetton-Ford	61	1h 33m 52.8s	3
3	Brundle	Ligier-Renault	60		10
4	Lehto	Sauber-Ilmor	59	engine	16
5	Alliot	Larrousse-Lamborghini	59		14
6	Barbazza	Minardi-Ford	59		25
7	Badoer	Lola-Ferrari	58		24
8	Herbert	Lotus-Ford	57	engine	12
9	A Suzuki	Footwork-Mugen Honda	54		21
	Zanardi	Lotus-Ford	53	accident	20
	Wendlinger	Sauber-Ilmor	48	engine	5
	Senna	McLaren-Ford	42	hydraulics	4

San Marino Grand Prix (cont)

Place	Driver	Car	Laps	Time/reason for retiring	Grid
	Alesi	Ferrari	40	clutch	9
	C Fittipaldi	Minardi-Ford	36	steering	23
	Andretti	McLaren-Ford	32	spun	6
	Warwick	Footwork-Mugen Honda	29	spun	15
	Katayama	Tyrrell-Yamaha	22	engine	22
	D Hill	Williams-Renault	20	spun	2
	Comas	Larrousse-Lamborghini	18	oil pressure	17
	de Cesaris	Tyrrell-Yamaha	18	gearbox	18
	Barrichello	Jordan-Hart	17	spun	13
	Berger	Ferrari	8	gearbox	8
	Boutsen	Jordan-Hart	1	gearbox	19
	Patrese	Benetton-Ford	0	accident	11
	Blundell	Ligier-Renault	0	accident	7

Fastest Lap: Prost, 1m 26.13s, 130.9mph/210.1kph

Spanish Grand Prix: Barcelona, 9 May, 1993

65 laps of 2.95 mile/4.75 km circuit

Place	Driver	Car	Laps	Time/Reason for retiring	Grid
1	Prost	Williams-Renault	65	1h 32m 27.7s	1
2	Senna	McLaren-Ford	65	1h 32m 44.6s	3
3	M Schumacher	Benetton-Ford	65	1h 32m 54.8s	4
4	Patrese	Benetton-Ford	64		5
5	Andretti	McLaren-Ford	64		7
6	Berger	Ferrari	63		11
7	Blundell	Ligier-Renault	63		12
8	C Fittipaldi	Minardi-Ford	63		20
9	Comas	Larrousse-Lamborghini	63		14
10	A Suzuki	Footwork-Mugen Honda	63		19
11	Boutsen	Jordan-Hart	62		21
12	Barrichello	Jordan-Hart	62		17
13	Warwick	Footwork-Mugen Honda	62		16
14	Zanardi	Lotus-Ford	60	engine	15
	Lehto	Sauber-Ilmor	53	engine	9
	Badoer	Lola-Ferrari	43	clutch	22
	Wendlinger	Sauber-Ilmor	42	fuel pressure	6
	de Cesaris	Tyrrell-Yamaha	42	disqualified: push start	24
	D Hill	Williams-Renault	41	engine	2
	Alesi	Ferrari	40	engine	8
	Barbazza	Minardi-Ford	37	accident	25
	Alliot	Larrousse-Lamborghini	26	gearbox	13
	Brundle	Ligier-Renault	11	accident	18
	Katayama	Tyrrell-Yamaha	11	accident	23
	Herbert	Lotus-Ford	2	suspension	10

Fastest Lap: M Schumacher, 1m 20.99s, 131.11mph/211.01kph

Monaco Grand Prix: Monte Carlo, 23 May, 1993

78 laps of 2.07 mile/3.33 km circuit

Place	Driver	Car	Laps	Time/Reason for retiring	Grid
1	Senna	McLaren-Ford	78	1h 52m 11s	3
2	D Hill	Williams-Renault	78	1h 53m 03.1s	4
3	Alesi	Ferrari	78	1h 53m 14.3s	5
4	Prost	Williams-Renault	77		1
5	C Fittipaldi	Minardi-Ford	76		17
6	Brundle	Ligier-Renault	76		13
7	Zanardi	Lotus-Ford	76		20
8	Andretti	McLaren-Ford	76		9
9	Barrichello	Jordan-Hart	76		16
10	de Cesaris	Tyrrell-Yamaha	76		19
11	Barbazza	Minardi-Ford	75		25
12	Alliot	Larrousse-Lamborghini	75		15
13	Wendlinger	Sauber-Ilmor	74		8
14	Berger	Ferrari	70	accident	7
	Herbert	Lotus-Ford	61	accident	14
	Patrese	Benetton-Ford	53	engine	6
	Comas	Larrousse-Lamborghini	51	accident	10
	A Suzuki	Footwork-Mugen Honda	46	accident	18
	Warwick	Footwork-Mugen Honda	43	throttle	12
	M Schumacher	Benetton-Ford	32	suspension	2
	Katayama	Tyrrell-Yamaha	31	oil	22
	Alboreto	Lola-Ferrari	28	gearbox	24
	Lehto	Sauber-Ilmor	23	accident	11
	Boutsen	Jordan-Hart	12	suspension	23
	Blundell	Ligier-Renault	3	suspension	21

Fastest Lap: Prost, 1m 23.6s, 89.05mph/143.3kph

Canadian Grand Prix: Montreal, 13 June, 1993

69 laps of 2.75 mile/4.43 km circuit

Place	Driver	Car	Laps	Time/Reason for retiring	Grid
1	Prost	Williams-Renault	69	1h 36m 41.8s	1
2	M Schumacher	Benetton-Ford	69	1h 36m 56.4s	3
3	D Hill	Williams-Renault	69	1h 37m 34.5s	2
4	Berger	Ferrari	68		5
5	Brundle	Ligier-Renault	68		7
6	Wendlinger	Sauber-Ilmor	68		9
7	Lehto	Sauber-Ilmor	68		11
8	Comas	Larrousse-Lamborghini	68		13
9	C Fittipaldi	Minardi-Ford	67		17
10	Herbert	Lotus-Ford	67		20
11	Zanardi	Lotus-Ford	67		21
12	Boutsen	Jordan-Hart	67		24

Canadian Grand Prix (cont)

Place	Driver	Car	Laps	Time/reason for retiring	Grid
13	A Suzuki	Footwork-Mugen Honda	66		16
14	Andretti	McLaren-Ford	66		12
15	Badoer	Lola-Ferrari	65		25
16	Warwick	Footwork-Mugen Honda	65		18
17	Katayama	Tyrrell-Yamaha	64		22
18	Senna	McLaren-Ford	62	alternator	8
	Patrese	Benetton-Ford	52	driver	4
	de Cesaris	Tyrrell-Yamaha	45	accident	19
	Barbazza	Minardi-Ford	33	gearbox	23
	Alesi	Ferrari	23	engine	6
	Blundell	Ligier-Renault	13	accident	10
	Barrichello	Jordan-Hart	10	electrical	14
	Alliot	Larrousse-Lamborghini	46	gearbox	15

Fastest Lap: M Schumacher, 1m 21.5s, 121.59mph/195.68kph

French Grand Prix: Magny-Cours, 4 July, 1993

72 laps of 2.64 mile/4.25 km circuit

Place	Driver	Car	Laps	Time/Reason for retiring	Grid
1	Prost	Williams-Renault	72	1h 38m 35.24s	2
2	D Hill	Williams-Renault	72	1h 38m 35.58s	1
3	M Schumacher	Benetton-Ford	72	1h 38m 56.5s	7
4	Senna	McLaren-Ford	72	1h 39m 07.7s	5
5	Brundle	Ligier-Renault	72	1h 39m 09s	3
6	Andretti	McLaren-Ford	71		16
7	Barrichello	Jordan-Hart	71		8
8	C Fittipaldi	Minardi-Ford	71		23
9	Alliot	Larrousse-Lamborghini	70		10
10	Patrese	Benetton-Ford	70		12
11	Boutsen	Jordan-Hart	70		20
12	A Suzuki	Footwork-Mugen Honda	70		13
13	Warwick	Footwork-Mugen Honda	70		15
14	Berger	Ferrari	70		14
15	de Cesaris	Tyrrell-Yamaha	68		25
16	Comas	Larrousse-Lamborghini	66	gearbox	9
	Alesi	Ferrari	47	engine	6
	Badoer	Lola-Ferrari	28	suspension	22
	Wendlinger	Sauber-Ilmor	25	gearbox	11
	Lehto	Sauber-Ilmor	22	gearbox	18
	Blundell	Ligier-Renault	20	spun	4
	Herbert	Lotus-Ford	16	spun	19
	Barbazza	Minardi-Ford	16	gearbox	24
	Katayama	Tyrrell-Yamaha	9	oil	21
	Zanardi	Lotus-Ford	3	suspension	17

Fastest Lap: M Schumacher, 1m 29.26s, 119.95mph/193.05kph

British Grand Prix: Silverstone, 11 July, 1993

59 laps of 3.25mile/5.23 km circuit

Place	Driver	Car	Laps	Time/Reason for retiring	Grid
1	Prost	Williams-Renault	59	1h 25m 38.2s	1
2	M Schumacher	Benetton-Ford	59	1h 25m 45.9s	3
3	Patrese	Benetton-Ford	59	1h 26m 55.7s	5
4	Herbert	Lotus-Ford	59	1h 26m 56.6s	7
5	Senna	McLaren-Ford	58	fuel	4
6	Warwick	Footwork-Mugen Honda	58		8
7	Blundell	Ligier-Renault	58		9
8	Lehto	Sauber-Ilmor	58		16
9	Alesi	Ferrari	58		12
10	Barrichello	Jordan-Hart	58		15
11	Alliot	Larrousse-Lamborghini	57		24
12	C Fittipaldi	Minardi-Ford	56	gearbox	19
13	Katayama	Tyrrell-Yamaha	55		22
14	Brundle	Ligier-Renault	53	gearbox	6
	de Cesaris	Tyrrell-Yamaha	43	running	21
	D Hill	Williams-Renault	41	engine	2
	Zanardi	Lotus-Ford	41	engine	14
	Boutsen	Jordan-Hart	41	spun	23
	Badoer	Lola-Ferrari	32	wheel	25
	Martini	Minardi-Ford	31	driver	20
	Wendlinger	Sauber-Ilmor	24	accident	18
	Berger	Ferrari	10	suspension	13
	A Suzuki	Footwork-Mugen Honda	8	spun	10
	Andretti	McLaren-Ford	0	spun	11
	Comas	Larrousse-Lamborghini	0	transmission	17

Fastest Lap: Hill, 1m 22.52s, 141.67mph/228kph

German Grand Prix: Hockenheim, 25 July, 1993

45 laps of 4.24 mile/6.82 km circuit

Place	Driver	Car	Laps	Time/Reason for retiring	Grid
1	Prost	Williams-Renault	45	1h 18m 40.9s	1
2	M Schumacher	Benetton-Ford	45	1h 18m 57.6s	3
3	Blundell	Ligier-Renault	45	1h 19m 40.2s	5
4	Senna	McLaren-Ford	45	1h 19m 49.1s	4
5	Patrese	Benetton-Ford	45	1h 20m 12.4s	7
6	Berger	Ferrari	45	1h 20m 15.6s	9
7	Alesi	Ferrari	45	1h 20m 16.7s	10
8	Brundle	Ligier-Renault	44		6
9	Wendlinger	Sauber-Ilmor	44		14
10	Herbert	Lotus-Ford	44		13
11	C Fittipaldi	Minardi-Ford	44		20
12	Alliot	Larrousse-Lamborghini	44		23

German Grand Prix (cont)

Place	Driver	Car	Laps	Time/reason for retiring	Grid
13	Boutsen	Jordan-Hart	44		24
14	Martini	Minardi-Ford	44		22
15	D Hill	Williams-Renault	43	tyre	2
16	Alboreto	Lola-Ferrari	43		26
17	Warwick	Footwork-Mugen Honda	43		11
	Barrichello	Jordan-Hart	34	wheel	17
	Katayama	Tyrrell-Yamaha	28	spun	21
	Lehto	Sauber-Ilmor	22	throttle	18
	Zanardi	Lotus-Ford	19	spun	15
	A Suzuki	Footwork-Mugen Honda	9	gearbox	8
	Andretti	McLaren-Ford	4	accident	12
	Badoer	Lola-Ferrari	4	suspension	25
	de Cesaris	Tyrrell-Yamaha	1	gearbox	19
	Comas	Larrousse-Lamborghini	0	clutch	16

Fastest Lap: M Schumacher, 1m 41.86s, 149.67mph/240.86kph

Hungarian Grand Prix: Hungaroring, 15 August, 1993

77 laps of 2.47 mile/3.97 km circuit

Place	Driver	Car	Laps	Time/Reason for retiring	Grid
1	D Hill	Williams-Renault	77	1h 47m 39.1s	2
2	Patrese	Benetton-Ford	77	1h 48m 51s	5
3	Berger	Ferrari	77	1h 48m 57.1s	6
4	Warwick	Footwork-Mugen Honda	76		9
5	Brundle	Ligier-Renault	76		13
6	Wendlinger	Sauber-Ilmor	76		17
7	Blundell	Ligier-Renault	76		12
8	Alliot	Larrousse-Lamborghini	75		19
9	Boutsen	Jordan-Hart	75		24
10	Katayama	Tyrrell-Yamaha	73		23
11	de Cesaris	Tyrrell-Yamaha	72		22
12	Prost	Williams-Renault	70		1
	Martini	Minardi-Ford	59	accident	7
	Comas	Larrousse-Lamborghini	54	oil	18
	Zanardi	Lotus-Ford	45	gearbox	21
	A Suzuki	Footwork-Mugen Honda	41	spun	10
	Alboreto	Lola-Ferrari	39	engine	25
	Herbert	Lotus-Ford	38	spun	20
	Badoer	Lola-Ferrari	37	spun	26
	M Schumacher	Benetton-Ford	26	spun	3
	C Fittipaldi	Minardi-Ford	22	accident	14
	Alesi	Ferrari	22	accident	8
	Lehto	Sauber-Ilmor	18	engine	15

Hungarian Grand Prix (cont)

Place	Driver	Car	Laps	Time/reason for retiring	Grid
	Senna	McLaren-Ford	17	throttle	4
	Andretti	McLaren-Ford	15	throttle	11
	Barrichello	Jordan-Hart	0	accident	16

Fastest Lap: Prost, 1m 19.63s, 111.46mph/179.38kph

Belgian Grand Prix: Spa, 29 August, 1993

44 laps of 4.33 mile/6.97 km circuit

Place	Driver	Car	Laps	Time/Reason for retiring	Grid
1	D Hill	Williams-Renault	44	1h 24m 32.1s	2
2	M Schumacher	Benetton-Ford	44	1h 24m 35.8s	3
3	Prost	Williams-Renault	44	1h 24m 47.1s	1
4	Senna	McLaren-Ford	44	1h 26m 11.9s	5
5	Herbert	Lotus-Ford	43		10
6	Patrese	Benetton-Ford	43		8
7	Brundle	Ligier-Renault	43		11
8	Andretti	McLaren-Ford	43		14
9	Lehto	Sauber-Ilmor	43		9
10	Berger	Ferrari	42	accident	16
11	Blundell	Ligier-Renault	42	accident	15
12	Alliot	Larrousse-Lamborghini	42		18
13	Badoer	Lola-Ferrari	42		24
14	Alboreto	Lola-Ferrari	41		25
15	Katayama	Tyrrell-Yamaha	40		23
	Comas	Larrousse-Lamborghini	37	fuel pump	19
	Warwick	Footwork-Mugen Honda	28	electrical	7
	Wendlinger	Sauber-Ilmor	27	engine	12
	de Cesaris	Tyrrell-Yamaha	24	engine	17
	C Fittipaldi	Minardi-Ford	15	accident	22
	Martini	Minardi-Ford	15	spun	21
	A Suzuki	Footwork-Mugen Honda	14	suspension	6
	Barrichello	Jordan-Hart	11	wheel	13
	Alesi	Ferrari	4	suspension	4
	Boutsen	Jordan-Hart	0	gearbox	20

Fastest Lap: Prost, 1m 51.1s, 140.42mph/226kph

Italian Grand Prix: Monza, 12 September, 1993

53 laps of 3.6 mile/5.8 km circuit

Place	Driver	Car	Laps	Time/Reason for retiring	Grid
1	D Hill	Williams-Renault	53	1h 17m 07.5s	2
2	Alesi	Ferrari	53	1h 17m 47.5s	3
3	Andretti	McLaren-Ford	52		9
4	Wendlinger	Sauber-Ilmor	52		15
5	Patrese	Benetton-Ford	52		10
6	Comas	Larrousse-Lamborghini	51		20
7	Martini	Minardi-Ford	51	accident	22
8	C Fittipaldi	Minardi-Ford	51	accident	24
9	Alliot	Larrousse-Lamborghini	51		16
10	Badoer	Lola-Ferrari	51		25
11	Lamy	Lotus-Ford	49	engine	26
12	Prost	Williams-Renault	48	engine	1
13	de Cesaris	Tyrrell-Yamaha	47	oil	18
14	Katayama	Tyrrell-Yamaha	47		17
	Alboreto	Lola-Ferrari	23	suspension	21
	M Schumacher	Benetton-Ford	21	engine	5
	Blundell	Ligier-Renault	20	accident	14
	Berger	Ferrari	15	suspension	6
	Herbert	Lotus-Ford	14	accident	7
	Brundle	Ligier-Renault	8	accident	12
	Senna	McLaren-Ford	8	accident	4
	A Suzuki	Footwork-Mugen Honda	0	accident	8
	Warwick	Footwork-Mugen Honda	0	accident	11
	Lehto	Sauber-Ilmor	0	accident	13
	Barrichello	Jordan-Hart	0	accident	19
	Apicella	Jordan-Hart	0	accident	23

Fastest Lap: Hill, 1m 23.58s, 159.82mph/257.21kph

Portuguese Grand Prix: Estoril, 26 September, 1993

71 laps of 2.7 mile/4.35 km circuit

Place	Driver	Car	Laps	Time/Reason for retiring	Grid
1	M Schumacher	Benetton-Ford	71	1h 32m 46.3s	6
2	Prost	Williams-Renault	71	1h 32m 47.3s	2
3	D Hill	Williams-Renault	71	1h 32m 54.5s	1
4	Alesi	Ferrari	71	1h 33m 53.9s	5
5	Wendlinger	Sauber-Ilmor	70		13
6	Brundle	Ligier-Renault	70		11
7	Lehto	Sauber-Ilmor	69		12
8	Martini	Minardi-Ford	69		19
9	C Fittipaldi	Minardi-Ford	69		24

Portuguese Grand Prix (cont)

Place	Driver	Car	Laps	Time/reason for retiring	Grid
10	Alliot	Larrousse-Lamborghini	69		20
11	Comas	Larrousse-Lamborghini	68		22
12	de Cesaris	Tyrrell-Yamaha	68		17
13	Barrichello	Jordan-Hart	68		15
14	Badoer	Lola-Ferrari	68		26
15	Warwick	Footwork-Mugen Honda	63	accident	9
16	Patrese	Benetton-Ford	63	accident	7
	Lamy	Lotus-Ford	61	accident	18
	Herbert	Lotus-Ford	60	accident	14
	Blundell	Ligier-Renault	51	accident	10
	Alboreto	Lola-Ferrari	38	gearbox	25
	Berger	Ferrari	35	suspension	8
	Hakkinen	McLaren-Ford	32	accident	3
	A Suzuki	Footwork-Mugen Honda	27	gearbox	16
	Senna	McLaren-Ford	19	engine	4
	Katayama	Tyrrell-Yamaha	12	accident	21
	Naspetti	Jordan-Hart	8	engine	23

Fastest Lap: Hill, 1m 14.86s, 129.99mph/209.19kph

Japanese Grand Prix: Suzuka, 24 October, 1993

53 laps of 3.64 mile/5.86 km circuit

Place	Driver	Car	Laps	Time/Reason for retiring	Grid
1	Senna	McLaren-Ford	53	1h 40m 27.9s	2
2	Prost	Williams-Renault	53	1h 40m 39.4s	1
3	Hakkinen	McLaren-Ford	53	1h 40m 54s	3
4	D Hill	Williams-Renault	53	1h 41m 51.5s	6
5	Barrichello	Jordan-Hart	53	1h 42m 03s	12
6	Irvine	Jordan-Hart	53	1h 42m 14.3s	8
7	Blundell	Ligier-Renault	52		17
8	Lehto	Sauber-Ilmor	52		11
9	Brundle	Ligier-Renault	51	accident	15
10	Martini	Minardi-Ford	51		22
11	Herbert	Lotus-Ford	51		19
12	T Suzuki	Larrousse-Lamborghini	51		23
13	Lamy	Lotus-Ford	49	accident	20
14	Warwick	Footwork-Mugen Honda	48	accident	7
	Patrese	Benetton-Ford	45	accident	10
	Berger	Ferrari	40	engine	5
	A Suzuki	Footwork-Mugen Honda	28	spun	9
	Katayama	Tyrrell-Yamaha	26	engine	13
	Gounon	Minardi-Ford	26	withdrawn	24
	Wendlinger	Sauber-Ilmor	25	throttle	16

Japanese Grand Prix (cont)

Place	Driver	Car	Laps	Time/reason for retiring	Grid
	Comas	Larrousse-Lamborghini	17	engine	21
	M Schumacher	Benetton-Ford	10	accident	4
	Alesi	Ferrari	7	electrical	14
	de Cesaris	Tyrrell-Yamaha	0	accident	18

Fastest Lap: Prost, 1m 41.18s, 129.65mph/208.65kph

Australian Grand Prix: Adelaide, 7 November, 1993

79 laps of 2.35 mile/3.78 km circuit

Place	Driver	Car	Laps	Time/Reason for retiring	Grid
1	Senna	McLaren-Ford	79	1h 43m 27.5s	1
2	Prost	Williams-Renault	79	1h 43m 36.7s	2
3	D Hill	Williams-Renault	79	1h 44m 01.4s	3
4	Alesi	Ferrari	78		7
5	Berger	Ferrari	78		6
6	Brundle	Ligier-Renault	78		8
7	A Suzuki	Footwork-Mugen Honda	78		10
8	Patrese	Benetton-Ford	77	fuel pressure	9
9	Blundell	Ligier-Renault	77		14
10	Warwick	Footwork-Mugen Honda	77		17
11	Barrichello	Jordan-Hart	76		13
12	Comas	Larrousse-Lamborghini	75		21
13	de Cesaris	Tyrrell-Yamaha	74		15
14	T Suzuki	Larrousse-Lamborghini	73		24
15	Wendlinger	Sauber-Ilmor	56	brakes	11
	Lehto	Sauber-Ilmor	34	throttle	12
	Gounon	Minardi-Ford	28	spun	22
	Hakkinen	McLaren-Ford	19	brake	5
	M Schumacher	Benetton-Ford	11	engine	4
	Katayama	Tyrrell-Yamaha	10	accident	18
	Irvine	Jordan-Hart	9	accident	19
	Herbert	Lotus-Ford	5	suspension	20
	Martini	Minardi-Ford	0	gearbox	16
	Lamy	Lotus-Ford	0	accident	23

Fastest Lap: Hill, 1m 15.38s, 112.17mph/180.52kph

World Championship 1993

1	Prost	99
2	Senna	73
3	D Hill	69
4	M Schumacher	52
5	Patrese	20
6	Alesi	16
7	Brundle	13
8	Berger	12
9	Herbert	11
10	Blundell	10
11 =	Andretti, Wendlinger	7
13 =	C Fittipaldi, Lehto	5
15 =	Hakkinen, Warwick	4
17 =	Alliot, Barrichello, Barbazza	2
20 =	Comas, Irvine, Zanardi	1

Constructors' Championship

1	Williams-Renault	168
2	McLaren-Ford	84
3	Benetton-Ford	72
4	Ferrari	28
5	Ligier-Renault	23
6 =	Lotus-Ford, Sauber-Ilmor	12
8	Minardi-Ford	4
9 =	Jordan-Hart, Larrousse-Lamborghini	3

1994

Roland Ratzenberger and Ayrton Senna were both killed at the San Marino Grand Prix. Senna was one of the greatest drivers of all time but his forceful and abrasive approach sometimes became intimidatory. The year was also marked by a serious accident to Karl Wendlinger at Monaco. Refuelling returned in order to introduce greater excitement into what were becoming increasingly processional races. Jos Verstappen survived a brief but spectacular pit stop refuelling fire in Germany. It was also a political year with Schumacher and Hill engaged in a war of words and clashes on the track: Schumacher was disqualified from the British race after overtaking Hill on the parade lap and lost his Belgian Grand Prix win when the skid block under the car was deemed to have worn beyond the permitted tolerances. Banned for two races, he returned to take the title from Hill after a controversial coming together in Australia that left both contenders sidelined. Mansell returned from a less successful second season in Indycars to take the second Williams seat on occasion, winning the Australian Grand Prix.

Brazilian Grand Prix: Interlagos, 27 March, 1994

71 laps of 2.69 mile/4.33 km circuit

Place	Driver	Car	Laps	Time/Reason for retiring	Grid
1	M Schumacher	Benetton-Ford	71	1h 35m 38.8s	2
2	D Hill	Williams-Renault	70		4
3	Alesi	Ferrari	70		3
4	Barrichello	Jordan-Hart	70		14
5	Katayama	Tyrrell-Yamaha	69		10
6	Wendlinger	Sauber-Mercedes	69		7
7	Herbert	Lotus-Mugen Honda	69		21
8	Martini	Minardi-Ford	69		15
9	Comas	Larrousse-Ford	68		13
10	Lamy	Lotus-Mugen Honda	68		24
11	Panis	Ligier-Renault	68		19
12	D Brabham	Simtek-Ford	67		26
	Senna	Williams-Renault	55	spun	1
	Brundle	McLaren-Peugeot	34	accident	18

Brazilian Grand Prix (cont)

Place	Driver	Car	Laps	Time/reason for retiring	Grid
	Irvine	Jordan-Hart	34	accident	16
	Verstappen	Benetton-Ford	34	accident	9
	Bernard	Ligier-Renault	33	accident	20
	Blundell	Tyrrell-Yamaha	21	accident	12
	C Fittipaldi	Footwork-Ford	21	gearbox	11
	Frentzen	Sauber-Mercedes	15	spun	5
	Hakkinen	McLaren-Peugeot	13	fire	8
	Alboreto	Minardi-Ford	7	electrical	22
	Morbidelli	Footwork-Ford	5	gearbox	6
	Berger	Ferrari	5	engine	17
	Beretta	Larrousse-Ford	2	accident	23
	Gachot	Pacific-Ilmor	1	accident	25

Fastest Lap: M Schumacher, 1m 18.46s, 123.32mph/198.46kph

Pacific Grand Prix: Aida, 17 April 1994

83 laps of 2.3 mile/3.7 km circuit

Place	Driver	Car	Laps	Time/Reason for retiring	Grid
1	M Schumacher	Benetton-Ford	83	1h 47m 01.7s	2
2	Berger	Ferrari	83	1h 47m 17s	5
3	Barrichello	Jordan-Hart	82		8
4	C Fittipaldi	Footwork-Ford	82		9
5	Frentzen	Sauber-Mercedes	82		11
6	Comas	Larrousse-Ford	80		16
7	Herbert	Lotus-Mugen Honda	80		23
8	Lamy	Lotus-Mugen Honda	79		24
9	Panis	Ligier-Renault	78		22
10	Bernard	Ligier-Renault	78		18
11	Ratzenberger	Simtek-Ford	78		26
	Morbidelli	Footwork-Ford	69	engine	13
	Wendlinger	Sauber-Mercedes	69	accident	19
	Alboreto	Minardi-Ford	69	accident	15
	Brundle	McLaren-Peugeot	67	engine	6
	Martini	Minardi-Ford	63	brakes	17
	Verstappen	Benetton-Ford	54	spun	10
	D Hill	Williams-Renault	49	transmission	3
	A Suzuki	Jordan-Hart	44	steering	20
	Katayama	Tyrrell-Yamaha	42	engine	14
	Hakkinen	McLaren-Peugeot	19	gearbox	4
	Beretta	Larrousse-Ford	14	electrical	21
	D Brabham	Simtek-Ford	2	engine	25
	Senna	Williams-Renault	0	accident	1
	Blundell	Tyrrell-Yamaha	0	accident	12
	Larini	Ferrari	0	accident	7

Fastest Lap: M Schumacher, 1m 14.02s, 111.9mph/180.09kph

San Marino Grand Prix: Imola, 1 May 1994

58 laps of 3.13 mile/5.04 km circuit

Place	Driver	Car	Laps	Time/Reason for retiring	Grid
1	M Schumacher	Benetton-Ford	58	1h 28m 28.6s	2
2	Larini	Ferrari	58	1h 29m 23.6s	6
3	Hakkinen	McLaren-Peugeot	58	1h 29m 39.3s	8
4	Wendlinger	Sauber-Mercedes	58	1h 29m 42.3s	10
5	Katayama	Tyrrell-Yamaha	57		9
6	D Hill	Williams-Renault	57		4
7	Frentzen	Sauber-Mercedes	57		7
8	Brundle	McLaren-Peugeot	57		13
9	Blundell	Tyrrell-Yamaha	56		12
10	Herbert	Lotus-Mugen Honda	56		20
11	Panis	Ligier-Renault	56		19
12	Bernard	Ligier-Renault	56		17
13	C Fittipaldi	Footwork-Ford	54	brakes	16
	de Cesaris	Jordan-Hart	49	accident	21
	Alboreto	Minardi-Ford	44	wheel	15
	Morbidelli	Footwork-Ford	40	engine	11
	Martini	Minardi-Ford	37	spun	14
	D Brabham	Simtek-Ford	27	tyre	24
	Gachot	Pacific-Ilmor	23	oil pressure	25
	Beretta	Larrousse-Ford	17	engine	23
	Berger	Ferrari	16	handling	3
	Senna	Williams-Renault	5	fatal accident	1
	Comas	Larrousse-Ford	5	accident	18
	Lehto	Benetton-Ford	0	accident	5
	Lamy	Lotus-Mugen Honda	0	accident	22

Fastest Lap: Hill, 1m 24.34s, 133.68mph/215.14kph
* Ratzenberger killed in practice crash

Monaco Grand Prix: Monte Carlo, 15 May 1994

78 laps of 2.07 mile/3.33 km circuit

Place	Driver	Car	Laps	Time/Reason for retiring	Grid
1	M Schumacher	Benetton-Ford	78	1h 49m 55.4s	1
2	Brundle	McLaren-Peugeot	78	1h 50m 32.7s	8
3	Berger	Ferrari	78	1h 51m 12.2s	3
4	de Cesaris	Jordan-Hart	77		14
5	Alesi	Ferrari	77		5
6	Alboreto	Minardi-Ford	77		12
7	Lehto	Benetton-Ford	77		17
8	Beretta	Larrousse-Ford	76		18
9	Panis	Ligier-Renault	76		20
10	Comas	Larrousse-Ford	75		13
11	Lamy	Lotus-Mugen Honda	73		19
	Herbert	Lotus-Mugen Honda	68	gearbox	16

Monaco Grand Prix (cont)

Place	Driver	Car	Laps	Time/reason for retiring	Grid
	Belmondo	Pacific-Ilmor	53	driver	24
	Gachot	Pacific-Ilmor	49	gearbox	23
	C Fittipaldi	Footwork-Ford	47	gearbox	6
	D Brabham	Simtek-Ford	45	accident	22
	Blundell	Tyrrell-Yamaha	40	engine	10
	Katayama	Tyrrell-Yamaha	38	gearbox	11
	Bernard	Ligier-Renault	34	spun	21
	Barrichello	Jordan-Hart	27	electrical	15
	D Hill	Williams-Renault	0	accident	4
	Hakkinen	McLaren-Peugeot	0	accident	2
	Morbidelli	Footwork-Ford	0	accident	7
	Martini	Minardi-Ford	0	accident	9

Fastest Lap: M Schumacher, 1m 21.08s, 91.82mph/147.77kph

Spanish Grand Prix: Barcelona, 29 May 1994

65 laps of 2.95 mile/4.75 km circuit

Place	Driver	Car	Laps	Time/Reason for retiring	Grid
1	D Hill	Williams-Renault	65	1h 36m 14.4s	2
2	M Schumacher	Benetton-Ford	65	1h 36m 38.5s	1
3	Blundell	Tyrrell-Yamaha	65	1h 37m 41.3s	11
4	Alesi	Ferrari	64		6
5	Martini	Minardi-Ford	64		18
6	Irvine	Jordan-Hart	64		13
7	Panis	Ligier-Renault	63		19
8	Bernard	Ligier-Renault	62		20
9	Zanardi	Lotus-Mugen Honda	62		23
10	D Brabham	Simtek-Ford	61		24
11	Brundle	McLaren-Peugeot	59	transmission	8
	Lehto	Benetton-Ford	53	engine	4
	Hakkinen	McLaren-Peugeot	48	engine	3
	Herbert	Lotus-Mugen Honda	41	spun	22
	Barrichello	Jordan-Hart	39	gearbox	5
	C Fittipaldi	Footwork-Ford	35	engine	21
	Coulthard	Williams-Renault	32	electrical	9
	Gachot	Pacific-Ilmor	32	wing	25
	Berger	Ferrari	27	gearbox	7
	Morbidelli	Footwork-Ford	24	fuel system	15
	Frentzen	Sauber-Mercedes	21	gearbox	12
	Comas	Larrousse-Ford	19	water	16
	Katayama	Tyrrell-Yamaha	16	engine	10
	Alboreto	Minardi-Ford	4	engine	14
	Belmondo	Pacific-Ilmor	2	spun	26
	Beretta	Larrousse-Ford	0	did not start: engine	17

Fastest Lap: M Schumacher, 1m 25.16s, 124.7mph/200.68kph

Canadian Grand Prix: Montreal, 12 June 1994

69 laps of 2.77 mile/4.45 km circuit

Place	Driver	Car	Laps	Time/Reason for retiring	Grid
1	M Schumacher	Benetton-Ford	69	1h 44m 31.9s	1
2	D Hill	Williams-Renault	69	1h 45m 11.6s	4
3	Alesi	Ferrari	69	1h 45m 45.3s	2
4	Berger	Ferrari	69	1h 45m 47.5s	3
5	Coulthard	Williams-Renault	68		5
	C Fittipaldi	Footwork-Ford	68	disqualified: under weight	16
6	Lehto	Benetton-Ford	68		20
7	Barrichello	Jordan-Hart	68		6
8	Herbert	Lotus-Mugen Honda	68		17
9	Martini	Minardi-Ford	68		15
10	Blundell	Tyrrell-Yamaha	67	accident	13
11	Alboreto	Minardi-Ford	67		18
12	Panis	Ligier-Renault	67		19
13	Bernard	Ligier-Renault	66		24
14	D Brabham	Simtek-Ford	65		25
15	Zanardi	Lotus-Mugen Honda	62	engine	23
	Hakkinen	McLaren-Peugeot	61	engine	7
	Beretta	Larrousse-Ford	57	engine	22
	Morbidelli	Footwork-Ford	50	gearbox	11
	Gachot	Pacific-Ilmor	47	oil pressure	26
	Comas	Larrousse-Ford	45	clutch	21
	Katayama	Tyrrell-Yamaha	44	spun	9
	Irvine	Jordan-Hart	40	accident	8
	de Cesaris	Sauber-Mercedes	24	oil	14
	Frentzen	Sauber-Mercedes	5	accident	10
	Brundle	McLaren-Peugeot	3	electrical	12

Fastest Lap: M Schumacher, 1m 28.93s, 111.94mph/180.15kph

French Grand Prix: Magny-Cours, 3 July 1994

72 laps of 2.64 mile/4.25 km circuit

Place	Driver	Car	Laps	Time/Reason for retiring	Grid
1	M Schumacher	Benetton-Ford	72	1h 38m 35.7s	3
2	D Hill	Williams-Renault	72	1h 38m 48.4s	1
3	Berger	Ferrari	72	1h 39m 28.5s	5
4	Frentzen	Sauber-Mercedes	71		10
5	Martini	Minardi-Ford	70		16
6	de Cesaris	Sauber-Mercedes	70		11
7	Herbert	Lotus-Mugen Honda	70		19
8	C Fittipaldi	Footwork-Ford	70		18
9	Gounon	Simtek-Ford	68		26
10	Blundell	Tyrrell-Yamaha	67		17

French Grand Prix (cont)

Place	Driver	Car	Laps	Time/reason for retiring	Grid
11	Comas	Larrousse-Ford	66	engine	20
	Katayama	Tyrrell-Yamaha	53	spun	14
	Hakkinen	McLaren-Peugeot	48	engine	9
	Mansell	Williams-Renault	45	transmission	2
	Alesi	Ferrari	41	accident	4
	Barrichello	Jordan-Hart	41	accident	7
	Bernard	Ligier-Renault	40	gearbox	15
	Beretta	Larrousse-Ford	36	engine	25
	Brundle	McLaren-Peugeot	29	engine	12
	Morbidelli	Footwork-Ford	28	accident	22
	Panis	Ligier-Renault	28	accident	13
	D Brabham	Simtek-Ford	28	engine	24
	Verstappen	Benetton-Ford	25	spun	8
	Irvine	Jordan-Hart	24	spun	6
	Alboreto	Minardi-Ford	21	engine	21
	Zanardi	Lotus-Mugen Honda	20	engine	23

Fastest Lap: Hill, 1m 19.68s, 119.32mph/192.02kph

British Grand Prix: Silverstone, 10 July 1994

60 laps of 3.14 mile/5.06 km circuit

Place	Driver	Car	Laps	Time/Reason for retiring	Grid
1	D Hill	Williams-Renault	60	1h 30m 03.6s	1
	M Schumacher	Benetton-Ford	60	disqualified: overtook on parade lap	2
2	Alesi	Ferrari	60	1h 31m 11.77s	4
3	Hakkinen	McLaren-Peugeot	60	1h 31m 44.3s	5
4	Barrichello	Jordan-Hart	60	1h 31m 45.4s	6
5	Coulthard	Williams-Renault	59		7
6	Katayama	Tyrrell-Yamaha	59		8
7	Frentzen	Sauber-Mercedes	59		13
8	Verstappen	Benetton-Ford	59		10
9	C Fittipaldi	Footwork-Ford	58		20
10	Martini	Minardi-Ford	58		14
11	Herbert	Lotus-Mugen Honda	58		21
12	Panis	Ligier-Renault	58		15
13	Bernard	Ligier-Renault	58		23
14	Beretta	Larrousse-Ford	58		24
15	D Brabham	Simtek-Ford	57		25
16	Gounon	Simtek-Ford	57		26
	Alboreto	Minardi-Ford	48	engine	17
	Berger	Ferrari	32	engine	3
	Blundell	Tyrrell-Yamaha	20	gearbox	11
	Brundle	McLaren-Peugeot	29	engine	9

British Grand Prix (cont)

Place	Driver	Car	Laps	Time/reason for retiring	Grid
	Zanardi	Lotus-Mugen Honda	20	engine	19
	Comas	Larrousse-Ford	12	engine	22
	de Cesaris	Sauber-Mercedes	11	engine	18
	Morbidelli	Footwork-Ford	5	fuel system	16
	Irvine	Jordan-Hart	0	did not start: engine	12

Fastest Lap: Hill, 1m 27.1s, 129.88mph/209.02kph

German Grand Prix: Hockenheim, 31 July 1994

45 laps of 4.24 mile/6.82 km circuit

Place	Driver	Car	Laps	Time/Reason for retiring	Grid
1	Berger	Ferrari	45	1h 30m 03,6s	1
2	Panis	Ligier-Renault	45	1h 31m 11.77s	12
3	Bernard	Ligier-Renault	45	1h 31m 44.3s	14
4	C Fittipaldi	Footwork-Ford	45	1h 31m 45.4s	17
5	Morbidelli	Footwork-Ford	45		16
6	Comas	Larrousse-Ford	45		22
7	Beretta	Larrousse-Ford	44		24
8	D Hill	Williams-Renault	44		3
	Gounon	Simtek-Ford	39	gearbox	26
	D Brabham	Simtek-Ford	37	clutch	25
	M Schumacher	Benetton-Ford	20	engine	4
	Brundle	McLaren-Peugeot	19	engine	13
	Coulthard	Williams-Renault	17	electrical	6
	Verstappen	Benetton-Ford	15	fire	19
	Katayama	Tyrrell-Yamaha	6	throttle	5
	Alesi	Ferrari	0	electrical	2
	Frentzen	Sauber-Mercedes	0	accident	9
	Herbert	Lotus-Mugen Honda	0	accident	15
	Barrichello	Jordan-Hart	0	accident	11
	Irvine	Jordan-Hart	0	accident	10
	Blundell	Tyrrell-Yamaha	0	accident	7
	Hakkinen	McLaren-Peugeot	0	accident	8
	Zanardi	Lotus-Mugen Honda	0	accident	21
	Martini	Minardi-Ford	0	accident	20
	Alboreto	Minardi-Ford	0	accident	23
	de Cesaris	Sauber-Mercedes	0	accident	18

Fastest Lap: Coulthard, 1m 46.21s, 143.7mph/231.26kph

Hungarian Grand Prix: Hungaroring, 14 August 1994

77 laps of 2.47 mile/3.97 km circuit

Place	Driver	Car	Laps	Time/Reason for retiring	Grid
1	M Schumacher	Benetton-Ford	77	1h 48m 00.2s	1
2	D Hill	Williams-Renault	77	1h 48m 21s	2
3	Verstappen	Benetton-Ford	77	1h 49m 10.5s	12
4	Brundle	McLaren-Peugeot	76	electrical	6
5	Blundell	Tyrrell-Yamaha	76		11
6	Panis	Ligier-Renault	76		9
7	Alboreto	Minardi-Ford	75		20
8	Comas	Larrousse-Ford	75		21
9	Beretta	Larrousse-Ford	75		25
10	Bernard	Ligier-Renault	75		18
11	D Brabham	Simtek-Ford	74		23
12	Berger	Ferrari	72		4
13	Zanardi	Lotus-Mugen Honda	72		22
14	C Fittipaldi	Footwork-Ford	69	gearbox	16
	Coulthard	Williams-Renault	59	accident	3
	Alesi	Ferrari	58	gearbox	13
	Martini	Minardi-Ford	58	spun	15
	Frentzen	Sauber-Mercedes	39	gearbox	8
	Herbert	Lotus-Mugen Honda	34	electrical	24
	de Cesaris	Sauber-Mercedes	30	accident	17
	Morbidelli	Footwork-Ford	30	accident	19
	Alliot	McLaren-Peugeot	21	water	14
	Gounon	Simtek-Ford	9	handling	26
	Katayama	Tyrrell-Yamaha	0	accident	5
	Barrichello	Jordan-Hart	0	accident	10
	Irvine	Jordan-Hart	0	accident	7

Fastest Lap: M Schumacher, 1m 20.88s, 109.7mph/176.62kph

Belgian Grand Prix: Spa, 28 August 1994

44 laps of 4.35 mile/7 km circuit

Place	Driver	Car	Laps	Time/Reason for retiring	Grid
	M Schumacher	Benetton-Ford	44	disqualified: skidblock illegal	2
1	D Hill	Williams-Renault	44	1h 28m 47.2s	3
2	Hakkinen	McLaren-Peugeot	44	1h 29m 38.6s	8
3	Verstappen	Benetton-Ford	44	1h 29m 57.6s	6
4	Coulthard	Williams-Renault	44	1h 30m 33s	7
5	Blundell	Tyrrell-Yamaha	43		12
6	Morbidelli	Footwork-Ford	43		14
7	Panis	Ligier-Renault	43		17
8	Martini	Minardi-Ford	43		10

Belgian Grand Prix (cont)

Place	Driver	Car	Laps	Time/reason for retiring	Grid
9	Alboreto	Minardi-Ford	43		18
10	Bernard	Ligier-Renault	42		16
11	Gounon	Simtek-Ford	42		25
12	Herbert	Lotus-Mugen Honda	41		20
13	Irvine	Jordan-Hart	40	electrical	4
	C Fittipaldi	Footwork-Ford	33	engine	24
	D Brabham	Simtek-Ford	29	wheel	21
	de Cesaris	Sauber-Mercedes	27	throttle	15
	Brundle	McLaren-Peugeot	24	spun	13
	Barrichello	Jordan-Hart	19	spun	1
	Katayama	Tyrrell-Yamaha	18	engine	23
	Adams	Lotus-Mugen Honda	15	spun	26
	Berger	Ferrari	11	engine	11
	Alliot	Larrousse-Ford	11	engine	19
	Frentzen	Sauber-Mercedes	10	spun	9
	Comas	Larrousse-Ford	3	engine	22
	Alesi	Ferrari	2	engine	5

Fastest Lap: Hill, 1m 57.12s, 133.72mph/215.2kph

Italian Grand Prix: Monza, 11 September 1994

53 laps of 3.6 mile/5.8 km circuit

Place	Driver	Car	Laps	Time/Reason for retiring	Grid
1	D Hill	Williams-Renault	53	1h 18m 02.8s	3
2	Berger	Ferrari	53	1h 18m 07.7s	2
3	Hakkinen	McLaren-Peugeot	53	1h 18m 28.4s	7
4	Barrichello	Jordan-Hart	53	1h 18m 53.4s	16
5	Brundle	McLaren-Peugeot	53	1h 19m 28.3s	15
6	Coulthard	Williams-Renault	52	out of fuel	5
7	Bernard	Ligier-Renault	52		12
8	Comas	Larrousse-Ford	52		24
9	Lehto	Benetton-Ford	52		20
10	Panis	Ligier-Renault	51		6
	D Brabham	Simtek-Ford	46	brakes	26
	Katayama	Tyrrell-Yamaha	45	brakes	14
	C Fittipaldi	Footwork-Ford	43	engine	19
	Irvine	Jordan-Hart	41	engine	9
	Blundell	Tyrrell-Yamaha	39	brakes	21
	Martini	Minardi-Ford	30	spun	18
	Alboreto	Minardi-Ford	28	gearbox	22
	Frentzen	Sauber-Mercedes	22	engine	11
	de Cesaris	Sauber-Mercedes	20	engine	8
	Gounon	Simtek-Ford	20	transmission	25
	Dalmas	Larrousse-Ford	18	spun	23

Italian Grand Prix (cont)

Place	Driver	Car	Laps	Time/reason for retiring	Grid
	Alesi	Ferrari	14	gearbox	1
	Herbert	Lotus-Mugen Honda	13	engine	4
	Verstappen	Benetton-Ford	0	tyre	10
	Zanardi	Lotus-Mugen Honda	0	accident	13
	Morbidelli	Footwork-Ford	0	tyre	17

Fastest Lap: Hill, 1m 25.93s, 150.99mph/242.99kph

Portuguese Grand Prix: Estoril, 25 September 1994

71 laps of 2.71 mile/4.36 km circuit

Place	Driver	Car	Laps	Time/Reason for retiring	Grid
1	D Hill	Williams-Renault	71	1h 41m 10.2s	2
2	Coulthard	Williams-Renault	71	1h 41m 10.8s	3
3	Hakkinen	McLaren-Peugeot	71	1h 41m 30.4s	4
4	Barrichello	Jordan-Hart	71	1h 41m 38.2s	8
5	Verstappen	Benetton-Ford	71	1h 41m 39.6s	10
6	Brundle	McLaren-Peugeot	71	1h 42m 02.9s	7
7	Irvine	Jordan-Hart	70		13
8	C Fittipaldi	Footwork-Ford	70		11
	Panis	Ligier-Renault	70	disqualified: skidblock illegality	15
9	Morbidelli	Footwork-Ford	70		16
10	Bernard	Ligier-Renault	70		21
11	Herbert	Lotus-Mugen Honda	70		20
12	Martini	Minardi-Ford	69		18
13	Alboreto	Minardi-Ford	69		19
14	Dalmas	Larrousse-Ford	69		23
15	Gounon	Simtek-Ford	67		26
16	Adams	Lotus-Mugen Honda	67		25
	Blundell	Tyrrell-Yamaha	61	engine	12
	Lehto	Benetton-Ford	60	spun	14
	de Cesaris	Sauber-Mercedes	54	spun	17
	Alesi	Ferrari	38	accident	5
	D Brabham	Simtek-Ford	36	accident	24
	Frentzen	Sauber-Mercedes	31	transmission	9
	Comas	Larrousse-Ford	27	accident	22
	Katayama	Tyrrell-Yamaha	26	gearbox	6
	Berger	Ferrari	7	gearbox	1

Fastest Lap: Coulthard, 1m 22.45s, 118.29mph/190.38kph

European Grand Prix: Jerez, 16 October 1994

69 laps of 2.75 mile/4.43 km circuit

Place	Driver	Car	Laps	Time/Reason for retiring	Grid
1	M Schumacher	Benetton-Ford	69	1h 40m 26.7s	1
2	D Hill	Williams-Renault	69	1h 40m 51.4s	2
3	Hakkinen	McLaren-Peugeot	69	1h 41m 36.3s	9
4	Irvine	Jordan-Hart	69	1h 41m 45.1s	10
5	Berger	Ferrari	68		6
6	Frentzen	Sauber-Mercedes	68		4
7	Katayama	Tyrrell-Yamaha	68		13
8	Herbert	Ligier-Renault	68		7
9	Panis	Ligier-Renault	68		11
10	Alesi	Ferrari	68		16
11	Morbidelli	Footwork-Ford	68		8
12	Barrichello	Jordan-Hart	68		5
13	Blundell	Tyrrell-Yamaha	68		14
14	Alboreto	Minardi-Ford	67		20
15	Martini	Minardi-Ford	67		17
16	Zanardi	Lotus-Mugen Honda	67		21
17	C Fittipaldi	Footwork-Ford	66		19
18	Bernard	Lotus-Mugen Honda	66		22
19	Schiattarella	Simtek-Ford	64		26
	Mansell	Williams-Renault	47	spun	3
	D Brabham	Simtek-Ford	42	engine	25
	de Cesaris	Sauber-Mercedes	37	throttle	18
	Comas	Larrousse-Ford	37	electrical	23
	Verstappen	Benetton-Ford	15	spun	12
	Noda	Larrousse-Ford	10	gearbox	24
	Brundle	McLaren-Peugeot	8	engine	15

Fastest Lap: M Schumacher, 1m 25.04s, 116.48mph/187.45kph

Japanese Grand Prix: Suzuka, 6 November 1994

50 laps of 3.64 mile/5.86 km circuit

Place	Driver	Car	Laps	Time/Reason for retiring	Grid
1	D Hill	Williams-Renault	50	1h 55m 53.5s	2
2	M Schumacher	Benetton-Ford	50	1h 55m 56.9s	1
3	Alesi	Ferrari	50	1h 56m 45.6s	7
4	Mansell	Williams-Renault	50	1h 56m 49.6s	4
5	Irvine	Jordan-Hart	50	1h 57m 35.6s	6
6	Frentzen	Sauber-Mercedes	50	1h 57m 53.4s	3
7	Hakkinen	McLaren-Peugeot	50	1h 57m 36.5s	8
8	C Fittipaldi	Footwork-Ford	49		18
9	Comas	Larrousse-Ford	49		22
10	Salo	Lotus-Mugen Honda	49		25

Japanese Grand Prix (cont)

Place	Driver	Car	Laps	Time/reason for retiring	Grid
11	Panis	Ligier-Renault	49		19
12	D Brabham	Simtek-Ford	48		24
13	Zanardi	Lotus-Mugen Honda	48		17
	Blundell	Tyrrell-Yamaha	26	engine	13
	Barrichello	Jordan-Hart	16	gearbox	10
	Brundle	McLaren-Peugeot	13	accident	9
	Morbidelli	Footwork-Ford	10	accident	12
	Berger	Ferrari	10	electrical	11
	Lagorce	Ligier-Renault	10	accident	20
	Martini	Minardi-Ford	10	accident	16
	Alboreto	Minardi-Ford	3	spun	21
	Herbert	Benetton-Ford	3	spun	5
	Katayama	Tyrrell-Yamaha	3	accident	14
	Inoue	Simtek-Ford	0	accident	26
	Noda	Larrousse-Ford	0	fuel injection	23
	Lehto	Sauber-Mercedes	0	engine	15

Fastest Lap: Hill, 1m 56.6s, 112.5mph/181.05kph

Australian Grand Prix: Adelaide, 13 November 1994

81 laps of 2.35 mile/3.78 km circuit

Place	Driver	Car	Laps	Time/Reason for retiring	Grid
1	Mansell	Williams-Renault	81	1h 47m 51.5s	1
2	Berger	Ferrari	81	1h 47m 54s	11
3	Brundle	McLaren-Peugeot	81	1h 48m 44s	9
4	Barrichello	Jordan-Hart	81	1h 49m 02s	5
5	Panis	Ligier-Renault	80		12
6	Alesi	Ferrari	80		8
7	Frentzen	Sauber-Mercedes	80		10
8	C Fittipaldi	Footwork-Ford	80		19
9	Martini	Minardi-Ford	79		18
10	Lehto	Sauber-Mercedes	79		17
11	Lagorce	Ligier-Renault	79		20
12	Hakkinen	McLaren-Peugeot	76	brakes	4
	Alboreto	Minardi-Ford	69	accident	16
	Blundell	Tyrrell-Yamaha	66	accident	13
	Deletraz	Larrousse-Ford	56	gearbox	25
	Salo	Lotus-Mugen Honda	49	electrical	22
	D Brabham	Simtek-Ford	49	engine	24
	Zanardi	Lotus-Mugen Honda	40	throttle	14
	D Hill	Williams-Renault	35	accident	3
	M Schumacher	Benetton-Ford	35	accident	2
	Schiattarella	Simtek-Ford	21	gear lever	26
	Katayama	Tyrrell-Yamaha	19	spun	15

Australian Grand Prix (cont)

Place	Driver	Car	Laps	Time/reason for retiring	Grid
	Noda	Larrousse-Ford	18	oil	23
	Morbidelli	Footwork-Ford	17	oil system	21
	Irvine	Jordan-Hart	15	spun	6
	Herbert	Benetton-Ford	13	gearbox	7

Fastest Lap: M Schumacher, 1m 17.14s, 109.61mph/176.41kph

World Championship 1994

1	M Schumacher	92
2	D Hill	91
3	Berger	41
4	Hakkinen	26
5	Alesi	24
6	Barrichello	19
7	Brundle	16
8	Coulthard	14
9	Mansell	13
10	Verstappen	10
11	Panis	9
12	Blundell	8
13	Frentzen	7
14 =	C Fittipaldi, Irvine, Larini	6
17	Katayama	5
18 =	Bernard, de Cesaris, Martini, Wendlinger	4
22	Morbidelli	3
23	Comas	2
24 =	Alboreto, Lehto	1

Constructors' Championship

1	Williams-Renault	118
2	Benetton-Ford	103
3	Ferrari	71
4	McLaren-Peugeot	42
5	Jordan-Hart	28
6 =	Ligier-Renault, Tyrrell-Yamaha	13
8	Sauber-Mercedes	12
9	Footwork-Ford	9
10	Minardi-Ford	5
11	Larrousse-Ford	2

1995

Schumacher dominated the season, taking his second title by a very clear margin. Nigel Mansell's brief relationship with McLaren began badly when he couldn't fit into the car and stopped after two undistinguished races. Mansell was one of the great racers: although his relationship with the press was always difficult, he had a natural affinity with the public who recognised his determination to succeed in the face of great difficulties and his sheer competitiveness. Alesi, Coulthard and Herbert won their first grand prix. Engine size was reduced to three litres. Larrousse and Lotus withdrew before the season and Simtek after Monaco. Juan Manuel Fangio, five times world champion and one of the very greatest drivers of all time, died.

Brazilian Grand Prix: Interlagos, 26 March, 1995

71 laps of 2.69 mile/4.33 km circuit

Place	Driver	Car	Laps	Time/reason for retiring	Grid
1	M Schumacher	Benetton-Renault	71	1h 38m 34.2s	2
2	Coulthard	Williams-Renault	71	1h 38m 42.2s	3
3	Berger	Ferrari	70		5
4	Hakkinen	McLaren-Mercedes	70		7
5	Alesi	Ferrari	70		6
6	Blundell	McLaren-Mercedes	70		9
7	Salo	Tyrrell-Yamaha	69		12
8	Suzuki	Ligier-Mugen Honda	69		15
9	Montermini	Pacific-Ford	65		22
10	Diniz	Forti-Ford	64		25
	Morbidelli	Footwork-Hart	62	fuel system	13
	Inoue	Footwork-Hart	48	fire	21
	Badoer	Minardi-Ford	47	gearbox	18
	Moreno	Forti-Ford	47	spun	23
	Wendlinger	Sauber-Ford	41	electrical	19
	D Hill	Williams-Renault	30	suspension	1
	Herbert	Benetton-Renault	30	accident	4
	Gachot	Pacific-Ford	23	gearbox	20

Brazilian Grand Prix (cont)

Place	Driver	Car	Laps	Time/reason for retiring	Grid
	Barrichello	Jordan-Peugeot	16	gearbox	16
	Verstappen	Simtek-Ford	16	clutch	24
	Katayama	Tyrrell-Yamaha	15	spun	11
	Irvine	Jordan-Peugeot	15	gearbox	8
	Schiattarella	Simtek-Ford	12	steering	26
	Frentzen	Sauber-Ford	10	electrical	14
	Panis	Ligier-Mugen Honda	0	accident	10
	Martini	Minardi-Ford	0	did not start: gearbox	17

Fastest Lap: M Schumacher, 1m 20.92s. 119.56mph/192.41kph
* no constructors' championship points awarded to first two finishers: fuel irregularities

Argentinian Grand Prix: Buenos Aires, 9 April 1995

72 laps of 2.65 mile/4.26 km circuit

Place	Driver	Car	Laps	Time/reason for retiring	Grid
1	D Hill	Williams-Renault	72	1h 53m 14.5s	2
2	Alesi	Ferrari	72	1h 53m 20.9s	6
3	M Schumacher	Benetton-Renault	72	1h 53m 47.9s	3
4	Herbert	Benetton-Renault	71		11
5	Frentzen	Sauber-Ford	70		9
6	Berger	Ferrari	70		8
7	Panis	Ligier-Mugen Honda	70		18
8	Katayama	Tyrrell-Yamaha	69		15
9	Schiattarella	Simtek-Ford	68		20
	Diniz	Forti-Ford	63	running	25
	Moreno	Forti-Ford	63	running	24
	Salo	Tyrrell-Yamaha	48	accident	7
	A Suzuki	Ligier-Mugen Honda	47	accident	19
	Martini	Minardi-Ford	44	spun	16
	Morbidelli	Footwork-Hart	43	electrical	12
	Inoue	Footwork-Hart	40	spun	26
	Barrichello	Jordan-Peugeot	33	engine	10
	Verstappen	Simtek-Ford	23	gearbox	14
	Coulthard	Williams-Renault	16	throttle	1
	Blundell	McLaren-Mercedes	9	gearbox	17
	Irvine	Jordan-Peugeot	6	engine	4
	Montermini	Pacific-Ford	1	accident	22
	Hakkinen	McLaren-Mercedes	0	accident	5
	Gachot	Pacific-Ford	0	accident	23
	Wendlinger	Sauber-Ford	0	accident	21
	Badoer	Minardi-Ford	0	accident	13

Fastest Lap: M Schumacher, 1m 30.52s. 105.25mph/169.38kph
* restarted after first lap accident; Badoer eliminated after first start

San Marino Grand Prix: Imola, 30 April 1995

63 laps of 3.04 mile/4.9 km circuit

Place	Driver	Car	Laps	Time/reason for retiring	Grid
1	D Hill	Williams-Renault	63	1h 41m 42.6s	4
2	Alesi	Ferrari	63	1h 42m 01.1s	5
3	Berger	Ferrari	63	1h 42m 25.7s	2
4	Coulthard	Williams-Renault	63	1h 42m 34.4s	3
5	Hakkinen	McLaren-Mercedes	62		6
6	Frentzen	Sauber-Ford	62		14
7	Herbert	Benetton-Renault	61		8
8	Irvine	Jordan-Peugeot	61		7
9	Panis	Ligier-Mugen Honda	61		12
10	Mansell	McLaren-Mercedes	61		9
11	A Suzuki	Ligier-Mugen Honda	60		16
12	Martini	Minardi-Ford	59		18
13	Morbidelli	Footwork-Hart	59		11
14	Badoer	Minardi-Ford	59		20
15	Diniz	Forti-Ford	56		26
16	Moreno	Forti-Ford	56		25
	Wendlinger	Sauber-Ford	43	wheel	21
	Gachot	Pacific-Ford	36	gearbox	22
	Schiattarella	Simtek-Ford	35	accident	23
	Barrichello	Jordan-Peugeot	31	gearbox	10
	Katayama	Tyrrell-Yamaha	23	spun	15
	Salo	Tyrrell-Yamaha	19	engine	13
	Montermini	Pacific-Ford	15	gearbox	24
	Verstappen	Simtek-Ford	14	gearbox	17
	Inoue	Footwork-Hart	12	spun	19
	M Schumacher	Benetton-Renault	10	accident	1

Fastest Lap: Berger, 1m 29.57s. 122.25 mph/196.74 kph

Spanish Grand Prix: Barcelona, 14 May 1995

65 laps of 2.94 mile/4.73 km circuit

Place	Driver	Car	Laps	Time/reason for retiring	Grid
1	M Schumacher	Benetton-Renault	65	1h 34m 20.5s	1
2	Herbert	Benetton-Renault	65	1h 35m 12.5s	7
3	Berger	Ferrari	65	1h 35m 25.7s	3
4	D Hill	Williams-Renault	65	1h 36m 22.3s	5
5	Irvine	Jordan-Peugeot	64		6
6	Panis	Ligier-Mugen Honda	64		15
7	Barrichello	Jordan-Peugeot	64		8
8	Frentzen	Sauber-Ford	64		12
9	Brundle	Ligier-Mugen Honda	64		11
10	Salo	Tyrrell-Yamaha	64		13

Spanish Grand Prix (cont)

Place	Driver	Car	Laps	Time/reason for retiring	Grid
11	Morbidelli	Footwork-Hart	63		14
12	Verstappen	Simtek-Ford	63		16
13	Wendlinger	Sauber-Ford	63		20
14	Martini	Minardi-Ford	62		19
15	Schiattarella	Simtek-Ford	61		22
	Katayama	Tyrrell-Yamaha	56	engine	17
	Coulthard	Williams-Renault	54	gearbox	4
	Hakkinen	McLaren-Mercedes	53	fuel pressure	9
	Inoue	Footwork-Hart	43	engine	18
	Gachot	Pacific-Ford	43	fire	24
	Moreno	Forti-Ford	39	water system	25
	Alesi	Ferrari	25	engine	2
	Badoer	Minardi-Ford	21	gearbox	21
	Mansell	McLaren-Mercedes	18	handling	10
	Diniz	Forti-Ford	17	gearbox	26
	Montermini	Pacific-Ford	0	did not start: gearbox	23

Fastest Lap: Hill, 1m 24.53s. 125.09mph/201.31kph

Monaco Grand Prix: Monte Carlo, 28 May 1995

78 laps of 2.07 mile/3.33 km circuit

Place	Driver	Car	Laps	Time/reason for retiring	Grid
1	M Schumacher	Benetton-Renault	78	1h 53m 11.3s	2
2	D Hill	Williams-Renault	78	1h 53m 46.1s	1
3	Berger	Ferrari	78	1h 54m 22.7s	4
4	Herbert	Benetton-Renault	77		7
5	Blundell	McLaren-Mercedes	77		10
6	Frentzen	Sauber-Ford	76		14
7	Martini	Minardi-Ford	76		18
8	Boullion	Sauber-Ford	74	accident	19
9	Morbidelli	Footwork-Hart	74		13
10	Diniz	Forti-Ford	72		22
	Badoer	Minardi-Ford	68	accident	16
	Panis	Ligier-Mugen Honda	65	accident	12
	Salo	Tyrrell-Yamaha	63	engine	17
	Barrichello	Jordan-Peugeot	60	throttle	11
	Gachot	Pacific-Ford	42	gearbox	21
	Alesi	Ferrari	41	accident	5
	Brundle	Ligier-Mugen Honda	40	accident	8
	Inoue	Footwork-Hart	27	gearbox	26
	Katayama	Tyrrell-Yamaha	26	accident	15
	Montermini	Pacific-Ford	23	disqualified: late for penalty	25
	Irvine	Jordan-Peugeot	22	wheel	9
	Coulthard	Williams-Renault	16	throttle	3

Monaco Grand Prix (cont)

Place	Driver	Car	Laps	Time/reason for retiring	Grid
	Moreno	Forti-Ford	9	brakes	24
	Hakkinen	McLaren-Mercedes	8	engine	6
	Schiattarella	Simtek-Ford	0	accident	20
	Verstappen	Simtek-Ford	0	accident	23

Fastest Lap: Alesi, 1m 24.62s. 87.98mph/141.58kph
* restarted after first lap accident; Schiattarella and Verstappen eliminated after first start

Canadian Grand Prix: Montreal, 11 June 1995

68 laps of 2.75 mile/4.43 km circuit

Place	Driver	Car	Laps	Time/reason for retiring	Grid
1	Alesi	Ferrari	68	1h 46m 31.3s	5
2	Barrichello	Jordan-Peugeot	68	1h 47m 03.s	9
3	Irvine	Jordan-Peugeot	68	1h 47m 04.6s	8
4	Panis	Ligier-Mugen Honda	68	1h 47m 07.8s	11
5	M Schumacher	Benetton-Renault	68	1h 47m 08.4s	1
6	Morbidelli	Footwork-Hart	67		13
7	Salo	Tyrrell-Yamaha	67		15
8	Badoer	Minardi-Ford	67		19
9	Inoue	Footwork-Hart	66		22
10	Brundle	Ligier-Mugen Honda	61	accident	14
11	Berger	Ferrari	61	accident	4
	Martini	Minardi-Ford	60	throttle	17
	Moreno	Forti-Ford	54	out of fuel	23
	D Hill	Williams-Renault	50	gearbox	2
	Blundell	McLaren-Mercedes	47	engine	10
	Katayama	Tyrrell-Yamaha	42	engine	16
	Gachot	Pacific-Ford	36	battery	20
	Frentzen	Sauber-Ford	26	engine	12
	Diniz	Forti-Ford	26	gearbox	24
	Boullion	Sauber-Ford	19	spun	18
	Montermini	Pacific-Ford	5	gearbox	21
	Coulthard	Williams-Renault	1	spun	3
	Herbert	Benetton-Renault	0	accident	6
	Hakkinen	McLaren-Mercedes	0	accident	7

Fastest Lap: M Schumacher, 1m 29.17s. 111.13mph/178.84kph

French Grand Prix: Magny-Cours, 2 July 1995

72 laps of 2.64 mile/4.25 km circuit

Place	Driver	Car	Laps	Time/reason for retiring	Grid
1	M Schumacher	Benetton-Renault	72	1h 38m 28.4s	2
2	D Hill	Williams-Renault	72	1h 38m 59.7s	1

French Grand Prix (cont)

Place	Driver	Car	Laps	Time/reason for retiring	Grid
3	Coulthard	Williams-Renault	72	1h 39m 31.255s	3
4	Brundle	Ligier-Mugen Honda	72	1h 39m 31.722s	9
5	Alesi	Ferrari	72	1h 39m 46.3s	4
6	Barrichello	Jordan-Peugeot	71		5
7	Hakkinen	McLaren-Mercedes	71		8
8	Panis	Ligier-Mugen Honda	71		6
9	Irvine	Jordan-Peugeot	71		11
10	Frentzen	Sauber-Ford	71		12
11	Blundell	McLaren-Mercedes	70		13
12	Berger	Ferrari	70		7
13	Badoer	Minardi-Ford	69		17
14	Morbidelli	Footwork-Hart	69		16
15	Salo	Tyrrell-Yamaha	69		14
16	Moreno	Forti-Ford	66		24
	Montermini	Pacific-Ford	62	running	21
	Boullion	Sauber-Ford	48	transmission	15
	Gachot	Pacific-Ford	24	gearbox	22
	Martini	Minardi-Ford	23	gearbox	20
	Herbert	Benetton-Renault	2	accident	10
	Katayama	Tyrrell-Yamaha	0	accident	19
	Inoue	Footwork-Hart	0	accident	18
	Diniz	Forti-Ford	0	accident	23

Fastest Lap: M Schumacher, 1m 20.22s. 118.51mph/190.73kph

British Grand Prix: Silverstone, 16 July 1995

61 laps of 3.14 mile/5.06 km circuit

Place	Driver	Car	Laps	Time/reason for retiring	Grid
1	Herbert	Benetton-Renault	61	1h 34m 35.1s	5
2	Alesi	Ferrari	61	1h 34m 51.6s	6
3	Coulthard	Williams-Renault	61	1h 34m 59s	3
4	Panis	Ligier-Mugen Honda	61	1h 36m 08.3s	13
5	Blundell	McLaren-Mercedes	61	1h 39m 23.3s	10
6	Frentzen	Sauber-Ford	60		12
7	Martini	Minardi-Ford	60		15
8	Salo	Tyrrell-Yamaha	60		23
9	Boullion	Sauber-Ford	60		16
10	Badoer	Minardi-Ford	60		18
11	Barrichello	Jordan-Peugeot	59	accident	9
12	Gachot	Pacific-Ford	58		21
	Moreno	Forti-Ford	48	engine	22
	M Schumacher	Benetton-Renault	45	accident	17
	D Hill	Williams-Renault	45	accident	14
	Papis	Footwork-Hart	28	accident	24
	Katayama	Tyrrell-Yamaha	22	fuel system	14

British Grand Prix (cont)

Place	Driver	Car	Laps	Time/reason for retiring	Grid
	Montermini	Pacific-Ford	21	spun	24
	Hakkinen	McLaren-Mercedes	20	gearbox	8
	Berger	Ferrari	20	wheel	4
	Brundle	Ligier-Mugen Honda	16	spun	11
	Inoue	Footwork-Hart	16	spun	19
	Diniz	Forti-Ford	13	gearbox	20
	Irvine	Jordan-Peugeot	2	engine	7

Fastest Lap: Hill, 1m 29.75s. 126.04mph/202.84kph

German Grand Prix: Hockenheim, 30 July 1995

45 laps of 4.24 mile/6.82 km circuit

Place	Driver	Car	Laps	Time/reason for retiring	Grid
1	M Schumacher	Benetton-Renault	45	1h 22m 56s	2
2	Coulthard	Williams-Renault	45	1h 23m 02s	3
3	Berger	Ferrari	45	1h 24m 04.1s	4
4	Herbert	Benetton-Renault	45	1h 24m 19.5s	9
5	Boullion	Sauber-Ford	44		14
6	A Suzuki	Ligier-Mugen Honda	44		18
7	Katayama	Tyrrell-Yamaha	44		17
8	Montermini	Pacific-Ford	42		23
9	Irvine	Jordan-Peugeot	41	throttle	6
	Hakkinen	McLaren-Mercedes	33	engine	7
	Frentzen	Sauber-Ford	32	engine	11
	Badoer	Minardi-Ford	28	gearbox	16
	Lavaggi	Pacific-Ford	27	gearbox	24
	Moreno	Forti-Ford	27	transmission	22
	Barrichello	Jordan-Peugeot	20	engine	5
	Blundell	McLaren-Mercedes	17	engine	8
	Panis	Ligier-Mugen Honda	13	water pipe	12
	Alesi	Ferrari	12	engine	10
	Martini	Minardi-Ford	11	engine	20
	Inoue	Footwork-Hart	9	gearbox	19
	Diniz	Forti-Ford	8	brakes	21
	D Hill	Williams-Renault	1	accident	1
	Salo	Tyrrell-Yamaha	0	transmission	13
	Papis	Footwork-Hart	0	gearbox	15

Fastest Lap: M Schumacher, 1m 48.82s. 140.25mph/225.71kph

Hungarian Grand Prix: Hungaroring, 13 August 1995

77 laps of 2.47 mile/3.97 km circuit

Place	Driver	Car	Laps	Time/reason for retiring	Grid
1	D Hill	Williams-Renault	77	1h 46m 25.7s	1
2	Coulthard	Williams-Renault	77	1h 46m 59.1s	2
3	Berger	Ferrari	76		4
4	Herbert	Benetton-Renault	76		9
5	Frentzen	Sauber-Ford	76		11
6	Panis	Ligier-Mugen Honda	76		10
7	Barrichello	Jordan-Peugeot	76		14
8	Badoer	Minardi-Ford	75		12
9	Lamy	Minardi-Ford	74		15
10	Boullion	Sauber-Ford	74		19
11	M Schumacher	Benetton-Renault	73	fuel system	3
12	Montermini	Pacific-Ford	73		22
13	Irvine	Jordan-Peugeot	70	clutch	7
	Brundle	Ligier-Mugen Honda	67	engine	8
	Salo	Tyrrell-Yamaha	58	throttle	16
	Blundell	McLaren-Mercedes	54	engine	13
	Katayama	Tyrrell-Yamaha	46	accident	17
	Papis	Footwork-Hart	45	brakes	20
	Alesi	Ferrari	42	engine	6
	Diniz	Forti-Ford	32	engine	23
	Inoue	Footwork-Hart	13	fire	18
	Moreno	Forti-Ford	8	gear lever	21
	Lavaggi	Pacific-Ford	5	spun	24
	Hakkinen	McLaren-Mercedes	3	engine	5

Fastest Lap: Hill, 1m 20.43s. 110.61mph/178.01kph

Belgian Grand Prix: Spa, 27 August 1995

44 laps of 4.33 mile/6.97 km circuit

Place	Driver	Car	Laps	Time/reason for retiring	Grid
1	M Schumacher	Benetton-Renault	44	1h 36m 47.9s	16
2	D Hill	Williams-Renault	44	1h 37m 07.4s	8
3	Brundle	Ligier-Mugen Honda	44	1h 37m 12.9s	13
4	Frentzen	Sauber-Ford	44	1h 37m 14.9s	10
5	Blundell	McLaren-Mercedes	44	1h 37m 21.7s	6
6	Barrichello	Jordan-Peugeot	44	1h 37m 27.6s	12
7	Herbert	Benetton-Renault	44	1h 37m 41.9s	4
8	Salo	Tyrrell-Yamaha	44	1h 37m 42.4s	11
9	Panis	Ligier-Mugen Honda	44	1h 37m 54.1s	9
10	Lamy	Minardi-Ford	44	1h 38m 07.7s	17
11	Boullion	Sauber-Ford	43		14
12	Inoue	Footwork-Hart	43		18
13	Diniz	Forti-Ford	42		24

Belgian Grand Prix (cont)

Place	Driver	Car	Laps	Time/reason for retiring	Grid
14	Moreno	Forti-Ford	42		22
	Katayama	Tyrrell-Yamaha	28	spun	15
	Lavaggi	Pacific-Ford	27	gearbox	23
	Badoer	Minardi-Ford	23	accident	19
	Berger	Ferrari	22	electrical	1
	Irvine	Jordan-Peugeot	21	fire	7
	Papis	Footwork-Hart	20	spun	20
	Montermini	Pacific-Ford	18	fuel system	21
	Coulthard	Williams-Renault	13	gearbox	5
	Alesi	Ferrari	4	suspension	2
	Hakkinen	McLaren-Mercedes	1	spun	3

Fastest Lap: Coulthard, 1m 53.41s. 137.56mph/221.37kph

Italian Grand Prix: Monza, 10 September 1995

53 laps of 3.6 mile/5.8 km circuit

Place	Driver	Car	Laps	Time/reason for retiring	Grid
1	Herbert	Benetton-Renault	53	1h 16m 27.9s	8
2	Hakkinen	McLaren-Mercedes	53	1h 18m 45.7s	7
3	Frentzen	Sauber-Ford	53	1h 18m 52.2s	10
4	Blundell	McLaren-Mercedes	53	1h 18m 56.1s	9
5	Salo	Tyrrell-Yamaha	52		16
6	Boullion	Sauber-Ford	52		14
7	Papis	Footwork-Hart	52		15
8	Inoue	Footwork-Hart	52		20
9	Diniz	Forti-Ford	50		23
10	Katayama	Tyrrell-Yamaha	47		17
	Alesi	Ferrari	45	wheel	5
	Barrichello	Jordan-Peugeot	43	hydraulics	6
	Irvine	Jordan-Peugeot	40	engine	12
	Berger	Ferrari	32	suspension	3
	Badoer	Minardi-Ford	26	accident	18
	M Schumacher	Benetton-Renault	23	accident	2
	D Hill	Williams-Renault	23	accident	4
	Panis	Ligier-Mugen Honda	20	spun	13
	Coulthard	Williams-Renault	13	wheel	1
	Brundle	Ligier-Mugen Honda	10	tyre	11
	Lavaggi	Pacific-Ford	6	spun	24
	Lamy	Minardi-Ford	0	transmission	19
	Moreno	Forti-Ford	0	accident	22
	Montermini	Pacific-Ford	18	accident	21

Fastest Lap: Berger, 1m 26.42s. 149.36mph/240.36kph
* restarted after first lap accident; Moreno and Montermini eliminated after first start

Portuguese Grand Prix: Estoril, 24 September 1995

71 laps of 2.71 mile/4.36 km circuit

Place	Driver	Car	Laps	Time/reason for retiring	Grid
1	Coulthard	Williams-Renault	71	1h 41m 52.2s	1
2	M Schumacher	Benetton-Renault	71	1h 41m 59.4s	3
3	D Hill	Williams-Renault	71	1h 42m 14.3s	2
4	Berger	Ferrari	71	1h 43m 17s	4
5	Alesi	Ferrari	71	1h 43m 17.6s	7
6	Frentzen	Sauber-Ford	70		5
7	Herbert	Benetton-Renault	70		6
8	Brundle	Ligier-Mugen Honda	70		9
9	Blundell	McLaren-Mercedes	70		12
10	Irvine	Jordan-Peugeot	70		10
11	Barrichello	Jordan-Peugeot	70		8
12	Boullion	Sauber-Ford	70		14
13	Salo	Tyrrell-Yamaha	69		15
14	Badoer	Minardi-Ford	68		18
15	Inoue	Footwork-Hart	68		19
16	Diniz	Forti-Ford	66		22
17	Moreno	Forti-Ford	64		23
	Montermini	Pacific-Ford	53	gearbox	21
	Hakkinen	McLaren-Mercedes	44	engine	13
	Deletraz	Pacific-Ford	14	driver	24
	Panis	Ligier-Mugen Honda	10	spun	11
	Lamy	Minardi-Ford	7	gearbox	17
	Katayama	Tyrrell-Yamaha	0	accident	16
	Papis	Footwork-Hart	0	gearbox	20

Fastest Lap: Coulthard, 1m 23.22s. 117.2mph/188.61kph
* restarted after first lap accident; Katayama and Papis eliminated after first start

European Grand Prix: Nürburgring, 1 October 1995

67 laps of 2.83 mile/4.56 km circuit

Place	Driver	Car	Laps	Time/reason for retiring	Grid
1	M Schumacher	Benetton-Renault	67	1h 39m 59.04s	3
2	Alesi	Ferrari	67	1h 40m 01.73s	6
3	Coulthard	Williams-Renault	67	1h 40m 34.4s	1
4	Barrichello	Jordan-Peugeot	66		11
5	Herbert	Benetton-Renault	66		7
6	Irvine	Jordan-Peugeot	66		5
7	Brundle	Ligier-Mugen Honda	66		12
8	Hakkinen	McLaren-Mercedes	65		9
9	Lamy	Minardi-Ford	64		16
10	Salo	Tyrrell-Yamaha	64		15
11	Badoer	Minardi-Ford	64		18
12	Papis	Footwork-Hart	64		17

European Grand Prix (cont)

Place	Driver	Car	Laps	Time/reason for retiring	Grid
13	Diniz	Forti-Ford	62		22
14	Tarquini	Tyrrell-Ford	61		19
	Deletraz	Pacific-Ford	60	running	24
	D Hill	Williams-Renault	58	accident	2
	Montermini	Pacific-Ford	45	out of fuel	20
	Boullion	Sauber-Ford	44	accident	13
	Berger	Ferrari	40	electrical	4
	Moreno	Forti-Ford	22	gearbox	23
	Frentzen	Sauber-Ford	17	accident	8
	Panis	Ligier-Mugen Honda	14	spun	14
	Blundell	McLaren-Mercedes	14	spun	10
	Inoue	Footwork-Hart	0	electrical	21

Fastest Lap: M Schumacher 1m 21.18s. 125.42mph/202.04kph

Pacific Grand Prix: Aida, 22 October 1995

83 laps of 2.3 mile/3.7 km circuit

Place	Driver	Car	Laps	Time/reason for retiring	Grid
1	M Schumacher	Benetton-Renault	83	1h 48m 50s	3
2	Coulthard	Williams-Renault	83	1h 49m 04.9s	1
3	D Hill	Williams-Renault	83	1h 49m 38.3s	2
4	Berger	Ferrari	82		5
5	Alesi	Ferrari	82		4
6	Herbert	Benetton-Renault	82		7
7	Frentzen	Sauber-Ford	82		8
8	Panis	Ligier-Mugen Honda	81		9
9	Blundell	McLaren-Mercedes	81		10
10	Magnussen	McLaren-Mercedes	81		12
11	Irvine	Jordan-Peugeot	81		6
12	Salo	Tyrrell-Yamaha	80		18
13	Lamy	Minardi-Ford	80		14
14	Katayama	Tyrrell-Ford	80		17
15	Badoer	Minardi-Ford	80		16
16	Moreno	Forti-Ford	78		22
17	Diniz	Forti-Ford	77		21
	Barrichello	Jordan-Peugeot	67	electrical	11
	Morbidelli	Footwork-Hart	53	engine	19
	Inoue	Footwork-Hart	38	engine	20
	Montermini	Pacific-Ford	14	gearbox	23
	A Suzuki	Ligier-Mugen Honda	10	spun	13
	Boullion	Sauber-Ford	7	spun	15
	Gachot	Pacific-Ford	2	gearbox	24

Fastest Lap: M Schumacher 1m 16.37s. 108.46mph/174.55kph

Japanese Grand Prix: Suzuka, 29 October 1995

53 laps of 3.64 mile/5.86 km circuit

Place	Driver	Car	Laps	Time/reason for retiring	Grid
1	M Schumacher	Benetton-Renault	53	1h 36m 52.9s	1
2	Hakkinen	McLaren-Mercedes	53	1h 37m 12.3s	3
3	Herbert	Benetton-Renault	53	1h 38m 16.7s	9
4	Irvine	Jordan-Peugeot	53	1h 38m 35.1s	7
5	Panis	Ligier-Mugen Honda	52		11
6	Salo	Tyrrell-Yamaha	52		12
7	Blundell	McLaren-Mercedes	52		23
8	Frentzen	Sauber-Ford	52		8
9	Badoer	Minardi-Ford	51		17
10	Wendlinger	Sauber-Ford	51		15
11	Lamy	Minardi-Ford	51		16
12	Inoue	Footwork-Hart	51		18
	D Hill	Williams-Renault	40	spun	4
	Coulthard	Williams-Renault	39	accident	6
	Diniz	Forti-Ford	32	spun	20
	Alesi	Ferrari	24	transmission	2
	Montermini	Pacific-Ford	23	spun	19
	Berger	Ferrari	16	electrical	5
	Barrichello	Jordan-Peugeot	15	accident	10
	Katayama	Tyrrell-Yamaha	12	accident	13
	Gachot	Pacific-Ford	6	transmission	22
	Moreno	Forti-Ford	1	gearbox	21
	Morbidelli	Footwork-Hart	0	spun	14

Fastest Lap: M Schumacher 1m 43s. 127.38mph/205kph

Australian Grand Prix: Adelaide, 12 November 1995

81 laps of 2.35 mile/3.78 km circuit

Place	Driver	Car	Laps	Time/reason for retiring	Grid
1	D Hill	Williams-Renault	81	1h 49m 16s	1
2	Panis	Ligier-Mugen Honda	79		12
3	Morbidelli	Footwork-Hart	79		13
4	Blundell	McLaren-Mercedes	79		10
5	Salo	Tyrrell-Yamaha	78		14
6	Lamy	Minardi-Ford	78		17
7	Diniz	Forti-Ford	77		21
8	Gachot	Pacific-Ford	76		23
	Katayama	Tyrrell-Yamaha	70	engine	16
	Herbert	Benetton-Renault	69	transmission	8
	Irvine	Jordan-Peugeot	62	engine	9
	Frentzen	Sauber-Ford	39	gearbox	6
	Berger	Ferrari	34	engine	4
	Brundle	Ligier-Mugen Honda	29	accident	11

Australian Grand Prix (cont)

Place	Driver	Car	Laps	Time/reason for retiring	Grid
	M Schumacher	Benetton-Renault	25	accident	3
	Alesi	Ferrari	23	accident	5
	Moreno	Forti-Ford	21	accident	20
	Barrichello	Jordan-Peugeot	20	accident	7
	Coulthard	Williams-Renault	19	accident	2
	Inoue	Footwork-Hart	15	accident	19
	Wendlinger	Sauber-Ford	8	driver	18
	Montermini	Pacific-Ford	2	gearbox accident	22
	Badoer	Minardi-Ford		did not start: electrical	15

Fastest Lap: Hill, 1m 17.94s. 108.49mph/174.59kph

World Championship 1995

1	M Schumacher	102
2	D Hill	69
3	Coulthard	49
4	Herbert	45
5	Alesi	42
6	Berger	31
7	Hakkinen	17
8	Panis	16
9	Frentzen	15
10	Blundell	13
11	Barrichello	11
12	Irvine	10
13	Brundle	7
14 =	Morbidelli, Salo	5
16	Boullion	3
17 =	Lamy, A Suzuki	1

Constructors' Championship

1	Benetton-Renault	137
2	Williams-Renault	112
3	Ferrari	73
4	McLaren-Mercedes	30
5	Ligier-Mugen Honda	24
6	Jordan-Peugeot	21
7	Sauber-Ford	18
8 =	Footwork-Hart, Tyrrell-Yamaha	5
10	Minardi-Ford	1

1996

Damon Hill won the championship fairly comfortably but Williams decided to replace him with Heinz-Harald Frentzen for 1997, another interesting example of the team's driver management techniques. Hill's cause was helped by Michael Schumacher's move to Ferrari who were not as competitive as Benetton had been. Hill's main challenge came from his Williams team mate, another son of a famous father, Jacques Villeneuve, son of Gilles. Unlike another Indycar champion and son of a famous father, Michael Andretti, Villeneuve was an immediate success, leading his first grand prix until forced to ease off by engine problems. Panis scored his first grand prix win in the rain at Monaco with a fast and accomplished drive. Pacific withdrew before the season and Forti did not survive it.

Australian Grand Prix: Melbourne, 10 March 1996

58 laps of 3.3 mile/5.3 km circuit

Place	Driver	Car	Laps	Time/reason for retiring	Grid
1	D Hill	Williams-Renault	58	1h 32m 50.5s	2
2	J Villeneuve	Williams-Renault	58	1h 33m 28.5s	1
3	Irvine	Ferrari	58	1h 33m 53.1s	3
4	Berger	Benetton-Renault	58	1h 34m 07.5s	7
5	Hakkinen	McLaren-Mercedes	58	1h 34m 25.6s	5
6	Salo	Tyrrell-Yamaha	57		10
7	Panis	Ligier-Mugen Honda	57		11
8	Frentzen	Sauber-Ford	57		9
9	Rosset	Footwork-Hart	56		18
10	Diniz	Ligier-Mugen Honda	56		20
11	Katayama	Tyrrell-Yamaha	55		15
	Lamy	Minardi-Ford	42	accident	17
	M Schumacher	Ferrari	34	engine	4
	Fisichella	Minardi-Ford	32	brakes	16
	Barrichello	Jordan-Peugeot	29	engine	8
	Coulthard	McLaren-Mercedes	24	throttle	13
	Verstappen	Footwork-Hart	15	engine	12

Australian Grand Prix (cont)

Place	Driver	Car	Laps	Time/reason for retiring	Grid
	Alesi	Benetton-Renault	9	accident	6
	Brundle	Jordan-Peugeot	1	spun	19
	Herbert	Sauber-Ford	0	accident	14

Fastest Lap: Villeneuve, 1m 33.42s. 126.96mph/204.31kph
* restarted after first lap accident; Herbert eliminated after first start

Brazilian Grand Prix: Interlagos, 31 March 1996

71 laps of 2.69 mile/4.33 km circuit

Place	Driver	Car	Laps	Time/reason for retiring	Grid
1	D Hill	Williams-Renault	71	1h 49m 53s	1
2	Alesi	Benetton-Renault	71	1h 50m 11a	5
3	M Schumacher	Ferrari	70		4
4	Hakkinen	McLaren-Mercedes	70		7
5	Salo	Tyrrell-Yamaha	70		11
6	Panis	Ligier-Mugen Honda	70		15
7	Irvine	Ferrari	70		10
8	Diniz	Ligier-Mugen Honda	69		22
9	Katayama	Tyrrell-Yamaha	69		16
10	Lamy	Minardi-Ford	68		18
11	Badoer	Forti-Ford	67		19
12	Brundle	Jordan-Peugeot	64	spun	6
	Barrichello	Jordan-Peugeot	59	spun	2
	Frentzen	Sauber-Ford	36	engine	9
	Coulthard	McLaren-Mercedes	29	spun	14
	Herbert	Sauber-Ford	28	engine	12
	J Villeneuve	Williams-Renault	26	spun	3
	Berger	Benetton-Renault	26	hydraulics	8
	Montermini	Forti-Ford	26	spun	20
	Rosset	Footwork-Hart	24	accident	17
	Verstappen	Footwork-Hart	19	engine	13
	Marques	Minardi-Ford	0	spun	21

Fastest Lap: Hill, 1m 21.55s. 118.64mph/190.93kph

Argentinian Grand Prix: Buenos Aires, 7 April, 1996

72 laps of 2.65 mile/4.26 km circuit

Place	Driver	Car	Laps	Time/reason for retiring	Grid
1	D Hill	Williams-Renault	72	1h 54m 55.3s	1
2	J Villeneuve	Williams-Renault	72	1h 55m 07.49s	3
3	Alesi	Benetton-Renault	72	1h 55m 10.08s	4
4	Barrichello	Jordan-Peugeot	72	1h 55m 50.5s	6

Argentinian Grand Prix (cont)

Place	Driver	Car	Laps	Time/reason for retiring	Grid
5	Irvine	Ferrari	72	1h 56m 00.31s	10
6	Verstappen	Footwork-Hart	72	1h 56m 04.24s	7
7	Coulthard	McLaren-Mercedes	72	1h 56m 08.72s	9
8	Panis	Ligier-Mugen Honda	72	1h 56m 09.62s	12
9	Herbert	Sauber-Ford	71		17
10	Montermini	Forti-Ford	69		22
	Berger	Benetton-Renault	56	suspension	5
	M Schumacher	Ferrari	46	wing	2
	Lamy	Minardi-Ford	39	transmission	19
	Salo	Tyrrell-Yamaha	36	throttle	16
	Brundle	Jordan-Peugeot	34	accident	15
	Marques	Minardi-Ford	33	accident	14
	Frentzen	Sauber-Ford	32	spun	11
	Diniz	Ligier-Mugen Honda	29	fire	18
	Katayama	Tyrrell-Yamaha	28	transmission	13
	Rosset	Footwork-Hart	24	fuel system	20
	Badoer	Forti-Ford	24	accident	21
	Hakkinen	McLaren-Mercedes	19	throttle	8

Fastest Lap: Alesi, 1m 29.41s. 106.45mph/171.48kph

European Grand Prix: Nürburgring, 28 April 1996

67 laps of 2.83 mile/4.56 km circuit

Place	Driver	Car	Laps	Time/reason for retiring	Grid
1	J Villeneuve	Williams-Renault	67	1h 33m 26.47s	2
2	M Schumacher	Ferrari	67	1h 33m 27.24s	3
3	Coulthard	McLaren-Mercedes	67	1h 33m 59.31s	6
4	D Hill	Williams-Renault	67	1h 33m 59.98s	1
5	Barrichello	Jordan-Peugeot	67	1h 34m 00.19s	5
6	Brundle	Jordan-Peugeot	67	1h 34m 22.04s	11
7	Herbert	Sauber-Ford	67	1h 34m 44.5s	12
8	Hakkinen	McLaren-Mercedes	67	1h 34m 44.91s	9
9	Berger	Benetton-Renault	67	1h 34m 47.53s	8
	Salo	Tyrrell-Yamaha	66	disqualified: under weight	14
10	Diniz	Ligier-Mugen Honda	66		17
	Katayama	Tyrrell-Yamaha	65	disqualified: push start	16
11	Rosset	Footwork-Hart	65		20
12	Lamy	Minardi-Ford	65		19
13	Fisichella	Minardi-Ford	65		18
	Frentzen	Sauber-Ford	59	spun	10
	Verstappen	Footwork-Hart	38	gearbox	13
	Panis	Ligier-Mugen Honda	6	accident	15
	Irvine	Ferrari	6	spun	7
	Alesi	Benetton-Renault	1	accident	4

Fastest Lap: Hill, 1m 21.36s. 125.26mph/201.59kph

San Marino Grand Prix: Imola, 5 May 1996

63 laps of 3.04 mile/4.89 km circuit

Place	Driver	Car	Laps	Time/reason for retiring	Grid
1	D Hill	Williams-Renault	63	1h 35m 26.2s	2
2	M Schumacher	Ferrari	63	1h 35m 42.6s	1
3	Berger	Benetton-Renault	63	1h 36m 13.1s	7
4	Irvine	Ferrari	63	1h 36m 27.7s	6
5	Barrichello	Jordan-Peugeot	63	1h 36m 44.7s	9
6	Alesi	Benetton-Renault	62		5
7	Diniz	Ligier-Mugen Honda	62		17
8	Hakkinen	McLaren-Mercedes	61	engine	11
9	Lamy	Minardi-Ford	61		18
10	Badoer	Forti-Ford	59		21
11	J Villeneuve	Williams-Renault	57	suspension	3
	Panis	Ligier-Mugen Honda	54	gearbox	13
	Katayama	Tyrrell-Yamaha	45	transmission	16
	Coulthard	McLaren-Mercedes	44	gearbox	4
	Rosset	Footwork-Hart	40	engine	20
	Verstappen	Footwork-Hart	38	refuelling hose	14
	Brundle	Jordan-Peugeot	36	spun	12
	Frentzen	Sauber-Ford	32	brakes	10
	Fisichella	Minardi-Ford	30	engine	19
	Herbert	Sauber-Ford	25	electrical	15
	Salo	Tyrrell-Yamaha	23	engine	8

Fastest Lap: Hill, 1m 28.93s. 123.05mph/198.03kph

Monaco Grand Prix: Monte Carlo, 19 May 1996

75 laps of 2.07 mile/3.33 km circuit

Place	Driver	Car	Laps	Time/reason for retiring	Grid
1	Panis	Ligier-Mugen Honda	75	2h 00m 45.63s	14
2	Coulthard	McLaren-Mercedes	75	2h 00m 50.46s	5
3	Herbert	Sauber-Ford	75	2h 01m 23.1s	13
4	Frentzen	Sauber-Ford	74		9
5	Salo	Tyrrell-Yamaha	70	accident	11
6	Hakkinen	McLaren-Mercedes	70	accident	8
7	Irvine	Ferrari	68	accident	7
	J Villeneuve	Williams-Renault	66	accident	10
	Alesi	Benetton-Renault	60	suspension	3
	Badoer	Forti-Ford	60	accident	21
	D Hill	Williams-Renault	40	engine	2
	Brundle	Jordan-Peugeot	30	accident	16
	Berger	Benetton-Renault	9	gearbox	4
	Diniz	Ligier-Mugen Honda	5	transmission	17
	Rosset	Footwork-Hart	3	accident	20
	Katayama	Tyrrell-Yamaha	2	throttle	15

Monaco Grand Prix (cont)

Place	Driver	Car	Laps	Time/reason for retiring	Grid
	M Schumacher	Ferrari	0	accident	1
	Barrichello	Jordan-Peugeot	0	accident	6
	Verstappen	Footwork-Hart	0	spun	12
	Lamy	Minardi-Ford	0	accident	19
	Fisichella	Minardi-Ford	0	accident	18

Fastest Lap: Alesi, 1m 25.21s. 87.37mph/140.61kph

Spanish Grand Prix: Barcelona, 2 June 1996

65 laps of 2.94 mile/4.73 km circuit

Place	Driver	Car	Laps	Time/reason for retiring	Grid
1	M Schumacher	Ferrari	65	1h 59m 49.3s	3
2	Alesi	Benetton-Renault	65	2h 00m 34.6s	4
3	J Villeneuve	Williams-Renault	65	2h 00m 37.7s	2
4	Frentzen	Sauber-Ford	64		11
5	Hakkinen	McLaren-Mercedes	64		10
6	Diniz	Ligier-Mugen Honda	63		17
	Verstappen	Footwork-Hart	47	spun	13
	Barrichello	Jordan-Peugeot	45	transmission	7
	Berger	Benetton-Renault	44	spun	5
	Herbert	Sauber-Ford	20	spun	9
	Brundle	Jordan-Peugeot	17	transmission	15
	Salo	Tyrrell-Yamaha	16	disqualified: changed car	12
	D Hill	Williams-Renault	10	spun	1
	Katayama	Tyrrell-Yamaha	8	electrical	16
	Irvine	Ferrari	1	spun	6
	Panis	Ligier-Mugen Honda	1	accident	8
	Fisichella	Minardi-Ford	1	accident	19
	Coulthard	McLaren-Mercedes	0	accident	14
	Rosset	Footwork-Hart	0	accident	20
	Lamy	Minardi-Ford	0	accident	18

Fastest Lap: M Schumacher, 1m 45.52s. 100.21mph/161.27kph

Canadian Grand Prix: Montreal, 16 June 1996

69 laps of 2.75 mile/4.42 km circuit

Place	Driver	Car	Laps	Time/reason for retiring	Grid
1	D Hill	Williams-Renault	69	1h 36m 03.465s	1
2	J Villeneuve	Williams-Renault	69	1h 36m 07.648s	2
3	Alesi	Benetton-Renault	69	1h 36m 58.1s	4

Canadian Grand Prix (cont)

Place	Driver	Car	Laps	Time/reason for retiring	Grid
4	Coulthard	McLaren-Mercedes	69	1h 37m 07.1s	10
5	Hakkinen	McLaren-Mercedes	68		6
6	Brundle	Jordan-Peugeot	68		9
7	Herbert	Sauber-Ford	68		15
8	Fisichella	Minardi-Ford	67		16
	Lamy	Minardi-Ford	44	accident	19
	Badoer	Forti-Ford	44	gearbox	20
	Berger	Benetton-Renault	42	spun	7
	M Schumacher	Ferrari	41	transmission	3
	Panis	Ligier-Mugen Honda	39	electrical	11
	Salo	Tyrrell-Yamaha	39	engine	14
	Diniz	Ligier-Mugen Honda	38	engine	18
	Barrichello	Jordan-Peugeot	22	clutch	8
	Montermini	Forti-Ford	22	handling	22
	Frentzen	Sauber-Ford	19	gearbox	12
	Verstappen	Footwork-Hart	10	engine	13
	Rosset	Footwork-Hart	6	accident	21
	Katayama	Tyrrell-Yamaha	6	accident	17
	Irvine	Ferrari	1	steering	5

Fastest Lap: Villenueve, 1m 21.92s. 120.73mph/194.29kph

French Grand Prix: Magny-Cours, 30 June 1996

72 laps of 2.64 mile/4.25 km circuit

Place	Driver	Car	Laps	Time/reason for retiring	Grid
1	D Hill	Williams-Renault	72	1h 36m 28.8s	2
2	J Villeneuve	Williams-Renault	72	1h 36m 36.9s	6
3	Alesi	Benetton-Renault	72	1h 37m 15.237s	3
4	Berger	Benetton-Renault	72	1h 37m 15.654s	4
5	Hakkinen	McLaren-Mercedes	72	1h 37m 31.6s	5
6	Coulthard	McLaren-Mercedes	71		7
7	Panis	Ligier-Mugen Honda	71		9
8	Brundle	Jordan-Peugeot	71		8
9	Barrichello	Jordan-Peugeot	71		10
10	Salo	Tyrrell-Yamaha	70		13
	Herbert	Sauber-Ford	70	disqualified: bodywork	16
11	Rosset	Footwork-Hart	69		19
12	Lamy	Minardi-Ford	69		18
	Frentzen	Sauber-Ford	56	throttle	12
	Katayama	Tyrrell-Yamaha	33	engine	14
	Badoer	Forti-Ford	29	fuel system	20
	Diniz	Ligier-Mugen Honda	28	engine	11
	Verstappen	Footwork-Hart	10	steering	15
	Irvine	Ferrari	5	gearbox	22

French Grand Prix (cont)

Place	Driver	Car	Laps	Time/reason for retiring	Grid
	Fisichella	Minardi-Ford	2	fuel system	17
	Montermini	Forti-Ford	2	electrical	21
	M Schumacher	Ferrari	0	did not start, engine	1

Fastest Lap: Villenueve, 1m 18.61s. 120.94mph/194.63kph

British Grand Prix: Silverstone, 14 July 1996

61 laps of 3.15 mile/5.07 km circuit

Place	Driver	Car	Laps	Time/reason for retiring	Grid
1	J Villeneuve	Williams-Renault	61	1h 33m 00.9s	2
2	Berger	Benetton-Renault	61	1h 33m 19.9s	7
3	Hakkinen	McLaren-Mercedes	61	1h 33m 51.7s	4
4	Barrichello	Jordan-Peugeot	61	1h 34m 07.6s	6
5	Coulthard	McLaren-Mercedes	61	1h 34m 23.4s	9
6	Brundle	Jordan-Peugeot	60		8
7	Salo	Tyrrell-Yamaha	60		14
8	Frentzen	Sauber-Ford	60		11
9	Herbert	Sauber-Ford	60		13
10	Verstappen	Footwork-Hart	60		15
11	Fisichella	Minardi-Ford	59		18
	Alesi	Benetton-Renault	44	wheel	5
	Panis	Ligier-Mugen Honda	40	handling	16
	Diniz	Ligier-Mugen Honda	38	engine	17
	D Hill	Williams-Renault	26	wheel	1
	Lamy	Minardi-Ford	33	gearbox	19
	Rosset	Footwork-Hart	28	electrical	20
	Katayama	Tyrrell-Yamaha	10	engine	12
	Irvine	Ferrari	5	transmission	10
	M Schumacher	Ferrari	3	gearbox	3

Fastest Lap: Villenueve, 1m 29.28s. 127.07mph/204.5kph

German Grand Prix: Hockenheim, 28 July 1996

45 laps of 4.24 mile/6.82 km circuit

Place	Driver	Car	Laps	Time/reason for retiring	Grid
1	D Hill	Williams-Renault	45	1h 21m 43.4s	1
2	Alesi	Benetton-Renault	45	1h 21m 54.9s	5
3	J Villeneuve	Williams-Renault	45	1h 22m 17.3s	6
4	M Schumacher	Ferrari	45	1h 22m 24.9s	3
5	Coulthard	McLaren-Mercedes	45	1h 22m 25.6s	7

German Grand Prix (cont)

Place	Driver	Car	Laps	Time/reason for retiring	Grid
6	Barrichello	Jordan-Peugeot	45	1h 23m 25.5s	9
7	Panis	Ligier-Mugen Honda	45	1h 23m 27.3s	12
8	Frentzen	Sauber-Ford	44		13
9	Salo	Tyrrell-Yamaha	44		15
10	Brundle	Jordan-Peugeot	44		10
11	Rosset	Footwork-Hart	44		19
12	Lamy	Minardi-Ford	43		18
13	Berger	Benetton-Renault	42	engine	2
	Irvine	Ferrari	34	gearbox	8
	Herbert	Sauber-Ford	25	gearbox	14
	Diniz	Ligier-Mugen Honda	19	throttle	11
	Katayama	Tyrrell-Yamaha	19	accident	16
	Hakkinen	McLaren-Mercedes	13	gearbox	4
	Verstappen	Footwork-Hart	0	accident	17

Fastest Lap: Hill, 1m 46.5s. 143.31mph/230.63kph

Hungarian Grand Prix: Hungaroring, 11 August 1996

77 laps of 2.47 mile/3.97 km circuit

Place	Driver	Car	Laps	Time/reason for retiring	Grid
1	J Villeneuve	Williams-Renault	77	1h 46m 21.134s	3
2	D Hill	Williams-Renault	77	1h 46m 21.905s	2
3	Alesi	Benetton-Renault	77	1h 47m 45.4s	5
4	Hakkinen	McLaren-Mercedes	76		7
5	Panis	Ligier-Mugen Honda	76		11
6	Barrichello	Jordan-Peugeot	75		13
7	Katayama	Tyrrell-Yamaha	74		14
8	Rosset	Footwork-Hart	74		18
9	M Schumacher	Ferrari	70	throttle	1
10	Lavaggi	Minardi-Ford	69	spun	20
	Berger	Benetton-Renault	64	engine	6
	Frentzen	Sauber-Ford	50	electrical	10
	Herbert	Sauber-Ford	35	engine	8
	Irvine	Ferrari	31	gearbox	4
	Lamy	Minardi-Ford	24	accident	19
	Coulthard	McLaren-Mercedes	23	water system	9
	Verstappen	Footwork-Hart	10	spun	17
	Brundle	Jordan-Peugeot	5	accident	12
	Diniz	Ligier-Mugen Honda	1	accident	15
	Salo	Tyrrell-Yamaha	0	accident	16

Fastest Lap: Hill, 1m 20.09s. 110.82mph/178.35kph

Belgian Grand Prix: Spa, 25 August 1996

44 laps of 4.33 mile/6.97 km circuit

Place	Driver	Car	Laps	Time/reason for retiring	Grid
1	M Schumacher	Ferrari	44	1h 28m 15.1s	3
2	J Villeneuve	Williams-Renault	44	1h 28m 20.7s	1
3	Hakkinen	McLaren-Mercedes	44	1h 28m 30.8s	6
4	Alesi	Benetton-Renault	44	1h 28m 34.3s	7
5	D Hill	Williams-Renault	44	1h 28m 44.3s	2
6	Berger	Benetton-Renault	44	1h 28m 45s	5
7	Salo	Tyrrell-Yamaha	44	1h 29m 15.9s	13
8	Katayama	Tyrrell-Yamaha	44	1h 29m 55.4s	17
9	Rosset	Footwork-Hart	43		18
10	Lamy	Minardi-Ford	43		19
	Coulthard	McLaren-Mercedes	37	spun	4
	Brundle	Jordan-Peugeot	34	engine	8
	Irvine	Ferrari	29	gearbox	9
	Barrichello	Jordan-Peugeot	29	accident	10
	Diniz	Ligier-Mugen Honda	22	engine	15
	Verstappen	Footwork-Hart	11	suspension	16
	Panis	Ligier-Mugen Honda	0	accident	14
	Herbert	Sauber-Ford	0	accident	12
	Frentzen	Sauber-Ford	0	accident	11

Fastest Lap: Berger, 1m 53.07s. 137.86mph/221.86kph

Italian Grand Prix: Monza, 8 September 1996

53 laps of 3.59 mile/5.77 km circuit

Place	Driver	Car	Laps	Time/reason for retiring	Grid
1	M Schumacher	Ferrari	53	1h 17m 43.6s	3
2	Alesi	Benetton-Renault	53	1h 18m 01.9s	6
3	Hakkinen	McLaren-Mercedes	53	1h 18m 50.3s	4
4	Brundle	Jordan-Peugeot	53	1h 19m 08.849s	9
5	Barrichello	Jordan-Peugeot	53	1h 19m 09.107s	10
6	Diniz	Ligier-Mugen Honda	52		14
7	J Villeneuve	Williams-Renault	52		2
8	Verstappen	Footwork-Hart	52		15
9	Herbert	Sauber-Ford	51	engine	12
10	Katayama	Tyrrell-Yamaha	51		16
	Rosset	Footwork-Hart	36	accident	19
	Irvine	Ferrari	23	accident	7
	Lamy	Minardi-Ford	12	engine	18
	Salo	Tyrrell-Yamaha	9	engine	17
	Frentzen	Sauber-Ford	7	accident	13
	D Hill	Williams-Renault	5	accident	1
	Lavaggi	Minardi-Ford	5	engine	20

Italian Grand Prix (cont)

Place	Driver	Car	Laps	Time/reason for retiring	Grid
	Berger	Benetton-Renault	4	gearbox	8
	Panis	Ligier-Mugen Honda	2	accident	11
	Coulthard	McLaren-Mercedes	1	accident	5

Fastest Lap: M Schumacher, 1m 26.11s. 149.89mph/241.23kph

Portuguese Grand Prix: Estoril, 22 September 1996

70 laps of 2.71 mile/4.36 km circuit

Place	Driver	Car	Laps	Time/reason for retiring	Grid
1	J Villeneuve	Williams-Renault	70	1h 40m 22.9s	2
2	D Hill	Williams-Renault	70	1h 40m 42.9s	1
3	M Schumacher	Ferrari	70	1h 41m 16.68s	4
4	Alesi	Benetton-Renault	70	1h 41m 18.024s	3
5	Irvine	Ferrari	70	1h 41m 50.3s	6
6	Berger	Benetton-Renault	70	1h 41m 56.1s	5
7	Frentzen	Sauber-Ford	69		11
8	Herbert	Sauber-Ford	69		12
9	Brundle	Jordan-Peugeot	69		10
10	Panis	Ligier-Mugen Honda	69		15
11	Salo	Tyrrell-Yamaha	69		13
12	Katayama	Tyrrell-Yamaha	68		14
13	Coulthard	McLaren-Mercedes	68		8
14	Rosset	Footwork-Hart	67		17
15	Lavaggi	Minardi-Ford	65		20
16	Lamy	Minardi-Ford	65		19
	Hakkinen	McLaren-Mercedes	52	accident	7
	Verstappen	Footwork-Hart	47	engine	16
	Diniz	Ligier-Mugen Honda	46	spun	18
	Barrichello	Jordan-Peugeot	41	spun	9

Fastest Lap: Villeneuve, 1m 22.87s. 117.69mph/189.4kph

Japanese Grand Prix: Suzuka, 13 October 1996

52 laps of 3.64 mile/5.86 km circuit

Place	Driver	Car	Laps	Time/reason for retiring	Grid
1	D Hill	Williams-Renault	52	1h 32m 33.791s	2
2	M Schumacher	Ferrari	52	1h 32m 35.674s	3
3	Hakkinen	McLaren-Mercedes	52	1h 32m 37.003s	5
4	Berger	Benetton-Renault	52	1h 33m 00.3s	4
5	Brundle	Jordan-Peugeot	52	1h 33m 40.9s	10

Japanese Grand Prix (cont)

Place	Driver	Car	Laps	Time/reason for retiring	Grid
6	Frentzen	Sauber-Ford	52	1h 33m 55s	7
7	Panis	Ligier-Mugen Honda	52	1h 33m 58.301s	12
8	Coulthard	McLaren-Mercedes	52	1h 33m 59.024s	8
9	Barrichello	Jordan-Peugeot	52	1h 34m 14.856s	11
10	Herbert	Sauber-Ford	52	1h 34m 15.59s	13
11	Verstappen	Footwork-Hart	51		17
12	Lamy	Minardi-Ford	50		18
13	Rosset	Footwork-Hart	50		19
	Irvine	Ferrari	39	accident	6
	Katayama	Tyrrell-Yamaha	37	engine	14
	J Villeneuve	Williams-Renault	36	wheel	1
	Salo	Tyrrell-Yamaha	20	engine	15
	Diniz	Ligier-Mugen Honda	13	spun	16
	Alesi	Benetton-Renault	0	accident	9

Fastest Lap: Villeneuve, 1m 44.04s. 126.08mph/202.9kph

World Championship 1996

1	D Hill	97
2	J Villeneuve	78
3	M Schumacher	59
4	Alesi	47
5	Hakkinen	31
6	Berger	21
7	Coulthard	18
8	Barrichello	14
9	Panis	13
10	Irvine	11
11	Frentzen	8
12	Brundle	7
13	Salo	5
14	Herbert	4
15	Diniz	2
16	Verstappen	1

Constructors' Championship

1	Williams-Renault	175
2	Ferrari	70
3	Benetton-Renault	68
4	McLaren-Mercedes	49
5	Jordan-Peugeot	22
6	Ligier-Mugen Honda	15
7	Sauber-Ford	11
8	Tyrrell-Yamaha	5
9	Footwork-Hart	1

1997

One of the most closely contested championships saw the lead change between Michael Schumacher and Jacques Villeneuve throughout the season. Schumacher's phenomenal control in the wet saw him to brilliant wins in Monaco and Belgium in what was generally regarded as the inferior car. Schumacher's sixth in Austria after a stop and go penalty for not complying with a yellow flag matched Villeneuve's disqualification for a similar but repeated offence in Japan, thus ensuring that the championship battle extended to the final race. Schumacher crashed out after colliding with Villeneuve who was attempting to overtake him for the lead of the race and the championship. Villeneuve finished the race and took the title, but Schumacher's second place in the Drivers' Championship was disallowed by the FIA after the end of the season.

Footwork reverted to the name Arrows, Ligier became Prost, and Jackie Stewart started a new team. Sauber raced Ferrari engines badged with the name of their sponsor Petronas. Damon Hill's move to Arrows was largely unsuccessful but he led comfortably in Hungary before problems forced him to settle for second. Hakkinen and Frentzen won their first grand prix. Trulli and Wurz starred in their races as understudies. Gerhard Berger retired from grand prix racing at the end of the season.

Australian Grand Prix: Melbourne, 9 March 1997

58 laps of 3.3 mile/5.3 km circuit

Place	Driver	Car	Laps	Time/reason for retiring	Grid
1	Coulthard	McLaren-Mercedes	58	1h 30m 28.7s	4
2	M Schumacher	Ferrari	58	1h 30m 48.8s	3
3	Hakkinen	McLaren-Mercedes	58	1h 30m 50.9s	6
4	Berger	Benetton-Renault	58	1h 31m 29s	10
5	Panis	Prost-Mugen Honda	58	1h 32m 04.8s	9
6	Larini	Sauber-Petronas	58	1h 32m 11.6s	13
7	Nakano	Prost-Mugen Honda	56		16
8	Frentzen	Williams-Renault	55	brakes	2
9	Trulli	Minardi-Hart	55		17
10	Diniz	Arrows-Yamaha	54		22

Australian Grand Prix (cont)

Place	Driver	Car	Laps	Time/reason for retiring	Grid
	Barrichello	Stewart-Ford	49	engine	11
	Salo	Tyrrell-Ford	42	electrical	18
	Magnussen	Stewart-Ford	36	suspension	19
	Alesi	Benetton-Renault	34	out of fuel	8
	Katayama	Minardi-Hart	32	fuel system	15
	Fisichella	Jordan-Peugeot	14	accident	14
	Verstappen	Tyrrell-Ford	2	accident	21
	R Schumacher	Jordan-Peugeot	0	transmission	12
	Irvine	Ferrari	0	accident	5
	J Villeneuve	Williams-Renault	0	accident	1
	Herbert	Sauber-Petronas	0	accident	7
	D Hill	Arrows-Yamaha	0	did not start: throttle	20

Fastest Lap: Frentzen, 1m 30.59s. 130.94mph/209.5kph

Brazilian Grand Prix: Interlagos, 30 March 1997

72 laps of 2.66 mile/4.26 km circuit

Place	Driver	Car	Laps	Time/reason for retiring	Grid
1	J Villeneuve	Williams-Renault	72	1h 36m 06.9s	1
2	Berger	Benetton-Renault	72	1h 36m 11.2s	3
3	Panis	Prost-Mugen Honda	72	1h 36m 22.9s	5
4	Hakkinen	McLaren-Mercedes	72	1h 36m 40.023s	4
5	M Schumacher	Ferrari	72	1h 36m 40.721s	2
6	Alesi	Benetton-Renault	72	1h 36m 41.01s	6
7	Herbert	Sauber-Petronas	72	1h 36m 57.9s	13
8	Fisichella	Jordan-Peugeot	72	1h 37m 07.6s	7
9	Frentzen	Williams-Renault	72	1h 37m 22.4s	8
10	Coulthard	McLaren-Mercedes	71		12
11	Larini	Sauber-Petronas	71		19
12	Trulli	Minardi-Hart	71		17
13	Salo	Tyrrell-Ford	71		22
14	Nakano	Prost-Mugen Honda	71		15
15	Verstappen	Tyrrell-Ford	70		21
16	Irvine	Ferrari	70		14
17	D Hill	Arrows-Yamaha	68		9
18	Katayama	Minardi-Hart	67		18
	R Schumacher	Jordan-Peugeot	52	electrical	10
	Barrichello	Stewart-Ford	16	suspension	11
	Diniz	Arrows-Yamaha	15	spun	16
	Magnussen	Stewart-Ford	0	accident	20

Fastest Lap: Villenueve, 1m 18.4s. 122.47mph/195.95kph

1997

Argentinian Grand Prix: Buenos Aires, 7 April, 1997

72 laps of 2.65 mile/4.26 km circuit

Place	Driver	Car	Laps	Time/reason for retiring	Grid
1	J Villeneuve	Williams-Renault	72	1h 52m 01.715s	1
2	Irvine	Ferrari	72	1h 52m 02.694s	7
3	R Schumacher	Jordan-Peugeot	72	1h 52m 13.8s	6
4	Herbert	Sauber-Petronas	72	1h 52m 32.066s	8
5	Hakkinen	McLaren-Mercedes	72	1h 52m 33.108s	17
6	Berger	Benetton-Renault	72	1h 52m 48.1s	12
7	Alesi	Benetton-Renault	72	1h 52m 58.5s	11
8	Salo	Tyrrell-Ford	71		19
9	Trulli	Minardi-Hart	71		18
10	Magnussen	Stewart-Ford	66		15
	Larini	Sauber-Petronas	53	spun	14
	Diniz	Arrows-Yamaha	50	engine	22
	Nakano	Prost-Mugen Honda	49	engine	20
	Verstappen	Tyrrell-Ford	43	engine	16
	Katayama	Minardi-Hart	37	spun	21
	D Hill	Arrows-Yamaha	33	engine	13
	Fisichella	Jordan-Peugeot	24	accident	9
	Barrichello	Stewart-Ford	24	throttle	5
	Panis	Prost-Mugen Honda	16	hydraulics	3
	Frentzen	Williams-Renault	5	clutch	2
	M Schumacher	Ferrari	0	accident	4
	Coulthard	McLaren-Mercedes	0	accident	10

Fastest Lap: Berger, 1m 27.98s. 108.29mph/173.26kph

San Marino Grand Prix: Imola, 27 April 1997

62 laps of 3.04 mile/4.89 km circuit

Place	Driver	Car	Laps	Time/reason for retiring	Grid
1	Frentzen	Williams-Renault	62	1h 31m 00.673s	2
2	M Schumacher	Ferrari	62	1h 31m 01.91s	3
3	Irvine	Ferrari	62	1h 32m 19s	9
4	Fisichella	Jordan-Peugeot	62	1h 32m 24.1s	6
5	Alesi	Benetton-Renault	61		14
6	Hakkinen	McLaren-Mercedes	61		8
7	Larini	Sauber-Petronas	61		12
8	Panis	Prost-Mugen Honda	61		4
9	Salo	Tyrrell-Ford	71		19
10	Verstappen	Tyrrell-Ford	60		21
11	Katayama	Minardi-Hart	59		22
	Diniz	Arrows-Yamaha	53	exhaust	17
	J Villeneuve	Williams-Renault	40	gearbox	1
	Coulthard	McLaren-Mercedes	38	engine	10

San Marino Grand Prix (cont)

Place	Driver	Car	Laps	Time/reason for retiring	Grid
	Barrichello	Stewart-Ford	32	engine	13
	Herbert	Sauber-Petronas	18	electrical	7
	R Schumacher	Jordan-Peugeot	17	transmission	5
	Nakano	Prost-Mugen Honda	11	accident	18
	D Hill	Arrows-Yamaha	11	accident	15
	Berger	Benetton-Renault	4	spun	11
	Magnussen	Stewart-Ford	2	spun	16
	Trulli	Minardi-Hart	0	hydraulics	20

Fastest Lap: Frentzen, 1m 25.53s. 128.94mph/206.3kph

Monaco Grand Prix: Monte Carlo, 11 May 1997

62 laps of 2.09 mile/3.34 km circuit

Place	Driver	Car	Laps	Time/reason for retiring	Grid
1	M Schumacher	Ferrari	62	2h 00m 05.7s	2
2	Barrichello	Stewart-Ford	62	2h 00m 59s	10
3	Irvine	Ferrari	62	2h 01m 27.8s	15
4	Panis	Prost-Mugen Honda	62	2h 01m 50.1s	12
5	Salo	Tyrrell-Ford	61		14
6	Fisichella	Jordan-Peugeot	61		4
7	Magnussen	Stewart-Ford	61		19
8	Verstappen	Tyrrell-Ford	60		22
9	Berger	Benetton-Renault	60		17
10	Katayama	Minardi-Hart	60		20
	Frentzen	Williams-Renault	39	accident	1
	Nakano	Prost-Mugen Honda	36	accident	21
	Larini	Sauber-Petronas	24	accident	11
	Alesi	Benetton-Renault	16	spun	9
	J Villeneuve	Williams-Renault	16	accident	3
	R Schumacher	Jordan-Peugeot	10	accident	6
	Herbert	Sauber-Petronas	9	accident	7
	Trulli	Minardi-Hart	7	accident	18
	Coulthard	McLaren-Mercedes	1	accident	5
	Hakkinen	McLaren-Mercedes	1	accident	8
	D Hill	Arrows-Yamaha	1	accident	13
	Diniz	Arrows-Yamaha	0	spun	16

Fastest Lap: Schumacher, 1m 53.32s. 66.45mph/106.32kph

1997

Spanish Grand Prix: Barcelona, 25 May 1997

64 laps of 2.94 mile/4.73 km circuit

Place	Driver	Car	Laps	Time/reason for retiring	Grid
1	J Villeneuve	Williams-Renault	64	1h 30m 35.9s	1
2	Panis	Prost-Mugen Honda	64	1h 30m 41.7s	12
3	Alesi	Benetton-Renault	64	1h 30m 48.4s	4
4	M Schumacher	Ferrari	64	1h 30m 54s	7
5	Herbert	Sauber-Petronas	64	1h 31m 03.882s	10
6	Coulthard	McLaren-Mercedes	64	1h 31m 05.64s	3
7	Hakkinen	McLaren-Mercedes	64	1h 31m 24.7s	5
8	Frentzen	Williams-Renault	64	1h 31m 40.035s	2
9	Fisichella	Jordan-Peugeot	64	1h 31m 40.663s	8
10	Berger	Benetton-Renault	64	1h 31m 41.6s	6
11	Verstappen	Tyrrell-Ford	63		19
12	Irvine	Ferrari	63		11
13	Magnussen	Stewart-Ford	63		22
14	Morbidelli	Sauber-Petronas	62		13
15	Trulli	Minardi-Hart	62		18
	Diniz	Arrows-Yamaha	53	engine	21
	R Schumacher	Jordan-Peugeot	50	engine	9
	Barrichello	Stewart-Ford	37	engine	17
	Salo	Tyrrell-Ford	35	tyre	14
	Nakano	Prost-Mugen Honda	34	gearbox	16
	D Hill	Arrows-Yamaha	18	engine	15
	Katayama	Minardi-Hart	11	hydraulics	20

Fastest Lap: Fisichella, 1m 22.24s. 128.6mph/205.76kph

Canadian Grand Prix: Montreal, 15 June 1997

54 laps of 2.75 mile/4.42 km circuit

Place	Driver	Car	Laps	Time/reason for retiring	Grid
1	M Schumacher	Ferrari	54	1h 17m 40.7s	1
2	Alesi	Benetton-Renault	54	1h 17m 43.21s	8
3	Fisichella	Jordan-Peugeot	54	1h 17m 43.87s	6
4	Frentzen	Williams-Renault	54	1h 17m 44.41s	4
5	Herbert	Sauber-Petronas	54	1h 17m 45.36s	13
6	Nakano	Prost-Mugen Honda	54	1h 18m 17.3s	19
7	Coulthard	McLaren-Mercedes	54	1h 18m 18.4s	5
8	Diniz	Arrows-Yamaha	53		16
9	D Hill	Arrows-Yamaha	53		15
10	Morbidelli	Sauber-Petronas	53		18
11	Panis	Prost-Mugen Honda	51	accident	10
	Salo	Tyrrell-Ford	46	engine	17
	Verstappen	Tyrrell-Ford	42	gearbox	14
	Wurz	Benetton-Renault	35	transmission	11
	Barrichello	Stewart-Ford	33	gearbox	3

Canadian Grand Prix (cont)

Place	Driver	Car	Laps	Time/reason for retiring	Grid
	Trulli	Minardi-Hart	32	engine	20
	R Schumacher	Jordan-Peugeot	14	accident	7
	Katayama	Minardi-Hart	5	accident	22
	J Villeneuve	Williams-Renault	1	accident	2
	Irvine	Ferrari	0	accident	12
	Hakkinen	McLaren-Mercedes	0	accident	9
	Magnussen	Stewart-Ford	0	accident	21

Fastest Lap: Coulthard, 1m 19.64s. 124.19mph/198.7kph

French Grand Prix: Magny-Cours, 29 June 1997

72 laps of 2.64 mile/4.25 km circuit

Place	Driver	Car	Laps	Time/reason for retiring	Grid
1	M Schumacher	Ferrari	72	1h 38m 50.5s	1
2	Frentzen	Williams-Renault	72	1h 39m 14s	2
3	Irvine	Ferrari	72	1h 40m 05.3s	5
4	J Villeneuve	Williams-Renault	72	1h 40m 12.3s	4
5	Alesi	Benetton-Renault	72	1h 40m 13.2s	8
6	R Schumacher	Jordan-Peugeot	72	1h 40m 20.4s	3
7	Coulthard	McLaren-Mercedes	71		9
8	Herbert	Sauber-Petronas	71		14
9	Fisichella	Jordan-Peugeot	71		11
10	Trulli	Prost-Mugen Honda	70		6
11	Katayama	Minardi-Hart	70		21
12	D Hill	Arrows-Yamaha	69		17
	Salo	Tyrrell-Ford	61	electrical	19
	Wurz	Benetton-Renault	60	spun	7
	Diniz	Arrows-Yamaha	58	spun	16
	Fontana	Sauber-Petronas	40	spun	20
	Barrichello	Stewart-Ford	36	engine	13
	Magnussen	Stewart-Ford	33	brakes	15
	Hakkinen	McLaren-Mercedes	18	engine	10
	Verstappen	Tyrrell-Ford	15	throttle	18
	Nakano	Prost-Mugen Honda	7	spun	12
	Marques	Minardi-Hart	5	engine	22

Fastest Lap: M Schumacher, 1m 17.91s. 122.03mph/195.25kph

British Grand Prix: Silverstone, 13 July 1997

59 laps of 3.19 mile/5.1 km circuit

Place	Driver	Car	Laps	Time/reason for retiring	Grid
1	J Villeneuve	Williams-Renault	59	1h 28m 01.7s	1
2	Alesi	Benetton-Renault	59	1h 28m 11.87s	11
3	Wurz	Benetton-Renault	59	1h 28m 12.96s	8
4	Coulthard	McLaren-Mercedes	59	1h 28m 32.89s	6
5	R Schumacher	Jordan-Peugeot	59	1h 28m 33.55s	5
6	D Hill	Arrows-Yamaha	59	1h 29m 15.2s	12
7	Fisichella	Jordan-Peugeot	58		10
8	Trulli	Prost-Mugen Honda	58		13
9	Fontana	Sauber-Petronas	58		22
10	Marques	Minardi-Hart	58		20
11	Nakano	Prost-Mugen Honda	57		14
	Hakkinen	McLaren-Mercedes	52	engine	3
	Magnussen	Stewart-Ford	50	engine	15
	Verstappen	Tyrrell-Ford	45	engine	19
	Irvine	Ferrari	44	transmission	7
	Salo	Tyrrell-Ford	44	engine	17
	Herbert	Sauber-Petronas	42	electrical	9
	M Schumacher	Ferrari	38	wheel	4
	Barrichello	Stewart-Ford	37	engine	21
	Diniz	Arrows-Yamaha	29	engine	16
	Frentzen	Williams-Renault	0	accident	2
	Katayama	Minardi-Hart	0	accident	18

Fastest Lap: M Schumacher, 1m 24.48s. 136.12mph/217.79kph

German Grand Prix: Hockenheim, 27 July 1997

45 laps of 4.24 mile/6.82 km circuit

Place	Driver	Car	Laps	Time/reason for retiring	Grid
1	Berger	Benetton-Renault	45	1h 20m 59.1s	1
2	M Schumacher	Ferrari	45	1h 21m 16.6s	4
3	Hakkinen	McLaren-Mercedes	45	1h 21m 23.8s	3
4	Trulli	Prost-Mugen Honda	45	1h 21m 26.2s	11
5	R Schumacher	Jordan-Peugeot	45	1h 21m 29s	7
6	Alesi	Benetton-Renault	45	1h 21m 33.8s	6
7	Nakano	Prost-Mugen Honda	45	1h 22m 18.8s	17
8	D Hill	Arrows-Yamaha	44		13
9	Fontana	Sauber-Petronas	44		18
10	Verstappen	Tyrrell-Ford	44		20
11	Fisichella	Jordan-Peugeot	40		2
	J Villeneuve	Williams-Renault	33	spun	9
	Barrichello	Stewart-Ford	33	engine	12
	Salo	Tyrrell-Ford	33	clutch	19
	Magnussen	Stewart-Ford	27	engine	15

German Grand Prix (cont)

Place	Driver	Car	Laps	Time/reason for retiring	Grid
	Katayama	Minardi-Hart	23	fuel	22
	Herbert	Sauber-Petronas	8	accident	14
	Diniz	Arrows-Yamaha	8	accident	16
	Coulthard	McLaren-Mercedes	1	accident	8
	Frentzen	Williams-Renault	1	accident	5
	Irvine	Ferrari	1	accident	10
	Marques	Minardi-Hart	0	transmission	21

Fastest Lap: Berger, 1m 45.75s. 144.34mph/230.94kph

Hungarian Grand Prix: Hungaroring, 10 August 1997

77 laps of 2.47 mile/3.97 km circuit

Place	Driver	Car	Laps	Time/reason for retiring	Grid
1	J Villeneuve	Williams-Renault	77	1h 45m 47.2s	2
2	D Hill	Arrows-Yamaha	77	1h 45m 56.3s	3
3	Herbert	Sauber-Petronas	77	1h 46m 07.6s	10
4	M Schumacher	Ferrari	77	1h 46m 17.650s	1
5	R Schumacher	Jordan-Peugeot	77	1h 46m 17.864s	14
6	Nakano	Prost-Mugen Honda	77	1h 46m 28.7s	16
7	Trulli	Prost-Mugen Honda	77	1h 47m 02.7s	12
8	Berger	Benetton-Renault	77	1h 47m 03.6s	7
9	Irvine	Ferrari	76		5
10	Katayama	Minardi-Hart	76		20
11	Alesi	Benetton-Renault	76		9
12	Marques	Minardi-Hart	75		22
13	Salo	Tyrrell-Ford	75		21
	Coulthard	McLaren-Mercedes	65	electrical	8
	Verstappen	Tyrrell-Ford	61	gearbox	18
	Diniz	Arrows-Yamaha	53	electrical	19
	Fisichella	Jordan-Peugeot	42	spun	13
	Frentzen	Williams-Renault	29	fuel system	6
	Barrichello	Stewart-Ford	29	engine	11
	Hakkinen	McLaren-Mercedes	12	hydraulics	4
	Morbidelli	Sauber-Petronas	7	engine	15
	Magnussen	Stewart-Ford	5	steering	17

Fastest Lap: Frentzen, 1m 18.37s. 113.26mph/181.22kph

Belgian Grand Prix: Spa, 24 August 1997

44 laps of 4.33 mile/6.97 km circuit

Place	Driver	Car	Laps	Time/reason for retiring	Grid
1	M Schumacher	Ferrari	44	1h 33m 46.7s	3
2	Fisichella	Jordan-Peugeot	44	1h 34m 13.5s	4
	Hakkinen	McLaren-Mercedes	44	disqualified: fuel	5
3	Frentzen	Williams-Renault	44	1h 34m 18.9s	7
4	Herbert	Sauber-Petronas	44	1h 34m 25.7s	11
5	J Villeneuve	Williams-Renault	44	1h 34m 28.8s	1
6	Berger	Benetton-Renault	44	1h 34m 50.5s	15
7	Diniz	Arrows-Yamaha	44	1h 35m 12.7s	9
8	Alesi	Benetton-Renault	44	1h 35m 28.7s	2
9	Morbidelli	Sauber-Petronas	44	1h 35m 29.3s	13
10	Irvine	Ferrari	43		17
11	Salo	Tyrrell-Ford	43		19
12	Magnussen	Stewart-Ford	43		18
13	D Hill	Arrows-Yamaha	42		9
14	Katayama	Minardi-Hart	42		20
15	Trulli	Prost-Mugen Honda	42		14
	Verstappen	Tyrrell-Ford	25	spun	21
	R Schumacher	Jordan-Peugeot	21	spun	6
	Coulthard	McLaren-Mercedes	19	spun	10
	Marques	Minardi-Hart	18	spun	22
	Barrichello	Stewart-Ford	8	steering	12
	Nakano	Prost-Mugen Honda	5	electrical	16

Fastest Lap: Villenueve, 1m 52.69s. 138.32mph/221.31kph

Italian Grand Prix: Monza, 7 September 1997

53 laps of 3.59 mile/5.77 km circuit

Place	Driver	Car	Laps	Time/reason for retiring	Grid
1	Coulthard	McLaren-Mercedes	53	1h 17m 04.6s	6
2	Alesi	Benetton-Renault	53	1h 17m 06.6s	1
3	Frentzen	Williams-Renault	53	1h 17m 09s	2
4	Fisichella	Jordan-Peugeot	53	1h 17m 10.5s	3
5	J Villeneuve	Williams-Renault	53	1h 17m 11s	4
6	M Schumacher	Ferrari	53	1h 17m 16.1s	9
7	Berger	Benetton-Renault	53	1h 17m 17.1s	7
8	Irvine	Ferrari	53	1h 17m 22.3s	10
9	Hakkinen	McLaren-Mercedes	53	1h 17m 54s	5
10	Trulli	Prost-Mugen Honda	53	1h 18m 07.315s	16
11	Nakano	Prost-Mugen Honda	53	1h 18m 07.936s	15
12	Morbidelli	Sauber-Petronas	52		18
13	Barrichello	Stewart-Ford	52		11
14	Marques	Minardi-Hart	50		22

Italian Grand Prix (cont)

Place	Driver	Car	Laps	Time/reason for retiring	Grid
	D Hill	Arrows-Yamaha	46	engine	14
	R Schumacher	Jordan-Peugeot	39	accident	11
	Herbert	Sauber-Petronas	38	accident	12
	Salo	Tyrrell-Ford	33	engine	19
	Magnussen	Stewart-Ford	31	transmission	13
	Verstappen	Tyrrell-Ford	12	hydraulics	20
	Katayama	Minardi-Hart	8	accident	21
	Diniz	Arrows-Yamaha	4	suspension	17

Fastest Lap: Hakkinen, 1m 24.81s. 152.2mph/243.52kph

Austrian Grand Prix: A1-Ring, 21 September 1997

71 laps of 2.67 mile/4.27 km circuit

Place	Driver	Car	Laps	Time/reason for retiring	Grid
1	J Villeneuve	Williams-Renault	71	1h 27m 36s	1
2	Coulthard	McLaren-Mercedes	71	1h 27m 38.91s	10
3	Frentzen	Williams-Renault	71	1h 27m 39.96s	4
4	Fisichella	Jordan-Peugeot	71	1h 27m 48.1s	14
5	R Schumacher	Jordan-Peugeot	71	1h 28m 07.9s	11
6	M Schumacher	Ferrari	71	1h 28m 09.4s	9
7	D Hill	Arrows-Yamaha	71	1h 28m 13.2s	7
8	Herbert	Sauber-Petronas	71	1h 28m 25.1s	12
9	Morbidelli	Sauber-Petronas	71	1h 28m 42.5s	13
10	Berger	Benetton-Renault	70		18
11	Katayama	Minardi-Hart	69		19
12	Verstappen	Tyrrell-Ford	69		20
13	Diniz	Arrows-Yamaha	64	suspension	17
14	Barrichello	Stewart-Ford	64	accident	5
	Trulli	Prost-Mugen Honda	58	engine	3
	Magnussen	Stewart-Ford	58	engine	6
	Nakano	Prost-Mugen Honda	57	engine	16
	Salo	Tyrrell-Ford	48	gearbox	21
	Irvine	Ferrari	38	accident	8
	Alesi	Benetton-Renault	37	accident	15
	Hakkinen	McLaren-Mercedes	1	engine	2

Fastest Lap: Villenueve, 1m 11.81s. 135.44mph/216.7kph

Luxembourg Grand Prix: Nürburgring, 28 September 1997

67 laps of 2.83 mile/4.56 km circuit

Place	Driver	Car	Laps	Time/reason for retiring	Grid
1	J Villeneuve	Williams-Renault	67	1h 31m 27.8s	2
2	Alesi	Benetton-Renault	67	1h 31m 39.6s	10
3	Frentzen	Williams-Renault	67	1h 31m 41.3s	3
4	Berger	Benetton-Renault	67	1h 31m 44.3s	7
5	Diniz	Arrows-Yamaha	67	1h 32m 10.99s	15
6	Panis	Prost-Mugen Honda	67	1h 32m 11.59s	11
7	Herbert	Sauber-Petronas	67	1h 32m 12.2s	16
8	D Hill	Arrows-Yamaha	67	1h 32m 12.62s	13
9	Morbidelli	Sauber-Petronas	66		19
10	Salo	Tyrrell-Ford	66		20
	Verstappen	Tyrrell-Ford	50	engine	21
	Hakkinen	McLaren-Mercedes	43	engine	1
	Barrichello	Stewart-Ford	43	hydraulics	9
	Coulthard	McLaren-Mercedes	42	engine	6
	Magnussen	Stewart-Ford	40	transmission	12
	Irvine	Ferrari	22	engine	14
	Nakano	Prost-Mugen Honda	16	engine	17
	M Schumacher	Ferrari	2	suspension	5
	Marques	Minardi-Hart	1	engine	18
	Katayama	Minardi-Hart	1	accident	22
	R Schumacher	Jordan-Peugeot	0	accident	8
	Fisichella	Jordan-Peugeot	0	accident	4

Fastest Lap: Frentzen, 1m 18.81s. 129.31mph/206.89kph

Japanese Grand Prix: Suzuka, 12 October 1997

53 laps of 3.64 mile/5.96 km circuit

Place	Driver	Car	Laps	Time/reason for retiring	Grid
1	M Schumacher	Ferrari	53	1h 29m 48.45s	2
2	Frentzen	Williams-Renault	53	1h 29m 49.82s	6
3	Irvine	Ferrari	53	1h 30m 14.83s	3
4	Hakkinen	McLaren-Mercedes	53	1h 30m 15.583s	4
	J Villeneuve	Williams-Renault	53	*disqualified	1
5	Alesi	Benetton-Renault	53	1h 30m 28.85s	7
6	Herbert	Sauber-Petronas	53	1h 30m 30.1s	8
7	Fisichella	Jordan-Peugeot	53	1h 30m 45.3s	9
8	Berger	Benetton-Renault	53	1h 30m 48.9s	5
9	R Schumacher	Jordan-Peugeot	53	1h 31m 10.5s	13
10	Coulthard	McLaren-Mercedes	52		11
11	D Hill	Arrows-Yamaha	52		17
12	Diniz	Arrows-Yamaha	52		16

Japanese Grand Prix (cont)

Place	Driver	Car	Laps	Time/reason for retiring	Grid
13	Verstappen	Tyrrell-Ford	52		21
	Marques	Minardi-Hart	46	gearbox	20
	Salo	Tyrrell-Ford	46	engine	22
	Panis	Prost-Mugen Honda	36	engine	10
	Nakano	Prost-Mugen Honda	22	wheel	15
	Katayama	Minardi-Hart	8	engine	19
	Barrichello	Stewart-Ford	6	spun	12
	Magnussen	Stewart-Ford	3	spun	14
	Morbidelli	Sauber-Petronas		did not start: practice accident	18

Fastest Lap: Frentzen, 1m 38.94s. 130.66mph/209.06kph
* Villeneuve, initially excluded after a practice rule infringement, was allowed to race under appeal. The appeal was later withdrawn.

European Grand Prix: Jerez, 26 October 1997

69 laps of 2.75 mile/4.4 km circuit

Place	Driver	Car	Laps	Time/reason for retiring	Grid
1	Hakkinen	McLaren-Mercedes	69	1h 38m 57.77s	5
2	Coulthard	McLaren-Mercedes	69	1h 38m 59.425s	6
3	J Villeneuve	Williams-Renault	69	1h 38m 59.54s	1
4	Berger	Benetton-Renault	69	1h 38m 59.69s	8
5	Irvine	Ferrari	69	1h 39m 01.56s	7
6	Frentzen	Williams-Renault	69	1h 39m 02.31s	3
7	Panis	Prost-Mugen Honda	69	1h 40m 04.92s	9
8	Herbert	Sauber-Petronas	69	1h 40m 10.7s	14
9	Magnussen	Stewart-Ford	69	1h 40m 15.26s	11
10	Nakano	Prost-Mugen Honda	69	1h 40m 15.99s	15
11	Fisichella	Jordan-Peugeot	68		17
12	Salo	Tyrrell-Ford	68		21
13	Alesi	Benetton-Renault	68		10
14	Fontana	Sauber-Petronas	68		18
15	Marques	Minardi-Hart	68		20
16	Verstappen	Tyrrell-Ford	68		22
17	Katayama	Minardi-Hart	68		19
	D Hill	Arrow-Yamaha	47	hydraulics	4
	M Schumacher	Ferrari	47	accident	2
	R Schumacher	Jordan-Peugeot	44	engine	16
	Barrichello	Stewart-Ford	30	gearbox	12
	Diniz	Arrows-Yamaha	11	spun	13

Fastest Lap: Frentzen, 1m 25.14s 119.15 mph/191.75 kph

World Championship 1997

1	Villeneuve	81
	M Schumacher	78 (disqualified)
2	Frentzen	42
3 =	Alesi, Coulthard	36
5 =	Berger, Hakkinen	27
7	Irvine	24
8	Fisichella	20
9	Panis	16
10	Herbert	15
11	R Schumacher	13
12	D Hill	7
13	Barrichello	6
14	Wurz	4
15	Trulli	3
16 =	Diniz, Nakano, Salo	2
19	Larini	1

Constructors' Championship

1	Williams-Renault	123
2	Ferrari	102
3	Benetton-Renault	67
4	McLaren-Mercedes	63
5	Jordan-Peugeot	33
6	Prost-Mugen Honda	21
7	Sauber-Petronas	16
8	Arrows-Yamaha	9
9	Stewart-Ford	6
10	Tyrrell-Ford	2

Part 2:
Drivers' Career Records

Abbreviations

Arg	:	Argentina
Austral	:	Australia
Aus	:	Austria
Bel	:	Belgium
Bra	:	Brazil
CH	:	Switzerland
Can	:	Canada
Eur	:	Europe
Fr	:	France
GB	:	Britain
Ger	:	Germany
Hol	:	Holland
Hun	:	Hungary
Indy	:	Indianapolis
It	:	Italy
Jap	:	Japan
Lux	:	Luxembourg
Mex	:	Mexico
Mon	:	Monaco
Pac	:	Pacific
Por	:	Portugal
SA	:	South Africa
SM	:	San Marino
Sp	:	Spain
Swe	:	Sweden
US	:	United States

Drivers' Results and Biographies A–Z

1 Drivers are only treated as competing in a race if they actually started (ie drivers who fail to complete warm-up laps are deemed not to have started the race).
2 Bracketed figures after world championship positions indicate points scored.
3 Where two finishes are given for one race it means the driver competed in more than one car.
4 Dates of birth have been given where possible. Readers are invited to contact the Author via the Publisher with any further details if known.
5 An asterisk [*] indicates results in the German Grand Prix F2 section 1967 and 1969, which started from separate grids.
6 Information given in brief biographies is selective.
7 Disqualifications, retirements and unclassified finishes are indicated by –.

Abecassis, George   Great Britain
Born: 21 Mar 1913   **Died:** 18 Dec 1991
Co-founder of the HWM team.
Contested: 1951, CH –; **1952**, CH –
Total contested: 2

Acheson, Kenny   Great Britain
Born: 27 Nov 1957
Contested: 1983, SA 12; **1985**, Aus –, It –
Total contested: 3

Adams, Philippe   Belgium
Born: 19 Nov 1969
1994 Bel –, Por 16
Total contested: 2

Ader, Walt   United States
Born: 15 Dec 1913   **Died:** 25 Nov 1982
Contested: 1950, Indy 22
Total contested: 1

Adolff, Kurt   Germany
Born: 5 Nov 1921
Contested: 1953, Ger –
Total contested: 1

Agabashian, Freddie   United States
Born: 21 Aug 1913   **Died:** 13 Oct 1989

Contested: 1950, Indy 28, Indy 25; **1951**, Indy 17; **1952**, Indy 27; **1953**, Indy 4; **1954**, Indy 6; **1955**, Indy 32; **1956**, Indy 12; **1957**, Indy 22
Total contested: 8 **Poles:** 1
World championship position: 1953, 18th (1.5)

Ahrens, Kurt   Germany
Born: 19 Apr 1940
Formula 2 and Porsche sports car driver with annual outings in his home grand prix.
Contested: 1966, Ger –; **1967**, Ger –*; **1968**, Ger 12; **1969**, Ger 3*
Total contested: 4

Alboreto, Michele   Italy
Born: 23 Dec 1956
Le Mans winner 1997.
Contested: 1981, SM –, Bel 12, Mon –, Fr 16, GB –, Aus –, Hol 9, It –, Can 11, US Las Vegas –; **1982**, SA 7, Bra 4, US West 4, SM 3, Bel –, Mon –, US East –, Can –, Hol 7, GB –, Fr 6, Ger 4, Aus –, CH 7, It 5, US Las Vegas 1; **1983**, Bra –, US West 9, Fr 8, SM –, Mon –, Bel 14, US East 1, Can 8, GB 13, Ger –, Aus –, Hol 6, It –, Eur 17, SA –; **1984**, Bra –, SA 11, Bel 1, SM –, Fr –, Mon 6, Can –, US East –, US Dallas –, GB 5, Ger –, Aus 3, Hol –, It 2, Eur 2, Por 4; **1985**, Bra 2, Por 2,

[487]

SM –, Mon 2, Can 1, US 3, Fr –, GB 2, Ger 1, Aus 3, Hol 4, It 13, Bel –, Eur –, SA –, Austral –; **1986**, Bra –, Spa –, SM 10, Mon –, Bel 4, Can 8, Detroit 4, Fr 8, GB –, Ger –, Hun –, Aus 2, It –, Por 5, Mex –, Austral –; **1987**, Bra 8, SM 3, Bel –, Mon 3, US –, Fr –, GB –, Ger –, Hun –, Aus –, It –, Por –, Spa 15, Mex –, Jap 4, Austral 2; **1988**, Bra 5, SM 18, Mon 3, Mex 4, Can –, Detroit –, Fr 3, GB 17, Ger 4, Hun –, Bel –, It 2, Por 5, Spa –, Jap 11, Austral –; **1989**, Bra 10, Mon 5, Mex 3, US –, Can –, Ger –, Hun –, Bel –, It –, Por 11; **1990**, US 10, Bra –, Can –, Mex 17, Fr 10, GB –, Ger –, Hun 12, Bel 13, It 12, Por 9, Spa 10, Jap –; **1991**, US –, Mon –, Can –, Mex –, Fr –, GB –, Por 15, Spa –, Austral 13; **1992**, SA 10, Mex 13, Bra 6, Spa 5, SM 5, Mon 7, Can 7, Fr 7, GB 7, Ger 9, Hun 7, Bel –, It 7, Por 6, Jap 15, Austral –; **1993**, SA –, Bra 11, Eur 11, Mon –, Ger 16, Hun –, Bel 14, It –, Por –; **1994**, Bra –, Pac –, SM –, Mon 6, Sp –, Can 11, Fr –, GB –, Ger –, Hun 7, Bel 9, It –, Por 13, Eur 14, Jap –, Austral –

Total contested: 194 Won: 5 Poles: 2

World championship position: 1982, 7th (25); 1983, 12th (10); 1984, 4th (30.5); 1985, 2nd (53); 1986, 8th (14); 1987, 7th (17); 1988, 5th (24); 1989, 11th (6); 1992, 10th (6); 1994, 24th (1)

Fastest laps: 5

Alesi, Jean   France
Born: 11 Jun 1964

1989 F3000 champion whose highly promising first year with Tyrrell led to a Ferrari contract and a stalled career. Eventually won a grand prix in 1995.

Contested: 1989, Fr 4, GB –, Ger 10, Hun 9, It 5, Spa 4, Jap –, Austral –; **1990**, US 2, Bra 7, SM 6, Mon 2, Can –, Mex 7, Fr –, GB 8, Ger 11, Hun –, Bel 8, It –, Por 8, Spa –, Austral 8; **1991**, US 12, Bra 6, SM –, Mon 3, Can –, Mex –, Fr 4, GB –, Ger 3, Hun 5, Bel –, It –, Por 3, Spa 4, Jap –, Austral –; **1992**, SA –, Mex –, Bra 4, Spa 3, SM –, Mon –, Can 3, Fr –, GB –, Ger 5, Hun –, Bel –, It –, Por –, Jap 5, Austral 4; **1993**, SA –, Bra 8, Eur –, SM –, Sp –, Mon 3, Can –, Fr –, GB 9, Ger 7, Hun –, Bel –, It 2, Por 4, Jap –, Austral 4; **1994**, Bra 3, Mon 5, Sp 4, Can 3, Fr –, GB 2, Ger –, Hun –, Bel –, It –, Por –, Eur 10, Jap 3, Austral 6; **1995**, Bra 5, Arg 2, SM 2, Sp –, Mon –, Can 1, Fr 5, GB 2, Ger –, Hun –, Bel –, It –, Por 5, Eur 2, Pac 5,

Jap –, Austral –; **1996**, Austral –, Bra 2, Arg 3, Eur –, SM 6, Mon –, Sp 2, Can 3, Fr 3, GB –, Ger 2, Hun 3, Bel 4, It 2, Por 4, Jap –; **1997**, Austral –, Bra 6, Arg 7, SM 5, Mon –, Sp 3, Can 2, Fr 5, GB 2, Ger 6, Hun 11, Bel 8, It 2, Aus –,   Lux 2, Jap 5, Eur 13

Total contested: 5 Won: 1 Poles: 2

World championship position: 1989, 9th (8); 1990, 9th (13); 1991, 7th (21); 1992, 7th (18); 1993, 6th (16); 1994, 5th (24); 1995, 5th (42); 1996, 4th (47); 1997, 3rd (36)

Fastest laps: 4

Alliot, Phillippe   France
Born: 27 Jul 1954

Contested: 1984, Bra –, SA –, SM 10, Fr –, Can 10, US East –, GB –, Ger –, Aus 11, Hol 10, It –, Eur –, Por –; **1985**, Bra 9, Por –, SM –, Can –, US –, Fr –, GB –, Ger –, Aus –, Hol –, It –, Bel –, Eur –; **1986**, Ger –, Hun 9, Aus –, It –, Por –, Mex 6, Austral 8; **1987**, SM 10, Bel 8, Mon –, US –, Fr –, GB –, Ger 6, Hun –, Aus 12, It –, Por –, Spa 6, Mex 6, Jap –, Austral –; **1988**, Bra –, SM 17, Mon –, Mex –, Can 10, Detroit –, Fr –, GB 14, Ger –, Hun 12, Bel 9, It –, Por –, Spa 14, Jap 9, Austral –; **1989**, Bra 12, SM –, Mon –, Mex –, US –, Can –, Fr –, GB –, Ger –, Bel 16, It –, Por 9, Spa 6, Jap –, Austral –; **1990**, Bra 12, SM 9, Mon –, Can –, Mex 18, Fr 9, GB 13, Ger –, Hun 14, It 13, Por –, Spa –, Jap 10, Austral 11; **1993**, SA –, Bra 7, Eur –, SM 5, Sp –, Mon 12, Can –, Fr 9, GB 11, Ger 12, Hun 8, Bel 12, It 9, Por 10 **1994**, Hun –, Bel –

Total contested: 109

World championship position: 1986, 18th (1); 1987, 16th (3); 1989, 26th (1); 1993, 17th (2)

Allison, Cliff   Great Britain
Born: 8 Feb 1932

Promising driver who retired after serious crashes in 1960 and 1961.

Contested: 1958, Mon 6, Hol 6, Bel 4, Fr –, GB –, Ger –, Por –, It 7, Moroccan 10; **1959**, Mon –, Hol 9, Ger –, It 5, US –; **1960**, Arg 2; **1961**, Mon 8

Total contested: 16

World championship position: 1958, 18th (3); 1959, 17th (2); 1960, 12th (6)

Amick, George   United States
Born: 24 Oct 1924   **Died:** 9 Apr 1959

Killed at Daytona.

Contested: 1958, Indy 2

Total contested: 1
World championship position: 1958, 15th (6)

Amick, Red   United States
Born: 19 Jan 1929
Contested: 1959, Indy 31; **1960**, Indy 11
Total contested: 2

Amon, Chris   New Zealand
Born: 20 Jul 1943
Probably the best driver never to win a championship grand prix, Amon had an uncanny knack of being with the right team in the wrong season. Won Le Mans in 1966.
Contested: 1963, Bel –, Hol –, Fr 7, GB 7, Ger –, Mex –; **1964**, Hol 5, Bel –, Fr 10, GB –, Ger –, Aus –, US –, Mex –; **1965**, Fr –, Ger –; **1966**, Fr 8; **1967**, Mon 3, Hol 4, Bel 3, Fr –, GB 3, Ger 3, Can 6, It 7, US –, Mex 9; **1968**, SA 4, Spa –, Bel –, Hol 6, Fr 10, GB 2, Ger –, It –, Can –, US –, Mex –; **1969**, SA –, Spa –, Mon –, Hol 3, Fr –, GB –; **1970**, SA –, Spa –, Mon –, Bel 2, Hol –, Fr 2, GB 5, Ger –, Aus 8, It 7, Can 3, US 5, Mex 4; **1971**, SA 5, Spa 3, Mon –, Hol –, Fr 5, GB –, Ger –, It 6, Can 10, US 12; **1972**, SA 15, Spa –, Mon 6, Bel 6, Fr 3, GB 4, Ger 15, Aus 5, It –, Can 6, US 15; **1973**, Bel 6, Mon –, GB –, Hol –, Can 10; **1974**, Spa –, Can –, US 9; **1975**, Aus 12, It 12; **1976**, SA 14, US West 8, Spa 5, Bel –, Mon 13, Swe –, GB –, Ger –
Total contested: 96 **Poles:** 5
World championship position: 1964, 16th (2); 1967, 4th (20); 1968, 10th (10); 1969, 12th (4); 1970, 7th (23); 1971, 9th (9); 1972, 9th (12); 1973, 19th (1); 1976, 18th (2)
Fastest laps: 3

Anderson, Bob   Great Britain
Born: 19 May 1931   **Died:** 14 Aug 1967
Former motorcycle racer who won the non-championship Rome Grand Prix in 1963 and was awarded the von Trips Memorial Trophy as the most successful private entrant of 1964. Killed in a testing crash at Silverstone.
Contested: 1963, GB 12, It 12; **1964**, Mon 7, Hol 6, Fr 12, GB 7, Ger –, Aus 3, It 11; **1965**, SA 16, Mon 9, Fr –, GB –, Hol –; **1966**, Mon –, Fr 7, GB –, Hol –, Ger –, It 6; **1967**, SA 5, Hol 9, Bel 8, Fr –, GB –
Total contested: 25
World championship position: 1964, 11th (5); 1966, 17th (1); 1967, 16th (2)

Andersson, Conny   Sweden
Born: 28 Dec 1939
Contested: 1976, Hol –
Total contested: 1

Andretti, Mario   United States
Born: 28 Feb 1940
One of the greatest and most versatile drivers of all time. Winner of Indianapolis and the World Championship, the Indycar championship 4 times, the Daytona 500 for American NASCAR stock cars, and the Sebring 12 Hours, Andretti was still competitive in Indycars in 1992.
Contested: 1968, US –; **1969**, SA –, Ger –, US –; **1970**, SA –, Spa 3, GB –, Ger –, Aus –; **1971**, SA 1, Spa –, Hol –, Ger 4, Can 13; **1972**, Arg –, SA 4, Spa –, It 7, US 6; **1974**, Can 7, US –; **1975**, Arg –, Bra 7, SA 17, Spa –, Mon –, Swe 4, Fr 5, GB 12, Ger 10, Aus –, It –, US –; **1976**, Bra –, SA 6, US West –, Spa –, Bel –, Swe –, Fr 5, GB –, Ger 12, Aus 5, Hol 3, It –, Can 3, US East –, Jap 1; **1977**, Arg 5, Bra –, SA –, US West 1, Spa 1, Mon 5, Bel –, Swe 6, Fr 1, GB 14, Ger –, Aus –, Hol –, It 1, US East 2, Can 9, Jap –; **1978**, Arg 1, Bra 4, SA 7, US West 2, Mon 11, Bel 1, Spa 1, Swe –, Fr 1, GB –, Ger 1, Aus –, Hol 1, It 6, US East –, Can 10; **1979**, Arg 5, Bra –, SA 4, US West 4, Spa 3, Bel –, Mon –, Fr –, GB –, Ger –, Aus –, Hol –, It 5, Can 10, US East –; **1980**, Arg –, Bra –, SA 12, US West –, Bel –, Mon 7, Fr –, GB –, Ger 7, Aus –, Hol 8, It –, Can –, US East 6; **1981**, US West 4, Bra –, Arg 8, SM –, Bel 10, Mon –, Spa 8, Fr 8, GB –, Ger 9, Aus –, Hol –, It –, Can 7, US Las Vegas –; **1982**, US West –, It 3, US Las Vegas –
Total contested: 128 **Won:** 12 **Poles:** 17
World championship position: 1970, 15th (4); 1971, 8th (12); 1972, 12th (4); 1975, 14th (5); 1976, 6th (22); 1977, 3rd (47); 1978, 1st (64); 1979, 10th (14); 1980, 20th (1); 1981, 17th (3); 1982, 19th (4)
Fastest laps: 10

Andretti, Michael   United States
Son of Mario, Michael's brief grand prix career punctuated a very successful Indycar record which included the championship in 1991. He also finished third at Le Mans with Mario and Alliot in 1983.
Born: 5 Oct 1962
1993, SA –, Bra –, Eur –, SM –, Sp 5, Mon 8, Can 14, Fr 6, GB –, Ger –, Hun –, Bel –, It 3

Drivers' Career Records

Total contested: 13
World championship position: 1993, 11th (7)

Andrews, Keith   United States
Born: 15 Jun 1920   Died: 15 May 1957
Contested: **1955**, Indy 20; **1956**, Indy 26
Total contested: 2

Apicella, Marco   Italy
Born: 7 Oct 1965
1993, It –
Total contested: 1

Armi, Frank   United States
Born: 12 Oct 1918   Died: 28 Nov 1992
Contested: **1954**, Indy 19
Total contested: 1

Arnold, Chuck   United States
Born: 30 May 1926
Contested: **1959**, Indy 15
Total contested: 1

Arnoux, René   France
Born: 4 Jul 1948
Contested: **1978**, Bel 9, Fr 14, Aus 9, Hol –,
US East 9, Can –; **1979**, Arg –, Bra –, SA –,
Spa 9, Bel –, Mon –, Fr 3, GB 2, Ger –, Aus 6,
Hol –, It –, Can –, US East 2; **1980**, Arg –, Bra
1, SA 1, US West 9, Bel 4, Mon –, Fr 5, GB –,
Ger –, Aus 9, Hol 2, It 10, Can –, US East 7;
1981, US West 8, Bra –, Arg 5, SM 8, Mon –,
Spa 9, Fr 4, GB 9, Ger 13, Aus 2, Hol –, It –,
Can –, US Las Vegas –; **1982**, SA 3, Bra –, US
West –, SM –, Bel –, Mon –, US East 10, Can –,
Hol –, GB –, Fr 1, Ger 2, Aus –, CH –, It 1, US
Las Vegas –; **1983**, Bra 10, US West 3, Fr 7,
SM 3, Mon –, Bel –, US East –, Can 1, GB 5,
Ger 1, Aus 2, Hol 1, It 2, Eur 9, SA –; **1984**,
Bra –, SA –, Bel 3, SM 2, Fr 4, Mon 3, Can 5,
US East –, US Dallas 2, GB 6, Ger 6, Aus 7,
Hol 11, It –, Eur 5, Por 9; **1985**, Bra 4; **1986**,
Bra 4, Spa –, SM –, Mon 5, Bel –, Can 6,
Detroit –, Fr 5, GB 4, Ger 4, Hun –, Aus
10, It –, Por 7, Mex 15, Austral 7; **1987**, Bel
6, Mon 11, US 10, Fr –, GB –, Ger –, Hun –,
Aus 10, It 10, Por –, Spa –, Mex –, Jap –,
Austral –; **1988**, Bra –, Mon –, Mex –, Can –,
Detroit –, GB 18, Ger 17, Hun –, Bel –, It 13,
Por 10, Spa –, Jap 17, Austral –; **1989**, Mon
12, Mex 14, Can 5, Fr –, Ger 11, Bel –, It 9,
Por 13, Austral –
Total contested: 149 **Won:** 7 **Poles:** 18

World championship position: 1979, 8th (17);
1980, 6th (29); 1981, 9th (11); 1982, 6th (28);
1983, 3rd (49); 1984, 6th (27); 1985, 17th (3);
1986, 8th (14); 1987, 19th (1); 1989, 23rd (2)
Fastest laps: 12

Arundell, Peter   Great Britain
Born: 8 Nov 1933
Severely injured in a crash in 1964, Arundell
returned to Lotus in 1966 when the team
struggled with uncompetitive cars. He was
replaced by Graham Hill in 1967.
Contested: **1964**, Mon 3, Hol 3, Bel 9, Fr 4;
1966, Fr –, GB –, Hol –, Ger 12, It 8, US 6,
Mex 7
Total contested: 11
World championship position: 1964, 8th (11);
1966, 17th (1)

Ascari, Alberto   Italy
Born: 13 July 1918   Died: 26 May 1955
One of the greatest drivers of all time, son of
Antonio who drove for Alfa Romeo in the
twenties, his career included a record nine
straight wins in grand prix. His last seasons
were ruined by Lancia's unpreparedness,
although he did win the Mille Miglia in
1954. After surviving a crash into the harbour at Monte Carlo, he was killed in a
testing accident at Monza.
Contested: **1950**, Mon 2, CH –, Bel 5, It –, It 2;
1951, CH 6, Bel 2, Fr 2, Fr –, GB –, Ger 1, It 1,
Spa 4; **1952**, Indy 31, Bel 1, Fr 1, GB 1, Ger 1,
Hol 1, It 1; **1953**, Arg 1, Hol 1, Bel 1, Fr 4, GB
1, Ger 8, Ger 15, CH 1, It –; **1954**, Fr –, GB 2,
GB –, It –, Spa –; **1955**, Arg –, Mon –
Total contested: 32 **Won:** 13 **Poles:** 14
World championship position: 1950, 5th (11);
1951, 2nd (25, total 28); 1952, 1st (36, total
53.5); 1953, 1st (34.5, total 46.5); 1954, 25th
(1.14)
Fastest laps: 13

Ashdown, Peter   Great Britain
Born: 16 Oct 1934
Contested: **1959**, GB 12
Total contested: 1

Ashley, Ian   Great Britain
Born: 26 Oct 1947
Contested: **1974**, Ger 14, Aus –; **1976**, Bra –;
1977, US East 17
Total contested: 4

[490]

Ashmore, Gerry Great Britain
Born: 25 Jul 1936
Contested: 1961, GB –, Ger 17, It –
Total contested: 3

Aston, Bill Great Britain
Born: 29 Mar 1900 **Died:** 4 Mar 1974
Contested: 1952, Ger –
Total contested: 1

Attwood, Dickie Great Britain
Born: 4 Apr 1940
A nearly man who showed great potential when given competitive grand prix rides, his greatest success was winning Le Mans in 1971.
Contested: 1965, Mon –, Bel –, GB 13, Hol 12, Ger –, It 6, US 10, Mex 6; **1967**, Can 10; **1968**, Mon 2, Bel –, Hol 7, Fr 7, Ger 14, GB –; **1969**, Mon 4, Ger 2*
Total contested: 17
World championship position: 1965, 14th (2); 1968, 13th (6); 1969, 13th (3)

Ayulo, Manny United States
Born: 20 Oct 1921 **Died:** 16 May 1955
Contested: 1951, Indy 3; **1952**, Indy 20; **1953**, Indy 13; **1954**, Indy 13
Total contested: 4
World championship position: 1951, 15th (2)

Badoer, Luca Italy
European F3000 champion 1992
Born: 25 Jan 1971
1993, SA –, Bra 12, SM 7, Sp –, Can 15, Fr –, GB –, Ger –, Hun –, Bel 13, It 10, Por 14; **1995**, Bra –, Arg –, SM 14, Sp –, Mon –, Can 8, Fr 13, GB 10, Ger –, Hun 8, Bel –, It –, Por 14, Eur11, Pac 15, Jap 9; **1996**, Bra 11, Arg –, SM 10, Mon –, Can –, Fr –
Total contested: 34

Baghelti, Giancario Italy
Born: 25 Dec 1934 **Died:** 27 Nov 1995
After winning his first three formula one races, including the French Grand Prix, his career petered out into sporadic sports car appearances and guest drives at his home grand prix.
Contested: 1961, Fr 1, GB –; It –, **1962**, Hol 4, Bel –, Ger 10, It 5; **1963**, Bel –, Hol –, It 15, US –, Mex –; **1964**, Hol 10, Bel 8, GB 12, Ger –, Aus 7, It 8; **1965**, It –; **1966**, It –; **1967**, It –

Total contested: 21 **Won:** 1
World championship position: 1961, 9th (9); 1962, 11th (5)
Fastest laps: 1

Balley, Julian Great Britain
Born: 9 Oct 1961
Contested: 1988, SM –, Can –, Detroit 9, GB 16, It 12, Jap 14; **1991**, SM 6
Total contested: 7
World championship position: 1991, 18th (1)

Baldi, Mauro Italy
Born: 31 Jan 1954
World sports car champion in 1990. Le Mans winner 1994.
Contested: 1982, Bra 10, Bel –, US East –, Can 8, Hol 6, GB 9, Fr –, Ger –, Aus 6, It 12, US Las Vegas 11; **1983**, Bra –, US West –, Fr –, SM 10, Mon 6, Bel –, US East 12, Can 10, GB 7, Ger –, Aus –, Hol 5, It –, Eur –, SA –; **1984**, Bra –, SA 8, Bel –, SM 8, Fr –, Eur 8, Por 15; **1985**, Bra –, Por –, SM –
Total contested: 36
World championship position: 1982, 22nd (2); 1983, 16th (3)

Bali, Bobby United States
Born: 26 Aug 1925 **Died:** 27 Feb 1954
Contested: 1951, Indy 5; **1952**, Indy 32
Total contested: 2
World championship position: 1951, 16th (2)

Balsa, Marcel France
Born: 1 Jan 1909 **Died:** 11 Aug 1984
Contested: 1952, Ger –
Total contested: 1

Bandini, Lorenzo Italy
Born: 21 Dec 1935 **Died:** 10 May 1967
The leading Italian driver of his period, he won Le Mans in 1963. Succumbed to burns after crashing at Monaco.
Contested: 1961, Bel –, GB 12, Ger –, It 8; **1962**, Mon 3, Ger –, It 8; **1963**, Fr 10, GB 5, Ger –, It –, US 5, Mex –, SA 5; **1964**, Mon –, Hol –, Bel –, Fr 9, GB 5, Ger 3, Aus 1, It 3, US –, Mex 3; **1965**, SA 15, Mon 2, Bel 9, Fr –, GB –, Hol 9, Ger 6, It 4, US 4, Mex 8; **1966**, Mon 2, Bel 3, Fr –, Hol 6, Ger 6, It –, US –; **1967**, Mon –
Total contested: 42 **Won:** 1 **Poles:** 1
World championship position: 1962, 12th (4);

1963, 9th (6); 1964, 4th (23); 1965, 6th (13); 1966 8th (12)
Fastest laps: 2

Banks, Henry United States
Born: 14 Jun 1913
English-born 1950 American Champion, also worked as a film extra, losing the race to Clark Gable in *To Please a Lady*.
Contested: 1950, Indy 25; **1951,** Indy 6; **1952,** Indy 19
Total contested: 3

Barbazza, Fabrizio Italy
Born: 2 Apr 1963
1993, SA –, Bra –, Eur 6, SM 6, Sp –, Mon 11, Can –, Fr –
Total contested: 8
World championship position: 1993, 17th (2)

Barber, John Great Britain
Contested: 1953, Arg 8
Total contested: 1

Barber, Skip United States
Born: 16 Nov 1936
Took in several formula one races with a car bought for Formula A racing in the USA. Now runs highly successful racing schools and the Barber Challenge series for up and coming drivers.
Contested: 1971, Can –, Hol –, US –; **1972,** Can –, US 16
Total contested: 5

Barilla, Paulo Italy
Born: 20 Apr 1961
Le Mans winner, 1985.
Contested: 1989, Jap –; **1990,** US –, Bra –, SM 11, Mon –, Mex 14, GB 12, Hun 15, Bel –
Total contested: 9

Barrichello, Rubens Brazil
Born: 23 May 1972
1993, SA –, Bra –, Eur 10, SM –, Sp 12, Mon 9, Can –, Fr 7, GB 10, Ger –, Hun –, Bel –, It –, Por 13, Jap 5, Austral 11; **1994,** Bra 4, Pac 3, Mon –, Sp –, Can 7, Fr –, GB 4, Ger –, Hun –, Bel –, It 4, Por 4, Eur 12, Jap –, Austral 4; **1995,** Bra –, Arg –, SM –, Sp 7, Mon –, Can 2, Fr 6, GB 11, Ger –, Hun 7, Bel 6, It –, Por 11, Eur 4, Pac –, Jap –, Austral –; **1996,** Austral –, Bra –, Arg 4, Eur 5, SM 5, Mon –, Sp –, Can –,

Fr 9, GB 4, Ger 6, Hun 6, Bel –, It 5, Por –, Jap 9; **1997,** Austral –, Bra –, Arg –, SM –, Mon 2, Sp –, Can –, Fr –, GB –, Ger –, Hun –, Bel –, It 13, Aus 14, Lux –, Jap –, Eur –
Total contested: 81 **Poles:** 1
World championship position: 1993, 17th (2); 1994, 6th (19); 1995, 11th (11); 1996, 8th (14); 1997, 13th (16)

Barth, Edgar Germany
Born: 26 Jan 1917 **Died:** 20 May 65
Invited by Porsche to drive for them in 1957, Barth left East Germany and enjoyed a successful career as European Hill Climb Champion in 1959, 1963 and 1964, also winning the Targa Florio in 1959.
Contested: 1953, Ger –; **1957,** Ger 12; **1958,** Ger 6; **1960,** It 7; **1964,** Ger –
Total contested: 5

Bassi, Giorgio Italy
Born: 20 Jan 1934
Contested: 1965, It –
Total contested: 1

Bauer, Erwin Germany
Born: 17 Jul 1912 **Died:** 3 Jun 1958
Contested: 1953, Ger –
Total contested: 1

Bayol, Élie France
Born: 28 Feb 1914
Contested: 1952, It –; **1953,** Fr –, It –; **1954,** Arg 5; **1955,** Arg –, Mon –; **1956,** Mon 6
Total contested: 7
World championship position: 1954, 19th (2)

Beauman, Don Great Britain
Born: 26 Jul 1928 **Died:** 9 Jul 1955
Contested: 1954, GB 11
Total contested: 1

Bechem, Gunther (also raced as Bernd Nacke) Germany
Born: 21 Dec 1921
1952, Ger –; **1953,** Ger –
Total contested: 2

Behra, Jean France
Born: 16 Feb 1921 **Died:** 1 Aug 1959
One of the best drivers never to win a championship grand prix, Behra achieved Gordini's greatest victory when he beat the Ferraris

at Rheims in 1952. He was killed in a sports car race in Berlin.

Contested: 1952, CH 3, Bel –, Fr 7, Ger 5, Hol –, It 18; **1953**, Arg 6, Bel –, Fr 10, GB –, Ger –, CH –; **1954**, Arg –, Bel –, Fr 6, GB 17, Ger 10, CH –, It –, Spa –; **1955**, Arg 6, Arg –, Arg –, Mon 3, Mon 8, Bel 5, Bel –, Hol 6, GB –, It 4; **1956**, Arg 2, Mon 3, Bel 7, Fr 3, GB 3, It 11, It –; **1957**, Arg 2, Fr 5, GB –, Ger 6, Pescara –, It –; **1958**, Arg 5, Mon –, Hol 3, Bel –, Fr 11, GB –, Ger –, Por 4, It –, Moroccan –; **1959**, Mon –, Hol 5, Fr –
Total contested: 52
World championship position: 1952, 10th (6); 1954, 26th (0.14); 1955, 9th (6); 1956, 4th (22); 1957, 10th (6); 1958, 10th (9); 1959, 17th (2)
Fastest laps: 1

Bell, Derek   Great Britain
Born: 31 Oct 1941
Although his grand prix career never took off, Bell became an outstanding sports car driver with five Le Mans wins and two world championships.
Contested: 1968, It –, US –; **1969**, GB –; **1970**, Bel –, US 6; **1971**, GB –; **1972**, Ger –, US –; **1974**, Ger 11
Total contested: 9
World championship position: 1970, 22nd (1)

Bellof, Stefan   Germany
Born: 20 Nov 1957   **Died:** 1 Sep 1985
World Sports Car Champion in 1984, killed in a sports car race at Spa.
Contested: 1984, Bra –, SA –, Bel –, SM –, Fr –, Mon –, Can –, US East –, US Dallas –, GB –, Hol –; **1985**, Por 6, SM –, Can 11, US 4, Fr 13, GB 11, Ger 8, Aus 7, Hol –
Total contested: 20
World championship position: 1985, 15th (4) (Bellof scored 5 points in 1984 before the Tyrrell team were disqualified from the championship.)

Belmondo, Paul   France
Born: 23 Apr 1963
Contested: 1992, Spa 12, SM 13, Can 14, Ger 13, Hun 9; **1994**, Mon –, Sp –
Total contested: 7

Belso, Tom   Denmark
Born: 27 Aug 1942
Contested: 1974, SA –, Swe 8
Total contested: 2

Beltoise, Jean-Pierre   France
Born: 26 Apr 1937
Beltoise's only grand prix win was BRM's last Cevert's brother-in-law.
Contested: 1966, Ger 8; **1967**, US 7, Mex 7; **1968**, SA 6, Spa 5, Mon –, Bel 8, Hol 2, Fr 9, GB –, Ger –, It 5, Can –, US –, Mex –; **1969**, SA 6, Spa 3, Mon –, Hol 8, Fr 2, GB 9, Ger 6, It 3, Can 4, US –, Mex 5; **1970**, SA 4, Spa –, Mon –, Bel 3, Hol 5, Fr 13, GB –, Ger –, Aus 6, It 3, Can 8, US –, Mex 5; **1971**, Spa 6, Mon –, Hol 9, Fr 7, GB 7, Can –, US 8; **1972**, SA –, Spa –, Mon 1, Bel –, Fr 15, GB 11, Ger 9, Aus 8, It 8, Can –, US –; **1973**, Arg –, Bra –, SA –, Spa 5, Bel –, Mon –, Swe –, Fr 11, GB –, Hol 5, Ger –, Aus 5, It 13, Can 4, US 9; **1974**, Arg 5, Bra 10, SA 2, Spa –, Bel 5, Mon –, Swe –, Hol –, Fr 10, GB 12, Ger –, Aus –, It –, Can –
Total contested: 86 Won: 1
World Championship position: 1968, 9th (11); 1969, 5th (21); 1970, 9th (16); 1971, 22nd (1); 1972, 11th (9); 1973, 10th (9); 1974, 13th (10)
Fastest laps: 4

Beretta, Olivier   Monaco
Born: 23 Nov 1969
1994, Bra –, Pac –, SM –, Mon 8, Can –, Fr –, GB 14, Ger 7, Hun 9
Total contested: 9

Berg, Allen   Canada
Born: 1 Aug 1961
Contested: 1986, Detroit –, Fr –, GB –, Ger 12, Hun –, Aus –, Por 13, Mex 16, Austral –
Total contested: 9

Berger, Georges   Belgium
Born: 14 Sep 1918   **Died:** 23 Aug 1967
Contested: 1953, Bel –; **1954**, Fr –
Total contested: 2

Berger, Gerhard   Austria
Born: 27 Aug 1959
Contested: 1984, Aus 12, It 6, Eur –, Por 13; **1985**, Bra –, Por –, SM –, Mon –, Can 13, US 11, Fr –, GB 8, Ger 7, Aus –, Hol 9, It –, Bel 7, Eur 10, SA 5, Austral 6; **1986**, Bra 6, Spa 6, SM 3, Mon –, Bel 10, Can –, Detroit –, Fr –, GB –, Ger 10, Hun –, Aus 7, It 5, Por –, Mex 1, Austral –; **1987**, Bra 4, SM –, Bel –, Mon 4, US 4, Fr –, GB –, Ger –, Hun –, Aus –, It 4, Por 2, Spa –, Mex –, Jap 1, Austral 1; **1988**, Bra 2, SM 5, Mon 2, Mex 3, Can –, Detroit –, Fr 4,

Drivers' Career Records

GB 9, Ger 3, Hun 4, Bel –, It 1, Por –, Spa 6, Jap 4, Austral –; **1989**, Bra –, SM –, Mex –, US –, Can –, Fr –, GB –, Ger –, Hun –, Bel –, It 2, Por 1, Spa 2, Jap –, Austral –; **1990**, US –, Bra 2, SM 2, Mon 3, Can 4, Mex 3, Fr 5, GB 14, Ger 3, Hun –, Bel 3, It 3, Por 4, Spa –, Jap –, Austral 4; **1991**, US –, Bra 3, SM 2, Mon –, Can –, Mex –, Fr –, GB 2, Ger 4, Hun 4, Bel 2, It 4, Por –, Spa –, Jap 1, Austral 3; **1992**, SA 5, Mex 4, Bra –, Spa 4, SM –, Mon –, Can 1, Fr –, GB 5, Ger –, Hun 3, Bel –, It 4, Por 2, Jap 2, Austral 1; **1993**, SA 6, Bra –, Eur –, SM –, Sp 6, Mon 14, Can 4, Fr 14, GB –, Ger 6, Hun 3, Bel 10, It –, Por –, Jap –, Austral 5; **1994**, Bra –, Pac 2, SM –, Mon 3, Sp –, Can 4, Fr 3, GB –, Ger 1, Hun 12, Bel –, It 2, Por –, Eur 5, Jap –, Austral 2; **1995**, Bra 3, Arg 6, SM 3, Sp 3, Mon 3, Can 11, Fr 12, GB –, Ger 3, Hun 3, Bel –, It –, Por 4, Eur –, Pac 4, Jap –, Austral –; **1996**, Austral 4, Bra –, Arg –, Eur 9, SM 3, Mon –, Sp –, Can –, Fr 4, GB 2, Ger 13, Hun –, Bel 6, It –, Por 6, Jap 4; **1997**, Austral 4, Bra 2, Arg 6, SM –, Mon 9, Sp 10, Ger 1, Hun 8, Bel 6, It 7, Aus 10, Lux 4, Jap 8, Eur 4
Total contested: 210 Won: 10 Poles: 12
World championship position: 1985, 17th (3); 1986, 5th (36); 1987, 5th (36); 1988, 3rd (41); 1989, 7th (21); 1990, 3rd (43); 1991, 4th (43); 1992, 5th (49); 1993, 8th (12); 1994, 3rd (41); 1995, 6th (31); 1996, 6th (21); 1997, 5th (27)
Fastest laps: 21

Bernard, Eric France
Born: 28 Aug 1964
Contested: 1989, Fr 11, GB –; **1990**, US 8, Bra –, SM 13, Mon 6, Can 9, Mex –, Fr 8, GB 4, Ger –, Hun 6, Bel 9, It –, Por –, Spa –, Jap –, Austral –; **1991**, US –, Bra –, SM –, Mon 9, Can –, Mex 6, Fr –, GB –, Ger –, Hun –, Bel –, It –, Spa –; **1994**, Bra –, Pac 10, SM 12, Mon –, Sp 8, Can 13, Fr –, GB 13, Ger 3, Hun 10, Bel 10, It 7, Por 10, Eur 18
Total contested: 45
World championship position: 1990, 13th (5); 1991, 18th (1); 1994, 18th (4)

Bettenhausen, Tony United States
Born: 12 Sep 1916 **Died:** 12 May 1961
One of the great Indycar champions, Bettenhausen was never to win the 500. He died testing Paul Russo's car.
Contested: 1950, Indy 31, Indy 5; **1951**, Indy

9; **1952**, Indy 24; **1953**, Indy 9; **1954**, Indy 29, Indy –; **1955**, Indy 2; **1956**, Indy 22; **1957**, Indy 15; **1958**, Indy 4; **1959**, Indy 4; **1960**, Indy 23
Total contested: 11
World championship position: 1955, 13th (3); 1958, 16th (4); 1959, 15th (3)
Fastest laps: 1

Beuttler, Mike Great Britain
Born: 13 Apr 1940 **Died:** 29 Dec 1988
Contested: 1971, GB –, Ger –, Aus –, It –, Can –; **1972**, Mon 13, Bel –, Fr –, GB 13, Ger 8, Aus –, It 10, Can –, US 13; **1973**, Arg 10, Bra –, SA –, Spa 7, Bel 11, Mon –, Swe 8, GB 11, Hol –, Ger 16, Aus –, It –, Can –, US 10
Total contested: 28

Bianchi, Lucien Belgium
Born: 10 Nov 1934 **Died:** 30 Mar 1969
Better known for his rallying and sports car successes – he won the Liège-Sofia-Liège in 1961 and Le Mans in 1968 – Bianchi's early grand prix career with Belgian teams reaped few rewards, but he had a reasonably competitive season with the last of the Coopers in 1968. He was killed testing an Alfa Romeo at Le Mans.
Contested: 1960, Bel 6, Fr –, GB –; **1961**, Bel –, Fr –, GB –; **1962**, Bel 9, Ger 16; **1963**, Bel –; **1965**, Bel 12; **1968**, Mon 3, Bel 6, Hol –, Ger –, Can 10, US –, Mex –
Total contested: 17
World championship position: 1960, 24th (1); 1968, 17th (5)

Bianco, Gino Brazil
Contested: 1952, GB 18, Ger –, Hol –, It 17
Total contested: 4

Binder, Hans Austria
Born: 12 Jun 1948
Contested: 1976, Aus –, Jap –; **1977**, Arg –, Bra –, SA 11, US West 11, Spa 9, Mon –, Aus 12, Hol 8, US East 11, Can –, Jap –
Total contested: 13

Biondetti, Clemente Italy
Born: 18 Aug 1898 **Died:** 24 Feb 1955
Although he only drove in one championship race, Biondetti had a distinguished pre-war career and won the Mille Miglia four times.

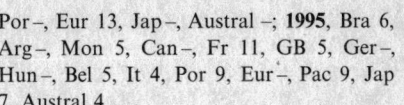

Contested: **1950**, It –
Total contested: 1

Bira, B   Thailand
Born: 15 Jul 1914   Died: 23 Dec 1985
A Siamese prince who raced on a British licence, Bira was a highly successful private owner both pre- and post-war.
Contested: **1950**, GB –, Mon 5, CH 4, It –; **1951**, Spa –; **1952**, CH –, Bel 10, Fr –, GB 11; **1953**, Fr –, GB 7, Ger –, It 13; **1954**, Arg 7, Bel 6, Fr 4, GB 19, Ger –, Spa 9
Total contested: 19
World championship position: 1950, 8th (5); 1954, 17th (3)

Birger, Pablo   Argentina
Born: 6 Jan 1924   Died: 9 Mar 1966
Contested: **1953**, Arg –; **1955**, Arg –
Total contested: 2

Bisch, Art   United States
Born: 10 Nov 1926   Died: 6 Jul 1958
Contested: **1958**, Indy 33
Total contested: 1

Blanchard, Harry   United States
Died: 31 Jan 1960
Contested: **1959**, US 7
Total contested: 1

Bleekemolen, Michael   Holland
Born: 2 Oct 1949
Contested: **1978**, US East –
Total contested: 1

Blokdyk, Trevor   South Africa
Born: 30 Nov 1935   Died: 19 Mar 1995
Contested: **1963**, SA 12
Total contested: 1

Blundell, Mark   Great Britain
Born: 8 April 1966
Without a grand prix drive in 1992, Blundell shared the winning Peugeot at Le Mans. Now a successful Indycar driver.
Contested: **1991**, US –, Bra –, SM 8, Mon –, Mex –, Fr –, GB –, Ger 12, Hun –, Bel 6, It 12, Por –, Spa –, Austral 17; **1993**, SA 3, Bra 5, Eur –, SM –, Sp 7, Mon –, Can –, Fr –, GB 7, Ger 3, Hun 7, Bel 11, It –, Por –, Jap 7, Austral 9; **1994**, Bra –, Pac –, SM 9, Mon –, Sp 3, Can 10, Fr 10, GB –, Ger –, Hun 5, Bel 5, It –,

Por –, Eur 13, Jap –, Austral –; **1995**, Bra 6, Arg –, Mon 5, Can –, Fr 11, GB 5, Ger –, Hun –, Bel 5, It 4, Por 9, Eur –, Pac 9, Jap 7, Austral 4
Total contested: 61
World championship position: 1991 18th (1); 1993, 10th (10); 1994, 12th (8); 1995, 10th (13)

Boesel, Raul   Brazil
Born: 4 Dec 1957
World sportscar champion 1987, switched to Indycar racing.
Contested: **1982**, SA 15, Bra –, US West 9, Bel 8, US East –, Can –, Hol –, Ger –, CH –, US Las Vegas 13; **1983**, Bra –, US West 7, Fr –, SM 9, Mon –, Bel 13, US East 10, Can –, GB –, Ger –, Hol 10, Eur 15, SA –
Total contested: 23

Bondurant, Bob   United States
Born: 27 Apr 1933
An occasional grand prix driver, Bondurant's career in sports and Can-Am cars led to the successful Bondurant School of High Performance Driving.
Contested: **1965**, US 9, Mex –; **1966**, Mon 4, Bel –, GB 9, Ger –, It 7, US –, Mex –
Total contested: 9
World championship position: 1966, 14th (3)

Bonetto, Felice   Italy
Born: 9 Jun 1903   Died: 21 Nov 1953
An occasional Alfa team driver, Bonetto enjoyed his greatest successes in sports cars, pushing his Lancia uphill to win the 1952 Targa Florio. He was killed in the 1953 Carrera Pan-Americana.
Contested: **1950**, CH 5, France –; **1951**, GB 4, Ger –, It 3, Spa 5; **1952**, Ger –, It 5; **1953**, Arg –, Hol 3, Fr –, GB 6, Ger 4, CH 4, CH –, It 6
Total contested: 15 **Poles:** 1
World championship position: 1950, 19th (2); 1951, 8th (7); 1952, 16th (2); 1953, 9th (6.5)

Bonnier, Jo   Sweden
Born: 31 Jan 1930   Died: 11 Jun 1972
His greatest achievement in a long grand prix career was to score BRM's first championship win. An influential member of the Grand Prix Driver's Association, he continued in formula one for too long. His sports car wins included Sebring, the Targa Florio, and the

Drivers' Career Records

Nürburgring 1000 Kilometres. He was killed at Le Mans in 1972.

Contested: 1956, It –; **1957**, Arg 7, GB–, Pescara–, It –; **1958**, Mon–, Hol 10, Bel 9, Fr 8, GB–, Ger–, Por–, It–, Moroccan 4; **1959**, Mon–, Hol 1, Fr–, GB–, Ger 5, Por–, It 8; **1960**, Arg 7, Mon 5, Hol–, Bel–, Fr–, GB–, Por–, US 5; **1961**, Mon 12, Hol 11, Bel 7, Fr 7, GB 5, Ger–, It–, US 6; **1962**, Hol 7, Mon 5, Fr–, GB–, Ger 7, It 6, US 13; **1963**, Mon 7, Bel 5, Hol 13, Fr 15, GB–, Ger 6, It 7, US 8, Mex 5, SA 6; **1964**, Mon 5, Hol 9, Bel–, GB–, Ger–, Aus 6, It 12, US–, Mex –; **1965**, SA–, Mon 7, Bel–, Fr–, GB 7, Hol–, Ger 7, It 7, US 8, Mex –; **1966**, Mon–, Bel–, Fr–, GB–, Hol 7, Ger–, It–, US –, Mex 6; **1967**, SA –, Bel–, GB–, Ger 5, Can 8, It –, US 6, Mex 10; **1968**, SA–, Bel–, Hol 8, GB–, It 6, Can–, US–, Mex 5; **1969**, GB–, Ger –; **1970**, US –; **1971**, SA –, It 10, US 16

Total contested: 104 **Won:** 1 **Poles:** 1

World championship position: 1958, 18th (3); 1959, 8th (10); 1960, 15th (4); 1961, 13th (3); 1962, 14th (3); 1963, 9th (6); 1964, 15th (3); 1966, 17th (1); 1967, 14th (3); 1968, 21st (3)

Bonomi, Roberto   Argentina
Born: 30 Sep 1919
Contested: 1960, Arg 11
Total contested: 1

Borgudd, Silm   Sweden
Born: 25 Nov 1946
One time pop drummer and truck racer.
Contested: 1981, SM 13, GB 6, Ger–, Aus–, Hol 10, It–, Can –; **1982**, SA 16, Bra 7, US West 10
Total contested: 10
World championship position: 1981, 18th (1)

Botha, Luki   South Africa
Born: 16 Jan 1930
Contested: 1967, SA –
Total contested: 1

Boullion, Jean-Christophe (Jules)   France
European F3000 champion 1994
Born: 27 Dec 1969
1995, Mon 8, Can–, Fr–, GB 9, Ger 5, Hun 10, Bel 11, It 6, Por 12, Eur–, Pac –
Total contested: 11
World championship position: 1995, 16th (3)

Boutsen, Thierry   Belgium
Born: 13 July 1957
Contested: 1983, Bel–, US East 7, Can 7, GB 15, Ger 9, Aus 13, Hol 14, It–, Eur 11, SA 9; **1984**, Bra 6, SA 12, Bel–, SM 5, Fr 11, Can–, US East–, US Dallas–, GB–, Ger–, Aus 5, Hol–, It 10, Eur 9, Por –; **1985**, Bra 11, Por–, SM 2, Mon 9, US 7, Fr 9, GB–, Ger 4, Aus 8, Hol–, It 9, Bel 10, Eur 6, SA 6, Austral–, Can 9; **1986**, Bra–, Spa 7, SM 7, Mon 8, Bel–, Can–, Detroit–, Fr–, GB–, Ger–, Hun–, Aus–, It 7, Por 10, Mex 7, Austral –; **1987**, Bra 5, SM–, Bel–, Mon–, US–, Fr–, GB 7, Ger–, Hun 4, Aus 4, It 5, Por 14, Spa 16, Mex–, Jap 5, Austral 3; **1988**, Bra 7, SM 4, Mon 8, Mex 8, Can 3, Detroit 3, Fr–, GB–, Ger 6, Hun 3, Bel–, It 6, Por 3, Spa 9, Jap 3, Austral 5; **1989**, Bra–, SM 4, Mon 10, Mex–, US 6, Can 1, Fr–, GB 10, Ger–, Hun 3, Bel 4, It 3, Por–, Spa –, Jap 3, Austral 1; **1990**, US 3, Bra 5, SM –, Mon 4, Can–, Mex 5, Fr–, GB 2, Ger 6, Hun 1, Bel–, It–, Por–, Spa 4, Jap 5, Austral 5; **1991**, US–, Bra 10, SM 7, Mon 7, Can–, Mex 8, Fr 12, GB–, Ger 9, Hun 17, Bel 11, It–, Por 16, Spa–, Jap 9, Austral –; **1992**, SA–, Mex 10, Bra–, Spa–, SM–, Mon 12, Can 10, Fr–, GB 10, Ger 7, Hun–, Bel–, It–, Por 8, Jap–, Austral 5; **1993**, Eur–, SM –, Sp 11, Mon–, Can 12, Fr 11, GB–, Ger 13, Hun 9, Bel –

Total contested: 162 **Won:** 3 **Poles:** 1
World championship position: 1984, 14th (5); 1985, 11th (11); 1987, 8th (16); 1988, 4th (27); 1989, 5th (37); 1990, 6th (34); 1992, 14th (2)
Fastest laps: 1

Boyd, Johnny   United States
Born: 19 Aug 1926
Contested: 1955, Indy 29; **1956**, Indy 30; **1957**, Indy 6; **1958**, Indy 3; **1959**, Indy 6; **1960**, Indy 27
Total contested: 6
World championship position: 1958, 16th (4)

Brabham, David   Australia
Born: 5 Sept 1965
Son of Jack.
Contested: 1990, Mon–, Mex–, Fr 15, Ger–, Bel–, Por–, Jap–, Austral –; **1994**, Bra 12, Pac–, SM–, Mon–, Sp 10, Can 14, Fr–, GB 15, Ger–, Hun 11, Bel–, It–, Por–, Eur–, Jap 12, Austral –
Total contested: 22

Brabham, Jack   Australia
Born: 2 Apr 1926
Triple world champion who made history as
the first driver to win the championship in a
rear-engined car (in 1959) and as the first
person to win a race (and a championship)
in a car he designed (1966). Although he
seldom raced sports cars he co-drove Moss's
winning Aston Martin at the Nürburgring in
1958. His Indianapolis foray with Cooper in
1961 started the revolution in Indycar design.
Father of David, Geoffrey and Gary, all of
whom race. The Brabham team was sold
several times after Brabham himself retired.
Contested: 1955, GB –; **1956**, GB –; **1957**,
Mon 6, Fr –, Fr 7, GB 8, Ger –, Pescara 7;
1958, Mon 4, Hol 8, Bel –, Fr 6, GB 6, Ger –,
Por 7, It –, Moroccan 11; **1959**, Mon 1, Hol 2,
Fr 3, GB 1, Ger –, Por –, It 3, US 4; **1960**, Arg –,
Mon –, Hol 1, Bel 1, Fr 1, GB 1, Por 1, US 4;
1961, Mon –, Hol 6, Bel –, Fr –, GB 4, Ger –,
It –, US –; **1962**, Hol –, Mon –, Bel 6, Fr –, GB
5, Ger –, US 4, SA 4; **1963**, Mon 9, Bel –, Hol
11, Fr 4, GB –, Ger 7, It 5, US 4, Mex 2, SA 13;
1964, Mon –, Hol –, Bel 3, Fr 3, GB 4, Ger –,
Aus 9, It –, US –, Mex –; **1965**, SA 8, Mon –,
Bel 4, Ger 5, US 3, Mex 2; **1966**, Mon –, Bel 4,
Fr 1, GB 1, Hol 1, Ger 1, It –, US –, Mex 2;
1967, SA 6, Mon –, Hol 2, Bel –, Fr 1, GB 4,
Ger 2, Can 1, It 2, US 5, Mex 2; **1968**, SA –,
Mon –, Bel –, Hol –, Fr –, GB –, Ger 5, It –,
Can –, US –, Mex –; **1969**, SA –, Spa –, Mon –,
Hol 6, It –, Can 2, US 4, Mex 3; **1970**, Sa 1,
Spa –, Mon 2, Bel –, Hol 11, Fr 3, GB 2, Ger –,
Aus 13, It –, Can 16, US –, Mex –
Total contested: 126 **Won:** 14 **Poles:** 13
World championship position: 1958, 18th (3);
1959, 1st (31, total 34); 1960, 1st (43); 1961,
11th (4); 1962, 9th (9); 1963, 7th (14); 1964,
8th (11); 1965, 10th (9); 1966, 1st (42, total
45); 1967, 2nd (46, total 48); 1968, 23rd (2);
1969, 10th (14); 1970, 5th (25)
Fastest laps: 12

Brack, Bill   Canada
Born: 26 Dec 1935
Contested: 1968, Can –; **1969**, Can 8; **1972**,
Can –
Total contested: 3

Brambilla, Vittorio   Italy
Born: 11 Nov 1937
His only grand prix win, in the rain-shortened

1975 Austrian race, ended with a spin after he
crossed the line.
Contested: 1974, SA 10, Bel 9, Mon –, Swe 10,
Hol 10, Fr 11, GB –, Ger 13, Aus 6, It –, US –;
1975, Arg 9, Bra –, SA –, Spa 5, Mon –, Bel –,
Swe –, Hol –, Fr –, GB 6, Ger –, Aus 1, It –, US
7; **1976**, Bra –, SA 8, US West –, Spa –, Bel –,
Mon –, Swe 10, Fr –, GB –, Ger –, Aus –, Hol
6, It 7, Can 14, US East –, Jap –; **1977**, Arg 7,
Bra –, SA 7, US West –, Spa –, Mon 8, Bel 4,
Swe –, Fr 13, GB 8, Ger 5, Aus 15, Hol 12, It –,
US East 19, Can 6, Jap 8; **1978**, Arg 18, SA
12, US West –, Bel 13, Spa 7, Swe –, Fr 17, GB
9, Ger –, Aus 6, Hol –, It –; **1979**, It 12, Can –;
1980, Hol –, It –
Total contested: 74 **Won:** 1 **Poles:** 1
World championship position: 1974, 18th (1);
1975, 11th (6.5); 1976, 19th (1); 1977, 15th (6);
1978, 19th (1)
Fastest laps: 1

Branca, Toni   Switzerland
Born: 15 Sep 1916   **Died:** 10 May 1985
Contested: 1950, CH 11, Bel 10; **1951**, Ger –
Total contested: 3

Brandon, Eric   Great Britain
Born: 18 Jul 1920   **Died:** 8 Aug 1982
Contested: 1952, CH 8, Bel 9, GB 20, It 13;
1954, GB –
Total contested: 5

Branson, Don   United States
Born: 6 Jun 1920   **Died:** 12 Nov 1966
Killed in a crash in a race in California.
Contested: 1959, Indy 24; **1960**, Indy 4
Total contested: 2
World championship position: 1960, 19th (3)

Bridger, Tom   Great Britain
Born: 24 Jun 1934   **Died:** 30 Jul 1991
Contested: 1958, Moroccan –
Total contested: 1

Brise, Tony   Great Britain
Born: 28 Mar 1952   **Died:** 29 Nov 75
A very promising driver killed when Graham
Hill's plane crashed returning from a test
session in France.
Contested: 1975, Spa 7, Bel –, Swe 6, Hol 7,
Fr 7, GB 15, Ger –, Aus 15, It –, US –
Total contested: 10
World championship position: 1975, 19th (1)

Drivers' Career Records

Bristow, Chris   Great Britain
Born: 2 Dec 1937   **Died:** 19 Jun 1960
A dashing driver killed in the Belgian Grand Prix.
Contested: 1959, GB 10; **1960**, Mon –, Hol –, Bel –
Total contested: 4

Broeker, Peter   Canada
Born: 15 May 1929
The driver of the only Canadian car to appear in a grand prix.
Contested: 1963, US 7
Total contested: 1

Brooks, Tony   Great Britain
Born: 25 Feb 1932
His Connaught victory at Syracuse in 1955 was the first grand prix win by a British car since 1923. Brooks was one of the finest drivers of his generation.
Contested: 1956, GB –; **1957**, Mon 2, GB 1, GB –, Ger 9, Pescara –, It 7; **1958**, Mon –, Hol –, Bel 1, Fr –, Fr 13, GB 7, Ger 1, Por –, It 1, Moroccan –; **1959**, Mon 2, Hol –, Fr 1, GB –, Ger 1, Por 9, It –, US 3; **1960**, Mon 4, Hol –, Bel –, Fr –, GB 5, Por 5, US –; **1961**, Mon 13, Hol 9, Bel 13, Fr –, GB 9, Ger –, It 5, US 3
Total contested: 38 **Won:** 6 **Poles:** 4
World championship position: 1957, 5th (11); 1958, 3rd (24); 1959, 2nd (27); 1960, 11th (7); 1961, 10th (6)
Fastest laps: 3

Brown, Alan   Great Britain
Born: 20 Nov 1919
Contested: 1952, CH 5, Bel 6, It 15, GB 23; **1953**, Arg 9, GB –, Ger 16, It 15
Total contested: 8
World championship position: 1952, 16th (2)

Brown, Walt   United States
Born: 30 Dec 1911   **Died:** 29 Jul 1951
Contested: 1950, Indy 19; **1951**, Indy 26
Total contested: 2

Brown, Warwick   Australia
Born: 24 Dec 1949
Contested: 1976, US East 14
Total contested: 1

Brudes, Adolf   Germany
Born: 15 Oct 1899   **Died:** 5 Nov 1986

Contested: 1952, Ger –
Total contested: 1

Brundle, Martin   Great Britain
Born: 1 Jun 1959
In 1984 Brundle actually finished 5th in Brazil and 2nd in Detroit, but his placings were annulled when the Tyrrell team was excluded from the championship. In 1988 (world champion) and 1990 (Le Mans winner) he competed in sports cars rather than taking an uncompetitive grand prix drive.
Contested: 1984, Bra –, SA –, Bel –, SM –, Fr –, Can –, US East –; **1985**, Bra 8, Por –, SM 9, Mon 10, Can 12, US –, Fr –, GB 7, Ger 10, Hol 7, It 8, Bel 13, Eur –, SA 7, Austral –; **1986**, Bra 5, Spa –, SM 8, Mon –, Bel –, Can 9, Detroit –, Fr 10, GB 5, Ger –, Hun 6, Aus –, It 10, Por –, Mex 11, Austral 4; **1987**, Bra –, SM 5, Bel –, Mon 7, US –, Fr –, GB –, Ger –, Hun –, Aus 14, It –, Por –, Spa 11, Mex –, Jap –, Austral –; **1988**, Bel 7; **1989**, Bra –, SM –, Mon 6, Mex 9, US –, GB –, Ger 8, Hun 12, Bel –, It 6, Por 8, Spa –, Jap 5, Austral –; **1991**, US 11, Bra 12, SM 11, Can –, Mex –, Fr –, GB –, Ger 11, Hun –, Bel 9, It 13, Por 12, Spa 10, Jap 5; **1992**, SA –, Mex –, Bra –, Spa –, SM 4, Mon 5, Can –, Fr 3, GB 3, Ger 4, Hun 5, Bel 4, It 2, Por 4, Jap 3, Austral 3; **1993**, SA –, Bra –, Eur –, SM 3, Sp –, Mon 6, Can 5, Fr 5, GB 14, Ger 8, Hun 5, Bel 7, It –, Por 6, Jap 9, Austral 6; **1994**, Bra –, Pac –, SM 8, Mon 2, Sp 11, Can –, Fr –, GB –, Ger –, Hun 4, Bel –, It 5, Por 6, Eur –, Jap –, Austral 3; **1995**, Sp 9, Mon –, Can 10, Fr 4, GB –, Hun –, Bel 3, It –, Por 8, Eur 7, Austral –; **1996**, Austral –, Bra 12, Arg –, Eur 6, SM –, Mon –, Sp –, Can 6, Fr 8, GB 6, Ger 10, Hun –, Bel –, It 4, Por 9, Jap 5
Total Contested: 158
World championship position: 1986, 11th (8); 1987, 18th (2); 1989, 16th (4); 1991, 15th (2); 1992, 6th (38); 1993, 7th (13); 1994, 7th (16); 1995, 13th (7); 1996, 12th (7)

Bryan, Jimmy   United States
Born: 28 Jan 1927   **Died:** 19 Jun 1960
Three times American champion, he died in a crash at Langhorne.
Contested: 1952, Indy 6; **1953**, Indy 14; **1954**, Indy 2; **1955**, Indy 24; **1956**, Indy 19; **1957**, Indy 3; **1958**, Indy 1; **1959**, Indy 33; **1960**, Indy 19

Total contested: 9 Won: 1
World championship position: 1954, 8th (6);
1957, 14th (4); 1958, 13th (8)

Bucci, Clemar   Argentina
Born: 4 Sep 1920
Contested: 1954, GB–, Ger–, CH–, It –; **1955**,
Arg –
Total contested: 5

Bucknum, Ronnie   United States
Born: 5 Apr 1936   **Died:** 14 Apr 1992
A versatile driver chosen to give Honda its
grand prix debut, he also won in sports cars
and Indycars.
Contested: 1964, Ger–, It–, US –; **1965**,
Mon–, Bel–, Fr–, It–, US 13, Mex 5; **1966**,
US –, Mex 8
Total contested: 11
World championship position: 1965, 14th (2)

Bueb, Ivor   Great Britain
Born: 6 Jun 1923   **Died:** 1 Aug 1959
Twice a Le Mans winner, he died after a crash
in a F2 race in France.
Contested: 1957, Mon –, GB 9; **1958**, GB–,
Ger 11; **1959**, GB 13
Total contested: 5

Bueno, Luis   Brazil
Contested: 1973 Bra 12
Total contested: 1

Burgess, Ian   Great Britain
Born: 6 Jul 1930
Contested: 1958, GB–, Ger 7; **1959**, Fr–,
GB–, Ger 6, It 14; **1960**, Fr 10, GB–, US –
; **1961**, Fr 14, GB 14, Ger 12; **1962**, GB 12,
Ger 11; **1963**, GB–, Ger –
Total contested: 16

Bussinello, Roberto   Italy
Born: 4 Oct 1927
Contested: 1961, It –; **1965**, It –
Total contested: 2

Byrne, Tommy   Ireland
Born: 6 May 1958
Contested: 1982, Aus –, US Las Vegas –
Total contested: 2

Cabianca, Giulio   Italy
Born: 19 Feb 1923   **Died:** 15 Jun 1961

Contested: 1958, It –; **1959**, It 15; **1960**, It 4
Total contested: 3
World championship position: 1960, 19th (3)

Cabral, Mario   Portugal
Born: 15 Jan 1934
Contested: 1959, Por 10; **1960**, Por –; **1963**,
Ger –; **1964**, It –
Total contested: 4

Caffi, Alex   Italy
Born: 18 Mar 1964
Contested: 1986, It 11; **1987**, Bra–, SM 12,
Bel–, Mon–, US–, Fr–, GB–, Ger–, Hun–,
Aus–, It–, Por–, Mex–, Jap –; **1988**, SM –,
Mon–, Mex–, Detroit 8, Fr 12, GB 11, Ger
15, Hun–, Bel 8, It–, Por 7, Spa 10, Jap–,
Austral –; **1989**, SM 7, Mon 4, Mex 13,
US–, Can 6, Fr–, Ger–, Hun 7, Bel–, It
11, Por–, Spa–, Jap 9, Austral –; **1990**,
Bra–, Mon 5, Can 8, Fr–, GB 7, Ger 9,
Hun 9, Bel 10, It 9, Por 13, Jap 9; **1991**, Jap
10, Austral 15
Total contested: 56
World championship position: 1989, 16th (4);
1990, 16th (2)

Campbell-Jones, John   Great Britain
Born: 21 Jan 1930
Contested: 1962, Bel 16; **1963**, GB 13
Total contested: 2

Campos, Adrian   Spain
Born: 17 Jun 1960
Contested: 1987, Bra–, SM–, Bel–, US–, Fr–,
GB–, Ger–, Hun–, Aus–, It–, Por–, Spa 14,
Mex–, Jap–, Austral –; **1988**, Bra–, SM 16
Total contested: 17

Cannon, John   Canada
Born: 21 Jun 1937
Contested: 1971, US 14
Total contested: 1

Cantoni, Heini   Uruguay
Contested: 1952, GB–, Ger–, It 11
Total contested: 3

Cantrell, Bill   United States
Born: 31 Jan 1908
Contested: 1950, Indy 27
Total contested: 1

Drivers' Career Records

Capelli, Ivan Italy
Born: 24 May 1963
Contested: 1985, Eur–, Austral 4; **1986**, It–, Por –; **1987**, SM –, Bel–, Mon 6, US–, Fr–, GB–, Ger–, Hun 10, Aus 11, It 13, Por 9, Spa 12, Mex–, Jap–, Austral –; **1988**, Bra–, SM–, Mon 10, Mex 16, Can 5, Fr 9, GB–, Ger 5, Hun–, Bel 3, It 5, Por 2, Spa–, Jap–, Austral 6; **1989**, Bra–, SM–, Mon 11, Mex–, US–, Can–, Fr–, GB–, Ger–, Hun–, Bel 12, It–, Por–, Spa–, Jap–, Austral –; **1990**, US–, SM–, Mon–, Can 10, Fr 2, GB–, Ger 7, Hun–, Bel 7, It–, Por–, Spa–, Jap–, Austral –; **1991**, US–, Bra–, SM–, Mon–, Can–, Mex–, Fr–, GB–, Ger–, Hun 6, Bel–, It 8, Por 17, Spa –; **1992**, SA–, Mex–, Bra 5, Spa 10, SM–, Mon–, Can–, Fr–, GB 9, Ger–, Hun 6, Bel–, It–, Por –; **1993**, SA –
Total contested: 93
World championship position: 1985, 17th (3); 1987, 19th (1); 1988, 7th (17); 1990, 10th (6); 1991, 18th (1); 1992, 12th (3)

Carini, Piero Italy
Born: 6 Mar 1921   **Died:** 30 May 1957
Contested: 1952, Fr–, Ger –; **1953**, It –
Total contested: 3

Carter, Duane United States
Born: 5 May 1913   **Died:** 8 Mar 1993
Contested: 1950, Indy 12; **1951**, Indy 8; **1952**, Indy 4; **1953**, Indy 24, Indy 3; **1954**, Indy 15, Indy 4; **1955**, Indy 11; **1959**, Indy 7; **1960**, Indy 12
Total contested: 8
World championship position: 1952, 13th (3)

Castellotti, Eugenio Italy
Born: 10 Oct 1930   **Died:** 14 Mar 1957
Killed in a testing crash at Modena, he was one of the leading Italian drivers of his day with a Mille Miglia win in 1956.
Contested: 1955, Arg–, Mon 2, Bel–, Hol 5, GB 6, GB–, It 3; **1956**, Arg–, Mon 4, Mon–, Bel–, Fr 2, GB 11, Ger–, Ger–, It 8, It –; **1957**, Arg –
Total contested: 14 **Poles:** 1
World championship position: 1955, 3rd (12); 1956, 6th (7.5)

Cecotto, Johnny Venezuela
Born: 25 Jan 1956
A former motorcycle champion who now races German touring cars.

Contested: 1983, Bra 14, US West 6, Fr 11, SM –, Bel 10, US East–, Can–, Ger 11, It 12; **1984**, Bra–, SA–, Bel–, SM 11, Fr–, Mon–, Can 9, US East–, US Dallas –
Total contested: 18
World championship position: 1983, 19th (1)

Cevert, François France
Born: 25 Feb 1944   **Died:** 6 Oct 1973
Beltoise's brother-in-law, he was promoted to Formula One after Servoz-Gavin retired. A formidable number two to Jackie Stewart, he crashed fatally in practice for the American Grand Prix.
Contested: 1969, Ger –*; **1970**, Hol–, Fr 11, GB 7, Ger 7, Aus–, It 6, Can 9, US–, Mex –; **1971**, SA–, Spa 7, Mon–, Hol–, Fr 2, GB 10, Ger 2, Aus–, It 3, Can 6, US 1; **1972**, Arg–, SA 9, Spa–, Mon –, Bel 2, Fr 4, GB–, Ger 10, Aus 9, It–, Can–, US 2; **1973**, Arg 2, Bra 10, SA –, Spa 2, Bel 2, Mon 4, Swe 3, Fr 2, GB 5, Hol 2, Ger 2, Aus–, It 5, Can –
Total contested: 47 **Won:** 1
World championship position: 1970, 22nd (1); 1971, 3rd (26); 1972, 6th (15); 1973, 4th (47)
Fastest laps: 2

Chaboud, Eugene France
Born: 12 Apr 1907   **Died:** 28 Dec 1983
Le Mans winner, 1938.
Contested: 1950, Bel–, France 5; **1951**, Fr 8
Total contested: 3
World championship position: 1950, 20th (1)

Chamberlain, Jay United States
Born: 29 Dec 1925
Contested: 1962, GB 15
Total contested: 1

Charlton, Dave South Africa
Born: 27 Oct 1936
Multiple South African champion who contested occasional European races.
Contested: 1967, SA –; **1968**, SA –; **1970**, SA –; **1971**, SA–, GB –; **1972**, SA–, GB–, Ger –; **1973**, SA –; **1974**, SA 19; **1975**, SA 14
Total contested: 11

Cheesbourg, Bill United States
Born: 12 Jun 1927
Contested: 1957, Indy 26; **1958**, Indy 10; **1959**, Indy 21
Total contested: 3

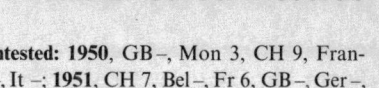

Cheever, Eddie   United States
Born: 10 Jan 1958
After a long but relatively unsuccessful grand prix career, Cheever switched to Indycars without a major change in fortune.
Contested: 1978, SA –; **1980**, SA –, US West –, Fr –, GB –, Ger –, Aus –, Hol –, It 12, Can –, US East –; **1981**, US West 5, Bra –, Arg –, SM –, Bel 6, Mon 5, Spa –, Fr 13, GB 4, Ger 5, Hol –, It –, Can 12, US Las Vegas –; **1982**, SA –, Bra –, US West –, Bel 3, Mon –, US East 2, Can 10, GB –, Fr 16, Ger –, Aus –, CH –, It 6, US Las Vegas 3; **1983**, Bra –, US West –, Fr 3, SM –, Mon –, Bel 3, US East –, Can 2, GB –, Ger –, Aus 4, Hol –, It 3, Eur 10, SA 6; **1984**, Bra 4, SA –, Bel –, SM 7, Fr –, Can 11, US East –, US Dallas –, GB –, Ger –, Aus –, Hol 13, It 9, Eur –, Por 17; **1985**, Bra –, Por –, SM –, Mon –, Can 17, US 9, Fr 10, GB –, Ger –, Aus –, Hol –, It –, Bel –, Eur 11, SA –, Austral –; **1986**, Detroit –; **1987**, Bra –, SM –, Bel 4, Mon –, US 6, Fr –, GB –, Ger –, Hun 8, Aus –, It –, Por 6, Spa 8, Mex 4, Jap 9, Austral –; **1988**, Bra 8, SM 7, Mon –, Mex 6, Can –, Detroit –, Fr 11, GB 7, Ger 10, Hun –, Bel 6, It 3, Por –, Spa –, Jap –, Austral –; **1989**, Bra –, SM 9, Mon 7, Mex 7, US 3, Can –, Fr 7, Ger 12, Hun 5, Bel –, Por –, Spa –, Jap 8, Austral –
Total contested: 132
World championship position: 1981, 11th (10); 1982, 12th (15); 1983, 6th (22); 1984, 16th (3); 1987, 10th (8); 1988, 12th (6); 1989, 11th (6)

Chiesa, Andrea   Switzerland
Born: 6 May 1964
Contested: 1992, Mex –, Spa –, Fr –
Total contested: 3

Chimeri, Ettore   Venezuela
Born: 4 Jun 1921   **Died:** 27 Feb 1960
Contested: 1960, Arg –
Total contested: 1

Chiron Louis   Monaco
Born: 3 Aug 1899   **Died:** 22 Jun 1979
Competed from 1923 to 1959. One of the great pre-war drivers. Chiron was past his prime by the time the championship was inaugurated but won the Monte Carlo Rally in 1954. On retirement, he ran both the rally and the Monaco Grand Prix. He was the oldest driver to start a grand prix.

Contested: 1950, GB –, Mon 3, CH 9, France –, It –; **1951**, CH 7, Bel –, Fr 6, GB –, Ger –, It –, Spa –, **1953**, Fr 15, It 12; **1955**, Mon 6
Total contested: 15
World championship position: 1950, 9th (4)

Chitwood, Joie   United States
Born: 14 Apr 1912   **Died:** 3 Jan 1988
A Cherokee who became a millionaire through running stunt car shows.
Contested: 1950, Indy 5
Total contested: 1
World championship position: 1950, 20th (1)

Christie, Bob   United States
Born: 4 Apr 1924
Contested: 1956, Indy 13; **1957**, Indy 13; **1958**, Indy 14; **1959**, Indy 25; **1960**, Indy 10
Total contested: 5

Claes, Johnnie   Belgium
Born: 11 Aug 1916   **Died:** 3 Feb 1956
Contested: 1950, GB 11, Mon 7, CH 10, Bel 8, France –, It –; **1951**, CH 14, Bel 7, Fr –, GB 13, Ger 12, It –, Spa –; **1952**, Bel 8, Fr –, GB 14, Ger 10; **1953**, Hol 13, Bel –, Fr 12, Ger –, It –; **1955**, Hol 11
Total contested: 23

Clark, Jim   Great Britain
Born: 4 Mar 1936   **Died:** 7 Apr 1968
The outstanding driver of his generation, the first European to win Indianapolis in modern times (1965). Broke Fangio's record for grand prix wins. Killed in a F2 race at Hockenheim.
Contested: 1960, Hol –, Bel 5, Fr 5, GB 17, Por 3, US 16; **1961**, Mon 10, Hol 3, Bel 12, Fr 3, GB 17, Ger 4, It –, US 8; **1962**, Hol 11, Mon –, Bel 1, Fr –, GB 1, Ger 4, It –, US 1, SA –; **1963**, Mon 8, Bel 1, Hol 1, Fr 1, GB 1, Ger 2, It 1, US 3, Mex 1, SA 1; **1964**, Mon 4, Hol 1, Bel 1, Fr –, GB 1, Ger –, Aus –, It –, US –, Mex 5; **1965**, SA 1, Bel 1, Fr 1, GB 1, Hol 1, Ger 1, It –, US –, Mex –; **1966**, Mon –, Bel –, GB 4, Hol 3, Ger –, It –, US 1, Mex –; **1967**, SA –, Mon –, Hol 1, Bel 6, Fr –, GB 1, Ger –, Can –, It 3, US 1, Mex 1; **1968**, SA 1
Total contested: 72 **Won:** 25 **Poles:** 33
World championship position: 1960, 8th (8); 1961, 7th (11); 1962, 2nd (30); 1963, 1st (54, total 73); 1964, 3rd (32); 1965, 1st (54); 1966, 6th (16); 1967, 3rd (41); 1968, 11th (9)
Fastest laps: 28

Drivers' Career Records

Collins, Peter Great Britain
Born: 6 Nov 1931 Died: 3 Aug 1958
Talented and sporting driver, killed in the
German Grand Prix.
Contested: 1952, CH –, Bel –, Fr 6, GB 22;
1953, Hol 8, Bel –, Fr 13, GB –; 1954, GB –, It
7; 1955, GB –, It –; 1956, Arg –, Mon 2, Bel 1,
Fr 1, GB 2, GB –, Ger –, Ger –, It 2; 1957, Arg
6, Arg –, Mon –, Fr 3, GB 4, GB –, Ger 3, It –;
1958, Arg –, Mon 3, Hol –, Bel –, Fr 5, GB 1,
Ger –
Total contested: 32 Won: 3
World championship position: 1956, 3rd (25);
1957, 8th (8); 1958, 5th (14)

Collomb, Bernard France
Born: 7 Oct 1930
Contested: 1961, Fr –, Ger –; 1962, Ger –;
1963, Ger 10
Total contested: 4

Comas, Erik France
Born: 28 Sep 1963
European F3000 champion 1990
Contested: 1991, Bra –, SM 9, Mon 10, Can 8,
Fr 11, Ger –, Hun 10, Bel –, It 11, Por 11,
Spa –, Jap –, Austral 18; 1992, SA 7, Mex 9,
Bra –, Spa –, SM –, Mon 10, Can 6, Fr 5, GB
8, Ger 6, Hun –, It –, Por –, Jap –, Austral –;
1993, SA –, Bra 10, Eur 9, SM –, Sp 9, Mon –,
Can 8, Fr 16, GB –, Ger –, Hun –, Bel –, It 6,
Por 11, Jap –, Austral 12; 1994, Bra 9, Pac 6,
SM –, Mon 10, Sp –, Can –, Fr 11, GB –, Ger
6, Hun 8, Bel –, It 8, Por –, Eur –, Jap 9
Total contested: 59
World championship position: 1992, 11th (4);
1993, 20th (1); 1994, 23rd (2)

Comotti, Franco Italy
Born: 24 Jul 1906 Died: 10 May 1963
Contested: 1950, It –; 1952, Fr 12
Total contested: 2

Connor, George United States
Born: 16 Aug 1908
Contested: 1950, Indy 8; 1951, Indy 30; 1952,
Indy 8
Total contested: 3

Constantine, George United States
Born: 22 Feb 1918
Contested: 1969, US –
Total contested: 1

Cordts, John Canada
Born: 23 Jul 1935
Contested: 1969, Can –
Total contested: 1

Coulthard, David Great Britain
Born: 27 Mar 1971
1994, Sp –, Can 5, Fr –, Ger –, Hun –, Bel 4, It 6,
Por 2; 1995, Bra 2, Arg –, SM 4, Sp –, Mon –,
Can –, Fr 3, GB 3, Ger 2, Hun 2, Bel –, It –, Por
1, Eur 3, Pac 2, Jap –, Austral –; 1996, Aus-
tral –, Bra –, Arg 7, Eur 3, SM –, Mon 2, Sp –,
Can 4, Fr 6, GB 5, Ger 5, Hun –, Bel –, It –, Por
13, Jap 8; 1997, Austral 1, Bra 10, Arg –, SM –,
Mon –, Sp 6, Can 7, Fr 7, GB 4, Ger –, Hun –,
Bel –, It 1, Aus 2, Lux –, Jap 10, Eur 2
Total contested: 58 Won: 3 Poles: 5
World championship position: 1994, 8th (14);
1995 3rd (49); 1996, 7th (18); 1997, 3rd (36)
Fastest laps: 5

Courage, Piers Great Britain
Born: 27 May 1942 Died: 21 Jun 1970
A member of the brewing family, he was
becoming increasingly competitive when he
died in a crash at Zandvoort.
Contested: 1996, Ger –; 1967, SA –, Mon –;
1968, Spa –, Mon –, Bel –, Hol –, Fr 6, GB 8,
Ger 8, It 4, Can –, US –, Mex –; 1969, Spa –,
Mon 2, Hol –, Fr –, GB 5, Ger –, It 5, Can –,
US 2, Mex 10; 1970, SA –, Mon –, Bel –,
Hol –
Total contested: 28
World championship position: 1968, 19th (4);
1969, 8th (16)

Craft, Chris Great Britain
Born: 17 Nov 1939
Contested: 1971, US –
Total contested: 1

Crawford, Jim Great Britain
Born: 13 Feb 1948
A talented driver whose grand prix career
coincided with one of Lotus's lows.
Contested: 1975, GB –, It 13
Total contested: 2

Crawford, Ray United States
Born: 26 Oct 1915
Contested: 1955, Indy 23; 1956, Indy 29; 1959,
Indy 23
Total contested: 3

Creus, Antonio   Spain
Contested: 1960, Arg –
Total contested: 1

Crockett, Larry   United States
Born: 23 Oct 1926   **Died:** 20 Mar 1955
Contested: 1954, Indy 9
Total contested: 1

Crook, Tony   Great Britain
Born: 16 Feb 1920
Contested: 1952, GB 21; **1953**, GB –
Total contested: 2

Cross, Art   United States
Born: 24 Jan 1918
Contested: 1952, Indy 5; **1953**, Indy 2; **1954**, Indy 11; **1955**, Indy 17
Total contested: 4
World championship position: 1952, 16th (2); 1953, 10th (6)

Crossley, Geoff   Great Britain
Born: 11 May 1921
Contested: 1950, GB –, Bel 9
Total contested: 2

Daigh, Chuck   United States
Born: 29 Nov 1923
Contested: 1960, Bel –, GB –, US 10
Total contested: 3

Dalmas, Yannick   France
Born: 28 Jul 1961
1992 sports car World Champion and Le Mans winner, 1992, 1994 and 1995.
Contested: 1987, Mex 9, Jap 14, Austral 5; **1988**, Bra –, SM 12, Mon 7, Mex 9, Detroit 7, Fr 13, GB 13, Ger 19, Hun 9, Bel –, It –, Por –, Spa 11; **1989**, SM –; **1990**, Bra –, Fr 17, It –, Por –, Spa 9; **1994**, It –, Por 14
Total contested: 24

Daly, Derek   Ireland
Born: 11 Mar 1953
Contested: 1978, GB –, Aus –, Hol –, It 10, US East 8, Can 6; **1979**, Arg 11, Bra 13; US West –, Aus 8, Can –, US East –; **1980**, Arg 4, Bra 14, SA –, US West 8, Bel 9, Mon –, Fr 11, GB 4, Ger 10, Aus –, Hol –, It –, Can –, US East –; **1981**, Spa 16, Fr –, GB 7, Ger –, Aus 11, Hol –, It –, Can 8; **1982**, SA 14, Bra –, US West –, Bel –, Mon 6, US East 5, Can 7, Hol 5,

GB 5, Fr 7, Ger –, Aus –, CH 9, It –, US Las Vegas 6
Total contested: 49
World championship position: 1978, 19th (1); 1980, 10th (6); 1982, 13th (8)

Danner, Christian   Germany
Born: 4 Apr 1958
Contested: 1985, Bel –, Eur –; **1986**, Bra –, Spa –, SM –, Bel –, Can –, Detroit –, Fr 11, GB –, Ger 13, Hun –, Aus 6, It 8, Por 11, Mex 9, Austral –; **1987**, Bra 9, SM 7, Bel –, US 8, Fr –, GB –, Ger –, Hun –, Aus 9, It 9, Por –, Spa –, Mex –, Jap –, Austral 7; **1989**, Bra 14, Mex 12, US 4, Can 8
Total contested: 36
World championship position: 1986, 18th (1); 1989, 21st (3)

Daponte, Jorge   Argentina
Born: 5 Jun 1923   **Died:** 9 Mar 1963
Contested: 1954, Arg –, It 11
Total contested: 2

da Silva Ramos, Nano   Brazil/France
Born: 7 Dec 1925
Contested: 1955, Hol 8, GB –, It –; **1956**, Mon 5, Fr 8, GB –, It –
Total contested: 7
World championship position: 1956, 19th (2)

Davies, Jimmy   United States
Born: 8 Aug 1923   **Died:** 11 Jun 1966
Contested: 1950, Indy 17; **1951**, Indy 16; **1953**, Indy 10; **1954**, Indy 20; **1955**, Indy 3
Total contested: 5
World championship position: 1955, 12th (4)

Davis, Colin   Great Britain
Born: 29 Jul 1933
Contested: 1959, Fr –, It 11
Total contested: 2

Daywalt, Jimmy   United States
Born: 28 Aug 1924   **Died:** 4 Apr 1966
Contested: 1953, Indy 6; **1954**, Indy 24, Indy 27; **1955**, Indy 9; **1956**, Indy 24; **1957**, Indy 28; **1959**, Indy 14
Total contested: 6

de Adamich, Andrea   Italy
Born: 3 Oct 1941
Contested: 1968, SA –; **1970**, Fr –, Aus 12, It

8, Can –; **1971**, SA 13, Spa–, Fr–, GB–, Ger–, It–, US 11; **1972**, Arg–, SA–, Spa 4, Mon 7, Bel –, Fr 14, GB –, Ger 13, Aus 14, It –, Can–, US –; **1973**, SA 8, Spa –, Bel 4, Mon 7, Fr–, GB –

Total contested: 30

World championship position: 1972, 16th (3); 1973, 15th (3)

de Angelis, Elio Italy
Born: 26 Mar 1958   **Died:** 15 May 1986
Killed in testing at Paul Ricard.
Contested: 1979, Arg 7, Bra 12, SA –, US West 7, Spa–, Bel–, Fr 16, GB 12, Ger 11, Aus–, Hol–, It–, Can–, US East 4; **1980**, Arg–, Bra 2, SA–, US West–, Bel 10, Mon 9, Fr–, GB–, Ger 16, Aus 6, Hol–, It 4, Can 10, US East 4; **1981**, US West–, Bra 5, Arg 6, Bel 5, Mon–, Spa 5, Fr 6, GB–, Ger 7, Aus 7, Hol 5, It 4, Can 6, US Las Vegas –; **1982**, SA 8, Bra–, US West 5, Bel 4, Mon 5, US East–, Can 4, Hol–, GB 4, Fr–, Ger–, Aus 1, CH 6, It–, US Las Vegas –; **1983**, Bra–, US West–, Fr–, SM–, Mon–, Bel 9, US East–, Can–, GB–, Ger–, Aus–, Hol–, It 5, Eur–, SA –; **1984**, Bra 3, SA 7, Bel 5, SM 3, Fr 5, Mon 5, Can 4, US East 2, US Dallas 3, GB 4, Ger–, Aus–, Hol 4, It–, Eur–, Por 5; **1985**, Bra 3, Por 4, SM 1, Mon 3, Can 5, US 5, Fr 5, GB–, Ger–, Aus 5, Hol 5, It 6, Bel–, Eur 5, SA–, Austral –; **1986**, Bra 8, Spa –, SM –, Mon –

Total contested: 108 **Won:** 2 **Poles:** 3

World championship position: 1979, 15th (3); 1980, 7th (13); 1981, 8th (14); 1982, 9th (23); 1983, 17th (2); 1984, 3rd (34); 1985, 5th (33)

de Beaufort, Carel Godin Holland
Born: 10 Apr 1934   **Died:** 3 Aug 1964
A true amateur who drove without shoes, he campaigned the same Porsche for many years before his fatal crash in practice for the German Grand Prix.
Contested: 1957, Ger 14; **1958**, Hol 11, Ger –; **1959**, Hol 10, Fr 9; **1960**, Hol 8; **1961**, Hol 14, Bel 11, Fr –, GB 16, Ger 14, It 7; **1962**, Hol 6, Bel 7, Fr 6, GB 14, Ger 13, It 10, US –, SA 11; **1963**, Bel 6, Hol 9, GB 10, Ger–, US 6, Mex 10, SA 10; **1964**, Hol –

Total contested: 28

World championship position: 1962, 16th (2); 1963, 14th (2)

de Cesaris, Andrea Italy
Born: 31 May 1959
Competed in more grand prix without winning one than any other driver.
Contested: 1980, Can–, US East –; **1981**, US West–, Bra –, Arg 11, SM 6, Bel –, Mon–, Spa –, Fr 11, GB –, Ger –, Aus 8, It 7, Can –, US Las Vegas 12; **1982**, SA 13, Bra–, US West –, SM –, Bel –, Mon 3, US East –, Can 6, Hol –, GB –, Fr –, Ger –, Aus –, CH 10, It 10, US Las Vegas 9; **1983**, US West –, Fr 12, SM –, Mon –, Bel –, US East –, Can –, GB 8, Ger 2, Aus –, Hol –, It –, Eur 4, SA 2; **1984**, Bra –, SA 5, Bel –, SM 6, Fr 10, Mon –, Can –, US East –, US Dallas –, GB 10, Ger 7, Aus –, Hol –, It –, Eur 7, Por 12; **1985**, Bra –, Por –, SM –, Mon 4, Can 14, US 10, Fr –, GB –, Ger –, Aus –, Hol –; **1986**, Bra –, Spa –, SM –, Bel –, Can –, Detroit –, Fr –, GB –, Ger –, Hun –, Aus –, It –, Por –, Mex 8, Austral –; **1987**, Bra –, SM –, Bel 3, Mon –, US –, Fr –, GB –, Ger –, Hun –, Aus –, It –, Por –, Spa –, Mex –, Jap –, Austral 8; **1988**, Bra –, SM –, Mon –, Mex –, Can 9, Detroit 4, Fr 10, GB –, Ger 13, Hun –, Bel –, It –, Por –, Spa –, Jap –, Austral 8; **1989**, Bra 13, SM 10, Mon 13, Mex –, US 8, Can 3, GB –, Ger 7, Hun –, Bel 11, It –, Por –, Spa 7, Jap 10, Austral –; **1990**, US –, Bra –, SM –, Mon –, Can –, Mex 13, Fr –, GB –, Hun –, Bel –, It 10, Por –, Spa –, Jap –, Austral –; **1991**, Bra –, SM –, Mon –, Can 4, Mex 4, Fr 6, GB –, Ger 5, Hun 7, Bel 13, It 7, Por 8, Spa –, Jap –, Austral 8; **1992**, SA –, Mex 5, Bra –, Spa –, SM 14, Mon –, Can 5, Fr –, GB –, Ger –, Hun 8, Bel 8, It 6, Por 9, Jap 4, Austral –; **1993**, SA –, BRa –, Eur –, SM –, Sp –, Mon 10, Can –, Fr 15, GB –, Ger –, Hun 11, Bel –, It 13, Por 12, Jap –, Austral 13; **1994**, SM –, Mon 4, Can –, Fr 6, GB –, Ger –, Hun –, Bel –, It –, Por –, Eur –

Total contested: 208 **Poles:** 1

World championship position: 1981, 18th (1); 1982, 17th (5); 1983, 8th (15); 1984, 16th (3); 1985, 17th (3); 1987, 14th (4); 1988, 15th (3); 1989, 16th (4); 1991, 9th (9); 1992, 9th (8); 1994, 18th (4)

Fastest laps: 1

de Filippis, Maria Teresa Italy
Born: 11 Nov 1926
The first woman to compete in the championship.

Contested: 1958, Bel 10, Por –, It –
Total contested: 3

de Graffenried, Toulo   Switzerland
Born: 18 May 1914
Still active in the sport, he was most successful in the early post-war period, winning the 1949 British Grand Prix.
Contested: 1950, GB–, Mon–, CH 6, It 6; **1951**, CH 5, Fr–, Ger–, It–, Spa 6; **1952**, CH 6, Fr–, GB 19; **1953**, Hol 5, Bel 4, Fr 7, GB–, Ger 5, CH –, It 14; **1954**, Arg 8, Spa –; **1956**, It 7
Total contested: 22
World championship position: 1951, 15th (2); 1953, 8th (7)

de Klerk, Peter   South Africa
Born: 16 Mar 1935
Contested: 1963, SA –; **1965**, SA 10; **1969**, SA –; **1970**, SA 11
Total contested: 4

de Portago, Alfonso   Spain
Born: 11 Oct 1928   **Died:** 12 May 1957
Something of a playboy, his fatal crash in the Mille Miglia killed nine spectators and his co-driver and spelled the end of open road racing.
Contested: 1956, Fr–, GB 2, Ger–, It –; **1957**, Arg 5
Total contested: 5
World championship position: 1956, 15th (3); 1957, 20th (1)

de Terra, Max   Switzerland
Born: 6 Oct 1918   **Died:** 29 Dec 1982
Contested: 1952, CH –; **1953**, CH 10
Total contested: 2

de Tomaso, Alessandro   Argentina
Born: 10 Jul 1928
An Argentinian who settled in Italy, he constructed cars for both the 1½ and 3 litre formulas and supercars for the road.
Contested: 1957, Arg 9; **1959**, US –
Total contested: 2

de Tornaco, Charles   Belgium
Born: 7 Jun 1927   **Died:** 18 Sep 1953
Contested: 1952, Bel 7, Hol –
Total contested: 2

Deletraz, Jean-Denis   Switzerland
Born: 1 Oct 1963
1994, Austral –; **1995**, Por–, Eur –
Total contested: 3

Depailler, Patrick   France
Born: 9 Aug 1944   **Died:** 1 Aug 1980
Killed in testing at Hockenheim.
Contested: 1972, Fr 20, US 7; **1974**, Arg 6, Bra 8, SA 4, Spa 8, Bel–, Mon 9, Swe 2, Hol 6, Fr 8, GB–, Ger–, Aus–, It 11, Can 5, US 6; **1975**, Arg 5, Bra–, SA 3, Spa–, Mon 5, Bel 4, Swe 12, Hol 9, Fr 6, GB 9, Ger 9, Aus 11, It 7, US –; **1976**, Bra 2, SA 9, US West 3, Spa–, Bel–, Mon 3, Swe 2, Fr 2, GB–, Ger–, Aus–, Hol 7, It 6, Can 2, US East–, Jap 2; **1977**, Arg–, Bra–, SA 3, US West 4, Spa–, Mon–, Bel 8, Swe 4, Fr–, GB–, Ger–, Aus 13, Hol–, It–, US East 14, Can 2, Jap 3; **1978**, Arg 3, Bra–, SA 2, US West 3, Mon 1, Bel–, Spa–, Swe–, Fr–, GB 4, Ger–, Aus 2, Hol–, It 11, US East–, Can 5; **1979**, Arg 4, Bra 2, SA–, US West 5, Spa 1, Bel–, Mon 5; **1980**, Arg–, Bra–, SA–, US West–, Bel–, Mon–, Fr–, GB –
Total contested: 95 Won: 2 Poles: 1
World championship position: 1974, 9th (14); 1975, 9th (12); 1976, 4th (39); 1977, 8th (20); 1978, 5th (34); 1979, 6th (20, total 22)
Fastest laps: 4

Diniz, Pedro   Brazil
Born: 22 May 1970
1995, Bra 10, Arg–, SM 15, Sp–, Mon 10, Can–, Fr–, GB–, Ger–, Hun–, Bel 13, It 9, Por 16, Eur 13, Pac 17, Jap–, Austral 7; **1996**, Austral 10, Bra 8, Arg–, Eur 10, SM 7, Mon–, Sp 6, Can–, Fr–, GB–, Ger–, Hun–, Bel–, It 6, Por–, Jap –; **1997**, Austral–, Bra–, Arg–, SM–, Mon–, Sp–, Can 8, Fr–, GB–, Ger–, Hun–, Bel 7, It–, Aus 13, Lux 5, Jap 12, Eur –
Total contested: 50
World championship position: 1996, 15th (2); 1997, 16th (2)

Dinsmore, Duke   United States
Born: 10 Apr 1913   **Died:** 12 Oct 1985
Contested: 1950, Indy 33; **1951**, Indy 24; **1953**, Indy 16; **1956**, Indy 17
Total contested: 4

Dolhem, José   France
Born: 26 Apr 1944   **Died:** 16 Apr 1988
Contested: 1974, US –
Total contested: 1

Drivers' Career Records

Donnelly, Martin   Great Britain
Born: 26 Mar 1964
Survived a near fatal crash in practice for the Spanish Grand Prix.
Contested: 1989, Fr 12; **1990,** US –, Bra –, SM 8, Mon –, Can –, Mex 8, Fr 12, GB –, Ger –, Hun 7, Bel 12, It –, Por –
Total contested: 14

Donohue, Mark   United States
Born: 18 Mar 1937   **Died:** 19 Aug 1975
A winner, usually for Roger Penske, in Can-Am, Trans-Am, Indycars (he won Indianapolis in 1972) and NASCAR, Donohue was killed in practice for the Austrian Grand Prix.
Contested: 1971, Can 3; **1974,** Can 12, US –; **1975,** Arg 7, Bra –, SA 8, Spa –, Mon –, Bel 11, Swe 5, Hol 8, Fr –, GB 5, Ger –
Total contested: 14
World championship position: 1971, 16th (4); 1975, 15th (4)

d'Orey, Fritz   Brazil
Born: 25 Mar 1938   **Died:** 1961
Contested: 1959, Fr 10, GB –, US –
Total contested: 3

Downing, Ken   Great Britain
Born: 5 Dec 1917
Contested: 1952, GB 9, Hol –
Total contested: 2

Drake, Bob   United States
Born: 14 Dec 1919   **Died:** 18 Apr 1990
Contested: 1960, US 13
Total contested: 1

Driver, Paddy   South Africa
Born: 13 May 1934
Contested: 1974, SA –
Total contested: 1

Drogo, Piero   Venezuela
Born: 8 Aug 1926   **Died:** 28 Apr 1973
Contested: 1960, It 8
Total contested: 1

Dumfries, Johnny   Great Britain
Born: 26 Apr 1958
A Scottish Earl, he did well enough in his one Lotus season but the arrival of Honda engines also meant the arrival of a Japanese driver. Le Mans winner in 1988.

Contested: 1986, Bra 9, Spa –, SM –, Bel –, Can –, Detroit 7, Fr –, GB 7, Ger –, Hun 5, Aus –, It –, Por 9, Mex –, Austral 6
Total contested: 15
World championship position: 1986, 13th (3)

Duncan, Len   United States
Born: 25 Jul 1911
Contested: 1954, Indy 31
Total contested: 1

Eaton, George   Canada
Born: 12 Nov 1945
A member of the Canadian department store family.
Contested: 1969, US –, Mex –; **1970,** SA –, Hol –, Fr 12, GB –, Aus 11, It –, Can 10, US –; **1971,** Can 15
Total contested: 11

Edmunds, Don   United States
Born: 23 Sep 1930
Contested: 1957, Indy 19
Total contested: 1

Edwards, Guy   Great Britain
Born: 30 Dec 1942
Contested: 1974, Arg 11, Bra –, Bel 12, Mon 8, Swe 7, Hol –, Fr 15; **1976,** Fr 17, GB –, Ger 15, Can 20
Total contested: 11

Elford, Vic   Great Britain
Born: 10 Jun 1935
His Porsche rally drives (he won the Monte Carlo rally in 1968) led to a distinguished endurance racing career including wins at Daytona (1968), Nürburgring (1968, 1970), and in the Targo Florio (1968) but he never had a truly competitive grand prix drive.
Contested: 1968, Fr 4, GB –, Ger –, It –, Can 5, US –, Mex 8; **1969,** Mon 7, Hol 10, Fr 5, GB 6, Ger –; **1971,** Ger 11
Total contested: 13
World championship position: 1968, 17th (5); 1969, 13th (3)

Elisian, Ed   United States
Born: 9 Dec 1926   **Died:** 30 Aug 1959
Contested: 1954, Indy 18; **1955,** Indy 30; **1956,** Indy 23; **1957,** Indy 29; **1958,** Indy 28
Total contested: 5

Drivers' Career Records

Emery, Paul   Great Britain
Born: 12 Nov 1916 **Died:** 3 Feb 93
An indefatigable builder of specials including
the cars raced by the Ecurie Nationale Belge
in 1961.
Contested: 1956, GB –
Total contested: 1

England, Paul   Australia
Born: 28 Mar 1929
Contested: 1957, Ger –
Total contested: 1

Erti, Harald   Austria
Born: 31 Aug 1948   **Died:** 7 Apr 1982
Contested: 1975, Ger 8, Aus–, It 9; **1976**, SA
15, Bel–, Swe–, Fr–, GB 7, Ger–, Aus 8,
Hol–, It 16, US East 13, Jap 8; **1977**, Spa–,
Bel 9, Swe 16; **1978**, Ger 11,–, Aus –
Total contested: 19

Estefano, Nasif   Argentina
Born: 18 Nov 1932   **Died:** 21 Oct 1973
Contested: 1960, Arg 14
Total contested: 1

Etancelin, Philippe   France
Born: 28 Dec 1896   **Died:** 13 Oct 1981
The oldest driver to score world championship points, Etancelin raced from 1926 to
1953, always as an independent. He won
the 1930 French Grand Prix and Le Mans
in 1934.
Contested: 1950, GB 8, Mon–, CH–, Bel–, Fr
5, It 5; **1951**, CH 10, Bel–, Fr–, Ger–, Spa 8;
1952, Fr 8
Total contested: 12
World championship position: 1950, 13th (3)

Evans, Bob   Great Britain
Born: 11 Jun 1947
Contested: 1975, SA 15, Spa–, Bel 9, Swe 13,
Hol–, Fr 17, Aus–, It –; **1976**, SA 10, GB –
Total contested: 10

Fabi, Corrado   Italy
Born: 12 Apr 1961
Brother of Teo.
Contested: 1983, Bra–, Fr–, SM–, Bel–,
Can–, It–, SA–, Aus 10, Hol 11; **1984**,
Mon–, Can–, US 7
Total contested: 12

Fabi, Teo   Italy
Born: 9 Mar 1955
Brother of Corrado. World sportscar cham-
pion in 1991.
Contested: 1982, SM–, Bel–, GB–, Fr–,
Aus–, CH–, It –; **1984**, Bra–, SA–, Bel–,
SM–, GB–, Ger–, It–, Eur–, US 3, Aus 4,
Hol 5, Fr 9; **1985**, Mon–, Can–, US–, GB–,
Fr 14, Ger–, Aus–, Hol–, Bel–, Eur–, SA–,
Austral–, It 12; **1986**, Bra 10, Spa 5, SM–,
Mon–, Bel 7, Can–, Detroit–, Fr–, GB–,
Ger–, Hun–, Aus–, It–, Por 8, Mex–, Aus-
tral 10; **1987**, Bra–, SM–, Bel–, US–, Ger–,
Hun–, Spa–, Jap–, Austral–, Aus 3, Por 4, Fr
5, Mex 5, GB 6, It 7, Mon 8
Total contested: 64 **Poles:** 3
World championship position: 1984, 12th (9);
1986, 15th (2); 1987, 9th (12)
Fastest laps: 2

Fabre, Pascal   France
Born: 9 Jan 1960
Contested: 1987, Bra 12, SM 13, Bel 10, Mon
13, US 12, Fr 9, GB 9, Ger–, Hun 13, It–,
Spa –
Total contested: 11

Fagioli, Luigi   Italy
Born: 9 Jun 1898   **Died:** 20 Jun 1952
Pre-war ace whose shared drive with Fangio
in the 1951 French Grand Prix made him the
oldest driver to win a championship race. He
died after a practice crash at Monaco.
Contested: 1950, GB 2, Mon–, CH 2, Bel 2,
France 2, It 3; **1951**, Fr 1
Total contested: 7 **Won:** 1
World championship position: 1950, 3rd (24,
total 28); 1951, 11th (4)

Fairman, Jack   Great Britain
Born: 15 Mar 1913
Contested: 1953, GB–, It 20; **1956**, GB 4, It 5;
1957, GB –; **1958**, GB–, Moroccan 8; **1959**,
GB–, It –; **1960**, GB –; **1961**, GB–, It –
Total contested: 12
World championship position: 1956, 10th (5)

Fangio, Juan Manuel   Argentina
Born: 24 Jun 1911   **Died:** 17 Jul 1995
The outstanding Grand Prix driver of the
1950s and one of the best of all time, his
five championships remain a record.
Contested: 1950, GB 12, Mon 1, CH–, Bel 1,

Drivers' Career Records

France 1, It–, It –; **1951**, CH 1, Bel 9, Fr 11, GB 2, Ger 2, It–, Spa 1; **1953**, Arg–, Hol–, Bel–, Bel–, Fr 2, GB 2, Ger 2, CH 4, CH–, It 1; **1954**, Arg 1, Bel 1, Fr 1, GB 4, Ger 1, CH 1, It 1, Spa 3; **1955**, Arg 1, Mon–, Bel 1, Hol 1, GB 2, It 1; **1956**, Arg 1, Arg–, Mon 2, Mon 4, Bel–, Fr 4, GB 1, Ger 1, It 8; **1957**, Arg 1, Mon 1, Fr 1, GB–, Ger 1, Pescara 2, It 2; **1958**, Arg 4, Fr 4

Total contested: 51 **Won:** 24 **Poles:** 29
World championship position: 1950, 2nd (27); 1951, 1st (31, total 37); 1953, 2nd (27.5, total 29); 1954, 1st (42, total 57.14); 1955, 1st (40, total 41); 1956, 1st (30, total 33); 1957, 1st (40, total 46); 1958, 14th (7)
Fastest laps: 23

Farina, Nino   Italy
Born: 30 Oct 1906   **Died:** 30 Jun 1966
The first world champion, he died in a road accident.
Contested: 1950, GB 1, Mon–, CH 1, Bel 4, France 7, It 1; **1951**, CH 3, Bel 1, Fr 5, GB 14, Ger–, Spa 3, It–, It 3; **1952**, CH–, CH –, Bel 2, Fr 2, GB 6, Ger 2, Hol 2, It 4; **1953**, Arg–, Hol 2, Bel–, Fr 5, GB 3, Ger 1, CH 2, It 2; **1954**, Arg 2, Bel –; **1955**, Arg 3, Mon 4, Bel 3
Total contested: 33 **Won:** 5 **Poles:** 5
World championship position: 1950, 1st (30); 1951, 4th (19, total 22); 1952, 2nd (24, total 27); 1953, 3rd (26, total 32); 1954, 8th (6); 1955, 10th (10.33)
Fastest laps: 5

Faulkner, Walt   United States
Born: 16 Feb 1920   **Died:** 22 Apr 1956
Contested: 1950, Indy 7; **1951**, Indy 15; **1953**, Indy 17; **1954**, Indy 12; **1955**, Indy 5
Total contested: 5 **Poles:** 1
World championship position: 1955, 22nd (1)

Fischer, Rudi   Switzerland
Born: 19 Apr 1912   **Died:** 30 Dec 1976
Contested: 1951, CH 11, Ger 6; **1952**, CH 2, Fr 11, GB 13, Ger 3, It –
Total contested: 7
World championship position: 1952, 4th (10)

Fisher, Mike   United States
Born: 13 Mar 1943
Contested: 1967, Can 11
Total contested: 1

Fisichella, Giancarlo   Italy
Born: 14 Jan 1973
1996, Austral–, Eur 13, SM–, Mon–, Sp–, Can 8, Fr–, GB 11; **1997**, Austral–, Bra 8, Arg–, SM 4, Mon 6, Sp 9, Can 3, Fr 9, GB 7, Ger 11, Hun–, Bel 2, It 4, Aus 4, Lux–, Jap 7, Eur 11
Total contested: 25
World championship position: 1997, 8th (20)
Fastest laps: 1

Fitch, John   United States
Born: 4 Aug 1917
Contested: 1953, It –; **1955**, It 9
Total contested: 2

Fittipaldi, Christian   Brazil
Born: 18 Jan 1971
Son of Wilson, nephew of Emerson. Now a successful Indycar racer. European F3000 Champion 1991.
Contested: 1992, SA –, Mex–, Bra–, Spa 11, SM –, Mon 8, Can 13, Por 12, Jap 6, Austral 9; **1993**, SA 4, Bra–, Eur 7, SM–, Sp 8, Mon 5, Can 9, Fr 8, GB 12, Ger 11, Hun–, Bel–, It 8, Por 9; **1994**, Bra–, Pac 4, SM 13, Mon–, Sp–, Can–, Fr 8, GB 9, Ger 4, Hun 14, Bel–, It–, Por 8, Eur 17, Jap 8, Austral 8
Total contested: 40
World championship position: 1992, 17th (1); 1993, 13th (5); 1994, 14th (6)

Fittipaldi, Emerson   Brazil
Born: 12 Dec 1946
His grand prix career went into decline after he left McLaren to drive for his brother Wilson's team, but he has since become a major Indycar driver, winning both the 500 and the championship in 1989. He won Indianapolis again in 1993.
Contested: 1970, GB 8, Ger 4, Aus 15, US 1, Mex –; **1971**, SA –, Spa–, Mon 5, Fr 3, GB 3, Ger–, Aus 2, It 8, Can 7, US –; **1972**, Arg–, SA 2, Spa 1, Mon 3, Bel 1, Fr 2, GB 1, Ger–, Aus 1, It 1, Can 11, US –; **1973**, Arg 1, Bra 1, SA 3, Spa 1, Bel 3, Mon 2, Swe 12, Fr–, GB–, Hol–, Ger 6, Aus 11, It 2, Can 2, US 6; **1974**, Arg 10, Bra 1, SA 7, Spa 3, Bel 1, Mon 5, Swe 4, Hol 3, Fr–, GB 2, Ger–, Aus–, It 2, Can 1, US 4; **1975**, Arg 1, Bra 2, SA–, Mon 2, Bel 7, Swe 8, Hol–, Fr 4, GB 1, Ger–, Aus 9, It 2, US 2; **1976**, Bra 13, SA–, US West 6, Spa–, Mon 6, Swe–, Fr–, GB 6, Ger 13, Aus–,

Hol–, It 15, Can–, US East 9, Jap –; **1977,**
Arg 4, Bra 4, SA 10, US West 5, Spa 14,
Mon–, Bel–, Swe 18, Fr 11, GB–, Aus 11,
Hol 4, US East 13, Can –; **1978,** Arg 9, Bra 2,
SA–, US West 8, Mon 9, Bel–, Spa–, Swe 6,
Fr–, GB–, Ger 4, Aus 4, Hol 5, It 8, US East
5, Can –; **1979,** Arg 6, Bra 11, SA 13, US
West–, Spa 11, Bel 9, Mon–, Fr–, GB–,
Ger–, Aus–, Hol–, It 8, Can 8, US East 7;
1980, Arg–, Bra 15, SA 8, US West 3, Bel–,
Mon 6, Fr 13, GB 12, Ger–, Aus 11, Hol–,
It–, Can–, US East –
Total contested: 144 **Won:** 14 **Poles:** 6
World championship position: 1970, 10th (12);
1971, 6th (16); 1972, 1st (61); 1973, 2nd (55);
1974, 1st (58); 1975, 2nd (45); 1976, 16th (3);
1977, 12th (11); 1978, 9th (17); 1979, 21st (1);
1980, 15th (5)
Fastest laps: 6

Fittipaldi, Wilson   Brazil
Born: 25 Dec 1943
Brother of Emerson, father of Christian,
constructor of the Fittipaldi cars.
Contested: 1972, Spa 7, Mon 9, Bel–, Fr 8, GB
12, Ger 7, Aus–, It–, Can–, US –; **1973,** Arg
6, Bra–, SA–, Spa 10, Bel–, Mon 11, Swe–,
Fr 16, GB–, Hol–, Ger 5, Aus–, It–, Can 11,
US –; **1975,** Arg–, Bra 13, Spa–, Bel 12, Swe
17, Hol 11, Fr–, GB 19, Ger–, US 10
Total contested: 35
World championship position: 1973, 15th (3)

Fitzau, Theo   Germany
Born: 10 Feb 1923   **Died:** 18 Mar 1982
Contested: 1953, Ger –
Total contested: 1

Flaherty, Pat   United States
Born: 6 Jan 1926
Contested: 1950, Indy 10; **1953,** Indy 22; **1954,**
Indy 28; **1955,** Indy 10; **1956,** Indy 1; **1959,**
Indy 19
Total contested: 6 **Won:** 1 **Poles:** 1
World championship position: 1956, 5th (8)

Flinterman, Jan   Holland
Born: 2 Oct 1919   **Died:** 26 Dec 1992
Contested: 1952, Hol–, Hol 9
Total contested: 1

Flockhart, Ron   Great Britain
Born: 16 Jun 1923   **Died:** 12 Apr 1962

Le Mans winner 1956 and 1957. Killed in an
air crash.
Contested: 1954, GB 19; **1956,** GB–, It 3; **1957,**
Mon–, Fr –; **1958,** Moroccan –; **1959,** Mon–,
Fr 6, GB–, Por 7, It 13; **1960,** Fr 6, US –
Total contested: 13
World championship position: 1956, 11th (4);
1960, 24th (1)

Fohr, Myron   United States
Born: 17 Jun 1912
Contested: 1950, Indy 11
Total contested: 1

Foitek, Gregor   Switzerland
Born: 27 Mar 1965
Contested: 1990, US–, Bra–, SM–, Mon 7,
Can–, Mex 15, Ger –
Total contested: 7

Folimer, George   United States
Born: 27 Jan 1934
Contested: 1973, SA 6, Spa 3, Bel–, Swe 14,
Fr–, GB–, Hol 10, Ger–, Aus–, It 10, Can 17,
US 14
Total contested: 12
World championship position: 1973, 13th (5)

Fonder, George   United States
Born: 22 Jun 1917   **Died:** 14 Jun 1958
Contested: 1952, Indy 15; **1954,** Indy 31, Indy
19
Total contested: 3

Fontana, Norberto   Argentina
Born: 20 Jan 1975
1997, Fr–, GB 9, Ger 9, Eur 14
Total contested: 4

Forberg, Carl   United States
Born: 4 Mar 1911
Contested: 1951, Indy 7
Total contested: 1

Force, Gene   United States
Born: 15 Jun 1916   **Died:** 21 Aug 1983
Contested: 1951, Indy 11; **1960,** Indy 28
Total contested: 2

Forini, Franco   Switzerland
Born: 22 Sep 1958
Contested: 1987, It–, Por –
Total contested: 2

Drivers' Career Records

Fotheringham-Parker, Philip   Great Britain
Born: 22 Sep 1907   **Died:** 15 Oct 1981
Contested: 1951, GB –
Total contested: 1

Foyt, A J   United States
Born: 16 Jan 1935
One of the all time Indycar greats with four victories at Indianapolis, Le Mans winner 1967.
Contested: 1958, Indy 16; **1959,** Indy 10; **1960,** Indy 25
Total contested: 3

Freeland, Don   United States
Born: 25 Mar 1925
Contested: 1953, Indy 27; **1954,** Indy 7; **1955,** Indy 15; **1956,** Indy 3; **1957,** Indy 17; **1958,** Indy 7; **1959,** Indy 22; **1960,** Indy 22
Total contested: 8
World championship position: 1956, 11th (4)

Frentzen, Heinz-Harald   Germany
Born: 18 May 1967
1994, Bra –, –, Pac 5, SM 7, Sp –, Can –, Fr 4, GB 7, Ger –, Hun –, Bel –, It –, Por –, Eur 6, Jap 6, Austral 7; **1995,** Bra –, Arg 5, SM 6, Sp 8, Mon 6, Can –, Fr 10, GB 6, Ger –, Hun 5, Bel 4, It 3, Por 6, Eur –, Pac 7, Jap 8, Austral –; **1996,** Austral 8, Bra –, Arg –, Eur –, SM –, Mon 4, Sp 4, Can –, Fr –, GB 8, Ger 8, Hun –, Bel –, It –, Por 7, Jap 6; **1997,** Austral 8, Bra 9, Arg –, SM 1, Mon –, Sp 8, Can 4, Fr 2, GB –, Ger –, Hun –, Bel 3, It 3, Aus 3, Lux 3, Jap 2, Eur 6
Total contested: 65 **Won:** 1 **Poles:** 1
World championship position: 1994, 13th (7); 1995, 9th (15); 1996, 11th (8); 1997, 2nd (42)
Fastest laps: 6

Frere, Paul   Belgium
Born: 30 Jan 1917
Journalist and technical writer, Le Mans winner 1960.
Contested: 1952, Bel 5, Ger –, Hol –; **1953,** Bel 10, CH –; **1954,** Bel –, Fr –, Ger –; **1955,** Bel 4, Mon 9; **1956,** Bel 2
Total contested: 11
World championship position: 1952, 16th (2); 1955, 13th (3); 1956, 7th (6)

Fry, Joe   Great Britain
Born: 26 Oct 1915   **Died:** 29 Jul 1950

Contested: 1950, GB 10
Total contested: 1

Gabbiani, Bebe   Italy
Born: 2 Jan 1957
Contested: 1981, US West –, SM –, Bel –
Total contested: 3

Gachot, Bertrand   Belgium
Born: 23 Dec 1962
Le Mans winner 1991, returned to grand prix racing after being imprisoned in Britain for an assault on a taxi driver.
Contested: 1989, Fr 13, GB 12, Hun –, Bel –, It –; **1991,** US 10, Bra 13, SM –, Mon 8, Can 5, Mex –, Fr –, GB 6, Ger 6, Hun 9; **1992,** SA –, Mex 11, Bra –, Spa –, SM –, Mon 6, Can –, Fr –, GB –, Ger 14, Hun –, Bel 18, It –, Por –, Jap –, Austral –; **1994,** Bra –, SM –, Mon –, Sp –, Can –; **1995,** Bra –, Arg –, SM –, Sp –, Mon –, Can –, Fr –, GB 12, Pac –, Jap –, Austral 8
Total contested: 47
World championship position: 1991, 13th (3); 1992, 17th (1)
Fastest laps: 1

Gaillard, Patrick   France
Born: 12 Feb 1952
Contested: 1979, GB 13, Aus –
Total contested: 2

Galli   see Nanni Galli

Galvez, Oscar   Argentina
Born: 17 Aug 1913   **Died:** 16 Dec 1989
Contested: 1953, Arg 5
Total contested: 1
World championship position: 1953, 13th (2)

Gamble, Fred   United States
Born: 17 Mar 1932
Contested: 1960, It 10
Total contested: 1

Ganley, Howden   New Zealand
Born: 24 Dec 1941
Latterly manufacturer with Tim Schenken of Tiga cars.
Contested: 1971, SA –, Spa 10, Hol 7, Fr 10, GB 8, Ger –, Aus –, It 5, US 4; **1972,** Arg 9, SA –, Spa –, Mon –, Bel 8, Ger 4, Aus 6, It 11, Can 10, US –; **1973,** Arg –, Bra 7, SA 10, Spa –, Bel –, Mon –, Swe 11, Fr 14, GB 9,

Hol 9, Aus –, It –, Can 6, US 12; **1974**, Arg 8, Bra –
Total contested: 35
World championship position: 1971, 14th (5); 1972, 12th (4); 1973, 19th (1)

Gardner, Frank   Australia
Born: 1 Oct 1930
Contested: 1964, GB –; **1965**, SA 12, Mon –, Bel –, GB 8, Hol 11, Ger –, It –
Total contested: 8

Garrett, Billy   United States
Born: 24 Apr 1933
Contested: 1956, Indy 16; **1958**, Indy 21
Total contested: 2

Gartner, Jo   Austria
Born: 24 Jan 1954   **Died:** 1 Jun 1986
Killed at Le Mans.
Contested: 1984, SM –, GB –, Ger –, Aus –, Hol 12, It 5, Eur 12, Por 16
Total contested: 8

Gaze, Tony   Australia
Born: 3 Feb 1920
Contested: 1952, Bel 15, GB –, Ger –
Total contested: 3

'Geki', (Giacomo Russo)   Italy
Born: 23 Oct 1937   **Died:** 18 Jun 1967
Contested: 1965, It –; **1966**, It 9
Total contested: 2

Gendebien, Olivier   Belgium
Born: 12 Jan 1924
A truly great sports car driver with multiple wins at Le Mans (1958, 1960–2), the Targa Florio, and Sebring, Gendebien had relatively few grand prix drives.
Contested: 1956, Arg 5, Fr –; **1958**, Bel 6, It –, Moroccan –; **1959**, Fr 4, It 6; **1960**, Bel 3, Fr 2, GB 9, Por 7, US 12; **1961**, Bel 4, US 12
Total contested: 14
World championship position: 1956, 19th (2); 1959, 15th (3); 1960, 6th (10); 1961, 13th (3)

George, Elmer   United States
Born: 15 Jul 1928   **Died:** 30 May 1976
Contested: 1957, Indy 33
Total contested: 1

Gerard, Bob   Great Britain
Born: 19 Jan 1914   **Died:** 26 Jan 1990
Contested: 1950, GB 6, Mon 6; **1951**, GB 11; **1953**, Fr 11, GB –; **1954**, GB 10; **1956**, GB 12; **1957**, GB 6
Total contested: 8

Gerini, Gerino   Italy
Born: 10 Aug 1928
Contested: 1956, It 10, Arg 4; **1958**, Fr 9, GB –, It –, Moroccan 13
Total contested: 6
World championship position: 1956, 25th (1.5)

Gethin, Peter   Great Britain
Born: 21 Feb 1940
His only grand prix win was the fastest and one of the closest, with five cars covered by less than a second.
Contested: 1970, Hol –, Ger –, Aus 10, It –, Can 6, US 14, Mex –; **1971**, SA –, Spa 8, Mon –, Hol –, Fr 9, GB –, Ger –, Aus 10, It 1, Can 14, US 9; **1972**, Arg –, SA –, Spa –, Mon –, Bel –, GB –, Aus 13, It 6, Can –, US –; **1973**, Can –; **1974**, GB –
Total contested: 30 **Won:** 1
World championship position: 1970, 22nd (1); 1971, 9th (9); 1972, 20th (1)

Ghinzani, Piercarlo   Italy
Born: 16 Jan 1952
One of the least successful drivers with 76 starts (admittedly in less than competitive machinery) resulting in only one points scoring finish.
Contested: 1981, Bel 13; **1983**, US East –, GB –, Ger –, Aus 11, It –, Eur –, SA –; **1984**, Bra –, Bel –, Fr 12, Mon 7, Can –, US East –, US Dallas 5, GB 9, Ger –, Aus –, Hol –, It 7, Eur –, Por –; **1985**, Bra 12, Por 9, SM –, Can –, US –, Fr 15, GB –, Aus –, Hol –, It –, Bel –, Eur –, SA –, Austral –; **1986**, Bra –, Spa –, SM –, Bel –, Can –, Detroit –, Fr –, GB –, Ger –, Hun –, Aus 11, It –, Por –, Mex –, Austral –; **1987**, SM –, Bel 7, Mon 12, US –, Fr –, Ger –, Hun 12, Aus 8, It 8, Por –, Spa –, Mex –, Jap 13, Austral –; **1988**, SM –, Mon –, Mex 15, Can 14, Ger 14, Bel –, It –, Austral –; **1989**, Hun –, Spa –, Austral –
Total contested: 76
World championship position: 1984, 19th (2)

Drivers' Career Records

Giacomelli, Bruno Italy
Born: 10 Sep 1952
Contested: 1977, It –; **1978**, Bel 8, Fr –, GB 7, Hol –, It 14; **1979**, Bel –, Fr 17, It –, US East –; **1980**, Arg 5, Bra 13, SA –, US West –, Bel –, Mon –, Fr –, GB –, Ger 5, Aus –, Hol –, It –, Can –, US East –; **1981**, US West –, Bra –, Arg 10, SM –, Bel 9, Mon –, Spa 10, Fr 15, GB –, Ger 15, Aus –, Hol –, It 8, Can 4, US Las Vegas 3; **1982**, SA 11, Bra –, US West –, SM –, Bel –, Mon –, US East –, Can –, Hol 11, GB 7, Fr 9, Ger 5, Aus –, CH 12, It –, US Las Vegas 10; **1983**, Bra –, US West –, Fr 13, SM –, Bel 8, US East 9, Can –, GB –, Ger –, Aus –, Hol 13, It 7, Eur 6, SA –
Total contested: 69 **Poles:** 1
World championship position: 1980, 17th (4); 1981, 15th (7); 1982, 22nd (2); 1983, 19th (1)

Gibson, Dick Great Britain
Born: 16 Apr 1918
Contested: 1957, Ger –; **1958**, Ger –
Total contested: 2

Ginther, Richie United States
Born: 5 Aug 1930 **Died:** 20 Sept 1989
A versatile and highly rated development driver, he gave Honda their first grand prix win.
Contested: 1960, Mon 6, Hol 6, It 2; **1961**, Mon 2, Hol 5, Bel 3, Fr –, GB 3, Ger 8, It –; **1962**, Hol 9, Mon –, Bel 13, Fr 3, GB 13, Ger 8, It 2, US –; SA 7; **1963**, Mon 2, Bel 4, Hol 5, Fr –, GB 4, Ger 3, It 2, US 2, Mex 3, SA –; **1964**, Mon 2, Hol 11, Bel 4, Fr 5, GB 8, Ger 7, Aus 2, It 4, US 4, Mex 8; **1965**, Mon –, Bel 6, Fr –, GB –, Hol 6, It –, US 7, Mex 1; **1966**, Mon –, Bel 5, It –, US –, Mex 4
Total contested: 52 **Won:** 1
World championship position: 1960, 8th (8); 1961, 5th (16); 1962, 8th (10); 1963, 2nd (29, total 34); 1964, 4th (23); 1965, 7th (11); 1966, 11th (5)
Fastest laps: 3

Giraud-Cabantous, Yves France
Born: 8 Oct 1904 **Died:** 30 Mar 1973
Contested: 1950, GB 4, CH –, Bel –, France 8; **1951**, CH –, Bel 5, Fr 7, Ger 11, It 8, Spa –; **1952**, Fr 10; **1953**, Fr 14, It 18
Total contested: 13
World championship position: 1950, 13th (3); 1951, 15th (2)

Giunti, Ignazio Italy
Born: 30 Aug 1941 **Died:** 10 Jan 1971
A highly promising driver killed in a sports car race in Buenos Aires.
Contested: 1970, Bel 4, Fr 14, Aus 7, It –
Total contested: 4
World championship position: 1970, 17th (3)

Godia, Francisco Spain
Born: 21 Mar 1921 **Died:** 28 Nov 1990
Contested: 1951, Spa 10; **1954**, Spa 6; **1956**, Bel –, Fr 7, GB 8, Ger 4, It 4; **1957**, Ger –, Pescara –, It 9; **1958**, Arg 8, Bel –, Fr –
Total contested: 13
World championship position: 1956, 7th (6)

Goethais, Christian Belgium
Born: 4 Aug 1928
Contested: 1958, Ger –
Total contested: 1

Goldsmith, Paul United States
Born: 2 Oct 1927
Contested: 1958, Indy 30; **1959**, Indy 5; **1960**, Indy 3
Total contested: 3
World championship position: 1959, 17th (2); 1960, 15th (4)

Gonzalez, Froilan Argentina
Born: 5 Oct 1922
A very well built man who would not fit into one of today's cars, he was a highly competitive grand prix driver and won Le Mans in 1954.
Contested: 1950, Mon –, France –; **1951**, CH –, Fr 2, GB 1, Ger 3, It 2, Spa 2; **1952**, It 2; **1953**, Arg 3, Hol 3, Hol –, Bel –, Fr 3, GB 4; **1954**, Arg 3, Fr –, GB 1, Ger 2, CH 2, It 3; **1955**, Arg 2; **1956**, Arg –, GB –; **1957**, Arg 5; **1960**, Arg 10
Total contested: 26 **Won:** 2 **Poles:** 3
World championship position: 1951, 3rd (24, total 27); 1952, 9th (6.5); 1953, 6th (13.5, total 14.5); 1954, 2nd (25.14, total 26.14); 1955, 17th (2); 1957, 20th (1)
Fastest laps: 6

Gonzalez, Oscar Uruguay
Contested: 1956, Arg 6
Total contested: 1

Gordini, Aldo France
Born: 20 May 1921 **Died** 28 Jan 1995

Son of the constructor Amèdée Gordini.
Contested: **1951**, Fr –
Total contested: 1

Gould, Horace   Great Britain
Born: 20 Sep 1921   Died: 4 Nov 1968
Contested: **1954**, GB 20; **1955**, Hol –, GB –,
It –; **1956**, Mon 8, Bel –, GB 5, Ger –; **1957**,
Mon –, Fr –, Ger –, Pescara –, It 10; **1958**, Arg
9
Total contested: 14
World championship position: 1956, 19th (2)

Gounon, Jean-Marc   France
Born: 1 Jan 1963
1993, Jap –, Austral –; **1994**, Fr 9, GB 16,
Ger –, Hun –, Bel 11, It –, Por 15
Total contested: 9

Green, Cecil   United States
Born: 30 Sep 1919   Died: 29 Jul 1951
Contested: **1950**, Indy 4; **1951**, Indy 22
Total contested: 2
World championship position: 1950, 13th (3)

Greene, Keith   Great Britain
Born: 5 Jan 1938
Contested: **1960**, GB –; **1961**, GB 15; **1962**,
Ger –
Total contested: 3

Gregory, Masten   United States
Born: 29 Feb 1932   Died: 8 Nov 1985
Survived several serious crashes to win Le
Mans in 1965.
Contested: **1957**, Mon 3, Ger 8, Pescara 4, It 4;
1958, Hol –, Bel –, It 4, Moroccan 6; **1959**,
Mon –, Hol 3, Fr –, GB 7, Ger –, Por 2; **1960**,
Arg 12, Fr 9, GB 15, Por –; **1961**, Bel 10, Fr
12, GB 11, It –, US –, US 12; **1962**, Hol 13,
Bel –, Fr –, GB 7, It 12, US 6; **1963**, Fr –, GB
11, It –, US –, Mex –; **1965**, Bel –, GB 12, Ger
8, It –
Total contested: 38
World championship position: 1957, 6th (10);
1959, 8th (10); 1962, 18th (1)

Griffith, Cliff   United States
Born: 6 Feb 1916
Contested: **1951**, Indy 28; **1952**, Indy 9; **1956**,
Indy 10
Total contested: 3

Grignard, Georges   France
Born: 25 Jul 1905   Died: 7 Dec 1977
Contested: **1951**, Spa –
Total contested: 1

Grim, Bobby   United States
Born: 4 Sep 1924   Died: 14 Jun 1995
Contested: **1959**, Indy 26; **1960**, Indy 16
Total contested: 2

Grouillard, Ollvier   France
Born: 2 Sep 1958
Contested: **1989**, Bra 9, SM –, Mon –, Mex 8,
Fr 6, GB 7, Ger –, Bel 13, It –, Spa –, Jap –,
Austral –; **1990**, US –, Bra –, SM –, Can 13,
Mex 19, Bel 16, It –, Spa –, Austral 13; **1991**,
Mex –, Fr –, Bel 10, It –; **1992**, SA –, Mex –,
Bra –, Spa –, SM 8, Mon –, Can 12, Fr 11, GB
11, Ger –, Hun –, Bel –, It –, Por –, Jap –,
Austral –
Total contested: 41

Guelfi, André   France
Born: 6 May 1919
Contested: **1958**, Moroccan 15
Total contested: 1

Guerra, Miguel-Angel   Argentina
Born: 31 Aug 1953
Contested: **1981**, SM –
Total contested: 1

Guerrero, Roberto   Colombia
Born: 16 Nov 1958
Switched to Indycars.
Contested: **1982**, US West –, US East –, Can –,
GB –, Ger 8, Aus –, CH –, It –; **1983**, Bra –, US
West –, Fr –, SM –, Bel –, US East –, Can –, GB
16, Ger –, Aus –, Hol 12, It 13, Eur 12
Total contested: 21

Gugelmin, Mauricio   Brazil
Born: 20 Apr 1963
Contested: **1988**, Bra –, SM 15, Mon –, Mex –,
Can –, Detroit –, Fr 8, GB 4, Ger 8, Hun 5,
Bel –, It 8, Por –, Spa 7, Jap 10, Austral –;
1989, Bra 3, SM –, Mon –, US –, Can –, Fr –,
GB –, Ger –, Hun –, Bel 7, It –, Por 10, Spa –,
Jap 7, Austral 7; **1990**, US 14, SM –, Fr –,
Ger –, Hun 8, Bel 6, It –, Por 12, Spa 8, Jap –,
Austral –; **1991**, US –, Bra –, SM 12, –, Mon –,
Can –, Mex –, Fr 7, GB –, Ger –, Hun 11, Bel –,
It 15, Por 7, Spa 7, Jap 8, Austral 14; **1992**, SA

11, Mex –, Bra –, Spa –, SM 7, Mon –, Can –, Fr –, GB –, Ger 15, Hun 10, Bel 14, It –, Por –, Jap –, Austral –
Total contested: 74
World championship position: 1988, 13th (5); 1989, 16th (4); 1990, 18th (1)
Fastest laps: 1

Gurney, Dan   United States
Born: 13 Apr 1931
Won the Belgian Grand Prix in his own Eagle and Le Mans on successive weekends in 1967. One of the best and most versatile American drivers, he also gave Porsche and Brabham their first championship victories. His Eagles were a mainstay of Indycar racing in the seventies.
Contested: 1959, Fr –, Ger 2, Por 3, It 4; **1960,** Mon –, Hol –, Bel –, Fr –, GB 10, Por –, US –; **1961,** Mon 5, Hol 10, Bel 6, Fr 2, GB 7, Ger 7, It 2, US 2; **1962,** Hol –, Mon –, Fr 1, GB 9, Ger 3, It –, US 5; **1963,** Mon –, Bel 3, Hol 2, Fr 5, GB –, Ger –, It 14, US –, Mex 6, SA 2; **1964,** Mon –, Hol –, Bel 6, Fr 1, GB 13, Ger 10, Aus –, It 10, US 9, Mex 1; **1965,** SA –, Bel 10, Fr –, GB 6, Hol 3, Ger 3, It 3, US 2, Mex 2; **1966,** Bel –, Fr 5, GB –, Hol –, Ger 7, It –, US –, Mex 5; **1967,** SA –, Mon –, Hol –, Bel 1, Fr –, GB –, Ger –, Can 3, It –, US –, Mex –; **1968,** SA –, Mon –, Hol –, GB –, Ger 9, It –, Can –, US 4, Mex –; **1970,** Hol –, Fr 6, GB –
Total contested: 86 **Won:** 4 **Poles:** 3
World championship position: 1959, 7th (13); 1961, 3rd (21); 1962, 5th (15); 1963, 5th (19); 1964, 6th (19); 1965, 4th (25); 1966, 12th (4); 1967, 8th (13); 1968, 21st (3); 1970, 22nd (1)
Fastest laps: 6

Hahne, Hubert   Germany
Born: 28 Mar 1935
Contested: 1966, Ger 9; **1967,** Ger –; **1968,** Ger 10
Total contested: 3

Hailwood, Mike   Great Britain
Born: 2 Apr 1940   **Died:** 23 Mar 1981
One of the great motorcycle racers, Hailwood had a less successful career in cars, although he won the 1972 F2 championship. He died in a road accident.
Contested: 1963, GB 8, It 10; **1964,** Mon 6, Hol 12, Fr 8, GB –, Ger –, Aus 8, It –, US 8,

Mex –; **1965,** Mon –; **1971,** It 4, US 15; **1972,** SA –, Spa –, Mon –, Bel 4, Fr 6, GB –, Ger –, Aus 4, It 2, US 17; **1973,** Arg –, Bra –, SA –, Spa –, Bel –, Mon 8, Swe –, Fr –, GB –, Hol –, Ger 14, Aus 10, It 7, Can 9, US –; **1974,** Arg 4, Bra 5, SA 3, Spa 9, Bel 7, Mon –, Swe –, Hol 4, Fr 7, GB –, Ger 15
Total contested: 50
World championship position: 1964, 19th (1); 1971, 18th (3); 1972, 8th (13); 1974, 10th (12)
Fastest laps: 1

Hakkinen, Mika   Finland
Born: 28 Sept 1968
Contested: 1991, US –, Bra 9, SM 5, Mon –, Can –, Mex 9, GB 12, Ger –, Hun 14, Bel –, It 14, Por 14, Spa –, Jap –, Austral 19; **1992,** SA 9, Mex 6, Bra 10, Spa –, Mon –, Can –, Fr 4, GB 6, Ger –, Hun 4, Bel 6, It –, Por 5, Jap –, Austral 7; **1993,** Por –, Jap 3, Austral –; **1994,** Bra –, Pac –, SM 3, Mon –, Sp –, Can –, Fr –, GB 3, Ger –, Bel 2, It 3, Por 3, Eur 3, Jap 7, Austral 12; **1995,** Bra 4, Arg –, SM 5, Sp –, Mon –, Can –, Fr 7, GB –, Ger –, Hun –, Bel –, It 2, Por –, Eur 8, Pac –, Jap 2; **1996,** Austral 5, Bra 4, Arg –, Eur 8, SM 8, Mon 6, Sp 5, Can 5, Fr 5, GB 3, Ger –, Hun 4, Bel 3, It 3, Por –, Jap 3; **1997,** Austral 3, Bra 4, Arg 5, SM 6, Mon –, Sp 7, Can –, Fr –, GB –, Ger 3, Hun –, Bel –, It 9, Aus –, Lux –, Jap 4, Eur 1
Total contested: 96 **Won:** 1 **Poles:** 1
World championship position: 1991, 15th (2); 1992, 8th (11), 1993, 25th (4); 1994, 4th (26); 1995, 7th (17); 1996, 5th (31), 1997, 5th (27)
Fastest laps: 1

Halford, Bruce   Great Britain
Born: 18 May 1931
A stalwart private owner who later competed in historic races.
Contested: 1956, GB –, Ger –, It –; **1957,** Ger 11, Pescara –, It –; **1959,** Mon –; **1960,** Fr 8
Total contested: 8

Hall, Jim   United States
Born: 23 Jul 1935
Constructor of the revolutionary Chaparral cars, Hall was also a talented driver.
Contested: 1960, US 7; **1961,** US –; **1963,** Mon –, Bel –, Hol 8, Fr 11, GB 6, Ger 5, It 8, US –, Mex 8
Total contested: 11
World championship position: 1963, 12th (3)

Hamilton, Duncan   Great Britain
Born: 30 Apr 1920   **Died:** 13 May 1994
Won Le Mans in 1953, with a hangover as his car had been disqualified before the race and later reinstated.
Contested: 1951, GB 12, Ger –; **1952**, GB–, Hol 7; **1953**, GB –
Total contested: 5

Hampshire, David   Great Britain
Born: 29 Dec 1917   **Died:** 25 Aug 1990
Contested: 1950, GB 9, France –
Total contested: 2

Hanks, Sam   United States
Born: 13 Jul 1914   **Died:** 27 Jun 1994
Contested: 1950, Indy 30; **1951**, Indy 12; **1952**, Indy 3; **1953**, Indy 3; **1954**, Indy 20, Indy 11; **1955**, Indy 19; **1956**, Indy 2; **1957**, Indy 1
Total contested: 8 **Won:** 1
World championship position: 1952, 12th (4); 1953, 13th (2); 1956, 7th (6); 1957, 7th (8)

Hansgen, Walt   United States
Born: 28 Oct 1919   **Died:** 7 Apr 1996
Fatally injured in Le Mans trials.
Contested: 1961, US –; **1964**, US 5
Total contested: 2
World championship position: 1964, 16th (2)

Harris, Mike   Zimbabwe
Born: 25 May 1939
Contested: 1962, SA –
Total contested: 1

Harrison, T C   Great Britain
Born: 6 Jul 1906 · **Died:** 21 Jan 1981
Contested: 1950, GB 7, Mon –, It –
Total contested: 3

Hart, Brian   Great Britain
Born: 7 Sep 1936
Better known as an engine builder.
Contested: 1967, Ger 4*
Total contested: 1

Hartley, Gene   United States
Born: 28 Jan 1926
Contested: 1950, Indy 16; **1952**, Indy 28; **1953**, Indy 28; **1954**, Indy 23; **1956**, Indy 11; **1957**, Indy 10; **1959**, Indy 11; **1960**, Indy 14
Total contested: 8

Hasemi, Masahiro   Japan
Born: 13 Nov 1945
Set his fastest lap on qualifying tyres after a pit stop.
Contested: 1976, Jap 11
Total contested: 1
Fastest laps: 1

Hawkins, Paul   Australia
Born: 12 Oct 1937   **Died:** 26 May 1969
The second driver (after Ascari) to survive a Monte Carlo harbour crash, Hawkins was a rugged and versatile driver who won the Targa Floria in 1967. He died in a crash in the Tourist Trophy.
Contested: 1965, SA 9, Mon –, Ger –
Total contested: 3

Hawthorn, Mike   Great Britain
Born: 10 Apr 1929   **Died:** 22 Jan 1959
Britain's first world champion and a Le Mans winner in 1955, he retired as champion but died in a road crash within months.
Contested: 1952, Bel 4, Fr –, GB 3, Hol 4, It 19; **1953**, Arg 4, Hol 4, Bel 6, Fr 1, GB 5, Ger 3, CH 3, It 4; **1954**, Arg –, Bel 4, Fr –, GB 2, Ger 2, Ger –, CH –, It 2, Spa 1; **1955**, Mon –, Bel –, Hol 7, GB 6, It –; **1956**, Arg 3, Fr 10, GB –; **1957**, Arg –, Mon –, Mon –, Fr 4, GB 3, Ger 2, It 6; **1958**, Arg 3, Mon –, Hol 5, Bel 2, Fr 1, GB 2, Ger –, Por 2, It 2, Moroccan 2
Total contested: 45 **Won:** 3 **Poles:** 4
World championship position: 1952, 4th (10); 1953, 4th (19, total 27); 1954, 3rd (24.64); 1956, 11th (4); 1957, 4th (13); 1958, 1st (42, total 49)
Fastest laps: 6

Hayje, Boy   Holland
Born: 3 May 1949
Contested: 1976, Hol –; **1977**, SA –, Bel 15
Total contested: 3

Heeks, Willi   Germany
Born: 13 Feb 1922
Contested: 1952, Ger –; **1953**, Ger –
Total contested: 2

Helfrich, Theo   Germany
Born: 13 May 1913   **Died:** 29 Apr 1978
Contested: 1952, Ger –; **1953**, Ger 12; **1954**, Ger –
Total contested: 3

Drivers' Career Records

Hellings, Mack   United States
Born: 14 Sept 1917   **Died:** 11 Nov 1951
Contested: 1950, Indy 13; **1951**, Indy 31
Total contested: 2

Henton, Brian   Great Britain
Born: 19 Sept 1946
Contested: 1975, GB 16, US –; **1977**, US West
10, Hol –; **1981**, It 10; **1982**, US West –, SM –,
Bel –, Mon 8, US East 9, Can –, Hol –, GB 8,
Fr 10, Ger 7, Aus –, CH 11, It –, US Las Vegas
8
Total contested: 19
Fastest laps: 1

Herbert, Johnny   Great Britain
Born: 25 Jun 1964
Le Mans winner, 1991.
Contested: 1989, Bra 4, SM 11, Mon 14, Mex
15, US 5, Bel –; **1990**, Jap –, Austral –; **1991**,
Mex 10, Fr 10, GB 14, Bel 7, Por –, Jap –,
Austral 11; **1992**, SA 6, Mex 7, Bra –, Spa –,
SM –, Mon –, Can –, Fr 6, GB –, Ger –, Hun –,
Bel 13, It –, Por –, Jap –, Austral 13; **1993**,
SA –, Bra 4, Eur 4, SM 8, Sp –, Mon –, Can
10, Fr –, GB 4, Ger 10, Hun –, Bel 5, It –,
Por –, Jap 11, Austral –; **1994**, Bra 7, Pac 7,
SM 10, Mon –, Sp –, Can 8, Fr 7, GB 11,
Ger –, Hun –, Bel 12, It –, Por 11, Eur 8, Jap –,
Austral –; **1995**, Bra –, Arg 4, SM 7, Sp 2,
Mon 4, Can –, Fr –, GB 1, Ger 4, Hun 4, Bel 7,
It 1, Por 7, Eur 5, Pac 6, Jap 3, Austral –;
1996, Austral –, Bra –, Arg 9, Eur 7, SM –,
Mon 3, Sp –, Can 7, Fr –, GB 9, Ger –, Hun –,
Bel –, It 9, Por 8, Jap 10; **1997**, Austral –, Bra
7, Arg 4, SM –, Mon –, Sp 5, Can 5, Fr 8,
GB –, Ger –, Hun 3, Bel 4, It –, Aus 8, Lux 7,
Jap 6, Eur 8
Total contested: 113 **Won:** 2
World championship position: 1989, 14th (5);
1992, 14th (2); 1993, 9th (11); 1995, 4th (45);
1996, 14th (3), 1997, 10th (15)

Herman, Al   United States
Born: 15 Mar 1927   **Died:** 18 Jun 1960
Contested: 1955, Indy 7; **1956**, Indy 28; **1957**,
Indy 21; **1959**, Indy 13; **1960**, Indy 32
Total contested: 5

Herrmann, Hans   Germany
Born: 23 Feb 1928
A crash at Monaco in 1955 ended Herr-
mann's Mercedes career but he developed
into a very successful all rounder. After an
agonisingly close second at Le Mans in 1969
he won in 1970 with another nearly man,
Richard Attwood.
Contested: 1953, Ger 9; **1954**, Fr –, Ger –, CH
3, It 4, Spa –; **1955**, Arg 4; **1957**, Ger –; **1958**,
Ger –, It –, Moroccan 9; **1959**, GB –, Ger –;
1960, It 6; **1961**, Mon 9, Hol 15, Ger 13; **1966**,
Ger 11
Total contested: 18
World championship position: 1954, 6th (8);
1955, 22nd (1); 1960, 24th (1)
Fastest laps: 1

Hesnault, François   France
Born: 30 Dec 1956
Contested: 1984, Bra –, SA 10, Bel –, SM –,
Mon –, Can –, US East –, US Dallas –, GB –,
Ger 8, Aus 8, Hol 7, It –, Eur 10, Por –; **1985**,
Bra –, Por –, SM –, Ger –
Total contested: 19

Heyer, Hans   Germany
Heyer, who was a reserve, started his only
grand prix illegally but retired.
Born: 16 Mar 1943
Contested: 1977, Ger –
Total contested: 1

Hill, Damon   Great Britain
Born: 17 Sep 1960
Son of Graham.
Contested: 1992, GB 16, Hun 11; **1993**, SA –,
Bra 2, Eur 2, SM –, Sp –, Mon 2, Can 3, Fr 2,
GB –, Ger 15, Hun 1, Bel 1, It 1, Por 3, Jap 4,
Austral 3; **1994**, Bra 2, Pac –, SM 6, Mon –, Sp
1, Can 2, Fr 2, GB 1, Ger 8, Hun 2, Bel 1, It 1,
Por 1, Eur 2, Jap 1, Austral –; **1995**, Bra –,
Arg 1, SM 1, Sp 4, Mon 2, Can –, Fr 2, GB –,
Ger –, Hun 1, Bel 2, It –, Por 3, Eur –, Pac 3,
Jap –, Austral 1; **1996**, Austral 1, Bra 1, Arg 1,
Eur 4, SM 1, Mon –, Sp –, Can 1, Fr 1, GB –,
Ger 1, Hun 2, Bel 5, It –, Por 2, Jap 1; **1997**,
Austral –, Bra 17, Arg –, SM –, Mon –, Sp –,
Can 9, Fr 12, GB 6, Ger 8, Hun 2, Bel 13, It –,
Aus 7, Lux 8, Jap 11, Eur –
Total contested: 83 **Won:** 21 **Poles:** 20
World championship position: 1993, 3rd (69);
1994, 2nd (91); 1995, 2nd (69); 1996, 1st (97);
1997, 12th (7)
Fastest laps: 19

Hill, Graham   Great Britain
Born: 15 Feb 1929   **Died:** 29 Nov 1975

The only driver to win the championship, Le Mans, and Indianapolis, Hill retired from driving to run his highly promising team with driver Tony Brise. Hill, Brise and other members of the team were killed when Hill's plane crashed returning from a testing session. Father of Damon, no relation of Phil.
Contested: 1958, Mon–, Hol–, Bel–, Fr–, GB–, Ger–, Por–, It 6, Moroccan 16; **1959**, Mon–, Hol 7, Fr–, GB 9, Ger–, Por–, It –; **1960**, Arg–, Mon 7, Hol 3, Bel–, Fr–, GB 14, Por–, US –; **1961**, Mon–, Hol 8, Bel–, Fr 6, GB–, Ger–, It–, US 5; **1962**, Hol 1, Mon 6, Bel 2, Fr 9, GB 4, Ger 1, It 1, US 2, SA 1; **1963**, Mon 1, Bel –, Hol 10, Fr 3, GB 3, Ger–, It–, US 1, Mex 4, SA 3; **1964**, Mon 1, Hol 4, Bel 5, Fr 2, GB 2, Ger 2, Aus–, It–, US 1, Mex 11; **1965**, SA 3, Mon 1, Bel 5, Fr 5, GB 2, Hol 4, Ger 2, It 2, US 1, Mex –; **1966**, Mon 3, Bel–, Fr–, GB 3, Hol 2, Ger 4, It–, US–, Mex –; **1967**, SA–, Mon 2, Hol–, Bel–, Fr–, GB–, Ger–, Can 4, It–, US 2, Mex –; **1968**, SA 2, Spa 1, Mon 1, Bel–, Hol 9, Fr–, GB–, Ger 2, It–, Can 4, US 2, Mex 1; **1969**, SA 2, Spa–, Mon 1, Hol 7, Fr 6, GB 7, Ger 4, It 9, Can–, US –; **1970**, SA 6, Spa 4, Mon 5, Bel–, Hol–, Fr 10, GB 6, Ger–, Can–, US–, Mex –; **1971**, SA 9, Spa–, Mon–, Hol 10, Fr–, GB–, Ger 9, Aus 5, It–, Can–, US 7; **1972**, Arg–, SA 6, Spa 10, Mon 12, Bel–, Fr 10, GB–, Ger 6, Aus–, It 5, Can 8, US 11; **1973**, Spa–, Bel 9, Mon–, Swe–, Fr 10, GB–, Hol–, Ger 13, Aus–, It 14, Can 16, US 13; **1974**, Arg–, Bra 11, SA 12, Spa –, Bel 8, Mon 7, Swe 6, Hol–, Fr 13, GB 13, Ger 9, Aus 12, It 8, Can 14, US 8; **1975**, Arg 10, Bra 12
Total contested: 176 Won: 14 Poles: 13
World championship position: 1960, 15th (4); 1961, 13th (3); 1962, 1st (42, total 52); 1963, 2nd (29); 1964, 2nd (39, total 41); 1965, 2nd (40, total 47); 1966, 5th (17); 1967, 6th (15); 1968, 1st (48); 1969, 7th (19); 1970, 13th (7); 1971, 21st (2); 1972, 12th (4); 1974, 18th (1)
Fastest laps: 10

Hill, Phil United States
Born: 20 Apr 1927
The forgotten champion, Hill's victory was overshadowed by von Trips's death at Monza and a subsequent grand prix career ruined by the non-competitiveness of his cars. A consummate sports car driver, he won Le Mans three times.

Contested: 1958, Fr 7, Ger 9, It 3, Moroccan 3; **1959**, Mon 4, Hol 6, Fr 2, Ger 3, Por–, It 2, US –; **1960**, Arg 8, Mon 3, Hol–, Bel 4, Fr–, GB 7, Por–, It 1, US 6; **1961**, Mon 3, Hol 2, Bel 1, Fr 9, GB 2, Ger 3, It 1; **1962**, Hol 3, Mon 2, Bel 3, GB–, Ger–, It 11; **1963**, Bel–, Hol–, Fr 14, It 11, US–, Mex –; **1964**, Mon–, Hol 8, Bel–, Fr 7, GB 6, Ger–, Aus–, US–, Mex 9
Total contested: 48 Won: 3 Poles: 6
World championship position: 1958, 10th (9); 1959, 4th (20); 1960, 5th (16); 1961, 1st (34, total 38); 1962, 6th (14); 1964, 19th (1)
Fastest laps: 6

Hirt, Peter Switzerland
Born: 30 Mar 1910 **Died:** 28 Jun 1992
Contested: 1951, CH –; **1952**, CH 7, GB–, Fr 11; **1953**, CH –
Total contested: 5

Hobbs, David Great Britain
Born: 9 Jun 1939
Hobbs never had very competitive rides in formula one but displayed his versatility in many types of racing, mainly in the USA.
Contested: 1967, GB 8, Ger 3*, Can 9; **1968**, It –; **1971**, US 10; **1974**, Aus 7, It 9
Total contested: 7

Hoffman, Ingo Brazil
Born: 18 Feb 1953
Contested: 1976, Bra 11; **1977**, Arg–, Bra 7
Total contested: 3

Holland, Bill United States
Born: 18 Dec 1907 **Died:** 20 May 1984
Contested: 1950, Indy 2; **1953**, Indy 15
Total contested: 2
World championship position: 1950, 7th (6)
Fastest laps: 1

Holmes, Jackie United States
Born: 4 Sep 1920
Contested: 1950, Indy 23; **1953**, Indy 19
Total contested: 2

Homeier, Bill United States
Born: 31 Aug 1918
Contested: 1954, Indy 33; **1955**, Indy 5; **1960**, Indy 13
Total contested: 3
World championship position: 1955, 22nd (1)

Drivers' Career Records

Hoshino, Kazuyoshi   Japan
Born: 1 Jul 1947
Contested: 1976, Jap –; **1977**, Jap 11
Total contested: 2

Hoyt, Jerry   United States
Born: 29 Jan 1929   **Died:** 10 Jul 1955
Contested: 1950, Indy 21; **1953**, Indy 23; **1954**, Indy 26, Indy 8; **1955**, Indy 31
Total contested: 4 **Poles:** 1

Hulme, Denny   New Zealand
Born: 18 Jun 1936   **Died:** 4 Oct 1992
Hulme was highly competitive in grand prix cars and Can-Am cars but he also finished second at Le Mans (in a staged Ford finish). He died of a heart attack while competing in a touring car race in Australia.
Contested: 1965, Mon 8, Fr 4, GB –, Hol 5, Ger –, It –; **1966**, Mon –, Bel –, Fr 3, GB 2, Hol –, Ger –, It 3, US –, Mex 3; **1967**, SA 4, Mon 1, Hol 3, Bel –, Fr 2, GB 2, Ger 1, Can 2, It –, US 3, Mex 3; **1968**, SA 5, Spa 2, Mon 5, Bel –, Hol –, Fr 5, GB 4, Ger 7, It 1, Can 1, US –, Mex –; **1969**, SA 3, Spa 4, Mon 6, Hol 4, Fr 8, GB –, Ger –, It 7, Can –, US –, Mex 1; **1970**, SA 2, Spa –, Mon 4, Fr 4, GB 3, Ger 3, Aus –, It 4, Can –, US 7, Mex 3; **1971**, SA 6, Spa 5, Mon 4, Hol 12, Fr –, GB –, Ger –, Aus –, Can 4, US –; **1972**, Arg 2, SA 1, Spa –, Mon 15, Bel 3, Fr 7, GB 5, Ger –, Aus 2, It 3, Can 3, US 3; **1973**, Arg 5, Bra 3, SA 5, Spa 6, Bel 7, Mon 6, Swe 1, Fr 8, GB 3, Hol –, Ger 12, Aus 8, It 15, Can 13, US 4; **1974**, Arg 1, Bra 12, SA 9, Spa 6, Bel 6, Mon –, Swe –, Hol –, Fr 6, GB 7, Ger –, Aus 2, It 6, Can 6, US –
Total contested: 112 **Won:** 8 **Poles:** 1
World championship position: 1965, 11th (5); 1966, 4th (18); 1967, 1st (51); 1968, 3rd (33); 1969, 6th (20); 1970, 4th (27); 1971, 9th (9); 1972, 3rd (39); 1973, 6th (26); 1974, 7th (20)
Fastest laps: 9

Hunt, James   Great Britain
Born: 29 Aug 1947   **Died:** 15 Jun 1993
Won his first grand prix with Lord Hesketh's colourful team, became champion in an extraordinary contest characterised by off-track politics and Niki Lauda's near fatal crash. Subsequently a television commentator.
Contested: 1973, Mon 9, Fr 6, GB 4, Hol 3, Aus –, Can 7, US 2; **1974**, Arg –, Bra 9, SA –,

Spa 10, Bel –, Mon –, Swe 3, Hol –, Fr –, GB –, Ger –, Aus 3, It –, Can 4, US 3; **1975**, Arg 2, Bra 6, SA –, Spa –, Mon –, Bel –, Swe –, Hol 1, Fr 2, GB 4, Ger –, Aus 5, It 5, US 4; **1976**, Bra –, SA 2, US West –, Spa 1, Bel –, Mon –, Swe 5, Fr 1, GB –, Ger 1, Aus 4, Hol 1, It –, Can 1, US East 1, Jap 3; **1977**, Arg –, Bra 2, SA 4, US West 7, Spa –, Mon –, Bel 7, Swe 12, Fr 3, GB 1, Ger –, Aus –, Hol –, It –, US East 1, Can –, Jap 1; **1978**, Arg 4, Bra –, SA –, US West –, Mon –, Bel –, Spa 6, Swe 8, Fr 3, GB –, Ger –, Aus –, Hol 10, It –, US East 7, Can –; **1979**, Arg –, Bra –, SA 8, US West –, Spa –, Bel –, Mon –
Total contested: 92 **Won:** 10 **Poles:** 14
World championship position: 1973, 8th (14); 1974, 8th (15); 1975, 4th (33); 1976, 1st (69); 1977, 5th (40); 1978, 13th (8)
Fastest laps: 8

Hurtubuise, Jim   United States
Born: 5 Dec 1932   **Died:** 6 Jan 1989
Contested: 1960, Indy 18
Total contested: 1

Hutchison, Gus   United States
Born: 26 Apr 1937
Contested: 1970, US –
Total contested: 1

Ickx, Jacky   Belgium
Born: 1 Jan 1945
A record breaking six times Le Mans winner, Ickx was one of the best grand prix drivers of the late sixties/early seventies. After his grand prix career he took up long distance rallying, winning the 1983 Paris-Dakar. World Sports Car Champion 1982, 1983.
Contested: 1966, Ger –; **1967**, Ger –*, It 6, US –; **1968**, SA –, Spa –, Bel 3, Hol 4, Fr 1, GB 3, Ger 4, It 3, Mex –; **1969**, SA –, Spa 6, Mon –, Hol 5, Fr 3, GB 2, Ger 1, It 10, Can 1, US –, Mex 2; **1970**, SA –, Spa –, Mon –, Bel 8, Hol 3, Fr –, GB –, Ger 2, Aus 1, It –, Can 1, US 4, Mex 1; **1971**, SA 8, Spa 2, Mon 3, Hol 1, Fr –, GB –, Ger –, Aus –, It –, Can 8, US –; **1972**, Arg 3, SA 8, Spa 2, Mon 2, Bel –, Fr 11, GB –, Ger 1, Aus –, It –, Can 12, US 5; **1973**, Arg 4, Bra 5, SA –, Spa 12, Bel –, Mon –, Swe 6, Fr 5, GB 8, Ger 3, It 8, US 7; **1974**, Arg –, Bra 3, SA –, Spa –, Bel –, Mon –, Swe –, Hol 11, Fr 5, GB 3, Ger 5, Aus –, It –, Can 13, US –; **1975**, Arg 8, Bra 9, SA 12, Spa 2, Mon

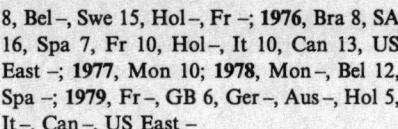

8, Bel –, Swe 15, Hol –, Fr –; **1976**, Bra 8, SA 16, Spa 7, Fr 10, Hol –, It 10, Can 13, US East –; **1977**, Mon 10; **1978**, Mon –, Bel 12, Spa –; **1979**, Fr –, GB 6, Ger –, Aus –, Hol 5, It –, Can –, US East –

Total contested: 116 Won: 8 Poles: 13

World championship position: 1967, 19th (1); 1968, 4th (27); 1969, 2nd (37); 1970, 2nd (40); 1971, 4th (19); 1972, 4th (27); 1973, 9th (12); 1974, 10th (12); 1975, 16th (3); 1979, 15th (3)

Fastest laps: 14

Iglesias, Julio   Argentina
Born: 22 Feb 1922
Contested: 1955, Arg –
Total contested: 1

Inoue, Taki   Japan
Born: 5 Sep 1963
1994, Jap –; **1995**, Bra –, Arg –, SM –, Sp –, Mon –, Can 9, Fr –, GB –, Ger –, Hun –, Bel 12, It 8, Por 15, Eur –, Pac –, Jap 12, Austral –
Total contested: 18

Ireland, Innes   Great Britain
Born: 12 Jun 1930   **Died:** 22 Oct 1993
Fired by Colin Chapman after giving the Lotus team its first championship victory, Ireland never again had truly competitive formula one machinery.
Contested: 1959, Hol 4, Fr –, Ger –, Por –, It –, US 5; **1960**, Arg 6, Mon 9, Hol 2, Bel –, Fr 7, GB 3, Por 6, US 2; **1961**, Bel –, Fr 4, GB 10, Ger –, It –, US 1; **1962**, Hol 12, Mon –, Bel –, Fr –, GB 16, It –, US 8, SA 5; **1963**, Mon –, Bel –, Hol 4, Fr 9, GB –, Ger –, It 4; **1964**, Bel 10, Fr –, GB 10, Aus 5, It 5, US –, Mex 12; **1965**, Bel 13, Fr –, GB –, Hol 10, It 9, US –; **1966**, US –, Mex –
Total contested: 50 Won: 1
World championship position: 1959, 12th (5); 1960, 4th (18); 1961, 6th (12); 1962, 16th (2); 1963, 9th (6); 1964, 12th (4)
Fastest laps: 1

Irvine, Eddie   Northern Ireland
Born: 10 Nov 1965
1993, Jap 6, Austral –; **1994**, Bra –, Sp 6, Can –, Fr –, GB –, Ger –, Hun –, Bel 13, It –, Por 7, Eur 4, Jap 5, Austral –; **1995**, Bra –, Arg –, SM 8, Sp 5, Mon –, Can 3, Fr 9, GB –, Ger 9, Hun 13, Bel –, It –, Por 10, Eur 6, Pac 11, Jap 4, Austral –; **1996**, Austral 3, Bra 7,

Arg 5, Eur –, SM 4, Mon 7, Sp –, Can –, Fr –, GB –, Ger –, Hun –, Bel –, It –, Por 5, Jap –; **1997**, Austral –, Bra 16, Arg 2, SM 3, Mon 3, Sp 12, Can –, Fr 3, GB –, Ger –, Hun 9, Bel 10, It 8, Aus –, Lux –, Jap 3, Eur 5
Total contested: 65
World championship position: 1993, 20th (1); 1994, 14th (6), 1995, 12th (10); 1996, 10th (11); 1997, 7th (24)

Irwin, Chris   Great Britain
Born: 27 Jun 1942
A serious crash at Nürburgring in 1968 terminated a promising career.
Contested: 1966, GB 7; **1967**, Hol 7, Bel –, Fr 5, GB 7, Ger 7, Can –, It –, US –, Mex –
Total contested: 10
World championship position: 1967, 16th (2)

Jabouille, Jean-Pierre   France
Born: 1 Oct 1942
A talented engineer, Jabouille played a large part in the development of the turbocharged Renault, but retired from grand prix driving as a result of injuries from a crash at the 1980 Canadian Grand Prix.
Contested: 1975, Fr 12; **1977**, GB –, Hol –, It –, US East –; **1978**, SA –, US West –, Mon 10, Bel –, Spa 13, Swe –, Fr –, GB –, Ger –, Aus –, Hol –, It –, US East 4, Can 12; **1979**, Arg –, Bra 10, SA –, Spa –, Bel –, Mon 8, Fr 1, GB –, Ger –, Aus –, Hol –, It 14, Can –, US East –; **1980**, Arg –, Bra –, SA –, US West 10, Bel –, Mon –, Fr –, GB –, Ger –, Aus 1, Hol –, It –, Can –; **1981**, SM –, Bel –, Spa –
Total contested: 49 Won: 2 Poles: 6
World championship position: 1978, 17th (3); 1979, 13th (9); 1980, 8th (9)

Jackson, Jimmy   United States
Born: 25 Jul 1910   **Died:** 24 Nov 1984
Contested: 1950, Indy 29; **1954**, Indy –
Total contested: 2

James, Joe   United States
Born: 23 May 1925   **Died:** 5 Nov 1952
Contested: 1951, Indy 33; **1952**, Indy 13
Total contested: 2

James, John   Great Britain
Born: 10 May 1914
Contested: 1951, GB –
Total contested: 1

Drivers' Career Records

Jarier, Jean-Pierre France
Born: 10 Jul 1946
Contested: 1971, It –; **1973**, Arg –, Bra –, SA –, Bel –, Mon –, Swe –, Fr –, Aus –, Can –, US 11; **1974**, Arg –, Bra –, Spa –, Bel 13, Mon 3, Swe 5, Hol –, Fr 12, GB –, Ger 8, Aus 8, It –, Can –, US 10; **1975**, Bra –, SA –, Spa 4, Mon –, Bel –, Swe –, Hol –, Fr 8, GB 14, Ger –, Aus –, It –, US –; **1976**, Bra –, SA –, US West 7, Spa –, Bel 9, Mon 8, Swe 12, Fr 12, GB 9, Ger 11, Aus –, Hol 10, It 19, Can 18, US East 10, Jap 10; **1977**, US West 6, Mon 11, Bel 11, Swe 8, Fr –, GB 8, Ger –, Aus 14, Hol –, It –, US East 9, Jap –; **1978**, Arg 12, SA 8, US West 11, US East 15, Can –; **1979**, Arg –, SA 3, US West 6, Spa 5, Bel 11, Mon –, Fr 5, GB 3, Hol –, It 6, Can –, US East –; **1980**, Arg –, Bra 12, SA 7, US West –, Bel 5, Mon –, Fr 14, GB 5, Ger 15, Aus –, Hol 5, It 13, Can 7, US East –; **1981**, US West –, Bra 7, GB 8, Ger 8, Aus 10, Hol –, It 9, Can –, US Las Vegas –; **1982**, SA –, Bra 9, US West –, SM 4, Bel –, US East –, Can –, Hol 14, GB –, Fr –, Ger –, CH –, It –; **1983**, Bra –, US West –, Fr 9, SM –, Mon –, Bel –, US East –, Can –, GB 10, Ger 8, Aus 7, Hol –, It 9, Eur –, SA 10
Total contested: 134 **Poles:** 3
World championship position: 1974, 14th (4); 1975, 18th (1.5); 1977, 19th (1); 1979, 10th (14); 1980, 10th (6); 1982, 20th (3)
Fastest laps: 3

Johansson, Stefan Sweden
Born: 8 Sep 1956
Senna's arrival at McLaren in 1988 pushed Johansson into a downward spiral of increasingly uncompetitive cars, but a move to Indycars in 1992 revived his career. Le Mans winner 1997.
Contested: 1983, GB –, Ger –, Aus 12, Hol 7, It –, Eur 14; **1984**, GB –, Ger –, Hol –, It 4, Eur –, Por 11; **1985**, Bra 7, Por 8, SM 6, Mon –, Can 2, US 2, Fr 4, GB –, Ger 9, Aus 4, Hol –, It 5, Bel –, Eur –, SA 4, Austral 5; **1986**, Bra –, Spa –, SM 4, Mon 10, Bel 3, Can –, Detroit –, Fr –, GB –, Ger 11, Hun 4, Aus 3, It 3, Por 6, Mex 12, Austral 3; **1987**, Bra 3, SM 4, Bel 2, Mon –, US 7, Fr 8, GB –, Ger 2, Hun –, Aus 7, It 6, Por 5, Spa 3, Mex –, Jap 3, Austral –; **1988**, Bra 9, Mon –, Mex 10, Can –, Detroit –, Hun –, Bel 11, Por –, Spa –, Austral 8; **1989**, Mex –, US –, Can –, Fr 5, Ger –, Hun –, Bel 8, Por 3; **1991**, Can –

Total contested: 79
World championship position: 1984, 16th (3); 1985, 7th (26); 1986, 5th (23); 1987, 6th (30); 1989, 11th (6)

Johnson, Eddie United States
Born: 10 Feb 1919 **Died:** 30 Jun 1974
Contested: 1952, Indy 16; **1953**, Indy 7; **1954**, Indy 22; **1955**, Indy 13; **1956**, Indy 15; **1957**, Indy 25; **1958**, Indy 9; **1959**, Indy 8; **1960**, Indy 6
Total contested: 9
World championship position: 1960, 24th (1)

Johnson, Leslie Great Britain
Born 22 Mar 1912 **Died:** 8 Jun 1959
Contested: 1950, GB –
Total contested: 1

Johnstone, Bruce South Africa
Born: 30 Jan 1937
Contested: 1962, SA 9
Total contested: 1

Jones, Alan, Australia
Born: 2 Nov 1946
Williams's first world champion, he still competes in touring cars in Australia.
Contested: 1975, Spa –, Mon –, Bel –, Swe 11, Hol 13, Fr 16, GB 10, Ger 5; **1976**, US West –, Spa 9, Bel 5, Mon –, Swe 13, Fr –, GB 5, Ger 10, Aus –, Hol 8, It 12, Can 16, US East 8, Jap 4; **1977**, US West –, Spa –, Mon 6, Bel 5, Swe 17, Fr –, GB 7, Ger –, Aus 1, Hol –, It 3, US East –, Can 4, Jap 4; **1978**, Arg –, Bra 11, SA 4, US West 7, Mon –, Bel 10, Spa 8, Swe –, Fr 5, GB –, Ger –, Aus –, Hol –, It 13, US East 2, Can 9; **1979**, Arg 9, Bra –, SA –, US West 3, Spa –, Bel –, Mon –, Fr 4, GB –, Ger 1, Aus 1, Hol 1, It 9, Can 1, US East –; **1980**, Arg 1, Bra 3, SA –, US West –, Bel 2, Mon –, Fr 1, GB 1, Ger 3, Aus 2, Hol 11, It 22, Can 1, US East 1; **1981**, US West 1, Bra 2, Arg 4, SM 12, Bel –, Mon 2, Spa 7, Fr 17, GB –, Ger 11, Aus 4, Hol 3, It 2, Can –, US Las Vegas 1; **1983**, US West –; **1985**, It –, Eur –, Austral –; **1986**, Detroit –, Fr –, GB –, Ger 9, Hun –, Aus 4, Bra –, Spa –, SM –, Mon –, Bel 11, Can 10, It 6, Por –, Mex –, Austral –
Total contested: 116 **Won:** 12 **Poles:** 6
World championship position: 1975, 17th (2); 1976, 14th (7); 1977, 7th (22); 1978, 11th (11);

1979, 3rd (40, total 43); 1980, 1st (67, total 71); 1981, 3rd (46); 1986 12th (4)
Fastest laps: 13

Karch, Oswald   Germany
Born: 6 Mar 1917
Contested: 1953, Ger –
Total contested: 1

Katayama, Ukyo   Japan
Born: 29 May 1963
Contested: 1992, SA 12, Mex 12, Bra 9, SM –, Can –, Fr –, GB –, Ger –, Hun –, Bel 17, It 9, Por –, Jap 11, Austral –; **1993**, SA –, Bra –, Eur –, SM –, Sp –, Mon –, Can 17, Fr –, GB 13, Ger –, Hun 10, Bel 15, It 14, Por –, Jap –, Austral –; **1994**, Bra 5, Pac –, SM 5, Mon –, Sp –, Can –, Fr –, GB 6, Ger –, Hun –, Bel –, It –, Por –, Eur 7, Jap –, Austral –; **1995**, Bra –, Arg 8, SM –, Sp –, Mon –, Can –, Fr –, GB –, Ger 7, Hun –, Bel –, It 10, Por –, Pac 14, Jap –, Austral –; **1996**, Austral 11, Bra 9, Arg –, Eur –, SM –, Mon –, Sp –, Can –, Fr –, GB –, Ger –, Hun 7, Bel 8, It 10, Por 12, Jap –; **1997**, Austral –, Bra 18, Arg –, SM 11, Mon 10, Sp –, Can –, Fr 11, GB –, Ger –, Hun 10, Bel 14, It –, Aus 11, Lux –, Jap –, Eur 17
Total contested: 95
World championship position: 1994, 16th (5)

Keegan, Rupert   Great Britain
Born: 26 Feb 1955
Contested: 1977, Spa –, Mon 12, Bel –, Swe 13, Fr 10, GB –, Ger –, Aus 7, Hol –, It 9, US East 8, Can –; **1978**, Arg –, Bra –, SA –, Mon –, Spa 11, Fr –; **1980**, GB 11, Aus 15, It 11, US East 9; **1982**, Aus –, CH –, US Las Vegas 12
Total contested: 25

Keizan, Eddie   South Africa
Born: 12 Sep 1944
Contested: 1973, SA –; **1974**, SA 14; **1975**, SA 13
Total contested: 3

Keller, Al   United States
Born: 11 Apr 1920   **Died:** 19 Nov 1961
Contested: 1955, Indy 27; **1956**, Indy 14; **1957**, Indy 27; **1958**, Indy 11; **1959**, Indy 18
Total contested: 5

Kelly, Joe   Ireland
Born: 13 Mar 1913   **Died:** 28 Nov 1993

Contested: 1950, GB 13; **1951**, GB 15
Total contested: 2

Kessel, Loris   Switzerland
Born: 1 Apr 1950
Contested: 1976, Bel 12, Swe –, Aus –
Total contested: 3

Kinnunen, Leo   Finland
Born: 5 Aug 1943
Co-drove Pedro Rodriguez to four sports car wins in 1970.
Contested: 1974, Swe –
Total contested: 1

Kladis, Danny   United States
Born: 10 Feb 1917
Contested: 1954, Indy 30
Total contested: 1

Klenk, Hans   Germany
Born: 18 Oct 1919
Contested: 1952, Ger 11
Total contested: 1

Kling, Karl   Germany
Born: 16 Sep 1910
Contested: 1954, Fr 2, GB 7, Ger 4, CH –, It –, Spa 5; **1955**, Arg –, Bel –, Hol –, GB 3, It –, Arg 4
Total contested: 11
World championship position: 1954, 5th (12); 1955, 11th (5)
Fastest laps: 1

Klodwig, Ernst   Germany
Born: 23 May 1903   **Died:** 15 Apr 1973
Contested: 1952, Ger 12; **1953**, Ger 17
Total contested: 2

Koinigg, Helmut   Austria
Born: 3 Nov 1948   **Died:** 6 Oct 1974
Killed in the American Grand Prix.
Contested: 1974, Can 10, US –
Total contested: 2

Krause, Rudolf   Germany
Born: 30 Mar 1907   **Died:** 11 Apr 1987
Contested: 1952, Ger –; **1953**, Ger 14
Total contested: 2

Lacaze, Robert   Morocco
Born: 26 Feb 1917

Drivers' Career Records

Contested: **1958**, Moroccan 14
Total contested: 1

Laffite, Jacques France
Born: 21 Nov 1943
Injured in the race in which he equalled Graham Hill's record number of grand prix starts, he never returned to formula one.
Contested: **1974**, Ger–, Aus–, It–, Can 15, US –; **1975**, Arg–, Bra 11, SA–, Bel–, Hol–, Fr 11, GB–, Ger 2, Aus–, It –; **1976**, Bra–, SA–, US West 4, Spa 12, Bel 3, Mon 12, Swe 4, Fr 14, GB–, Ger–, Aus 2, Hol–, It 3, Can–, US East–, Jap 7; **1977**, Arg–, Bra–, SA–, US West 9, Spa 7, Mon 7, Bel–, Swe 1, Fr 8, GB 6, Ger–, Aus–, Hol 2, It 8, US East 7, Can–, Jap 5; **1978**, Arg 16, Bra 9, SA 5, US West 5, Mon–, Bel 5, Spa 3, Swe 7, Fr 7, GB 10, Ger 3, Aus 5, Hol 8, It 4, US East 11, Can –; **1979**, Arg 1, Bra 1, SA–, US West–, Spa–, Bel 2, Mon–, Fra 8, GB–, Ger 3, Aus 3, Hol 3, It –, Can–, US East –; **1980**, Arg–, Bra–, SA 2, US West–, Bel 11, Mon 2, Fr 3, GB–, Ger 1, Aus 4, Hol 3, It 9, Can 8, US East 5; **1981**, Bra 6, Arg–, SM–, Bel 2, Mon 3, Spa 2, Fr–, GB 3, Ger 3, Aus 1, Hol–, It–, Can 1, US Las Vegas 6, US West –; **1982**, SA–, Bra–, US West–, Bel 9, Mon–, US East 6, Can–, Hol–, GB–, Fr 14, Ger–, Aus 3, CH–, It–, US Las Vegas –; **1983**, Bra 4, US West 4, Fr 6, SM 7, Mon–, Bel 6, US East 5, Can–, GB 12, Ger 6, Aus–, Hol–, SA –; **1984**, Bra–, SA–, Bel–, SM–, Fr 8, Mon 8, Can–, US East 5, US Dallas 4, GB–, Ger–, Aus–, Hol–, It–, Eur–, Por 14; **1985**, Bra 6, Por–, SM–, Mon 6, Can 8, US 12, Fr–, GB 3, Ger 3, Aus–, Hol–, It–, Bel 11, Eur–, Austral 2; **1986**, Bra 3, Spa–, SM–, Mon 6, Bel 5, Can 7, Detroit 2, Fr 6, GB –
Total contested: 176 **Won:** 6 **Poles:** 7
World championship position: 1975, 12th (6); 1976, 7th (20); 1977, 10th (18); 1978, 8th (19); 1979, 4th (36); 1980, 4th (34); 1981, 4th (44); 1982, 17th (5); 1983, 11th (11); 1984, 14th (5); 1985, 9th (16); 1986, 8th (14)

Lagorce, Franck France
Born: 1 Sep 1968
1994, Jap–, Austral 11
Total contested: 2

Lammers, Jan Holland
Born: 2 Jun 1956

Won Le Mans in 1988, returned to grand prix racing in 1992.
Contested: **1979**, Arg–, Bra 14, SA–, US West–, Spa 12, Bel 10, Fr 18, GB 11, Ger 10, Aus–, Hol–, Can 9; **1980**, US West–, Bel–, Mon–, Ger 14, Can 12, US East –; **1981**, US West–, Arg 12; **1982**, Hol –; **1992**, Jap–, Austral 12
Total contested: 23

Lamy, Pedro Portugal
Born: 20 Mar 1972
1993, It 11, Por–, Jap 13, Austral –; **1994**, Bra 10, Pac 8, SM–, Mon 11; **1995**, Hun 9, Bel 10, It–, Por–, Eur 9, Pac 13, Jap 11, Austral 6; **1996**, Austral–, Bra 10, Arg–, Eur 12, SM 9, Mon–, Sp–, Can–, Fr 12, GB–, Ger 12, Hun–, Bel 10, It–, Por 16, Jap 12
Total contested: 32
World championship position: 1995, 17th (1)

Landi, Chico Brazil
Born: 14 Jul 1907 **Died:** 7 Jun 1989
Contested: **1951**, It –; **1952**, Hol 9, It –; **1953**, CH–, It –; **1956**, Arg 4
Total contested: 6
World championship position: 1956, 25th (1.5)

Lang, Hermann Germany
Born: 6 Apr 1909 **Died:** 19 Oct 1987
One of the great pre-war Mercedes team, Lang was European champion in 1939 and Le Mans winner in 1952.
Contested: **1953**, CH 5; **1954**, Ger –
Total contested: 2
World championship position: 1953, 13th (2)

Larini, Nicola Italy
Born: 19 Mar 1964
Contested: **1987**, Spa –; **1988**, Mon 9, Detroit–, Fr–, GB 19, Ger–, Bel–, It–, Por 12, Spa–, Jap –; **1989**, Bra–, SM 12, Can–, GB–, It–, Spa–, Jap–, Austral –; **1990**, US–, Bra 11, SM 10, Mon–, Can–, Mex 16, Fr 14, GB 10, Ger 10, Hun 11, Bel 14, It 11, Por 10, Spa 7, Jap 7, Austral 10; **1991**, US 7, Ger–, Hun 16, It 16, Austral –; **1992**, Jap 12, Austral 11; **1994**, Pac–, SM 2; **1997**, Austral 6, Bra 11, Arg–, SM 7, Mon –
Total contested: 49
World championship position: 1994, 14th (6); 1997, 19th (1)

Larrauri, Oscar Argentina
Born: 19 Aug 1954
Contested: 1988, Bra –, Mon –, Mex 13, Can –, Detroit –, Fr –, Ger 16, Austral –
Total contested: 8

Larrousse, Gerard France
Born: 23 May 1940
A successful sports car driver with Le Mans wins in 1973 and 1974, he founded his own grand prix team in 1987, running Lolas until 1992.
Contested: 1974, Bel –
Total contested: 1

Larson, Jud United States
Born: 21 Jan 1923 **Died:** 11 Jun 1966
Contested: 1958, Indy 8; **1959**, Indy 29
Total contested: 2

Lauda, Niki Austria
Born: 22 Feb 1949
Lauda retired as a double world champion, promoted his airline Lauda Air, returned to win a third championship and retired again before returning to Ferrari as a consultant in 1992. He lost the 1976 championship to James Hunt by one point after his near fatal crash at the Nürburgring.
Contested: 1971, Aus –; **1972**, Arg 11, SA 7, Spa –, Mon 16, Bel 12, Fr –, GB 9, Ger –, Aus 10, It 13, Can –, US –; **1973**, Arg –, Bra 8, SA –, Spa –, Bel 5, Mon –, Swe 13, Fr 9, GB 12, Hol –, Ger –, It –, Can –, US –; **1974**, Arg 2, Bra –, SA 16, Spa 1, Bel 2, Mon –, Swe –, Hol 1, Fr 2, GB 5, Ger –, Aus –, It –, Can –, US –; **1975**, Arg 6, Bra 5, SA 5, Spa –, Mon 1, Bel 1, Swe 1, Hol 2, Fr 1, GB 8, Ger 3, Aus 6, It 3, US 1; **1976**, Bra 1, SA 1, US West 2, Spa 2, Bel 1, Mon 1, Swe 3, Fr –, GB 1, Ger –, It 4, Can 8, US East 3, Jap –; **1977**, Arg –, Bra 3, SA 4, US West 2, Mon 2, Bel 2, Swe –, Fr 5, GB 2, Ger 1, Aus 2, Hol 1, It 2, US East 4; **1978**, Arg 2, Bra 3, SA –, US West –, Mon 2, Bel –, Spa –, Swe 1, Fr –, GB 2, Ger –, Aus –, Hol 3, It 1, US East –, Can –; **1979**, Arg –, Bra –, SA 6, US West –, Spa –, Bel –, Mon –, Fr –, GB –, Ger –, Aus –, Hol –, It 4; **1982**, SA 4, Bra –, US West 1, Bel –, Mon –, US East –, Can –, Hol 4, GB 1, Fr 8, Aus 5, CH 3, It –, US Las Vegas –; **1983**, Bra 3, US West 2, Fr –, SM –, Bel –, US East –, Can –, GB 6, Ger –, Aus 6, Hol –, It –, Eur –, SA 11; **1984**, Bra –,

SA 1, Bel –, SM –, Fr 1, Mon –, Can 2, US East –, US Dallas –, GB 1, Ger 2, Aus 1, Hol 2, It 1, Eur 4, Por 2; **1985**, Bra –, Por –, SM 4, Mon –, Can –, US East –, Fr –, GB –, Ger 5, Aus –, Hol 1, It –, SA –, Austral –
Total contested: 171 **Won:** 25 **Poles:** 24
World championship position: 1973, 17th (2); 1974, 4th (38); 1975, 1st (64.5); 1976, 2nd (68); 1977, 1st (72); 1978, 4th (44); 1979, 14th (4); 1982, 5th (30); 1983, 10th (12); 1984, 1st (72); 1985 10th (14)
Fastest laps: 24

Laurent, Roger Belgium
Born: 21 Feb 1913
Contested: 1952, Bel 12, Ger 6
Total contested: 2

Lavaggi, Giovanni Italy
Born: 18 Feb 1958
Unlike many young hopefuls sponsored by rich families, the impecunious Lavaggi went out, made his own money and bought a grand prix drive in his late thirties.
1995, Ger –, Hun –, Bel –, It –; **1996**, Hun 10, It –, Por 15
Total contested: 7

Lawrence, Chris Great Britain
Born: 27 Jul 1933
Contested: 1966, GB 11, Ger –
Total contested: 2

Leclere, Michel France
Born: 18 Mar 1946
Contested: 1975, US –; **1976**, SA 13, Spa 10, Bel 11, Mon 11, Swe –, Fr 13
Total contested: 7

Lederle, Neville South Africa
Born: 25 Sep 1938
Contested: 1962, SA 6
Total contested: 1
World championship position: 1962, 18th (1)

Lees, Geoff Great Britain
Born: 1 May 1951
Contested: 1979, Ger 7; **1980**, SA 13, Hol –; **1982**, Can –, Fr 12
Total contested: 5

Legat, Arthur Belgium
Born: 1 Nov 1898 **Died:** 23 Feb 1960

Drivers' Career Records

Contested: **1952**, Bel 13; **1953**, Bel –
Total contested: 2

Lehto, J J   Finland
Born: 31 Jan 1966
Le Mans winner 1995
Contested: **1989**, Spa –, Austral –; **1990**, SM
12, Mon –, Can –, Mex –, Ger –; **1991**, US –,
Bra –, SM 3, Mon 11, Can –, Mex –, Fr –, GB
13, Ger –, Hun –, Bel –, It –, Por –, Spa 8, Jap –,
Austral 12; **1992**, SA –, Mex 8, Bra 8, Spa –,
SM 11, Mon 9, Can 9, Fr 9, GB 13, Ger 10,
Bel 7, It 11, Por –, Jap 9, Austral –; **1993**, SA
5, Bra –, Eur –, SM 4, Sp –, Mon –, Can 7, Fr –,
GB 8, Ger –, Hun –, Bel 9, It –, Por 7, Jap 8,
Austral –; **1994**, SM –, Mon 7, Sp –, Can 6, It
9, Por –, Jap –, Austral 10
Total contested: 62
World championship position: 1991, 13th (3);
1993, 13th (5); 1994, 24th (1)

Leoni, Lamberto   Italy
Born: 24 May 1953
Contested: **1978**, Arg –
Total contested: 1

Leston, Les   Great Britain
Born: 16 Dec 1920
Contested: **1956**, It –; **1957**, GB –
Total contested: 2

Levegh, Pierre   France
Born: 22 Dec 1905   **Died:** 11 Jun 1955
Drove for twenty three hours at Le Mans in
1952 before missing a gear change and retir-
ing. Crashed fatally at Le Mans in 1955,
killing eighty one spectators.
Contested: **1950**, Bel 7, France –, It –; **1951**,
Bel 8, Ger 9, It –
Total contested: 6

Levrett, Bayliss   United States
Born: 14 Feb 1913
Contested: **1950**, Indy 27
Total contested: 1

Lewis, Jack   Great Britain
Born: 1 Nov 1936
Contested: **1961**, Bel 9, Fr –, GB –, Ger 9, It 4;
1962, Hol 10, Fr –, GB 10, Ger –
Total contested: 9
World championship position: 1961, 13th (3)

Lewis-Evans, Stuart   Great Britain
Born: 20 Apr 1930   **Died:** 25 Oct 1958
Died from injuries in the Moroccan Grand
Prix.
Contested: **1957**, Mon 4, Fr –, GB 7, Ger –,
Pescara 5, It –; **1958**, Mon –, Hol –, Bel 3, Fr
13, GB 4, Por 3, It –, Moroccan –
Total contested: 14 Poles: 2
World championship position: 1957, 12th (5);
1958, 9th (11)

Ligier, Guy   France
Born: 12 Jul 1930
A former rugby star who entered formula one
as a privateer, he went on to build his own
successful grand prix cars.
Contested: **1966**, Mon –, Bel –, Fr 9, GB 10,
Hol 9; **1967**, Bel 10, Fr –, GB 10, Ger 6, It –,
US –, Mex 11
Total contested: 12
World championship position: 1967, 19th (1)

Linden, Andy   United States
Born: 5 Apr 1922   **Died:** 10 Feb 1987
Contested: **1951**, Indy 4; **1952**, Indy 33;
1953, Indy 33, Indy 16; **1954**, Indy 25,
Indy 24; **1955**, Indy 6; **1956**, Indy 27;
1957, Indy 5
Total contested: 7
World championship position: 1951, 12th (3);
1957, 18th (2)

Lippi, Roberto   Italy
Born: 17 Oct 1926
Contested: **1961**, It –
Total contested: 1

Lombardi, Lella   Italy
Born: 26 Mar 1943   **Died:** 3 Mar 1992
The first woman to score in the championship
with sixth in the shortened 1975 Spanish
Grand Prix.
Contested: **1975**, SA –, Spa 6, Bel –, Swe –, Hol
14, Fr 18, GB –, Ger 7, Aus 17, It –; **1976**, Bra
14, Aus 12
Total contested: 12
World championship position: 1975, 21st (0.5)

Loof, Ernst   Germany
Born: 4 Jul 1907   **Died:** 3 Mar 1956
Contested: **1953**, Ger –
Total contested: 1

Louveau, Henri   France
Born: 25 Jan 1910   **Died:** 7 Jan 1991
Contested: 1950, It –, **1951**, CH –
Total contested: 2

Love, John   Zimbabwe
Born: 7 Dec 1924
Multiple South African champion and 1962 British saloon car champion, Love's greatest moment came when he led the 1967 South African Grand Prix against all the contemporary machinery in his outdated Cooper but had to pit to take on fuel.
Contested: 1962, SA 8; **1963**, SA 9; **1965**, SA –; **1967**, SA 2; **1968**, SA 9; **1969**, SA –; **1970**, SA 8; **1971**, SA –; **1972**, SA 16
Total contested: 9
World championship position: 1967, 11th (6)

Lovely, Pete   United States
Born: 11 Apr 1926
Contested: 1960, US 11; **1969**, Can 7, US –; Mex 9; **1970**, GB –; **1971**, Can –, US –
Total contested: 7

Loyer, Roger   France
Born: 5 Aug 1907   **Died:** 24 Mar 1988
Contested: 1954, Arg –
Total contested: 1

Lucas, Jean   France
Born: 25 Apr 1917
Contested: 1955, It –
Total contested: 1

Lunger, Brett   United States
Born: 14 Nov 1945
Contested: 1975, Aus 13, It 10, US –; **1976**, SA 11, Bel –, Swe 15, Fr 16, GB –, Ger –, Aus 10, It 14, Can 15, US East 11; **1977**, SA 14, US West –, Spa 10, Swe 11, GB 13, Ger –, Aus 10, Hol 9, It –, US East 10, Can 11; **1978**, Arg 13, Bra –, SA 11, Bel 7, Fr –, GB 8, Aus 8, Hol –, It –, US East 13
Total contested: 34

Mackay-Fraser, Herbert   United States
Born: 23 Jun 1927   **Died:** 14 Jul 1957
Killed in a Formula 2 race the week after his grand prix debut.
Contested: 1957, Fr –
Total contested: 1

Mackey, Bill   United States
Born: 15 Dec 1927   **Died:** 29 Jul 1951
Contested: 1951, Indy 19
Total contested: 1

Macklin, Lance   Great Britain
Born: 2 Sep 1919
Contested: 1952, CH –, Bel 11, Fr 9, GB 15, Hol 8; **1953**, Hol –, Bel –, Fr –, GB –, CH –, It –; **1954**, Fr –; **1955**, GB 8
Total contested: 13

Magee, Damien   Great Britain
Born: 17 Nov 1945
Contested: 1975, Swe 14
Total contested: 1

Maggs, Tony   South Africa
Born: 9 Feb 1937
Contested: 1961, GB 13, Ger 11; **1962**, Hol 5, Mon –, Bel 14, Fr 2, GB 6, Ger 9, It 7, US 7, SA 3; **1963**, Mon 5, Bel –, Hol –, Fr 2, GB 9, Ger –, It 6, US –, Mex –, SA 7; **1964**, GB –, Ger 6, Aus 4; **1965**, SA 11
Total contested: 25
World championship position: 1962, 7th (13); 1963, 8th (9); 1964, 12th (4)

Magill, Mike   United States
Born: 18 Feb 1920
Contested: 1957, Indy 24; **1958**, Indy 17; **1959**, Indy 30
Total contested: 3

Maglioli, Umberto   Italy
Born: 5 Jun 1928
Mainly a sports car driver, with wins in the Targa Florio in 1954, 1956 and 1968.
Contested: 1953, It 10; **1954**, Arg 9, CH 7, It 3; **1955**, Arg 3, It 6; **1956**, GB –, Ger –, It 11; **1957**, Ger –
Total contested: 10
World championship position: 1954, 18th (2); 1955, 21st (1.33)

Magnussen, Jan   Denmark
Born: 4 Jul 1973
1995, Pac 10; **1997**, Austral –, Bra –, Arg 10, SM –, Mon 7, Sp 13, Can –, Fr –, GB –, Ger –, Hun –, Bel 12, It –, Aus –, Lux –, Jap –, Eur 9
Total contested: 18

Mairesse, Guy   France
Born: 10 Aug 1910   **Died:** 24 Apr 1954
Contested: 1950, It –; **1951,** Fr 9, CH 15
Total contested: 3

Mairesse, Willy   Belgium
Born: 1 Oct 1928   **Died:** 2 Sep 1969
A fast but erratic driver whose career was punctuated by crashes, he died of an overdose of sleeping pills.
Contested: 1960, Bel –, Fr –, It 3; **1961,** Bel –, Fr –, Ger 16; **1962,** Mon –, Bel 12, It **4**; **1963**; Mon –, Bel –, Ger –
Total contested: 12
World championship position: 1960, 15th (4); 1962, 14th (3)

Mansell, Nigel   Great Britain
Born: 8 Aug 1953
Fiercely competitive driver, one of the best of his generation, whose determination and talent finally netted a richly deserved championship in 1992. He also set a new record for wins in a season.
Contested: 1980, Aus –, Hol –; **1981,** US West –, Bra 11, Arg –, Bel 3, Mon –, Spa 6, Fr 7, Ger –, Aus –, Hol –, It –, Can –, US Las Vegas 4; **1982**; SA –, Bra 3, US West 7, Bel –, Mon 4, US East –, Can –, GB –, Ger 9, Aus –, CH 8, It 7, US Las Vegas –; **1983,** Bra 12, US West 12, Fr –, SM 12, Mon –, Bel –, US East 6, Can –, GB 4, Ger –, Aus 5, Hol –, It 8, Eur 3, SA –; **1984,** Bra –, SA –, Bel –, SM –, Fr 3, Mon –, Can 6, US East –, US Dallas 6, GB –, Ger 4, Aus –, Hol 3, It –, Eur –, Por –; **1985,** Bra –, Por 5, SM 5, Mon 7, Can 6, US –, GB –, Ger 6, Aus –, Hol 6, It 11, Bel 2, Eur 1, SA 1, Austral –; **1986,** Bra –, Spa 2, SM –, Mon 4, Bel 1, Can 1, Detroit 5, Fr 1, GB 1, Ger 3, Hun 3, Aus –, It 2, Por 1, Mex 5, Austral –; **1987,** Bra 6, SM 1, Bel –, Mon –, US 5, Fr 1, GB 1, Ger –, Hun 14, Aus 1, It 3, Por –, Spa 1, Mex 1; **1988,** Bra –, SM –, Mon –, Mex –, Can –, Detroit –, Fr –, GB 2, Ger –, Hun –, Por –, Spa 2, Jap –, Austral –; **1989,** Bra 1, SM –, Mon –, Mex –, US –, Can –, Fr 2, GB 2, Ger 3, Hun 1, Bel 3, It –, Por –, Jap –, Austral –; **1990,** US –, Bra 4, SM –, Mon –, Can 3, Mex 2, Fr 18, GB –, Ger –, Hun 17, –, Bel –, It 4, Por 1, Spa 2, Jap –, Austral 2; **1991,** US –, Bra –, SM –, Mon 2, Can 6, Mex 2, Fr 1, GB 1, Ger 1, Hun 2, Bel –, It 1, Por –, Spa 1, Jap –, Austral 2; **1992,** SA 1, Mex 1, Bra 1, Spa 1, SM 1, Mon 2, Can –, Fr 1, GB 1, Ger 1, Hun 2, Bel 2, It –, Por 1, Jap –, Austral –; **1994,** Fr –, Eur –, Jap 4, Austral 1; **1995,** SM 10, Sp –
Total contested: 187 **Won:** 31 **Poles:** 32
World championship position: 1981, 14th (8); 1982, 14th (7); 1983, 12th (10); 1984, 10th (13); 1985, 6th (31); 1986, 2nd (70, total 72); 1987, 2nd (61); 1988, 9th (12); 1989, 4th (38); 1990, 5th (37); 1991, 2nd (72); 1992, 1st (108); 1994, 9th (13)
Fastest laps: 30

Mantovani, Sergio   Italy
Born: 22 May 1929
Contested: 1953, It 8; **1954,** Bel 7, Ger 5, CH 5, It 9, Spa –; **1955,** Arg –, Arg 7
Total contested: 7
World championship position: 1954, 15th (4)

Mantz, Johnny   United States
Born: 18 Sep 1918   **Died:** 25 Oct 1972
Contested: 1953, Indy 17
Total contested: 1

Manzon, Robert   France
Born: 12 Apr 1917
Contested: 1950, Mon –, Fr 4, It –; **1951,** Fr –, Ger 7, It –, Spa 9; **1952,** CH –, Bel 3, Fr 4, GB –, Ger –, Hol 5, It 14; **1953,** Arg –; **1954,** Fr 3, GB –, Ger 9, It –, Spa; **1955,** Mon –, Hol –, GB –; **1956,** Mon –, Fr 9, GB 9, Ger –, It –
Total contested: 28
World championship position: 1950, 13th (3); 1952, 6th (9); 1954, 15th (4)

Marimon, Onofre   Argentina
Born: 19 Dec 1923   **Died:** 31 Jul 1954
Talented protegé of Fangio, killed in the German Grand Prix.
Contested: 1951, Fr –; **1953,** Bel 3, Fr 9, GB –, Ger –, CH –, It 9; **1954,** Arg –, Bel –, Fr –, GB 3
Total contested: 11
World championship position: 1953, 11th (4); 1954, 13th (4.14)
Fastest laps: 1

Marko, Helmut   Austria
Born: 27 Apr 1943
Le Mans winner in 1971, his career ended when a stone severely damaged his eye in the

French Grand Prix, though he is still active in the sport, running his own team.
Contested: 1971, Aus 11, It –, Can 12, US 13; **1972**, Arg 10, SA 14, Mon 8, Bel 10, Fr –
Total contested: 9

Marques, Tarso   Brazil
Born: 19 Jan 1976
1996, Bra –, Arg –; **1997**, Fr –, GB 10, Ger –, Hun 12, Bel –, It 14, Aus –, Lux –, Jap –, Eur 15
Total contested: 11

Marr, Leslie   Great Britain
Born: 14 Aug 1922
Contested: 1954, GB 13; **1955**, GB –
Total contested: 2

Marsh, Tony   Great Britain
Born: 20 Jul 1931
Multiple British Hill Climb Champion.
Contested: 1957, Ger 15; **1958**, Ger 8; **1961**, GB –, Ger 15
Total contested: 4

Martin, Eugene   France
Born: 24 Mar 1915
Contested: 1950, GB –, CH –
Total contested: 2

Martini, Pierluigi   Italy
Born: 23 Apr 1961
Contested: 1985, Bra –, Por –, SM –, Can –, US –, Fr –, GB –, Ger 11, Aus –, Hol –, It –, Bel 12, Eur –, SA –, Austral 8; **1988**, Detroit 6, Fr 15, GB 15, Hun –, It –, Por –, Spa –, Jap 13, Austral 7; **1989**, Bra –, SM –, Mon –, Mex –, US –, Can –, Fr –, GB 5, Ger 9, Hun –, Bel 9, It 7, Por 5, Spa –, Austral 6; **1990**, US 7, Bra 9, Mon –, Can –, Mex 12, Fr –, GB –, Ger –, Hun –, Bel 15, It –, Por 11, Spa –, Jap 8, Austral 9; **1991**, US 9, Bra –, SM 4, Mon 12, Can 7, Mex –, Fr 9, GB 9, Ger –, Hun –, Bel 12, It –, Por 4, Spa 13, Jap –, Austral –; **1992**, SA –, Mex –, Bra –, Spa 6, SM 6, Mon –, Can 8, Fr 10, GB 15, Ger 11, Hun –, Bel –, It 8, Por –, Jap 10, Austral –; **1993**, GB –, Ger 14, Hun –, Bel –, It 7, Por 8, Jap 10, Austral –; **1994**, Bra 8, Pac –, SM –, Mon –, Sp 5, Can 9, Fr 5, GB 10, Ger –, Hun –, Bel 8, It –, Por 12, Eur 15, Jap –, Austral 9; **1995**, Arg –, SM 12, Sp 14, Mon 7, Can –, Fr –, GB 7, Ger –
Total contested: 118
World championship position: 1988, 16th (1);

1989, 14th (5); 1991, 11th (6); 1992, 14th (2); 1994, 18th (4)

Mass, Jochen   Germany
Born: 30 Sept 1946
Le Mans winner in 1989, his only grand prix win was the shortened 1975 Spanish race.
Contested: 1973, GB –, Ger 7, US –; **1974**, Arg –, Bra 17, SA –, Spa –, Bel –, Swe –, Hol –, Fr –, GB 14, Ger –, Can 16, US 7; **1975**, Arg 14, Bra 3, SA 6, Spa 1, Mon 6, Bel –, Swe –, Hol –, Fr 3, GB 7, Ger –, Aus 4, It –, US 3; **1976**, Bra 6, SA 3, US West 5, Spa –, Bel 6, Mon 5, Swe 11, Fr 15, GB –, Ger 3, Aus 7, Hol 9, It –, Can 5, US East 4, Jap –; **1977**, Arg –, Bra –, SA 5, US West –, Spa 4, Mon 4, Bel –, Swe 2, Fr 9, GB 4, Ger –, Aus 6, Hol –, It 4, US East –, Can 3, Jap –; **1978**, Arg 11, Bra 7, SA –, US West –, Bel 11, Spa 9, Swe 13, Fr 13, GB –, Ger –; **1979**, Arg 8, Bra 7, SA 12, US West 9, Spa 8, Bel –, Mon 6, Fr 15, GB –, Ger 6, Aus –, Hol 6, It –; **1980**, Arg –, Bra 10, SA 6, US West 7, Bel –, Mon 4, Fr 10, GB 13, Ger 8, Can 11, US East –; **1982**, SA 12, Bra 8, US West 8, Bel –, US East 7, Can 11, Hol –, GB 10, Fr –
Total contested: 105 **Won:** 1
World championship position: 1975, 7th (20); 1976, 9th (19); 1977, 6th (25); 1979, 15th (3); 1980, 17th (4)
Fastest laps: 2

Max, Jean   France
Born: 27 Jul 1943
Contested: 1971, Fr –
Total contested: 1

May, Michael   Switzerland
Born: 18 Aug 1934
Contested: 1961, Mon –, Fr 11
Total contested: 2

Mayer, Timmy   United States
Born: 22 Feb 1938   **Died:** 28 Feb 1964
Brother of Teddy Mayer of McLaren, he was killed in practice for a race in Tasmania.
Contested: 1962, US –
Total contested: 1

Mazet, François   France
Born: 26 Feb 1943
Contested: 1971, Fr 13
Total contested: 1

Drivers' Career Records

McAlpine, Ken   Great Britain
Born: 21 Sept 1920
Patron of Connaught.
Contested: 1952, GB 16, It –; **1953**, Hol 11,
GB–, Ger 13, It 22; **1955**, GB –
Total contested: 7

McCoy, Ernie   United States
Born: 19 Feb 1921
Contested: 1953, Indy 8; **1954**, Indy 16
Total contested: 2

McDowell, Johnny   United States
Born: 29 Jan 1915   **Died:** 8 Jun 1952
Contested: 1950, Indy 18; **1951**, Indy 32; **1952**,
Indy 21
Total contested: 3

McDowell, Mike   Great Britain
Born: 13 Sept 1932
Contested: 1957, Fr 7
Total contested: 1

McGrath, Jack   United States
Born: 8 Oct 1919   **Died:** 6 Nov 1955
Contested: 1950, Indy 14; **1951**, Indy 3; **1952**,
Indy 11; **1953**, Indy 5; **1954**, Indy 3; **1955**,
Indy 26
Total contested: 6 **Poles:** 1
World championship position: 1951, 13th (2);
1953, 13th (2); 1954, 12th (5)
Fastest laps: 1

McLaren, Bruce   New Zealand
Born: 30 Aug 1937   **Died:** 2 Jun 1970
Successful driver/constructor who won Can-
Am championships, grand prix, and Le Mans
in 1966. The youngest driver to win a cham-
pionship grand prix (1952 Indianapolis win-
ner Troy Ruttman was 24 days younger), he
was killed testing at Goodwood.
Contested: 1958, Ger–, Moroccan 12; **1959**,
Mon 5, Fr 5, GB 3, Ger–, Por–, It–, US 1;
1960, Arg 1, Mon 2, Hol–, Bel 2, Fr 3, GB 4,
Por 2, US 3; **1961**, Mon 6, Hol 12, Bel–, Fr 5,
GB 8, Ger 6, It 3, US 4; **1962**, Hol–, Mon 1,
Bel 15, Fr 4, GB 3, Ger 5, It 3, US 3, SA 2;
1963, Mon 3, Bel 2, Hol–, Fr 12, GB–, Ger–,
It 3, US–, Mex–; **1964**, Mon–, Hol 7,
Bel 2, Fr 6, GB–, Ger–, Aus–, It 2, US–, Mex
7; **1965**, SA 5, Mon 5, Bel 3, Fr–, GB 10,
Hol–, Ger–, It 5, US–, Mex –; **1966**, Mon–,
GB 6, US 5, Mex –; **1967**, Mon 4, Hol–, Fr–,

GB–, Ger–, Can 7, It–, US–, Mex –; **1968**,
Spa –, Mon –, Bel 1, Hol –, Fr 8, GB 7, Ger 13,
It –, Can 2, US 6, Mex 2; **1969**, SA 5, Spa 2,
Mon 5, Hol–, Fr 4, GB 3, Ger 3, It 4, Can 5;
1970, SA –, Spa 2, Mon –
Total contested: 100 **Won:** 4
World championship position: 1959, 6th (16.5);
1960, 2nd (34, total 37); 1961, 7th (11); 1962,
3rd, (27, total 32); 1963, 6th (17); 1964, 7th
(13); 1965, 8th (10); 1966, 14th (3); 1967, 14th
(3); 1968, 5th (22); 1969, 3rd (26); 1970, 14th
(6)
Fastest laps: 3

McRae, Graham   New Zealand
Born: 5 Mar 1940
Contested: 1973, GB –
Total contested: 1

McWithey, Jim   United States
Born: 4 Jul 1927
Contested: 1959, Indy 16; **1960**, Indy 29
Total contested: 2

Menditeguy, Carlos   Argentina
Born: 10 Aug 1915   **Died:** 28 Apr 1973
Contested: 1953, Arg –; **1955**, Arg–, Arg–, It
5; **1956**, Arg –; **1957**, Arg 3, Mon–, Fr–,
GB –; **1958**, Arg 7; **1960**, Arg 4
Total contested: 11
World championship position: 1955, 17th (2);
1957, 14th (4); 1960, 20th (3)

Merzario, Arturo   Italy
Born: 11 Mar 1943
Former Ferrari driver who constructed his
own unsuccessful grand prix car.
Contested: 1972, GB 6, Ger 12; **1973**, Arg 9,
Bra 4, SA 4, Mon–, Fr 7, Aus 7, It–, Can 15,
US 16; **1974**, Arg–, Bra–, SA 6, Spa–, Bel–,
Mon–, Hol–, Fr 9, GB–, Ger–, Aus–, It 4,
Can–, US –; **1975**, Arg–, Bra–, SA–, Spa–,
Bel–, It 11; **1976**, Spa–, Bel–, Swe 14, Fr 9,
GB–, Ger–, Aus–, Hol–, Can–, US East–,
Jap –; **1977**, Spa–, Bel 14, Fr–, GB–, Aus –;
1978, Arg–, SA–, US West–, Swe–, GB–,
Hol–, It–, US East –; **1979**, Arg–, US West –
Total contested: 57
World championship position: 1972, 20th (1);
1973, 12th (6); 1974, 17th (4)

Mieres, Roberto   Argentina
Born: 3 Dec 1924

Contested: 1953, Hol –, Fr –, It 7; **1954**, Arg –, Bel –, Fr –, GB 6, Ger –, CH 4, It –, Spa 4; **1955**, Arg 5, Mon –, Bel 5, Hol 4, GB –, It 7
Total contested: 17
World championship position: 1954, 8th (6), 1955, 8th (7)
Fastest laps: 1

Migault, François   France
Born: 4 Dec 1944
Contested: 1972, Aus –; **1974**, Arg –, Bra 16, SA 15, Spa –, Bel 16, Mon –, Hol –, Fr 14, GB –, It –; **1975**, Spa –, Bel –
Total contested: 13

Miles, John   Great Britain
Born: 14 Jun 1943
Son of actor Bernard Miles, he still works for Lotus.
Contested: 1969, Fr –, GB 10, It –, Can –, Mex –; **1970**, SA 5, Bel –, Hol 7, Fr 8, GB –, Ger –, Aus –
Total contested: 12
World championship position: 1970, 19th (2)

Milhoux, André   Belgium
Born: 9 Dec 1928
Contested: 1956, Ger –
Total contested: 1

Miller, Chet   United States
Born: 19 Jul 1902   **Died:** 15 May 1953
Contested: 1951, Indy 25; **1952**, Indy 30
Total contested: 2

Mitter, Gerhard   Germany
Born: 30 Aug 1935   **Died:** 1 Aug 1969
Versatile hill climber (European champion 1966, 1967, 1968) and sports car driver (Targa Florio winner 1969), his single seater career never took off despite his debut 4th in one of de Beaufort's old Porsches. He was killed in practice for the German Grand Prix.
Contested: 1963, Hol –, Ger 4; **1964**, Ger 9;· **1965**, Ger –; **1967**, Ger –*
Total contested: 5
World championship position: 1963, 12th (3)

Modena, Stefano   Italy
Born: 12 May 1963
Contested: 1987, Austral –; **1988**, Bra –, SM –, Can 12, Detroit –, Fr 14, GB 12, Ger –, Hun 11, Spa 13, Austral –; **1989**, Bra –, SM –, Mon

3, Mex 10, US –, Can –, Fr –, GB –, Ger –, Hun 11, Bel –, Por 14, Spa –, Jap –, Austral 8; **1990**, US 5, Bra –, SM –, Mon –, Can 7, Mex 11, Fr 13, GB 9, Ger –, Hun –, Bel 17, It –, Por –, Spa –, Jap –, Austral 12; **1991**, US 4, Bra –, SM –, Mon –, Can 2, Mex 11, Fr –, GB 7, Ger 13, Hun 12, Bel –, It –, Por –, Spa 16, Jap 6, Austral 10; **1992**, Mex –, Bra –, SM –, Mon –, Can –, Fr –, GB –, Hun –, Bel 15, Por 13, Jap 7, Austral 6
Total contested: 70
World championship position: 1989, 16th (4); 1990, 16th (2); 1991, 8th (10); 1992, 17th (1)

Montermini, Andrea   Italy
Born: 30 May 1964
1995, Bra 9, Arg –, SM –, Mon –, Can –, Fr –, GB –, Ger 8, Hun 12, Bel –, It –, Por –, Eur –, Pac –, Jap –, Austral –; **1996**, Bra –, Arg 10, Can –, Fr –
Total contested: 20

Montgomerie-Charrington, Robin   Great Britain
Born: 22 Jun 1915
Contested: 1952, Bel –
Total contested: 1

Morbidelli, Gianni   Italy
Born: 13 Jan 1968
Contested: 1990, Bra 14, Jap –, Austral –; **1991**, US –, Bra 8, SM –, Mon –, Can –, Mex 7, Fr –, GB 11, Ger –, Hun 13, Bel –, It 9, Por 9, Spa 14, Jap –, Austral 6; **1992**, SA –, Mex –, Bra 7, Spa –, SM –, Mon –, Can 11, Fr 8, GB 17, Ger 12, Bel 16, It –, Por 14, Jap 14, Austral 10; **1994**, Bra –, Pac –, SM –, Mon –, Sp –, Can –, Fr –, GB –, Ger 5, Hun –, Bel 6, It –, Por 9, Eur 11, Jap –, Austral –; **1995**, Bra –, Arg –, SM 13, Sp 11, Mon 9, Can 6, Fr 14, Pac –, Jap –, Austral 3; **1997**, Sp 14, Can 10, Hun –, Bel 9, It 12, Aus 9, Lux 9
Total contested: 66
World championship position: 1991, 24th (0.5); 1994, 22nd (3)

Moreno, Roberto   Brazil
Born: 11 Feb 1959
A talented but underfinanced driver who showed his true capability when drafted into the Benetton team in 1990. European F3000 champion 1988.
Contested: 1987, Jap –, Austral 6; **1989**,

Drivers' Career Records

Mon –, Can –, GB –, Por –; **1990**, US 13, SM –, Jap 2, Austral 7; **1991**, US –, Bra 7, SM 13, –, Mon 4, Can –, Mex 5, Fr –, GB –, Ger 8, Hun 8, Bel 4, It –, Por 10, Austral 16; **1992**, Mon –; **1995**, Bra –, Arg –, SM 16, Sp –, Mon –, Can –, Fr 16, GB –, Ger –, Hun –, Bel 14, It –, Por 17, Eur –, Pac 16, Jap –, Austral –
Total contested: 42
World championship position: 1987, 19th (1); 1990, 10th (6); 1991, 10th (8)
Fastest laps: 1

Morgan, Dave   Great Britain
Born: 7 Aug 1944
Contested: 1975, GB 18
Total contested: 1

Moser, Silvio   Switzerland
Born: 24 Apr 1941   **Died:** 26 May 1974
Killed at Monza.
Contested: 1967, GB –; **1968**, Hol 5, GB –; **1969**, Mon –, Hol –, Fr 7, It –, Can –, US 6, Mex 11; **1970**, Aus –; **1971**, It –
Total contested: 12
World championship position: 1968, 23rd (2); 1969, 16th (1)

Moss, Stirling   Great Britain
Born: 17 Sep 1929
One of the greatest and most versatile of all drivers, and the best never to win the championship, Moss's grand prix career was ended by a crash at Goodwood in 1962. Among his greatest wins were the 1955 Mille Miglia (he was only the second non-Italian winner) and the two grand prix he won in 1961 against much more powerful Ferrari opposition.
Contested: 1951, CH 8; **1952**, CH –, Bel –, GB –, Hol 11, It 16; **1953**, Hol 9, Fr –, Ger 6, It 16; **1954**, Bel 3, GB 14, Ger –, CH –, It 10, Spa –; **1955**, Arg 4, Arg –, Mon 10, Bel 2, Hol 2, GB 1, It –; **1956**, Arg –, Mon 1, Bel 3, Bel –, Fr 5, Fr –, GB 10, Ger 2, It 1; **1957**, Arg 8, Mon –, GB 1, GB –, Ger 5, Pescara 1, It 1; **1958**, Arg 1, Mon –, Hol 1, Bel –, Fr 2, GB –, Ger –, Por 1, It –, Moroccan 1; **1959**, Mon –, Hol –, Fr –, GB 2, Ger –, Por 1, It 1, US –; **1960**, Arg 3, Arg –, Mon 1, Hol 4, Por –, US 1; **1961**, Mon 1, Hol 4, Bel 8, Fr –, GB –, GB –, Ger 1, It –, US –
Total contested: 66 **Won:** 16 **Poles:** 16
World championship position: 1954, 13th (4); 1955, 2nd (23); 1956, 2nd (27, total 28); 1957,

2nd (25); 1958, 2nd (41); 1959, 3rd (25.5); 1960, 3rd (19); 1961, 3rd (21)
Fastest laps: 19

Munaron, Gino   Italy
Born: 2 Apr 1928
Contested: 1960, Arg 13, Fr –, GB 16, It –
Total contested: 4

Murray, David   Great Britain
Born: 28 Dec 1909   **Died:** 5 Apr 1973
Contested: 1950, GB –, It –; **1951**, GB –; **1952**, GB –
Total contested: 4

Musso, Luigi   Italy
Born: 29 Jul 1924   **Died:** 6 Jul 1958
Shared the winning car with Fangio in the 1956 Argentinian Grand Prix. Killed in the French Grand Prix.
Contested: 1953, It 8; **1954**, It –, Spa 2; **1955**, Arg 7, Arg –, Mon –, Bel 7, Hol 3, GB 5, It –; **1956**, Arg 1, Mon –, Ger –, It 8; **1957**, Arg –, Fr 2, GB 2, Ger 4, Pescara –, It 8; **1958**, Arg 2, Mon 2, Hol 7, Bel –, Fr –
Total contested: 24 **Won:** 1
World championship position: 1954, 8th (6); 1955, 9th (6); 1956, 11th (4); 1957, 3rd (16); 1958, 7th (12)
Fastest laps: 1

Nacke, Bernd   pseudonym of Bechem, Gunther

Nakajima, Satoru   Japan
Born: 23 Feb 1953
Contested: 1987, Bra 7, SM 6, Bel 5, Mon 10, US –, Fr –, GB 4, Ger –, Hun –, Aus 13, It 11, Por 8, Spa 9, Mex –, Jap 6, Austral –; **1988**, Bra 6, SM 8, Mex –, Can 11, Fr 7, GB 10, Ger 9, Hun 7, Bel –, It –, Por –, Spa –, Jap 7, Austral –; **1989**, Bra 8, SM –, Mex –, US –, Fr –, GB 8, Ger –, Hun –, It 10, Por 7, Spa –, Jap –, Austral 4; **1990**, US 6, Bra 8, SM –, Mon –, Can 11, Mex –, Fr –, GB –, Ger –, Hun –, Bel –, It 6, Spa –, Jap 6, Austral –; **1991**, US 5, Bra –, SM –, Mon –, Can 10, Mex 12, Fr –, GB 8, Ger –, Hun 15, Bel –, It –, Por 13, Spa 17, Jap –, Austral –
Total contested: 74
World championship position: 1987, 11th (7); 1988, 16th (1); 1989, 21st (3); 1990, 14th (3); 1991, 15th (2)

Nakano, Shinji Japan
Born: 1 Apr 1971
1997, Austral 7, Bra 14, Arg–, SM–, Mon–, Sp–, Can 6, Fr–, GB 11, Ger 7, Hun 6, Bel–, It 11, Aus–, Lux–, Jap–, Eur 10
Total contested: 17
World championship position: 1997, 16th (2)

Nalon, Duke United States
Born: 12 Mar 1913
Contested: 1951, Indy 10; **1952,** Indy 25; **1953,** Indy 11
Total contested: 3 **Poles:** 1

Nanni Galli Italy
Born: 2 Oct 1940
'Nanni' was the pseudonym of Giovanni Giuseppe Gilberto Galli.
Contested: 1971, Hol–, GB 11, Ger 12, Aus–, It –, Can 16, US –; **1972,** Bel–, Fr 13, GB–, Aus 17, It –; **1973,** Arg–, Bra 9, Spa 11, Bel–, Mon –
Total contested: 17

Nannini, Alessandro Italy
Born: 7 Jul 1959
A very promising driver whose right arm was saved after being severed in a helicopter crash, he returned to touring car racing in 1992.
Contested: 1986, Bra–, Spa–, SM–, Bel–, Can–, Detroit–, Fr–, GB–, Ger–, Hun–, Aus–, It –, Por–, Mex 14, Austral –; **1987,** Bra–, SM–, Bel–, Mon–, US–, Fr–, GB–, Ger–, Hun 11, Aus–, It 16, Por 11, Spa–, Mex–, Jap–, Austral –; **1988,** Bra–, SM 6, Mon–, Mex 7, Can–, Detroit–, Fr 6, GB 3, Ger 18, Hun–, Bel–, It 9, Por–, Spa 3, Jap 5, Austral –; **1989,** Bra 6, SM 3, Mon 8, Mex 4, US–, Can–, Fr–, GB 3, Ger–, Hun–, Bel 5, It –, Por 4, Spa–, Jap 1, Austral 2; **1990,** US 11, Bra 10, SM 3, Mon–, Can–, Mex 4, Fr 16, GB–, Ger 2, Hun–, Bel 4, It 8, Por 6, Spa 3
Total contested: 77 **Won:** 1
World championship position: 1988, 9th (12); 1989, 6th (32); 1990, 8th (21)

Naspetti, Emanuele Italy
Born: 24 Feb 1968
Contested: 1992, Bel 12, It –, Por 11, Jap 13, Austral –; **1993,** Por –
Total contested: 6

Natili, Massimo Italy
Born: 28 Jul 1935
Contested: 1961, GB –
Total contested: 1

Naylor, Brian Great Britain
Born: 24 Mar 1923 **Died:** 9 Aug 1989
Contested: 1957, Ger 13; **1958,** Ger –; **1959,** GB –; **1960,** GB 13, It –, US –; **1961,** It –
Total contested: 7

Nazaruk, Mike United States
Born: 2 Oct 1921 **Died:** 1 May 1955
Contested: 1951, Indy 2; **1953,** Indy 21; **1954,** Indy 5
Total contested: 3
World championship position: 1951, 9th (6); 1954, 18th (2)

Needell, Tiff Great Britain
Born: 29 Oct 1951
Now a television presenter, his career started when he won a drive in an *Autosport* readers' competition.
Contested: 1980, Bel –
Total contested: 1

Neve, Patrick Belgium
Born: 13 Oct 1949
Contested: 1976, Bel–, Fr 18; **1977,** Spa 12, Bel 10, Swe 15, GB 10, Aus 9, It 7, US East 18, Can –
Total contested: 10

Nicholson, John New Zealand
Born: 6 Oct 1941
Also an engine builder.
Contested: 1975, GB 17
Total contested: 1

Niday, Cal United States
Born: 29 Apr 1916 **Died:** 14 Feb 1988
Contested: 1953, Indy 30; **1954,** Indy 10; **1955,** Indy 16
Total contested: 3

Niedermayr, Helmut Germany
Born: 29 Nov 1915 **Died:** 3 Apr 1985
Contested: 1952, Ger 9
Total contested: 1

Niemann, Brausch South Africa
Born: 7 Jan 1939

Drivers' Career Records

Contested: **1963**, SA 14
Total contested: 1

Nilsson, Gunnar Sweden
Born: 20 Nov 1948 Died: 20 Oct 1978
Highly promising driver who died of cancer.
Contested: **1976**, SA–, US West–, Spa 3, Bel–, Mon–, Swe–, Fr–, GB–, Ger 5, Aus 3, Hol–, It 13, Can 12, US East–, Jap 6; **1977**, Bra 5, SA 12, US West 8, Spa 5, Mon–, Bel 1, Swe 19, Fr 4, GB 3, Ger–, Aus–, Hol–, It–, US East–, Can–, Jap –
Total contested: 31 Won: 1
World championship position: 1976, 10th (11); 1977, 8th (20)
Fastest laps: 1

Noda, Hideki Japan
Born: 7 Mar 1969
1994, Eur–, Jap–, Austral –
Total contested: 3

Nuckey, Hodney Great Britain
Born: 26 Jun 1929
Contested: **1953**, Ger 11
Total contested: 1

O'Brien, Robert United States
Contested: **1952**, Bel 14
Total contested: 1

O'Connor, Pat United States
Born: 9 Oct 1928 Died: 30 May 1958
Contested: **1954**, Indy 21; **1955**, Indy 8; **1956**, Indy 18; **1957**, Indy 8; **1958**, Indy 29
Total contested: 5 Poles: 1

Oliver, Jackie Great Britain
Born: 14 Aug 1942
Le Mans winner in 1969, he played a leading part in the early days of both Shadow and Arrows.
Contested: **1967**, Ger 1*; **1968**, Mon–, Bel 5, Hol–, GB–, Ger 11, It–, Can–, Mex 3; **1969**, SA 7, Spa–, Mon–, Hol–, GB–, Ger–, It–, Can–, US–, Mex 6; **1970**, SA–, Spa–, Mon–, Bel–, Hol–, Fr–, GB–, Ger–, Aus 5, It–, Can–, US–, Mex 7; **1971**, GB–, Aus 9, It 7; **1972**, GB –; **1973**, SA–, Spa–, Bel–, Mon 10, Swe–, Fr–, GB–, Hol–, Ger 8, Aus–, It 11, Can 3, US 15; **1977**, Swe 9
Total contested: 50

World championship position: 1968, 13th (6); 1969, 16th (1); 1970, 19th (2); 1973, 14th (4)
Fastest laps: 1

Ongais, Danny United States
Born: 21 May 1942
Hawaian drag racer and Indycar driver.
Contested: **1977**, US East–, Can 7; **1978**, Arg–, Bra –
Total Contested: 4

Owen, Arthur Great Britain
Born: 23 Mar 1915
Contested: **1960**, It –
Total contested: 1

Pace, Carlos Brazil
Born: 6 Oct 1944 Died: 18 Mar 1977
Promising driver killed in a plane crash.
Contested: **1972**, SA 17, Spa 6, Mon 17, Bel 5, Fr–, GB–, Ger–, Aus–, It–, Can 9, US –; **1973**, Arg–, Bra–, SA–, Spa–, Bel 8, Mon–, Swe 10, Fr 13, GB–, Hol 7, Ger 4, Aus 3, It–, Can 18, US –; **1974**, Arg–, Bra 4, SA 11, Spa 13, Bel–, Mon–, Swe–, GB 9, Ger 12, Aus–, It 5, Can 8, US 2; **1975**, Arg–, Bra 1, SA 4, Spa–, Mon 3, Bel 8, Swe–, Hol 5, Fr–, GB 2, Ger–, Aus–, It–, US –; **1976**, Bra 10, SA–, US West 9, Spa 6, Bel–, Mon 9, Swe 8, Fr 4, GB 8, Ger 4, Aus–, Hol–, It–, Can 7, US East–, Jap –; **1977**, Arg 2, Bra–, SA 13
Total contested: 72 Won: 1 Poles: 1
World championship position: 1972, 16th (3); 1973, 11th (7); 1974, 12th (11); 1975, 6th (24); 1976, 14th (7); 1977, 15th (6)
Fastest laps: 5

Pagani, Nello Italy
Born: 11 Oct 1911
Contested: **1950**, CH 7
Total contested: 1

Paletti, Riccardo Italy
Born: 15 Jun 1958 Died: 13 Jun 1982
Killed in a startline accident in his second grand prix.
Contested: **1982**, SM–, Can –
Total contested: 2

Palm, Torsten Sweden
Born: 23 Jul 1947
Brother of the rally driver Gunnar Palm.
Contested: **1975**, Swe 10
Total contested: 1

Palmer, Jonathan   Great Britain
Born: 7 Nov 1956
Won the championship for normally aspirated cars in 1987.
Contested: 1983, Eur 13; **1984**, Bra 8, SA –, Bel 10, SM 9, Fr 13, US East –, US Dallas –, GB –, Ger –, Aus 9, Hol 9, It –, Eur –, Por –; **1985**, Por –, Mon 11, Fr –, GB –, Ger –, Aus –, Hol –; **1986**, Bra –, Spa –, SM –, Mon 12, Bel –, Can –, Detroit 8, Fr –, GB 9, Ger –, Hun 10, Aus –, It –, Por 12, Mex 10, Austral 9; **1987**, Bra 10, SM –, Bel –, Mon 5, US 11, Fr 7, GB 8, Ger 5, Hun 7, Aus 15, It 14, Por 10, Spa –, Mex 7, Jap 8, Austral 4; **1988**, Bra –, SM 14, Mon 5, Can 6, Detroit 5, Fr –, GB –, Ger 11, Hun –, Bel 12, Por –, Spa –, Jap 12, Austral –; **1989**, Bra 7, SM 6, Mon 9, Mex –, US 9, Can –, Fr 10, GB –, Ger –, Hun 13, Bel 14, It –, Por 6, Spa 10, Jap –
Total contested: 83
World championship position: 1987, 11th (7); 1988, 13th (5); 1989, 23rd (2)

Panis, Olivier   France
European F3000 champion 1993
Born: 2 Sept 1966
1994, Bra 11, Pac 9, SM 11, Mon 9, Sp 7, Can 12, Fr –, GB 12, Ger 2, Hun 6, Bel 7, It 10, Por –, Eur 9, Jap 11, Austral 5; **1995**, Bra –, Arg 7, SM 9, Sp 6, Mon –, Can 4, Fr 8, GB 4, Ger –, Hun 6, Bel 9, It –, Por –, Eur –, Pac 8, Jap 5, Austral 2; **1996**, Austral 7, Bra 6, Arg 8, Eur –, SM –, Mon 1, Sp –, Can –, Fr 7, GB –, Ger 7, Hun 5, Bel –, It –, Por 10, Jap 7; **1997**, Austral 5, Bra 3, Arg –, SM 8, Mon 4, Sp 2, Can 11, Lux 6, Jap –, Eur 7
Total contested: 59 **Won:** 1
World championship position: 1994, 11th (9); 1995, 8th (16); 1996, 9th (13); 1997, 9th (16)

Papis, Max   Italy
Born: 3 Oct 1969
1995, GB –, Ger –, Hun –, Bel –, It 7, Por –, Eur 12
Total contested: 7

Parkes, Mike   Great Britain
Born: 24 Sep 1931   **Died:** 28 Aug 1977
Ferrari engineer and sports car racer from 1963, drafted into the grand prix team in 1966. Killed in a road accident.

Contested: 1966, Fr 2, Hol –, Ger –, It 2; **1967**, Hol 5, Bel –
Total contested: 6 **Poles:** 1
World championship position: 1966, 8th (12); 1967, 16th (2)

Parnell, Reg   Great Britain
Born: 2 Jul 1911   **Died:** 7 Jan 1964
Leading British driver of the immediate postwar period, later team managed for Aston Martin and his own grand prix team. Father of Tim.
Contested: 1950, GB 3, Fr –; **1951**, Fr 4, GB 5; **1952**, GB 7; **1954**, GB –
Total contested: 6
World championship position: 1950, 9th (4); 1951, 10th (5)

Parnell, Tim   Great Britain
Born: 25 Jun 1932
Son of Reg, took over his father's team on his death.
Contested: 1961, GB –, It 10
Total contested: 2

Parsons, Johnnie   United States
Born: 4 Jul 1918   **Died:** 8 Sep 1984
Contested: 1950, Indy 1; **1951**, Indy 21; **1952**, Indy 10; **1953**, Indy 26; **1954**, Indy 32, Indy 11; **1955**, Indy 21; **1956**, Indy 4; **1957**, Indy 16; **1958**, Indy 12
Total contested: 9 **Won:** 1
World championship position: 1950, 6th (8); 1956, 15th (3)

Patrese, Riccardo   Italy
Born: 17 Apr 1954
First driver to compete in 200 grand prix, has driven in more grand prix than any other driver.
Contested: 1977, Mon 9, Bel –, Fr –, GB –, Ger 10, Hol 13, It –, Can 10, Jap 6; **1978**, Bra 10, SA –, US West 6, Mon 6, Bel –, Spa –, Swe 2, Fr 8, GB –, Ger 9, Aus –, Hol –, It –, Can 4; **1979**, Bra 9, SA 11, US West –, Spa 10, Bel 5, Mon –, Fr 14, GB –, Ger –, Aus –, Hol –, It 13, Can –, US East –; **1980**, Arg –, Bra 6, SA –, US West 2, Bel –, Mon 8, Fr 9, GB 9, Ger 9, Aus 14, Hol –, It –, Can –, US East –; **1981**, US West –, Bra 3, Arg 7, SM 2, Bel –, Mon –, Spa –, Fr 14, GB 10, Ger –, Aus –, Hol –, It –, Can –, US Las Vegas 11; **1982**, SA –, Bra –, US West 3, Bel –, Mon 1, US East –, Can 2, Hol

Drivers' Career Records

15, GB –, Fr –, Ger –, Aus –, CH 5, It –, US Las Vegas –; **1983**, Bra –, US West 10, Fr –, SM –, Mon –, Bel –, US East –, Can –, GB –, Ger 3, Aus –, Hol 9, It –, Eur 7, SA 1; **1984**, Bra –, SA 4, Bel –, SM –, Fr –, Mon –, Can –, US East –, US Dallas –, GB 12, Ger –, Aus 10, Hol –, It 3, Eur 6, Por 8; **1985**, Bra –, Por –, SM –, Mon –, Can 10, US –, Fr 11, GB 9, Ger –, Aus –, Hol –, It –, Bel –, Eur 9, SA –, Austral –; **1986**, Bra –, Spa –, SM 6, Mon –, Bel 8, Can –, Detroit 6, Fr 7, GB –, Ger –, Hun –, Aus –, It –, Por –, Mex 13, Austral –; **1987**, Bra –, SM 9, Bel –, Mon –, US 9, Fr –, GB –, Ger –, Hun 5, Aus –, It –, Por –, Spa 13, Mex 3, Jap 11, Austral 9; **1988**, Bra –, SM 13, Mon 6, Mex –, Can –, Detroit –, Fr –, GB 8, Ger –, Hun 6, Bel –, It 7, Por –, Spa 5, Jap 6, Austral 4; **1989**, Bra –, SM –, Mon 15, Mex 2, US 2, Can 2, Fr 3, GB –, Ger 4, Hun –, Bel –, It 4, Por –, Spa 5, Jap 2, Austral 3; **1990**, US 9, Bra 13, SM 1, Mon –, Can –, Mex 9, Fr 6, GB –, Ger 5, Hun 4, Bel –, It 5, Por 7, Spa 5, Jap 4, Austral 6; **1991**, US –, Bra 2, SM –, Mon –, Can 3, Mex 1, Fr 5, GB –, Ger 2, Hun 3, Bel 5, It –, Por 1, Spa 3, Jap 3, Austral 5; **1992**, SA 2, Mex 2, Bra 2, Spa –, SM 2, Mon 3, Can –, Fr 2, GB 2, Ger 8, Hun –, Bel 3, It 5, Por –, Jap 1, Austral –; **1993**, SA –, Bra –, Eur 5, SM –, Sp 4, Mon –, Can –, Fr 10, GB 3, Ger 5, Hun 2, Bel 6, It 5, Por 16, Jap –, Austral 8
Total contested: 256 **Won:** 6 **Poles:** 8
World championship position: 1977, 19th (1); 1978, 11th (11); 1979, 19th (2); 1980, 9th (7); 1981, 11th (10); 1982, 10th (21); 1983, 9th (13); 1984, 13th (8); 1986, 15th (2); 1987, 13th (6); 1988, 11th (8); 1989, 3rd (40); 1990, 7th (23); 1991, 3rd (53); 1992, 2nd (56); 1993, 5th (20)
Fastest laps: 13

Pease, Al   Canada
Born: 15 Oct 1921
Contested: 1967, Can –; **1969**, Can –
Total contested: 2

Penske, Roger   United States
Born: 20 Feb 1937
Team owner and constructor with multiple Indianapolis victories, whose cars have won in every form of racing he has entered.
Contested: 1961, US 9; **1962**, US 9
Total contested: 2

Perdisa, Cesare   Italy
Born: 21 Oct 1932
Contested: 1955, Mon 3, Mon 8, Bel 8; **1956**, Mon 7, Bel 3, Fr 5, GB 7; **1957**, Arg 6
Total contested: 7
World championship position: 1955, 17th (2); 1956, 15th (3)

Perkins, Larry   Australia
Born: 18 Mar 1950
Contested: 1976, Spa 13, Bel 8, Swe –, Hol –, It –, Can 17, US East –, Jap –; **1977**, Bra –, SA 15, Bel 12
Total contested: 11

Perrot, Xavier   Switzerland
Born: 1 Feb 1932
Contested: 1969, Ger 6*
Total contested: 1

Pescarolo, Henri   France
Born: 25 Sep 1942
Best known as a sports car driver, he won Le Mans three years running (1972–4) and took a fourth victory in 1984.
Contested: 1968, Can –, Mex 9; **1969**, Ger 1*; **1970**, SA 7, Spa –, Mon 3, Bel 6, Hol 8, Fr 5, GB –, Ger 6, Aus 14, It –, Can 7, US 8, Mex 9; **1971**, SA 11, Spa –, Mon 8, Hol –, Fr –, GB 4, Ger –, Aus 6, It –, US –; **1972**, Arg 8, SA 11, Spa 11, Mon –, Bel –, GB –, Ger –, Can 13, US 14; **1973**, Spa 8, Fr –, Ger 10; **1974**, Arg 9, Bra 14, SA 18, Spa 12, Bel –, Mon –, Swe –, Hol –, Fr –, GB 15, Ger 10, It –; **1976**, Fr –, GB –, Aus 9, Hol 11, It 17, Can 19, US East –
Total contested: 57
World championship position: 1970, 12th (8); 1971, 16th (4)
Fastest laps: 1

Pesenti-Rossi, Sandro   Italy
Born: 31 Aug 1942
Contested: 1976, Ger 14, Aus 11, It 18
Total contested: 3

Peters, Josef   Germany
Born: 16 Sep 1914
Contested: 1952, Ger –
Total contested: 1

Peterson, Ronnie   Sweden
Born: 14 Feb 1944   **Died:** 11 Sep 1978

One of the fastest drivers of his era, he was killed in the Italian Grand Prix.
Contested: 1970, Mon 7, Bel –, Hol 9, Fr –, GB 9, Ger–, It–, Can–, US 11; **1971**, SA 10, Spa–, Mon 2, Hol 4, Fr–, GB 2, Ger 5, Aus 8, It 2, Can 2, US 3; **1972**, Arg 6, SA 5, Spa–, Mon 11, Bel 9, Fr 5, GB 7, Ger 3, Aus 12, It 9, Can–, US 4; **1973**, Arg–, Bra–, SA 11, Spa–, Bel–, Mon 3, Swe 2, Fr 1, GB 2, Hol 11, Ger–, Aus 1, It 1, Can–, US 1; **1974**, Arg 13, Bra 6, SA–, Spa–, Bel–, Mon 1, Swe–, Hol 8, Fr 1, GB 10, Ger 4, Aus–, It 1, Can 3, US –; **1975**; Arg–, Bra 15, SA 10, Spa–, Mon 4, Bel–, Swe 9, Hol 15, Fr 10, GB–, Ger–, Aus 5, It–, US 5; **1976**, Bra–, SA–, US West 10, Spa–, Bel–, Mon–, Swe 7, Fr 19, GB–, Ger–, Aus 6, Hol–, It 1, Can 9, US East–, Jap –; **1977**, Arg–, Bra–, SA–, US West–, Spa 8, Mon–, Bel 3, Swe–, Fr 12, GB–, Ger 9, Aus 5, Hol–, It 6, US East 16, Can–, Jap –; **1978**, Arg 5, Bra–, SA 1, US West 4, Mon–, Bel 2, Spa 2, Swe 3, Fr 2, GB–, Ger–, Aus 1, Hol 2, It –
Total contested: 123 Won: 10 Poles: 14
World championship position: 1971, 2nd (33); 1972, 9th (12); 1973, 3rd (52); 1974, 5th (35); 1975, 12th (6); 1976, 11th (10); 1977, 14th (7); 1978, 2nd (51)
Fastest laps: 9

Picard, Francois   France
Born: 26 Apr 1921   **Died:** Jun 1996
Contested: 1958, Moroccan –
Total contested: 1

Pieterse, Ernie   South Africa
Born: 4 Jul 1938
Contested: 1962, SA 10; **1963**, SA –
Total contested: 2

Pietsch, Paul   Germany
Born: 20 Jun 1911
A leading pre-war driver.
Contested: 1950, It –; **1951**, Ger –; **1952**, Ger –
Total contested: 3

Pilette, André   Belgium
Born: 6 Oct 1918   **Died:** 27 Dec 1993
Father of Teddy.
Contested: 1951, Bel 6; **1953**, Bel 11; **1954**, Bel 5, GB 9, Ger –; **1956**, Mon 6, Bel 6, Fr 11; **1964**, Bel –

Total contested: 9
World championship position: 1954, 18th (2)

Pilette, Teddy   Belgium
Born: 26 Jul 1942
Son of André.
Contested: 1974, Bel 17
Total contested: 1

Piotti, Luigi   Italy
Born: 27 Oct 1913   **Died:** 19 Apr 1971
Contested: 1956, Arg–, Ger–, It 6; **1957**, Arg 10, Pescara –, It –
Total contested: 6

Piper, David   Great Britain
Born: 2 Dec 1930
Better known as a private entrant in sports car racing, lost part of a leg as the result of an accident during the filming of *Le Mans* but still enters and drives some of his original cars in historic racing.
Contested: 1959, GB –; **1960**, GB 12
Total contested: 2

Piquet, Nelson   Brazil
Born: 17 Aug 1952
The second driver to compete in 200 grand prix, triple world champion Piquet turned to Indycars in the absence of a competitive 1992 grand prix drive but was severely injured in an Indianapolis practice crash.
Contested: 1978, Ger–, Aus–, Hol–, It 9, Can 11; **1979**, Arg–, Bra–, SA 7, US West 8, Spa–, Bel–, Mon–, Fr–, GB–, Ger 12, Aus–, Hol 4, It–, Can–, US East –; **1980**, Arg 2, Bra–, SA 4, US West 1, Bel–, Mon 3, Fr 4, GB 2, Ger 4, Aus 5, Hol 1, It 1, Can–, US East –; **1981**, US West 3, Bra 12, Arg 1, SM 1, Bel–, Mon–, Spa–, Fr 3, GB–, Ger 1, Aus 3, Hol 2, It 6, Can 5, US Las Vegas 5; **1982**, SA–, Bra –, US West–, Bel 5, Mon–, Can 1, Hol 2, GB–, Fr–, Ger–, Aus–, CH 4, It–, US Las Vegas –; **1983**, Bra 1, US West–, Fr 2, SM–, Mon 2, Bel 4, US East 4, Can–, GB 2, Ger 13, Aus 3, Hol–, It 1, Eur 1, SA 3; **1984**, Bra –, SA–, Bel 9, SM –, Fr–, Mon–, Can 1, US East 1, US Dallas–, GB 7, Ger –, Aus 2, Hol–, It–, Eur 3, Por 6; **1985**, Bra –, Por–, SM 8, Mon–, Can–, US 6, Fr 1, GB 4, Ger–, Aus–, Hol 8, It 2, Bel 5, Eur–, SA –, Austral –; **1986**, Bra 1, Spa–, SM 2, Mon 7, Bel–, Can 3, Detroit–, Fr 3, GB 2, Ger 1, Hun 1, Aus–, It 1, Por 3, Mex 4,

Austral 2; **1987**, Bra 2, Bel –, Mon 2, US 2, Fr 2, GB 2, Ger 1, Hun 1, Aus 2, It 1, Por 3, Spa 4, Mex 2, Jap 15, Austral –; **1988**, Bra 3, SM 3, Mon –, Mex –, Can 4, Detroit –, Fr 5, GB 5, Ger –, Hun 8, Bel 4, It –, Por –, Spa 8, Jap –, Austral 3; **1989**, Bra –, SM –, Mon –, Mex 11, US –, Can 4, Fr 8, GB 4, Ger 5, Hun 6, It –, Por –, Spa 8, Jap 4, Austral –; **1990**, US 4, Bra 6, SM 5, Mon –, Can 2, Mex 6, Fr 4, GB 5, Ger –, Hun 3, Bel 5, It 7, Por 5, Spa –, Jap 1, Austral 1; **1991**, US 3, Bra 5, SM –, Mon –, Can 1, Mex –, Fr 8, GB 5, Ger –, Hun –, Bel 3, It 6, Por 5, Spa 11, Jap 7, Austral 4
Total contested: 204 **Won:** 23 **Poles:** 24
World championship position: 1979, 15th (3); 1980, 2nd (54); 1981, 1st, (50); 1982, 11th (20); 1983, 1st (59); 1984, 5th (29); 1985, 8th, (21); 1986, 3rd (69); 1987, 1st (73, total 76); 1988, 6th (22); 1989, 8th (12); 1990, 3rd (43, total 44); 1991, 6th (26.5)
Fastest laps: 23

Pirocchi, Renato   Italy
Born: 26 Mar 1933
Contested: 1961, It 12
Total contested: 1

Pironi, Didier   France
Born: 26 Mar 1952   **Died:** 23 Aug 87
Won Le Mans in 1978, retired from motor racing after a severe crash in practice for the German Grand Prix (for which he had taken pole position) but was killed power boat racing.
Contested: 1978, Arg 14, Bra 6, SA 6, US West –, Mon 5, Bel 6, Spa 12, Swe –, Fr 10, GB –, Ger 5, Aus –, Hol –, It –, US East 10, Can 7; **1979**, Arg –, Bra 4, SA –, US West –, Spa 6, Bel 3, Mon –, Fr –, GB 10, Ger 9, Aus 7, Hol –, It 10, Can 5, US East 3; **1980**, Arg –, Bra 4, SA 3, US West 6, Bel 1, Mon –, Fr 2, GB –, Ger –, Aus –, Hol –, It 6, Can 3, US East 3; **1981**, US West –, Bra –, Arg –, SM 5, Bel 8, Mon 4, Spa 15, Fr 5, GB –, Ger –, Aus 9, Hol –, It 5, Can –, US Las Vegas 9; **1982**, SA 18, Bra 6, US West –, SM 1, Mon 2, US East 3, Can 9, Hol 1, GB 2, Fr 3
Total contested: 70 **Won:** 3 **Poles:** 3
World championship position: 1978, 15th (7); 1979, 10th (14); 1980, 5th (32); 1981, 13th (9); 1982, 2nd (39)
Fastest laps: 6

Pirro, Emanuele   Italy
Born: 12 Jan 1962
Now competing in touring cars.
Contested: 1989, Fr 9, GB 11, Ger –, Hun 8, Bel 10, It –, Por –, Spa –, Jap –, Austral 5; **1990**, SM –, Mon –, Can –, Mex –, Fr –, GB 11, Ger –, Hun 10, Bel –, It –, Por 15, Spa –, Jap –, Austral –; **1991**, US –, Bra 11, Mon 6, Can 9, GB 10, Ger 10, Hun –, Bel 8, It 10, Por –, Spa 15, Jap –, Austral 7
Total contested: 37
World championship position: 1989, 23rd (2); 1981, 18th (1)

Pollet, Jacques   France
Born: 28 Jul 1932
Contested: 1954, Fr –, Spa –; **1955**, Mon 7, Hol 10, It –
Total contested: 5

Pon, Ben   Holland
Born: 9 Dec 1936
Contested: 1962, Hol –
Total contested: 1

Poore, Dennis   Great Britain
Born: 19 Aug 1916   **Died:** 12 Feb 1987
Contested: 1952, GB 4, It 12
Total contested: 2
World championship position: 1952, 13th (3)

Posey, Sam   United States
Born: 26 May 1944
Contested: 1971, US –; **1972**, US 12
Total contested: 2

Pozzi, Charles   France
Born: 27 Aug 1909
Contested: 1950, France 6
Total contested: 1

Pretorius, Jackie   South Africa
Born: 22 Nov 1934
Contested: 1968, SA –; **1971**, SA –; **1973**, SA –
Total contested: 3

Prophet, David   Great Britain
Born: 9 Oct 1937   **Died:** 29 Mar 1981
Contested: 1963, SA –; **1965**, SA 14
Total contested: 2

Prost, Alain   France
Born: 24 Feb 1955

Winner of the most grand prix, the triple world champion took a sabbatical in 1992.
Contested: 1980, Arg 6, Bra 5, Bel–, Mon–, Fr–, GB 6, Ger 11, Aus 7, Hol 6, It 7, Can –; **1981**, US West–, Bra–, Arg 3, SM–, Bel–, Mon–, Spa–, Fr 1, GB–, Ger 2, Aus–, Hol 1, It 1, Can–, US Las Vegas 2; **1982**, SA 1, Bra 1, US West–, SM–, Bel–, Mon 7, US East 12, Can–, Hol–, GB 6, Fr 2, Ger–, Aus–, CH 2, It–, US Las Vegas 4; **1983**, Bra 7, US West 11, Fr 1, SM 2, Mon 3, Bel 1, US East 8, Can 5, GB 1, Ger 4, Aus 1, Hol–, It–, Eur 2, SA –; **1984**, Bra 1, SA 2, Bel–, SM 1, Fr 7, Mon 1, Can 3, US East 4, US Dallas–, GB–, Ger 1, Aus–, Hol 1, It–, Eur 1, Por 1; **1985**, Bra 1, Por–, SM–, Mon 1, Can 3, US–, Fr 3, GB 1, Ger 2, Aus 1, Hol 2, It 1, Bel 3, Eur 4, SA 3, Austral –; **1986**, Bra–, Spa 3, SM 1, Mon 1, Bel 6, Can 2, Detroit 3, Fr 2, GB 3, Ger 6, Hun–, Aus 1, It–, Por 2, Mex 2, Austral 1; **1987**, Bra 1, SM–, Bel 1, Mon 9, US 3, Fr 3, GB–, Ger 7, Hun 3, Aus 6, It 15, Por 1, Spa 2, Mex–, Jap 7, Austral –; **1988**, Bra 1, SM 2, Mon 1, Mex 1, Can 2, Detroit 2, Fr 1, GB–, Ger 2, Hun 2, Bel 2, It–, Por 1, Spa 1, Jap 2, Austral 1; **1989**, Bra 2, SM 2, Mon 2, Mex 5, US 1, Can–, Fr 1, GB 1, Ger 2, Hun 4, Bel 2, It 1, Por 2, Spa 3, Jap–, Austral –; **1990**, US–, Bra 1, SM 4, Mon–, Can 5, Mex 1, Fr 1, GB 1, Ger 4, Hun–, Bel 2, It 2, Por 3, Spa 1, Jap–, Austral 3; **1991**, US 2, Bra 4, Mon 5, Can–, Mex–, Fr 2, GB 3, Ger–, Hun–, Bel–, It 3, Por–, Spa 2, Jap 4; **1993**, SA 1, Bra–, Eur 3, SM 1, Sp 1, Mon 4, Can 1, Fr 1, GB 1, Ger 1, Hun 12, Bel 1, It 12, Por 2, Jap 2, Austral 2
Total contested: 199 **Won:** 51 **Poles:** 33
World championship position: 1980, 15th (5); 1981, 5th (43); 1982, 4th (34); 1983, 2nd (59); 1984, 2nd (71.5); 1985, 1st (73, total 76); 1986, 1st (72, total 74); 1987, 4th (46); 1988, 2nd 87 (105); 1989, 1st 76 (81); 1990, 2nd (71, total 73); 1991, 5th (34); 1993, 1st (99)
Fastest laps: 41

Pryce, Tom Great Britain
Born: 11 Jun 1949 **Died:** 5 Mar 1977
Highly promising Welsh driver killed when a marshal ran into his car at Kyalami.
Contested: 1974, Bel–, Hol–, Fr–, GB 8, Ger 6, Aus–, It 10, Can–, US –; **1975**, Arg 12, Bra–, SA 9, Spa–, Mon–, Bel 6, Swe–, Hol 6, Fr–, GB–, Ger 4, Aus 3, It 5, US –; **1976**, Bra 3, SA 7, US West–, Spa 8, Bel 10, Mon 7, Swe

9, Fr 8, GB 4, Ger 8, Aus–, Hol 4, It 8, Can 11, US East–, Jap –; **1977**, Arg–, Bra–, SA –
Total contested: 42 **Poles:** 1
World championship position: 1974, 18th (1); 1975, 10th (8); 1976, 11th (10)

Purley, David Great Britain
Born: 26 Jan 1945 **Died:** 2 Jul 1985
A fearless competitor in many sports, he made heroic efforts to rescue Roger Williamson after his Dutch Grand Prix crash, competed in the LEC car built for his father's LEC Refrigeration company and died when his aerobatic plane crashed.
Contested: 1973, Mon–, Hol–, Ger 15, It 9; **1977**, Bel 13, Swe 14, Fr –
Total contested: 7

Quester, Dieter Austria
Born: 30 May 1939
Now competing in historic racing.
Contested: 1974, Aus 9
Total contested: 1

Raby, Ian Great Britain
Born: 22 Sep 1921 **Died:** 7 Nov 1967
Contested: 1963, GB –; **1964**, GB –; **1965**, GB 11
Total contested: 3

Rahal, Bobby United States
Born: 10 Jan 1953
Won Indianapolis in 1986.
Contested: 1978, US East 12, Can –
Total contested: 2

Raphanel, Pierre-Henri France
Born: 27 May 1961
Contested: 1989, Mon –
Total contested: 1

Rathmann, Dick United States
Born: 6 Jan 1926
Brother of Jim.
Contested: 1950, Indy 32; **1956**, Indy 5; **1958**, Indy 27; **1959**, Indy 20; **1960**, Indy 31
Total contested: 5 **Poles:** 1
World championship position: 1956, 19th (2)

Rathmann, Jim United States
Born: 16 Jul 1928
Brother of Dick.
Contested: 1950, Indy 24; **1952**, Indy 2; **1953**,

Drivers' Career Records

Indy 7, Indy 15; **1954**, Indy 28; **1955**, Indy 14; **1956**, Indy 20; **1957**, Indy 2; **1958**, Indy 5; **1959**, Indy 2; **1960**, Indy 1
Total contested: 10 **Won:** 1
World championship position: 1952, 10th (6); 1957, 11th (7); 1958, 21st (2); 1959, 11th (6); 1960, 8th (8)
Fastest laps: 2

Ratzenberger, Roland   Austria
Ratzenberger was killed in practice for the San Marino Grand Prix
Born: 4 Jul 1962   **Died:** 30 Apr 1994
1994, Pac 11
Total contested: 1

Rebaque, Hector   Mexico
Born: 5 Feb 1956
Contested: 1977, Ger –; **1978**, Bra –, SA 10, Spa –, Swe 12, GB –, Ger 6, Aus –, Hol 11, US East –; **1979**, Arg –, SA –, US West –, Spa –, Bel –, Fr 12, GB 9, Ger –, Hol 7, Can –; **1980**, GB 7, Ger –, Aus 10, Hol –, It –, Can 6, US East –; **1981**, US West –, Bra –, Arg –, SM 4, Bel –, Spa –, Fr 9, GB 5, Ger 4, Aus –, Hol 4, It –, Can –, US Las Vegas –
Total contested: 42
World championship position: 1978, 19th (1); 1980, 20th (1); 1981, 9th (11)

Redman, Brian   Great Britain
Born: 9 Mar 1937
A highly competitive sports car driver who never quite got the grand prix breaks he deserved.
Contested: 1968, SA –, Spa 3, Bel –; **1971**, SA 7; **1972**, Mon 5, Fr 9, Ger 5, US –; **1973**, US –; **1974**, Spa 7, Bel 18, Mon –
Total contested: 12
World championship position: 1968, 19th (4); 1972, 12th (4)

Reece, Jimmy   United States
Born: 17 Nov 1929   **Died:** 28 Sept 1958
Contested: 1952, Indy 7; **1954**, Indy 17; **1955**, Indy 33; **1956**, Indy 9; **1957**, Indy 18; **1958**, Indy 6
Total contested: 6

Rees, Alan   Great Britain
Born: 12 Jan 1938
One of the founders of March.
Contested: 1966, Ger –; **1967**, Ger –*, GB 9
Total contested: 3

Regazzoni, Clay   Switzerland
Born: 5 Sep 1939
Partially paralysed as a result of his crash in the US Grand Prix West.
Contested: 1970, Hol 4, GB 4, Ger –, Aus 2, It 1, Can 2, US 13, Mex 2; **1971**, SA 3, Spa –, Mon –, Hol 3, Fr –, GB –, Ger 3, Aus –, It –, Can –, US 6; **1972**, Arg 4, SA 12, Spa 3, Mon –, Bel –, Ger 2, Aus –, It –, Can 5, US 8; **1973**, Arg 7, Bra 6, SA –, Spa 9, Bel 10, Mon –, Swe 9, Fr 12, GB 7, Hol 8, Ger –, Aus 6, It –, US 8; **1974**, Arg 3, Bra 2, SA –, Spa 2, Bel 4, Mon 4, Swe –, Hol 2, Fr 3, GB 4, Ger 1, Aus 5, It –, Can 2, US 11; **1975**, Arg 4, Bra 4, SA 16, Spa –, Mon –, Bel 5, Swe 3, Hol 3, Fr –, GB 13, Ger –, Aus 7, It 1, US –; **1976**, Bra 7, SA –, US West 1, Spa 11, Bel 2, Mon –, Swe 6, Fr –, GB –, Ger 9, Hol 2, It 2, Can 6, US East 7, Jap 5; **1977**, Arg 6, Bra –, SA 9, US West –, Spa –, Bel –, Swe 7, Fr 7, Ger –, Aus –, Hol –, It 5, US East 5, Can –, Jap –; **1978**, Arg 15, Bra 5, US West 10, Bel –, Spa 15, Swe 5, Fr –, GB –, Aus –, It –, US East 14; **1979**, Arg 10, Bra 15, SA 9, US West –, Spa –, Bel –, Mon 2, Fr 6, GB 1, Ger 2, Aus 5, Hol –, It 3, Can 3, US East –; **1980**, Arg –, Bra –, SA 9, US West –
Total contested: 132 **Won:** 5 **Poles:** 5
World championship position: 1970, 3rd (33); 1971, 7th (13); 1972, 6th (15); 1973, 17th (2); 1974, 2nd (52); 1975, 5th (25); 1976, 5th (31); 1977, 17th (5); 1978, 16th (4); 1979, 5th (29, total 32)
Fastest laps: 15

Reutemann, Carlos   Argentina
Born: 12 Apr 1942
Fast but enigmatic driver, now a politician.
Contested: 1972, Arg 7, SA –, Bel 13, Fr 12, GB 8, Ger –, Aus –, It –, Can 4, US –; **1973**, Arg –, Bra 11, SA 7, Spa –, Bel –, Mon –, Swe 4, Fr 3, GB 6, Hol –, Ger –, Aus 4, It 6, Can 8, US 3; **1974**, Arg 7, Bra 7, SA 1, Spa –, Bel –, Mon –, Swe –, Hol 12, Fr –, GB 6, Ger 3, Aus 1, It –, Can 9, US 1; **1975**, Arg 3, Bra 8, SA 2, Spa 3, Mon 9, Bel 3, Swe 2, Hol 4, Fr 14, GB –, Ger 1, Aus 14, It 4, US –; **1976**, Bra 12, SA –, US West –, Spa 4, Bel –, Mon –, Swe –, Fr 11, GB –, Ger –, Aus –, Hol –, It 9; **1977**, Arg 3, Bra 1, SA 8, US West –, Spa 2, Mon 3, Bel –, Swe 3, Fr 6, GB 15, Ger 4, Aus 4, Hol 6, It –, US East 6, Can –, Jap 2; **1978**, Arg 7, Bra 1, SA –, US West 1, Mon 8, Bel 3, Spa –, Swe

10, Fr 18, GB 1, Ger–, Aus–, Hol 7, It 3, US East 1, Can 3; **1979**, Arg 2, Bra 3, SA 5, US West–, Spa 2, Bel 4, Mon 3, Fr 13, GB 8, Ger–, Aus–, Hol–, It 7, Can–, US East –; **1980**, Arg–, Bra–, SA 5, US West–, Bel 3, Mon 1, Fr 6, GB 3, Ger 2, Aus 3, Hol 4, It 3, Can 2 US East 2; **1981**, US West 2, Bra 1, Arg 2, SM 3, Bel 1, Mon–, Spa 4, Fr 10, GB 2, Ger–, Aus 5, Hol–, It 3, Can 10, US Las Vegas 8; **1982**, SA 2, Bra –
Total contested: 146 **Won:** 12 **Poles:** 6
World championship position: 1972, 16th (3); 1973, 7th (16); 1974, 6th (32); 1975, 3rd (37); 1976, 16th (3); 1977, 4th (42); 1978, 3rd (48); 1979, 6th (20, total 25); 1980, 3rd (42, total 49); 1981, 2nd (49); 1982, 15th (6)
Fastest laps: 5

Reventlow, Lance United States
Born: 24 Feb 1936 **Died:** 24 Jul 1972
Heir to the Woolworth fortune, Reventlow attempted to beat the established grand prix teams with his own Scarab cars with poor results. He was killed in a plane crash.
Contested: 1960, Bel –
Total contested: 1

Revson, Peter United States
Born: 27 Feb 1939 **Died:** 22 Mar 1974
Fared well in his second attempt at grand prix racing, but was killed testing for the South African race.
Contested: 1964, Bel–, GB–, Ger–, It 13; **1971**, US –; **1972**, Arg–, SA 3, Spa 5, Bel 7, GB 3, Aus 3, It 4, Can 2, US 18; **1973**, Arg 8, Bra–, SA 2, Spa 4, Bel–, Mon 5, Swe 7, GB 1, Hol 4, Ger 9, Aus–, It 3, Can 1, US 5; **1974**, Arg–, Bra –
Total contested: 30 **Won:** 2 **Poles:** 1
World championship position: 1972, 5th (23); 1973, 5th (38)

Rhodes, John Great Britain
Born: 18 Aug 1927
Contested: 1965, GB –
Total contested: 1

Ribeiro, Alex Brazil
Born: 7 Nov 1948
Contested: 1976, US East 12; **1977**, Arg–, Bra–, SA–, US West–, Ger 8, Hol 11, US East 15, Can 8, Jap 12
Total contested: 10

Riess, Fritz Germany
Born: 11 Jul 1922 **Died:** May 1991
1952 Le Mans winner.
Contested: 1952, Ger 7
Total contested: 1

Rigsby, Jim United States
Born: 6 Jun 1923 **Died:** 31 Aug 1952
Contested: 1952, Indy 12
Total contested: 1

Rindt, Jochen Austria
Born: 18 Apr 1942 **Died:** 5 Sep 1970
Le Mans winner in 1965. Posthumous world champion after a fatal crash in practice at Monza.
Contested: 1964, Aus –; **1965**, SA–, Bel 11, Fr–, GB–, Hol–, Ger 4, It 8, US 6, Mex –; **1966**, Mon–, Bel 2, Fr 4, GB 5, Hol–, Ger 3, It 4, US 2, Mex –; **1967**, SA–, Mon–, Hol–, Bel 4, Fr–, GB–, Ger–, Can–, It 4, US –; **1968**, SA 3, Spa–, Mon–, Bel–, Hol–, Fr–, GB–, Ger 3, It–, Can–, US–, Mex –; **1969**, SA–, Spa–, Hol–, Fr–, GB 4, Ger–, It 2, Can 3, US 1, Mex –; **1970**, SA–, Spa–, Mon 1, Bel–, Hol 1, Fr 1, GB 1, Ger 1, Aus –
Total contested: 60 **Won:** 6 **Poles:** 10
World championship position: 1965, 13th (4); 1966, 3rd (22, total 24); 1967, 11th (6); 1968, 12th (8); 1969, 4th (22); 1970, 1st (45)
Fastest laps: 3

Riseley-Prichard, John Great Britain
Born: 17 Jan 1924
Contested: 1954, GB –
Total contested: 1

Robarts, Richard Great Britain
Born: 22 Sep 1944
Contested: 1974, Arg–, Bra 15, SA 17
Total contested: 3

Rodriguez, Pedro Mexico
Born: 18 Jan 1940 **Died:** 11 Jul 1971
Outstanding sports car driver (Le Mans winner 1968), killed in a race in Germany. Brother of Ricardo.
Contested: 1963, US–, Mex –; **1964**, Mex 6; **1965**, US 5, Mex 7; **1966**, Fr–, Ger –*, US–, Mex –; **1967**, SA 1, Mon 5, Hol–, Bel 19, Fr 6, GB 5, Ger 8, Mex 6; **1968**, Fr–, GB–, Ger 6, It–, Can 3, US 13, Mex 4; **1969**, SA–, Spa–, Mon–, GB–, It 6, Can–, US 5, Mex 7; **1970**,

Drivers' Career Records

SA 9, Spa –, Mon 6, Bel 1, Hol 10, Fr –, GB –, Ger –, Aus 4, It –, Can 4, US 2, Mex 6; **1971**, SA –, Spa 4, Mon 9, Hol 2, Fr –
Total contested: 55 **Won:** 2
World championship position: 1964, 19th (1); 1965, 14th (2); 1967, 6th (15); 1968, 6th (18); 1969, 13th (3); 1970, 7th (23); 1971, 9th (9)
Fastest laps: 1

Rodriguez, Ricardo Mexico
Born: 14 Feb 1942 **Died:** 1 Nov 1962
Brother of Pedro. Youngest driver to score championship points, killed in practice for the Mexican Grand Prix.
Contested: 1961, It –; **1962**, Hol 8, Bel 4, Ger 6, It –
Total contested: 5
World championship position: 1962, 12th (4)

Rodriguez Larreta, Alberto Argentina
Born: 14 Jan 1934 **Died:** 11 Mar 1977
Contested: 1960, Arg 9
Total contested: 1

Rol, Franco Italy
Born: 5 Jun 1908 **Died:** 5 Jun 1977
Contested: 1950, Mon –, France –, It –; **1951**, It 9; **1952**, It –
Total contested: 5

Rolt, Tony Great Britain
Born: 16 Oct 1918
Le Mans winner in 1953.
Contested: 1950, GB –; **1953**, GB –; **1955**, GB –
Total contested: 3

Roos, Bertil Sweden
Born: 12 Oct 1943
Contested: 1974, Swe –
Total contested: 1

Rosberg, Keke Finland
Born: 6 Dec 1948
Highly competitive driver, often in inferior machinery, who only won one race in his championship year.
Contested: 1978, SA –, Swe 15, Fr 16, GB –, Ger 10, Aus –, Hol –, US East –, Can –; **1979**, Fr 9, GB –, Ger –, Aus –, Hol –, It –, US East –; **1980**, Arg 3, Bra 9, SA –, US West –, Bel 7, Fr –, Ger –, Aus 16, It 5, Can 9, US East 10; **1981**, US West –, Bra 9, Arg –, SM –, Bel –,

Spa 12, Fr –, GB –, US Las Vegas 10; **1982**, SA 5, Bra –, US West 2, Bel 2, Mon –, US East 4, Can –, Hol 3, GB –, Fr 5, Ger 3, Aus 2, CH 1, It 8, US Las Vegas 5; **1983**, Bra –, US West –, Fr 5, SM 4, Mon 1, Bel 5, US East 2, Can 4, GB 11, Ger 10, Aus 8, Hol –, It 11, Eur –, SA 5; **1984**, Bra 2, SA –, Bel 4, SM –, Fr 6, Mon 4, Can –, US East –, US Dallas 1, GB –, Ger –, Aus –, Hol 8, It –, Eur –, Por; **1985**, Bra –, Por –, SM –, Mon 8, Can 4, US 1, Fr 2, GB –, Ger 12, Aus –, Hol –, It –, Bel 4, Eur 3, SA 2, Austral 1; **1986**, Bra –, Spa 4, SM 5, Mon 2, Bel –, Can 4, Detroit –, Fr 4, GB –, Ger 5, Hun –, Aus 9, It 4, Por –, Mex –, Austral –
Total contested: 114 **Won:** 5 **Poles:** 5
World championship position: 1980, 10th (6); 1982, 1st (44); 1983, 5th (27); 1984, 8th (20.5); 1985, 3rd (40); 1986, 6th (22)
Fastest laps: 3

Rose, Mauri United States
Born: 26 May 1906 **Died:** 1 Jan 1981
Triple Indianapolis winner.
Contested: 1950, Indy 3; **1951**, Indy 14
Total contested: 2
World championship position: 1950, 9th (4)

Rosier, Louis France
Born: 5 Nov 1905 **Died:** 29 Oct 1956
One of the leading drivers of the immediate post-war period, he won Le Mans in 1950 co-driven (briefly) by his son Jean-Louis. Killed in a race in Paris.
Contested: 1950, GB 5, Mon –, CH 3, Bel 3, Fr 6, Fr –, It 4; **1951**, CH 9, Bel 4, Fr –, GB 10, Ger 8, It 7, Spa 7; **1952**, CH –, Bel –, Fr –, It 10; **1953**, Hol 7, Bel 8, Fr 8, GB 11, Ger 10, CH –, It 19; **1954**, Arg –, Fr –, GB –, Ger 8, It 8, Spa 7; **1955**, Mon –, Bel 9, Hol 9; **1956**, Mon –, Bel 8, Fr 6, GB –, Ger 5
Total contested: 38
World championship position: 1950, 4th (13); 1951, 12th (3); 1956, 19th (2)

Rosset, Ricardo Brazil
Born: 27 Jul 1968
1996, Austral 9, Bra –, Arg –, Eur 11, SM –, Mon –, Sp –, Can –, Fr 11, GB –, Ger 11, Hun 8, Bel 9, It –, Por 14, Jap 13
Total contested: 16

Rothengatter, Huub Holland
Born: 8 Oct 1954

Contested: **1984**, Can –, US Dallas –, GB 13, Ger 9, Aus –, Hol –, It 8; **1985**, Ger –, Aus 9, Hol –, It –, Bel –, SA –, Austral 7; **1986**, Fr –, GB –, Ger –, Hun –, Aus 8, SM –, Bel –, Can 12, It –, Por –, Austral –
Total contested: 25

Ruby, Lloyd   United States
Born: 12 Jan 1928
Contested: **1960**, Indy 7; **1961**, US –
Total contested: 2

Russo, Eddie   United States
Born: 19 Nov 1925
Contested: **1955**, Indy 22; **1956**, Indy 23; **1957**, Indy 32; **1960**, Indy 26
Total contested: 4

Russo, Paul   United States
Born: 10 Apr 1914   Died: 23 Jun 1976
Contested: **1950**, Indy 9; **1953**, Indy 4, Indy 25; **1954**, Indy 8; **1955**, Indy 2; **1956**, Indy 33; **1957**, Indy 4; **1958**, Indy 18; **1959**, Indy 9
Total contested: 8
World championship position: 1953, 18th (1.5); 1955, 10th (3); 1957, 17th (3)
Fastest laps: 1

Ruttman, Troy   United States
Born: 11 Mar 1930
One of the few Indycar drivers to try his hand at grand prix racing in the fifties, he remains the youngest driver to have won a race counting for the World Championship (Bruce McLaren is the youngest grand prix winner).
Contested: **1950**, Indy 15; **1951**, Indy 23; **1952**, Indy 1; **1954**, Indy 4; **1956**, Indy 31; **1957**, Indy 31; **1958**, Fr 10; **1960**, Indy 20
Total contested: 8 Won: 1
World championship position: 1952, 7th (8); 1954, 23rd (1.5)

Ryan, Peter   Canada
Born: 10 Jun 1940   Died: 2 Jul 1962
Contested: **1961**, US 10
Total contested: 1

Sachs, Eddie   United States
Born: 28 May 1927   Died: 30 May 1964
Contested: **1957**, Indy 23; **1958**, Indy 22; **1959**, Indy 17; **1960**, Indy 21
Total contested: 4 Poles: 1

Said, Bob   United States
Born: 5 May 1932
Contested: **1959**, US –
Total contested: 1

Sala, Luis   Spain
Born: 15 May 1959
Contested: **1988**, Bra –, SM 11, Mon –, Mex 11, Can 13, Detroit –, Fr –, GB –, Hun 10, It –, Por 8, Spa 12, Jap 15, Austral –; **1989**, Bra –, SM –, Mon –, US –, Can –, GB 6, Hun –, Bel 15, It 8, Por 12, Spa –, Jap –
Total contested: 26
World championship position: 1989, 26th (1)

Salazar, Eliseo   Chile
Born: 14 Nov 1954
Contested: **1981**, SM –, Spa 14, Fr –, Ger –, Aus –, Hol 6, It –, Can –, US Las Vegas –; **1982**, SA 9, Bra –, US West –, SM 5, Bel –, Mon –, US East –, Can –, Hol 13, Fr –, Ger –, CH 14, It 9; **1983**, Bra 15, US West –
Total contested: 24
World championship position: 1981, 18th (1); 1982, 22nd (2)

Salo, Mika   Finland
Born: 30 Nov 1966
1994, Jap 10, Austral –; **1995**, Bra 7, Arg –, SM –, Sp 10, Mon –, Can 7, Fr 15, GB 8, Ger –, Hun –, Bel 8, It 5, Por 13, Eur 10, Pac 12, Jap 6, Austral 5; **1996**, Austral 6, Bra 5, Arg –, Eur –, SM –, Mon 5, Sp –, Can –, Fr 10, GB 7, Ger 9, Hun –, Bel 7, It –, Por 11, Jap –; **1997**, Austral –, Bra 13, Arg 8, SM 9, Mon 5, Sp –, Can –, Fr –, GB –, Ger –, Hun 13, Bel 11, It –, Aus –, Lux 10, Jap –, Eur 12
Total contested: 52
World championship position: 1995, 14th (5); 1996, 13th (5); 1997, 16th (2)

Salvadori, Roy   Great Britain
Born: 12 May 1922
Le Mans winner in 1959.
Contested: **1952**, GB 8; **1953**, Hol –, Fr –, GB –, Ger –, It –; **1954**, Fr –, GB 18; **1955**, GB –; **1956**, GB –, Ger –, It 12; **1957**, Fr –, GB 5, Ger –, Pescara –; **1958**, Mon –, Hol 4, Bel 8, Fr 14, GB 3, Ger 2, Por 10, It 5, Moroccan 7; **1959**, Mon 6, Hol –, Fr –, GB 6, Por 6, It –, US –; **1960**, Mon –, GB –, US 8; **1961**, Fr 8, GB 6, Ger 10, It 6, US 7;

Drivers' Career Records

1962, Hol–, Mon–, Fr–, GB–, Ger–, It–, SA –
Total contested: 47
World championship position: 1957, 18th (2); 1958, 4th (15); 1961, 17th (2)

Sanesi, Consalvo Italy
Born: 28 Mar 1911
Contested: 1950, It –; **1951**, CH 4, Bel –, Fr 10, GB 6
Total contested: 5
World championship position: 1951, 12th (3)

Scarborough, Carl United States
Born: 3 Jul 1914 **Died:** 30 May 1953
Contested: 1951, Indy 18; **1953**, Indy 12
Total contested: 2

Scarfiotti, Ludovico Italy
Born: 18 Oct 1933 **Died:** 8 Jun 1968
Le Mans winner in 1963, European Hill Climb Champion in 1962 and 1965, he died in practice for the Rossfeld Hill Climb.
Contested: 1963, Hol 6; **1964**, It 9; **1966**, Ger –, It 1; **1967**, Hol 6, Bel –, It –; **1968**, SA –, Spa 4, Mon 4
Total contested: 10 **Won:** 1
World championship position: 1963, 15th (1); 1966, 10th (9); 1967, 19th (1); 1968, 13th (6)
Fastest laps: 1

Scarlatti, Giorgio Italy
Born: 2 Oct 1921
Contested: 1956, Ger –; **1957**, Mon –, Ger 10, Pescara 6, It 5; **1958**, Mon –, Hol –; **1959**, Fr 8, It 12; **1960**, Arg –, It –; **1961**, Fr – ·
Total contested: 12
World championship position: 1957, 20th (1)

Scheckter, Ian South Africa
Born: 22 Aug 1947
Brother of Jody.
Contested: 1974, SA 13; **1975**, SA–, Swe–, Hol 12; **1976**, SA –; **1977**, Arg–, Bra–, Spa 11, Bel–, Swe–, Fr–, GB–, Ger–, Aus–, Hol 10, It–, US–, Can –
Total contested: 18

Scheckter, Jody South Africa
Born: 29 Jan 1950
Brother of Ian.
Contested: 1974, Arg–, Bra 13, SA 8, Spa 5, Bel 3, Mon 2, Swe 1, Hol 5, Fr 4, GB 1, Ger 2, Aus–,

It 3, Can–, US –; **1975**, Arg 11, Bra–, SA 1, Spa–, Mon 7, Bel 2, Swe 7, Hol 16, Fr 9, GB 3, Ger–, Aus 8, It 8, US 6; **1976**, Bra 5, SA 4, US West –, Spa –, Bel 4, Mon 2, Swe 1, Fr 6, GB 2, Ger 2, Aus –, Hol 5, It 5, Can 4, US East 2, Jap –; **1977**, Arg 1, Bra–, SA 2, US West 3, Spa 3, Mon 1, Bel–, Swe–, Fr–, GB–, Ger 2, Aus–, Hol 3, It–, US East 3, Can 1, Jap 10; **1978**, Arg 10, Bra–, SA–, US West–, Mon 3, Bel–, Spa 4, Swe–, Fr 6, GB–, Ger 2, Aus–, Hol 12, It 12, US East 3, Can 2; **1979**, Arg–, Bra 6, SA 2, US West 2, Spa 4, Bel 1, Mon 1, Fr 7, GB 5, Ger 4, Aus 4, Hol 2, It 1, Can 4, US East –; **1980**, Arg–, Bra–, SA–, US West 5, Bel 8, Mon–, Fr 12, GB 10, Ger 13, Aus 13, Hol 9, It 8, US East 11
Total contested: 112 **Won:** 10 **Poles:** 3
World championship position: 1974, 3rd (45); 1975, 7th (20); 1976, 3rd (49); 1977, 2nd (55); 1978, 7th (24); 1979, 1st (51, total 60); 1980, 19th (2)
Fastest laps: 5

Schell, Harry United States
Born: 29 Jun 1921 **Died:** 13 May 1960
A leading second rank driver who debuted the first rear engined car in the championship at Monaco in 1950. Killed in practice at Silverstone.
Contested: 1950, Mon–, CH 8; **1951**, CH 12, Fr –; **1952**, CH–, Fr–, Fr–, GB 17; **1953**, Arg 7, Hol 12, Bel 7, Fr–, GB–, Ger–, It 11; **1954**, Arg 6, Fr–, GB 12, Ger 7, CH–, Spa –; **1955**, Arg 6, Arg–, Arg–, Mon–, GB 9, GB–, It –; **1956**, Mon–, Bel 4, Fr 10, Fr–, GB–, Ger–, It –; **1957**, Arg 4, Mon–, Mon–, Fr 6, GB–, Ger 7, Pescara 3, It–, It–, It 5; **1958**, Arg 6, Mon 5, Hol 2, Bel 5, Fr 12, GB 5, Ger–, Por 6, It–, Moroccan 5; **1959**, Mon–, Hol–, Fr 7, GB 4, Ger 7, Por 5, It 7, US –; **1960**, Arg –
Total contested: 56
World championship position: 1956, 15th (3); 1957, 7th (8); 1958, 5th (14); 1959, 12th (5)

Schenken, Tim Australia
Born: 26 Sep 1943
Manufacturer with Howden Ganley of Tiga racing cars.
Contested: 1970, Aus–, It–, Can–, US –; **1971**, Spa 9, Mon 10, Hol–, Fr 12, GB 12, Ger 6, Aus 3, It–, Can–, US –; **1972**, Arg 5, SA–, Spa 8, Mon–, Bel–, Fr 17, GB–, Ger 14, Aus 11, It–, Can 7, US –; **1973**, Can 14; **1974**, Spa 14, Bel 10, Mon–, GB–, Aus 10, It –

Total contested: 33
World championship position: 1971, 14th (5); 1972, 19th (2)

Scherrer, Albert   Switzerland
Born: 28 Feb 1908   **Died:** 5 Jul 1986
Contested: 1953, CH 9
Total contested: 1

Schiattarella, Domenico (Mimmo)   Italy
Born: 17 Nov 1967
1994, Eur 19, Austral –; **1995,** Bra –, Arg 9, SM –, Sp –, Mon
Total contested: 7

Schiller, Heinz   Switzerland
Born: 25 Jan 1930
Contested: 1962, Ger –
Total contested: 1

Schindler, Bill   United States
Born: 6 Mar 1909   **Died:** 20 Sep 1952
Raced with only one leg after a 1936 crash. Killed in a race in Pennsylvania.
Contested: 1950, Indy 26; **1951,** Indy 13; **1952,** Indy 14
Total contested: 3

Schlesser, Jean-Louis   France
Born: 12 Sep 1948
Cousin of Jo. World Sports Car Champion, 1989 and 1990.
Contested: 1988, It 11
Total contested: 1

Schlesser, Jo   France
Born: 18 May 1928   **Died:** 7 Jul 1968
Cousin of Jean-Louis. Killed in the French Grand Prix.
Contested: 1966, Ger 10; **1967,** Ger 10; **1968,** Fr –
Total contested: 3

Schneider, Bernd   Germany
Born: 20 Jul 1964
Contested: 1988, Mex –, Fr –, Ger 12, Bel 13, It –, Jap –; **1989,** Bra –, Jap –; **1990,** US 12
Total contested: 9

Schoeller, Rudolf   Switzerland
Born: 27 Apr 1902   **Died:** 7 Mar 1978
Contested: 1952, Ger –
Total contested: 1

Schroeder, Rob   United States
Born: 11 May 1926
Contested: 1962, US 10
Total contested: 1

Schumacher, Michael   Germany
Born: 3 Jan 1969
Contested: 1991, Bel –, It 5, Por 6, Spa 6, Jap –, Austral –; **1992,** SA 4, Mex 3, Bra 3, Spa 2, SM –, Mon 4, Can 2, Fr –, GB 4, Ger 3, Hun –, Bel 1, It 3, Por 7, Jap –, Austral 2; **1993,** SA –, Bra 3, Eur –, SM 2, Sp 3, Mon –, Can 2, Fr 3, GB 2, Ger 2, Hun –, Bel 2, It –, Por 1, Jap –, Austral –; **1994,** Bra 1, Pac 1, SM 1, Mon 1, Sp 2, Can 1, Fr 1, GB –, Ger –, Hun 1, Bel –, It –, Por –, Eur 1, Jap 2, Austral –; **1995,** Bra 1, Arg 3, SM –, Sp 1, Mon 1, Can 5, Fr 1, GB –, Ger 1, Hun 11, Bel 1, It –, Por 2, Eur 1, Pac 1, Jap 1, Austral –; **1996,** Austral –, Bra 3, Arg –, Eur 2, SM 2, Mon –, Sp 1, Can –, GB –, Ger 4, Hun 9, Bel 1, It 1, Por 3, Jap 2; **1997,** Austral 2, Bra 5, Arg –, SM 2, Mon 1, Sp 4, Can 1, Fr 1, GB –, Ger 2, Hun 4, Bel 1, It 6, Aus 6, Lux –, Jap 1, Eur –
Total contested: 101 **Won:** 27 **Poles:** 17
World championship position: 1991, 12th (4); 1992, 3rd (53); 1993, 4th (52); 1994, 1st (92); 1995, 1st (102); 1996, 3rd (59); 1997, 2nd, until disqualification from the championship (78)
Fastest laps: 28

Schumacher, Ralf   Germany
Younger brother of Michael
Born: 30 June 1975
1997, Austral –, Bra –, Arg 3, SM –, Mon –, Sp –, Can –, Fr 6, GB 5, Ger 5, Hun 5, Bel –, It –, Aus 5, Lux –, Jap 9, Eur –
Total contested: 17
World championship position: 1997, 11th (13)

Schuppan, Vern   Australia
Born: 19 Mar 1943
Le Mans winner, 1983.
Contested: 1974, Bel 15, Mon –, Hol –, Ger –; **1975,** Swe –; **1977,** GB 12, Ger 7, Aus 16
Total contested: 8

Schwelm Cruz, Adolfo   Argentina
Born: 28 Jun 1923
Contested: 1953, Arg –
Total contested: 1

Drivers' Career Records

Scott, Bob   United States
Born: 4 Oct 1928   **Died:** 5 Jul 1954
Contested: 1952, Indy 29; **1953,** Indy 31, Indy 12; **1954,** Indy 18, Indy 25
Total contested: 3

Scott-Brown, Archie   Great Britain
Born: 13 May 1927   **Died:** 19 May 1958
Born with a seriously malformed hand, Scott-Brown showed great promise but had difficulties in persuading continental organisers to accept his entries. He was killed in a race at Spa.
Contested: 1956, GB –
Total contested: 1

Scotti, Piero   Italy
Born: 11 Nov 1909   **Died:** 14 Feb 1976
Contested: 1956, Bel –
Total contested: 1

Seidel, Wolfgang   Germany
Born: 4 Jul 1926   **Died:** 1 Mar 1987
Contested: 1953, Ger 18; **1958,** Bel –, Ger –, Moroccan –; **1960,** It 9; **1961,** GB 18, Ger –, It –; **1962,** Hol 14, GB –
Total contested: 10

Senna, Ayrton   Brazil
Born: 21 Mar 1960   **Died:** 1 May 1994
Controversial multiple World Champion who took the record number of pole positions in grand prix racing.
Contested: 1984, Bra –, SA 6, Bel 6, Fr –, Mon 2, Can 7, US East –, US Dallas –, GB 3, Ger –, Aus –, Hol –, Eur –, Por 3; **1985,** Bra –, Por 1, SM 7, Mon –, Can 16, US –, Fr –, GB 10, Ger –, Aus 2, Hol 3, It 3, Bel 1, Eur 2, SA –, Austral –; **1986,** Bra 2, Spa 1, SM –, Mon 3, Bel 2, Can 5, Detroit 1, Fr –, GB –, Ger 2, Hun 2, Aus –, It –, Por 4, Mex 3, Austral –; **1987,** Bra –, SM 2, Bel –, Mon 1, US 1, Fr 4, GB 3, Ger 3, Hun 2, Aus 5, It 2, Por 7, Spa 5, Mex –, Jap 2, Austral –; **1988,** Bra –, SM 1, Mon –, Mex 2, Can 1, Detroit 1, Fr 2, GB 1, Ger 1, Hun 1, Bel 1, It 10, Por 6, Spa 4, Jap 1, Austral 2; **1989,** Bra 11, SM 1, Mon 1, Mex 1, US –, Can 7, Fr –, GB –, Ger 1, Hun 2, Bel 1, It –, Por –, Spa 1, Jap –, Austral –; **1990,** US 1, Bra 3, SM –, Mon 1, Can 1, Mex 20, Fr 3, GB 3, Ger 1, Hun 2, Bel 1, It 1, Por 2, Spa –, Jap –, Austral –; **1991,** US 1, Bra 1, SM 1, Mon 1, Can –, Mex 3, Fr 3, GB –, Ger 7, Hun 1, Bel 1, It 2, Por 2, Spa 5, Jap 2, Austral 1; **1992,** SA 3, Mex –, Bra –, Spa 9, SM 3, Mon 1, Can –, Fr –, GB –, Ger 2, Hun 1, Bel 5, It 1, Por 3, Jap –, Austral –; **1993,** SA 2, Bra 1, Eur 1, SM 2, Sp 3, Mon –, Can 18, Fr 4, GB 5, Ger 4, Hun –, Bel 4, It –, Por –, Jap 1, Austral 1; **1994,** Bra –, Pac –, SM –
Total contested: 161 **Won:** 41 **Poles:** 65
World championship position: 1984, 9th (13); 1985, 4th (38); 1986, 4th (55); 1987, 3rd (57); 1988, 1st (90, total 94); 1989, 2nd (60); 1990, 1st (78); 1991, 1st (96); 1992, 4th (50); 1993, 2nd (73)
Fastest laps: 19

Serafini, Dorino   Italy
Born: 22 Jul 1909
Contested: 1950, It 2
Total contested: 1
World championship position: 1950, 13th (3)

Serra, Chico   Brazil
Born: 3 Feb 1957
Contested: 1981, US West 7, Bra –, Arg –, Bel –, Spa 11; **1982,** SA 17, Bra –, Bel 6, US East 11, Hol –, GB –, Ger 11, Aus 7, It 11; **1983,** Bra 9, Fr –, SM 8, Mon 7
Total contested: 18
World championship position: 1982, 26th (1)

Serrurier, Doug   South Africa
Born: 9 Dec 1920
Contested: 1962, SA –; **1963,** SA 11
Total contested: 2

Servoz-Gavin, Johnny   France
Born: 18 Jan 1942
Contested: 1967, Mon –; **1968,** Mon –, Fr –, It 2, Can –, Mex –; **1969,** Ger –*, Can 6, US –, Mex 8; **1970,** SA –, Spa 5
Total contested: 12
World championship position: 1968, 13th (6); 1969, 16th (1); 1970, 19th (2)

Settember, Tony   United States
Born: 1930
Contested: 1962, GB 11, It –; **1963,** Bel –, Fr –, GB –, Ger –
Total contested: 6

Sharp, Hap   United States
Born: 1 Jan 1928   **Died:** 7 May 1993
Co-founder with Jim Hall of Chaparral cars.

Contested: 1961, US 11; **1962**, US 11; **1963**, US –, Mex 7; **1964**, US 10, Mex 13
Total contested: 6

Shawe-Taylor, Brian   Great Britain
Born: 29 Jan 1915
Contested: 1950, GB 10; **1951**, GB 8
Total contested: 2

Shelby, Carol   United States
Born: 11 Jan 1923
Winner of the 1959 Le Mans, he was also creator of the Shelby Cobra, instrumental in Ford's Le Mans efforts, and co-founder of All American Racers (manufacturer of the Eagle grand prix and Indianapolis cars) with Dan Gurney.
Contested: 1958, Fr –, GB 9, Por 9, It –, It 4; **1959**, Hol –, GB –, Por 8, It 10
Total contested: 8

Shelly, Tony   New Zealand
Born: 2 Feb 1937
Contested: 1962, GB –
Total contested: 1

Siffert, Jo   Switzerland
Born: 7 Jul 1936   **Died:** 24 Oct 1971
One of the great sports car drivers and winner of the 1968 British Grand Prix as a private entry for Rob Walker, he was killed in a non-championship Formula One race at Brands Hatch.
Contested: 1962, Bel 10, Fr –, Ger 12; **1963**, Mon –, Bel –, Hol 7, Fr 6, GB –, Ger 9, It –, US –, Mex 9; **1964**, Mon 8, Hol 13, Bel –, Fr –, GB 11, Ger 4, Aus –, It 7, US 3, Mex –; **1965**, SA 7, Mon 6, Bel 8, Fr 6, GB 9, Hol 13, Ger –, It –, US 11, Mex 4; **1966**, Mon –, Bel –, Fr –, GB –, Hol –, It –, US 4, Mex –; **1967**, SA –, Mon –, Hol 10, Bel 7, Fr 4, GB –, Ger –, It –, US 4, Mex 12; **1968**, SA 7, Spa –, Mon –, Bel 7, Hol –, Fr 11, GB 1, Ger –, It –, Can –, US 5, Mex 6; **1969**, SA 4, Spa –, Mon 3, Hol 2, Fr 9, GB 8, Ger 5, It 8, Can –, US –, Mex –; **1970**, SA 10, Mon 8, Bel 7, Hol –, Fr –, GB –, Ger –, Aus 9, It –, Can –, US 9, Mex –; **1971**, SA –, Spa –, Mon –, Hol 6, Fr 4, GB 9, Ger –, Aus 1, It 9, Can 9, US 2
Total contested: 96 **Won:** 2 **Poles:** 2
World championship position: 1963, 15th (1); 1964, 10th (7); 1965, 11th (5); 1966, 14th (3); 1967, 11th (6); 1968, 7th (12); 1969, 9th (15); 1971, 4th (19)

Fastest laps: 4

Simon, André   France
Born: 5 Jan 1920
Contested: 1951, Fr –, Ger –, It 6, Spa –; **1952**, CH –, It 6; **1955**, Mon –, GB –; **1956**, It 9, Fr –; **1957**, It 11
Total contested: 11

Solana, Moises   Mexico
Born: 1936   **Died:** 27 Jul 1969
Killed in a Mexican hill climb.
Contested: 1963, Mex –; **1964**, Mex 10; **1965**, US 12, Mex –; **1966**, Mex –; **1967**, US –, Mex –; **1968**, Mex –
Total contested: 8

Soler-Roig, Alex   Spain
Born: 29 Oct 1932
Contested: 1971, SA –, Spa –, Hol –, Fr –; **1972**, Arg –, Spa –
Total contested: 6

Sommer, Raymond   France
Born: 31 Aug 1906   **Died:** 10 Sep 1950
A leading pre-war driver (he won Le Mans in 1932 and 1933), he was killed in a race in France.
Contested: 1950, Mon 4, CH –, Bel –, France –, It –
Total contested: 5
World championship position: 1950, 13th (3)

Sparken, Mike   France
Born: 16 Jun 1930
Contested: 1955, GB 7
Total contested: 1

Spence, Mike   Great Britain
Born: 30 Dec 1936   **Died:** 7 May 1968
Killed in practice for Indianapolis.
Contested: 1963, It 13; **1964**, GB 9, Ger 8, Aus –, It 6, Mex 4, US 7, US –; **1965**, SA 4, Bel 7, Fr 7, GB 4, Hol 8, Ger –, It –, US –, Mex 3; **1966**, Mon –, Bel –, Fr –, GB –, Hol 5, Ger –, It 5, US 9; **1967**, SA –, Mon 6, Hol 8, Bel 5, Fr –, GB –, Ger –, Can 5, It 5, US –, Mex 5; **1968**, SA –
Total contested: 36 **Poles:** 1
World championship position: 1964, 12th (4); 1965, 8th (10); 1966, 12th (4); 1967, 10th (9)

Stacey, Alan   Great Britain
Born: 29 Aug 1933   **Died:** 19 Jun 1960

Competitive, despite an artificial leg, Stacey was killed when a bird hit him in the Belgian Grand Prix.
Contested: 1958, GB –; **1959**, GB 8, US –; **1960**, Arg–, Mon–, Hol–, Bel –
Total contested: 7

Starrabba, Gaetano Italy
Born: 3 Dec 1932
Contested: 1961, It –
Total contested: 1

Stevenson, Chuck United States
Born: 15 Oct 1919
American Champion in 1952.
Contested: 1951, Indy 20; **1952**, Indy 18; **1953**, Indy 29, Indy 9, Indy 23; **1954**, Indy 12; **1960**, Indy 15
Total contested: 5

Stewart, Ian Great Britain
Born: 15 Jul 1929
No relation of Jackie or Jimmy.
Contested: 1953, GB –
Total contested: 1

Stewart, Jackie Great Britain
Born: 11 Jun 1939
Triple World Champion who broke Jim Clark's record number of wins. Brother of Jimmy.
Contested: 1965, SA 6, Mon 3, Bel 2, Fr 2, GB 5, Hol 2, Ger–, It 1, US–, Mex –; **1966**, Mon 1, Bel–, GB–, Hol 4, Ger 5, It–, US–, Mex –; **1967**, SA–, Mon–, Hol–, Bel 2, Fr 3, GB–, Ger–, Can–, It–, US–, Mex –; **1968**, SA–, Bel 4, Hol 1, Fr 3, GB 6, Ger 1, It–, Can 6, US 1, Mex 7; **1969**, SA 1, Spa 1, Mon–, Hol 1, Fr 1, GB 1, Ger 2, It 1, Can–, US–, Mex 4; **1970**, SA 3, Spa 1, Mon–, Bel–, Hol 2, Fr 9, GB–, Ger–, Aus–, It 2, Can–, US–, Mex –; **1971**, SA 2, Spa 1, Mon 1, Hol 11, Fr 1, GB 1, Ger 1, Aus–, It–, Can 1, US 5; **1972**, Arg 1, SA–, Spa–, Mon 4, Fr 1, GB 2, Ger 11, Aus 7, It–, Can 1, US 1; **1973**, Bra 2, SA 1, Spa–, Bel 1, Mon 1, Swe 5, Fr 4, GB 10, Hol 1, Ger 1, Aus 2, It 4, Can 5
Total contested: 99 **Won:** 27 **Poles:** 17
World championship position: 1965, 3rd (33, total 34); 1966, 7th (14); 1967, 9th (10); 1968, 2nd (36); 1969, 1st (63); 1970, 5th (25); 1971, 1st (62); 1972, 2nd (45); 1973, 1st (75)
Fastest laps: 15

Stewart, Jimmy Great Britain
Born: 6 Mar 1931
Brother of Jackie.
Contested: 1953, GB 9
Total contested: 1

Stohr, Slegfried Italy
Born: 10 Oct 1952
Contested: 1981, Bra–, Arg 9, Bel–, Mon–, Spa–, GB–, Ger 12, Aus–, Hol 7
Total contested: 9

Stommelen, Rolf Germany
Born: 11 Jul 1943 **Died:** 24 Apr 1983
Led the 1975 Spanish Grand Prix until mechanical failure led to a crash which killed four spectators and severely injured Stommelen. Killed in a race at Riverside.
Contested: 1969, Ger 4[*]; **1970**, SA –, Spa –, Bel 5, Fr 7, Ger 5, Aus 3, It 5, Can–, US 12, Mex –; **1971**, SA 12, Spa –, Mon 6, Hol–, Fr 11, GB 5, Ger 10, Aus 7, Can –; **1972**, SA 13, Spa –, Mon 10, Bel 11, Fr 16, GB 10, Ger–, Aus 15; **1973**, Ger 11, Aus–, It 12, Can 12; **1974**, Aus–, It–, Can 11, US 12; **1975**, Arg 12, Bra 14, SA 7, Spa–, Aus 16, It –; **1976**, Ger 6, Hol 12, It –; **1978**, SA 9, US West 9, Mon–, Bel–, Spa 14, Swe 14, Fr 15, Ger–, US East 16
Total contested: 54
World championship position: 1970, 11th (10); 1971, 18th (3); 1976, 19th (1)

Strelff, Phillippe France
Born: 26 Jun 1955
Severely injured in a pre-season crash in 1989.
Contested: 1984, Por –; **1985**, It 10, Bel 9, Eur 8, SA –, Austral 3; **1986**, Bra 7, Spa–, SM –, Mon 11, Bel 12, Can 11, Detroit 9, Fr –, GB 6, Ger–, Hun 8, Aus–, It 9, Por–, Mex–, Austral 5; **1987**, Bra 11, SM 8, Bel 9, Mon–, US –, Fr 6, GB–, Ger 4, Hun 9, Aus–, It 12, Por 12, Spa 7, Mex 8, Jap 12, Austral –; **1988**, Bra–, SM 10, Mon–, Mex 12, Can–, Detroit–, Fr–, GB–, Ger–, Hun–, Bel 10, It–, Por 9, Spa–, Jap 8, Austral 11
Total contested: 54
World championship position: 1985, 15th (4); 1986, 13th (3); 1987, 14th (4)

Stuck, Hans Germany
Born: 27 Dec 1900 **Died:** 8 Feb 78
One of the great pre-war drivers, winning grand prix and hill climbs for Auto-Union,

Stuck won the German Hillclimb Championship as late as 1960. Father of Hans-Joachim.
Contested: 1952, CH –; **1953**, Ger –, It 17
Total contested: 3

Stuck, Hans-Joachim   Germany
Born: 1 Jan 1951
Son of Hans, won Le Mans in 1986 and 1987.
Contested: 1974, Arg –, Br –, SA 5, Sp 4, Bel –, Mon –, Hol –, GB –, Ger 7, Aus –, It –, Can –; **1975**, GB –, Ger –, Aus –, It –, US 8; **1976**, Br 4, SA 12, US West –, Spa –, Bel –, Mon 4, Swe –, Fr 7, GB –, Ger –, Aus –, Hol –, It –, Can –, US East 5, Jap –; **1977**, SA –, US West –, Spa 6, Mon –, Bel 6, Swe 10, Fr –, GB 5, Ger 3, Aus 3, Hol 7, It –, US East –, Can –, Jap 7; **1978**, Arg 17, Bra –, Mon –, Bel –, Spa –, Swe 11, Fr 11, GB 5, Ger –, Aus –, Hol –, It –, US East –, Can –; **1979**, Bra –, SA –, US West –, Spa 14, Bel 8, Mon –, Ger –, Aus –, Hol –, It 11, Can –, US East 5
Total contested: 74
World championship position: 1974, 16th (5); 1976, 13th (8); 1977, 11th (12); 1978, 18th (2); 1979, 19th (2)

Sullivan, Danny   United States
Born: 9 Mar 1950
Indianapolis winner in 1985.
Contested: 1983, Bra 11, US West 8, Fr –, SM –, Mon 5, Bel 12, US East –, Can –, GB 14, Ger 12, Aus –, Hol –, It –, Eur –, SA 7
Total contested: 15
World championship position: 1983, 17th (2)

Surer, Marc   Switzerland
Born: 18 Sep 1951
Injuries from a rally crash ended his grand prix career.
Contested: 1979, US East –; **1980**, Arg –, Bra 7, Fr –, GB –, Ger 12, Aus 12, Hol 10, It –, US East 8; **1981**, US West –, Bra 4, Arg –, SM 9, Bel 11, Mon 6, Fr 12, GB 11, Ger 14, Aus –, Hol 8, Can 9, US Las Vegas –; **1982**, Bel 7, Mon 9, US East 8, Can 5, Hol 10, GB –, Fr 13, Ger 6, Aus –, CH 15, It –, US Las Vegas 7; **1983**, Bra 6, US West 5, Fr 10, SM 6, Mon –, Bel 11, US East 11, Can –, GB 17, Ger 7, Aus –, Hol 8, It 10, Eur –, SA 8; **1984**, Bra 7, SA 9, Bel 8, SM –, Fr –, Can –, US East –, US Dallas –, GB 11, Ger –, Aus 6, Hol –, It –, Eur –, Por –; **1985**, Can 15, US 8, Fr 8, GB 6, Ger –, Aus 6, Hol 10, It 4, Bel 8, Eur –, SA –,

Austral –; **1986**, Bra –, Spa –, SM 9, Mon 9, Bel 9
Total contested: 82
World championship position: 1981, 16th (4); 1982, 20th (3); 1983, 15th (4); 1984, 20th (1); 1985, 13th (5)
Fastest laps: 1

Surtees, John   Great Britain
Born: 11 Feb 1934
World Champion on motorcycles and in cars, Surtees achieved less success as a constructor.
Contested: 1960, Mon –, GB 2, Por –, US –; **1961**, Mon 11, Hol 7, Bel 5, Fr –, GB –, Ger 5, It –, US –; **1962**, Hol –, Mon 4, Bel 5, Fr 5, GB 2, Ger 2, It –, US –, SA –; **1963**, Mon 4, Bel –, Hol 3, Fr –, GB 2, Ger 1, It –, US –, Mex –, SA –; **1964**, Mon –, Hol 2, Bel –, Fr –, GB 3, Ger 1, Aus –, It 1, US 2, Mex 2; **1965**, SA 2, Mon 4, Bel –, Fr 3, GB 3, Hol 7, Ger –, It –; **1966**, Mon –, Bel 1, Fr –, GB –, Hol –, Ger 2, It –, US 3, Mex 1; **1967**, SA 3, Mon –, Hol –, Bel –, GB 6, Ger 4, It 1, US –. Mex 4; **1968**, SA 8, Spa –, Mon –, Bel –, Hol –, Fr 2, GB 5, Ger –, It –, Can –, US 3, Mex –; **1969**, SA –, Spa 5, Mon –, Hol 9, GB –, It –, Can –, US 3, Mex –; **1970**, SA –, Spa –, Mon –, Hol 6, GB –, Ger –, Aus –, It –, Can 5, US –, Mex 8; **1971**, SA –, Spa 11, Mon 7, Hol 5, Fr 8, GB 6, Ger 7, Aus –, It –, Can 11, US 17; **1972**, It –
Total contested: 111 **Won:** 6 **Poles:** 8
World championship position: 1960, 12th (6); 1961, 11th (4); 1962, 4th (19); 1963, 4th (22); 1964, 1st (40); 1965, 5th (17); 1966, 2nd (28); 1967, 4th (20); 1968, 7th (12); 1969, 11th (6); 1970, 17th (3); 1971, 18th (3)
Fastest laps: 11

Sutton, Len   United States
Born: 9 Aug 1925
Contested: 1958, Indy 32; **1959**, Indy 32; **1960**, Indy 30
Total contested: 3

Suzuki, Aguri   Japanese
Born: 8 Sep 1960
Contested: 1988, Jap 16; **1990**, US –, Bra –, SM –, Mon –, Can 12, Mex –, Fr 7, GB 6, Ger –, Hun –, Bel –, It –, Por 14, Spa 6, Jap 3, Austral –; **1991**, US 6, SM –, Mon –, Can –, Mex –, Fr –, GB –, Ger –, Hun –, Jap –; **1992**, SA 8, Bra –, Spa 7, SM 10, Mon 11, Fr –, GB 12, Ger –, Hun –, Bel 9, It –, Por 10, Jap 8,

Drivers' Career Records

Austral 8; **1993**, SA –, Bra –, Eur –, SM 9, Sp 10, Mon –, Can 13, Fr 12, GB –, Ger –, Hun –, Bel –, It –, Por –, Jap –, Austral 7; **1994**, Pac –; **1995**, Bra 8, Arg –, SM 11, Ger 6, Pac –
Total contested: 64
World championship position: 1990, 12th (6); 1991, 18th (1); 1995, 17th (1)

Suzuki, Toshio   Japan
Born: 10 March 1955
1993, Jap 12, Austral 14
Total contested: 2

Swaters, Jacques   Belgium
Born: 30 Oct 1926
Contested: 1951, Ger 10, It –; **1953**, Ger 7, CH –; **1954**, Bel –, CH 8, Spa –
Total contested: 7

Swelkert, Bob   United States
Born: 20 May 1926   **Died:** 17 Jun 1956
American champion in 1955, killed in a race in America.
Contested: 1952, Indy 26; **1953**, Indy 20; **1954**, Indy 14; **1955**, Indy 1; **1956**, Indy 6
Total contested: 5 **Won:** 1
World championship position: 1955, 7th (8)

Takahara, Noritake   Japan
Born: 6 Jun 1951
Contested: 1976, Jap 9; **1977**, Jap –
Total contested: 2

Takahashi, Kunimitsu   Japan
Born: 29 Jan 1940
Contested: 1977, Jap 9
Total contested: 1

Tambay, Patrick   France
Born: 25 Jun 1949
Contested: 1977, GB –, Ger 6, Aus –, Hol 5, It –, Can 5, Jap –; **1978**, Arg 6, Bra –, SA –, US West 12, Mon 7, Spa –, Swe 4, Fr 9, GB 6, Ger –, Aus –, Hol 9, It 5, US East 6, Can 8; **1979**, Arg –, Bra –, SA 10, US West –, Spa 13, Fr 10, GB 7, Ger –, Aus 10, Hol –, It –, Can –, US East –; **1981**, US West 6, Bra 10, Arg –, SM 11, Mon 7, Spa 13, Fr –, GB –, Ger –, Aus –, Hol –, It –, Can –, US Las Vegas –; **1982**, Hol 8, GB 3, Fr 4, Ger 1, Aus 4, It 2; **1983**, Bra 5, US West –, Fr 4, SM 1, Mon 4, Bel 2, US East –, Can 3, GB 3, Ger –, Aus –, Hol 2, It 4, Eur –, SA –; **1984**, Bra 5, SA –, Bel

7, SM –, Fr 2, Mon –, US East –, US Dallas –, GB 8, Ger 5, Aus –, Hol 6, It –, Eur –, Por 7; **1985**, Bra 5, Por 3, SM 3, Mon –, Can 7, US –, Fr 6, GB –, Ger –, Aus 10, Hol –, It 7, Bel –, Eur 12, Austral –; **1986**, Fr –, GB –, Ger 8, Hun 7, Aus 5, Bra –, Spa 8, SM –, Mon –, Bel –, It –, Por 15, Mex –, Austral –
Total contested: 114 **Won:** 2 **Poles:** 5
World championship position: 1977, 17th (5); 1978, 13th (8); 1981, 18th (1); 1982, 7th (25); 1983, 4th (40); 1984, 11th (11); 1985, 12th (11); 1986, 15th (2)
Fastest laps: 2

Tarquini, Gabriele   Italy
Born: 2 Mar 1962
Contested: 1987, SM –; **1988**, Bra –, SM –, Mon –, Mex 14, Can 8, Hun 13, Bel –, Por 11; **1989**, SM 8, Mon –, Mex 6, US 7, Can –, Fr –; **1990**, GB –, Hun 13, Spa –, Austral –; **1991**, US 7, Bra –, Mon –, Spa 12, Jap 11; **1992**, SA –, Mex –, Bra –, Spa –, SM –, Mon –, Can –, Fr –, GB 14, Ger –, Hun –, Bel –, It –; **1995**, Eur 14
Total contested: 38
World championship position: 1989, 26th (1)

Taruffi, Piero   Italy
Born: 12 Oct 1906   **Died:** 12 Jan 1988
Winner of the last Mille Miglia, a versatile all rounder, and author of a classic guide to competition driving.
Contested: 1950, It –; **1951**, CH 2, Bel –, Ger 5, It 5, Spa –; **1952**, CH 1, Bel –, Fr 3, GB 2, Ger 4, It 7; **1954**, Ger 6; **1955**, Mon 9, GB 4, It 2; **1956**, Fr –, It –
Total contested: 18 **Won:** 1
World championship position: 1951, 6th (10); 1952, 3rd (22); 1955, 6th (9)
Fastest laps: 1

Taylor, Henry   Great Britain
Born: 16 Dec 1932
Later became Ford competition manager.
Contested: 1959, GB 11; **1960**, Fr 4, Hol 7, GB 8, US 14; **1961**, Fr 10, GB –, It 11
Total contested: 8
World championship position: 1960, 19th (3)

Taylor, John   Great Britain
Born: 23 Mar 1933   **Died:** 8 Sept 1966
Died of injuries sustained in the German Grand Prix.

Contested: 1964, GB 14; **1966**, Fr 6, GB 8, Hol 8, Ger –
Total contested: 5
World championship position: 1966, 17th (1)

Taylor, Michael   Great Britain
Born: 24 Apr 1934
Contested: 1959, GB –
Total contested: 1

Taylor, Trevor   Great Britain
Born: 26 Dec 1936
Contested: 1961, Hol 13; **1962**, Hol 2, Mon –, Bel 11, Fr 8, GB 8, Ger –, It –, US 12, SA –; **1963**, Mon 6, Bel –, Hol 10, Fr 13, GB –, Ger 8, US –, Mex –, SA 8; **1964**, Mon –, Bel 7, Fr –, GB –, Aus –, US 6, Mex –; **1966**, GB –
Total contested: 27
World championship position: 1962, 10th (6); 1963, 15th (1); 1964, 19th (1)

Teague, Marshall   United States
Born: 22 May 1921   **Died:** 11 Feb 1959
Killed in a record attempt at Daytona.
Contested: 1953, Indy 18; **1954**, Indy 15, Indy 23; **1957**, Indy 7
Total contested: 3

Templeman, Shorty   United States
Born: 12 Aug 1919   **Died:** 24 Aug 1962
Contested: 1955, Indy 18; **1958**, Indy 19; **1960**, Indy 17
Total contested: 3

Thackwell, Mike   New Zealand
Born: 30 Mar 1961
The youngest driver to start a championship race.
Contested: 1980, Can –; **1984**, Can –
Total contested: 2

Thiele, Alfonso   United States
Born: 1922
Contested: 1960, It –
Total contested: 1

Thompson, Eric   Great Britain
Born: 4 Nov 1919
Contested: 1952, GB 5
Total contested: 1
World championship position: 1952, 16th (2)

Thomson, Johnny   United States
Born: 9 Apr 1922   **Died:** 24 Sep 1960
Contested: 1953, Indy 32, Indy 19; **1954**, Indy 24; **1955**, Indy 4; **1956**, Indy 32; **1957**, Indy 12; **1958**, Indy 23; **1959**, Indy 3; **1960**, Indy 5
Total contested: 8 **Poles:** 1
World championship position: 1955, 13th (3); 1959, 12th (5); 1960, 23rd (2)
Fastest laps: 1

Thorne, Leslie   Great Britain
Born: 23 Jun 1916   **Died:** 13 Jul 1993
Contested: 1954, GB 15
Total contested: 1

Tingle, Sam   Zimbabwe
Born: 24 Aug 1921
Contested: 1963, SA –; **1965**, SA 13; **1967**, SA –; **1968**, SA –; **1969**, SA 8
Total contested: 5

Tinglestad, Bud   United States
Born: 4 Apr 1928   **Died:** 30 Jul 1981
Contested: 1960, Indy 9
Total contested: 1

Titterington, Desmond   Great Britain
Born: 1 May 1928
Contested: 1956, GB –
Total contested: 1

Tolan, Johnnie   United States
Born: 22 Oct 1918   **Died:** 6 Jun 1986
Contested: 1956, Indy 21; **1957**, Indy 20; **1958**, Indy 13
Total contested: 3

Trintignant, Maurice   France
Born: 30 Oct 1917
Viniculturist, sometime mayor of Vergeze, Le Mans winner in 1954.
Contested: 1950, Mon –, It –; **1951**, Fr –, Ger –, It –, Spa –; **1952**, Fr 5, GB –, Ger –, Hol 6, It –; **1953**, Arg 7, Hol 6, Bel 5, Fr –, GB –, Ger –, CH –, It 5; **1954**, Arg 4, Bel 2, Fr –, GB 5, Ger 3, CH –, It 5, Spa –; **1955**, Arg 2, Arg 3, Arg –, Mon 1, Bel 6, Hol –, GB –, It 8; **1956**, Mon –, Bel –, Fr –, GB –, It –; **1957**, Mon 5, Fr –, GB 4; **1958**, Mon 1, Hol 9, Bel 7, Fr –, GB 8, Ger 3, Por 8, It –, Moroccan –; **1959**, Mon 3, Hol 8, Fr 11, GB 5, Ger 4, Por 4, It 9, US 2; **1960**, Arg 3, Mon –, Hol –, Fr –, GB 11, US 15; **1961**, Mon 7, Bel –, Fr 13, Ger 18,

It 9; **1962**, Mon –, Bel 8, Fr 7, Ger –, It –, US –;
1963, Mon –, Fr 8, It 9; **1964**, Mon –, Fr 11,
Ger 5, It –
Total contested: 82 Won: 2
World championship position: 1952, 16th (2);
1953, 11th (4); 1954, 4th (17); 1955, 4th
(11,33); 1957, 12th (5); 1958, 7th (12); 1959,
5th (19); 1964, 16th (2)
Fastest laps: 1

Trulli, Jarno   Italy
Born: 13 July 1973
1997, Austral 9, Bra 12, Arg 9, SM –, Mon –,
Sp 15, Can –, Fr 10, GB 8, Ger 4, Hun 7, Bel
15, It 10, Aus –
Total contested: 14
World championship position: 1997, 15th (3)

Tunmer, Guy   South Africa
Born: 1 Dec 1948
Contested: 1975, SA 11
Total contested: 1

Turner, Jack   United States
Born: 12 Feb 1920
Contested: 1956, Indy 25; **1957**, Indy 11; **1958**,
Indy 25; **1959**, Indy 27
Total contested: 4

Ulmen, Toni   Germany
Born: 25 Jan 1906   **Died:** 4 Nov 76
Contested: 1952, CH –, Ger 8
Total contested: 2

Unser, Bobby   United States
Born: 20 Feb 1934
A great Indycar driver (he won Indianapolis in
1968, 1975, and 1981) who had a nightmare
grand prix career with BRM. Nephew of Jerry.
Contested: 1968, US –
Total contested: 1

Unser, Jerry   United States
Born: 15 Nov 1932   **Died:** 17 May 59
Uncle of Bobby, killed in practice at India-
napolis.
Contested: 1958, Indy 31
Total contested: 1

Uria, Alberto   Uruguay
Contested: 1955, Arg –; **1956**, Arg 6
Total contested: 2

Vaccarella, Nino   Italy
Born: 4 Mar 1933
Won Le Mans in 1964 and the 1965 and 1971
Targa Florio.
Contested: 1961, It –; **1962**, Ger 15, It 9; **1965**,
It –
Total contested: 4

van de Poele, Eric   Belgium
Born: 30 Sep 1961
Contested: 1991, SM 9; **1992**, SA 13, Hun –,
Bel 10, It –
Total contested: 5

van der Lof, Dries   Holland
Born: 23 Aug 1919   **Died:** 24 May 1990
Contested: 1952, Hol 12
Total contested: 1

van Lennep, Gijs   Holland
Born: 16 Mar 1942
Won Le Mans in 1971 and 1976.
Contested: 1971, Hol 8; **1973**, Hol 6, Aus 9,
It –; **1974**, Bel 14; **1975**, Hol 10, Fr 15, Ger 6
Total contested: 8
World championship position: 1973, 19th (1),
1975, 19th (1)

van Rooyen, Basil   South Africa
Born: 19 Apr 1938
Contested: 1968, SA –; **1969**, SA –
Total contested: 2

Veith, Bob   United States
Born: 1 Nov 1926
Contested: 1956, Indy 7; **1957**, Indy 9; **1958**,
Indy 26; **1959**, Indy 12; **1960**, Indy 8
Total contested: 5

Verstappen, Jos   Holland
Born: 4 Mar 1972
1994, Bra –, Pac –, Fr –, GB 8, Ger –, Hun 3,
Bel 3, It –, Por 5, Eur –; **1995**, Bra –, Arg –,
SM –, Sp 12, Mon –; **1996**, Austral –, Bra –,
Arg 6, Eur –, SM –, Mon –, Sp –, Can –, Fr –,
GB 10, Ger –, Hun –, Bel –, It 8, Por –, Jap 11;
1997, Austral –, Bra 15, Arg –, SM 10, Mon 8,
Sp 11, Can –, Fr –, GB –, Ger 10, Hun –, Bel –,
It –, Aus 12, Lux –, Jap 13, Eur 16
Total contested:
World championship position: 1994, 10th (10);
1996, 16th (1)

Villeneuve, Gilles Canada
Born: 18 Jan 1950 **Died:** 8 May 1982
Killed in practice for the Belgian Grand Prix.
Father of Jacques.
Contested: 1977, GB 11, Can 12, Jap –; **1978**,
Arg 8, Bra –, SA –, US West –, Mon –, Bel 4,
Spa 10, Swe 9, Fr 12, GB –, Ger 8, Aus 3, Hol
6, It 7, US East –, Can 1; **1979**, Arg –, Bra 5,
SA 1, US West 1, Spa 7, Bel 7, Mon –, Fr 2,
GB 14, Ger 8, Aus 2, Hol –, It 2, Can 2, US
East 1; **1980**, Arg –, Bra 16, SA –, US West –,
Bel 6, Mon 5, Fr 8, GB –, Ger 6, Aus 8, Hol 7,
It –, Can 5, US East –; **1981**, US West –, Bra –,
Arg –, SM 7, Bel 4, Mon 1, Spa 1, Fr –, GB –,
Ger 10, Aus –, Hol –, It –, Can 3, US Las
Vegas –; **1982**, SA –, Bra –, US West –, SM 2
Total contested: 67 **Won:** 6 **Poles:** 2
World championship position: 1978, 9th (17);
1979, 2nd (47, total 53); 1980, 10th (6); 1981,
7th (25); 1982, 15th (6)
Fastest laps: 8

Villeneuve, Jacques Canada
Son of Gilles. Indianapolis winner and Indy-
car Champion 1995.
Born: 9 April 1971
1996, Austral 2, Bra –, Arg 2, Eur 1, SM 11,
Mon –, Sp 3, Can 2, Fr 2, GB 1, Ger 3, Hun 1, Bel
2, It 7, Por 1, Jap –; **1997**, Austral –, Bra 1, Arg 1,
SM –, Mon –, Sp 1, Can –, Fr 4, GB 1, Ger –,
Hun 1, Bel 5, It 5, Aus 1, Lux 1, Jap –, Eur 3
Total contested: 33 **Won:** 11 **Poles:** 13
World championship position: 1996, 2nd (78);
1997, 1st (81)
Fastest laps: 9

Villoresi, Luigi Italy
Born: 16 May 1909 **Died:** 24 August 1997
A leading competitor in the immediate pre-
and post-war periods, with victories in the
Targa Florio (1939 and 1940), British Grand
Prix (1948), and Mille Miglia (1951).
Contested: 1950, Mon –, CH –, Bel 6; **1951**,
CH –, Bel 3, Fr 3, GB 3, Ger 4, It 4, Spa –;
1952, Hol 3, It 3; **1953**, Arg 2, Hol 10, Bel 2,
Fr 6, GB –, Ger 8, Ger 15, CH 6, It 3; **1954**, Fr
5, GB –, It –, Spa –; **1955**, Arg –, Arg –, Mon 5;
1956, Bel 5, Fr –, GB 6, Ger –, It –
Total contested: 31 **Poles:** 1
World championship position: 1951, 5th (15,
total 18); 1952, 7th (8); 1953, 5th (17); 1954,
18th (2); 1955, 17th (2); 1956, 19th (2)
Fastest laps: 1

Villota, Emilio de Spain
Born: 26 Jul 1946
Contested: 1977, Spa 13, Aus 17
Total contested: 2

Volonterio, Ottorino Switzerland
Born: 7 Dec 1917
Contested: 1954, Spa –; **1956**, Ger 6; **1957**, It
11
Total contested: 3

von Opel, Rikky Liechtenstein
Born: 14 Oct 1947
Contested: 1973, Fr 15, GB 13, Aus –, It –,
Can –, US –; **1974**, Spa –, Bel –, Swe 9, Hol 9
Total contested: 10

von Trips, Wolfgang Germany
Born: 4 May 1928 **Died:** 10 Sep 1961
In contention for the 1961 championship
when he crashed fatally at Monza, killing
fourteen spectators.
Contested: 1957, Arg 6, Mon –, It 3; **1958**,
Mon –, Fr 3, GB –, Ger 4, Por 5, It –; **1959**,
Mon –, US 6; **1960**, Arg 5, Mon 8, Hol 5,
Bel –, Fr –, GB 6, Por 4, It 5, US 9; **1961**,
Mon 4, Hol 1, Bel 2, Fr –, GB 1, Ger 2,
It –
Total contested: 27 **Won:** 2 **Poles:** 1
World championship position: 1957, 14th (4);
1958, 10th (9); 1960, 6th (10); 1961, 2nd (33)

Vonlanthen, Jo Switzerland
Born: 31 May 1942
Contested: 1975, Aus –
Total contested: 1

Vukovich, Bill United States
Born: 13 Dec 1918 **Died:** 30 May 1955
Killed at Indianapolis going for his third
consecutive win.
Contested: 1951, Indy 29; **1952**, Indy 17; **1953**,
Indy 1; **1954**, Indy 1; **1955**, Indy 25
Total contested: 5 **Won:** 2 **Poles:** 1
World championship position: 1952, 22nd (1);
1953, 7th (9); 1954, 6th (8)
Fastest laps: 2

Wacker, Fred United States
Born: 10 Jul 1918
Contested: 1953, Bel 9; **1954**, CH –, It 6
Total contested: 3

Drivers' Career Records

Walker, Dave   Australia
Born: 10 Jun 1941
Contested: 1971, Hol –; **1972**, Arg–, SA 10, Spa 9, Mon 14, Bel 14, Fr 18, GB–, Ger–, Aus–, US –
Total contested: 11

Walker, Peter   Great Britain
Born: 7 Dec 1912   **Died:** 1 Mar 1984
Le Mans winner 1951.
Contested: 1950, GB –; **1951**, GB 7; **1955**, Hol–, GB –
Total contested: 4

Wallard, Lee   United States
Born: 7 Sept 1910   **Died:** 28 Nov 1963
Contested: 1950, Indy 6; **1951**, Indy 1
Total contested: 2 **Won:** 1
World championship position: 1951, 7th (9)
Fastest laps: 1

Walter, Heini   Switzerland
Born: 28 Jul 1927
Contested: 1962, Ger 14
Total contested: 1

Ward, Rodger   United States
Born: 10 Jan 1921
One of the great Indycar drivers with Indianapolis wins in 1959 and 1962 he competed in the 1959 American Grand Prix in a midget racer.
Contested: 1951, Indy 27; **1952**, Indy 23; **1953**, Indy 16; **1954**, Indy 22; **1955**, Indy 28; **1956**, Indy 8; **1957**, Indy 30; **1958**, Indy 20; **1959**, Indy 1, US –; **1960**, Indy 2; **1963**, US –
Total contested: 12 **Won:** 1
World championship position: 1959, 10th (8)

Warwick, Derek   Great Britain
Born: 27 Aug 1954
Desperately unlucky not to win a grand prix, he won Le Mans and the World Sportscar Championship in 1992.
Contested: 1981, US Las Vegas –; **1982**, SA–, Bel–, Hol–, GB–, Fr 15, Ger 10, Aus–, CH–, It –, US Las Vegas –; **1983**, Bra 8, US West–, Fr–, SM–, Mon–, Bel 7, US East–, Can–, GB–, Ger–, Aus–, Hol 4, It 6, Eur 5, SA 4; **1984**, Bra–, SA 3, Bel 2, SM 4, Fr–, Mon–, Can–, US East–, US Dallas–, GB 2, Ger 3, Aus–, Hol–, It –, Eur 11, Por –; **1985**, Bra 10, Por 7, SM 10, Mon 5, Can –, US–, Fr 7, GB 5, Ger–, Aus–, It –, Bel 6, Eur–, Austral–, Hol –;

1986, Can–, Detroit 10, Fr 9, GB 8, Ger 7, Hun–, It –, Por–, Mex–, Austral –; **1987**, Bra–, SM 11, Bel–, Mon–, US–, Fr–, GB 5, Ger–, Hun 6, Aus–, It –, Por 13, Spa 10, Mex–, Jap 10, Austral –; **1988**, Bra 4, SM 9, Mon 4, Mex 5, Can 7, Detroit–, Fr–, GB 6, Ger 7, Hun –, Bel 5, It 4, Por 4, Spa –, Jap –, Austral –; **1989**, Bra 5, SM 5, Mon–, Mex–, US–, Can–, GB 9, Ger 6, Hun 10, Bel 6, It –, Por–, Spa 9, Jap 6, Austral –; **1990**, US–, Bra–, SM 7, Mon–, Can 6, Mex 10, Fr 11, GB–, Ger 8, Hun 5, Bel 11, It –, Por–, Spa–, Jap–, Austral –; **1993**, SA 7, Bra 9, Eur–, SM –, Sp 13, Mon–, Can 16, Fr 13, GB 6, Ger 17, Hun 4, Bel–, It –, Por 15, Jap 14, Austral 10
Total contested: 146
World championship position: 1983, 14th (9); 1984, 7th (23); 1985, 13th (5); 1987, 16th (3); 1988, 7th (17); 1989, 10th (7); 1990, 14th (3); **1993**, 15th (4)
Fastest laps: 2

Watson, John   Great Britain
Born: 4 May 1946
Contested: 1973, GB–, US –; **1974**, Arg 12, Bra–, SA–, Spa 11, Bel 11, Mon 6, Swe 11, Hol 7, Fr 16, GB 11, Ger–, Aus 4, It 7, Can–, US 5; **1975**, Arg–, Bra 10, SA –, Spa 8, Mon–, Bel 10, Swe 16, Hol–, Fr 13, GB 11, Ger–, Aus 10, US 9; **1976**, Bra–, SA 5, US West–, Spa–, Bel 7, Mon 10, Swe–, Fr 3, GB 3, Ger 7, Aus 1, Hol–, It 11, Can 10, US East 6, Jap –; **1977**, Arg–, Bra–, SA 6, US West–, Spa–, Mon–, Bel –, Swe 5, Fr 2, GB–, Ger–, Aus 8, Hol–, It –, US East 12, Can –, Jap –; **1978**, Arg–, Bra 8, SA 3, US West–, Mon 4, Bel–, Spa 5, Swe–, Fr 4, GB 3, Ger 7, Aus 7, Hol 4, It 2, US East–, Can –; **1979**, Arg 3, Bra 8, SA–, US West–, Spa–, Bel 6, Mon 4, Fr 11, GB 4, Ger 5, Aus 9, Hol –, It –, Can 6, US East 6; **1980**, Arg–, Bra 11, SA 11, US West 4, Bel–, Fr 7, GB 8, Ger–, Aus–, Hol–, It –, Can 4, US East –; **1981**, US West–, Bra 8, Arg–, SM 10, Bel 7, Mon–, Spa 3, Fr 2, GB 1, Ger 6, Aus 6, Hol–, It –, Can 2, US Las Vegas 7; **1982**, SA 6, Bra 2, US West 6, Bel 1, Mon–, US East 1, Can 3, Hol 9, GB–, Fr–, Ger–, Aus –, CH 13, It 4, US Las Vegas 2; **1983**, Bra–, US West 1, Fr–, SM 5, Bel–, US East 3, Can 6, GB 9, Ger 5, Aus 9, Hol 3, It –, Eur–, SA –; **1985**, Eur 7
Total contested: 152 **Won:** 5 **Poles:** 2
World championship position: 1974, 14th (6); 1976, 7th (20); 1977, 13th (9); 1978, 6th (25); 1979, 9th (15); 1980, 10th (6); 1981, 6th (27);

1982, 2nd (39); 1983, 6th (22)
Fastest laps: 5

Webb, Spider   United States
Born: 8 Oct 1910   **Died:** 29 Jan 1990
Contested: 1950, Indy 20; **1952,** Indy 22; **1953,**
Indy 19; **1954,** Indy 30
Total contested: 4

Weiler, Wayne   United States
Born: 9 Dec 1934
Contested: 1960, Indy 24
Total contested: 1

Wendlinger, Karl   Austria
Born: 20 Dec 1968
Contested: 1991, Jap –, Austral 20; **1992,** SA –,
Mex –, Bra –, Spa 8, SM 12, Mon –, Can 4, Fr –,
GB –, Ger 16, Hun –, Bel 11, It 10, Por –; **1993,**
SA –, Bra –, Eur –, SM –, Sp –, Mon 13, Can 6,
Fr –, GB –, Ger 9, Hun 6, Bel –, It 4, Por 5, Jap –,
Austral 15; **1994,** Bra 6, Pac –, SM 4; **1995,**
Bra –, Arg –, SM –, Sp 13, Jap 10, Austral –
Total contested: 41
World championship position: 1992, 12th (3);
1993, 11th (7); **1994,** 18th (4)

Westbury, Peter   Great Britain
Born: 26 May 1938
Multiple British Hillclimb Champion.
Contested: 1969, Ger 5*
Total contested: 1

Weyant, Chuck   United States
Born: 3 Apr 1923
Contested: 1955, Indy 12; **1957,** Indy 14; **1958,**
Indy 24; **1959,** Indy 28
Total contested: 4

Wharton, Ken   Great Britain
Born: 21 Mar 1916   **Died:** 12 Jan 1957
Killed in a race in New Zealand.
Contested: 1952, CH 4, Bel –, Hol 10, It 9;
1953, Hol –, Fr –, GB 8, CH 7, It 21; **1954,**
Fr –, GB 8, CH 6, Spa 8; **1955,** GB 9, It –
Total contested: 15
World championship position: 1952, 13th (3)

Whitehead, Graham   Great Britain
Born: 15 Apr 1922   **Died:** 15 Jan 1981
Half brother of Peter.
Contested: 1952, GB 12
Total contested: 1

Whitehead, Peter   Great Britain
Born: 12 Nov 1914   **Died:** 21 Sep 58
Le Mans winner 1951. Half brother of Gra-
ham, killed in the Tour de France.
Contested: 1950, France 3, It 7; **1951,** Fr –,
It –, GB 9, CH 13; **1952,** Fr –, GB 10; **1953,**
GB 10; **1954,** GB –
Total contested: 10
World championship position: 1950, 9th (4)

Whitehouse, Bill   Great Britain
Born: 1 Apr 1909   **Died:** 14 Jul 1957
Contested: 1954, GB 16
Total contested: 1

Widdows, Robin   Great Britain
Born: 27 May 1942
Contested: 1968, GB –
Total contested: 1

Wietzes, Eppie   Canada
Born: 28 May 1938
Contested: 1967, Can –; **1974,** Can –
Total contested: 2

Wilds, Mike   Great Britain
Born: 7 Jan 1946
Contested: 1974, US –; **1975,** Arg –, Bra –
Total contested: 3

Williams, Jonathan   Great Britain
Born: 26 Oct 1942
A promising driver whose career foundered
despite a Ferrari contract.
Contested: 1967, Mex 8
Total contested: 1

Williamson, Roger   Great Britain
Born: 2 Feb 1948   **Died:** 29 Jul 1973
Killed in the Dutch Grand Prix.
Contested: 1973, GB –, Hol –
Total contested: 2

Wilson, Dempsey   United States
Born: 11 Mar 1927   **Died:** 23 Apr 1971
Contested: 1958, Indy 15, **1960,** Indy 33
Total contested: 2

Wilson, Vic   South Africa
Born: 14 Apr 1931
1960, It –
Total contested: 1

Drivers' Career Records

Winkelhock, Manfred Germany
Born: 6 Oct 1951 **Died:** 12 Aug 1985
Killed in a race in Canada.
Contested: 1982, SA 10, Bra 5, US West –,
SM –, Bel –, Mon –, US East –, Hol 12, Fr
11, Ger –, Aus –, CH –, US Las Vegas –;
1983, Bra 16, US West –, Fr –, SM 11,
Mon –, Bel –, US East –, Can 9, GB –, Aus –,
Hol –, It –, Eur 8, SA –; **1984,** SA –, Bel –,
SM –, Fr –, Mon –, Can 8, US East –, US
Dallas 8, GB –, Ger –, Hol –, Por 10; **1985,**
Bra 13, Por –, SM –, Can –, US –, Fr 12,
GB –, Ger –
Total contested: 47
World championship position: 1982, 22nd (2)

Wissell, Reine Sweden
Born: 30 Sep 1941
Contested: 1970, US 3, Mex –; **1971,** SA 4,
Spa –, Mon –, Hol –, Fr 6, GB 13, Ger 8, Aus
4, Can 5, US –; **1972,** Arg –, Spa –, Mon –,
Fr –, Ger –, It 12, Can –, US 10; **1973,** Fr –;
1974, Swe –
Total contested: 22
World championship position: 1970, 15th (4);
1971, 9th (9)

Wunderink, Roelof Holland
Born: 12 Dec 1948
Contested: 1975, Spa –, Aus –, US –
Total contested: 3

Wurz, Alex Austria
Le Mans winner 1996.
Born: 15 Feb 1974
1997, Can –, Fr –, GB 3
Total contested: 3
World championship position: 1997, 14th (4)

Zanardi, Alessandro Italy
Born: 23 Oct 1966
Now a successful Indycar driver (1997 champion).
Contested: 1991, Spa 9, Jap –, Austral 9; **1992,**
Ger –; **1993,** SA –, Bra 6, Eur 8, SM –, Sp 14,
Mon 7, Can 11, Fr –, GB –, Ger –, Hun –;
1994, Sp 9, Can 15, Fr –, GB –, Ger –, Hun
13, It –, Eur 16, Jap 13, Austral –
Total contested: 25
World championship position: 1993, 20th (1)

Zorzi, Renzo Italy
Born: 12 Dec 1946
Contested: 1975, It 14; **1976,** Bra 9; **1977,**
Arg –, Bra 6, SA –, US West –, Spa –
Total contested: 7
World championship position: 1977, 19th (1)

Zunino, Ricardo Argentina
Born: 13 Apr 1949
Contested: 1979, Can 7, US East –; **1980,** Arg
7, Bra 8, SA 10, US West –, Bel –, Fr –; **1981,**
Bra 13, Arg 13
Total contested: 10

Part 3:
Constructors' Records

Constructors' Records A–Z

AFM
AFM 1952, CH ret 1; Ger 9, ret 1; **1953**, Ger ret 3; It 17
Total contested: 4

AGS
AGS–Ford 1987, Bra 12, SM 13; Bel 10; Mon 13; US Detroit 12; Fr 9; GB 9; Ger ret 1; Hun 13; Aus ret 1; Sp ret 1; Jap ret 1; Austral 6; **1988**, Bra ret 1; SM 10; Mon ret 1; Mex 12; Can ret 1; US Detroit ret 1; Fr ret 1; GB ret 1; Ger ret 1; Hun ret 1; Bel 10; It ret 1; Por 9; Sp ret 1; Jap 8; Austral 11; **1989**, SM 8; Mon ret 1; Mex 6; US Phoenix 7; Can ret 1; **1990**, Bra ret 1; Fr 17; GB ret 1; Hun 13; It ret 1; Por ret 1; Sp 9, ret 1; Austral ret 1; **1991**, US Phoenix 7; Bra ret 1; Mon ret 1
AGS – Motori Moderni 1986, It ret 1; Por ret 1
Total contested: 48
Best result: 6th, Austral 1987 and Mex 1989

Alfa Romeo
Alfa Romeo 1950, GB 1, 2, 3, 12; Mon 1, ret 2; CH 1, 2, ret 1; Bel 1, 2, 4; Fr 1, 2, 7; It 1, 3, ret 3; **1951**, CH 1, 3, 4, 5; Bel 1, 9, ret 1; Fr 1, 5, 10, 11; GB 2, 4, 6, 14; Ger 2, ret 3; It 3, ret 3; Sp 1, 3, 5, 6; **1979**, Bel ret 1; Fr 17; It 12, ret 1, Can ret 1; US East ret 1; **1980**, Arg 5, ret 1; Bra 13, ret 1; SA ret 1; US West ret 2; Bel ret 2; Mon ret 2; Fr ret 2; GB ret 2; Ger 5; Aus ret 1; Hol ret 2; It ret 2; Can ret 2; US ret 2; **1981**, US West 4, ret 1; Bra ret 2; Arg 8, 10; SM ret 2; Bel 9, 10; Mon ret 2; Sp 8, 10; Fr 8, 15; GB

ret 2; Ger 9, 15; Aus ret 2; Hol ret 2; It 8, ret 1; Can 4, 7; US Las Vegas 3, ret 1; **1982**, SA 11, 13; Bra ret 2; US West ret 2; SM ret 2; Bel ret 2; Mon 3, ret 1; US East ret 2; Can 6, ret 1; Hol 11, ret 1; GB 7, ret 1; Fr 9, ret 1; Ger 5, ret 1; Aus ret 2; CH 10, 12; It 10, ret 1; US Las Vegas 9, 10; **1983**, Bra ret 1; US West ret 2; Fr 12, ret 1; SM 10, ret 1; Mon 6, ret 1; Bel ret 2; US Detroit 12, ret 1; Can 10, ret 1; GB 7, 8; Ger 2, ret 1; Aus ret 2; Hol 5, ret 1; It ret 2; Eur 4, ret 1; SA 2, ret 1; **1984**, Bra 4, ret 1; SA 4, ret 1; Bel ret 2; SM 7, ret 1; Fr ret 2; Mon ret 1; Can 11, ret 1; US Detroit ret 2; US Dallas ret 1; GB 12, ret 1; Ger ret 2; Aus 10, ret 1; Hol 13, ret 1; It 3, 9; Eur 6, ret 1; Por 8, 17; **1985**, Bra ret 2; Por ret 2; SM, ret 2; Mon ret 2; Can 10, 17; US Detroit 9, ret 1; Fr 10, 11; GB 9, ret 1; Ger ret 2; Aus ret 2; Hol ret 2; It ret 2; Bel ret 2; Eur 9, 11; SA ret 2; Austral ret 2
Total contested: 110 Wins: 10 Poles: 12 Fastest laps: 14

Alfa Romeo Special
1963, SA ret 1; **1965**, SA 10
Total contested: 2

Alta
Alta 1950, GB 13, ret 1; Bel 9; **1951**, GB 15; **1952**, Fr ret 1; GB 12
Total contested: 5

Amon – Ford
Amon Ford 1974, Sp ret 1
Total contested: 1

Constructors' Records

Andrea Moda – Judd
Andrea Moda – Judd 1992, Mon ret 1
Total contested: 1

Arrows
Arrows – BMW 1984, Bel ret 1; SM ret 1; Fr
11; Can ret 1; US Detroit ret 1; US Dallas ret
2; GB 11, ret 1; Ger ret 2, Aus 5, 6; Hol ret 2;
It 10, ret 1; Eur 9, ret 1; Por ret 2; **1985**, Bra
11, ret 1; Por ret 2; SM 2, ret 1; Mon 9, ret 1;
Can 9, 13; US Detroit 7, 11; Fr 9, ret 1; GB 8,
ret 1; Ger 4, 7; Aus 8, ret 1; Hol 9, ret 1; It 9,
ret 1; Bel 7, 10; Eur 10; SA 5, 6; Austral 6, ret
1; **1986**, Bra ret 2; Sp 7, ret 1; SM 7, 9; Mon 8,
9; Bel 9, ret 1; Can ret 1; US Detroit ret 2; Fr
11, ret 1; GB ret 2; Ger ret 2; Hun ret 2; Aus 6,
ret 1; It 7, 8; Por 10, 11; Mex 7, 9; Austral ret 2
Arrows – Ford 1978, Bra 10; SA 9, ret 1; US
West 6, 9; Mon 6, ret 1; Bel ret 2; Sp 14, ret 1:
Swe 2, 14; Fr 8, 15; GB ret 1; Ger 9, ret 1; Aus
ret 1; Hol ret 1; It ret 1; US 16? Can 4; **1979**,
Arg 8; Bra 7, 9; Sa 11, 12; US West 9, ret 1; Sp
8, 10; Bel 5, ret 1; Mon 6, ret 1; Fr 14, 15; GB
ret 2; Ger 6, ret 1; Aus ret 2; Hol 6, ret 1; It 13,
ret 1; Can ret 1; US East ret 1; **1980**, Arg ret 2;
Bra 6, 10; SA 6, ret 1; US West 2, 7; Bel ret 2;
Mon 4, 8; Fr 9, 10; GB 9, 13; Ger 8, 9; Aus 14;
Hol ret 1; It ret 1; Can 11, ret 1; US ret 2;
1981, US West ret 1; Bra 3, ret 1; Arg 7, 9; SM
2; Bel ret 2; Mon ret 2; Sp ret 2; Fr 14; GB 10,
ret 1; Ger 12, ret 1; Aus ret 2; Hol 7, ret 1; It
ret 1; Can ret 1; US Las Vegas 11; **1982**, Bra
10; US West ret 1; Bel 7, ret 1; Mon 9; US
East 8, ret 1; Can 5, 8; Hol 6, 10; GB 9, ret 1;
Fr 13, ret 1; Ger 6, ret 1; Aus 6, ret 1; CH 15;
It 12, ret 1; US Las Vegas 7, 11; **1983**, Bra 6, 9;
US West 5, ret 1; Fr 10, ret 1; SM 6, 8; Mon 7,
ret 1; Bel 11, ret 1; US Detroit 7, 11; Can 7, ret
1; GB 15, 17; Ger 7, 9; Aus 13, ret 1; Hol 8, 14;
It 10, ret 1; Eur 11, ret 1; SA 8, 9; **1984**, Bra 6,
7; SA 9, 12; Bel 8; SM 5; Fr ret 1; Can ret 1;
US Detroit ret 1; **1989**, Bra 5, ret 1; SM 5, 9;
Mon 7, ret 1; Mex 7, ret 1; US Phoenix 3, ret
1; Can ret 2; Fr 7, 12; GB 9; Ger 6, 12; Hun 5,
10; Bel 6, ret 1; It ret 1; Por ret 2; Sp 9, ret 1;
Jap 6, 8; Austral ret 2; **1990**, US Phoenix 10,
12; Bra ret 2; Mon 5; Can 8, ret 1; Mex 17; Fr
10, ret 1; GB 7, ret 1; Ger 9, ret 1; Hun 9, 12;
Bel 10, 13; It 9, 12; Por 9, 13; Sp 10; Jap 9, ret
1
Arrows – Megatron 1987, Bra ret 2; SM 11,
ret 1; Bel 4, ret 1; Mon ret 2; US Detroit 6, ret
1; Fr ret 2; GB 5, ret 1; Ger ret 2; Hun 6, 8;
Aus ret 2; It ret 2; Por 6, 13; Sp 8, 10; Mex 4,
ret 1; Jap 9, 10; Austral ret 2; **1988**, Bra 4, 8;
SM 7, 9; Mon 4, ret 1; Mex 5, 6; Can 7, ret 1;
US Detroit ret 2; Fr 11, ret 1; GB 6, 7; Ger 7,
10; Hun ret 2; Bel 5, 6; It 3, 4; Por 4, ret 1; Sp
ret 2; Jap ret 2; Austral ret 2
Arrows-Yamaha, 1997, Austral 10, ret 1; Bra
17, ret 1; Arg ret 2; SM ret 2; Mon ret 2; Sp ret
2; Can 8, 9; Fr 12, ret 1; GB 6, ret 1; Ger 8, ret
1; Hun 2, ret 1; Bel 7, 13; It ret 2; Aus 7, 13;
Lux 5, 8; Jap 11, 12; Eur ret 2
Total contested:
Best result: 2nd, Swe 1978, US West 1980, SM
1981, SM 1985 **Poles:** 1
Fastest laps: 1
Continued as Footwork; reverted to Arrows,
1997

Aston – Butterworth
Aston – Butterworth 1952, Bel 1 ret; Ger ret 1
Total contested: 2

Aston Martin
Aston Martin 1959, Hol ret 2; GB 6, ret 1; Por
6, 8; It 10, ret 1; **1960**, GB 11, ret 1
Total contested: 5

ATS   (Italy)
ATS 1963, Bel ret 2; Hol ret 2; It 11, 15; US
ret 2; Mex ret 2; **1964**, It ret 1
Total contested: 6

ATS   (Germany)
ATS – BMW 1983, Bra 16; US West ret 1; Fr
ret 1; SM 11; Mon ret 1; Bel ret 1; US Detroit
ret 1; Can 9; GB ret 1; Aus ret 1; Hol ret 1; It
ret 1; Eur 8; SA ret 1; **1984**, SA ret 1; Bel ret 1;
SM ret 1; Fr ret 1; Mon ret 1; Can 8; US
Detroit ret 1; US Dallas 8; GB ret 1; Ger ret 1;
Aus 12; Hol ret 1; It 6; Eur ret 1; Por 13
ATS – Ford 1978, Arg 11, 12; Bra 7; SA 8, ret
1; US West 11, ret 1; Bel 11; Sp 9; Swe 13, 15;
Fr 13, 16; GB ret 2; Ger ret 1; US ret 2; Can
ret 1; **1979**, Bra ret 1; SA ret 1; US West ret 1;
Sp 14; Bel 8; Mon ret 1; Ger ret 1; Aus ret 1;
Hol ret 1; It 11; Can ret 1; US East 5; **1980**,
Arg ret 1; Bra 7; US West ret 1; Bel ret 1; Mon
ret 1; Fr ret 1; GB ret 1; Ger 12; Aus 12; Hol
10; It ret 1; US 8; **1981**, US West ret 1; Arg 12;
SM 13; GB 6; Ger ret 1; Aus ret 1; Hol 10; It
ret 1; Can ret 1; **1982**, SA 9, 10; Bra 5, ret 1;
US West ret 2; SM 5, ret 1; Bel ret 2; Mon ret
2; US East ret 2; Can ret 1; Hol 12, 13; Fr 11,

ret 1; Ger ret 2; Aus ret 1; CH 14, ret 1; It 9; US Las Vegas ret 1
Total contested: 89
Best result: 5th, US East 1979, Bra and SM 1982
(ATS raced Penske cars in 1977 – these are included in the Penske records)

Behra – Porsche
Behra – Porsche **1960**, Arg 12; It 10
Total contested: 2

Bellasi – Ford
Bellast – Ford **1970**, Aus ret 1; **1971**, It ret 1
Total contested: 2

Benetton
Benetton – BMW **1986**, Bra 6, 10; Sp 5, 6; SM 3, ret 1; Mon ret 2; Bel 7, 10; Can ret 2; US Detroit ret 2; Fr ret 2; GB ret 2; Ger 10, ret 1; Hun ret 2; Aus 7, ret 1; It 5, ret 1; Por 8, ret 1; Mex 1, ret 1; Austral 10, ret 1
Benetton – Ford **1987**, Bra 5, ret 1; SM ret 2; Bel ret 2; Mon 8, ret 1; US Detroit ret 2; Fr 5, ret 1; GB 6, 7; Ger ret 2; Hun 4, ret 1; Aus 3, 4; It 5, 7; Por 4, 14; Sp 16, ret 1; Mex 5, ret 1; Jap 5, ret 1; Austral 3, ret 1; **1988**, Bra 7, ret 1; SM 4, 6; Mon 8, ret 1; Mex 7, 8; Can 3, ret 1; US Detroit 3, ret 1; Fr 6, ret 1; GB 3, ret 1; Ger 6, 18; Hun 3, ret 1; Bel ret 2; It 6, 9; Por 3, ret 1; Sp 3, 9; Jap 3, 5; Austral 5, ret 1; **1989**, Bra 4, 6; SM 3, 11; Mon 8, 14, Mex 4, 15; US Phoenix 5, ret 1; Can ret 1; Fr 9, ret 1; GB 3, 11; Ger ret 2; Hun 8, ret 1; Bel 5, 10; It ret 2; Por 4, ret 1; Sp ret 2; Jap 2, ret 1; Austral 2, 5; **1990**, US Phoenix 4, 11; Bra 6, 10; SM 3, 5; Mon ret 2; Can 2, ret 1; Mex 4, 6; Fr 4, 16; GB 5, ret 1; Ger 2, ret 1; Hun 3, ret 1; Bel 4, 5; It 7, 8; Por 5, 6; Sp 3, ret 1; Jap 1, 2; Austral 1, 7; **1991**, US Phoenix 3, ret 1; Bra 5, 7; SM 13, ret 1; Mon 4, ret 1; Can 1, ret 1; Mex 5, ret 1; Fr 8, ret 1; GB 5, ret 1; Ger 8, ret 1; Hun 8, ret 1; Bel 3, 4; It 5, 6; Por 5, 6; Sp 6, 11; Jap 7, ret 1; Austral 4, ret 1; **1992**, SA 4, ret 1; Mex 3, ret 1; Bra 3, ret 1; Sp 2, ret 1; SM 4, ret 1; Mon 4, 5; Can 2, ret 1; Fr 3, ret 1; GB 3, 4; Ger 3, 4; Hun 5, ret 1; Bel 1, 4; It 2, 3; Por 4, 7; Jap 3, ret 1; Austral 2, 3; **1993**, SA ret 2; Bra 3, ret 1; Eur 5, ret 1; SM 2, ret 1; Sp 3, 4; Mon ret 2; Can 2, ret 1; Fr 3, 10; GB 2, 3; Ger 2, 5; Hun 2, ret 1; Bel 2, 6; It 5, ret 1; Por 1, 16; Jap ret 2; Austral 8, ret 1; **1994**, Bra 1, ret 1; Pac 1, ret 1; SM 1, ret 1; Mon 1, 7; Sp 2, ret 1; Can 1, 6; Fr 1, ret

1; GB 8, ret 1; Ger ret 2; Hun 1, 3; Bel 3, ret 1; It 9, ret 1; Por 5, ret 1; Eur 1, ret 1; Jap 2, ret 1; Austral ret 2;
Benetton-Renault, 1995, Bra 1, ret 1; Arg 3, 4; SM 7, ret 1; Sp 1, 2; Mon 1, 4; Can 5, ret 1; Fr 1, ret 1; GB 1, ret 1; Ger 1, 4; Hun 4, 11; Bel 1, 7; It 1, ret 1; Por 2, 7; Eur 1, 5; Pac 1, 6; Jap 1, 3; Austral ret 2; **1996**, Austral 4, ret 1; Bra 2, ret 1; Arg 3, ret 1; Eur 9, ret 1; SM 3, 6; Mon ret 2; Sp 2, ret 1; Can 3, ret 1; Fr 3, 4; GB 2, ret 1; Ger 2, 13; Hun 3, ret 1; Bel 4, 6; It 2, ret 1; Por 4, 6; Jap 4, ret 1; **1997**, Austral 4, ret 1; Bra 2, 6; Arg 6, 7; SM 5, ret 1; Mon 9, ret 1; Sp 3, 10; Can 2, ret 1; Fr 5, ret 1; GB 2, 3; Ger 1, 6; Hun 8, 11; Bel 6, 8; It 2, 7; Aus 10, ret 1; Lux 2, 4; Jap 5, 8; Eur 4, 1
Total contested: 194 **Wins:** 27 **Poles:** 13
Constructors' Championship: 1995
Fastest laps:

BMW
BMW **1952**, Ger 12, ret 3; **1953**, Ger 14, 17
Total contested: 2

Boro – Ford
Boro – Ford **1976**, Sp 13; Bel 8; Swe ret 1; Hol ret 1; It ret 1
Total contested: 5
The Boro was a renamed Ensign

Brabham
Brabham – Alfa Romeo **1976**, Bra 10, 12; SA ret 2; US West 9, ret 1; Sp 4, 6; Bel ret 2; Mon 9, ret 1; Swe 8, ret 1; Fr 4, 11; GB 8, ret 1; Ger 4, 6, ret 1; Aus ret 2; Hol ret 2; It ret 2; Can 7, 17; US ret 2; Jap 2; **1977**, Arg 2, ret 1; Bra ret 2; SA 6, 13; US West ret 2; Sp 6, ret 1; Mon ret 2; Bel 6, ret 1; Swe 5, 10; Fr 2, ret 1; GB 5, ret 1; Ger 3, ret 1; Aus 3, 8; Hol 7, ret 1; It 2, US 12, ret 1; Can ret 2; Jap 7, ret 1; **1978**, Arg 2, ret 1; Bra 3, 8; SA 3, ret 1; US West ret 2; Mon 2, 4; Bel ret 2; Sp 5, ret 1; Swe 1, ret 1; Fr 4, ret 1; GB 2, 3; Ger 7, ret 1; Aus 7, ret 1; Hol 3, 4; It 1, 2; US ret 2; Can 11, ret 2; **1979**, Arg ret 2; Bra ret 2; SA 6, 7; US West 8, ret 1; Sp ret 2; Bel ret 2; Mon 7 ret 1; Fr ret 2; GB ret 2; Ger 12, ret 1; Aus ret 2; Hol 4, ret 1; It 4, ret 1
Brabham – BMW **1982**, SA ret 2; Bel 5, ret 1; Mon ret 1; Can 1; Hol 2, 15; GB ret 2; Fr ret 2; Ger ret 2; Aus ret 2; CH 4, 5; It ret 2; US Las Vegas ret 2; **1983**, Bra 1, ret 1; US West 10, ret 1; Fr 2, ret 1; SM ret 2; Mon 2, ret 1; Bel 4, ret 1; US Detroit 4, ret 1; Can ret 2; GB 2, ret 1;

Constructors' Records

Ger 3, 13; Aus 3, ret 1; Hol 9, ret 1; It 1, ret 1; Eur 1, 7; SA 1, 3; **1984**, Bra ret 2; SA ret 2; Bel 9, ret 1; SM ret 2; Fr 9, ret 1; Mon ret 2; Can 1, ret 1; US Detroit 1, 3; US Dallas 7, ret 1; GB 7, ret 1; Ger ret 2; Aus 2, 4; Hol 5, ret 1; It ret 2; Eur 3, ret 1; Por 6, 10; **1985**, Bra ret 2; Por ret 2; SM 8, ret 1; Mon ret 1; Can 15, ret 1; US Detroit 6, 8; Fr 1, 8; GB 4, 6; Ger ret 2; Aus 6, ret 1; Hol 8, 10; It 2, 4; Bel 5, 8; Eur ret 2; SA ret 2; Austral ret 2; **1986**, Bra 8, ret 1; Sp ret 2; SM 6, ret 1; Mon ret 2; Bel 8; Can ret 2; US Detroit 6, 10; Fr 7, 9; GB 8, ret 1; Ger 7, ret 1; Hun ret 2; Aus ret 1; It ret 2; Por ret 2; Mex 13, ret 1; Austral ret 2; **1987**, Bra ret 2; SM 9, ret 1; Bel 3, ret 1; Mon ret 2; US Detroit 9, ret 1; Fr ret 2; GB ret 2; Ger ret 2; Hun 5, ret 1; Aus ret 2; It ret 2; Por ret 2; Sp 13, ret 1; Mex 3, ret 1; Jap 11, ret 1; Austral 8, ret 1

Brabham – BRM 1964, Hol 9, 13; Bel ret 2; Fr ret 1; GB 11, ret 2; Ger 4, ret 1; Aus ret 2; It 7; US 3, 10; Mex 13, ret 1; **1965**, SA 7, 12; Mon 6, ret 1; Bel 8, ret 1; Fr 6; GB 8, 9, 11; Hol 11, 13; Ger ret 2; It ret 2; US 11; Mex 4; **1966**, Mon ret 1; Fr 6; GB 8; Hol 8; Ger ret 1

Brabham – Climax 1962, Ger ret 1; US 3; SA 4; **1963**, Mon ret 1; Bel 3, ret 1; Hol 2, 11; Fr 4, 5; GB ret 2; Ger 7, ret 1; It 5, 14; US 4, ret 1; Mex 2, 6; SA 2, 13; **1964**, Mon 7, ret 2; Hol 6, ret 2; Bel 3, 6; Fr 1, 3, 12; GB 4, 7, 13; Ger 10, ret 2; Aus 3, 6, 9, ret 1; It 10, 11, 12, ret 1; US 9, ret 2, Mex 1, ret 2; **1965**, SA 8, 16, ret 2; Mon 7, 8, 9, ret 1; Bel 4, 10, ret 1; Fr 4, ret 3; GB 6, 7, ret 2; Hol 3, 5, ret 2; Ger 3, 5, 7, ret 1; It 3, 7, ret 2; US 2, 3, 8; Mex 2, ret 2; **1966**, Mon ret 2; Bel ret 1; Fr 7, ret 1; GB 7, ret 2; Hol ret 1; Ger ret 1; It 6; **1967**, SA 5, ret 2; Hol 9; Bel 8, Fr ret 1; GB ret 1; **1968**, SA ret 1; **1969**, Can ret 1

Brabham – Ford 1963, SA ret 1; **1964**, GB ret 1; **1965**, SA 9, 14; **1966**, Ger 11, ret 2; **1967**, *Ger 2, ret 1; **1969**, SA ret 2; Sp 6, ret 2; Mon 2, ret 3; Hol 5, 6, ret 2; Fr 7, ret 1; GB 2, 5; Ger 1, ret 1,* 2, 3, 5, 6; It 5, 10, ret 2; Can 1, 2, ret 2; US 2, 4, 6, ret 1; Mex 2, 3, 10, 11; **1970**, SA 1, 11, ret 1; Sp ret 2; Mon 2; Bel 5, ret 2; Hol 11; Fr 3, 7; GB 2; Ger 5, ret 1; Aus 3, 13; It 5, ret 1; Can ret 2; US 10, 12, ret 1; Mex ret 2; **1971**, SA 9, ret 2; Sp 9, ret 1; Mon 10, ret 1; Hol 10, ret 1; Fr 12, ret 1; GB 12, ret 1; Ger 6, 9; Aus 3, 5; It ret 1; Can ret 2; US 7, ret 2; **1972**, Arg 7, ret 1; SA 6, ret 1; Sp 7, 10; Mon 9, 12; Bel 13, ret 2; Fr 8, 10, 12; GB 8, 12, ret

1; Ger 6, 7, ret 1; Aus ret 3; It 5, ret 2; Can 4, 8, ret 1; US 11, ret 2; **1973**, Arg 6, ret 1; Bra 11, ret 1; SA 7, ret 1; Sp 10, ret 2; Bel 4, ret 2; Mon 7, 11, ret 1; Swe 4, ret 1; Fr 3, 16, ret 1; GB 6, ret 3; Hol ret 2; Ger 5, 11, ret 1; Aus 4, ret 2; It 6, 12, ret 1; Can 8, 11, 12; US 3, ret 2; **1974**, Arg 7, 12, ret 1; Bra 7, 15, ret 1; SA 1, ret 2; Sp 11, ret 2; Bel 11, 17, ret 3; Mon 6, ret 1; Swe 9, 11, ret 1; Hol 7, 9, 12; Fr 16, ret 1; GB 6, 9, 11; Ger 3, 12, ret 1; Aus 1, 4, ret 1; It 5, 7, ret 1; Can 8, 9, ret 2; US 1, 2, 5; **1975**, Arg 3, ret 1; Bra 1, 8; SA 2, 4; Sp 3, ret 1; Mon 3, 9; Bel 3, 8; Swe 2, ret 1; Hol 4, 5; Fr 14, ret 1; GB 2, ret 1; Ger 1, ret 1; Aus 14, ret 1, It 4, ret 1; US ret 2; **1976**, Bel 12, ret 1; Swe ret 1; GB ret 1; Aus 12, ret 1; **1979**, Can 7, ret 1; US East ret 2; **1980**, Arg, 2, 7; Bra 8, ret 1; SA 4, 10; US West 1, ret 1; Bel ret 2; Mon 3; Fr 4, ret 1; GB 2, 7; Ger 4, ret 1; Aus 5, 10; Hol 1, ret 1; It 1, ret 1; Can 6, ret 1; US ret 2; **1981**, US West 3, ret 1; Bra 12, ret 1; Arg 1, ret 1; SM 1, 4; Bel ret 2; Mon ret 1; Sp ret 2; Fr 3, 9; GB 5, ret 1; Ger 1, 4; Aus 3, ret 1; Hol 2, 4; It 6, ret 1; Can 5, ret 1; US Las Vegas 5, ret 1; **1982**, Bra ret 2; US West 3, ret 1; Mon 1; US East ret 1; Can 2

Brabham – Judd 1989, Bra ret 2; SM ret 2; Mon 3, 6; Mex 9, 10; US Phoenix ret 2; Can ret 1; Fr ret 1; GB ret 2; Ger 8, ret 1; Hun 11, 12; Bel ret 2; It 6; Por 8, 14; Sp ret 2; Jap 5, ret 1; Austral 8, ret 1; **1990**, US Phoenix 5, ret 1; Bra ret 2; SM ret 1; Mon ret 2; Can 7; Mex 11, ret 1; Fr 13, 15; GB 9; Ger ret 2; Hun ret 1; Bel 17, ret 1; It ret 1; Por ret 2; Sp ret 1; Jap ret 2; Austral 12, ret 1; **1992**, SA 13; GB 16; Hun 11

Brabham – Repco 1966, Mon ret 1; Bel 4; Fr 1, 3; GB 1, 2; Hol 1, ret 1; Ger 1, ret 1; It 3, ret 1; US ret 2; Mex 2, 3; **1967**, SA 4, 6; Mon 1, ret 1; Hol 2, 3; Bel ret 2; Fr 1, 2; GB 2, 4, 10; Ger 1, 2, 6; Can 1, 2; It 2, ret 2; US 3, 5, ret 1; Mex 2, 3, 11; **1968**, SA 3, 9, ret 2; Sp ret 1; Mon ret 2; Bel ret 2; Hol 5, ret 2; Fr ret 2; GB, ret 3; Ger 3, 5, 12; It ret 2; Can ret 2; US ret 2; Mex ret 2; **1969**, SA 8, ret 1

Brabham – Yamaha 1991, US Phoenix 11, ret 1; Bra 12, ret 1; SM 8, 11; Mon ret 1; Can ret 1; Mex ret 1; Fr ret 2; GB ret 2; Ger 11, 12; Hun ret 2; Bel 6, 9; It 12, 13; Por 12, ret 1; Sp 10, ret 1; Jap 5; Austral 17

Total contested: 394
Constructors' Championship: 1966 and 1967
Wins: 35 **Poles:** 39
Fastest laps: 41

BRM

BRM 1951, GB 5, 7; **1956**, GB ret 3; **1957**, Mon ret 1; Fr ret 2; GB ret 2; **1958**, Mon 5, ret 1; Hol 2, 3; Bel 5 ret 1; Fr 11, 12, ret 1; GB 5, ret 1; Ger ret 2; Por 4, 6; It ret 3; Moroccan 4, 5, ret 2; **1959**, Mon ret 3; Hol 1, ret 1; Fr 6, 7, ret 2; GB 2, 4, ret 2; Ger 5, 7, ret 1; Por 5, 7, ret 1; It 7, 8, 13; **1960**, Arg 7, ret 1; Mon 5, 7, ret 1; Hol 3, ret 2; Bel, ret 3; Fr ret 3; GB 10, 14, ret 1; Por ret 3; US 5, ret 2; **1962**, Hol 1, 9; Mon 6, ret 1; Bel 2, 13; Fr 3, 9; GB 4, 13; Ger 1, 8; It 1, 2; US 2, ret 1; SA 1, 7, 9; **1963**, Mon 1, 2; Bel 4, ret 1; Hol 5, 10; Fr 3, 10, ret 1; GB 3, 4, 5; Ger 3, ret 2; It 2, 9, ret 1; US 1, 2; Mex 3, 4, ret 1; SA 3, ret 1; **1964**, Mon 1, 2, ret 1; Hol 4, 10, 11; Bel 4, 5, 8; Fr 2, 5, 11; GB 2, 8, 12, ret 1; Ger 2, 5, 6, 7, ret 1; Aus 2, 4, 7, ret 1; It 4, 8, ret 2; US 1, 4; Mex 8, 11; **1965**, SA 3, 6; Mon 1, 3; Bel 2, 5, 12, ret 1; Fr 2, 5; GB 2, 5, 12; Hol 2, 4; Ger 2, 8, ret 1; It 1, 2, ret 3; US 1, ret 1; Mex ret 2; **1966**, Mon 1, 3, 4; Bel ret 3; Fr ret 1; GB 3, 9, ret 1; Hol 2, 4; Ger 4, 5, ret 1; It 7, ret 2; US ret 3; Mex ret 3; **1967**, SA ret 2; Mon 6, ret 2; Hol 8, ret 1; Bel 2, 5, ret 1; Fr 3, 5, ret 1; GB 7, 8, ret 2; Ger 7, ret 2; Can 5, 9, ret 2; It 5, ret 2; US ret 3; Mex ret 3; **1968**, SA ret 2; Sp ret 2; Mon 2, ret 2; Bel 2, ret 2; Hol 3, 7, ret 1; Fr 6, 7, ret 2; GB 8, ret 2; Ger 6, 8, 14; It 4, ret 1; Can 3, ret 1; US ret 3; Mex 4, ret 1; **1969**, SA 7, ret 2; Sp 5, ret 2; Mon ret 3; Hol 9, ret 1; GB ret 2; Ger ret 1; It 1 ret 2; Can 8, ret 2; US 3, ret 2; Mex 6, ret 2; **1970**, SA 9, ret 2; Sp ret 2; Mon 6, ret 1; Bel 1, ret 1; Hol 10, ret 2; Fr 12, ret 2; GB ret 3; Ger ret 2; Aus 4, 5, 11; It ret 3; Can 4, 10, ret 1; US 2, ret 2; Mex 6, 7; **1971**, SA ret 3; Sp 4, 10, ret 1; Mon 9, ret 1; Hol 2, 6, 7; Fr 4, 10, ret 1; GB 8, 9; Ger 11, ret 2; Aus 1, 10, 11, ret 1; It 1, 5, 9, ret 1; Can 9, 12, 14, 15; US 2, 4, 9, 13, 14; **1972**, Arg 9, 10, ret 3; SA 14, ret 3; Sp ret 5; Mon 1, 8, ret 3; Bel 8, 10, ret 2; Fr 15, ret 2; GB 11, ret 2; Ger 4, 9, ret 1; Aus 6, 8, 13; It 6, 8, 11, 12; Can 10, ret 3; US ret 4; **1973**, Arg 7, ret 2; Bra 6, 8, ret 1; SA ret 3; Sp 5, 9, ret 1; Bel 5, 10, ret 1; Mon ret 3; Swe 9, 13, ret 1; Fr 9, 11, 12; GB 7, 12, ret 1; Hol 5, 8, ret 1; Ger ret 3; Aus 5, 6; It 13, ret 2; Can 4, ret 2; US 8, 9, ret 1; **1974**, Arg 5, 9, ret 1; Bra 10, 15, 16; SA 2, 15, 18; Sp 12, ret 2; Bel 5, 16, ret 1; Mon ret 3; Swe ret 2; Hol ret 3; Fr 10, 14, ret 1; GB 12, ret 2; Ger 10, ret 1; Aus ret 1; It ret 3; Can ret 2; US 9; **1975**, Arg ret 1; Bra ret 1; SA 15; Sp ret 1; Bel 9; Swe 13; Hol ret 1; Fr 17; Aus ret 1; It ret 1; **1976**, Bra ret 1; **1977**, Bra ret 1; SA 15

BRM – Climax 1961, Mon 13, ret 1; Hol 8, 9; Bel 13, ret 1; Fr 6, ret 1; GB 9, ret 1; Ger ret 2; It 5, ret 1; US 3, 5

Total contested: 197 **Wins:** 17 **Poles:** 11

Fastest laps: 15

BRP – BRM

BRP – BRM 1963, Bel ret 1; Hol 4; Fr ret 1; GB ret 1; It 4; **1964**, Mon ret 1; Bel 7, 10; Fr ret 2; GB 10; Aus 5, ret 1; It 5; US 6, ret 1; Mex 12, ret 1

Total contested: 13

Best result: 4th, Hol and It 1964

Bugatti

Bugatti 1956, Fr ret 1

Total contested: 1

Coloni – Ford

Coloni – Ford 1987, Sp ret 1; **1988**, Bra ret 1; SM ret 1; Mon ret 1; Mex 14; Can 8; Hun 13; Bel 14, Por 11; **1989**, Mon ret 2; Can ret 1; GB ret 1; Por ret 1

Total contested: 13

Connaught

Connaught 1952, GB 4, 5, 9, 16; Hol ret 1; It 12, 16, ret 1; **1953**, Hol 9, 11, 13, ret 1; Bel 11; Fr 12, ret 2; GB 7, ret 4; Ger 13, ret 3; It 22, ret 2; **1954**, GB 11, 13, 15, 16, ret 1; **1955**, GB ret 3; **1956**, Bel ret 1; GB 4, ret 2; It 3, 5, ret 1; **1957**, Mon 4, ret 1; **1958**, GB ret 2; **1959**, US ret 1

Total contested: 17

Best result: 3rd, It 1956

Connew – Ford

Connew – Ford 1972, Aus ret 1

Total contested: 1

Cooper

Cooper – Alfa Romeo 1962, SA ret 1

Cooper – Alta 1953, Fr ret 1; GB 10; Ger 6; It 16; **1954**, GB ret 1

Cooper – ATS 1967, GB ret 1

Cooper – Borgward 1959, GB 10, 13

Cooper – Bristol 1952, CH 5, 8; Bel 4, 6, 9; Fr ret 1; GB 3, 7, 20, 23, ret 1; Hol 4; It 9, 13, 15, 19; **1953**, Arg 8, 9, ret 1; Hol ret 1; Fr 11, ret 1; GB 8, 9, ret 3; Ger 11, 16; CH 7; It 15, 21; **1954**, GB 10, 20, ret 1; **1955**, GB ret 1; **1956**, GB 12; **1957**, GB 6

Constructors' Records

Cooper – BRM 1968, Sp 3, 4; Mon 3, 4; Bel 6, ret 1; Hol ret 1; Fr 4, ret 1; GB ret 2; Ger ret 2; It ret 1; Can 5, ret 1; US ret 2; Mex 8, ret 1
Cooper – Climax 1957, Mon 6; Fr 7, ret 1; GB 5, 8; Ger 13, 15, ret 4; Pescara 7, ret 2; **1958**, Arg 1; Mon 1, 4, ret 1; Hol 4, 8, 9; Bel 8, ret 1; Fr 6, 14; GB 3, 6, 8, ret 1; Ger 2, 3, 5, 7, 8, ret 5; Por 7, 8, 10; It 5, ret 2; Moroccan 7, 8, 11, 12, 14, 15, ret 3; **1959**, Mon 1, 3, 5, ret 2; Hol 2, 3, 8, ret 1; Fr 3, 5, 11, ret 1; GB 1, 3, 5, 7, 11, 12, ret 2; Ger 4, ret 4; Por 1, 2, 4, ret 2; It 1, 3, 9, 12, ret 1; US 1, 2, 4, ret 3; **1960**, Arg 1, 3, ret 3; Mon 1, 2, 4, ret 3; Hol 1, 7, 8, ret 3; Bel, 1, 2, 3, 6, ret 2; Fr 1, 2, 3, 4, 8, ret 1; GB 1, 4, 5, 8, 9, ret 3; Por 1, 2, 5, 7; It 8, 9, ret 2; US 3, 4, 6, 8, 12, 14, ret 3; **1961**, Mon 6, 11, ret 1; Hol 6, 7, 12; Bel 5, 9, 10, ret 2; Fr 5, 8, 12, ret 4; GB 4, 6, 8, 11, ret 2; Ger 5, 6, 9, 10, 12, ret 2; It 3, 4, 6, ret 3; US 4, 7, 9, 11, ret 3; **1962**, Hol 5, 10, ret 1; Mon 1, ret 1; Bel 14, 15; Fr 2, 4, ret 1; GB 3, 6, 12; Ger 5, 9, 11, ret 2; It 3, 7, 11, ret 1; SA 2, 3, 8; **1963**, Mon 3, 5, 7; Bel 2, 5, ret 1; Hol 13, ret 2; Fr 2, 12, 15; GB 9, ret 2; Ger 6, ret 3; It 3, 6, 7; US 8 ret 2; Mex 5, ret 2; SA 4, 6, 7, 9; **1964**, Mon 5, ret 2; Hol 7, 8; Bel 2, ret 1; Fr 6, 7; GB 6, ret 1; Ger ret 3; Aus ret 2; It 2; US ret 2; Mex 7, 9; **1965**, SA 5, ret 2; Mon 5; Bel 3, 11; Fr ret 2; GB 10, ret 2; Hol ret 2; Ger 4, ret 1; It 5, 8; US 6, ret 1; Mex ret 2; **1967**, SA 2; **1968**, SA ret 1
Cooper – Ferrari 1960, Fr ret 1; GB 16; It 4, ret 1; US 11; **1966**, GB 11; Ger ret 1
Cooper – Ford 1964, GB 14
Cooper – JAP 1950, Mon ret 1
Cooper – Maserati 1959, Mon 6; Fr ret 3; GB ret 2; Ger 6; Por 10; It 11, 14, ret 1; US ret 1; **1960**, Arg 4, 11; Mon ret 1; Hol ret 1; Fr 9, 10, ret 1; GB 15, ret 2; Por ret 2; It ret 2; US 9, 15, ret 1; **1961**, Mon 7; Bel ret 2; Fr 13; GB 12, ret 1; Ger 18, ret 1; It 8, 9, 12; **1963**, SA 12; **1966**, Mon ret 4; Bel 2, 5, ret 3; Fr 4, 8, 9, ret 2; GB 5, 10, ret 2; Hol 7, 9, ret 3; Ger 2, 3, ret 1; It 4, ret 3; US 2, 3, 4, ret 1; Mex 1, 6, ret 3; **1967**, SA 1, ret 3; Mon 5, ret 2; Hol 10, ret 2; Bel 4, 7, 9, 10, ret 1; Fr 4, 6, ret 2; GB 5, 9, ret 3; Ger 5, 8, ret 2; Can 8, 10, ret 1; It 4, 6, ret 2; US 4, 6, ret 2; Mex 6, 10, ret 1; **1968**, SA 7, ret; **1969**, Mon 7
Cooper – OSCA 1959, US ret 1
Total contested: 129
Constructors' Championship: 1959, 1960
Wins: 16 **Poles:** 11
Fastest laps: 14

Dallara
Dallara – Ford 1988, SM ret 1; Mon ret 1; Mex ret 1; US Detroit 8; Fr 12; GB 11; Ger 15; Hun ret 1; Bel 8; It ret 1; Por 7; Sp 10; Jap ret 1; Austral ret 1; **1989**, Bra 13; SM 7, 10; Mon 4, 13; Mex 13, ret 1; US Phoenix 8, ret 1; Can 3, 6; Fr ret 1; GB ret 1; Ger 7, ret 1; Hun 7, ret 1; Bel 11, ret 1; It 11, ret 1; Por ret 2; Sp 7, ret 1; Jap 9, 10; Austral ret 2; **1990**, US Phoenix ret 1; Bra 14, ret 1; SM ret 2; Mon ret 2; Can ret 2; Mex 13, ret 1; Fr ret 2; GB 11, ret 1; Ger ret 1; Hun 10, ret 1; Bel ret 2; It 10, ret 1; Por 15, ret 1; Sp ret 2; Jap ret 2; Austral ret 2
Dallara – Ferrari 1992, SA ret 2; Mex 8, ret 1; Bra 8, ret 1; Sp 6, ret 1; SM 6, 11; Mon 9, ret 1; Can 8, 9; Fr 9, 10; GB 13, 15; Ger 10, 11; Hun ret 1; Bel 7, ret 1; It 8, 11; Por ret 2; Jap 9, 10; Austral ret 2
Dallara – Judd 1991, US Phoenix ret 2; Bra 12, ret 1; SM 3; Mon 6, 11; Can 9, ret 1; Mex ret 1; Fr ret 1; GB 10, 13; Ger 10, ret 1; Hun ret 2; Bel 8, ret 1; It 10, ret 1; Por ret 2; Sp 8, 15; Jap ret 2; Austral 7, 12
Total contested: 68
Best result: 3rd, Can 1989 and SM 1991

de Tomaso
de Tomaso – Conrero 1961, It ret 1
de Tomaso – Ford 1970, SA ret 1; Mon ret 1; Bel ret 1; Hol ret 1; Aus ret 1; It ret 1; Can ret 1; US ret 1
de Tomaso – OSCA 1961, Fr ret 1; It ret 2
Total contested: 10

Eagle
Eagle – Climax 1966, Bel ret 1; Fr 5; GB ret 1; Hol ret 1; Ger 7; US ret 1; Mex 5; **1967**, SA ret 1; Can ret 1; **1969**, Can ret 1
Eagle – Weslake 1966, It ret 1; US ret 1; Mex ret 1; **1967**; Mon ret 1; Hol ret 1; Bel 1; Fr ret 2; GB ret 2; Ger ret 2; Can 3; It ret 2; US ret 1; Mex ret 1; **1968**, SA ret 1; Mon ret 1; GB ret 1; Ger 9; It ret 1
Total contested: 25 **Wins:** 1
Fastest laps: 2

Emeryson
Emeryson 1956, GB ret 1
Emeryson – Climax 1962, Hol 14; GB 11; It ret 1
Total contested: 4

ret 1; Sp ret 1; Mon ret 1; Hol 3; Fr ret 1; GB ret 2; It ret 1; Can ret 1; US 5; Mex 7; **1970**, SA ret 1; Sp rep 1; Mon ret 1; Bel 4, 8; Hol 3, 4; Fr 14, ret 1; GB 4, ret 1; Ger 2, ret 1; Aus 1, 2, 7; It 1, ret 2; Can 1, 2; US 4, 13; Mex 1, 2; **1971**, SA 1, 3, 8; Sp 2, ret 2; Mon 3, ret 1; Hol 1, 3, ret 1; Fr ret 2; GB ret 2; Ger 3, 4, ret 1; Aus ret 2; It ret 2; Can 8, 13, ret 1; US 6, ret 1; **1972**, Arg 3, 4, ret 1; SA 4, 8, 12; Sp 2, 3, ret 1; Mon 2, ret 1; Bel ret 2; Fr 11, 13; GB 6, ret 1; Ger 1, 2, 12; Aus ret 2; It 7, ret 2; Can 5, 12; US 5, 6, 8; **1973**, Arg 4, 9; Bra 4, 5; SA 4, ret 1; Sp 12; Bel ret 1; Mon ret 2; Swe 6; Fr 5, 7; GB 8; Aus 7; It 8, ret 1; Can 15; US 16; **1974**, Arg 2, 3; Bra 2, ret 1; SA 16, ret 1; Sp 1, 2; Bel 2, 4; Mon 4, ret 1; Swe ret 2; Hol 1, 2; Fr 2, 3; GB 4, 5; Ger 1, ret 1; Aus 5, ret 1; It ret 2; Can 2, ret 1; US 11, ret 1; **1975**, Arg 4, 6; Bra 4, 5; SA 5, 16; Sp ret 2; Mon 1, ret 1; Bel 1, 5; Swe 1, 3; Hol 2, 3; Fr 1, ret 1; GB 8, 13; Ger 3, ret 1; Aus 6, 7; It 1, 3; US ret 1; **1976**, Bra 1, 7; SA 1, ret 1; US West 1, 2; Sp 2, 11; Bel 1, 2; Mon 1, ret 1; Swe 3, 6; Fr ret 2; GB 1, ret 1; Ger 9, ret 1; Hol 2; It 2, 4, 9; Can 6, 8; US 3, 7; Jap 5, ret 1; **1977**, Arg 3, ret 1; Bra 1, 3; SA 1, 8; US West 2, ret 1; Sp 2; Mon 2, 3; Bel 2, ret 1; Swe 3, ret 1; Fr 5, 6; GB 2, 15; Ger 1, 4; Aus 2, 4; Hol 1, 6; It 2, ret 1; US 4, 6; Can 12, ret 1; Jap 2, ret 1; **1978**, Arg 7, 8; Bra 1, ret 1; SA ret 2; US West 1, ret 1; Mon 8, ret 1; Bel 3, 4; Sp 10, ret 1; Swe 9, 10; Fr 12, 18; GB 1, ret 1; Ger 8, ret 1; Aus 3, ret 1; Hol 6, 7; It 3, 7; US 1, ret 1; Can 1, 3; **1979**, Arg ret 2; Bra 5, 6; SA 1, 2; US West 1, 2; Sp 4, 7; Bel 1, 7; Mon 1, ret 1; Fr 2, 7; GB 5, 14; Ger 4, 8; Aus 2, 4; Hol 2, ret 1; It 1, 2; Can 2, 4; US East 1, ret 1; **1980**, Arg ret 2; Bra 16, ret 1; SA ret 2; US West 5, ret 1; Bel 6, 8; Mon 5, ret 1; Fr 8, 12; GB 10, ret 1; Ger 6, 13; Aus 8, 13; Hol 7, 9; It 8, ret 1; Can 5; US 11, ret 1; **1981**, US West ret 2; Bra ret 2; Arg ret 2; SM 5, 7; Bel 4, 8; Mon 1, 4; Sp 1, 15; Fr 5, ret 1; GB ret 2; Ger 10, ret 1; Aus 9, ret 1; Hol ret 2; It 5, ret 1; Can 3, ret 1; US Las Vegas 9, ret 1; **1982**, SA 18, ret 1; Bra 6, ret 1; US West ret 2; SM 1, 2; Mon 2; US East 3; Can 9; Hol 1, 8; GB 2, 3; Fr 3, 4; Ger 1; Aus 4; It 2, 3; US Las Vegas ret 1; **1983**, Bra 5, 10; US West 3, ret 1; Fr 4, 7; SM 1, 3; Mon 4, ret 1; Bel 2, ret 1; US Detroit ret 2; Can 1, 3; GB 3, 5; Ger 1, ret 1; Aus 2, ret 1; Hol 1, 2; It 2, 4; Eur 9, ret 1; SA ret 2; **1984**, Bra ret 2; SA 11, ret 1; Bel 1, 3; SM 2, ret 1; Fr 4, ret 1; Mon 3, 6; Can 5, ret 1; US Detroit ret 2; US Dallas 2, ret 1; GB 5, 6; Ger 6, ret 1; Aus

3, 7; Hol 11, ret 1; It 2, ret 1; Eur 2, 5; Por 4, 9; **1985**, Bra 2, 4; Por 2, 8; SM 6, ret 1; Mon 2, ret 1; Can 1, 2; US Detroit 2, 3; Fr 4, ret 1; GB 2, ret 1; Ger 1, 9; Aus 3, 4; Hol 4, ret 1; GB 2, ret 1; Ger 1, 9; Aus 3, 4; Hol 4, ret 1; It 5, 13; Bel ret 2; Eur ret 2; SA 4, ret 1; Austral 5, ret 1; **1986**, Bra ret 2; Sp ret 2; SM 4, 10; Mon 10, ret 1; Bel 3, 4; Can 8, ret 1; US Detroit 4, ret 1; Fr 8, ret 1; GB ret 2; Ger 11, ret 1; Hun 4, ret 1; Aus 2, 3; It 3, ret 1; Por 5, 6; Mex 12, ret 1; Austral 3, ret 1; **1987**, Bra 4, 8; SM 3, ret 1; Bel ret 2; Mon 3, 4; US Detroit 4, ret 1; Fr ret 2; GB ret 2; Ger ret 2; Hun ret 2; Aus ret 2; It 4, ret 1; Por 2, ret 1; SP 15, ret 1; Mex ret 2; Jap 1, 4; Austral 1, 2; **1988**, Bra 2, 5; SM 5, 18; Mon 2, 3; Mex 3, 4; Can ret 2; US Detroit ret 2; Fr 3, 4; GB 9, 17; Ger 3, 4; Hun 4, ret 1; Bel ret 2; It 1, 2; Por 5, ret 1; Sp 6, ret 1; Jap 4, 11; Austral ret 2; **1989**, Bra 1, ret 1, SM ret 2; Mon ret 1; Mex ret 2; US Phoenix, ret 2; Can ret 2; Fr 2, ret 1; GB 2, ret 1; Ger 3, ret 1; Hun 1, ret 1; Bel 3, ret 1; It 2, ret 1; Por 1, ret 1; Sp 2; Jap ret 2; Austral ret 2; **1990**, US Phoenix ret 2; Bra 1, 4; SM 4, ret 1; Mon ret 2; Can 3, 5; Mex 1, 2; Fr 1, 18; GB 1, ret 1; Ger 4, ret 1; Hun 17, ret 1; Bel 2, ret 1; It 2, 4; Por 1, 3; Sp 1, 2; Jap ret 2; Austral 2, 3; **1991**, US Phoenix 2, 12; Bra 4, 6; SM ret 1; Mon 3, 5; Can ret 2; Mex ret 2; Fr 2, 4; GB 3, ret 1; Ger 3, ret 1; . Hun 5, ret 1; Bel ret 2; It 3, ret 1; Por 3, ret 1; Sp 2, 4; Jap 4, ret 1; Austral 6, ret 1; **1992**, SA ret 2; Mex ret 2; Bra 4, 5; Sp 3, 10; SM ret 2; Mon ret 2; Can 3, ret 1; Fr ret 2; GB 9, ret 1; Ger 5, ret 1; Hun 6, ret 1; Bel ret 2; It ret 2; Por ret 2; Jap 5, 12; Austral 4, 11; **1993**, SA 6, ret 1; Bra 8, ret 1; Eur ret 2; SM ret 2; Sp 6, ret 1; Mon 3, 14; Can 4, ret 1; Fr 14, ret 1; GB 9, ret 1; Ger 6, 7; Hun 3, ret 1; Bel 10, ret 1; It 2, ret 1; Por 4, ret 1; Jap 14, ret 1; Austral 4, 5; **1994**, Bra 3, ret 1; Pac 2, ret 1; SM 2, ret 1; Mon 3, 5; Sp 4, ret 1; Can 3, 4; Fr; GB 2, ret 1; Ger 1, ret 1; Hun 12, ret 1; Bel ret 2; It 2, ret 1; Por ret 2; Eur 5, 10; Jap 3, ret 1; Austral 2, 6; **1995**, Bra 3, 5; Arg 2, 6; SM 2, 3; Sp 3, ret 1; Mon 3, ret 1; Can 1, 11; Fr 5, 12; GB 2, ret 1; Ger 3, ret 1; Hun 3, ret 1; Bel ret 2; It ret 2; Por 4, 5; Eur 2, ret 1; Pac 4, 5; Jap ret 2; Austral ret 2; **1996**, Austral 3, ret 1; Bra 3, 7; Arg 5, ret 1; Eur 4, ret 1; SM 2, 4; Mon 7, ret 1; Sp 1, ret 1; Can ret 2; Fr ret 2; GB ret 2; Ger 4, ret 1; Hun 9, ret 1; Bel 1, ret 1; It 1, ret 1; Por 3, 5; Jap 3, ret 1; **1997**, Austral 2, ret 1; Bra 5, 16; Arg 2, ret 1; SM 2, 3; Mon 1, 3; Sp 4, 12; Can 1, ret 1; Fr 1,

3; GB ret 2; Ger 2, ret 1; Hun 4, 9; Bel 1, 10; It 6, 8; Aus 6, ret 1; Lux ret 2; Jap 1, 3; Eur 5, ret 1

Ferrari – Jaguar 1950, It ret 1

Total contested:

Constructors' Championship: 1961, 1964, 1975, 1976, 1977, 1979, 1982 and 1983

Wins: 113 **Poles:** 121

Fastest laps:

*1956 and 1957 results are for the Lancia-Ferraris except for 1 retirement in Germany (1956) and 9th in Argentina in 1957. The total contested does not include the works Ferrari entry at Indianapolis in 1952.

Fittipaldi – Ford

Fittipaldi – Ford 1975, Arg ret 1; Bra 13; Sp ret 1; Bel 12; Swe 17; Hol 11; Fr ret 1; GB 19; Ger ret 1; It 11; US 10; **1976**, Bra 11, 13; SA ret 1; US West 6, SP ret 1; Mon 6; Swe ret 1; Fr ret 1; GB 6; Ger 13; Aus ret 1; Hol ret 1; It 15; Can ret 1; US 9; Jap ret 1; **1977**, Arg 4, ret 1; Bra 4, 7; SA 10; US West 5; Sp 14; Mon ret 1; Bel ret 1; Swe 18; Fr 11; GB ret 1; Aus 11; Hol 4; US 13; Can ret 1; **1978**, Arg 9; Bra 2; SA ret 1; US West 8; Mon 9; Bel ret 1; Sp ret 1; Swe 6; Fr ret 1; GB ret 1; Ger 4; Aus 4; Hol 5; It 8; US 5; Can ret 1; **1979**, Arg 6; Bra 11; SA 13; US West ret 1; Sp 11; Bel 9; Mon ret 1; Fr ret 1; GB ret 1; Ger ret 1; Aus ret 1; Hol ret 1; It 8; Can 8; US East 7; **1980**, Arg 3, ret 1; Bra 9, 15; SA 8, ret 1; US West 3, ret 1; Bel 7, ret 1; Mon 6; Fr 13, ret 1; GB 12; Ger ret 2; Aus 11, 16; Hol ret 1; It 5, ret 1; Can 9, ret 1; US 10, ret 1; **1981**, US West 7, ret 1; Bra 9, ret 1; Arg ret 2; SM ret 1; Bel ret 2; Sp 11, 12; Fr ret 1; GB ret 1; US Las Vegas 10; **1982**, SA 17; Bra ret 1; Bel 6; US East 11; Hol ret 1; GB ret 1; Ger 11; Aus 7; It 11

Total contested: 103

Best result: 2nd, Bra 1978

Fondmetal – Ford

Fondmetal – Ford 1991, Mex ret 1; Fr ret 1; Bel 10, It ret 1; Sp 12; Jap 11; **1992**, SA ret 1; Mex ret 2; Bra ret 1; Sp ret 2; SM ret 1; Mon ret 1; Can ret 1; Fr ret 2; GB 14; Ger ret 1; Hun ret 2; Bel 10, ret 1; It ret 2

Total contested: 19

(successor to Osella)

Footwork

Footwork – Ford 1991, GB ret 1; Por 15; Sp ret 1; Jap 10; Austral 13, 15; **1994**, Bra ret 2; Pac 4, ret 1; SM 13, ret 1; Mon ret 2; Sp ret 2; Can ret 2; Fr 8, ret 1; GB 9, ret 1; Ger 4, 5; Hun 14, ret 1; Bel 6, ret 1; It ret 2; Por 8, 9; Eur 11, 17; Jap 8, ret 1; Austral 8, ret 1

Footwork-Hart, 1995, Bra ret 2; Arg ret 2; SM 13, ret 1; Sp 11, ret 1; Mon 9, ret 1; Can 6, 9; Fr 14, ret 1; GB ret 2; Ger ret 2; Hun ret 2; Bel 12, ret 1; It 7, 8; Por 15, ret 1; Eur 12, ret 1; Pac ret 2; Jap 12, ret 1; Austral 3, ret 1; **1996**, Austral 9, ret 1; Bra ret 2; Arg 6, ret 1; Eur 11, ret 1; SM ret 2; Mon ret 2; Sp ret 2; Can ret 2; Fr 11, ret 1; GB 10, ret 1; Ger 11, ret 1; Hun 8, ret 1; Bel 9, ret 1; It 8, ret 1; Por 14, ret 1; Jap 11, 13

Footwork–Mugen Honda 1992, SA 8, 10; Mex 13; Br 6, ret 1; SP 5, 7; SM 5, 10; Mon 7, 11; Can 7; Fr 7, ret 1; GB 7, 12; Ger 9, ret 1; Hun 7, ret 1; Bel 9, ret 1; It 7, ret 1; Por 6, 10; Jap 8, 15; Austral 8, ret 1; **1993**, SA 7, ret 1; Bra 9, ret 1; Eur ret 2; SM 9, ret 1; Sp 10, 13; Mon ret 2; Can 13, 16; Fr 12, 13; GB 6, ret 1; Ger 17, ret 1; Hun 4, ret 1; Bel ret 2; It ret 2; Por 15, ret 1; Jap ret 2; Austral 7, 10

Footwork – Porsche 1991, US Phoenix ret 1; Mon ret 1; Can ret 2; Mex ret 1; Fr ret 1

Total contested: 91

Best result: 3rd, Austral 1995

(successor to Arrows, continued as Arrows)

Forti

Forti-Ford, 1995, Bra 10, ret 1; Arg ret 2; SM 15, 16; Sp ret 2; Mon 10, ret 1; Can ret 2; Fr 16, ret 1; GB ret 2; Ger ret 2; Hun ret 2; Bel 13, 14; It 9, ret 1; Por 16, 17; Eur 13, ret 1; Pac 16, 17; Jap ret 2; Austral 7, ret 1; **1996**, Bra 11, ret 1; Arg 10, ret 1; SM 10; Mon ret 1; Can ret 2

Total contested: 22

Best Result: 7th, Austral 1995

Frazer Nash

Frazer Nash 1952, CH 4; Bel ret 1; GB 21; Hol 10

Total contested: 4

Best result: 4th, CH 1952

Gilby

Gilby – BRM 1962, Ger ret 1; **1963**, GB ret 1

Gilby – Climax 1961, GB 15

Total contested: 3

Gordini

Gordini 1950, Mon ret 2; Fr ret 4; It ret 2;

Constructors' Records

1951, Fr ret 4; Ger 7, ret 2; It 6, ret 3; Sp 9, ret 2; **1952**, CH 3, ret 3; Bel 3, 8, 10, 14, ret 1; Fr 4, 5, 7, ret 2; GB 11, 14, ret 2; Ger 5, ret 2; Hol 5, 6, ret 2; It 14, 18, ret 1; **1953**, Arg 6, 7, ret 3; Hol 6, 12, ret 1; Bel 5, 7, 9; Fr 10, ret 3; GB ret 3; Ger ret 3; CH ret 2; It 5, 7, 11; **1954**, Arg 5, ret 2; Bel 5, ret 2; Fr 6, ret 3; GB 9, 17, ret 1; Ger 10, ret 3; CH ret 3; It 6, ret 2; Sp ret 2; **1955**, Arg ret 3; Mon 7, ret 2; Hol 8, 10, 11; GB 7, ret 2; It ret 3; **1956**, Mon 5, 6; Fr 8, 9, 11, ret 1; GB 9, ret 1; Ger ret 2; It 9, ret 2
Total contested: 40
Best result: 3rd, CH and Bel 1952
Fastest laps: 1
(includes Simca – Gordini)

Hesketh – Ford
Hesketh – Ford 1974, SA ret 1; Sp 14; Bel ret 1; Mon ret 1; Swe 3; Hol ret 1; Fr ret 1; GB ret 1; Ger ret 1; Aus 3; It ret 1; Can 4; US 3; **1975**, Arg 2; Bra 6; SA ret 1; Sp ret 2; Mon ret 2; Bel ret 2; Swe 10, 11, ret 1; Hol 1; Fr 2; GB 4; Ger 8, ret 1; Aus 2, 13, ret 1; It 5, 9, 10; US 4, ret 1; **1976**, SA 15; Bel ret 1; Swe ret 1; Fr 17, ret 1; It 16; Can 20; US 12, 13; Jap 8; **1977**, Sp ret 2; Mon 12; Bel 9, ret 1; Swe 13, 16; Fr 10; GB ret 1; Ger ret 2; Aus 7; Hol ret 1; It 9; US 8, 18; Can ret 1; **1978**, SA ret 1
Total contested: 52 **Wins:** 1
Fastest laps: 1

Hill – Ford
Hill – Ford 1975, Sp ret 2; Bel ret 2; Swe 6, ret 1; Hol 7, 13; Fr 7, 16; GB 10, 15; Ger 5, ret 1; Aus 15, 16; It ret 2; US ret 1
Total contested: 10
Best result: 5th, Ger 1975
(see also Lola)

Honda
Honda 1964, Ger ret 1; It ret 1; US ret 1; **1965**, Mon ret 2; Bel 6, ret 1; Fr ret 2; GB ret 1; Hol 6; It ret 2; US 7, 13; Mex 1, 5; **1966**, It ret 1; US ret 2; Mex 4, 8; **1967**, SA 3; Mon ret 1; Hol ret 1; Bel ret 1; GB 6; Ger 4; It 1; US ret 1; Mex 4; **1968**, SA 8; Sp ret 1; Mon ret 1; Bel ret 1; Hol ret 1; Fr 2, ret 1; GB 5; Ger ret 1; It ret 2; Can ret 1; US 3; Mex 5, ret 1
Total contested: 35 **Wins:** 1 **Poles:** 1
Fastest laps: 2

HWM
HW 1951, CH 8, ret 1; **1952**, CH ret 4; Bel 5, 11, 12, 15, ret 1; Fr 6, 9, 10; GB 15, 22, ret 2;

Ger 10, ret 2; Hol 7, 8, 12; **1953**, Hol 8, ret 1; Bel 10, ret 1; Fr 13, 14, ret 1; GB ret 4; CH 9, ret 2; It 18, 20, ret 2; **1954**, Fr ret 1
Total contested: 14
Best result: 5th, Bel 1952

JBW
JBW – Climax 1961, It ret 1
JBW – Maserati 1959, GB ret 1; **1960**, GB 13; It ret 1; US ret 1
Total contested: 5

Jordan
Jordan – Ford 1991, US Phoenix 10; Bra 13, ret 1; SM ret 2; Mon 8, ret 1; Can 4, 5; Mex 4, ret 1; Fr 6, ret 1; GB 6, ret 1; Ger 5, 6; Hun 7, 9; Bel 13, ret 1; It 7, ret 1; Por 8, 10; Sp 9, ret 1; Jap ret 1; Austral 8, 9
Jordan-Hart, 1993, SA ret 2; Bra ret 1; Eur 10, ret 1; SM ret 2; Sp 11, 12; Mon 9, ret 1; Can 12, ret 1; Fr 7, 11; GB 10, ret 1; Ger 13, ret 1; Hun 9, ret 1; Bel ret 2; It ret 2; Por 13, ret 1; Jap 5, 6; Austral 11, ret 1; **1994**, Bra 4, ret 1; Pac 3, ret 1; SM ret 1; Mon 4, ret 1; Sp 6, ret 1; Can 7, ret 1; Fr ret 2; GB 4, ret 1; Ger ret 2; Hun ret 2; Bel 13, ret 1; It 4, ret 1; Por 4, 7; Eur 4, 12; Jap 5, ret 1; Austral 4, ret 1
Jordan-Peugeot, 1995, Bra ret 2; Arg ret 2; SM 8, ret 1; Sp 5, 7; Mon ret 2; Can 2, 3; Fr 6, 9; GB 11, ret 1; Ger 9, ret 1; Hun 7, 13; Bel 6, ret 1; It ret 2; Por 10, 11; Eur 4, 6; Pac 11, ret 1; Jap 4, ret 1; Austral ret 2; **1996**, Austral ret 2; Bra 12, ret 1; Arg 4, ret 1; Eur 5, 6; SM 5, ret 1; Mon ret 2; Sp ret 2; Can 6, ret 1; Fr 8, 9; GB 4, 6; Ger 6, 10; Hun 6, ret 1; Bel ret 2; It 4, 5; Por 9, ret 1; Jap 5, 9; **1997**, Austral ret 2; Bra 8, ret 1; Arg 3, ret 1; SM 4, ret 1; Mon 6, ret 1; Sp 9, ret 1; Can 3, ret 1; Fr 6, 9; GB 5, 7; Ger 5, 11; Hun 5, ret 1; Bel 2, ret 1; It 4, ret 1; Aus 4, 5; Lux ret 2; Jap 7, 9; Eur
Jordan – Yamaha 1992, SA 11; Mex ret 2; Bra ret 2; Sp ret 1; SM 7, ret 1; Mon ret 2; Can ret 2; Fr ret 2; GB ret 2; Ger 15; Hun 10, ret 1; Bel 14, 15; It ret 1; Por 13, ret 1; Jap 7, ret 1; Austral 6, ret 1
Total contested: 114
Poles: 1
Best result: 2nd, Can 1995 and Bel 1997
Fastest laps: 2

Klenk – Meteor
Klenk – Meteor 1954, Ger ret 1
Total contested: 1

Kojima – Ford
Kojima – Ford 1976; Jap 11; **1977**, Jap 11, ret
1
Total contested: 2
Fastest laps: 1

Kurtis Kraft – Offenhauser
Kurtis Kraft – Offenhauser 1959, US ret 1
Total contested: 1
(excluding Indianapolis)

Lamborghini
Lamborghini 1991, US Phoenix 7; SM 9; Ger
ret 1; Hun 16; It 16; Austral ret 1
Total contested: 6

Lancia
Lancia 1954, Sp ret 2; **1955**, Arg ret 3; Mon 2,
5, 6, ret 1; Bel ret 1
Total contested: 4
Best result: 2nd, Mon 1955 Poles: 2
Fastest laps: 1
(see also Ferrari 1956–7)

Larrousse
raced in 1992 as Venturi-Larrousse-Lamborghini
Larrousse-Lamborghini, 1992, SA 12, ret 1;
Mex 11, 12; Bra 9, ret 1; Sp ret 2; Mon 6;
Can ret 2; Fr ret 2; GB ret 2, Ger 14, ret 1;
Hun ret 2; Bel 17, 18; It 9, ret 1; Por ret 2,
Jap 11, ret 1; Austral ret 2; **1993**, SA ret 2;
Bra 7, 10; Eur 9, ret 1; SM 5, ret 1; Sp 9, ret
1; Mon 12, ret 1; Can 8, ret 1; Fr 9, 16; GB
11, ret 1; Ger 12, ret 1; Hun 8, ret 1; Bel 12,
ret 1; It 6, 9; Por 10, 11; Jap 12; Austral 12,
14
Larrousse-Ford, 1994, Bra 9, ret 1; Pac 6, ret 1;
SM ret 2; Mon 8, 10; Sp ret 2; Can ret 2; Fr 11,
ret 1; GB 14, ret 1; Ger 6, 7; Hun 8, 9; Bel ret
2; It 8, ret 1; Por 14, ret 1; Eur ret 2; Jap 9, ret
1; Austral ret 2
Total contested: 48
Best Result: 5th, SM 1993

LDS
LDS – Alfa Romeo 1962, SA ret 1; **1963**, SA
11, ret 1; **1965**, SA 13
LDS – Climax 1968, SA ret 1
LDS – Repco 1967, SA ret 1
Total contested: 5

Lec – Ford
Lec – Ford 1977, Bel 13; Swe 14; Fr ret 1
Total contested: 3

Leyton House
See March

Ligier
Ligier – Ford 1979, Arg 1, 4; Bra 1, 2; SA ret
2; US West 5, ret 1; Sp 1, ret 1; Bel 2, ret 1;
Mon 5, ret 1; Fr 8, ret 1; GB 6, ret 1; Ger 3, ret
1; Aus 3, ret 1; Hol 5; It ret 2; Can ret 2; US
East ret 2; **1980**, Arg ret 2; Bra 4, ret 1; SA 2,
3; US West 6, ret 1; Bel 1, 11; Mon 2, ret 1; Fr
2, 3; GB ret 2; Ger 1, ret 1; Aus 4, ret 1; Hol 3,
ret 1; It 6, 9; Can 3, 8; US 3, 5; **1983**, Bra ret 2;
US West 7, ret 1; Fr 9, ret 1; SM 9, ret 1; Mon
ret 2; Bel 13, ret 1; US Detroit 10, ret 1; Can
ret 2; GB 10, ret 1; Ger 8, ret 1; Aus 7; Hol 10,
ret 1; It 9; Eur 15, ret 1; SA 10, ret 1; **1989**, Bra
9; SM ret 1; Mon 12, ret 1; Mex 8, 14; Can 5;
Fr 6, ret 1; GB 7; Ger 12, ret 1; Bel 13, ret 1; It
9, ret 1; Por 13; Sp ret 1; Jap ret 1; Austral ret
2; **1990**, US Phoenix ret 1; Bra 11, 12; SM 9,
10; Mon ret 2; Can ret 2; Mex 16, 18; Fr 9, 14;
GB 10, 13; Ger 10, ret 1; Hun 11, 14; Bel 14; It
11, 13; Por 10, ret 1; Sp 7, ret 1; Jap 7, 10;
Austral 10, 11
Ligier – Judd 1988, Bra 9, ret 1; Mon ret 2;
Mex 10, ret 1; Can ret 2; US Detroit ret 2; GB
18, Ger 17; Hun ret 2; Bel 11, ret 1; It 13; Por
10, ret 1; Sp ret 2; Jap 17; Austral 9, ret 1
Ligier – Lamborghini 1991, US Phoenix ret 1;
Bra 10, ret 1; SM 7, 10; Mon 7, 10; Can 8, ret
1; Mex 8; Fr 11, 12; GB ret 1; Ger 9, ret 1;
Hun 10, 17; Bel 11, ret 1; It 11, ret 1; Por 11,
16; Sp ret 2; Jap 9, ret 1; Austral 18, ret 1
Ligier – Matra 1976, Bra ret 1; SA ret 1; US
West 4; Sp 12; Bel 3; Mon 12; Swe 4; Fr 14;
GB ret 1; Ger ret 1; Aus 2; Hol ret 1; It 3; Can
ret 1; US ret 1; Jap 7; **1977**, Arg ret 1; Bra ret
1; SA ret 1; US West 9; Sp 7; Mon 7; Bel ret 1;
Swe 1; Fr 8; GB 6; Ger ret 1; Aus ret 1; Hol 2;
It 8; US 7; Can ret 1; Jap 5, ret 1; **1978**, Arg
16; Bra 9; SA 5; US West 5; Mon ret 1; Bel 5;
Sp 3; Swe 7; Fr 7; GB 10; Ger 3; Aus 5; Hol 8;
It 4; US 11; Can ret 1; **1981**, US West ret 2;
Bra 6, 7; Arg ret 1; SM ret 2; Bel 2, ret 1; Mon
3; Sp 2, ret 1; Fr ret 1; GB 3, ret 1; Ger 3, ret 1;
Aus 1, ret 1; Hol ret 2; It ret 2; Can 1, ret 1; US
Las Vegas 6, ret 1; **1982**, SA ret 2; Bra ret 2;
US West ret 2; Bel 3, 9; Mon ret 2; US East 2,
6; Can 10, ret 1; Hol ret 1; GB ret 2; Fr 14, 16;

Constructors' Records

Ger ret 2; Aus 3, ret 1; CH ret 2; It 6, ret 1; US Las Vegas 3, ret 1

Ligier – Megatron 1987, SM ret 1; Bel 6, 7; Mon 11, 12; US Detroit 10, ret 1; Fr ret 2; GB ret 1; Ger ret 2; Hun 12, ret 1; Aus 8, 10; It 8, 10; Por ret 2; Sp ret 2; Mex ret 2; Jap 13, ret 1; Austral ret 2

Ligier – Mugen Honda, 1995, Bra 8, ret 1; Arg 7, ret 1; SM 9, 11; Sp 6, 9; Mon ret 2; Can 4, 10; Fr 4, 8; GB 4, ret 1; Ger 6, ret 1; Hun 6, ret 1; Bel 3, 9; It ret 2; Por 8, ret 1; Eur 7, ret 1; Pac 8, ret 1; Jap 5; Austral 2, ret 1; **1996**, Austral 7, 10; Bra 6, 8; Arg 8, 1; Eur 11, ret 1; SM 7, ret 1; Mon 1, ret 1; Sp 6, ret 1; Can ret 2; Fr 7, ret 1; GB ret 2; Ger 7, ret 1; Hun 5, ret 1; Bel ret 2; It 6, ret 1; Por 10, ret 1; Jap 7, ret 1

Ligier – Renault 1984, Bra ret 2; SA 5, 10; Bel ret 2; SM ret 1; Fr 10; Mon ret 2; Can ret 2; US Detroit ret 2; US Dallas ret 2; GB 10, ret 1; Ger 7, 8; Aus 8, ret 1; Hol 7, ret 1; It ret 2; Eur 7, 9; Por 12, ret 1; **1985**, Bra 6, ret 1; Por ret 2; SM ret 2; Mon 4, 6; Can 8, 14; US Detroit 10, 12; Fr ret 2; GB 3, ret 1; Ger 3, ret 1; Aus ret 2; Hol ret 2; It 10, ret 1; Bel 9, 11; Eur 8, ret 1; Austral 2, 3; **1986**, Bra 3, 4; Sp ret 2; SM ret 2; Mon 5, 6; Bel 5, ret 1; Can 6, 7; US Detroit 2, ret 1; Fr 5, 6; GB 4, ret 1; Ger 4, ret 1; Hun 9, ret 1; Aus 10, ret 1; It ret 2; Por 7, ret 1; Mex 6, 15; Austral 7, 8; **1992**, SA 7, ret 1; Mex 9, 10; Bra ret 2; Sp ret 2; SM 9, ret 1; Mon 10, 12; Can 6, 10; Fr 5, ret 1; GB 8, 10; Ger 6, 7; Hun ret 2; Bel ret 1; It ret 2; Por 8, ret 1; Jap ret 2; Austral 5, ret 1; **1993**, SA 3, ret 1; Bra 5, ret 1; Eur ret 2; SM 3, ret 1; Sp 7, ret 1; Mon 6, ret 1; Can 5, ret 1; Fr 5, ret 1; GB 7, 14; Ger 3, 8; Hun 5, 7; Bel 7, 11; It ret 2; Por 6, ret 1; Jap 7, 9; Austral 6, 9; **1994**, Bra 11, ret 1; Pac 9, 10; SM 11, 12; Mon 9, ret 1; Sp 7, 8; Can 12, 13; Fr ret 2; GB 12, 13; Ger 2, 3; Hun 6, 10; Bel 7, 10; It 7, 10; Por 10, ret 1; Eur 8, 9; Jap 11, ret 1; Austral 5, 11;

Total contested: 324 Wins: 9 Poles: 9

Fastest laps: 9

(continued as Prost)

Lola

Lola – BMW 1967, Ger ret 1, *3; **1968**, Ger 10

Lola – Climax 1962, Hol ret 2; Mon 4, ret 1; Bel 5; FR 5, ret 1; GB 2, ret 1; Ger 2, ret 1; It ret 2; US ret 1; SA ret 2; **1963**, Mon ret 1; Bel ret 2; Hol ret 1; Fr 7; GB 7, 12, 13; Ger ret 1; It 10, 12; US ret 1; Mex ret 1

Lola – Ferrari,

1993, SA ret 2; Bra 11, 12; Eur 11; SM 7; Sp ret 1; Mon ret 1; Can 15; Fr ret 1; GB ret 1; Ger 16, ret 1; Hun ret 2; Bel 13, 14; It 10, ret 1; Por 14, ret 1; Jap ret 2; Austral ret 2

Lola – Ford 1974, Arg 11, ret 1; Bra 11, ret 1; SA 12; Sp ret 1; Bel 8, 12; Mon 7, 8; Swe 6, 7; Hol ret 2; Fr 13, 15; GB 13, ret 1; Ger 9; Aus 12, ret 1; It 8, ret 1; Can 11, 14; US 8, 12; **1975**, Arg 10, 12; Bra 12, 14; SA 7; **1986**, SM ret 1; Mon ret 2; Bel 11, ret 1; Can 10; US Detroit ret 2; Fr ret 2; GB ret 2; Ger 8, 9; Hun 7, ret 1; Aus 4, 5; It 6, ret 1; Por, ret 2; Mex ret 2; Austral 2, ret 1; **1987**, SM 10; Bel 8; Mon ret 1; US Detroit ret 1; Fr ret 1; GB ret 1; Ger 6; Hun ret 1; Aus 12; It ret 1; Por ret 1; Sp 6; Mex 6, 9; Jap 14, ret 1; Austral 5, ret 1; **1988**, Bra ret 2; SM 12, 17, Mon 7, ret 1; Mex 9, ret 1; Can 10; US Detroit 7, ret 1; Fr 13, ret 1; GB 13, 14; Ger 19, ret 1; Hun 9, 12; Bel 9, ret 1; It ret 2; Por ret 2; Sp 11, 14; Jap 9, 16; Austral 10; **1991**, US Phoenix 6, ret 1; Bra ret 1; SM ret 2; Mon 9, ret 1; Can ret 2; Mex 6, ret 1; Fr ret 2; GB ret 2; Ger ret 2; Hun ret 2; Bel ret 1; It ret 1; Por ret 1; Sp ret 1; Jap ret 1

Lola – Hart 1985, It ret 1; Eur ret 1; Austral ret 1; **1986**, Bra ret 2; Sp 8, ret 1; SM ret 1

Lola – Lamborghini 1989, Bra ret 1; SM ret 2; Mon ret 1; Mex ret 1; US Phoenix ret 1; Can ret 1; Fr 11, ret 1; GB ret 2; Ger ret 2; Hun ret 1; Bel 16, ret 1; It ret 2, Por 9, 11; Sp 6; Jap ret 1; Austral ret 1; **1990**, US Phoenix ret 2; Bra ret 2; SM 13, ret 1; Mon 6, ret 1; Can 9, 12; Mex ret 2; Fr 7, 8; GB 4, 6; Ger ret 2; Hun 6, ret 1; Bel 9, ret 1; It ret 2; Por 14, ret 1; Sp 6, ret 1; Jap 3, ret 1; Austral ret 1

Total contested: 161

Best result: 2nd, GB and Ger 1962 **Poles:** 1 (total contested includes 10 races by the Hill team in 1975; see also Hill)

Lotus

Lotus – BRM 1962, Bel ret 1; Fr ret 2; GB ret 1; Ger ret 1; It 12; US 6; **1963**, Mon ret 3; Bel ret 2; Hol 7, 8; Fr 6, 11, 14, ret 1; GB 6, 11, ret 1; Ger 5, 9, ret 1; It 8, ret 2; US ret 4; Mex 7, 8, 9, ret 1; **1964**, Mon 6, 8; Hol 5, ret 1; Bel ret 2; Fr 8, 10; GB ret 4; Ger ret 3; Aus 8; It 13, ret 1; US 8, ret 1; Mex ret 2; **1965**, SA 11; Mon ret 2; Bel 13, ret 1; Fr ret 2; GB 13, ret 1; Hol 10, 12; Ger ret 2; It 6, 9; US 10, ret 1; Mex 6, ret 1; **1966**, Mon ret 1; Bel ret 1; Fr ret 2; GB ret 2; Hol 5, ret 1; Ger 12, ret 1; It 5, 8, ret 1; US 1, ret 3; Mex 7, ret 1; **1967**, SA ret 3; Mon 2; Hol 7; Can 11

Lotus – Climax 1958, Mon 6, ret 1; Hol 6, ret 1; Bel 4, ret 1; Fr ret 2; GB ret 3; Ger 10, 11, ret 1; Por ret 1; It 6, 7; Moroccan 10, 16; **1959**, Mon ret 2; Hol 4, 7; Fr ret 2; GB 8, 9, ret 1; Ger ret 2; Por ret 2; It ret 2; US 5, ret 1; **1960**, Arg 6, 9, ret 1; Mon 9, ret 2; Hol 2, 4, ret 2; Bel 5, ret 2; Fr 5, 6, 7; GB 2, 3, 12, 17; Por 3, 6, ret 2; US 1, 2, 7, 16, ret 1; **1961**, Mon 1, 8, 10, ret 1; Hol 3, 4, 13; Bel 8, 12, ret 3; Fr 3, 4, 10, 11, 14, ret 3; GB 10, 13, 14, 17, 18, ret 6; Ger 1, 4, 11, 15, 17, ret 2; It 10, 11, ret 6; US 1, 8, 10, 12, ret 4; **1962**, Hol 2, 11, 12, 13, ret 1; Mon ret 5; Bel 1, 6, 8, 9, 10, 11, 16, ret 1; Fr 7, 8, ret 3; GB 1, 5, 7, 8, 15, 16, ret 1; Ger 4, 12, ret 2; It 9, ret 4; US 1, 8, 9, 10, 12, ret 1; SA 5, 6, 10, ret 2; **1963**, Mon 6, 8, 9; Bel 1, ret 1; Hol 1, 12; Fr 1, 8, 13; GB 1, 8, ret 1; Ger 2, 8, 10; It 1, 13; US 3, ret 2; Mex 1, ret 2; SA 1, 8, ret 1; **1964**, Mon 3, 4; Hol 1, 3; Bel 1, 9; fr 4, ret 1; GB 1, 9; Ger 8, 9, ret 1; Aus ret 3; It 6, ret 1; US 5, 7, ret 1; Mex 4, 5, 10; **1965**, SA 1, 4; Mon ret 1; Bel 1, 7; Fr 1, 7; GB 1, 4; Hol 1, 8; Ger 1, ret 3; It ret 3; US ret 3; Mex 3, ret 2; **1966**, Mon ret 1; Bel ret 1; Fr ret 1; GB 4; Hol 3; Ger ret 1; It 9; US 6; Mex ret 1; **1967**, Mon ret 1

Lotus – Ford 1963, SA 12; **1966**, Ger ret 2; **1967**, Hol 1, ret 1; Bel 6, ret 1; Fr ret 2; GB 1, ret 1; Ger ret 2, *1; Can 4, ret 2; It 3, ret 2; US 1, 2, ret 1; Mex 1, ret 2; **1968**, SA 1, 2; Sp 1, ret 1; Mon 1, ret 2; Bel 5, 7, ret 1; Hol 9, ret 2; Fr 11, ret 1; GB 1, ret 2; Ger 2, 11, ret 1; It ret 3; Can 4, ret 3; US 2, 5, ret 1; Mex 1, 3, 6, ret 1; **1969**, SA 2, 4, ret 3; Sp ret 3; Mon 1, 3, 4; Hol 2, 7, ret 1; Fr 6, 9, ret 2; GB 4, 7, 8, 10, ret 1; Ger 4, 5, ret 3, *4; It 2, 8, 9, ret 1; Can 3, 7, ret 3; US 1, ret 4; Mex 9, ret 3; **1970**, SA 5, 6, 8, ret 2; Sp 4, ret 1; Mon 1, 5; Bel ret 3; Hol 1, 7, ret 1; Fr 1, 8, 10; GB 1, 6, 8, ret 2; Ger 1, 4, ret 2; Aus 13, ret 2; Can ret 1; US 1, 3, ret 1; Mex ret 3; **1971**, SA 4, ret 1; Sp ret 2; Mon 5, ret 1; Hol ret 1; Fr 3, 6; GB 3, ret 1; Ger 8, ret 1; Aus 2, 4; Can 5, 7, ret 1; US ret 3; **1972**, Arg 2; SA 2, 10, ret 1; Sp 1, 9; Mon 3, 14; Bel 1, 14; Fr 2, 18; GB 1, ret 2; Ger ret 3; Aus 1, ret 1; It 1; Can 11, ret 1; US 10, ret 2; **1973**, Arg 1, ret 1; Bra 1, ret 1; SA 3, 11, ret 1; Sp 1, ret 1; Bel 3, ret 1; Mon 2, 3; Swe 2, 12; Fr 1, ret 1; GB 2, ret 1; Hol 11, ret 1; Ger 6, ret 1; Aus 1, 11; It 1, 2; Can 2, ret 1; US 1, 6; **1974**, Arg 13, ret 1; Bra 3, 6; SA 13, ret 3; Sp ret 2; Bel ret 2; Mon 1, ret 1; Swe ret 2; Hol 8, 11; Fr 1, 5; GB 3, 10; Ger 4, 5; Aus ret 2; It 1, ret 1; Can 3, 13; US ret 2; **1975**, Arg 8, ret 1; Bra 9, 15; SA 10, 11, 12, 13; Sp 2, ret 1; Mon 4, 8; Bel ret 2; Swe 9, 15; Hol 15, ret 1; Fr 10, ret 1; GB 16, ret 2; Ger ret 2; Aus 5; It 13, ret 1; US 5, ret 1; **1976**, Bra ret 2; SA 10, ret 1; US West ret 1; Sp 3, ret 1; Bel ret 2; Mon ret 1; Swe ret 2; Fr 5, ret 1; GB ret 2; Ger 5, 12; Aus 3, 5; Hol 3, ret 1; It 13, ret 1; Can 3, 12; US ret 2; Jap 1, 6; **1977**, Arg 5; Bra 5, ret 1; SA 12, ret 1; US West 1, 8; Sp 1, 5; Mon 5, ret 1; Bel 1, ret 1; Swe 6, 19; Fr 1, 4; GB 3, 14; Ger ret 2; Aus ret 2; Hol ret 2; It 1, ret 1; US 2, ret 1; Can 9, ret 1; Jap ret 2; **1978**, Arg 1, 5; Bra 4, ret 2; SA 1, 7, 10; US West 2, 4; Mon 10, ret 1; Bel 1, 2; Sp 1, 2, ret 1; Swe 3, 12, ret 1; Fr 1, 2; GB ret 3; Ger 1, 6, ret 1; Aus 1, ret 2; Hol 1, 2, 12; It 6, ret 1; US 15, ret 2; Can 10, ret 1; **1979**, Arg 2, 5, ret 1; Bra 3, ret 1; SA 4, 5, ret 1; US West 4, ret 2; Sp 2, 3, ret 1; Bel 4, ret 2; Mon 3, ret 1; Fr 12, 13, ret 1; GB 8, 9, ret 1; Ger ret 3; Aus ret 2; Hol 7, ret 2; It 5, 7; Can 10, ret 1; US East ret 2; **1980**, Arg ret 2; Bra 2, ret 1; SA 12, ret 1; US West ret 2; Bel 10, ret 1; Mon 7, 9; Fr ret 2; GB ret 2; Ger 7, 16; Aus 6, ret 2; Hol 8, ret 2; It 4, ret 1; Can 10, ret 1; US 4, 6; **1981**, US West ret 2; Bra 5, 11; Arg 6, ret 1; Bel 3, 5; Mon ret 2; Sp 5, 6; Fr 6, 7; GB ret 1; Ger 7, ret 1; Aus 7, ret 1; Hol 5, ret 1; It 4, ret 1; Can 6, ret 1; US Las Vegas 4, ret 1; **1982**, SA 8, ret 1; Bra 3, ret 1; US West 5, 7; Bel 4, ret 1; Mon 4, 5; US East ret 2; Can 4, ret 1; Hol ret 1; GB 4, ret 1; Fr 12, ret 1; Ger 9, ret 1; Aus 1, ret 1; CH 6, 8; It 7, ret 1; US Las Vegas ret 2; **1983**, Bra 12, ret 1; US West 12; Fr ret 1; SM 12; Mon ret 1; Bel ret 1; US Detroit 6; Can ret 1; **1992**, SA 6, 9; Mex 6, 7; Bra 10, ret 1; Sp ret 2; SM ret 1; Mon ret 2; Can ret 2; Fr 4, 6; GB ret 2; Ger ret 2; Hun 4, ret 1; Bel 6, 13; It ret 2; Por 5, ret 1; Jap ret 2; Austral 7, 13; **1993**, SA ret 2; Bra 4, 6; Eur 4, 8; SM 8, ret 1; Sp 14, ret 1; Mon 7, ret 1; Can 10, 11; Fr ret 2; GB 4, ret 1; Ger 10, ret 1; Hun ret 2; Bel 5; It 11, ret 1; Por ret 2; Jap 11, 13; Austral ret 2

Lotus – Honda 1987, Bra 7, ret 1; SM 2, 6; Bel 5, ret 1; Mon 1, 10; US Detroit 1, ret 1; Fr 4, ret 1; GB 3, 4; Ger 3, ret 1; Hun 2, ret 1; Aus 5, 13; It 2; Por 7, 8; Sp 5; Mex ret 2; Jap 2, 6; Austral ret 2; **1988**, Bra 3, 6; SM 3, 8; Mon ret 1; Mex ret 2; Can 4, 11; US Detroit ret 1; Fr 5, 7; GB 5, 10; Ger 9, ret 1; Hun 7, 8; Bel 4, ret 1; It ret 2; Por ret 2; Sp 8, ret 1; Jap 7, ret 1; Austral 3, ret 1

Lotus – Judd 1989, Bra 8, ret 1; SM ret 2;

Mon ret 1; Mex 11, ret 1; US Phoenix ret 2; Can 4; Fr 8, ret 1; GB 4, 8; Ger 5, ret 1; Hun 6, ret 1; It 10, ret 1; Por 7, ret 1; Sp 8, ret 1; Jap 4, ret 1; Austral 4, ret 1; **1991**, US Phoenix ret 1; Bra 9; SM 5, 6; Mon ret 1; Can ret 1; Mex 9, 10; Fr 10; GB 12, 14; Ger ret 1; Hun 14; Bel 7, ret 1; It 14; Por 14, ret 1; Sp ret 1; Jap ret 2; Austral 11, 19

Lotus – Lamborghini 1990, US Phoenix ret 2; Bra ret 2; SM 7, 8; Mon ret 2; Can 6, ret 1; Mex 8, 10; Fr 11, 12; GB ret 2; Ger 8, ret 1; Hun 5, 7; Bell 11, 12; It ret 1; Por ret 2; Sp ret 1; Jap ret 2; Austral ret 2

Lotus – Maserati 1961, It ret 1

Lotus-Mugen Honda, 1994, Bra 7, 10; Pac 7, 8; SM 10, ret 1; Mon 11, ret 1; Sp 9, ret 1; Can 8, 15; Fr 7, ret 1; GB 11, ret 1; Ger ret 2; Hun 13, ret 1; Bel 12, ret 1; It ret 2; Por 11, 16; Eur 16, 18; Jap 10, 13; Austral ret 2

Lotus Pratt and Whitney turbine 1971, Hol ret 1; GB ret 1; It 8

Lotus – Renault 1983, US West ret 1; Fr ret 1; SM ret 1; Mon ret 1; Bel 9; US Detroit ret 1; Can ret 1; GB 4, ret 1; Ger ret 2; Aus 5, ret 1; Hol ret 2; It 5, 8; Eur 3, ret 1; SA ret 2; **1984**, Bra 3, ret 1; SA 7, ret 1; Bel 5, ret 1; SM 3, ret 1; Fr 3, 5; Mon 5, ret 1; Can 4, 6; US Detroit 2, ret 1; US Dallas 3, 6; GB 4, ret 1; Ger 4, ret 1; Aus ret 2; Hol 3, 4; It ret 2; Eur ret 2; Por 5, ret 1; **1985**, Bra 3, ret 1; Por 1, 4; SM 1, 7; Mon 3, ret 1; Can 5, 16; US Detroit 5, ret 1; Fr 5, ret 1; GB 10, ret 1; Ger ret 2; Aus 2, 5; Hol 3, 5; It 3, 6; Bel 1, ret 1; Eur 2, 5; SA ret 2; Austral ret 2; **1986**, Bra 2, 9; Sp 1, ret 1; SM ret 2; Mon 3; Bel 2, ret 1; Can 5, ret 1; US Detroit 1, 7; Fr ret 2; GB 7, ret 1; Hun 2, 5; Aus ret 2; It ret 2; Por 4, 9; Mex 3, ret 1; Austral 6, ret 1

Total contested: 491

Constructors' Championships: 1963, 1965, 1968, 1970, 1972, 1973, 1978

Wins: 79 **Poles:** 107

Fastest laps: 71

Lyncar – Ford

Lyncar – Ford 1975, GB 17

Total contested: 1

McLaren

McLaren – Alfa Romeo 1970, Fr ret 1; Aus 12; It 8; Can ret 1

McLaren – BRM 1967, Mon 4; Hol ret 1; Can 7; It ret 1; US ret 1; Mex ret 1; **1968**, SA 4; Bel ret 1; Hol 8; GB ret 1; It 6; Can ret 1; US ret 1

McLaren – Ford 1966, Mon ret 1; US 5; Mex ret 1; **1968**, Sp 2, ret 1; Mon 5, ret 1; Bel 1, ret 1; Hol ret 2; Fr 5, 8; GB 4, 7; Ger 7, 13; It 1, ret 1; Can 1, 2, ret 1; US 4, 6, ret 1; Mex 2, ret 2; **1969**, SA 3, 5, ret 1; Sp 2, 4; Mon 5, 6; Hol 4, 10, ret 1; Fr 4, 5, 8; GB 3, 6, ret 2; Ger 3, ret 2; It 4, 7; Can 5, ret 1; US ret 1; Mex 1; **1970**, SA 2, ret 2; Sp 2, ret 2; Mon 4, ret 2; Hol 6, ret 2; Fr 4, 6; GB 3, ret 1; Ger 3, ret 1; Aus 10, ret 1; It 4, ret 1; Can 6, ret 1; US 7, 14, ret 1; Mex 3, ret 1; **1971**, SA 6, ret 2; Sp 5, 8; Mon 4, ret 1; Hol 12, ret 1; Fr 9, ret 1; GB ret 3; Ger ret 2; Aus 9, ret 1; It 7, 10; Can 3, 4; US 10, 16, ret 1; **1972**, Arg 2, ret 1; SA 1, 3; Sp 5, ret 1; Mon 5, 15; Bel 3, 7; Fr 7, 9; GB 3, 5; Ger 5, ret 1; Aus 2, 3; It 3, 4; Can 2, 3; US 3, 9, 18; **1973**, Arg 5, 8; Bra 3, ret 1; SA 2, 5, 9; Sp 4, 6; Bel 7, ret 1; Mon 5, 6; Swe 1, 7; Fr 8, ret 1; GB 1, 3, ret 1; Hol 4, ret 1; Ger 3, 9, 12; Aus 8, ret 2; It 15; Can 1, 13, ret 1; US 4, 5, ret 1; **1974**, Arg 1, 4, 10; Bra 1, 5, 12; SA 3, 7, 9, 19; Sp 3, 6, 9; Bel 1, 6, 7; Mon 5, ret 2; Swe 4, ret 2; Hol 3, 4, ret 1; Fr 6, 7, ret 1; GB 2, 7, ret 1; Ger 15, ret 2; Aus 2, 7, ret 2; It 2, 6, 9; Can 1, 6; US 4, ret 1; **1975**, Arg 1, 14; Bra 2, 3; SA 6, 14, ret 1; Sp 1; Mon 2, 6; Bel 7, ret 1; Swe 8, ret 1; Hol ret 2; Fr 3, 4; GB 1, 7; Ger ret 2; Aus 4, 9; It 2, ret 1; US 2, 3; **1976**, Bra 6, ret 1; SA 2, 3; US West 5, ret 1; Sp 1, ret 1; Bel 6, ret 1; Mon 5, ret 1; Swe 5, 11; Fr 1, 15; GB ret 2; Ger 1, 3; Aus 4, 7; Hol 1, 9; It ret 1; Can 1, 5; US 1, 4; Jap 3, ret 1; **1977**, Arg ret 2; Bra 2, ret 1; SA 4, 5; US West 7, ret 1; Sp 4, 13, ret 1; Mon 4, ret 1; Bel 7, ret 1; Swe 2, 11, 12; Fr 3, 9; GB 1, 4, 11, 13; Ger ret 3; Aus 6, 10, 17, ret 1; Hol 9, ret 2; It 4, ret 3; US 1, 10, ret 1; Can 3, 11, ret 1; Jap 1, ret 1; **1978**, Arg 4, 6, 13; Bra ret 3; SA 11, ret 2; US West 12; Mon 7, ret 1; Bel 7, 8, ret 1; Sp 6, ret 1; Swe 4, 8; Fr 3, 9, ret 2; GB 6, 7, 8, ret 1; Ger ret 2; Aus 8, ret 3; Hol 9, 10, ret 3; It 5, 9, 14, ret 2; US 6, 7; Can 8, ret 1; **1979**, Arg 3, ret 1; Bra 8, ret 1; SA 10, ret 1; US West ret 2; Sp 13, ret 1; Bel 6; Mon 4; Fr 10, 11; GB 4, 7; Ger 5, ret 1; Aus 9, 10; Hol ret 2; It ret 2; Can 6, ret 1; US East 6, ret 1; **1980**, Arg 6, ret 1; Bra 5, 11; SA 11; US West 4; Bel ret 2; Mon ret 1; Fr 7, ret 1; GB 6, 8; Ger 11, ret 1; Aus 7, ret 1; Hol 6, ret 1; It 7, ret 1; Can 4, ret 1; US ret 1; **1981**, US West ret 2; Bra 8, ret 1; Arg 11, ret 1; SM 6, 10; Bel 7, ret 1; Mon ret 2; Sp 3, ret 1; Fr 2, 11; GB 1, ret 1; Ger 6, ret 1; Aus 6, 8; Hol ret 1; It 7, ret 1; Can 2, ret 1; US Las Vegas 7, 12;

1982, SA 4, 6; Bra 2, ret 1; US West 1, 6; Bel 1, ret 1; Mon ret 2; US East 1, ret 1; Can 3, ret 1; Hol 4, 9; GB 1, ret 1; Fr 8, ret 1; Ger ret 1; Aus 5, ret 1; CH 3, 13; It 4, ret 1; US Las Vegas 2, ret 1; **1983**, Bra 3, ret 1; US West 1, 2; Fr ret 2; SM 5, ret 1; Bel ret 2; US Detroit 3, ret 1; Can 6, ret 1; GB 6, 9; Ger 5, ret 1; Aus 6, 9; Hol 3; **1993**, SA 2, ret 1; Bra 1, ret 1; Eur 1, ret 1; SM ret 2; Sp 2, 5; Mon 1, 8; Can 14, 18; Fr 4, 6; GB 5, ret 1; Ger 4, ret 1; Hun ret 2; Bel 4, 8; It 3, ret 1; Por ret 2; Jap 3, 10; Austral 1, ret 1

McLaren – Honda 1988, Bra 1, ret 1; SM 1, 2; Mon 1, ret 1; Mex 1, 2; Can 1, 2; US Detroit 1, 2; Fr 1, 2; GB 1, ret 1; Ger 1, 2; Hun 1, 2; Bel 1, 2; It 10, ret 1; Por 1, 6; Sp 1, 4; Jap 1, 2; Austral 1, 2; **1989**, Bra 2, 11; SM 1, 2; Mon 1, 2; Mex 1, 5; US Phoenix 1, ret 1; Can 7, ret 1; Fr 1, ret 1; GB 1, ret 1; Ger 1, 2; Hun 1, 4; Bel 1, 2; It 1, ret 1; Por 2, ret 1; Sp 1, 3; Jap ret 2; Austral ret 2; **1990**, US Phoenix 1, ret 1; Bra 2, 3; SM 2, ret 1; Mon 1, 3; Can 1, 4; Mex 3, 20; Fr 3, 5; GB 3, 14; Ger 1, 3; Hun 2, 16; Bel 1, 3; It 1, 3; Pro 2, 4; Sp ret 2; Jap ret 2; Austral 4, ret 1; **1991**, US Phoenix 1, ret 1; Bra 1, 3; SM 1, 2; Mon 1, ret 1; Can ret 2; Mex 3, ret 1; Fr 3, ret 1; GB 2, 4; Ger 4, 7; Hun 1, 4; Bel 1, 2; It 2, 4; Por 2, ret 1; Sp 5, ret 1; Jap 1, 2; Austral 1, 3; **1992**, SA 3, 5; Mex 4, ret 1; Bra ret 2; Sp 4, 9; SM 3, ret 1; Mon 1, ret 1; Can 1, ret 1; Fr ret 2; GB 5, ret 1; Ger 2, ret 1; Hun 1, 3; Bel 5, ret 1; It 1, 4; Por 2, 3; Jap 2, ret 1; Austral 1, ret 1

McLaren-Mercedes, 1995, Bra 4, 6; Arg ret 2; SM 5, 10; Sp ret 2; Mon 5, ret 1; Can ret 2; Fr 7, 11; GB 5, ret 1; Ger ret 2; Hun ret 2; Bel 5, ret 1; It 2, 4; Por 9, ret 1; Eur 8, ret 1; Pac 9, 10; Jap 2, 7; Austral 4; **1996**, Austral 5, ret 1; Bra 4, ret 1; Arg 7, ret 1; Eur 3, 8; SM 8, ret 1; Mon 2, 6; Sp 5, ret 1; Can 4, 5; Fr 5, 6; GB 3, 5; Ger 5, ret 1; Hun 4, ret 1; Bel 3, ret 1; It 3, ret 1; Por 13, ret 1; Jap 3, 8; **1997**, Austral 1, 3; Bra 4, 10; Arg 5, ret 1; SM 6, ret 1; Mon ret 2; Sp 6, 7; Can 7, ret 1; Fr 7, ret 1; GB 4, ret 1; Ger 3, ret 1; Hun ret 2; Bel ret 2; It 1, 9; Aus 2, ret 1; Lux ret 2; Jap 4, 10; Eur

McLaren – Serenissima 1966, GB 6

McLaren-Peugeot, 1994, Bra ret 2; Pac ret 2; SM 3, 8; Mon 2, ret 1; Sp 11, ret 1; Can ret 2; Fr ret 2; GB 3, ret 1; Ger ret 2; Hun 4, ret 1; Bel 2, ret 1; It 3, 5; Por 3, 6; Eur 3, ret 1; Jap 7, ret 1; Austral 3, 12

McLaren – TAG 1983, Hol ret 1; It ret 2; Eur ret 2; SA 11, ret 1; **1984**, Bra 1, ret 1; SA 1, 2;

Bel ret 2; SM 1, ret 1; Fr 1, 7; Mon 1, ret 1; Can 2, 3; US Detroit 4, ret 1; US Dallas ret 2; GB 1, ret 1; Ger 1, 2; Aus 1, ret 1; Hol 1, 2; It 1, ret 1; Eur 1, 4; Por 1, 2; **1985**, Bra 1, ret 1; Por ret 2; SM 4, ret 1; Mon 1, ret 1; Can 3, ret 1; US Detroit ret 2; Fr 3, ret 1; GB 1, ret 1; Ger 2, 5; Aus 1, ret 1; Hol 1, 2; It 1, ret 1; Bel 3; Eur 4, 7; SA 3, ret 1; Austral ret 2; **1986**, Bra ret 2; Sp 3, 4; SM 1, 5; Mon 1, 2; Bel 6, ret 1; Can 2, 4; US Detroit 3, ret 1; Fr 2, 4; GB 3, ret 1; Ger 5, 6; Hun ret 2; Aus 1, 9; It 4, ret 1; Por 2, ret 1; Mex 2, ret 1; Austral 1, ret 1; **1987**, Bra 1, 3; SM 4, ret 1; Bel 1, 2; Mon 9, ret 1; US Detroit 3, 7; Fr 3, 8, GB ret 2; Ger 2, 7; Hun 3, ret 1; Aus 6, 7; It 6, 15; Por 1, 5; Sp 2, 3; Mex ret 2; Jap 3, 7; Austral ret 2

Total contested: 450

Constructor's Championships: 1974, 1984, 1985, 1988, 1989, 1990, 1991

Wins: 107 **Poles:** 80

Fastest laps: 71

March

March – Alfa Romeo 1971, SA 13; Sp ret 1; Hol ret 1; Fr ret 2; GB ret 2; Ger 12, ret 1; Aus 12; It ret 2; US 11

March – Ford 1970, SA 3, 10, ret 3; Sp 1, 3, 5, ret 1; Mon 7, 8, ret 2; Bel 2, 7, ret 2; Hol 2, 9, ret 3; Fr 2, 9, 11, ret 2; GB 5, 7, 9, ret 3; Ger 7, 8, ret 4; Aus 8, 9, ret 3; It 2, 6, 7, ret 2; Can 3, 9, ret 2; US 5, 9, 11, ret 1; Mex 4, ret 2; **1971**, SA 10, 11, ret 2; Sp ret 3; Mon 2, 8; Hol 4, ret 3; Fr 13, ret 3; GB 2, 4, 11, ret 1; Ger 5, ret 2; Aus 6, 8, ret 2; It 2, 12, ret 2; Can 2, 16, ret 2; US 3, ret 3; **1972**, Arg 6, 8, 11; SA 5, 7, 11, 13, 17; Sp 6, 11, ret 3; Mon 10, 11, 13, 16, 17, ret 1; Bel 5, 9, 11, 12, ret 2; Fr 5, 16, ret 3; GB 7, 9, 10, 13, ret 1; Ger 3, 8, ret 4; Aus 10, 12, 15, ret 2; It 9, 10, 13, ret 1; Can 9, 13, ret 4; US 4, 13, 14, 16, ret 2; **1973**, Arg 10, ret 1; Bra ret 2; SA ret 2; Sp 7, 8; Bel 11, ret 1; Mon 9, ret 3; Swe 8, ret 1; Fr 6, ret 3; GB 4, 11, ret 1; Hol 3, ret 3; Ger 10, 15, 16; Aus ret 3; It 9, ret 1; Can 7, ret 2; US 2, 10, 11; **1974**, Arg 8, ret 2; Bra 9, ret 2; SA 5, 10; Sp 4; Bel 9, ret 1; Mon ret 2; Swe 10, ret 1; Hol 10, ret 1; Fr 11; GB ret 2; Ger 7, 13; Aus 6, 11; It ret 2; Can ret 1; US ret 1; **1975**. Arg 9; Bra ret 1; SA ret 2; Sp 5, 6; Mon ret 1; Bel ret 2; Swe ret 2; Hol 14, ret 1; Fr 18, ret 1; GB 5, 6, ret 2; Ger 7, ret 3; Aus 1, 17, ret 1; It ret 3; US 7, 8; **1976**, Bra 4, 14, ret 1; SA 8, 12, ret 1; US West 10, ret 2; Sp ret 4; Bel ret 4; Mon 4, ret 2; Swe 7, 10, 14, ret 1; Fr

7, 9, 19, ret 1; GB ret 4; Ger ret 3; Aus 6, ret 2; Hol 6, ret 2; It 1, 7; ret 1; Can 9, 14, ret 1; US 5, ret 2; Jap ret 3; **1977**, Arg ret 2; Bra ret 2; SA 14, ret 3; US West 10, ret 2; Sp 10, 11, 12, ret 1; Bel 10, 14, 15, ret 1; Swe 15, ret 1; Fr ret 2; GB 10, ret 2; Ger 8, ret 1; Aus 9, ret 1; Hol 10, 11; It 7, ret 1; US 15, 18, ret 1; Can 8, ret 2; Jap 12; **1981**, SM ret 1; Sp 16; Fr ret 1; GB 7; Ger ret 1; Aus 11; Hol ret 1; It ret 1; Can 8; **1982**, SA 12, 15; Bra 8, ret 1; US West 8, 9; Bel 8, ret 1; US East 7, ret 1; Can 11, ret 1; Hol ret 2; GB 10; Fr ret 1; Ger ret 1; Aus ret 1; CH ret 2; US Las Vegas 12, 13; **1987**, SM ret 1; Bel ret 1; Mon 6; US Detroit ret 1; Fr ret 1; GB ret 1; Ger ret 1; Hun 10; Aus 11; It 13; Por 9; Sp 12; Mex ret 1; Jap ret 1; Austral ret 1

March – Ilmor 1991, US Phoenix ret 2; Bra ret 2; SM 12, ret 1; Mon ret 2; Can ret 2; Mex ret 2; Fr 7, ret 1; GB ret 2; Ger ret 2; Hun 6, 11; Bel ret 2; It 8, 15; Por 7, 17; Sp 7, ret 1; Jap 8, ret 1; Austral 14, 20; **1992**, SA ret 1; Mex ret 1; Bra ret 1; Sp 8, 12; SM 12, 13; Mex ret 1; Can 4, 14; Fr ret 1; GB ret 1; Ger 13, 16; Hun 9, ret 1; Bel 11, 12; It 10, ret 1; Por 11, ret 1; Jap 13, ret 1; Austral 12, ret 1

March – Judd 1988, Bra ret 2; SM 15, ret 1; Mon 10, ret 1; Mex 16, ret 1; Can 5, ret 1; US Detroit ret 1; Fr 8, 9; GB 4, ret 1; Ger 5, 8; Hun 5, ret 1; Bel 3, ret 1; It 5, 8; Por 2, ret 1; Sp 7, ret 1; Jap 10, ret 1; Austral 6, ret 1; **1989**, Bra 3, ret 1; SM ret 2; Mon 11, ret 1; Mex ret 1; US Phoenix ret 2; Can ret 2; Fr ret 2; GB ret 2; Ger ret 2; Hun ret 2; Bel 7, 12; It ret 2; Por 10, ret 1; Sp ret 2; Jap 7, ret 1; Austral 7, ret 1; **1990**, US Phoenix 14, ret 1; SM ret 2; Mon ret 1; Can 10; Fr 2, ret 1; GB ret 1; Ger 7, ret 1; Hun 8, ret 1; Bel 6, 7; It ret 2; Por 12, ret 1; Sp 8, ret 1; Jap ret 2; Austral ret 2

Total contested: 230 Wins: 3 Poles: 5
Fastest laps: 7
(includes Leyton House, 1990 and 1991; does not include RAM 1983)

Martini – Ford
Martini – Ford 1978, Bel 9; Fr 14; Aus 9; Hol ret 1
Total contested: 4

Maserati
Maserati 1950, GB 9, 10, ret 4; Mon 3, 5, ret 3; CH 4, 6, 7, 9, 11; Bel 10; Fr ret 5; It 6, ret 5; **1951**, CH 7, 12; Bel ret 1; Fr ret 2; GB ret 3;

Ger ret 2; Sp 10; **1952**, Fr 8; GB 18, ret 1; Ger ret 3; Hol 9, ret 2; It 2, 5, 8, 11, 17, ret 1; **1953**, Arg 3, 5, ret 2; Hol 3, 5, ret 2; Bel, 3, 4, ret 3; Fr 2, 3, 7, 9, ret 1; GB 2, 4, 6, ret 2; Ger 2, 4, 5, ret 1; CH 4, 5, 8, ret 3; It 1, 6, 8, 9, 13, 14, ret 1; **1954**, Arg 1, 6, 7, 8, ret 3; Bel 1, 3, 6, 7, ret 2; Fr 4, 5, ret 6; GB 3, 6, 8, 12, 14, 18, 19, ret 2; Ger 5, 7, ret 3; CH 4, 5, 6, ret 2; It 8, 9, 10, 11, ret 3; Sp 2, 4, 6, 7, 8, 9, ret 4; **1955**, Arg 5, 6, 7, ret 5; Mon 3, 8, ret 3; Bel, 5, 7, 8, 9, ret 1; Hol 3, 4, 6, 9, ret 2; GB 5, 8, ret 6; It 4, 5, 7, 9, ret 3; **1956**, Arg 2, 3, 4, 6, ret 4; Mon 1, 3, 7, 8, ret 1; Bel 3, 5, 7, 8, ret 3; Fr 3, 5, 6, 7, ret 4; GB 3, 5, 6, 7, 8, 10, ret 4; Ger 2, 3, 4, 5, 6, ret 7; It 1, 4, 6, 7, 10, 11, 12, ret 3; **1957**, Arg 1, 2, 3, 4, 7, 8, 10; Mon 1, 3, ret 4; Fr 1, 5, 6, ret 2; GB 9, ret 5; Ger 1, 6, 7, 8, 10, 11, ret 3; Pescara 2, 3, 4, 6, ret 5; It 2, 4, 5, 9, 10, 11, ret 5; **1958**, Arg 4, 5, 6, 7, 8, 9; Mon ret 2; Hol 10, ret 2; Bel 7, 9, 10, ret 3; Fr 4, 7, 8, 9, 10, ret 2; GB 9, ret 2; Ger ret 2; Por 9, ret 3; It 4, ret 5; Moroccan 6, 9, 13, ret 1; **1959**, Fr 8, 9, 10; GB ret 1; It ret 1; **1960**, Arg 13, 14, ret 3; US 13

Total contested: 68 Wins: 9 Poles: 10
Fastest laps: 15

Maserati – Milan
1950, CH 5; Fr ret 1; It ret 1; **1951**, Fr ret 1
Total contested: 4

Maserati – Platé
1952, CH 6, ret 1; Fr ret 2; GB 17, 19
Total contested: 3
Best result: 6th, CH 1952

Matra
Matra 1968, Mon ret 1; Bel 8; Hol 2; Fr 9; GB ret 1; Ger ret 1; It 5; Can ret 2; US ret 1; Mex 9, ret 1; **1970**, SA 4, 7; Sp ret 2; Mon 3, ret 1; Bel 3, 6; Hol 5, 8; Fr 5, 13; GB ret 2; Ger 6, ret 1; Aus 6, 14; It 3, ret 1; Can 7, 8; US 8, ret 1; Mex 5, 9; **1971**, SA 5; Sp 3, 6; Mon ret 2; Hol 9, ret 1; Fr 5, 7; GB 7, ret 1; It 6; Can 10, ret 1; US 8, 12; **1972**, SA 15; Sp ret 1; Mon 6; Bel 6; Fr 3; GB 4; Ger 15; Aus 5; It ret 1; Can 6; US 15

Matra – BRM 1966, Ger 9

Matra – Ford 1966, Ger 8, 10, ret 1; **1967**, Mon ret 1; Ger* ret 2; US 7; Mex 7; **1968**, SA 6, ret 1; Sp 5; Mon ret 1; Hol 1; Bel 4; Fr 3; GB 6; Ger 1; It 2, ret 1; Can 6, ret 1; US 1; Mex 7, ret 1; **1969**, SA 1, 6; Sp 1, 3; Mon ret 2; Hol 1, 8; Fr 1, 2; GB 1, 9; Ger 2, 6, *1, ret 1; It 1, 3;

Can 4, 6, ret 1; US 2, ret 3; Mex 4, 5, 8
Total contested: 62
Constructors' Championship: 1969
Wins: 9 **Poles:** 4
Fastest laps: 12

Mercedes

Mercedes 1954, Fr 1, 2, ret 1; GB 4, 7; Ger 1, 4, ret 2; CH 1, 3, ret 1; It 1, 4, ret 1; Sp 3, 5, ret 1; **1955,** Arg 1, 4, ret 2; Mon 10, ret 2; Bel 1, 2, ret 1; Hol 1, 2, ret 1; BG 1, 2, 3, 4; It 1, 2, ret 2
Total contested: 12 **Wins:** 9 **Poles:** 8
Fastest Laps: 12

Merzarlo – Ford

Merzarlo – Ford 1978, Arg ret 1; SA ret 1; US West ret 1; Swe ret 1; GB ret 1; Hol ret 1; It ret 1; US ret 1; **1979,** Arg ret 1; US West ret 1
Total contested: 10

Minardi

Minardi – Ferrari 1991, US Phoenix 9, ret 1; Bra 8, ret 1; SM 4, ret 1; Mon 12, ret 1; Can 7, ret 1; Mex 7, ret 1; Fr 9, ret 1; GB 9, 11; Ger ret 2; Hun 13, ret 1; Bel 12, ret 1; It 9, ret 1; Por 4, 9; Sp 13, 14; Jap ret 2; Austral 16, ret 1
Minardi – Ford 1985, Bra ret 1; Por ret 1; **1988,** Bra ret 2; SM 11, ret 1; Mon ret 1; Mex 11; Can 13; US Detroit 6, ret 1; Fr 15, 16; GB 15, ret 1; Hun 10, ret 1; It ret 2; Por 8, ret 1; Sp 12, ret 1; Jap 13, 15; Austral 7; **1989** Bra ret 2; SM ret 2; Mon ret 2; Mex ret 1; US Phoenix ret 2; Can ret 2; Fr ret 1; GB 5, 6; Ger 9; Hun ret 2; Bel 9, 15; It 7, 8; Por 5, 12; Sp ret 2; Jap ret 2; Austral 6; **1990,** US Phoenix 7, ret 1; Bra 9, ret 1; SM 11; Mon ret 2; Can ret 1; Mex 12, 14; Fr ret 1; GB 12, ret 1; Ger ret 1; Hun 15, ret 1; Bel 15, ret 1; It ret 1; Por 11; Sp ret 1; Jap 6, ret 1; Austral 9, ret 1; **1993,** SA 4, ret 1; Bra ret 2; Eur 6, 7; SM 6, ret 1; Sp 8, ret 1; Mon 5, ret 11; Can 9, ret 1; Fr 8, ret 1; GB 12, ret 1; Ger 11, 14; Hun ret 2; Bel ret 2; It 7, 8,; Por 8, 9; Jap 10, ret 1; Austral ret 2; **1994,** Bra 8, ret 1; Pac ret 2; SM ret 2; Mon 6, ret 1; Sp 5, rel 1; Can 9, 11; Fr 5, ret 1; GB 10 ret 1; Ger ret 2; Hun 7, ret 1; Bel 8, 9; It ret 2; Por 12, 13; Eur 14, 15; Jap ret 2; Austral 9, ret 1; **1995,** Bra ret 2; Arg ret 2; SM 12, 14; Sp, ret 1; Mon 7, ret 1; Can 8, ret 1; Fr 13, ret 1; GB 7, 10; Ger ret 2; Hun 8, 9; Bel 10, ret 1; It ret 2; Por 14, ret 1; Eur 9, 11; Pac 13, 15; Jap 9, 11; Austral 6; **1996,** Austral ret 2; Bra 10, ret 1; Arg ret 2; Eur 12, 13; SM 9, ret 1; Mon ret 2; Sp ret 2; Can 8, ret 1; Fr

12, ret 1; GB 11, ret 1; Ger 12; Hun 10, ret 1; Bel 10; It ret 2; Por 15, 16; Jap 12
Minardi – Hart 1997, Austral 9, ret 1; Bra 12, 18; Arg 9, ret 1; SM 11, ret 1; Mon 10, ret 1; Sp 15, ret 1; Can ret 2; Fr 11, ret 1; GB 10, ret 1; Ger ret 2; Hun 10, 12; Bel 14, ret 1; It 14, ret 1; Aus 11; Lux ret 2; Jap ret 2; Eur 15, 17
Minardi – Lamborghini 1992, SA ret 2; Mex ret 2; Bra 7, ret 1; Sp 11, ret 1; SM ret 2; Mon 8, ret 1; Can 11, 13; Fr 8; GB 17; Ger 12, ret 1; Bel 16; It ret 1; Por 12, 14; Jap 6, 14; Austral 9, 10
Minardi – Motori Moderni 1985, SM ret 1; Can ret 1; US Detroit ret 1; Fr ret 1; GB ret 1; Ger 11; Aus ret 1; Hol ret 1; It ret 1; Bel 12; Eur ret 1; SA ret 1; Ausral 8; **1986,** Bra ret 2; Sp ret 2; SM ret 2; Bel ret 2; Can ret 2; US detroit ret 2; Fr ret 2; GB ret 2; Hun ret 2; Aus ret 2; It ret 2; Por ret 2; Mex 8, 14; Austral ret 2; **1987,** Bra ret 2; SM ret 2; Bel ret 2; Mon ret 1; US Detroit ret 2; Fr ret 2; GB ret 2; Ger ret 2; Hun 11, ret 1; Aus ret 2; It 16, ret 1; Por 11, ret 1; Sp 14, ret 1; Mex ret 2; Jap ret 2; Austral ret 2
Total contested
Best result: 4th, GB 1989 and SM and Por 1991

Onyx – Ford

Onyx – Ford 1989, Mex ret 1; US Phoenix ret 1; Can ret 1; Fr 5, 13; GB 12; Ger ret 1; Hun ret 2; Bel 8, ret 1; It ret 1; Por 3; Sp ret 1; Austral ret 1; **1990,** SM 12, ret 1; Mon 7, ret 1; Can ret 2; Mex 15, ret 1; Ger 12, ret 1
Total contested: 17
Best result: 3rd, Por 1989

OSCA

OSCA 1951, Mon 9, Sp ret 1; **1952,** It ret 1; **1953,** Fr 15, ret 1; It 12, ret 1
Total contested: 5

Osella

Osella – Alfa Romeo 1983, US Detroit ret 1; GB ret 1; Aus 10, 11; Hol 11; It ret 2; Eur 18; SA ret 2; **1984,** Bra ret 1; Bel ret 1; SM ret 1; Fr 12; Mon 7; Can ret 1; US Detroit ret 1; US Dallas 5; GB 9, ret 1; Ger ret 2; Aus ret 2; Hol 12, ret 1; It 5, 7; Eur ret 2; Por 16, ret 1; **1985,** Bra 12; Por 9; SM 12; Can ret 1; US Detroit ret 1; Fr 15; GB ret 1; Ger ret 1; Aus 9; Hol 11; It ret 1; Bel 14; SA ret 1; Austral 7; **1986,** Bra ret 2; Sp ret 2; SM ret 2; Bel ret 2; Can ret 2;

US Detroit ret 2; Fr ret 2; GB ret 2; Ger 12, ret 1; Hun ret 2; Aus 11, ret 1; It 11, ret 1; Por 13, ret 1; Mex 16, ret 1; Austral 15, ret 1; **1987,** Bra ret 1; SM 12, ret 1; Bel ret 1; Mon 1; US Detroit ret 1; Fr ret 1; GB ret 1; Ger ret 1; Hun ret 1; Aus ret 1; It ret 2; Por ret 2; Mex ret 1; Jap ret 1; **1988,** Mon 9; US Detroit ret 1; Fr ret 1; GB 19; Ger ret 1; Bel ret 1; It ret 1; Por 12; Sp ret 1; Jap ret 1

Osella – Ford 1980, SA ret 1; US West ret 1; Fr ret 1; GB ret 1; Ger ret 1; Aus ret 1; Hol ret 1; It 12; Can ret 1; US ret 1; **1981,** US West ret 1; SM ret 2; Bel 13, ret 1; GB 8; Ger 8; Aus 10; Hol ret 1; It 9; Can ret 1; US Las Vegas ret 1; **1982,** SA ret 1; Bra 9; US West ret 1; SM 4, ret 1; Bel ret 1; US East ret 1; Can ret 2; Hol 14; GB ret 1; Fr ret 1; Ger ret 1; CH ret 1; It ret 1; **1983,** Bra ret 1; Fr ret 1; SM ret 1; Bel ret 1; Can ret 1; **1989,** Bra ret 1; SM 12; Can ret 1; GB ret 1; Hun ret 1; It ret 1; Sp ret 2; Jap ret 1; Austral ret 2; **1990,** US Phoenix ret 1; Bra ret 1; SM ret 1; Can 13; Mex 19; Bel 16; It ret 1; Sp ret 1; Austral 13

Total contested: 132
Best result: 4th, 1982
(see also Fondmetal)

Pacific –Ford, 1994, Bra ret 1; SM ret 1; Mon ret 2; Sp ret 2; Can ret 1; **1995,** Bra 9, ret 1; Arg ret 2; SM ret 2; Sp ret 2; Can ret 2; Fr ret 2; GB 12, ret 1; Ger 8, ret 1; Hun 12, ret 1; Bel ret 2; It ret 2; Por ret 2; Eur 15, ret 1; Pac ret 2; Jap ret 2; Austral 8, ret 1

Total contested: 22
Best Result: 8th, Ger and Austral 1995

Parnelli – Ford
Parnelli – Ford 1974, Can 7; US ret 1; **1975,** Arg ret 1; Bra 7; SA 17; Sp ret 1; Mon ret 1; Swe 4; Fr 5; GB 12; Ger 10; Aus ret 1; It ret 1; US ret 1; 1976, SA 6; US West ret 1

Total contested: 16
Best result: 4th, Swe 1975
Fastest laps: 1

Penske – Ford
Penske – Ford 1974, Can 12; US ret 1; **1975,** Arg 7, Bra ret 1; SA 8; Sp ret 1; Mon ret 1; Bel 11; Swe 5; Hol 8; Fr ret 1; US 9; **1976,** Bra ret 1; SA 5; US West 12; Sp ret 1; Bel 7; Mon 10; Swe ret 1; Fr 3; GB 3; Ger 7; Aus 1; Hol ret 2; It 11; Can 10; US 6; Jap ret 1; **1977,** US West 6; Mon 11; Bel 11; Swe 8; Fr ret 1; GB 8; Ger ret 1; Aus

12, 14; Hol 8, ret 1; It ret 1; US ret 1; Can 7
Total contested: 40 **Wins** 1

Porsche
Porsche **1957,** Ger 12, 14, ret 1; **1958,** Hol 11; Ger 6, ret 1; **1959,** Mon ret 1; Hol 10; US 7; **1960,** It 6, 7; **1961,** Mon 5, 9, 12; Hol 10, 11, 14, 15; Bel 6, 7, 11; Fr 2, 7, ret 1; GB 5, 7, 16; Ger 7, 13, 14 ret 1; It 2, 7, ret 1; US 2, 6; **1962,** Hol 6, 7, ret 2; Mon 5, ret 1; Bel 7; Fr 1, 6, ret 1; GB 9, 14, ret 1; Ger 3, 7, 13, 14, 15; It 6, 10, ret 1; US 5, 13, ret 1; SA 11; **1963,** Bel 6; Hol 9, ret 1; GB 10; Ger 4, ret 1; US 6; Mex 10; SA 10; **1964,** Hol ret 1

Total contested: 32 **Wins:** 1 **Poles:** 1

Prost-Mugen Honda
Prost-Mugen Honda, 1997, Austral 5, 7; Bra 3, 14; Arg ret 2; SM 8, ret 1; Mon 4, ret 1; Sp 2, ret 1; Can 6, 11; Fr 10, ret 1; GB 8, 11; Ger 4, 7; Hun 6, 7; Bel 15, ret 1; It 10, 11; Aus ret 2; Lux 6, ret 1; Jap ret 2; Eur 7, 10

Total contested: 17
Best Result: 2nd, Sp 1997

Protos – Ford
Protos – Ford 1967, Ger *4, ret 1
Total contested: 1

RAM
RAM – Ford **1983,** Bra 15; US West ret 1; SA 12
RAM – Hart 1984, Bra 8, ret 1; SA ret 2; Bel 10; SM 9, 10; Fr 13, ret 1; Can 10, ret 1; US Detroit ret 2; US Dallas ret 1; GB ret 2; Ger ret 2; Aus 9, 11; Hol 9, 10; It ret 2; Eur ret 2; Por ret 2; **1985,** Bra 9, 13; Por 9, ret 2; SM ret 2; Can ret 2; US Detroit ret 2; Fr 12, ret 1; GB ret 2; Ger ret 2; Aus ret 2; Hol ret 1; It ret 2; Bel ret 1; Eur ret 1

Total contested: 31

Rebaque – Ford
Rebaque – Ford 1979, Can ret 1
Total contested: 1

Renault
Renault 1977, GB ret 1; Hol ret 1; It ret 1; US ret 1; **1978,** SA ret 1; US West ret 1; Mon 10; Bel ret 1; Sp 13; Swe ret 1; Fr ret 1; GB ret 1; Ger ret 1; Aus ret 1; Hol ret 1; It ret 1; US 4; Can 12; **1979,** Arg ret 2; Bra 10, ret 1; SA ret 2; Sp 9, ret 1; Bel ret 2; Mon 8, ret 1; Fr 1, 3; GB 2, ret 1; Ger ret 2; Aus 6, ret 1; Hol ret 2; It 14, ret 1; Can ret 2; US East 2, ret 1; **1980,** Arg ret

2; Bra 1, ret 1; SA 1, ret 1; US West 9, 10; Bel 4, ret 1; Mon ret 2; Fr 5, ret 1; GB ret 2; Ger ret 2; Aus 1, 9; Hol 2, ret 1; It 10, ret 1; Can ret 2; US 7; **1981**, US West 8, ret 1; Bra ret 2; Arg 3, 5; SM 8, ret 1; Bel ret 1; Mon ret 2; Sp 9, ret 1; Fr 1, 4; GB 9, ret 1; Ger 2, 13; Aus 2, ret 1; Hol 1, ret 1; It 1, ret 1; Can ret 2; US Las Vegas 2, ret 1; **1982**, SA 1, 3; Bra 1, ret 1; US West ret 2; SM ret 2; Bel ret 2; Mon 7, ret 1; US East 10, 12; Can ret 2; Hol ret 2; GB 6, ret 1; Fr 1, 2; Ger 2, ret 1; Aus 8, ret 1; CH 2, ret 1; It 1, ret 1; US Las Vegas 4, ret 1; **1983**, Bra 7, ret 1; US West 11, ret 1; Fr 1, 3; SM 2, ret 1; Mon 3, ret 1; Bel 1, 3; US Detroit 8, ret 1; Can 2, 5; GB 1, ret 1; Ger 4, ret 1; Aus 1, 4; Hol ret 2; It 3, ret 1; Eur 2, 10; SA 6, ret 1; **1984**, Bra 5, ret 1; SA 3, ret 1; Bel 2, 7; SM 4, ret 1; Fr 2, ret 1; Mon ret 2; Can ret 1; US Detroit ret 2; US Dallas ret 2; GB 2, 8; Ger 3, 5; Aus 1 ret 2; Hol 6, ret 1; It ret 2; Eur 11, ret 1; Por 7, ret 2; **1985**, Bra 5, 10; Por 3, 7; SM 3, 10; Mon 5, ret 1; Can 7, ret 1; US Detroit ret 2; Fr 6, 7; GB 5, ret 1; Ger ret 3; Aus 10, ret 1; Hol ret 2; It 7, ret 1; Bel 6, ret 1; Eur 12, ret 1; Austral ret 2
Total contested: 123 Wins: 15 Poles: 31
Fastest laps: 18

Rial – Ford

Rial – Ford 1988, Bra ret 1; SM ret 1; Mon ret 1; Can 9; US Detroit 4; Fr 10; GB ret 1; Ger 13; Hun ret 1; Bel ret 1; It ret 1; Por ret 1; Sp ret 1; Jap ret 1; Austral 8; **1989**, Bra 14; Mex 12; US Phoenix 4; Can 8
Total contested: 20
Best result: 4th, US Detroit 1988 and US Phoenix 1989

Sauber

Sauber-Ford, 1995, Bra ret 2; Arg 5, ret 1; SM 6, ret 1; Sp 8, 13; Mon 6, 8; Can ret 2; Fr 10, ret 1; GB 6, 9; Ger 5, ret 1; Hun 5, 10; Bel 4, 11; It 3, 6; Por 6, 12; Eur ret 2; Pac 7, ret 1; Jap 8, 10; Austral ret 2; **1996**, Austral 8, ret 1; Bra ret 2; Arg 9, ret 1; Eur 7, ret 1; SM ret 2; Mon 3, 4; Sp 4, ret 1; Can 7, ret 1; Fr ret 2; GB 8, 9; Ger 8, ret 1; Hun ret 2; Bel ret 2; It 9, ret 1; Por 7, 8; Jap 6, 10;
Sauber-Ilmor, 1993, SA 5, ret 1; Bra 2; Eur ret 2; SM 4, ret 1; Sp ret 2; Mon 13, ret 1; Can 6, 7; Fr ret 2; GB 8, ret 1; Ger 9, ret 1; Hun 6, ret 1; Bel 9, ret 1; It 4, ret 1; Por 5, 7; Jap 8, ret 1; Austral 15, ret 1;
Sauber-Mercedes, 1994, Bra 5, ret 1; Pac ret 2;

SM 4, 7; Sp ret 1; Can ret 2; Fr 4, 6; GB 7, ret 1; Ger ret 2; Hun ret 2; Bel ret 2; It ret 2; Por ret 2; Eur 6, ret 1; Jap 6, ret 1; Austral 7, 10;
Sauber-Petronas (Ferrari), 1997, Austral 6, ret 1; Bra 7, 11; Arg 4, ret 1; SM 7, ret 1; Mon ret 2; Sp 5, 14; Can 5, 10; Fr 8, ret 1; GB 9, ret 1; Ger 9, ret 1; Hun 3, ret 1; Bel 4, 9; It 12, ret 1; Aus 8, 9; Lux 7, 9; Jap 6; Eur 8, 14
Total contested: 81
Best result: 3rd, 1995 and Mon 1996

Scarab

Scarab 1960, Bel ret 2; US 10
Total contested: 2

Scirocco

Scirocco – BRM 1963, Bel ret 1; Fr ret 1; GB ret 2; Ger ret 2
Scirocco – Climax 1964, Bel ret 1
Total contested: 5

Shadow

Shadow – Ford 1973, SA 6, ret 1; Sp 3, ret 2; Bel 9, ret 2; Mon 10, ret 1; Swe 14, ret 2; Fr 10, ret 2; GB ret 3; Hol 10, 12, ret 1; Ger 8, 13, ret 1; Aus ret 3; It 10, 11, 14; Can 3, 16, 17; US 13, 14, 15, ret 1; **1974**, Arg ret 2; Bra ret 2; Sp 7, ret 1; Bel 13, 18; Mon 3, ret 1; Swe 5, ret 1; Hol ret 2; Fr 12, ret 1; GB 8, ret 1; Ger 6, 8; Aus 8, ret 1; It 10, ret 1; Can 19, ret 1; US 10, 15; **1975**, Arg 12; Bra ret 2; SA 9, ret 1; Sp 4, ret 1; Mon ret 2; Bel 6, ret 1; Swe ret 2; Hol 6, ret 1; Fr 8, ret 1; GB 14, ret 1; Ger 4, ret 1; Aus 3; It 5; US ret 2; **1976**, Bra 3, ret 1; SA 7, ret 1; US West 7, ret 1; Sp 8, ret 1; Bel 9, 10; Mon 7, 8; Swe 9, 12; Fr 8, 12; GB 4, 9; Ger 8, 11; Aus ret 2; Hol 4, 10; It 8, 19; Can 11, 18; US 10, ret 1; Jap 10, ret 1; **1977**, Arg ret 2; Bra 6, ret 1; SA ret 2; US West ret 2; Sp ret 2; Mon 6, 9; Bel 5, ret 1; Swe 9, 17; Fr ret 2; GB 7, ret 1; Ger 10, ret 1; Aus 1, ret 1; Hol 13, ret 1; It 3, ret 1; US 9, ret 1; Can 4, 10; Jap 4, 6; **1978**, Arg 15, 17; Bra 5, ret 1; US West 10; Mon ret 1; Bel ret 2; Sp 15, ret 1; Swe 5, 11; Fr 11, ret 1; GB 5, ret 1; Ger ret 1; Aus ret 2; Hol ret 1; It ret 2; US 14, ret 1; Can ret 1; **1979**, Arg 7, ret 1; Bra 12, 14; SA ret 2; US West 7, ret 1; Sp 12, ret 1; Bel 10, ret 1; Fr 16, 18; GB 11, 12; Ger 10, 11; Aus ret 2; Hol ret 2; It ret 1; Can 9, ret 1; US East 4; **1980**, SA 13
Shadow – Matra 1975, Aus ret 1; It ret 1
Total contested: 104 Wins: 1 Poles: 3
Fastest laps: 2

Constructors' Records

Shannon – Climax
Shannon – Climax **1966**, GB ret 1
Total contested: 1

Simca – Gordini see Gordini

Simtek
Simtek-Ford, **1994**, Bra 12; Pac 11, ret 1; SM
ret 1; Mon ret 1; Sp 10; Can 14; Fr 9; GB 15,
16; Ger ret 2; Hun 11, ret 1; Bel 11, ret 1; It ret
2; Por 15, ret 1; Eur 19, ret 1; Jap 12, ret 1;
Austral ret 2; **1995**, Bra ret 2; Arg 9, ret 1; SM
ret 2; Sp 12, 15; Mon ret 2
Total contested: 21
Best Result: 9th, Fr 1992 and Arg 1993

Spirit
Spirit – Hart **1984.** Bra ret 1; SA 8; Bel ret 1;
SM 8; Fr ret 1; Can ret 1; US Dallas ret 1; GB
13; Ger 9; Aus ret 1; Hol ret 1; It 8; Eur 8; Por
15; **1985**, Bra ret 1; Por ret 1; SM ret 1
Spirit – Honda **1983**, GB ret 1; Ger ret 1; Aus
12; Hol 7; It ret 1; Eur 14
Total contested: 23

Stebro – Ford
Stebro – Ford **1963**, US 7
Total contested: 1

Stewart
Stewart-Ford, **1997**, Austral ret 2; Bra ret 2;
Arg 10, ret 1; SM ret 2; Mon 2, 7; Sp 13, ret 1;
Can ret 2; Fr ret 2; GB ret 2; Ger ret 2; Hun
ret 2; Bel 12, ret 1; It 13, ret 1; Aus 14 ret 1;
Lux ret 2; Jap ret 2; Eur 9, ret 1
Total contested: 17
Best Result: 2nd, Mon 1997

Surtees – Ford
Surtees – Ford **1970**, GB ret 1; Ger 9; Aus ret
1; It ret 1; Can 5; US 6, ret 1; Mex 8; **1971**, SA
7, 12, ret 1; Sp 11, ret 1; Mon 6, 7; Hol 5, 8,
ret 1; Fr 8, 11; GB 5, 6, ret 1; Ger 7, 10; Aus 7,
ret 1; It 4, ret 1; Can 11, ret 1; US 15, 17, ret 1;
1972, Arg 5, ret 1; SA 16, ret 3; Sp 4, 8, ret 1;
Mon 7, ret 2; Bel 4, ret 2; Fr 6, 14, 17; GB ret
3; Ger 13, 14, ret 1; Aus 4, 11, 14; It 2, ret 3;
Can 7, ret 1; US 12, 17, ret 2; **1973**, Arg ret 2;
Bra 12, ret 2; SA 8, ret 2; Sp ret 2; Bel 8, ret 1;
Mon 8, ret 1; Swe 10, ret 1; Fr 13, ret 1; GB
ret 3; Hol 7, ret 1; Ger 4, 7, 14; Aus 3, 10; It 7,
ret 1; Can 9, 18; US ret 3; **1974**, Arg ret 2; Bra
4, 17; SA 11, ret 1; Sp 13, ret 1; Bel ret 2; Mon

ret 1; Swe ret 3; Hol ret 1; Fr ret 1; GB 14;
Ger 11, ret 1; Aus 9; Can 10, 16; US 7, ret 2;
1975, Arg ret 1; Bra 10; SA ret 1; Sp 8; Mon
ret 1; Bel 10; Swe 16; Hol ret 1; Fr 13; GB 11,
18; Aus 10; **1976**, SA 11; US West ret 1, Sp 9;
Bel 5, ret 1; Mon ret 1; Swe 13, 15; Fr 16, ret
2; GB 5, ret 2; Ger 10, ret 2; Aus 9, 10, ret 1;
Hol 8, 11, ret 1; It 12, 14, 17; Can 15, 16, 19;
US 8, 11, ret 1; Jap 4, 9; **1977**, Arg 7, ret 2;
Bra ret 2; SA 7, 11; US West 11, ret 1; Sp 9,
ret 1; Mon 8, ret 1; Bel 4, 12; Swe ret 1; Fr 13;
GB 8, 12; Ger 5, 7; Aus 15, 16; Hol 12; It ret
1; US 11, 19; Can 6, ret 1; Jap 8, ret 1; **1978**,
Arg 18, ret 1; Bra ret 1; SA 12, ret 1; US West
ret 1; Mon ret 1; Bel 13; Sp 7, 11; Swe ret 1; Fr
17, ret 1; GB 9; Ger ret 1; Aus 6; Hol ret 1; It
ret 1; US 9; Can ret 1
Total contested: 118
Best result: 2nd, It 1972
Fastest laps: 3

Talbot
Talbot **1950**, GB 4, 5, 8, 11, ret 1; Mon 7, ret 2;
CH 3, 8, 10, ret 3; Bel 3, 7, 8, ret 4; Fr 5, 6, 8
ret 4; It 4, 5, ret 5; **1951**, CH 9, 10, 14, 15, ret 1;
Bel 4, 5, 6, 7, 8, ret 1; Fr 6, 7, 8, 9, ret 3; GB 10,
12, 13, ret 1; Ger 8, 9, 10, 11, 12, ret 3; It 7, 8,
ret 4; Sp 7, 8, ret 4
Total contested: 13
Best result: 3rd, CH and Bel 1950

Tec Mec Maserati
Tec Mec Maserati **1959**, US ret 1
Total contested: 1

Tecno
Tecno **1972**, Bel ret 1; GB ret 1; Ger ret 1; Aus
ret 1; It ret 1; US ret 1; **1973**, Bel 6; Mon ret 1;
GB ret 1; Hol ret 1
Tecno – Ford **1969**, Ger* ret 1
Total contested: 11
Best result: 6th, Bel 1973

Theodore – Ford
Theodore – Ford **1978**, SA ret 1; **1981**, US West
6; Bra 10; Arg ret 1; SM 11; Mon 7, Sp 13; Fr
12, ret 1; GB 11; Ger 14; Aus ret 1; Hol 8; Can
9; US Las Vegas ret 1; **1982**, SA 14; Bra ret 1;
US West ret 1; Can ret 1; Hol ret 1; Aus ret 1;
US Las Vegas ret 1; **1983**, Bra 14, 17; US West
6, ret 1; Fr 11, ret 1; SM ret 2; Bel 10, ret 1; US
Detroit 2, ret 1; Can ret 2; GB 16; Ger 11, ret 1;
Aus ret 1; Hol 12; It 12, 13; Eur 12

Total contested: 34
Best result: 6th, US West 1981 and 1983

Token – Ford
Token – Ford 1974, Bel ret 1; Ger 14; Aus ret 1
Total contested: 3

Toleman – Hart
Toleman – Hart 1981, It 10; US Las Vegas ret 1; **1982**, SA ret 1; SM ret 1; Bel ret 2; Hol ret 1; GB ret 2; Fr 15, ret 1; Ger 10; Aus ret 2; CH ret 2; It ret 2; US Las Vegas ret 1; **1983**, Bra 8, ret 1; US West ret 2; Fr 13 ret 1; SM ret 2; Mon ret 1; Bel 7, 8; US Detroit 9, ret 1; Can ret 2; GB ret 2; Ger ret 2; Aus ret 2; Hol 4, 13; It 6, 7; Eur 5, 6; SA 4, ret 1; **1984**, Bra ret 2; SA 6, ret 1; Bel 6, ret 1; SM 11; Fr ret 2; Mon 2, ret 1; Can 7, 9; US Detroit ret 2; US Dallas ret 2; GB 3; Ger ret 1; Aus ret 1; Hol ret 1; It 4; Eur ret 2; Por 3, 11; **1985**, Mon ret 1; Can ret 1; US Detroit ret 1; Fr 14; GB ret 1; Ger ret 1; Aus ret 2; Hol ret 2; It 12, ret 1; Bel ret 2; Eur ret 2; SA ret 2; Austral ret 2
Total contested: 57
Best result: 2nd, Mon 1984 **Poles:** 1
Fastest laps: 2

Trojan – Ford
Trojan – Ford 1974, Sp 14; Bel 10; Mon ret 1; GB ret 1; Aus 10; It ret 1
Total contested: 6

Tyrrell
Tyrell – Ford 1970, Can ret 1; US ret 1; Mex ret 1; **1971**, SA 2, ret 1; Sp 1, 7; Mon 1, ret 1; Hol 11, ret 1; Fr 1, 2; GB 1, 10; Ger 1, 2; Aus ret 2; It 3, ret 1; Can 1, 6; US 1, 5, ret 1; **1972**, Arg 1, ret 1; SA 9, ret 1; Sp ret 2; Mon 4, ret 1; Bel 2; Fr 1, 4, ret 1; GB 2, ret 1; Ger 10, 11; Aus 7, 9; It ret 2; Can 1, ret 1; US 1, 2, 7; **1973**, Arg 2, 3; Bra 2, 10; SA 1, ret 2; Sp 2, ret 1; Bel 1, 2; Mon 1, 4; Swe 3, 5; Fr 2, 4; GB 5, 10; Hol 1, 3; Ger 1, 2; Aus 2, ret 1; It 4, 5; Can 5, 10, ret 1; **1974**, Arg 6, ret 1; Bra 8, 13; SA 4, 8, 14; Sp 5, 8; Bel 3, ret 1; Mon 2, 9; Swe 1, 2; Hol 5, 6; Fr 4, 8; GB 1, ret 1; Ger 2, ret 1; Aus ret 2; It 3, 11; Can 5, ret 1; US 6, ret 1; **1975**, Arg 5, 11; Bra ret 2; SA 1, 3, ret 1; Sp ret 2; Mon 5, 7; Bel 2, 4; Swe 7, 12; Hol 9, 16; Fr 6, 9, 12; GB 3, 9; Ger 9, ret 1; Aus 8, 11; It 7, 8; US 6 ret 2; **1976**, Bra 2, 5; SA 4, 9, ret 1; US West 3, ret 1; Sp ret 2; Bel 4, ret 1; Mon 2, 3; Swe 1, 2; Fr 2, ret 1; GB 2, ret 1; Ger 2, 14, ret 1; Aus 11, ret

2; Hol 5, 7; It 5, 6, 18; Can 2, 4; US 2, ret 1; Jap 2, ret 2; **1977**, Arg ret 2; Bra ret 2; SA 3, ret 1; US West 4, ret 1; Sp 8, ret 1; Mon ret 2; Bel 3, 8; Swe 4, ret 1; Fr 12, ret 1; GB ret 2; Ger 9, ret 1; Aus 5, 13; Hol ret 2; It 6, ret 1; US 14, 16; Can 2, ret 1; Jap 3, 9, ret 1; **1978**, Arg 3, 14; Bra 6, ret 1; Sp 12, ret 1; Swe ret 2; Fr 10, ret 1; GB 4, ret 1; Ger 5, ret 1; Aus 2, ret 1; Hol ret 2; It 11, ret 1; US 10, ret 1; Can 5, 7; **1979**, Arg ret 2; Bra 4; SA 3, ret 1; US West 6, ret 1; Sp 5, 6; Bel 3, 11; Mon ret 2; Fr 5, ret 1; GB 3, 10; Ger 7, 9; Aus 7, 8; Hol ret 2; It 6, 10; Can 5, ret 2; US East 3, ret 2; **1980**, Arg 4, ret 1; Bra 12, 14; SA 7, ret 1; US West 8, ret 1; Bel 5, 9; Mon ret 2; Fr 11, 14; GB 4, 5; Ger 10, 15; Aus ret 2; Hol 5, ret 1; It ret 2; Can 7, ret 2; US ret 2; **1981**, US West 5; Bra 13, ret 1; Arg 13, ret 1; SM ret 2; Bel 6, 12; Mon 5, ret 1; Sp ret 1; Fr 13, 16; GB 4, ret 1; Ger 5; Aus ret 1; Hol 9, ret 1; It ret 2; Can 11, 12; US Las Vegas 13, ret 1; **1982**, SA 7, 16; **Bra 4**, 7; US West 4, 10; SM 3, ret 1; Bel ret 2; Mon 8, 10; US East 9, ret 1; Can ret 2; Hol 7, ret 1; GB 8, ret 1; Fr 6, 10; Ger 4, 7; Aus ret 2; CH 7, 11; It 5, ret 1; US Las Vegas 1, 8; **1983**, Bra 11, ret 1; US West 8, 9; Fr 8, ret 1; SM ret 2; Mon 5, ret 1; Bel 12, 14; US Detroit 1, ret 1; Can 8, ret 1; GB 13, 14; Ger 12, ret 1; Aus ret 2; Hol 6, ret 1; It ret 2; Eur, ret 2; SA 7, ret 1; **1984**, Bra 5, ret 1; SA 11, ret 1; Bel 6, ret 1; SM 5, 11; Fr 12, ret 1; Mon 3; Can 10, ret 1; US Detroit 2, ret 1; US Dallas ret 1; GB 11, ret 1; Ger 9; Hol 8, 9; **1985**, Bra 7, 8; Por 6, ret 1; SM 9, ret 1; Mon 10; Can 11, 12; US Detroit 4, ret 1; Fr 13; GB 11; **1987**, Bra 10, 11; SM 8, ret 1; Bel 9, ret 1; Mon 5, ret 1; US Detroit 11, ret 1; Fr 6, 7; GB 8, ret 1; Ger 4, 5; Hun 7, 9; Aus 15, ret 1; It 12, 14; Por 10, 12; Sp 7, ret 1; Mex 7, 8; Jap 8, 12; Austral 4, ret 1; **1988**, Bra ret 1; SM 14, ret 1; Mon 5; Can 6, ret 1; US Detroit 5, 9; Fr ret 1; GB 16, ret 1; Ger 11; Hun ret 1; Bel 12; It 12; Por ret 1; Sp ret 1; Jap 12, 14; Austral ret 1; **1989**, Bra 7, 10; SM 6; Mon 5, 9; Mex 3, ret 1; US Phoenix 9, ret 1; Can ret 2; Fr 4, 10; GB ret 2; Ger 10, ret 1; Hun 9, 13; Bel 14, ret 1; It 5, ret 1; Por 6; Sp 4, 10; Jap ret 2; Austral ret 1; **1990**, US Phoenix 2, 6; Bra 7, 8; SM 6, ret 1; Mon 2, ret 1; Can 11, ret 1; Mex 7, ret 1; Fr ret 2; GB 8, ret 1; Ger 11, ret 1; Hun ret 2; Bel 8, ret 1; It 6, ret 1; Por 8; Sp ret 2; Jap 6; Austral 8, ret 1; **1997**, Austral ret 2; Bra 13, 15; Arg 8, ret 1; SM 9, 10; Mon 5, 8; SP 11, ret 1; Can ret 2; Fr ret 2; GB ret 2; Ger 10, ret 1; Hun 13, ret

Constructors' Records

1; Bel 11, ret 1; It ret 2; Aus 12 ret 1; Lux 10, ret 1; Jap 13 ret 1; Eur 12, 16

Tyrrell – Honda 1991, US Phoenix 4, 5; Bra ret 2; SM ret 2; Mon ret 2; Can 2, 10; Mex 11, 12; Fr ret 2; GB 7, 8; Ger 13, ret 1; Hun 12, 15; Bel ret 2; It ret 2; Por 13, ret 1; Sp 16, 17; Jap 6, ret 1; Austral 10, ret 1

Tyrrell – Ilmor 1992, SA ret 2; Mex 5, ret 1; Bra ret 2; Sp ret 2; SM 8, 14; Mon ret 2; Can 5, 12; Fr 11, ret 1; GB 11, ret 1; Ger ret 2; Hun 8, ret 1; Bel 8, ret 1; It 6, ret 1; Por 9, ret 1; Jap 4, ret 1; Austral ret 2

Tyrell – Renault 1985, Fr ret 1; GB 7; Ger 8, 10; Aus 7; Hol 7, ret 1; It 8; Bel 13; Eur ret 2; SA 7, ret 1; Austral 4, ret 1; **1986**, Bra 5, 7; Sp ret 2; SM 8, ret 1; Mon 11, ret 1; Bel ret 2; Can 9, 11; US Detroit 9, ret 1; Fr 10, ret 1; GB 5, 6; Ger ret 2; Hun 6, 8; Aus ret 2; It 9, 10; Por ret 2; Mex 11, ret 1; Austral 4, 5

Tyrrell-Yamaha, 1993, SA ret 2; Bra ret 2; Eur ret 2; SM ret 2; Sp ret 2; Mon 10, ret 1; Can 17, ret 1; Fr 15, ret 1; GB 13, ret 1; Ger ret 2; Hun 10, 11; Bel 15, ret 1; It 13, 14; Por 12, ret 1; Jap ret 2; Austral 13, ret 1; **1994**, Bra 5, ret 1; Pac ret 2; SM 5, 9; Mon ret 2; SP 3, ret 1; Can 10, ret 1; Fr 10, ret 1; GB 6, ret 1; Ger ret 2; Hun 5, ret 1; Bel 5, ret 1; It ret 2; Por ret 2; Eur 7, 13; Jap ret 2; Austral ret 2; **1995**, Bra 7, ret 1; Arg 8, ret 1; SM ret 2; Sp 10, ret 1; Mon ret 2; Can 7, ret 1; Fr 15, ret 1; GB 8, ret 1; Ger 7, ret 1; Hun ret 2; Bel 8, ret 1; It 5, 10; Por 13, ret 1; Eur 10, 14; Pac 12, 14; Jap 6, ret 1; Austral 5, ret 1; **1996**, Austral 6, 11; Bra 5, 9; Arg ret 2; Eur 10, ret 1; SM ret 2; Mon 5, ret 1; SP ret 2; Can ret 2; Fr 10, ret 1; GB 7, ret 1; Ger 9, ret 1; Hun 7, ret 1; Bel 7, 8; It 10, ret 1; Por 11, 12; Jap ret 2

Total contested: 416
Constructors' Championships: 1971
Wins: 23 **Poles:** 14
Fastest laps: 20
(includes the 12 races in 1984 from which Tyrrell were disqualified)

Vanwall
Vanwall 1954, GB ret 1; It 7; **1955**, Mon ret 1; Bel ret 1; GB 9, ret 1; It ret 2; **1956**, Mon ret 2; Bel 4, ret 1; Fr 10, ret 1; GB ret 3; It ret 2; **1957**, Mon 2, ret 1; Fr ret 2; GB 1, 7, ret 1; Ger 5, ret 1; Pescara 1, 5, ret 1; It 1, 7, ret 1; **1958**, Mon ret 3; Hol 1, ret 2; Bel 1, 3, ret 1; Fr 2, 13, ret 1; GB 4, 7, ret 1; Ger 1, ret 1; Por 1, 3, ret 1; It 1, ret 2; Moroccan 1, ret 2; **1959**, GB ret 1; **1960**, Fr ret 1

Total contested: 28
Constructors' Championships: 1958
Wins: 9 **Poles:** 7
Fastest laps: 6

Venturi see Larrousse

Veritas
Veritas 1951, CH ret 1; **1952**, CH ret 1; Bel 13; Ger 7, 8, 11, ret 4; **1953**, Bel ret 1; Ger 9, 12, 18, ret 4
Total contested: 6

Williams
Williams – Ford 1972, GB ret 1; **1973**, Arg ret 2; Bra 7, 9; SA 10, ret 1; Sp 11, ret 1; Bel ret 2; Mon ret 2; Swe 11; Fr 14; GB 9, ret 1; Hol 6, 9; Aus 9, 12; It ret 2; Can 6, 14; US 7, 12; **1974**, Arg ret 1; Bra ret 1; SA 6, ret 1; Sp ret 1; Bel 14, ret 1; Mon ret 1; Swe 8; Hol ret 1; Fr 9; GB ret 1; Ger ret 2; Aus ret 2; It 4, ret 1; Can 15, ret 1; US ret 2; **1975**, Arg ret 2; Bra 11, ret 1; SA ret 2; Sp 7, ret 1; Bel ret 2; Swe 14, ret 1; Hol 12, ret 1; Fr 11; GB ret 1; Ger 2; Aus ret 2; It 14, ret 1; **1976**, Bra 8, 9; SA 13, 16; Sp 7, 10; Bel 11; Mon 11; Swe ret 1; Fr 10, 13; Ger ret 1; Aus ret 1; Hol ret 1; Can ret 1; US 14, ret 1; Jap ret 2; **1978**, Arg ret 1; Bra 11; SA 4; US West 7; Mon ret 1; Bel 10; Sp 8; Swe ret 1; Fr 5; GB ret 1; Ger ret 1; Aus ret 1; Hol ret 1; It 13; US 2; Can 9; **1979**, Arg 9, 10; Bra 15, ret 1; SA 9, ret 1; US West 3, ret 1; Sp ret 2; Bel ret 2; Mon 2, ret 1; Fr 4, 6; GB 1, ret 1; Ger 1, 2; Aus 1, 5; Hol 1, ret 1; It 3, 9; Can 1, 3; US East ret 2; **1980**, Arg 1, ret 1; Bra 3, ret 1; SA 5, ret 1; US West ret 2; Bel 2, 3; Mon 1, ret 1; Fr 1, 6; GB 1, 3, 11; Ger 2, 3; Aus 2, 3, 15; Hol 4, 11; It 2, 3, 11; Can 1, 2; US 1, 2, 9; **1981**, US West 1, 2; Bra 1, 2; Arg 2, 4; SM 3, 12; Bel 1, ret 1; Mon 2, ret 1; Sp 4, 7; Fr 10, 17; GB 2, ret 1; Ger 11, ret 1; Aus 4, 5; Hol 3, ret 1; It 2, 3; Can 10, ret 1; US Las Vegas 1, 8; **1982**, SA 2, 5; Bra ret 2; US West 2, ret 1; Bel 2, ret 1; Mon 6, ret 1; US East 4, 5; Can 7, ret 1; Hol 3, 5; GB 5, ret 1; Fr 5, 7; Ger 3, ret 1; Aus 2, ret 1; CH 1, 9; It 8, ret 1; US Las Vegas 5, 6; **1983**, Bra 1, 4; US West 4, ret 1; Fr 5, 6; SM 4, 7; Mon 1, ret 1; Bel 5, 6; US Detroit 2, 5; Can 4, ret 1; GB 11, 12; Ger 6, 10; Aus 8, ret 1; Hol ret 2; It 11; Eur 13, ret 1

Williams – Honda 1983, SA 5, ret 1; **1984**, Bra 2, ret 1; SA ret 2; Bel 4, ret 1; SM ret 2; Fr 6, 8; Mon 4, 8; Can ret 2; US Detroit 5, ret 1; US Dallas 1, 4; GB ret 2; Ger ret 2; Aus ret 2; Hol

8, ret 1; It ret 2; Eur ret 2; Por 14, ret 1; **1985**, Bra ret 2; Por 5, ret 1; SM 5, ret 1; Mon 7, 8; Can 4, 6; US Detroit 1, ret 1; Fr 2; GB ret 2; Ger 6, 12; Aus ret 2; Hol 6, ret 1; It 11, ret 1; Bel 2, 4; Eur 1, 3; SA 1, 2; Austral 1, ret 1; **1986**, Bra 1, ret 1; Sp 2, ret 1; SM 2, ret 1; Mon 4, 7; Bel 1, ret 1; Can 1, 3; US Detroit 5, ret 1; Fr 1, 3; GB 1, 2; Ger 1, 3; Hun 1, 3; Aus ret 2; It 1, 2; Por 1, 3; Mex 4, 5; Austral 2, ret 1; **1987**, Bra 2, 6; SM 1; Bel ret 1; Mon 2, ret 1; US Detroit 2, 5; Fr 1, 2; GB 1, 2; Ger 1, ret 1; Hun 1, 14; Aus 1, 2; It 1, 3; Por 3, ret 1; Sp 1, 4; Mex 1, 2; Jap ret 1; Austral 9, ret 1

Williams – Judd 1988, Bra ret 2; SM 13, ret 1; Mon 6, ret 1; Mex ret 2; Can ret 2; US Detroit ret 2; Fr ret 2; GB 2, 8; Ger ret 2; Hun 6, ret 1; Bel 7, ret 1; It 7, 11; Por ret 2; Sp 2, 5; Jap 6, ret 1; Austral 4, ret 1

Williams – Renault 1989, Bra ret 2; SM 4 ret 1; Mon 10, 15; Mex 2, ret 1; US Phoenix 2, 6; Can 1, 2; Fr 3, ret 1; GB 10, ret 1; Ger 4, ret 1; Hun 3, ret 1; Bel 4, ret 1; It 3, 4; Por ret 2; Sp 5, ret 1; Jap 2, 3; Austral 1, 3; **1990**, US Phoenix 3, 9; Bra 5, 13; SM 1, ret 1; Mon 4, ret 1; Can ret 2; Mex 5, 9; Fr 6, ret 1; GB 2, ret 1; Ger 5, 6; Hun 1, 4; Bel ret 2; It 5, ret 1; Por 7, ret 1; Sp 4, 5; Jap 4, 5; Austral 5, 6; **1991**, US Phoenix ret 2; Bra 2, ret 1; SM ret 2; Mon 2, ret 1; Can 3, 6; Mex 1, 2; Fr 1, 5; GB 1, ret 1; Ger 1, 2; Hun 2, 3; Bel 5, ret 1; It 1, ret 1; Por 1, ret 1; Sp 1, 3; Jap 3, ret 1; Austral 2, 5; **1992**, SA 1, 2; Mex 1, 2; Bra 1, 2; Sp 1, ret 1; SM 1, 2; Mon 2, 3; Can ret 2; Fr 1, 2; GB 1, 2; Ger 1, 8; Hun 2, ret 1; Bel 2, 3; It 5, ret 1; Por 1, ret 1; Jap 1, ret 1; Austral ret 2; **1993**, SA 1, ret 1; Bra 2, ret 1; Eur 2, 3; SM 1, ret 1; Sp 1, ret 1; Mon 2, 4; Can 1, 3; Fr 1, 15; GB 1, ret 1; Ger 1, 15; Hun 1, 12; Bel 1, 3; It 1, 12; Por 2, 3; Jap 2, 4; Austral 2, 3; **1994**, Bra 2, ret 1; Pac ret 2; SM 6, ret 1; Mon ret 1; Sp 1, ret 1; Can 2, 5; Fr 2, ret 1; GB 1, 5; Ger 8, ret 1; Hun 2, ret 1; Bel 1, 4; It 1, 6; Por 1, 2; Eur 2, ret 1; Jap 1, 4; Austral 1, ret 1; **1995**, Bra 2, ret 1; Arg 1, ret 1; SM 1, 4; Sp 4, ret 1; Mon 2, ret 1; Can ret 2; Fr 2, 3; GB 3, ret 1; Ger 2, ret 1; Hun 1, 2; Bel 2, ret 1; It ret 2; Por 1, 3; Eur 3, ret 1; Pac 2, 3; Jap ret 2; Austral 1, ret 1; **1996**, Austral 1, 2; Bra 1, ret 1; Arg 1, 2; Eur 1, 4;

SM 1, 11; Mon ret 2; Sp 3, ret 1; Can 1, 2; Fr 1, 2; GB 1, ret 1; Ger 1, 3; Hun 1, 2; Bel 2, 5; It 7, ret 1; Por 1, 2; Jap 1, ret 1; **1997**, Austral 8, ret 1; Bra 1, 9; Arg 1 ret 1; SM 1, ret 1; Mon ret 2; Sp 1, 8; Can 4, ret 1; Fr 2, ret 4; GB 1, ret 1; Ger ret 2; Hun 1, ret 1; Bel 3, 5; It 3, 5; Aus 1, 3; Lux 1, 3; Jap 2, ret 1; Eur 3, 6

Total contested: 371

Constructors' Championships: 1980, 1981, 1986, 1987, 1992, 1993, 1994, 1996, 1997, **Wins:** 103 **Poles:** 107

Fastest laps: 110

(does not include cars raced by the Williams team in 1977)

Wolf-Ford

Wolf-Ford 1977, Arg 1; Bra ret 1; SA 2; US West 3; Sp 3; Mon 1; Bel ret 1; Swe ret 1; Fr ret 1; GB ret 1; Ger 2; Aus ret 1; Hol 3; It ret 1; US 3; Can 1; Jap 10; **1978**, Arg 10; Bra ret 1; SA ret 1; US West ret 1; Mon 3; Bel ret 1; Sp 4; Swe ret 1; Fr 6; GB ret 1; Ger 2, 10; Aus ret 2; Hol 12, ret 1; It 12, US 3, 12; Can 1, ret 1; **1979**, Arg ret 1; Bra ret 1; SA 8; US West ret 1; Sp ret 1; Bel ret 1; Mon ret 1; Fr 9; GB ret 1; Ger ret 1; Aus ret 1; Hol ret 1; It ret 1; US East ret 1

Total contested: 47 **Wins:** 3 **Poles:** 1

Fastest laps: 2

Zakspeed

Zakspeed 1985, Por ret 1; Mon 11; Fr ret 1; GB ret 1; Ger ret 1; Aus ret 1; Hol ret 1; Bel ret 1; Eur ret 1; **1986**, Bra ret 1; Sp ret 1; SM ret 2; Mon 12; Bel ret 2; Can 12, ret 1; US Detroit 8; Fr ret 2; GB 9, ret 1; Ger 2 ret 1; Hun 10, ret 1; Aus 8, ret 1; It ret 2; Por 12, ret 1; Mex 10; Austral 9, ret 1; **1987**, Bra 9, ret 1; SM 5, 7; Bel ret 2; Mon 7; US Detroit 8, ret 1; Fr ret 2; GB ret 2; Ger ret 2; Hun ret 2; Aus 9, 14; It 9, ret 1; Por ret 2; Sp 9, 11, ret 1; Mex ret 2; Jap ret 2; Austral 7, ret 1; **1988**, SM ret 1; Mon ret 1; Mex 15, ret 1; Can 14; Fr ret 1; Ger 12, 14; Bel 13, ret 1; It ret 2; Jap ret 1; Austral ret 1

Zakspeed-Yamaha 1989, Bra ret 1; Jap ret 1

Total contested: 53

Best result: 5th, SM 1987

Constructors' Championship

1958	Vanwall	1978	Lotus-Ford
1959	Cooper-Climax	1979	Ferrari
1960	Cooper-Climax	1980	Williams-Ford
1961	Ferrari	1981	Williams-Ford
1962	BRM	1982	Ferrari
1963	Lotus-Climax	1983	Ferrari
1964	Ferrari	1984	McLaren-TAG
1965	Lotus-Climax	1985	McLaren-TAG
1966	Brabham-Repco	1986	Williams-Honda
1967	Brabham-Repco	1987	Williams-Honda
1968	Lotus-Ford	1988	McLaren-Honda
1969	Matra-Ford	1989	McLaren-Honda
1970	Lotus-Ford	1990	McLaren-Honda
1971	Tyrrell-Ford	1991	McLaren-Honda
1972	Lotus-Ford	1992	Williams-Renault
1973	Lotus-Ford	1993	Williams-Renault
1974	McLaren-Ford	1994	Williams-Renault
1975	Ferrari	1995	Benetton-Renault
1976	Ferrari	1996	Williams-Renault
1977	Ferrari	1997	Williams-Renault

There was no championship for constructors before 1958

Constructors' Victories

Ferrari	113	Matra	9
McLaren	107	Mercedes	9
Williams	103	Vanwall	9
Lotus	79	March	3
Brabham	35	Wolf	3
Benetton	27	Honda	2
Tyrrell	23	Eagle	1
BRM	17	Hesketh	1
Cooper	16	Penske	1
Renault	15	Porsche	1
Alfa Romeo	10	Shadow	1
Ligier	9		
Maserati	9	(excluding Indianapolis)	

Grand Prix Winners

The World Champions

1950	Farina	1974	Emerson Fittipaldi
1951	Fangio	1975	Lauda
1952	Ascari	1976	Hunt
1953	Ascari	1977	Lauda
1954	Fangio	1978	Andretti
1955	Fangio	1979	Jody Scheckter
1956	Fangio	1980	Jones
1957	Fangio	1981	Piquet
1958	Hawthorn	1982	Rosberg
1959	Brabham	1983	Piquet
1960	Brabham	1984	Lauda
1961	Phil Hill	1985	Prost
1962	Graham Hill	1986	Prost
1963	Clark	1987	Piquet
1964	Surtees	1988	Senna
1965	Clark	1989	Prost
1966	Brabham	1990	Senna
1967	Hulme	1991	Senna
1968	Graham Hill	1992	Mansell
1969	Stewart	1993	Prost
1970	Rindt	1994	Michael Schumacher
1971	Stewart	1995	Michael Schumacher
1972	Emerson Fittipaldi	1996	Damon Hill
1973	Stewart	1997	Jacques Villeneuve

Wins per Driver

Prost	51	Surtees	6	Beltoise	1
Senna	41	G Villeneuve	6	Bonnier	1
Mansell	31	Alboreto	5	Brambilla	1
M Schumacher	25	Farina	5	Bryan	1
Stewart	27	Regazzoni	5	Cevert	1
Clark	25	Rosberg	5	Fagioli	1[1]
Lauda	25	Watson	5	Flaherty	1
Fangio	24[1, 2]	Gurney	4	Frentzen	1
Piquet	23	McLaren	4	Gethin	1
D Hill	21	Boutsen	3	Ginther	1
Moss	16[3]	Collins	3	Hakkinen	1
J Brabham	14	Coulthard	3	Hanks	1
E Fittipaldi	14	P Hill	3	Ireland	1
G Hill	14	Hawthorn	3	Mass	1
Ascari	13	Pironi	3	Musso	1[2]
Andretti	12	de Angelis	2	Nannini	1
Jones	12	Depailler	2	Nilsson	1
Reutemann	12	Gonzalez	2	Pace	1
J Villeneuve	11	Herbert	2	Panis	1
G Berger	10	Jabouille	2	Parsons	1
Hunt	10	Revson	2	J Rathmann	1
Peterson	10	P Rodriguez	2	Ruttman	1
J Scheckter	10	Siffert	2	Scarfiotti	1
Hulme	8	Tambay	2	Sweikert	1
Ickx	8	Trintignant	2	Taruffi	1
Arnoux	7	von Trips	2	Wallard	1
Brooks	6[3]	Vukovich	2	Ward	1
Laffite	6	Alesi	1		
Patrese	6	Baghetti	1	[1] ,[2] ,[3] shared victories
Rindt	6	Bandini	1		

Race Winners

Argentinian Grand Prix

1953	Ascari	Ferrari
1954	Fangio	Maserati
1955	Fangio	Mercedes
1956	Musso/Fangio	Lancia-Ferrari
1957	Fangio	Maserati
1958	Moss	Cooper-Climax
1960	McLaren	Cooper-Climax
1972	Stewart	Tyrrell-Ford
1973	Fittipaldi	Lotus-Ford
1974	Hulme	McLaren-Ford
1975	Fittipaldi	McLaren-Ford
1977	Scheckter	Wolf-Ford
1978	Andretti	Lotus-Ford
1979	Laffite	Ligier-Ford
1980	Jones	Williams-Ford
1981	Piquet	Brabham-Ford
1995	D Hill	Williams-Renault
1996	D Hill	Williams-Renault
1997	J Villeneuve	Williams-Renault

Australian Grand Prix

1985	Rosberg	Williams-Honda
1986	Prost	McLaren-TAG
1987	Berger	Ferrari
1988	Prost	McLaren-Honda
1989	Boutsen	Williams-Renault
1990	Piquet	Benetton-Ford
1991	Senna	McLaren-Honda
1992	Berger	McLaren-Honda
1993	Senna	McLaren-Ford
1994	Mansell	William-Renault
1995	D Hill	Williams-Renault
1996	D Hill	Williams-Renault
1997	Coulthard	McLaren-Mercedes

Austrian Grand Prix

1964	Bandini	Ferrari
1970	Ickx	Ferrari
1971	Siffert	BRM

1972	Fittipaldi	Lotus-Ford
1973	Peterson	Lotus-Ford
1974	Reutemann	Brabham-Ford
1975	Brambilla	March-Ford
1976	Watson	Penske-Ford
1977	Jones	Shadow-Ford
1978	Peterson	Lotus-Ford
1979	Jones	Williams-Ford
1980	Jabouille	Renault
1981	Laffite	Ligier-Matra
1982	de Angelis	Lotus-Ford
1983	Prost	Renault
1984	Lauda	McLaren-TAG
1985	Prost	McLaren-TAG
1986	Prost	McLaren-TAG
1987	Mansell	Wiliams-Honda
1997	J Villeneuve	Williams-Renault

Belgian Grand Prix

1950	Fangio	Alfa Romeo
1951	Farina	Alfa Romeo
1952	Ascari	Ferrari
1953	Ascari	Ferrari
1954	Fangio	Maserati
1955	Fangio	Mercedes
1956	Collins	Lancia-Ferrari
1958	Brooks	Vanwall
1960	Brabham	Cooper-Climax
1961	P Hill	Ferrari
1962	Clark	Lotus-Climax
1963	Clark	Lotus-Climax
1964	Clark	Lotus-Climax
1965	Clark	Lotus-Climax
1966	Surtees	Ferrari
1967	Gurney	Eagle-Weslake
1968	McLaren	McLaren-Ford
1970	Rodriguez	BRM
1972	Fittipaldi	Lotus-Ford
1973	Stewart	Tyrrell-Ford
1974	Fittipaldi	McLaren-Ford

Grand Prix Winners

1975	Lauda	Ferrari
1976	Lauda	Ferrari
1977	Nilsson	Lotus-Ford
1978	Andretti	Lotus-Ford
1979	Scheckter	Ferrari
1980	Pironi	Ligier-Ford
1981	Reutemann	Williams-Ford
1982	Watson	McLaren-Ford
1983	Prost	Renault
1984	Alboreto	Ferrari
1985	Senna	Lotus-Renault
1986	Mansell	Williams-Honda
1987	Prost	McLaren-TAG
1988	Senna	McLaren-Honda
1989	Senna	McLaren-Honda
1990	Senna	McLaren-Honda
1991	Senna	McLaren-Honda
1992	Schumacher	Benetton-Ford
1993	D Hill	Williams-Renault
1994	D Hill	Williams-Renault
1995	Schumacher	Benetton-Renault
1996	Schumacher	Ferrari
1997	Schumacher	Ferrari

Brazilian Grand Prix

1973	Fittipaldi	Lotus-Ford
1974	Fittipaldi	McLaren-Ford
1975	Pace	Brabham-Ford
1976	Lauda	Ferrari
1977	Reutemann	Ferrari
1978	Reutemann	Ferrari
1979	Laffite	Ligier-Ford
1980	Arnoux	Renault
1981	Reutemann	Williams-Ford
1982	Prost	Renault
1983	Piquet	Brabham-BMW
1984	Prost	McLaren-TAG
1985	Prost	McLaren-TAG
1986	Piquet	Williams-Honda
1987	Prost	McLaren-TAG
1988	Prost	McLaren-Honda
1989	Mansell	Ferrari
1990	Prost	Ferrari
1991	Senna	McLaren-Honda
1992	Mansell	Williams-Renault
1993	Senna	McLaren-Ford
1994	Schumacher	Benetton-Ford
1995	Schumacher	Benetton-Renault
1996	D Hill	Williams-Renault
1997	J Villeneuve	Williams-Renault

British Grand Prix

1950	Farina	Alfa Romeo

1951	Gonzalez	Ferrari
1952	Ascari	Ferrari
1953	Ascari	Ferrari
1954	Gonzalez	Ferrari
1955	Moss	Mercedes
1956	Fangio	Lancia-Ferrari
1957	Brooks/Moss	Vanwall
1958	Collins	Ferrari
1959	Brabham	Cooper-Climax
1960	Brabham	Cooper-Climax
1961	von Trips	Ferrari
1962	Clark	Lotus-Climax
1963	Clark	Lotus-Climax
1964	Clark	Lotus-Climax
1965	Clark	Lotus-Climax
1966	Brabham	Brabham-Repco
1967	Clark	Lotus-Ford
1968	Siffert	Lotus-Ford
1969	Stewart	Matra-Ford
1970	Rindt	Lotus-Ford
1971	Stewart	Tyrrell-Ford
1972	Fittipaldi	McLaren-Ford
1973	Revson	McLaren-Ford
1974	Scheckter	Tyrrell-Ford
1975	Fittipaldi	McLaren-Ford
1976	Lauda	Ferrari
1977	Hunt	McLaren-Ford
1978	Reutemann	Ferrari
1979	Regazzoni	Williams-Ford
1980	Jones	Williams-Ford
1981	Watson	McLaren-Ford
1982	Lauda	McLaren-Ford
1983	Prost	Renault
1984	Lauda	McLaren-TAG
1985	Prost	McLaren-TAG
1986	Mansell	Williams-Honda
1987	Mansell	Williams-Honda
1988	Senna	McLaren-Honda
1989	Prost	McLaren-Honda
1990	Prost	Ferrari
1991	Mansell	Williams-Renault
1992	Mansell	Williams-Renault
1993	Prost	Williams-Renault
1994	D Hill	Williams-Renault
1995	Herbert	Benetton-Renault
1996	J Villeneuve	Williams-Renault
1997	J Villeneuve	Williams-Renault

Canadian Grand Prix

1967	Brabham	Brabham-Repco
1968	Hulme	McLaren-Ford
1969	Ickx	Brabham-Ford
1970	Ickx	Ferrari

Grand Prix Winners

1971	Stewart	Tyrrell-Ford
1972	Stewart	Tyrrell-Ford
1973	Revson	McLaren-Ford
1974	Fittipaldi	McLaren-Ford
1976	Hunt	McLaren-Ford
1977	Scheckter	Wolf-Ford
1978	G Villeneuve	Ferrari
1979	Jones	Williams-Ford
1980	Jones	Williams-Ford
1981	Laffite	Ligier-Matra
1982	Piquet	Brabham-BMW
1983	Arnoux	Ferrari
1984	Piquet	Brabham-BMW
1985	Alboreto	Ferrari
1986	Mansell	Williams-Honda
1988	Senna	McLaren-Honda
1989	Boutsen	Williams-Renault
1990	Senna	McLaren-Honda
1991	Piquet	Brabham-Ford
1992	Berger	McLaren-Honda
1993	Prost	Williams-Renault
1994	Schumacher	Benetton-Ford
1995	Alesi	Ferrari
1996	D Hill	Williams-Renault
1997	Schumacher	Ferrari

Dutch Grand Prix

1952	Ascari	Ferrari
1953	Ascari	Ferrari
1955	Fangio	Mercedes
1958	Moss	Vanwall
1959	Bonnier	BRM
1960	Brabham	Cooper-Climax
1961	von Trips	Ferrari
1962	G Hill	BRM
1963	Clark	Lotus-Climax
1964	Clark	Lotus-Climax
1965	Clark	Lotus-Climax
1966	Brabham	Brabham-Repco
1967	Clark	Lotus-Ford
1968	Stewart	Matra-Ford
1969	Stewart	Matra-Ford
1970	Rindt	Lotus-Ford
1971	Ickx	Ferrari
1973	Stewart	Tyrrell-Ford
1974	Lauda	Ferrari
1975	Hunt	Hesketh-Ford
1976	Hunt	McLaren-Ford
1977	Lauda	Ferrari
1978	Andretti	Lotus-Ford
1979	Jones	Williams-Ford
1980	Piquet	Brabham-Ford
1981	Prost	Renault

1982	Pironi	Ferrari
1983	Arnoux	Ferrari
1984	Prost	McLaren-TAG
1985	Lauda	McLaren-TAG

European Grand Prix

1983	Piquet	Brabham-BMW
1984	Prost	McLaren-TAG
1985	Mansell	Williams-Honda
1993	Senna	McLaren-Ford
1994	Schumacher	Benetton-Ford
1995	Schumacher	Benetton-Renault
1996	J Villeneuve	William-Renault
1997	Hakkinen	McLaren-Mercedes

French Grand Prix

1950	Fangio	Alfa Romeo
1951	Fagioli/Fangio	Alfa Romeo
1952	Ascari	Ferrari
1953	Hawthorn	Ferrari
1954	Fangio	Mercedes
1956	Collins	Lancia-Ferrari
1957	Fangio	Maserati
1958	Hawthorn	Ferrari
1959	Brooks	Ferrari
1960	Brabham	Cooper-Climax
1961	Baghetti	Ferrari
1962	Gurney	Porsche
1963	Clark	Lotus-Climax
1964	Gurney	Brabham-Climax
1965	Clark	Lotus-Climax
1966	Brabham	Brabham-Repco
1967	Brabham	Brabham-Repco
1968	Ickx	Ferrari
1969	Stewart	Matra-Ford
1970	Rindt	Lotus-Ford
1971	Stewart	Tyrrell-Ford
1972	Stewart	Tyrrell-Ford
1973	Peterson	Lotus-Ford
1974	Peterson	Lotus-Ford
1975	Lauda	Ferrari
1976	Hunt	McLaren-Ford
1977	Andretti	Lotus-Ford
1978	Andretti	Lotus-Ford
1979	Jabouille	Renault
1980	Jones	Williams-Ford
1981	Prost	Renault
1982	Arnoux	Renault
1983	Prost	Renault
1984	Lauda	McLaren-TAG
1985	Piquet	Brabham-BMW
1986	Mansell	Williams-Honda
1987	Mansell	Williams-Honda

Grand Prix Winners

1988	Prost	McLaren-Honda
1989	Prost	McLaren-Honda
1990	Prost	Ferrari
1991	Mansell	Williams-Renault
1992	Mansell	Williams-Renault
1993	Prost	Williams-Renault
1994	Schumacher	Benetton-Ford
1995	Schumacher	Benetton-Renault
1996	D Hill	Williams-Renault
1997	Schumacher	Ferrari

German Grand Prix

1951	Ascari	Ferrari
1952	Ascari	Ferrari
1953	Farina	Ferrari
1954	Fangio	Mercedes
1956	Fangio	Lancia-Ferrari
1957	Fangio	Maserati
1958	Brooks	Vanwall
1959	Brooks	Ferrari
1961	Moss	Lotus-Climax
1962	G Hill	BRM
1963	Surtees	Ferrari
1964	Surtees	Ferrari
1965	Clark	Lotus-Climax
1966	Brabham	Brabham-Repco
1967	Hulme	Brabham-Repco
1968	Stewart	Matra-Ford
1969	Ickx	Brabham-Ford
1970	Rindt	Lotus-Ford
1971	Stewart	Tyrrell-Ford
1972	Ickx	Ferrari
1973	Stewart	Tyrrell-Ford
1974	Regazzoni	Ferrari
1975	Reutemann	Brabham-Ford
1976	Hunt	McLaren-Ford
1977	Lauda	Ferrari
1978	Andretti	Lotus-Ford
1979	Jones	Williams-Ford
1980	Laffite	Ligier-Ford
1981	Piquet	Brabham-Ford
1982	Tambay	Ferrari
1983	Arnoux	Ferrari
1984	Prost	McLaren-TAG
1985	Alboreto	Ferrari
1986	Piquet	Williams-Honda
1987	Piquet	Williams-Honda
1988	Senna	McLaren-Honda
1989	Senna	McLaren-Honda
1990	Senna	McLaren-Honda
1991	Mansell	Williams-Renault
1992	Mansell	Williams-Renault
1993	Prost	Williams-Renault

1994	Berger	Ferrari
1995	Schumacher	Benetton-Renault
1996	Hill	Williams-Renault
1997	Berger	Benetton-Renault

Hungarian Grand Prix

1986	Piquet	Williams-Honda
1987	Piquet	Williams-Honda
1988	Senna	McLaren-Honda
1989	Mansell	Ferrari
1990	Boutsen	Williams-Renault
1991	Senna	McLaren-Honda
1992	Senna	McLaren-Honda
1993	D Hill	Williams-Renault
1994	Schumacher	Benetton-Ford
1995	D Hill	Williams-Renault
1996	J Villeneuve	Williams-Renault
1997	J Villeneuve	Williams-Renault

Indianapolis

1950	Parsons
1951	Wallard
1952	Ruttman
1953	Vukovich
1954	Vukovich
1955	Sweikert
1956	Flaherty
1957	Hanks
1958	Bryan
1959	Ward
1960	Rathmann

Italian Grand Prix

1950	Farina	Alfa Romeo
1951	Ascari	Ferrari
1952	Ascari	Ferrari
1953	Fangio	Maserati
1954	Fangio	Mercedes
1955	Fangio	Mercedes
1956	Moss	Maserati
1957	Moss	Vanwall
1958	Brooks	Vanwall
1959	Moss	Cooper-Climax
1960	P Hill	Ferrari
1961	P Hill	Ferrari
1962	G Hill	BRM
1963	Clark	Lotus-Climax
1964	Surtees	Ferrari
1965	Stewart	BRM
1966	Scarfiotti	Ferrari
1967	Surtees	Honda
1968	Hulme	McLaren-Ford
1969	Stewart	Matra-Ford

1970	Regazzoni	Ferrari
1971	Gethin	BRM
1972	Fittipaldi	Lotus-Ford
1973	Peterson	Lotus-Ford
1974	Peterson	Lotus-Ford
1975	Regazzoni	Ferrari
1976	Peterson	March-Ford
1977	Andretti	Lotus-Ford
1978	Lauda	Brabham-Alfa
1979	Scheckter	Ferrari
1980	Piquet	Brabham-Ford
1981	Prost	Renault
1982	Arnoux	Renault
1983	Piquet	Brabham-BMW
1984	Lauda	McLaren-TAG
1985	Prost	McLaren -TAG
1986	Piquet	Williams-Honda
1987	Piquet	Williams-Honda
1988	Berger	Ferrari
1989	Prost	McLaren-Honda
1990	Senna	McLaren-Honda
1991	Mansell	Williams-Renault
1992	Senna	McLaren-Honda
1993	D Hill	Williams-Renault
1994	D Hill	Williams-Renault
1995	Herbert	Benetton-Renault
1996	Schumacher	Ferrari
1997	Coulthard	McLaren-Mercedes

Japanese Grand Prix

1976	Andretti	Lotus-Ford
1977	Hunt	McLaren-Ford
1987	Berger	Ferrari
1988	Senna	McLaren-Ford
1989	Nannini	Benetton-Ford
1990	Piquet	Benetton-Ford
1991	Berger	McLaren-Ford
1992	Patrese	Williams-Renault
1993	Senna	McLaren-Ford
1994	D Hill	Williams-Renault
1995	Schumacher	Benetton-Renault
1996	D Hill	Williams-Renault
1997	Schumacher	Ferrari

Luxembourg Grand Prix

1997	J Villeneuve	Williams-Renault

Mexican Grand Prix

1963	Clark	Lotus-Climax
1964	Gurney	Brabham-Climax
1965	Ginther	Honda
1966	Surtees	Cooper-Maserati
1967	Clark	Lotus-Ford

1968	G Hill	Lotus-Ford
1969	Hulme	McLaren-Ford
1970	Ickx	Ferrari
1986	Berger	Benetton-BMW
1987	Mansell	Williams-Renault
1988	Prost	McLaren-Honda
1989	Senna	McLaren-Honda
1990	Prost	Ferrari
1991	Patrese	Williams-Renault
1992	Mansell	Williams-Renault

Monaco Grand Prix

1950	Fangio	Alfa Romeo
1955	Trintignant	Ferrari
1956	Moss	Maserati
1957	Fangio	Maserati
1958	Trintignant	Cooper-Climax
1959	Brabham	Cooper-Climax
1960	Moss	Lotus-Climax
1961	Moss	Lotus-Climax
1962	McLaren	Cooper-Climax
1963	G Hill	BRM
1964	G Hill	BRM
1965	G Hill	BRM
1966	Stewart	BRM
1967	Hulme	Brabham-Repco
1968	G Hill	Lotus-Ford
1969	G Hill	Lotus-Ford
1970	Rindt	Lotus-Ford
1971	Stewart	Tyrrell-Ford
1972	Beltoise	BRM
1973	Stewart	Tyrrell-Ford
1974	Peterson	Lotus-Ford
1975	Lauda	Ferrari
1976	Lauda	Ferrari
1977	Scheckter	Wolf-Ford
1978	Depailler	Tyrrell-Ford
1979	Scheckter	Ferrari
1980	Reutemann	Williams-Ford
1981	G Villeneuve	Ferrari
1982	Patrese	Brabham-Ford
1983	Rosberg	Williams-Ford
1984	Prost	McLaren-TAG
1985	Prost	McLaren-TAG
1986	Prost	McLaren-TAG
1987	Senna	McLaren-Honda
1988	Prost	McLaren-Honda
1989	Senna	McLaren-Honda
1990	Senna	McLaren-Honda
1991	Senna	McLaren-Honda
1992	Senna	McLaren-Honda
1993	Senna	McLaren-Ford
1994	Schumacher	Benetton-Ford

Grand Prix Winners

1995	Schumacher	Benetton-Renault
1996	Panis	Ligier-Mugen
1997	Schumacher	Ferrari

Moroccan Grand Prix
1958	Moss	Vanwall

Pacific Grand Prix
1994	Schumacher	Benetton-Ford
1995	Schumacher	Benetton-Renault

Pescara Grand Prix
1957	Moss	Vanwall

Portuguese Grand Prix
1958	Moss	Vanwall
1959	Moss	Cooper-Climax
1960	Brabham	Cooper-Climax
1984	Prost	McLaren-TAG
1985	Senna	Lotus-Renault
1986	Mansell	Williams-Honda
1987	Prost	McLaren-TAG
1988	Prost	McLaren-Honda
1989	Berger	Ferrari
1990	Mansell	Ferrari
1991	Patrese	Williams-Renault
1992	Mansell	Williams-Renault
1993	Schumacher	Benetton-Ford
1994	D Hill	Williams-Renault
1995	Coulthard	Williams-Renault
1996	J Villeneuve	Williams-Renault

San Marino Grand Prix
1981	Piquet	Brabham-Ford
1982	Pironi	Ferrari
1983	Tambay	Ferrari
1984	Prost	McLaren-TAG
1985	de Angelis	Lotus-Renault
1986	Prost	McLaren-TAG
1987	Mansell	Williams-Honda
1988	Senna	McLaren-Honda
1989	Senna	McLaren-Honda
1990	Patrese	Williams-Renault
1991	Senna	McLaren-Honda
1992	Mansell	Williams-Renault
1993	Prost	Williams-Renault
1994	Schumacher	Benetton-Ford
1995	D Hill	Williams-Renault
1996	D Hill	Williams-Renault
1997	Frentzen	Williams-Renault

South African Grand Prix
1962	G Hill	BRM
1963	Clark	Lotus-Climax

1965	Clark	Lotus-Climax
1967	Rodriguez	Cooper-Maserati
1968	Clark	Lotus-Ford
1969	Stewart	Matra-Ford
1970	Brabham	Brabham-Ford
1971	Andretti	Ferrari
1972	Hulme	McLaren-Ford
1973	Stewart	Tyrrell-Ford
1974	Reutemann	Brabham-Ford
1975	Scheckter	Tyrrell-Ford
1976	Lauda	Ferrari
1977	Lauda	Ferrari
1978	Peterson	Lotus-Ford
1979	G Villeneuve	Ferrari
1980	Arnoux	Renault
1982	Prost	Renault
1983	Patrese	Brabham-BMW
1984	Lauda	McLaren-TAG
1985	Mansell	Williams-Honda
1992	Mansell	Williams-Renault
1993	Prost	Williams-Renault

Spanish Grand Prix
1951	Fangio	Alfa Romeo
1954	Hawthorn	Ferrari
1968	G Hill	Lotus-Ford
1969	Stewart	Matra-Ford
1970	Stewart	March-Ford
1971	Stewart	Tyrrell-Ford
1972	Fittipaldi	Lotus-Ford
1973	Fittipaldi	Lotus-Ford
1974	Lauda	Ferrari
1975	Mass	McLaren-Ford
1976	Hunt	McLaren-Ford
1977	Andretti	Lotus-Ford
1978	Andretti	Lotus-Ford
1979	Depailler	Ligier-Ford
1981	G Villeneuve	Ferrari
1986	Senna	Lotus-Renault
1987	Mansell	Williams-Honda
1988	Prost	McLaren-Honda
1989	Senna	McLaren-Honda
1990	Prost	Ferrari
1991	Mansell	Williams-Renault
1992	Mansell	Williams-Renault
1993	Prost	Williams-Renault
1994	D Hill	Williams-Renault
1995	Schumacher	Benetton-Renault
1996	Schumacher	Ferrari
1997	J Villeneuve	Williams-Renault

Swedish Grand Prix
1973	Hulme	McLaren-Ford

1974	Scheckter	Tyrrell-Ford
1975	Lauda	Ferrari
1976	Scheckter	Tyrrell-Ford
1977	Laffite	Ligier-Matra
1978	Lauda	Brabham-Alfa

Swiss Grand Prix
1950	Farina	Alfa Romeo
1951	Fangio	Alfa Romeo
1952	Taruffi	Ferrari
1953	Ascari	Ferrari
1954	Fangio	Mercedes
1982	Rosberg	Williams-Ford

US Grand Prix
1959	McLaren	Cooper-Climax
1960	Moss	Lotus-Climax
1961	Ireland	Lotus-Climax
1962	Clark	Lotus-Climax
1963	G Hill	BRM
1964	G Hill	BRM
1965	G Hill	BRM
1966	Clark	Lotus-BRM
1967	Clark	Lotus-Ford
1968	Stewart	Matra-Ford
1969	Rindt	Lotus-Ford
1970	Fittipaldi	Lotus-Ford
1971	Cevert	Tyrrell-Ford
1972	Stewart	Tyrrell-Ford
1973	Peterson	Lotus-Ford
1974	Reutemann	Brabham-Ford
1975	Lauda	Ferrari
1976	Hunt	McLaren-Ford
1977	Hunt	McLaren-Ford

1978	Reutemann	Ferrari
1979	G Villeneuve	Ferrari
1980	Jones	Williams-Ford

Dallas
| 1984 | Rosberg | Williams-Honda |

Detroit
1982	Watson	McLaren-Ford
1983	Alborteo	Tyrrell-Ford
1984	Piquet	Brabham-BMW
1985	Rosberg	Williams-Honda
1986	Senna	Lotus-Renault
1987	Senna	Lotus-Honda
1988	Senna	McLaren-Honda

Phoenix
1989	Prost	McLaren-Honda
1990	Senna	McLaren-Honda
1991	Senna	McLaren-Honda

Las Vegas
| 1981 | Jones | Williams-Ford |
| 1982 | Alborteo | Tyrrell-Ford |

US Grand Prix West (Long Beach)
1976	Regazzoni	Ferrari
1977	Andretti	Lotus-Ford
1978	Reutemann	Ferrari
1979	G Villeneuve	Ferrari
1980	Piquet	Brabham-Ford
1981	Jones	Williams-Ford
1982	Lauda	McLaren-Ford
1983	Watson	McLaren-Ford

Select Bibliography

Books

Cimarosti, Adriano, *The Complete History of Grand Prix Motor Racing*, MRP, 1990

Crombac, Gerard, *Colin Chapman: The Man and his Cars*, Patrick Stephens, 1986

Cutter, Robert, and Bob Fendell, *Encyclopaedia of Auto Racing Greats*, Prentice-Hall, 1973

Deschenaux, Jacques, *Marlboro Grand Prix Guide*, Marlboro, 1992

Hayhoe, David, and David Milland, *Grand Prix Data Book 1997*, Duke, 1996

Henry, Alan, *Williams – the Business of Grand Prix Racing*, Patrick Stephens, 1991

Henry, Alan, *Formula One Driver by Driver*, Crowood, 1992

Hodges, David, *The French Grand Prix*, Temple Press, 1967

Hodges, David, *The Monaco Grand Prix*, Temple Press, 1964

Kettlewell, Mike, *The Champion Book of World Championship Facts and Figures*, Mill House Books, 1982

Lang, Mike, *Grand Prix! Volumes 1 & 2, 1950 to 1973*, Haynes, combined and revised edn 1990 (*1950 to 1965* first published 1981, *1966 to 1973* first published 1982)

Lang, Mike, *Grand Prix! Volume 3, 1974–1980*, Haynes, 1983

Lang, Mike, *Grand Prix! Volume 4, 1980–1984*, Haynes, 1992

Lawrence, Mike, *Grand Prix Cars 1945–65*, Aston, 1989

Nye, Doug, *McLaren: the Grand Prix, Can-Am and Indy Cars*, new edn, Hazleton, 1988

Posthumus, Cyril, *The German Grand Prix*, Temple Press, 1966

Pritchard, Anthony, *Directory of Formula One Cars 1966–1986*, Aston, 1986

Pritchard, Anthony, *Formula One*, Allen and Unwin, 1966

Sheldon, Paul with Yves de La Gorce and Duncan Rabagliati, *A Record of Grand Prix and Voiturette Racing, Volume 5 1950–1953*, St Leonard's Press, 1988

Sheldon, Paul with John Humphreys and Duncan Rabagliati, *A Record of Grand Prix and Voiturette Racing, Volume 6 1954–1959*, St Leonard's Press, 1987

Sheldon, Paul with Duncan Rabagliati, *A Record of Grand Prix and Voiturette Racing, Volume 7 1960–1964*, St Leonard's Press, 1991

Small, Steve, *The Grand Prix Who's Who*, Guinness, 2nd ed, 1996

Tanner, Hans and Doug Nye, *Ferrari*, 6th edn, Haynes, 1984

Journals and Annuals

Autocar
Autocourse
Autosport
Formula One: FIA yearbook
Formula One: FOCA yearbook

Grand Prix International
Motor
Motor Sport
Motoring News